STREAMS OF CIVILIZATION

Volume Two
Cultures in Conflict Since the Reformation Until the Third Millennium After Christ

Revised and Updated by

Garry J. Moes

Christian Liberty Press

Editors: Eric D. Bristley

Lars R. Johnson

Michael J. McHugh

Originally written by Robert G. Clouse and Richard V. Pierard
and edited by Mott Media

Library of Congress Cataloging in Publication Data

Moes, Garry J.

STREAMS OF CIVILIZATION

Vol. 2 Cultures in Conflict Since the Reformation

Includes indexes

1. Civilization—History—Juvenile literature. 2. Civilization—History.
3. History—World.

I. Moes, Garry J. 1944– II. Title

ISBN 978-1-930367-46-3 (v. 2 Cultures in Conflict Since the Reformation)

ISBN 978-1-930367-43-2 (v. 1 Earliest Times to the Discovery of the New World)

Set in Adobe Garamond and Formata

Printed in the United States of America

Table of Contents

Foreword:
A Christian View of History

The meaning and interpretation of history is a vital and continuing concern for every Christian, whatever his calling may be. While some are very interested in prophecy and place an emphasis on future events, they may fail to see the relationship between the future and the past. Some may insist that history is a secular study since it is under the control of satanic power. Yet the Christian has the duty of rightly interpreting the events of history in the light of Scripture. He must not only ask himself what the meaning of history is, but must also face the problem of interpreting it in accordance with biblical principles. The Christian dare not accept the interpretation imposed on history by unbelievers who find their frame of reference either in man himself (humanism) or in nature (materialism).

Non-Christian Views of History. The result of non-Christian attempts to interpret history apart from the Bible demonstrates their inability to find any meaning and purpose in history. The pagan Greeks believed that history is a repetitive cycle of events, which lead to the conclusion that it is an irrational riddle. When they spoke of a god they referred to an impersonal force of fate which determined history in a mechanical way. The humanism of the Renaissance built upon these ancient pagan ideas and further developed a secular approach to history. Believing in the inherent goodness of man, humanist historians assumed that history was nothing more than the story of man's increasing perfection. Eventually the fatalistic determinism of the ancient pagans was reworked in the Darwinian theory of evolution, and history was seen as being under the control of irrational forces. The conclusion was made that evolutionary progress was inevitable.

But the reality of human depravity could not be hidden, as modern culture produced two world wars and unspeakable mass murders. Some non-Christians began to embrace various forms of pessimism and became skeptical about the possibility of discovering any real meaning to history. Some even denied that a philosophy of history is possible since man is struggling with forces which he cannot understand. Yet Marxism, in the form of economic determinism continued to push evolutionary idealism forward.

Instead of abandoning the study of history because he could not find objectivity; the non-Christian historian began to reconstruct the past to promote a humanistic worldview. History is now used by many as a tool of manipulation and propaganda. The events of the past are merely occasions for redirecting public opinion in the present. And many secular writers explain historical events as the result merely of geographical, national, political, economic, or biological forces. Their secular worldview demonstrates a peculiar prejudice against the role of the Christian faith and the church in history.

The Biblical View of History

If the Christian dare not accept the optimism of such a humanistic view of history, neither may he accept the pessimistic conclusions to which it leads. The Christian student of history must not compromise with the view that the meaning of history cannot be known, and that men must interpret history as they see fit. The Christian student must learn to confront the unbelieving world with a biblical interpretation of history. He should emphasize anew that it has one purpose which God has decreed for it,

> He made known to us the mystery of His will, according to His kind intention which He purposed in Him with a view to an administration suitable to the fullness of the times, the summing up of all things in Christ, things in the heavens and things upon the earth (Eph. 1:9-10).

The Christian should endeavor to cleanse his mind by the Word of God from the spirit of the age. To help him, he may profit greatly from those Christians in the past who have sought to interpret history from a biblical perspective. With the fall of the Roman Empire, when pagan culture had reached the depths of disintegration, Augustine searched the Bible to understand the events of his time. He found that the Bible is the key to interpreting the whole of history—the events of his time were to be understood as a part of God's comprehensive plan. In his book *The City of God* (410), Augustine set forth a biblical philosophy of history.

The Origin of History. The Bible teaches that God the Father originated history when He created all things. By His creation of time, and placing man on the earth He set history into motion. The Christian therefore views history by faith in the all-wise and sovereign God, who works all historical events after the counsel of His will (Eph. 1:11). The history of all men, all peoples, all nations, are held together by the unity of His decree. "It is He who changes the times and the epochs; He removes kings and establishes kings; He gives wisdom to wise men, and knowledge to men of understanding." (Dan. 2:21) While human actions form the bulk of historical events, God's acts are the center of its meaning. God is the primary actor in history, bringing his judgements and his salvation on men and nations. He redirects the course of events to fulfill His purpose.

The Direction of History. The providence of God in the affairs of men, as it is taught in the Bible, provides us with the understanding that all events are under His care and direction. The God of the Bible is clearly separated from any idea of fate or chance. There are no accidents in history, and all events are meaningful as part of his plan of the ages to sum up all things in Christ.

God gave meaning and purpose to human actions by creating man in His own image and defining his relationship to Himself and the earth by a covenant. The Scriptures teach us that the unity of humanity does not exclude, but rather includes, the differences of race, in character, in attainment, in calling, and nationality. The meaning of every man and nation is derived from the place assigned to them by God in his plan. The unity of the human race is a presupposition of all history, and this has been made known to us only in the Bible.

The Center of History. The Bible teaches that the center focus of God's plan in history is the cross of Christ. All events are moving, not in an endless cycle, but in a linear direction from creation to consummation. Herman Bavinck writes,

Furthermore revelation gives us a division of history. There is no history without division of time, without periods, without progress and development. But now take Christ away. The thing is impossible, history falls to pieces, for he has lived and died, has risen from the dead, and lives to all eternity; and these facts cannot be eliminated,—they belong to history, they are the heart of history. But *think* Christ away for a moment, with all that he has spoken and done and wrought. Immediately history falls to pieces. It has lost its heart, its kernel, and its center, its distribution. It loses itself in a history of races and nations, of nature and culture-peoples. It becomes a chaos, without a center, and therefore without a circumference; without distribution and therefore without beginning or end; without principle and goal; a stream rolling down from the mountains, nothing more. But revelation teaches that as God is the Lord of the ages, Christ is the turning point of these ages. And thus it brings into history unity and plan, progress and aim. This aim is not this or that special idea, not the idea of freedom, or of humanity, or of material well-being. But it is the fullness of the Kingdom of God, the all-sided, all-containing dominion of God, which embraces heaven and earth, angels and men, mind and matter, cultus and culture, the specific and the generic; in a word, all in all. (Herman Bavinck, *The Philosophy of Revelation* [Grand Rapids: Baker, 1979], p. 141.)

Because the incarnation of Christ is the focal point of history we must relate all historical events to Him. Every person and movement must be evaluated by how they respond to Christ.

The Conflict of History. This response to Christ creates a conflict in history. "Do not think that I came to bring peace on the earth; I did not come to bring peace, but a sword" (Matt. 11:34). The Bible teaches that the drama of history consists in the spiritual battle between the kingdom of Christ and the kingdom of Satan. The non-Christian knows nothing of this and fails to grasp the terribly tragic seriousness of the central conflict of history. While he sees history as the development of one human civilization evolving itself by a series of revolutions, the Bible presents history as the conflict between the City of God and the City of (unredeemed) Man. The essence of history lies in the mighty conflict between the kingdoms of darkness and light, between sin and grace, between heaven and hell. Augustine declared that grace and election are the mystery and essence of history, as all events redound ultimately to the glory of God. Thus all the events of history must be understood in relationship to church history and its conflict with the powers of darkness.

The Goal of History. Scripture concludes that the culmination of history occurs at the coming of Christ. Guided by the sovereign God, the conflict between the two kingdoms will end in the triumph of Christ, when Jesus Christ comes to judge unbelievers and vindicate His people. At that time He will judge the nations and bring a final resolution to all issues of history. If all events look backward to the incarnation, they also look forward to this final event (2 Thess. 1:6–10).

The Theological Interpretation of History

The interpretation of history is subject to Him who has revealed Himself during history in the Bible. The Bible, being an historical book, provides us with a clear example of how God interprets history. We should learn from it how to study the past in the light of His eternal truth. It is the Bible which enables the Christian to view history as something greater than a mere human or natural process.

The Christian acknowledges the complexity of history, that there are many factors at work in it. Yet he never loses sight of the One who directs all of these factors. He will therefore avoid the attempt to explain the entire process of history from purely biological, psychological, economic, or other factors. Does this mean that the Christian historian should ignore the other influences on the development of history? Not at all. He should pay due attention to all the factors that play a role. But all these factors must be subordinated to the fundamental principles of interpretation which we find in the Scriptures.

While the Christian student of history can understand the ultimate meaning of history he does not always know the role of every event in the historical process. We will never understand history perfectly now. But we must seek to be faithful in bringing the interpretation of history captive to the obedience of Christ (2 Cor. 10:5).

The Christian student is enabled by the Word of God to make great progress in evaluating history in the light of Scripture. For example he knows that the rise of Communist Russia, Nazi Germany, and other totalitarian states were not accidents but part of God's plan for the chastening of an impenitent West and for the purifying of a church which had become apostate in great measure. He can learn that the decline of Western culture, as the fall of the Roman Empire, is not a tragedy but part of the sovereign purpose of God to bring to nothing the pagan philosophies and plans of the world. He can understand that this decline itself is the direct result of the triumph of the Renaissance over the Reformation in Western culture. He is under an obligation to make it very clear that the Enlightenment of the later seventeenth and eighteenth centuries was only superficially a period of enlightenment, but in reality it was a period in which the latent darkness of the Renaissance was popularized. He affirms that the French Revolution was the result of a rejection of the Reformation and an expression of unbelief. It is not Christianity but modern secular thought in all of its varieties which is the source of the decay in Western civilization.

From the Bible, the Christian learns that one's relationship to God is the determining factor of life. Therefore understanding the intellectual and religious history of any nation becomes a valuable tool in evaluating a people's culture and politics. The Christian will therefore interpret history in a God-centered or theological manner. Says C. Gregg Singer,

> Too seldom have these historians given theology its proper place as a determining factor in intellectual life. The recognition of the importance of intellectual forces in the stream of history must be followed by one other step, namely, the realization that the intellectual development of a people is not an entity in itself, but, in turn, depends upon their theology, or lack thereof. (C. Gregg Singer, *A Theological Interpretation of American History* [Philadelphia: Presbyterian and Reformed, 1964] p. 5)

Guillaume Groen van Prinsterer (1801–1876) was a Dutch Christian historian who published the archives of the House of Orange, and wrote a penetrating analysis of the French Revolution in *Unbelief and Revolution*, 1847.

Western Culture and Christianity. The period under study in this book treats the conflict between a culture which exalts Christ and a culture which exalts man. The constructive achievements of Western European culture resulted primarily from a Christian worldview and values.

Among these values is the belief that history is guided by a sovereign God toward the goal of the return of Jesus Christ. All things have been created by God and exist for His glory. Things visible and invisible were created by God, exist in God-defined relationships, and are equally affected by man's sin. Grace does not destroy creation but rather restores it.

Another Christian value is based on the teaching that men and women are created in the image of God. He placed them on the earth to serve as caretakers of His creation. They are so important to God that, when they sinned and were cut off from Him, He sent His only Son, Jesus Christ, to redeem men from every nation. This underlies the high regard given to the dignity of man and value of human life.

One key biblical value that has influenced Western civilization is that all men are subject to God's law. The biblical teachings on the sinfulness and depravity of man show that God alone can define the limits of human behavior. In addition, the Christian understanding of God's law is that it can be fulfilled only by God's grace out of a heart of charity. Those Western societies that have received the Christian covenantal perspective have been societies governed by a temperate system of law rather than by the arbitrary tyrannical display of raw power.

As these and other values flowed out of the biblical tradition, they came into conflict with pagan ideas and values flowing from the pagan Greco-Roman and Germanic societies. The Greco-Roman culture emphasized the autonomy of man and sought to idealize its humanism in political power. The deepest conflict in modern history is the struggle between these two world-views. This conflict is expressed at times in the power of paganism to dilute the impact of Christian values. We find then, at many points, the attempt to construct a synthesis from the key elements of the Christian (and Hebraic) and the pagan Greco-Roman (and Germanic) societies. In recent years, the influence of non-Western pagan societies, such as those from Asia and Africa, have further eroded the Christian influence in Western societies so that it is more and more difficult to identify that which is truly Christian. These non-Christian influences explain why the church, as well as individual Christians, have so frequently acted in ways that deviate widely from the basic principles of the Christian faith.

By the twentieth century, most of these Christian distinctives had become so humanized and secularized that they were effectively cut off from their spiritual roots. Europeans, once so successful in gaining political, economic, and cultural mastery over the world, found themselves without an effective defense against the threats of human depravity—world war, totalitarian ideologies, enslavement to technology, and the destruction of the earth's environment. These factors explain the decline in Western power and order. Yet, through the spread of the gospel, many Christian values have been transmitted to other cultures. And God has continued to revive His church and awaken His people to the fact that they must be distinct from the world.

The Christian must not be naive. He must become aware that every historian interprets history on the basis of his own relationship to God. The Christian historian will seek by God's grace to interpret history in a God-honoring fashion and exalt Christ as the Lord of History. He will not seek to be neutrally objective, as if he had no faith. The Christian is able to be truly objective when he interprets history in the light of God's unchanging Word. Nevertheless, because the Christian historian is not yet perfect and is still beset with much sin and ignorance, he will never write a perfect history. Yet he must seek by God's mercy to fulfill his responsibility to God in presenting as faithful an account as he is able in order to equip Christian students to fight the good fight on the terrain of historical studies.

(Portions of this section were adapted from C. Gregg Singer, "The Christian View of the Philosophy of History," in *Christian Approaches to Philosophy and History*. [Memphis, TN: Christian Studies Center, 1978].)

This political poster appeared in the Netherlands in 1922 to promote the election of Dr. Hendrik Colijn. It reflected the view of the Christian Anti-Revolutionary Party which had as its motto "Against the Revolution, the Gospel." Colijn was prime minister from 1925–1926, and again from 1933–1939. He was arrested by the Nazis for resistance activities.

The Benefits of Studying History

The Christian student should be especially interested in a study of modern history. He can learn how God manifests His justice and grace in His providential direction of the course of human affairs. Believers gain encouragement for the present when they see how Christ has caused His eternal Kingdom to spread among the nations. And by looking at the lives of His people in the past the Christian student can find an example of how he should and should not follow Christ in the present. Also, by looking at the lives of those who are outside of Christ he is warned of the results of unbelief.

By studying history he will be enabled to more clearly evaluate biblically the various teachings and practices that he might find in the church today. This holds true for every area of study; politics, science, economics, etc. A knowledge of history demonstrates the axiom that ideas have consequences.

History provides the Christian student with the background to current events. Without a proper understanding of history the Christian student will be easily manipulated by modern opinion in the secular media. A Christian study of history will enable the believer to be prepared to act as a Christian citizen and properly promote the building of Christ's kingdom in his nation and throughout world.

It will help him to have compassion on those who do not know God. By studying the developments in culture since the sixteenth century he will be able to understand better why people think and act the way they do. In a time when transportation and communication technology has brought the peoples of the world closer and closer, it is vital to know the traditions, values, and background of the nations that we might reach them with the message of the cross of Christ.

Organization of the Book

This book covers the events of world history with an emphasis on European and American culture since the Reformation. Each chapter traces a particular theme within a particular time-period. The principal themes include the history of Christianity and philosophy with their results in culture, politics; economics, society, science, and technology.

Several features have been included to enhance the student's understanding. First, a time line at the beginning of each chapter will help the reader to see the chronological relationships between the events discussed in the text. Throughout the text, particular points of interest, focusing on specific individuals and events, provide further information. Maps and photographs, as well as artwork of a particular period, add to the overall impact of the book. Thought-provoking questions given at the end of each chapter will encourage students to think through the Christian implications of the material and its relevance for today's world. In addition, a list of important words and concepts at the end of the chapter will aid the student in focusing on the most significant ideas discussed in the chapter. Suggested projects can also enliven the topics being covered as a particular activity is carried out by an individual or a class. A reading list, found on the next page, is provided to suggest resources for further study. An extensive index will also enable the student to use the book for reference in years to come.

Acknowledgments

It is difficult to sufficiently acknowledge the efforts of each individual who helped to make this world history text possible. It is only fitting that we begin by acknowledging the One who is the giver of all wisdom, knowledge, and grace—the Lord of history—Jesus Christ.

In addition, the publishers would like to thank the following staff members for their participation in preparing and finalizing this volume. The project coordinator and chief editor was Michael J. McHugh, from Christian Liberty Press. The text, originally written by Robert G. Clouse and Richard V. Pierard and edited by Mott Media, was thoroughly revised and supplemented by Garry J. Moes. General editorial work was done by Lars Johnson, who copyedited the text, maps, and timelines. The book was typeset by Edward J. Shewan who also prepared the timelines, maps, and index. Eric Bristley provided the layout and design for the book, handled the cover and text illustrations, and helped in the final review of the manuscript.

To all the others—named and unnamed—who played at least a minor role in the preparation of this history text, we are grateful.

Further Reading

Blair, William and Hunt, Bruce. *The Korean Pentecost and the Sufferings Which Followed*. Edinburgh: Banner of Truth Trust, 1977. The story of 20th century missions in Korea.

Cook, Harold R. *Highlights of Christian Missions*. Chicago: Moody Press, 1967. A history of Christian missions.

Cryer, France, Legg, Miller, and Thornbury. *Five Pioneer Missionaries*. Edinburgh: Banner of Truth Trust, 1965. This book includes short biographies of Brainerd, Burns, Eliot, Martyn, and Paton.

Douglas, J. D., ed. *The New International Dictionary of the Christian Church*. Grand Rapids: Zondervan, 1974. Provides useful information on the people, events, movements, and teachings that have shaped the Church throughout the ages.

Gray, Janet Glenn. *The French Huguenots: Anatomy of Courage*. Grand Rapids: Baker Book House, 1981. A history of the Huguenot movement through the Revocation of the Edict of Nantes.

Hooykaas, R. *Religion and the Rise of Modern Science*. Grand Rapids: William B. Eerdmans, 1972. A consideration of the Christian origins of modern science.

Houghton, S. M. *Sketches from Church History: An Illustrated Account of 20 Centuries of Christ's Power*. Edinburgh: Banner of Truth Trust, 1980. A short history of the Church, focusing on Europe and North America.

Hyma, Albert, Ph.D. *Renaissance to Reformation*. Grand Rapids: William B. Eerdmans, 1951. This book provides background information to modern history.

Lee, Francis Nigel. *A Christian Introduction to the History of Philosophy*. Nutley, NJ: The Craig Press, 1969. A concise history of Christian and non-Christian philosophy.

Machen, J. Gresham. *Christianity and Liberalism*. Grand Rapids: William B. Eerdmans, 1923. Shows the difference between historic Christianity and liberalism.

Morris, Henry M. *Men of Science–Men of God*. San Diego, CA: Master Books, 1982, 1988.

Morris, Henry M. *The Bible and Modern Science*. Chicago: Moody Press, 1951.

Murray, Ian. *The Forgotten Spurgeon*. Edinburgh: Banner of Truth Trust, 1966.

Murray, Ian. *The Puritan Hope*. Edinburgh: Banner of Truth Trust, 1971. A study of revivals and missions.

Noebel, David A. *Understanding the Times: The Story of the Biblical Christian, Marxist/Leninist, and Secular Humanist Worldviews*. Manitou Springs, CO: Summit Press, 1991.

Olasky, Marvin. *The Tragedy of American Compassion*. Wheaton, IL: Crossway Books, 1992. An examination of welfare in America from the 19th century to the present.

Praamsma, L. *Let Christ Be King*. St. Catherines, Ontario, Canada: Paideia Press, 1985. Chronicles the life of Abraham Kuyper.

Reid, W. Stanford, ed. *John Calvin: His Influence In the Western World*. Grand Rapids: Zondervan, 1982. Describes one of the key influences on world culture.

Rian, Edwin H. *The Presbyterian Conflict*. Philadelphia: Orthodox Presbyterian Church, 1992 (1940). Chronicles the battle between modernists and evangelicals in the Presbyterian Church during the early part of the 20th century.

Rookmaaker, H. R. *Modern Art and the Death of a Culture*. Downers Grove, IL: InterVarsity Press, 1970. This is an analysis of modern art by a Christian art historian.

Rose, Tom. *Economics: Principles and Policy from a Christian Perspective*. Mercer, PA: American Enterprise Publications, 1986.

Rushdoony, Rousas J. *The Biblical Philosophy of History*. Phillipsburg, NJ: Presbyterian and Reformed, 1979.

Rushdoony, Rousas J. *The Messianic Character of American Education*. Nutley, NJ: The Craig Press, 1963. Discussion of the history of secular education.

Rushdoony, Rousas J. *The One and the Many*. Fairfax, VA: Thoburn Press, 1971. Traces the impact of Christianity on the development of Western culture.

Ryle, J. C. *Christian Leaders of the 18th Century*. Edinburgh: Banner of Truth Trust, 1978 (1885). Contains short biographies of men who were part of the Evangelical Awakening.

Schaeffer, Edith. *L'Abri*. Wheaton, IL: Tyndale House Publishers, 1969. The story about L'Abri and its formation.

Schaeffer, Francis A. *How Should We Then Live? The Rise and Decline of Western Thought and Culture*. Old Tappen, NJ: Fleming H. Revell Company, 1976. A Christian analysis of world history.

Schaeffer, Francis A. *The Complete Works of Francis A. Schaeffer: A Christian Worldview*. Wheaton, IL: Crossway Books, 1982. Includes all of Francis Schaeffer's writings on religion, philosophy, culture, and history.

Scott, Otto. *Robespierre, the Voice of Virtue*. New York: Mason and Lipscomb, 1974. Explores a key figure in the French Revolution.

Singer, C. Gregg. *A Theological Interpretation of American History.*, Phillipsburg, NJ: Presbyterian and Reformed, 1964. Interprets the theological forces in American history.

Smith, Gary Scott, ed. *God and Politics: Four Views on the Reformation of Civil Government*. Phillipsburg, NJ: Presbyterian and Reformed, 1989. Considers theonomy, principled pluralism, Christian America, and national confessionalism.

Smith, Jane Stuart and Carlson, Betty. *A Gift of Music: Great Composers and Their Influence*. Westchester, IL: Good News Publishers, 1978. Short biographies of various composers.

Stonehouse, Ned B. *J. Gresham Machen: A Biographical Memoir.*, Edinburgh: Banner of Truth Trust, 1987 (1954). A study on the life and times of J. Gresham Machen.

Tracy, Joseph. *The Great Awakening: A History of the Revival of Religion In the Time of Edwards and Whitefield*. Edinburgh: Banner of Truth Trust, 1976 (1842).

Van Dyke, Harry. *Groen Van Prinsterer's Lectures on Unbelief and Revolution*. Jordan Station, Ontario, Canada: Wedge Pub. Foundation, 1989. A Christian analysis of the French Revolution.

Van Til, Henry R. *The Calvinistic Concept of Culture*. Grand Rapids: Baker Book House, 1959, 1970. Discusses the historical background of developing a Christian view of culture.

Introduction: Religion and Culture of the 16th Century World

In the first volume of *Streams of Civilization*, the history of the world was traced to the sixteenth century Reformation, the beginning of what is sometimes known as the modern era (A.D. 1500–present). Before the narrative is continued to contemporary times, it is well to review what has already been presented.

History began, of course, in the Garden of Eden and had a new beginning, so to speak, following the Great Flood, as recorded in the book of *Genesis*. Eventually men sought for a humanistic unity at the Tower of Babel. However, God confused their language and scattered them over the face of the earth. Because the Bible focuses on God's central purposes in history, it provides sketchy information about many of the peoples that were separated at Babel. The earliest civilization developed at Sumer in the southeastern corner of the Fertile Crescent (in the area believed to be the site of the Tower of Babel) around 3500 B.C. Sumeria was the beginning of a society that, with variations, eventually encompassed all of the Middle East.

This area was connected not only to Europe and Asia but also North Africa. While God had separated mankind into different languages there were still contacts between these various societies. These interchanges spread technology, institutions, material goods, and ideas. Eventually other major areas of the globe were settled with signifi-cant populations, such as North and South America, Australia, and Sub-Saharan Africa, but they were kept from these cultural exchanges by wide geographic barriers.

God's dispersion of man brought many to locate in fertile valleys such as those of the Nile, Tigris-Euphrates, Indus, and Yellow rivers. Irrigation in the river valleys and large desert oases made possible the production of an agricultural surplus even with primitive farming methods. The cooperative social effort of farming and trade led to the development of the specialized skills necessary for complex society. By 2000 B.C., more advanced life-styles also existed in rain-watered lands; and during the period 1700–500 B.C., a cosmopolitan society arose in the Middle East. This area was home to many societies featured in the Old Testament—the Hebrews, Philistines, and Chaldeans, as well as the great Egyptian, Assyrian, and Persian empires. By 500 B.C., the ancient cultures of the Middle East were united under the Persians.

On the Persians' northwestern frontier lived the Greeks. Greek society, formed in the years following 1500 B.C., developed the main institution of classical life—the **city-state**. By 500 B.C., the humanistic culture generated within this structure had made a permanent stamp on European civilization. The Greeks expanded militarily and commercially, but it was the Romans who enlarged the scope of Greek influence to include the entire Mediterranean basin. The Romans played a major role in world events for more than a thousand years and established what was perhaps the greatest civilization of the ancient world. Roman leaders imposed a single system of government upon the people of their vast realm, establishing first a republic (509 B.C.) and then an empire (31 B.C.).

The leaders of the Roman Republic were not particularly power-hungry and had no strong desires to conquer lands. Yet they found themselves in a long series of wars, resulting in victories and acquisition of new territory. Internal governing problems and the difficulty of defending its vast territory led to the demise of the republic and the rise of the Roman Empire. When Caesar Augustus became the first Roman emperor in about 30 B.C., the Romans began to enjoy a period of peace and prosperity, a period known as the *Pax Romana*.

It was during this period of the Roman Empire that Jesus Christ was born, ministered in Palestine, died, rose, and commissioned His disciples to evangelize the world. Christianity, which was to become the primary religion of Western society, began to spread its influence worldwide during the days of the Roman Empire.

After the fall of the Roman Empire in the West, the people of Europe sought to establish stability in social life and government. Christianity played the key role in meeting that need. As a result, the Christian faith spread rapidly throughout the old Roman Empire. Defective forms of Christianity also spread under the influence of the Coptic Church in North Africa and of Greek Orthodoxy in the Near East. The rise of Islam, however, was a challenge to their corruption of the gospel. Numerous clashes, including the Crusades in the Holy Land, resulted between the forces of Islam and Christianity.

Renaissance Humanism Versus the Reformation

During the fifteenth and sixteenth centuries, Europe experienced changes which made it into a society prepared for global exploration. The impact of the Reformation changed European society so much that the kind of culture that developed in the West is frequently referred to as *"modern"* society. There the quality of cultural development became much different from the traditional agricultural life elsewhere. Further, the cultural results of the Reformation in the area of science and technology gave the Europeans an advantage over other cultures by providing them with superior economic, technical, military, and political power. The Europeans became the world leaders in the modern era. The Western rise to **global hegemony** began with the Reformation, and its cultural results were spread through voyages of discovery. The Reformation played the leading part in causing the development of Western Europe to differ from that of other cultures. But there was another force at work—the rebirth of pre-Christian paganism, i.e., the Renaissance.

The Renaissance. The term *Renaissance* refers to the period from c. 1350 to c. 1650 in European history, when there was a renewed interest in the ancient pagan Greek and Roman classics and a shift in emphasis to the power of human achievement. Man became the measure of all things. The Renaissance began in Italy, where Roman Catholicism was centered. There such leading families as the Sforza of Milan and the Médici of Florence, and a series of popes such as Nicholas V, Pius II, Julius II, and Leo X patronized writers and artists who sought out ancient pagan ideas. The Italian Renaissance declined after 1550, largely due to the impact of the Reformation, but many of the values and ideas of humanism eventually spread into other parts of Europe among those who sought to destroy the influence of the gospel.

Renaissance humanism, with its emphasis on classical Greco-Roman culture, gave rise to the development of state absolutism. As humanistic philosophies replaced the Christian theology of earlier times as the source of true knowledge, the dream of developing a golden age through human reason and planning became a key element of apostate Western thought.

The Reformation. But God in his mercy counteracted the paganism of the Renaissance by bringing the *Protestant Reformation*. While some of the Protestants borrowed from the Renaissance an emphasis on careful analysis and a return to the original sources in pursuit of knowledge, they returned to the original sources of Christianity; the Hebrew Old Testament and the Greek New Testament. As a result the Reformation turned Renaissance secularism upside down by viewing all life activities as callings from God. In fact, the secularism of the Renaissance popes was a key factor behind the demands for reform. The tension between Renaissance humanism and the spirit of Reformation may perhaps be seen as a war between civil secularism and statism, on one hand, and the advancement of the Kingdom of God on the earth, on the other.

In 1517, a German monk and professor of theology, **Martin Luther**, began to criticize certain Roman Catholic church practices. He had been trained under the influence of the Christian Renaissance which stressed the study of the Bible as foundational to education. At first, most of his statements were rather mild, although he did state that the Bible rather than the church was the ultimate authority in religious matters. Then Luther discovered in the Bible the doctrine of **justification by faith**; that is, a person is made right with God through reliance on the atoning work of Jesus Christ and not through good deeds or the keeping of religious ceremonies. Although the German people responded enthusiastically to his teaching, in 1521 he was declared an outlaw and excommunicated from the church. In the years that followed, much of Western Europe was won over to the Protestant faith.

The Reformed Faith. The new movement did not center exclusively around Luther. And because Luther's successor, Melanchthon, made many compromises with the Roman Catholic church, the leadership of the Protestant cause shifted from Lutheran lands to those under the guidance of the followers of **John Calvin** (1509–1564). They were called **Calvinists** or Reformed. Calvin and his fellow laborers **William Farel** (1489–1565), **Theodore Beza** (1519–1605), **Pierre Viret** (1511–1571), **John Knox** (1513–1572), **Guido de Brès** (1522–1567), **Caspar Olevianus** (1536–1587), **Heinrich Bullinger** (1504–1575), **Peter Martyr Vermigli** (1499–1562) emphasized the absolute sovereignty of God and His word over all of life and thought. They taught that man's chief aim was to bring glory to God in every endeavor.

The Calvinistic understanding of the world as created and governed in every detail by God contributed much to the rise of modern science.

Europeans inherited from the Reformation a desire for a serious pursuit of truth and knowledge—not only in the area of salvation, but also in every area of society and culture. For them, all things existed for the glory of God.

Calvin believed it was the duty of the state to encourage and protect the church and it was the duty of the church to proclaim divine truth to society. These two institutions, the state and the church, were not to usurp each other's roles; however, Calvin helped to create a governmental system in Geneva, Switzerland, designed to demonstrate how the law of God could serve as the basis for civil order. Genevan leaders, against Calvin's views, entwined church and state affairs, resulting in what critics say was harsh treatment by the civil authorities for essentially religious offenses.

Calvin's ideas, known as **Calvinism**, spread to France, Switzerland, Germany, Hungary, the Netherlands, England, and Scotland. As espoused by the **Puritans**, these beliefs eventually became central to the construction of colonial American society and culture. Because America was settled in this period by people from these backgrounds, the influence of Calvinism on American culture can hardly be overstated.

The Calvinists encouraged the people to reject papal and state absolutism, appealing rather to God's sovereignty as absolute. The law of God was, therefore, considered king, not the state. This led to the rise of constitutional republics in Calvinistic countries. In many instances, the traditional powers of Europe were challenged in their claim of absolute sovereignty by these faithful Christians.

Rise of Dynastic States. By the time of the Reformation European governments had come under the power of monarchies. In the Middle Ages,

Europe had become divided into numerous fortified manors, each trying desperately to survive in a world of violence. The **feudal system** basically consisted of small territories (fiefs) ruled by nobles (vassals) under grant from a king. The local noble, in return, pledged loyalty to the king and supported him with an army of knights. The fief was maintained by serfs, or peasants, who earned their meager living and protection by working the fief under a kind of indentured servitude to the noble.

By marriage, by inheritance, and by constant conquest, the kings increased their holdings, thus depriving the feudal nobles of much of their authority, and causing scattered territories to combine to form stronger nations. The monarchs of these various lands became closely identified with the dynastic states they ruled.

The two greatest powers in the sixteenth century, Spain and the Holy Roman Empire (Germany), were united early in the century in the person of the Hapsburg heir, Charles V. The **Holy Roman Empire** consisted of more than 300 independent states in central and northern Europe, which were mostly German governments made up of feudal principalities, ecclesiastical states, and free cities. Unlike other European monarchies, the imperial crown was not hereditary, but elective. In addition to an emperor, another unifying element was an assembly, called a **diet**, made up of delegates from the various political units. However, the decisions of the Diet were not binding upon all the states.

During the later Middle Ages, the **Hapsburg family** established itself as the leading German dynasty and in 1519 Charles V became the emperor. As a result of some important marriage alliances, Charles inherited vast holdings in Austria, Germany, the Netherlands, and Spain. He became the most important leader in Europe

since Charlemagne (Charles the Great), the great Christian warrior king of the Franks (A.D. 742-814). It was Charles V who eventually declared Luther an outlaw, as he feared religious division might jeopardize the unity of the Holy Roman Empire, especially in light of the fact that Muslims were again at Europe's door.

The commercial wealth of the Netherlands and the riches flowing to Spain from the New World helped to finance Hapsburg power. Because Hapsburg possessions surrounded France, a long series of wars followed. The religious differences resulting from the growth of Lutheranism in Germany also contributed to the wars. Discouraged with his many problems, Charles turned over his Spanish possessions to his son Philip II and surrendered the Holy Roman Empire to his brother Ferdinand. He formally abdicated his throne in 1558. This action permanently separated Spain from the rest of the Empire under two different branches of the Hapsburg family.

In spite of the presence of many minority groups, by 1500 France was the most centralized of all the European monarchies. Her kings had extended their control over many feudal holdings and had increased the revenues of the crown. By 1453, the French had defeated the English in the **Hundred Years' War**, and a strong spirit of nationalism prevailed. At this time, Italy, although still wealthy, was in decline. Throughout the fifteenth century, its numerous city-states had been constantly at war with one another. This situation was encouraged by Spain, France, and Austria because they wanted to control the peninsula. In 1494, France began a half century of war to extend control over Italy. The French king, Francis I, determined that his country should not be controlled by the Hapsburgs and looked on the conflict as a way to counter that threat.

England, although not as large as France, was an influential state because it was quite well organized. The modern era came to England when Henry VII took the throne (1485) and founded the Tudor Dynasty. The rulers of England, aided by the middle class townspeople, gained control over the feudal barons. Henry reorganized the government, worked closely with Parliament, rebuilt the financial resources of the crown, and promoted foreign trade. He also gained respect among the continental powers by marrying his son to Catherine of Aragon, daughter of Ferdinand and Isabella of Spain. When Henry VIII came to the throne in 1509, he inherited a strong royal government. The Tudor monarchs tried to avoid large-scale continental wars. They attempted to maintain the "balance of power" in Europe by changing their alliances from one side to the other, depending on whether the Hapsburgs or the French were weaker at the moment.

Other major areas of Europe included Scandinavia and the states of Eastern Europe. The Scandinavians, during the fifteenth century, were ruled primarily by two monarchs, the king of Sweden and the king of Denmark. Various alliances and wars transpired until Sweden emerged as a major European power under the Vasa Dynasty. The Swedish empire extended far into Russia. Scandinavia became Lutheran and, with strong merchant classes, developed modern royal governments.

Eastern Europe was partially occupied by the Ottoman Turks at the dawn of the modern era. The most important independent state in the area was Poland. After overcoming the eastward drive of the Germans in the fifteenth century, the Poles expanded their rule over a vast region extending from the Baltic Sea to the Black Sea. An elected monarchy and an independent nobility kept the Poles from forming a strong nation-state. Poland was destroyed by weak government; by foreign enemies such as the Germans, Swedes, Turks, and Russians; and by the lack of natural defensible boundaries. The other major state in the east, Russia, did not become a factor in European politics until the late seventeenth century.

Islamic Culture

In the early sixteenth century, the lands from Morocco in the west to Indonesia in the east encompassed the Islamic culture and society. This overland growth was rivaled only by the European expansion by sea. The area was controlled by three dominant groups—the Ottoman Turks, rulers of the Middle East and North Africa, and conquerors of much of eastern Europe; the Mogul of India, who advanced southward; and the Safavids, who held Persia. Other areas of Africa and Asia also fell to Islam during the era of Western expansion.

This expansion also led to a rash of new converts, some of whom were coerced by sword into accepting the Muslim faith. Others were converted through contact with Islamic traders and preachers. Many Muslims, especially merchants, married local women who were persuaded to embrace the Islamic religion. Muslim schools were then started to educate their children. Often non-Muslims attended these schools, later converting to the faith.

Ottoman Empire. The Ottoman Empire reached its height after conquering Constantinople in 1453. **Suleiman the Magnificent**, their greatest ruler, led the Turks across the Danube River to destroy the Hungarian state (1526). Three years later they laid siege to Vienna, but were defeated. Undaunted, they pushed on and captured Cyprus, Crete, and the Polish Ukraine. Approximately 50 million people of many religions, languages, and nationalities lived within their realm.

The Ottoman Empire's large, well-trained army made it a first-class military power. However, in the sixteenth and seventeenth centuries the Ottomans lagged behind in military technology. To man their artillery, they imported Western gunners.

When Suleiman died in 1566, the long era of Ottoman victories and expansion ended. The empire slipped into a period of decline, punctuated by brief times of recovery. The first great Ottoman defeat came at the Battle of Lepanto in 1571. There a combined Spanish-Venetian fleet demolished the Turkish navy.

Political disputes, corruption, economic decline, and nationalistic rivalry further reduced Turkish power. The old practice of executing all but one of the sultan's sons was abandoned, and the resulting intrigues produced weak and degenerate rulers. The lower levels of government eventually became corrupt, following the example of their leaders.

Safavid Empire. The Moguls controlled Persia (modern Iran) from 1258 until 1500. Then Ismail I, a Muslim, set up the Safavid Dynasty. He spent his 24-year reign uniting Persia religiously and politically. The secret of his success lay in the religious zeal of his soldiers, dedicated Shiite Muslims.

Islam had divided into many sects, but they all descended from two main groups. One was the **Shiites**, who believed that Muhammad's authority passed down only through his son-in-law, Ali. The other was the **Sunnis**, who recognized the authority of all of the first four caliphs and their successors. The Ottoman Empire was part of the Sunni group. However, the Persians adopted Shiite doctrine, which gave the country a sense of unity. In time, a violent quarrel between the two factions of Islam led to a series of Ottoman-Persian Wars.

The Safavid Empire reached its height during the reign of **Shah Abbas I**. He modernized the army and increased contacts with other countries. During the sixteenth century, some European rulers asked for Persian help against the Turks. While Francis I of France gained Turkish cooperation, the Holy Roman Emperor, **Charles V**, urged the Persians to attack the Turks. Eventually, the same forces of decline at work in the Ottoman Empire led to Persia's ruin.

Mogul Empire. Two remarkable leaders, Babur and Akbar, founded the third great Islamic empire. Muslims had invaded India in the eighth and eleventh centuries. These invaders set up several Islamic kingdoms in northern India, but the south remained a varied mix of Hindu states. Even in the north, most people still followed the Hindu religion. The invaders formed such a tiny minority that they had little effect on the overall culture of India.

In 1500 **Babur** (the Tiger), a direct descendant of the great Turkish conqueror Tamerlane, moved into India. With artillery and firearms supplied by the Ottomans, his force of 12,000 men defeated an Indian army of 100,000. Babur's empire, called the Mogul, grew rapidly. It covered the most territory during a period ruled by Babur's grandson, **Akbar**, who led the empire from 1556 to 1605.

Akbar had an amazing range of interests—art, music, sports (he liked polo), and mechanical things. But religion and philosophy fascinated him most. He allowed freedom of worship because he realized that religious conflicts would weaken his empire. Though a Muslim, he believed that every religion had some truth. He built a Hall of Worship for religious discussion. Also he made up a new religion which he felt included the best features of the major faiths. Vainly he tried to convert Hindus and Muslims to his new faith and thus forge a united India.

Mogul architecture stands as one of the empire's greatest achievements. Tombs, palaces, mosques, and forts blended several elements. Intricate mosaics adorned floors, walls, and ceilings. Cupolas clung to sides of the buildings, which were crowned with bulging domes. Vaulted gateways and doorways led from one part to another. Formal gardens featured parks and fountains. The **Taj Mahal** remains the finest example of Mogul art.

However, the empire began to falter in the middle 1600s. **Shah Jahan** promoted the Muslim faith by persecuting Hindus and Christians. The decline set in even more rapidly after Shah Jahan's reign.

Confucian Culture

Chinese and Islamic societies were somewhat alike. Philosophically, both looked inward rather than out to the rest of the world, and both depended mainly on agriculture until the modern era. Change did not come easily to either. But in the years following Confucius, East Asia was much more united than the Islamic world. Confucianism in China influenced military, cultural, and political affairs.

Chinese society has maintained a feeling of cohesiveness for thousands of years. One of the main reasons for the survival and continuity of Chinese culture was its geographical isolation from other great civilizations. During much of its history, deserts, mountains, and oceans cut China off from contact with the Middle East and Europe. Consequently, the Chinese developed their culture with fewer interruptions.

But it is Confucianism, more than anything else that accounts for the lasting unity of Chinese civilization. This outlook came from the teachings of **Confucius**, who lived from around 551 to 479 B.C. during the **Chou Dynasty** (1027-256 B.C.), and his disciples. Confucianism did not begin as a religion, but rather as a political and social philosophy concerned mainly with good government.

Asked by a disciple what the functions of government should be, Confucius answered—to provide food, to maintain an army, and to have people's confidence. To achieve these goals, government should be in the hands of the most capable, regardless of social class, he taught. Ability resulted from character, which was shaped by education. All were to have the chance to learn. But in practice, only the wealthy could afford the years of study and preparation. To gain a government post, a person had to pass a difficult examination on the Confucian classics.

As a result of this system, the Chinese people developed an exaggerated respect for the past. They began to feel that their ancient scholars had had all wisdom and had explained everything bearing on the present and future. Constantly looking backward, the Chinese had no desire to keep up with progressive Western Europe.

A second great philosopher-leader who arose during the Chou Dynasty was **Lao-tze**, also known as the "Old Master." His teachings, called **Taoism**, emphasized contemplation on the *yin* and the *yang*, the opposing and balancing factors in all of life.

Certain patterns emerged during China's long history. Generally, each new dynasty, an aristocratic family, began by ruling the country well, bringing a time of peace and prosperity. It encouraged cultural life and protected the frontier from nomads. Almost without fail, however, corrupt rulers and rivalry among the leading groups would weaken the dynasty. Eventually corruption and inefficiency would lead to civil revolts. Often after nomadic invasions had occurred, the old dynasty would be replaced by a new one.

Ming Dynasty. The last two dynasties, the Ming (A.D. 1368–1644) and the Manchu or Ch'ing (1644–1912), controlled China during the era of Western expansion. The Ming dynasty forced the Mongols out of China and brought back the Confucian system, which the Mongols had set aside. However, Ming rulers were the cruelest of masters. Palace eunuchs, who depended completely on the emperor's favor, wielded great power. People who disobeyed the emperor received harsh punishments.

During the previous Mongol era, the Chinese disliked and suspected anything foreign. However, during the Ming period, Chinese fleets did sail as far as the east coast of Africa. Although they brought back items of interest and knowledge of strange lands, they were eventually forbidden to go beyond coastal waters because they did not contribute to China's wealth. China shut itself off from the world at about the same time European influence began to spread across the globe.

Ch'ing Dynasty. The Ming Dynasty slowly lost control of the land during the seventeenth century. In 1621, barbarians from the Manchurian forests and steppes began raiding across Chinese borders. While the Ming Dynasty decayed, the Manchus set up a strong confederacy. At first

they captured Chinese settlements in southern Manchuria, then in 1644, they moved deep into the empire and seized Peking. By 1683, the Manchus ruled all China, and the land returned to peace, order, and prosperity.

The Manchus allowed the Chinese to run civic affairs but kept the military in their own hands. Field units of the army were stationed at strategic places. China, during early modern times, was orderly and stable. The ancient institutions and the agricultural way of life worked smoothly under Manchu control. Such order might seem ideal, but, in fact, it was not.

During these years, Europe experienced the Renaissance, the Reformation, the Commercial and Industrial Revolutions (or more precisely "Reformations"), and the growth of national states which preceded to extend their control over the globe.

The Chinese dealt with all foreigners the way they had handled nomads on their northern and western boundaries. Russians were moving into Siberia and the steppe lands of central and eastern Asia. After a few conflicts with the Chinese, the Russians came to terms with them. Each would stay out of the other's territory, and conditions were laid down for trade between Siberia and Peking.

Pirates and European explorers also seriously threatened China's coasts. By trading with the European merchants, both the Ming and Manchus played them off against the pirates. The Portuguese, and later the Dutch and English, bought Chinese goods—silks, wood carvings, lacquerware, and porcelain—in return for spices from the East Indies and India. The Europeans took the role of middlemen in the Asian trade, and by the nineteenth century, England controlled trade with China.

Japan. Because it borrowed many aspects of Chinese culture, Japan is considered a part of Confucian civilization. During early modern times, the country went through a period of transition. In its system of feudalism, the **shogun** (military commander-in-chief) held the highest power. However, great lords (the **daimyo**) ruled their own territories. They were under the shogun's authority, yet had considerable independence—too much independence in the view of shoguns who wanted to bring the daimyo completely under their power and unite Japan.

Ieyasu Tokugawa, who became shogun in 1603, achieved this goal. His dynasty absorbed Japan's feudal institutions into the administration. Actually, Japan had a dual system of government. The *emperor* had the status of a divine rule. The *shoguns* claimed that they were carrying out his will. By this, they made their position more secure. However, the emperor exercised no political power and depended on the shogun, the real power in the country, for financial support.

The Europeans posed the main problem for the Tokugawa Dynasty in the seventeenth century. Western traders had come in large numbers to the islands. The Portuguese brought firearms, which played a role in the feudal wars and encouraged the building of huge stone castles.

The growth of Roman Catholicism created a greater headache for the Tokugawa. Francis Xavier, the great Jesuit proselytizer at the time, had arrived in 1549. Soon he had won 2,000 converts, and more proselytizers followed him. By the early seventeenth century, at least 300,000 Japanese were Roman Catholics, a larger percentage of the total population than today.

Eventually the Tokugawa began a ruthless persecution of Roman Catholics. Japan's story of religious persecution and martyrdom rivaled anything taking place in Europe's religious wars at that time. In 1637, a peasant revolt against high taxes developed into a sizable rebellion. The shogun wiped out the Roman Catholic communities in southern Japan and all but obliterated the influence of this religion.

The Tokugawa cut off contact with the West, allowing only one Dutch ship per year to come to Nagasaki with trade goods and news of the outside world. Japanese citizens were forbidden to leave the country and foreigners were barred from entering. Behind closed doors, the Tokugawa gave Japan a long period of peace and a class-structured society where the warrior had a place of great honor.

Japan made progress economically in spite of its isolation. Merchants grew wealthy as commerce and agriculture prospered. Cities grew—Edo (today known as Tokyo) had a million people in the eighteenth century—and a thriving culture developed as a result. The Kabuki—a realistic drama performed by men in formalized pantomime, dance, and song—delighted the middle and lower classes.

Like the Chinese, the Japanese did not make changes easily. Feudalism and two centuries of isolation kept the country in a backward state. However, it did have a custom of borrowing from the Chinese, and when the world forced Japan to open its doors in the nineteenth century, it was easier for Japan to adapt to the new order than China.

African Cultures

A Variety of Cultures. Ancient African society first developed in three regions of the continent: the Nile River Valley, North Africa, and the African interior. Along the Nile, the great cultures of Egypt and Kush (also known as Nubia; today's Sudan) developed, possibly by direct descendants of Noah. Settlement of the Nile Valley began as early as 3800 B.C.

Egyptian culture had its beginning in about 3000 B.C., when early wanderers, descendants of Ham, Noah's son, came across the Red Sea and were attracted by the rich, fertile Nile Valley. As people settled in the area, cities formed and the river served as a route of transportation. The rulers of Egypt, known as *pharaohs*, held absolute power and were worshipped as deities. Egyptian civilization covered three periods, known as the Old Kingdom (3000–2100 B.C.), the Middle Kingdom (2100–1545 B.C.), and the New Kingdom (1545–1200 B.C.)

The kingdom of Kush was a thriving civilization by 2000 B.C. When Egypt took over the kingdom of Kush to the south in about 1500 B.C., the Egyptians encouraged the Kushites to live in cities, and gradually the old nomadic way of life died out. Kush became the avenue by which Egyptian culture was spread into the African interior, with which Kush had long traded. Kush conquered Egypt in 725 B.C., after Egypt had gone into decline. But in a short time, both Egypt and Kush were taken by the Assyrians.

The Kingdom of Kush came to an end about 300 A.D., when it was conquered by the army of Axum, a power in the area of modern Ethiopia that had been settled by people migrating across the Red Sea in about 1000 B.C. In the fourth century A.D., Axum was Christianized but this Christian nation was isolated when Islam spread across North Africa.

The Nok culture developed in West Africa about 800 B.C. This culture was noted for its art. The Nok people eventually blended in with other peoples of the area, and by A.D. 400 they became part of the great trading empire of Ghana.

In the interior, various cultures and numerous languages developed among the Negroid, Nilo-Sudanic, Bantu, Pygmy, and Hottentot peoples. Much of the interior remained a mystery until Europeans began to explore there in the 1700s.

By the fifteenth century A.D., Africa was a land of great variety. Islamic culture dominated the northern part around the Mediterranean Sea. Large states and even empires—Ghana, Mali, and Songhai—rose one after another in the savanna (an area of grassland and bushes) south of the Sahara Desert. Muslims ruled these wealthy and powerful states, mixing their culture with that of black Africa. Their merchants coaxed heavily laden camels across the desert in a busy trade with the north.

The East African coast traded with other lands around the Indian Ocean. Ships sailed regularly from the coastal towns to Persia and India. Goods came from a far away as Malaya, Indonesia, and even China. A large number of city-states controlled this commerce and their own small domains. Through the influence of Arab traders, the people of the towns had adopted Islam. Nevertheless, these were African settlements, not Arab colonies.

A culture and language known as **Swahili** developed in the eastern part of the continent. This term applies to both the coastal peoples and their language. Mainly African, but with a large number of Arabic words, Swahili first came into use as the "trade language" along the coast. In the African interior, with no close links to either the Mediterranean or the Indian Ocean, cultures began to form. Some did trade a great deal with the Islamic states, such as the gold miners in the West African forest. Many other rulers, however, built their states on the payment of tribute (a type of tax) rather than on trade. The most important of these were the Rwanda, the Kongo, and the Benin empires.

Lineages. African politics became increasingly complex. As populations increased and land became scarce, states worked out new and better ways to make decisions and use power. This process was extremely slow, and historians are not exactly sure how it took place. Most believe it came out of the lineage or clan systems that were (and still are) a common feature of African society.

Although Islam made inroads into the Sudan, North Africa, and East Africa, the vast majority of Africans followed their own pagan and animistic religions. These religions helped a king retain his power. When a leader failed or got into trouble, people thought he had lost touch with the divine powers. That made it easier to replace him. The only exceptions to this fifteenth century religious pattern were some pockets of Christianity in the upper Nile and Ethiopia.

Opening of the Oceans. The most profound changes came to Africa when Europeans began arriving by sea. Eager for West African gold, Portuguese sailors tried to bypass Songhai Kingdom middlemen. By 1482, they made contact with a trading post name Elmina (the Mine). The Portuguese eventually rounded southern Africa and seized control of the Indian Ocean.

Several things resulted. As the Atlantic became a new highway for commerce, the Mediterranean lost importance. Now the trade which had sent caravans plodding across the Sahara went to the fast-sailing ships. The economy of states in the West Sudan, especially the Songhai, depended on the Sahara trade. These empires had once had a level of civilization equal to that of Europe.

Scholars from many parts of the Arab world had come to study in their libraries and schools. But the loss of the Sahara trade so weakened Songhai Berbers that they fell to a Moroccan army in 1591. Other enemy invasions followed, and, coupled with isolation, they ended the era of great empires in West Africa.

The Slave Trade. The trade in human lives forms what many consider to be a great blot on the pages of history. Slavery was well established before the first days of recorded history in Mesopotamia and Egypt. It has been a characteristic of cultures throughout the world and throughout time, including among ancient African peoples.

As to European slave trading, the Portuguese took the first African slaves in 1440 and controlled the trade for the next 150 years. Then the Dutch took over, followed by Britain and France in the late 1600s. The first African slaves went to Portugal and islands off the African coast, but soon most were shipped to America. Slaves from the east coast became household servants in the Muslim lands of Asia.

Slavery existed in Africa just as it did in other parts of the world. African slavery resembled European serfdom. Slaves performed tasks like child care, housework, preparation of meals, and gardening. Tribal law and custom protected the rights of slaves to marry and raise children, to gain their freedom, and to improve their position. Although the first slaves used by the Portuguese had many of these same rights, before long a human slave came to be viewed as a piece of property to be bought and sold at will. He lost all rights—to have a family, own property, receive fair treatment, or for that matter, even to live.

The slave trade did contribute to the growth of the states in West Africa, such as Oyo, Dahomey, and the Ashanti nation. But they practiced vio-

lence against their neighbors and their own people. Other states such as the Kongo were weakened or ruined by slave-raiding. A few like Benin, probably the most powerful of the West African forest states, were able to regulate both the Europeans and the extent of slaving.

It should be stressed that the arrival of the Europeans in Africa did not damage the native cultures as extensively as it did in America, Australia, and the Pacific islands. The Africans traded with Europeans on African terms. They restricted the foreigners to coastal trading posts, with some exception in the south. Since whites suffered a death rate of 50 percent from tropical diseases, they dealt with Africans from a position of weakness.

Even with Europeans coming and going, life in much of Africa went on as it had before. Thus, Western visitors to Benin in the seventeenth century were deeply impressed with the size and wealth of its capital city. States rose and fell in the Sudan, and the world took no notice.

When the influence of Islam waned, a number of prophets appeared to call the rulers back to the faith. In what is now Nigeria, the Fulani people were the sparkplug for a great Muslim revival which spread throughout central and western Sudan. They launched a series of "holy wars" and set up Islamic states in the area. The most famous of the leaders, **Usuman dan Fodio**, put together a program to purify worship, reform social practices, and renew Islamic culture.

Africans had been able to resist European control. However, changes sweeping the West would eventually make it possible to break through barriers of climate, geography, and political power. Europeans would one day conquer and subdivide the continent.

North and South American Indian Cultures

Because most of the inhabitants of the Western Hemisphere had arrived from Asia by way of the Bering Sea long before Columbus landed on western shores, several different kinds of cultural patterns developed in the Americas. Some of the most prominent cultures were those of the Mayas, the Incas, the Aztecs, and the so-called "Indians" of North America.

North American Patterns. Cultural characteristics of the Indians in North America reflected the geographical area in which they lived. Foods ranged from the fish, seals, and deer of the Northwest to the caribou of the Far North to corn, squash, and beans in other places. Houses were made of wood or skins, dug out of a cliff, or partially submerged below the ground.

There were no large-scale civilizations featuring cities with complex governments, but different tribes had their own chiefs and particular social-class divisions. Because many tribes were nomadic, few lasting monuments remain. Some Indians worshiped particular gods or spirits, including Manitou, the great spirit of nature who had remade the world from mud after a flood. There were also some elaborate religious rituals in the Southwest. Eventually a sign language had to be developed because so many different languages were spoken in the plains area.

Mayas. Much of the early history of the Mayas of Central America is still unknown because their hieroglyphic writing has not yet been deciphered. Archaeological discoveries have provided information about their impressive stone architecture and their scientific advancement. It is known that they had an accurate calendar and a mathematical system, that their religion encouraged them to capture victims as prisoners of war for human sacrifices, and that their agriculture included the cultivation of maize as an important food crop.

Eventually, a confederation of three cities, the **League of Mayapan**, provided stability during the thirteenth to the fifteenth centuries. In 1441, a revolt by the Xiu people caused the decline of the league. Cities were abandoned, weakening the society before the Spaniards arrived.

Incas. The Incas of Peru began to establish their power in the Cuzco Valley about the year A.D. 1000. Their highly organized system took control of the surrounding areas, ultimately including Ecuador. Their despotic state viewed every thing as belonging to the emperor, who was responsible for the needs of the citizens.

Well-constructed public works included roads, some of which still exist. Buildings and roads were built of carefully measured blocks which needed no mortar to hold them together. The Incas had no written records, but they made intricate models of proposed constructions or of their surveys of newly conquered territories.

Important leaders of the fifteenth century were **Pachacuti** and his son **Topa Inca**, who continued great conquests. The succeeding emperor, **Huayna Capac**, died in 1525 of smallpox brought by the Europeans. A civil war between two contenders for the throne followed, but the winner was executed by the Spanish explorer **Francisco Pizarro** in 1539. Many warriors, including the emperor, had been killed in the war which allowed the Spanish to overcome the Incas easily. Without the emperor, the social system lacked a strong focus to keep the society functioning.

Aztecs. The Aztecs of Mexico and Yucatan were somewhat nomadic until the founding of their capital city Tenochtitlán around 1325. From there they conquered of surrounding areas, and eventually 38 provinces sent regular tribute. The Aztecs developed a relatively centralized government but left some power in the provinces they conquered. The explorer **Hernando Cortez** ruled through Montezuma II, who was killed in 1520. Direct Spanish control began after the death of the last emperor **Cuauhtémoc** in 1525.

Aztec culture included craftsmen who made jewelry and carved designs on public monuments and merchants who traveled to distant cities. Warriors were especially honored as they could provide the prisoners of war needed to supply the human hearts for sacrifice to the Aztec god.

For your consideration

Questions

1. Discuss how biblical values affected the development of Western civilization (see foreword).

2. Why is it important to study history (see foreword)?

3. What is a civilization? How do the terms *culture* and *civilization* relate to each other?

4. What was Confucius' view of government and good social order?

5. How did Islam spread? Name some factors leading to the decline of Islamic empires.

Word List

caliph	hegemony
city-state	imperial
civilization	lineage
Confucianism	modern era
cosmopolitan	Renaissance
culture	republic
dynasty	shogun
feudalism	The Reformation

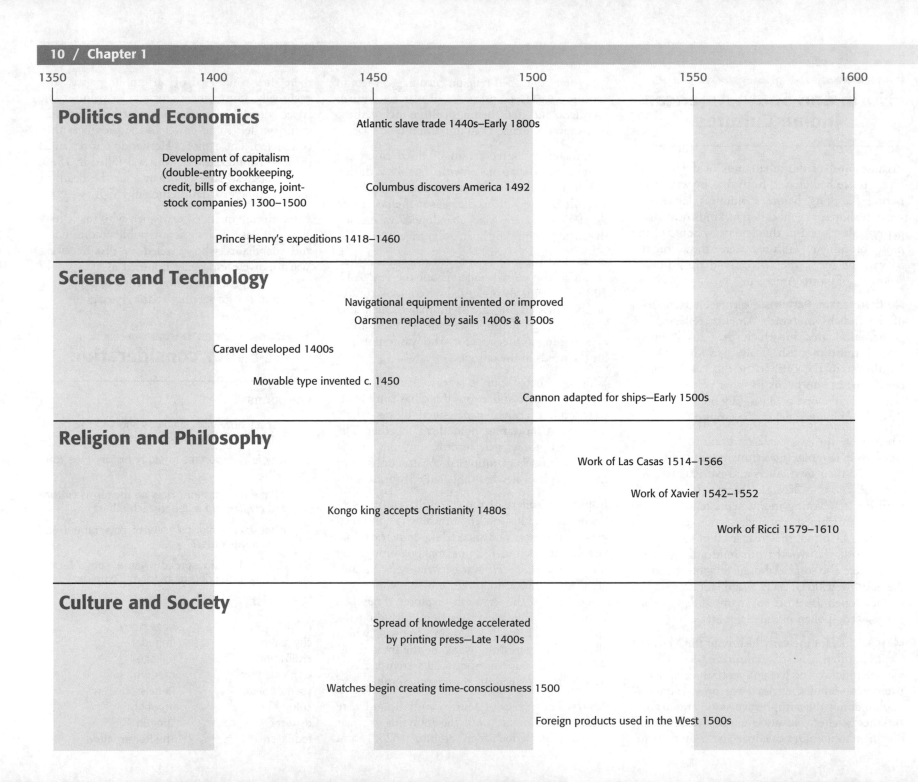

1350 1400 1450 1500 1550 1600

Politics and Economics

Atlantic slave trade 1440s–Early 1800s

Development of capitalism
(double-entry bookkeeping,
credit, bills of exchange, joint-
stock companies) 1300–1500

Columbus discovers America 1492

Prince Henry's expeditions 1418–1460

Science and Technology

Navigational equipment invented or improved
Oarsmen replaced by sails 1400s & 1500s

Caravel developed 1400s

Movable type invented c. 1450

Cannon adapted for ships—Early 1500s

Religion and Philosophy

Work of Las Casas 1514–1566

Work of Xavier 1542–1552

Kongo king accepts Christianity 1480s

Work of Ricci 1579–1610

Culture and Society

Spread of knowledge accelerated
by printing press—Late 1400s

Watches begin creating time-consciousness 1500

Foreign products used in the West 1500s

European Exploration and its Motives

About 600 years ago, people from the continent of Europe began to move out to the rest of the world. They already knew that other continents existed, but they knew very few specific details. Travelers who had visited in distant lands brought back fascinating stories, exotic spices, and other products. Current technological advances made sea travel possible for traders wanting to acquire these goods faster and more easily than by land routes.

Some Europeans, from Spain and France, sought to spread Roman Catholic beliefs. Many went as proselytizing priests to bring pagan peoples into submission to Catholic traditions.

Still others were motivated by the possibility of great wealth, since trade and exploration could be very profitable. New economic arrangements in different parts of Europe caused improved financing of long-distance trade. As exploration and conquest continued, large amounts of gold were brought back from the New World.

This map, issued in the 1600s, shows the American continents as they were known at the time. Geographers thought that Australia lay just south of Latin America and stretched across the earth's southern part.

New Technology

In order to launch what we now call the Age of Exploration, we need to understand the development of Western **technology**. *Technology* is the science of applying knowledge to practical purposes. Several kinds of inventions affected social and intellectual life. More seaworthy vessels and reliable navigational instruments made long ocean voyages possible. Without these, East Asia and the Western Hemisphere would have been beyond reach.

All through the Middle Ages, people found ways to improve their tools and methods of doing

A peece mounted at 6. points or 72. minutes.

This early cannon is being raised to its maximum elevation. The gunner's quadrant is being used to determine the correct elevation for the desired range.

work. They invented the crank, the wheelbarrow, and the canal lock. A major breakthrough came with inventions that are now taken for granted. Windmills and watermills began to take over jobs like cutting wood, grinding grain, and draining swamps and mines. Also in this period came the nailed horseshoe and the **tandem** harness. With its hoofs now protected from breaking, the horse replaced slow-moving oxen for pulling plows and heavy loads. The tandem harness hitched pairs of horses, one behind the other, to a load. Animals pulled more effectively this way. Another invention, the heavy plow, made farming more efficient and cut down on the labor required. This tendency of Europeans to think of labor-saving devices helped shift the whole basis of their economy from human labor to machines.

Metals. During the Renaissance, Europe also made notable improvements in mining and metallurgy. By the fourteenth century, surface ores were exhausted, and it became necessary to dig shafts deep into the ground. Because under-

ground shafts often filled up with water, mine operators had to find some way to drain them. The drainage designs and machines that were developed brought a mining boom to central Europe. By 1525, more than 100,000 workers were employed by the mining industry in the Holy Roman Empire. People worked out better ways to smelt, cast, roll, and forge metals. They used water power to make metals and published illustrated books which aided the miners in this work. These changes greatly increased the amount of metal in Europe.

Clocks. Some of the new Renaissance technology caused dramatic changes in Europe's life-style. Take clocks, for example. Although people had used sundials and hourglasses to tell time for thousands of years, mechanical clocks did not become common in Europe until the fifteenth century. Installed in churches or city halls, these clocks struck on the hour or quarter hour, telling the townspeople the time of day or night. People began to regulate their lives by exact time rather than by dawn, noon, and sunset, which changed with the seasons. Because early mechanical clocks were driven by weights, they were too heavy to be moved. In about 1500, however, spring-driven watches were invented. These were much larger and heavier than modern pocket watches, and they gained or lost fifteen minutes a day, but they enabled each person who could afford to buy one to have his own timepiece. While early clocks did not immediately cause society to schedule everything precisely, they laid the groundwork for the unique time-conscious approach to our modern world.

Movable type. Even greater changes in the way people lived came with the invention of the printing press. As early as the sixth century, the Chinese had made prints by pressing linen paper against inked wooden blocks. It took centuries

Gunpowder and Guns

Just as guns enabled the West to conquer native peoples and dominate the world, these weapons hastened an enormous change in the West itself. The early discoverers of gunpowder seemed to sense its significance. When Roger Bacon first wrote down the formula for it, he used a code, so dangerous did he consider this substance. But the secret could not be kept. Someone invented the cannon. Historians do not agree on whom to credit for this development, but the first time these noisy, undependable weapons appeared in battle was in 1346 at Crécy, France.

After that, attackers pointed the great guns at castle walls, an act which helped bring the medieval way of life to an end. No longer safe within his castle, the noble had to join with other lords when he was threatened. The vast number of small kingdoms gave way to larger units, and these would later form nations. Since the serfs and villagers could no longer count on the lord's castle for protection, their ties to him weakened. Thus while guns and gunpowder changed the nature of warfare both on land and at sea, these weapons also helped change the structure of Western society.

All through history, people have used weapons to help them force their will upon others. As nations developed, they took up this practice on a larger scale. It is ironic that before nations made serious attempts to change this habit, a weapon powerful enough to destroy all life had to appear.

for this process to reach Europe, but by 1400 wood engravings and block-printed books were being produced. Each page had to be carved separately, which made books very expensive. Only the church or a few rich people could afford them.

About 1450, **Johann (John) Gutenberg** of Mainz, Germany, began to make individual

Printing in the 16th Century

Ship Building in the 16th Century

helped by those in another. New insights can also be communicated by the printed word.

The Protestant Reformation clearly showed the new power of the press to bring changes. Martin Luther's ideas spread very quickly through the printed page. Calling the printing press one of God's greatest gifts to mankind, Luther published something every two weeks.

Besides the works of Luther and other Reformers, people could also own a copy of the Bible for themselves. Gutenberg's first Bible was very large, but soon copies were smaller and more affordable. From this developed a great interest in having the Bible in the **vernacular**, or one's own language, instead of only in Latin, Greek, and Hebrew.

Navigation. As the Portuguese did more sailing, they began to modify their ships to cope with new conditions. During the fifteenth century, the Portuguese developed a sturdy ship that could sail down the west coast of Africa and then return to Europe. This was not easy because of the winds and tides. Combining features from Roman, Viking, and Arab ships, the Portuguese gave their *caravel* a long hull, or frame, and a stern-post rudder. Placing the rudder at the back made the ship easier to maneuver than other craft. The vessel had two types of sails, square and triangular, giving it unusual speed. By the sixteenth century, the Europeans were building larger *galleons* with bulging hulls to carry troops and cannons.

Besides these changes in the ships themselves, sailors could also use new instruments such as the *astrolabe* and the *quadrant*. These plotted a ship's position, direction, and speed. Accurate coastal maps called **portolani** were also drawn. Seamen had already charted the coast of the Mediterranean Sea on such maps. They noted exact compass bearings and careful details about landmarks,

metal letters instead of wood-block pages. Since these letters were **interchangeable** and could be used many times, the process was much cheaper. Also, large numbers of books could be printed. Society soon felt the impact of this invention.

By 1501, there were printing presses in 110 European towns and cities. Printing with movable type enabled new ideas, art forms, and information to travel rapidly throughout Europe. In the past, it often took centuries for a change to become widespread. With such limited communication, only a privileged few were able to enjoy the work of poets, artists, and philosophers. However, once printing became common, the pace of change and progress speeded up greatly.

Sharing new information and ideas with other people is one of the significant *streams of civilization*. Diagrams of inventions or instructions for new procedures can be spread more easily than the inventions or the instructors themselves. In this way, people in one part of the world can be

soundings, and harbors. The outstanding achievement of the Portuguese **mariners** who sailed under Prince Henry in the fifteenth century was their *portolan* of the west coast of Africa.

In order to gain control of Asia, the Europeans also needed good weapons. They used an invention of the Chinese—*gunpowder*. The Chinese had used gunpowder for firecrackers and for starting fires, not for weapons. The Byzantines borrowed it to make the "Greek Fire" used to defend Constantinople. During the thirteenth century, an English monk, **Roger Bacon**, carried on many experiments with gunpowder. By the fifteenth century, Europeans had designed cannons fired by gunpowder, but these were too heavy for ships. Then in the early sixteenth century, they made lighter cannons. The cannon balls from these could be effective at a range of 300 yards.

Cannons and the new ships built to carry them won the seas for Europe. Until the sixteenth century, most ships still used oarsmen and battering rams. In battle, commanders tried to ram the enemy ship and sink it or board it and fight hand to hand. Such slow, awkward, and risky methods still used in Asia were no match for the new technology of the Europeans.

The Missionary Motives of Catholicism

While considering the reasons Western explorers set out on their quest, one must not overlook religion, for it too played an important part. Many people knew that Christians were supposed to preach throughout the whole earth (Matthew 28:19-20). Some had specifically studied the Bible to see what it had to say about the rest of the world. Not only does the Bible teach *evangelization*, but, as Christian scholars, especially some of the Reformers, discovered anew, it also calls upon man to have general *dominion* over all creation—to discover it, explore and study it, use it for his benefit, and carefully husband, manage, steward, and replenish it (Genesis 1:27-28, 9:1-2,7).

Columbus and Prince Henry. The Italian-born, pre-Reformation mariner Christopher Columbus (1451–1506) was one explorer who sailed into new worlds partly because of a vision drawn from the Bible. He compiled verses from the Bible into his *Book of Prophecies*. It includes biblical teachings about the earth, the seas, undiscovered tribes, the spread of the Gospel, the second coming of Christ, and the nature of His Kingdom.

Columbus believed that the Kingdom of God would not come until all the lands of the earth had heard the Gospel. He felt that God had chosen him to discover the unreached tribes so that the Gospel could be preached to them. In order that he might complete this task, the Holy Spirit had given him special aid in understanding the Scriptures and the science of navigation. Later,

Christopher Columbus, 1451–1506

after he had discovered new lands, he wrote to Pope Alexander VI asking for priests and friars to help him teach the natives.

Prince Henry the Navigator of Portugal (1394–1460) had previously become involved in exploration because of his Christian faith. Entrusted with the defense of the Portuguese foothold on the North African coast, he was convinced of the need to **outflank** Islam. Stretching in a great crescent from the Russian Steppe to the Atlantic coast of Morocco, Muslim lands hemmed in and threatened Christian Europe.

However, Europeans believed that beyond Islam to the east and south were non-Islamic peoples, many of whom were Christians. If the Europeans could work their way around the Muslims and contact the African Christians, it would be possible to take the enemy from the rear in a new crusade. The only way to do that was to sail down the west coast of Africa.

The Legend of Prester John. Henry, like other Europeans, believed that the Eastern Christians were led by a great king, Prester John. The legend

of Prester (Priest) John probably began in the 12th century with some Asian Christian priest and king who was an enemy of the Muslims. Later, the story placed him in Ethiopia, which was ruled by a Coptic Christian. Some of this ruler's priests had chapels at Jerusalem, and his **envoys** occasionally came to Rome. Europeans were able in their thinking to transfer the king from central Asia to eastern Africa because both lands lay "somewhere toward the Indies: on the borders between myth and reality."

In the marvelous kingdom of Prester John one could find **unicorns**, giants, and men whose heads grew beneath their shoulders. In the midst of these wonders, the king lived in a fantastic castle surrounded by a moat of precious stones. His throne room contained a magic mirror in which he could see at will any part of the world. Dozens of lesser kings obeyed him. His army had millions of foot soldiers, hundreds of thousands of horsemen, and thousands of war elephants.

The descriptions of Prester John vary, but they have one central theme—he was extremely wealthy and powerful. Representatives of the Ethiopian emperor who reached the West encouraged this idea. As the Portuguese embarked on their voyages to the East, they wished to increase their knowledge, convert the heathen, and share in the riches of the Orient. But the main goal was to find Prester John and reunite broken Christendom in a great crusade to crush Islam.

Missionary motives. Most of the missionary zeal fueling early Western expansion came from the Spanish and Portuguese Roman Catholics. Columbus first sailed to the New World 25 years before the beginning of the Reformation. The Protestants were first busy in Europe, and later became involved in English colonies in North America. Beginning in the eighteenth century and then increasing dramatically in the nineteenth and twentieth centuries, many Protestant groups also became involved in worldwide missions.

Catholic missionary activity had to face many non-Christian religions. It should not be surprising, then, that Christianity and Islam clashed, since the latter religion instructs its adherents to conquer territory for its God, Allah. By way of contrast, followers of most Asian religions did not try to win converts. Confucianism does not include the teaching that it should be spread to other cultures. So a follower of that system would have had no religious motivation to explore the rest of the world. But the beliefs of Christianity gave Europeans a drive to contact other peoples.

Kongo Kingdom. One of the earliest European missionary efforts of this period took place in the African kingdom of Kongo. Portuguese seamen came upon this realm in the 1480s, baptized the ruler, and helped him in struggles with neighboring tribes. When his son **Afonso** became king in 1507, the new ruler established close relations with the king of Portugal and asked for technical aid.

A strong Catholic, Afonso renamed his capital São Salvador, which means "holy savior." He made Catholicism the state religion and based his royal authority on it. He asked for more missionaries but few actually came. Because of Portuguese slaving in his domains and meddling in local politics, he soon grew disgusted with the Europeans. Vainly he protested to the pope and Portuguese king. He may have been one of the first Africans to learn that not all Europeans followed the Christian principles which they supposedly believed.

After Afonso's death in 1545, Roman Catholicism slowly declined in Kongo. His successor at

The Indians' Protector

A priest named Bartolomé de Las Casas was the strongest defender of the rights of the native people of the New World. Horrified by Spanish atrocities, he began to speak out against the colonial system which gave large grants of land to settlers. The Indians who lived on the land became virtual slaves of the new owners. In 1514, Las Casas gave up his own land and set his Indians free.

Father de Las Casas also protested the Spaniards' use of military conquest to Christianize the Indians. Rather than forcing the native people to become Christians, the priest insisted that the settlers should live among them and set an example, using love, reason, and persuasion. Twice he gathered groups of settlers to try to put this idea into practice, but circumstances were against him. The first attempt failed completely. The second was more successful, lasting for twenty years.

In 1540, Las Casas carried his fight for reform to Spain where he endlessly petitioned for a change in the laws. One day he read to the court from a book he was writing. With shocked dismay, the nobles listened to stories of the cruelty of "Christian" settlers.

Las Casas told of one Indian ruler named Hatuey who heard that the Spaniards were coming. Glancing at a basket of gold and jewels near him, he said, "Behold, here is the god of the Christians. Let us perform Areytos (worshipful dances) before him and perhaps we shall please him, and he will command that they do us no harm."

The people did as Hatuey suggested, but the Spaniards captured them anyway and prepared to burn Hatuey alive at the stake. Before lighting the fire, the conquistadors allowed a monk to talk to the chieftain about his soul. The monk explained heaven and hell.

"Do the Spanish go to heaven," Hatuey asked.

"Some do."

"Then I want to go to hell," declared the chief. "I don't want to be with such cruel people."

Stories like this caused such a sensation that the emperor changed the laws as Las Casas requested. Unfortunately, the New World was far away, and the colonial administrators did not enforce the new laws. To his death, Las Casas continued to fight for his beloved Indians, upholding the dignity and freedom of all men.

Material on Hatuey is based on "The Brevissima Relacion," in: Francis A. McNutt, **Bartholomew de Las Cases** (New York: G.P. Putnam's Sons, 1909) Appendix I.

first worked with the church, especially to obtain better schools; but the newly arrived Jesuit missionaries did not show him proper respect. Still, Kongo kept its diplomatic ties with the Vatican and won papal support in a quarrel with Portugal over nearby Angola in the 1620s. An Africanized form of Catholicism thrived for a short time in Kongo. The sect claimed that God and His angels were black and that Christ had lived in the area. Eventually, all that survived of that faith was the use of the cross and images of saints as charms.

Catholicism in the New World. The missionary outreach that began in Africa continued in other parts of the world. As the Spanish took control in the Western Hemisphere, a friar named **Bartolomé de Las Casas** came to the New World to preach to the Indians. Las Casas not only tried to win the native people to Catholicism, but he also taught the Spanish that the Indians were human beings who should be treated with kindness and consideration. Some of the other friars, however, did not join Las Casas in his crusade. Many were content to follow the practice of **Toribino**, archbishop of Lima from 1580 to 1606. Although he tried to defend the Indians, he must have spent most of his time baptizing and **confirming** them. Mass baptisms led to converts who had very little knowledge of Christianity. By 1594, he claimed to have confirmed 800,000 people.

To deal with the problems caused by contact between Indians and Europeans, separate villages were set up for Catholic Indians. These villages resembled the reservations started later in the United States. In Paraguay, for example, there were 30 villages, each with a church, hospital, convent, and a school where children could learn Latin. Governed by priests, these communities offered Indians an eight-hour workday and recreational activities. Church attendance was required. However, most Indians of South and Central America did not live on reservations but attended parish churches modeled after those of Spain and Portugal.

Spanish friars were also active in Asia. A Spanish proselyte effort came to the Philippines, which by 1620 had an archbishop, a Catholic university, and more than 300,000 baptized converts. The success in this land raised hopes that other victories would soon follow.

St. Francis Xavier.
Among those who tried to produce such miracles was the Basque priest Francis Xavier (1506–1562). One of the founders of the Jesuit Order, his work demonstrated that Roman Catholic proselyting was headed by the Jesuits. Formed with military patterns, the Jesuits were the key opponents in the Roman Catholic Church to combat the Reformation. This autocratic order stressed exact discipline and salvation by human effort. Their missionary or proselyting activity was marked by formalism and syncretism. Syncretism meant that they did not seek for the gospel to transform culture and society but to mix with pagan cultures as an supplement. As a result there was no real long term leavening influence of the gospel. Instead their defective form of Christianity was mixed up with pagan false religions. Xavier went on a mission to India in 1542

and later to Malacca in the East Indies and Japan. Although mastering none of the languages which he encountered, he felt at home among Hindus, Muslims, and Buddhists. He used the technique of formalized mass **conversion**. Working under the protection of the government, he would gather a crowd to hear him. Then he would recite the Apostles' Creed, the Ten Commandments, the Rosary, and the Lord's Prayer. After repeating this process many times, he would baptize those who had simply memorized these statements and expressed faith in God. Then he would move onto another place, leaving behind some of his more dedicated followers to care for the new converts.

In the Orient, Jesuit missionaries faced the challenge of strong, competing religions. Often they found their worship welcome in the temples, but Hindu and Buddhist worship continued along with it. While the Bible teaches that idols must be destroyed and non-Christian worship stopped, in India and China, the Jesuits modified this view. They built on the idolatry of Roman Catholicism, as evident in the worship of the crucifix, images and mariolatry, and accommodated to other pagan forms of idolatry.

Jesuits also applied their syncretist approach to Asian beliefs and traditions, hoping that such action would aid the spread of Catholicism. These proselytizers analyzed Japanese, Chinese, or Indian customs. They determined which were merely social or civil and which had religious significance opposed to Christianity. Previous missionaries had condemned the old traditions of emperor worship and veneration of Confucius and forebears as pagan and incompatible with Christian faith. The Jesuits argued that many of these old rites were not religious but merely related to legitimate respect for one's ancestors. They contended that the Chinese and other Ori-

entals influenced by Confucian culture would never accept Catholicism if these rites were forbidden. The Jesuits made great progress, by the late 1600s, in converting the Chinese emperor, and they hoped that if the old traditions could be absorbed into Christianity, the whole of Chinese culture would follow the emperor into Christianity. One Italian Jesuit leading this effort in its early days was Matteo (Matthew) Ricci.

Matthew Ricci.
Trained in science at Rome, Matteo Ricci (1552–1610) spent four years in India before going to China in 1583. Typical of his accommodating approach, he began a lecture by showing clocks, scientific instruments, maps, and books. He then spent hours discussing with his hearers the areas of agreement between Confucian wisdom and Catholic Christianity. Hundreds of thousands of copies of his dialogue between a Chinese scholar and a European priest were distributed to the Chinese. By the year of his death, 1610, there were more than 2,000 converts to Roman Catholicism in China.

Jesuit missionaries found a great array of gods being worshipped in China and simply added Jesus Christ to the list.

For more than a century, the issue of adapting to ancient customs as Ricci had done was debated by church officials. There were occasional persecutions and occasional periods of growth in the number of Catholics in China. Finally, after 50 years of debate, Pope Clement XI declared it wrong to value Confucian tradition too highly or pay undue respect to one's ancestors. The next two emperors exiled most missionaries from China and intensified restrictions on Chinese Catholics. Because Chinese culture was so influential throughout the Far East, the decision of the pope effectively shut the door to Christianity in that part of the world for years to come.

Roman Catholics in Japan. Another major oriental land, Japan, seemed to offer a chance to repeat the Philippine success. By 1617, there were at least 300,000 Catholics in Japan. Fearing that the priests would help Westerners take over the land, the government halted the rapid spread of this religion. In a series of horrible persecutions marked by savage tortures, the Catholic church of Japan was all but destroyed. A decree in 1638 closed the land to all foreigners, and by the end of the century few Christians of any kind remained.

The fate of the Japanese church illustrates the problems of early Roman Catholic missions in the Orient. Despite early success, the work of winning people to the Catholic religion did not go as well in South and East Asia as it did in the Americas. The fundamental problem with such Jesuit missions was that it was not true biblical evangelism in its message or method. It was but an extension of the Roman Catholic formalism that sought to add religious ceremonies to culture rather than see the truth of Christ make all things new.

Golden Temple in Kyoto, Japan

Economic Motives

European technology and the desire to spread Christianity were significant factors in European expansion around the globe. But there were other reasons for the Western success—reasons that had to do with money, production, and trade.

All during the Middle Ages, European trade increased greatly. By the time the Renaissance started, many merchants had grown very rich. Farmers, craftsmen, and others had to increase production to supply this growing trade. During the fourteenth and fifteenth centuries this increase in production and wealth in Italy led to a new type of economy—capitalism.

What is Capitalism? Capitalism is an economic system characterized by the voluntary exchange of goods and services among individuals who are free and self-governing. In a capitalistic economy, private individuals invest sums of money in commercial, industrial, and banking ventures. Under capitalism, private persons own property or the means of production. Capitalistic enterprises produce goods for sale on the open market, in contrast to the early medieval manor which produced only enough goods for its own use. In a capitalistic economy, decisions are in the hands of people most closely related to the individual enterprise—those whose resources have been invested in it. The capitalist expects to receive a profit on his investment. These ideas are based on the biblical concept that God created man to be self-responsible under His law and intends man to enjoy the fruits of his own productive efforts, which encompass his material investment and his labor.

During the Middle Ages, a master craftsman generally would not have been a capitalist. He did not have a large investment in his business, and he worked closely with his journeymen and apprentices. But the Médici bank of fifteenth-century Florence was definitely a capitalistic enterprise.

Italians' New Business Methods. The Italians worked out many of the techniques of capitalism during the Renaissance era. They developed **double-entry** (credits and debits) **bookkeeping**, which helped businessmen keep track of what they owed and the money owed to them. With these records, they could decide whether to take on new ventures. Italians also invented a kind of insurance for ships, which greatly reduced the risk of loss. They experimented with various types of companies, some of which became the forerunners of modern corporations. Earlier traders had gone from place to place to trade, but the new companies built a base of operations and stayed in one spot. Run by groups of merchants, these companies conducted business from a cen-

Spanish galleons carried much of the wealth taken from the New World to Spain.

tral office by means of agents or partners located in distant cities.

One of the largest of these early companies belonged to the Médici family. A series of partnerships, it operated three businesses in Florence and had several foreign branches. The Médici supplied more than half the capital to each partnership so that they could keep control. They traded in many types of goods, engaged in industry and mining, and operated large banks. **Foreign exchange** and credit also brought great profits for the Médici. The use of credit began during this period and made it unnecessary for merchants to carry large amounts of cash. Then too, credit made borrowing easier.

Since it was expensive and dangerous to move gold and silver from one part of Europe to another, the bill of exchange was created. If a merchant in London wanted to purchase goods in Florence, he could go to the Médici bank branch in London and buy a bill of exchange payable in Florence several months later. On the agreed date, he or his agent in Florence would make purchases in London with a bill of exchange, the one would cancel the other. Very little actual gold or silver had to be transferred. These bills of exchange, the beginning of paper currency, were also used by travelers just as people today use travelers' checks.

The papacy also had the Médici bank transfer funds from various parts of Europe to Rome. The bank made a profit on these operations due to the difference in the rate at which one currency could be changed into another. While the Roman Catholic Church forbade the charging of interest, Italian bankers used currency exchange and many other methods to dodge the rules.

Capitalism In Northern Europe. Capitalism spread from Italy to the rest of Europe when a series of crises swept across the continent. In 1315 and 1316, crops failed and famines resulted. Then the Black Death plague snuffed out countless lives in 1348 and 1349. These events caused changes in normal social activities. Many people also perished in the Hundred Years' War between England and France. Constant fighting made it hard to hold medieval trade fairs any longer. However, the new Italian money economy soon replaced both the fairs and the medieval barter economy.

Capitalism affected all aspects of European life. No previous society had dreamed so boldly of boundless growth. Most only wished to keep their present standard of living, not better it. But capitalism provided a new frame of mind. Driven by the profit motive, the capitalist reinvested his increase so that production would grow.

Jacob Fugger, the wealthiest man in sixteenth century Europe, expressed the spirit of capitalism: "Let me earn as long as I am able." Fugger got his wish. Compare the Fugger family fortune with those of earlier capitalist families.

Fugger	(1546)	$160,000,000
Médici	(1440)	30,000,000
Peruzzi	(1300)	3,200,000

The north Europeans improved on the Italian way of doing business. They developed joint-stock companies, which work something like our modern corporations. Few businessmen had enough money to acquire a ship, crew, cargo, and supplies for the long voyage to Asia. Moreover, many ships never returned from this dangerous journey. Such a loss would normally wipe out a merchant's whole fortune. So a great many merchants pooled their money for these voyages through joint-stock companies. By purchasing shares of stock, each became part owner in the business venture. Not only did this method provide large amounts of money, it also reduced the risk for each investor. He did not have to invest everything he owned, only a small part.

Joint-stock companies such as the Dutch, English, and French East India companies raised enormous sums of money this way. With few individual merchants able to compete, these

Bankruptcy

The word **bank** comes from the Italian word **banca**, which means "bench." In medieval times, an Italian moneylender sat on a bench in the marketplace to conduct his business. If he lost all his money, the people broke his bench. That is how the word **bankrupt** came into use. It means "broken bench."

By the time of the Renaissance, the money lenders had moved into buildings. As financial dealings increased in size and complexity, these new banks took an even more important place in a country's economic life.

The Fuggers

Although history gives few bankers more than honorable mention, the behind-the-scenes activities of these men of finance have often greatly influenced historical events. For example, the wealthy Fugger banking family of Germany put up money for bribes which affected the election of two popes and made Charles V the Holy Roman Emperor. Bishops, kings, businessmen, towns, and even European countries financed operations with enormous loans from Fugger banks.

Starting as cloth makers, the Fuggers, through several generations, expanded their business to include spices, metals, and jewels. They opened branches in all the large cities of Central and Western Europe and by 1473 counted the Hapsburg rulers of Austria among their clients. Under Jacob the Rich, the Fuggers gained control of the silver, copper, and iron production in much of Central Europe.

As his fortune increased, Jacob loaned money to businessmen and then to political rulers as well. He accepted deposits, handled foreign exchange, and transferred money over long distances. A major user of this last service was the pope, who needed money transferred from Northern Europe to Rome. The Fugger enterprises utilized the most advanced bookkeeping methods of the day, developed their own credit rating system, and kept careful watch on events in the business world. When Jacob died, he was the richest man in Europe.

In the following years, the loans to political rulers proved the Fuggers' undoing. Spain and France defaulted on their debts in 1557. Then other borrowers also failed to repay their loans. The firm went bankrupt in 1607.

firms became the tool by which Europe gained economic control of the globe.

From remote, mysterious lands came products to enrich European life and to spur even further growth of capitalism. In the sixteenth century, Eastern spices and American gold and silver filled the holds of most ships sailing from colonial lands. By the seventeenth and eighteenth centuries other items replaced these. Tea, coffee, cocoa, exotic dyes such as **indigo**, and new products such as tobacco began to change European patterns of **consumption**. Cotton and sugar, although known earlier, became widely available for the first time.

The Slave Trade. One branch of the new commerce was not admirable, because it dealt in human beings—the slave trade. Beginning in the 1440s, ships often returned to Portugal with a few African captives. They were used mainly as house servants and craftsmen. But before long, they were put to work on sugar plantations.

The production of sugar posed unusual problems. It was partly agriculture, growing cane, and partly manufacturing, making the cane juice into refined sugar. Moreover, the whole process required large numbers of people to work a small piece of land. Nowhere in Europe was the farm population large enough to provide workers for a plantation, so owners used slave labor. The slaves were usually war prisoners and black Africans. Unlike the other forms of slavery and forced labor in use at the time, the unskilled plantation workers were scarcely considered human beings.

As Europeans ventured out into the Atlantic, the plantation idea moved with them. Eventually, gold and silver in the New World began to run out. Then the colonists discovered that many areas were suitable for plantations. After first working American Indians on the plantations, the Europeans began bringing Africans over. Unlike the Indians, most of whom were hunters and gatherers, the Africans were experienced tropical farmers. They had had more contact with European diseases and thus did not die off

as quickly as the Indians. Being black-skinned, they could not run away and blend into the population. Finally, Africa seemed to have an endless supply of human beings.

The flow of slaves across the Atlantic was not large until the middle of the seventeenth century. Then the Dutch took charge of supplying the rapidly growing plantations in the West Indies and Brazil. Soon British and French slave shippers displaced the Dutch. From about 2,000 slaves imported per year in the sixteenth century, the figures peaked at more than 80,000 annually in the 1780s. Close to 10 million Africans landed in the Western Hemisphere during the 400-year history of the Atlantic slave trade.

This traffic in human beings proceeded through several steps. First, ships from Europe carrying manufactured items, rum, cloth, and other trade goods came to the West African coast. There the captains exchanged these for slaves provided by African middlemen. The native middlemen had obtained the slaves from the interior either through kidnapping or by purchase. Forced to

African slaves were brought to the New World under very inhumane conditions.

The Middle Passage

Capture by slavers was a frightening experience for Africans. But slaves faced their most terrible ordeal on the ships which carried them across the Atlantic, a journey called the Middle Passage. It lasted from three weeks to three months, depending on the distance covered and the winds. Inadequate food, disease, and overcrowding took the lives of about 13 percent of the slaves before they reached the Americas. Sometimes the ship would be attacked by competitors, and the slaves would drown during the fighting. If severe storms came up, the sailors often threw their captives overboard to lighten the ship. John Newton, an English slaver who himself became a slave of an African queen and later was converted to Christianity, becoming an evangelical minister, described conditions on these ships this way:

"Approximately 200 to 250 slaves can be carried in the hold of a 100-ton vessel. Their lodging rooms below deck are in three parts (for the men, the boys, and the women) and are around five feet high. They are divided toward the middle and the slaves lie in two rows, one above the other, on each side of the ship, close to each other like books upon a shelf. I have seen them so close that the shelf would not easily contain one more.

"The poor creatures, thus cramped, are likewise kept in iron chains which makes it difficult for them to turn or move or attempt to rise or lie down without hurting themselves or each other. Almost every morning instances are found of the living and dead fastened together."

Adapted from John Newton, ***Thoughts Upon the African Slave Trade*** (London: J. Buckland, 1788)

walk to the coast bound by heavy ropes or chains, the captives then waited in dungeons or floating prison ships until a trader came by.

After purchase, the slaves were crammed into the ship's hold, with scarcely room to move, and taken as quickly as possible to an American port before too many of them died. Deaths, of course, meant lost profits. Yet conditions on the voyage were dreadful. Chained together in the dank hold with its stale air and lack of sanitation, the captives suffered from hunger and brutal treatment. The shock of being torn from homes and loved ones still gripped them. During capture, journey to the coast, and shipment across the Atlantic, the loss of life was appalling.

When the slave cargoes landed in the New World, planters bought the Africans at auctions. Then the ships picked up plantation products, especially raw sugar and molasses, and returned to Europe. Merchants made a large profit at each stage of this three-cornered trade.

Growing Wealth. Above all of the world's exotic goods, Europeans hungered for gold and silver most. Said the conquistador, Hernando Cortez, "We, the Spanish, suffer an affliction (sickness) of the heart which can only be cured by gold.... I came in search of gold and not to work the land as a laborer." Between 1591 and 1595, the flow of silver pesos into Spain reached a peak of 35,184,863. Great quantities of gold also reached Spain and began to move through trade channels to the rest of Europe. Soon these precious metals flooded the continent and started a price revolution. During the sixteenth century, prices jumped fourfold, fivefold, and even sixfold.

Because prices rose more rapidly than wages, this inflation made capitalism grow even faster. Profits increased, giving capitalists more desire, as well as more money, to invest. The real income of workers dropped while the middle class grew wealthy. The growth of the middle class gave Europe a decided advantage in its economic conquest of the globe.

Not Altogether a European Innovation

To be sure, the African slave trade was not altogether a European innovation. Some form of slavery had existed in Africa, among Africans, for centuries. Prisoners of war and convicted criminals were often treated as "wageless labor," liable to be bought and sold. However, there was one important distinction. They were not chattels as they came to be in the mines and plantations of the Americas. In African society there was no clear and rigid division between bond and free. Every African was a working member of some domestic group, attached normally through the bond of kinship. The slave, too, was a working member of a group, but since he was not kin, his status was lower. It need not, however, remain so. A slave could advance through work; he could buy his freedom with the produce of the plot of land assigned to him for cultivation. Or he could advance through good fortune, by inheriting goods or marrying his master's daughter. Through such means it was not at all unusual for slaves to acquire positions of great influence and power.

But in many cases it was this reservoir of "captive labor" within African society that opened the gates to overseas slavery. African chiefs and kings sold their slaves to Europeans just as they had always sold them to one another. In this respect, moreover, they were behaving no differently from people in other cultures. For centuries the strong people in Europe had bought and sold their weaker brethren: even during the comparatively enlightened Renaissance, the pope more than once had occasion to excommunicate Venetian and Genoese merchants for selling Christian captives into Muslim slavery in Egypt and the Middle East.

From Basil Davidson, ***African Kingdoms: Great Ages of Man—A History of the World's Cultures*** (New York: Time-Life Books, Time Inc., 1966)

For your consideration

Questions

1. What effect did technology have on individual freedom?

2. How might the increase of metal in Europe have influenced progress?

3. Have you ever thought of any ideas for inventions? If so, list a few. What kind of thinking leads to new ideas? What other factors are necessary for the process of invention? What are some modern impediments to the spirit of invention?

4. In what ways may the invention of the printing press have aided the Age of Exploration?

5. Compare and evaluate the evangelistic approaches of Toribino, Xavier, and Ricci. Which do you think would have produced the strongest converts?

6. What actions of the Europeans may have hindered their missionary efforts?

7. What problems face a person who converts from one religion to another?

8. Does religion have any part in motivating people to attempt great projects today? Illustrate.

9. What are some strengths and weaknesses of capitalism?

10. Did the slave trade increase racial prejudice? Is any form of slavery justifiable?

11. Why did inflation in the sixteenth century increase business profits? How would inflation have affected craftsmen?

Projects

1. Choose one of the following headlines and write a newspaper article to go with it:

   Florence Bank Announces New Credit Services

   Local Merchant Concerned Over Trade Fair Decline

   Fugger Tells Graduates How to Succeed

   Inventor Demonstrates Windmill

   Old Timer Describes Life Before Clocks

   Caravels Sink Arab Fleet

   Pope Receives Protest from Kongo King

   Las Casas Scolds Conquistadors

   Japan Moves into Isolation

2. Create a newspaper advertisement for the new products brought to Europe by traders. Put together a bulletin board using the news stories above and the advertisements or actually put out a newspaper.

3. Do some research on one of the Asian religions such as Hinduism, Buddhism, or Confucianism. Prepare a report explaining the basic beliefs and practices.

4. Imagine you are a sixteenth century missionary in South America. Write a letter to a friend in Spain telling about your experiences.

5. Make a model or drawing (perhaps cutaway) of one of the inventions mentioned in this chapter. Basic materials for models might be clay, pieces of wood, or paper. Explain to the class how the invention worked and why it was important.

Word List

tandem

interchangeable

vernacular

portolani

mariners

outflank

envoys

unicorn

confirm

conversion

evangelistic

foreign exchange

indigo

consumption

People and Groups

Johann Gutenberg

Christopher Columbus

Prince Henry the Navigator

Prester John

Afonso

Bartholomew de Las Casas

Archbishop Toribino

Francis Xavier

Matteo Ricci

The Jesuits

Jacob Fugger and the Fugger Family

Médici Family

Hernando Cortez

Roger Bacon

Alhazen

Pere Marquette

Hatuey

1450	1500	1550	1600	1650	1700

Politics and Economics

Prince Henry's
expeditions 1418–1460

Pizarro conquers Incas 1530s

French found Quebec 1608

English Pilgrims found Plymouth 1620

Glorious Revolution in England 1688

Richelieu takes power 1624

Diaz rounds Africa's southern tip 1487

Holy Roman Empire splits 1556

Russian rule reaches Pacific 1640

Columbus discovers America 1492
Da Gama reaches India 1498

The Netherlands declares independence 1581

Fredrick the Great of Prussia 1740–1786

Cortez conquers Aztecs 1519–1521

England wins Seven Years' War 1763

Magellan sails around the globe 1519–1522

Reign of Louis XIV 1661–1715

Science and Technology

Caravel developed 1400s

In 1543 Copernicus publishes book:
Concerning the Revolutions of the Celestial Spheres

Movable type invented c. 1450

Peter the Great imports Western
technology to Russia 1700–1727

Navigational equipment invented or improved
Oarsmen replaced by sails 1400s & 1500s

Work of Galileo 1584–1642

Cannon adapted for ships—Early 1500s

Religion and Philosophy

Edict of Nantes 1598

Work of Xavier 1542–1552

Louis XIV revokes Edict of Nantes 1685

Work of Ricci 1579–1610

Peace of Augsburg 1555

Hapsburgs lose Thirty Years' War 1648

Work of Las Casas 1514–1566

Philip II uses Inquisition 1560s–1590s

Culture and Society

Spread of knowledge accelerated
by printing press—Late 1400s

Foreign products used in the West 1500s

French culture dominates Europe 1660s–1720s

Watches begin creating time-consciousness 1500

Peter the Great modernizes Russia 1700–1727

Spanish culture brought to Latin America;
Slavery begins in Western Hemisphere—Early 1500s

European Expansion and Counter Reformation

The focus now shifts from the *reasons* for Western expansion to the *West itself*. So begins the story of a quest—a quest for exotic Eastern wares, adventure, religious converts, wealth, and fame. Driven by these aims, Western sailors faced unknown oceans and defied countless perils sailing around Africa to Asia. Meanwhile, other Western explorers crossed the Atlantic Ocean, discovered a "New World," and **circumnavigated** the globe as the Russians moved overland across Siberia to the Pacific Ocean.

During this same period of time, there were many developments in the European nations themselves. National governments became stronger as kings and their advisers consolidated their power. A series of religious wars disturbed the peace of Europe for many years. They began as Protestantism spread from Germany and Switzerland to other countries. Often political motives went along with the religious reasons for the struggles.

Portuguese Exploration

Portugal was the first European nation to begin explorations. Its plans for expansion forced the Portuguese to take to the sea, since their inland neighbor, mighty Spain, was not about to give up one foot of soil to Portugal. Mariners from many lands often put into ports along the seacoast of the small country. The Italians, who sailed past on their way to Flanders, also stopped by to visit and share their knowledge of navigational techniques with Portuguese sailors.

Henry the Navigator. Prince Henry, a younger son of the king of Portugal, devoted his life to the quest. One project especially interested him—exploring the West African coast in hopes of reaching the Indian Ocean. At his castle, he gathered map makers, geographers, and navigators of all **nationalities** to help in this project. From 1418 until the end of his life, he sent out dozens

of expeditions, each one exploring a bit more of the African coast. The navigators and captains of these ships drew charts and began trading with the natives. By the time of Henry's death, his ships had reached Sierra Leone; and he had launched the Age of Exploration.

Diaz and da Gama. At first no one in Henry's family seemed interested in carrying on his work. The Portuguese were already busy getting rich from a gold, ivory, and slave trade with the kingdom of Ghana. But when **King John II** came to the throne in 1481, he renewed Prince Henry's quest. Within a few years, his explorers approached the tip of Africa.

In 1487, he sent out two expeditions. One, under **Bartholomew Diaz**, sailed down the west coast and rounded Africa's southern tip. The other went through the Mediterranean, then overland to the Red Sea, and sailed through the Indian Ocean to the Malabar coast of India. The groundwork was now complete for the famous voyage of **Vasco da Gama** around Africa to India. Charts made by the earlier explorers and a well-known Arab pilot guided him across the Indian Ocean.

Arab traders already in India did not want any competition and tried to prevent da Gama from completing trade agreements with the Indians. Complicating the negotiations was the lack of understanding by the Portuguese of the advanced level of the Indian culture. It left the Portuguese without anything to bargain with as the Indians neither needed nor wanted what they had to trade. However, da Gama did manage to return to Portugal with a cargo of pepper and cinnamon which sold for sixty times the cost of the voyage.

Portugal Takes Over Eastern Trade. The prospect of profits like that lured the Portuguese to the East in such force that within a dozen years they had destroyed Arab trade in the Indian Ocean. A chain of fortified Portuguese trading ports stretched from Mozambique on Africa's east coast to the Persian Gulf to Indonesia.

Under the leadership of **Afonso de Albuquerque**, the Portuguese governor general of India from 1509 to 1515, the Portuguese captured the islands at the entries to the Persian Gulf and the Red Sea. Thus they gained control of the narrow sea passages leading to the Indian Ocean, which meant they controlled the Indian Ocean as well. In India, Albuquerque seized the coastal port of Goa and made it his headquarters. The Portuguese also captured a few islands and ports in the Pacific. From these locations, they were able to control most of the trade routes for Eastern spices and other goods.

The Portuguese dominated the European spice trade throughout the sixteenth century. However, a good percentage still came to Europe through the Middle East as Arab traders managed to bring their cargoes to the eastern Mediterranean.

Portugal's Power Fades. Although the Portuguese gained great wealth from their empire, they did not use it to develop a sound commercial system. Perhaps the nation was too small and had exhausted its energy and manpower in voyages to the Orient. At any rate, all trade with the East became a royal monopoly with the profits going to the king and his favorites. The Portuguese did

not set up a system to market the spices and other Eastern products to the rest of Europe. Instead, they allowed the Dutch, Flemish, and Italians to do so. Most of the profits from the trade went to these middlemen. Thus, in the long run, the rich Portuguese monopoly strengthened other lands more than Portugal.

Then in 1580, **Philip II** of Spain took over Portugal. He was more interested in protecting the Spanish Empire than the Portuguese. By the end of the sixteenth century, the Dutch and English, forbidden to trade with Portugal because of their conflict with Spain, began to deal directly with Asia. After that, the Portuguese Empire withered away.

Spanish Conquests

Columbus Finds the New World. In 1484, while the Portuguese were still working their way down the coast of Africa, an Italian named **Christopher Columbus** asked for an audience with Portugal's king. Columbus needed financial backing for a voyage across the Atlantic to reach the East by sailing west. The idea was not new, for most scholars agreed that the earth is a globe. But King John II and his advisers decided against Columbus because they felt the distance was too great. Their view of the size of the globe was more accurate than that of Columbus.

Not one to give up easily, Columbus next brought his request to **King Ferdinand and Queen Isabella** of Spain. Although impressed with his ideas, they were busy fighting a war and could not spare the money he needed. But finally, in 1492, they were able to finance a small fleet and Columbus set sail. After many anxious weeks at sea, he landed at one of the Bahamian Islands, which he named San Salvador.

Until the end of his life, Columbus was sure he had landed in Asia. He made four voyages to the New World, landing on various islands as well as the coasts of Central and South America. Spain poured money into his voyages, but not until later did it receive any return on the investment. At the time, the discoveries were a great disappointment.

Soon Spain and Portugal began quarreling over ownership of the newly discovered lands. Both nations believed that since the souls of non-Christians were doomed, Christians had a right to take their lands. To strengthen their claim to these territories, Roman Catholic rulers wanted the pope's permission. In 1454, the pope had granted the Portuguese title to the African lands they had discovered. To settle the dispute between Spain and Portugal in 1493, the pope drew an imaginary line of demarcation through the world, giving the Spanish all land west of the line and the Portuguese all areas to the east. Based on this papal authority, the Treaty of Tordesillas was drawn up in 1494. Under it, Spain, basically, received the New World except for Brazil. Portugal received Brazil, Africa, and the eastern route to the Indies. Since the meridian that was designated as the dividing line circled the globe, some disputes arose between Spain and Portugal over certain islands in the Far East. Maps were drawn by each side showing the islands in one or the other territory. In 1529, Spanish King Charles V settled the dispute for much needed cash, selling his country's rights to the disputed lands, including the Moluccas and the Philippines.

Meanwhile, explorers of other nations soon followed up the news of Columbus's discovery. **Amerigo Vespucci**, agent of an Italian bank, explored South America's coast. From his studies of the plants and wildlife there, he realized that the continent could not be Asia. Later the New World continents were called by his name.

Magellan Expedition Circles the World. In 1513, a Spanish conquistador, Vasco Nuñez de Balboa hacked his way through the jungles of Panama to discover the eastern shore of the Pacific Ocean. By 1525, European navigators had explored the east coasts of North and South America from Labrador to Argentina. It was clear that Columbus had not discovered the Indies and that there was no easy passage through the new continents to Asia.

Was there a way around them? Ferdinand Magellan, a Portuguese mariner sailing for Spain, was determined to find out. Magellan did not dream of sailing around the world, for he believed that

Amerigo Vespucci, 1451–1512

Asia was a short distance beyond Panama. After a fearful, stormy passage through the straits at the southern tip of South America, he emerged into a calm sea, to which he gave the name *Pacific*, which means "peaceful."

Sailing on to the west, the expedition reached the Philippines. Hostile natives there killed Magellan, but one of his ships continued the journey. In 1522, after three years of starvation and disease, the remainder of his crew reached Spain. They were the first men to sail entirely around the earth.

Spain In The New World. For awhile, the Spanish Empire looked less profitable than the Portuguese. Despite their disappointment at not finding spices, the Spanish kept looking for a passage to India. In the course of their search, they stumbled upon wealthy civilizations in Mexico and South America. Here at last were the riches that Spain, like other European nations, had sought. Between 1519 and 1521, **Hernando Cortez** (Hernan Cortés) conquered the Aztecs in Mexico. Then in the 1530s, **Francisco Pizarro** overcame the Incas in Peru. By the end of the sixteenth century, the Spanish controlled almost the whole Western Hemisphere.

An accurate history of Spanish rule in the New World has been somewhat elusive over the centuries. This is despite the fact that the Spanish kept an unprecedented amount of official and unofficial records of their dealings in the Americas. That vast record has been overshadowed, however, by a historical phenomenon known as **The Black Legend**. This term describes a successful propaganda effort (perhaps the first in history) which was waged against mighty Spain by its European rivals and enemies, principally the Dutch and English. The propaganda effort was designed to depict Spanish conquerors as mad for gold, greedy, and indescribably cruel in their world exploits.

This propaganda effort was fueled by the writing of the Dominican friar and missionary **Bartolomé** (Bartholomew) **de Las Casas**, who published volumes of highly sensational reports of alleged atrocities by Spaniards against what he invariably described as noble and peaceful natives. The Las Casas version of early Spanish American history was reinforced in the American mind during the early twentieth century, when champions of the poor during the Mexican Revolution of 1910, inspired by Marxist class-conflict ideas, eagerly advanced the distorted, negative views of colonial Spain.

Las Casas was so successful in his campaign on behalf of the Indians that his sometimes outrageous charges have, to this day, been widely

The Ambush

Pizarro's small band of conquistadors could not hope to defeat the army of the Inca empire in an ordinary battle; thus they resorted to trickery. Inviting the Inca ruler to meet with him, Pizarro promised to receive him as a friend and brother. Unfortunately, the Incas believed him and walked right into an ambush.

Pizarro saw that the hour had come. He waved a white scarf in the air. The fatal gun was fired from the fortress.... Rushing from the avenues of the great halls in which they were concealed, the Spaniards poured into the plaza, horse and foot, and threw themselves into the midst of the Indians. The Incas, stunned by the report of artillery and muskets which echoed like thunder from the surrounding buildings, and blinded by the smoke which rolled along the square, were seized with panic.

...Nobles and commoners—all were trampled down under the fierce charge of the cavalry, who dealt their blows, right and left, without sparing; while their swords, flashing through the thick gloom, carried dismay into the hearts of the wretched natives. Now for the first time the Incas saw the horse and rider in all their terrors.

They made no resistance—as indeed, they had no weapons with which to make it. Every avenue to escape was closed, for the entrance to the square was choked with dead bodies....

The struggle now became fiercer than ever round the royal litter (platform on which the ruler was carried). It reeled more and more, and at length, several of the nobles who supported it having been slain, it overturned. The Indian prince would have fallen to the ground had not Pizarro and several others caught him in their arms. They placed him in a neighboring building under heavy guard.

Adapted from William H. Prescott, *The Conquest of Peru* (New York: Harper and Brothers, 1847).

accepted as fact. Due to his crusades, the Spanish government of that time eventually enacted what became known as the **New Laws**, protecting Indians in the Americas. However, there is ample historical evidence that much in Las Casas' reports was distorted, unfounded, overly sensationalized, or grossly false, including the famous story of a Cuban Indian chief who allegedly preferred hell to heaven if Spaniards were going to heaven (see Chapter 1).

To be sure, the initial years of the Spanish conquest of the Americas included harsh and even atrocious actions. In some cases, the wealth of native peoples was simply **plundered**. On the other hand, many atrocities were committed by the Indians as well. Furthermore, reliable records indicate that some of the atrocities against Indians were perpetrated by other Indians, as various rival tribes allied themselves with the Spanish to vanquish old enemies. Moreover, in true Spanish tradition of deference to the rule of law, those who perpetrated atrocities were, as often as possible, viewed as criminals and brought to justice.

The initial harshness of the early years of conquest gave way to an orderly, scholarly, civilized, and highly competent administration of the New World during the rest of the 300 years of Spanish rule in the New World. During this period, the Spanish scored astonishing cultural achievements, considering the vastness of their Western empire, including the establishment of many universities, hospitals, churches, schools, and thriving economic enterprises. There are few parallels in history—other than the Roman and British empires—to compare with Spain's successful entrenchment of its culture over such a vast territory, with such a lasting legacy.

In the economic realm, Spain introduced European mining methods to the rich silver deposits in the New World. Although Spain was casti-

In this old engraving, Spaniards are shown working their Indian and African laborers unmercifully. According to accompanying accounts, inadequate food, clothing, and medical attention added to their misery and caused many deaths.

gated for greediness in its search for gold, it was probably doing only what other nations wish they could have done, for riches were sought by all. It was gold and silver that made the Spanish colonial empire pay off. The law required that all precious metals be taxed at one-fifth of their value. Between 1503 and 1660, Spain officially received from the Americas 18,600 tons of silver and 200 tons of gold. In addition, as much as 50 percent of those amounts may have been smuggled into the country during the same years.

Gold and silver from the New World made Spain extremely rich during the sixteenth century. Before this time, Spain had been outside the mainstream of European history, or at least it has historically been depicted that way. In fact, Spain had been Christendom's strongest wall of defense against the Muslim hordes which frequently threatened Europe. After the sixteenth century, it again drifted into Europe's backwaters, partly because of the propaganda campaign which had been waged against it by the enemies it acquired while it ruled Western civilization. But during its "golden age" in the sixteenth century, Spain had the largest empire and became the wealthiest and most powerful nation in the world.

Spanish Colonies. From the beginning, the Spanish colonized and settled the areas they conquered, contrary to common claims that the only purpose for their expansion was to plunder and exploit. They brought Catholicism and European ways to the native peoples, with mixed methods and mixed results. Many new products such as wheat, sugar cane, coffee, vegetables, and fruits came to the Americas with the Spanish settlers. The only **domesticated** animals the Indians had were dogs and llamas, but the Spanish brought horses, cattle, sheep, goats, pigs, and poultry to the Western Hemisphere.

The Spanish also brought firearms, liquor, smallpox, measles, and typhus—against which the Indians had little resistance. In addition, many natives died from forced labor in mines and on plantations. Some scholars estimate that there were 10 million to 12 million Indians in Mexico before the Europeans arrived, and that by 1650 their numbers were down to 1.5 million. Other scholars, both of that time and today, argue that such allegations could not possibly be true. According to one view, every Spaniard who came to the New World would have had to kill a native every day and three on Sundays to have massacred as many Indians as Las Casas and other advocates of the natives claimed were killed. Indeed, there is evidence of a decline in native populations in some areas, but this decline likely was due to factors in addition to killings by the conquistadors. In some places where there was a

labor shortage among natives, the Spanish imported African slaves as other nations had been doing during this period of history.

Spanish officials continually were puzzled over how to handle the Indians. The king had given several conquistadors, known as protectors, the right to collect taxes and to demand forced labor from certain Indian villages. In return the protectors had to serve in the military forces and to pay the salaries of parish priests. Some protectors abused the system, and eventually all of them lost the right to demand forced labor.

The Spanish established farms and raised livestock in America. They started plantations on which African slaves worked to raise one main crop for the European market. The West Indies (and Brazil, which was owned by Portugal) produced sugar. Later, North and South American plantations grew tobacco, cotton, and coffee.

The Glory Fades. Its vast wealth made Spain such a major power that the legend of Spanish might did not die for two centuries. Strange as it may seem, however, Spain's decline came from the

Montezuma (1480–1520), ruler of the Aztecs of Mexico, was killed for betraying his people to the Spanish conquest.

same process that brought it great wealth. Like Portugal, the country lagged behind in developing a strong home economy. It depended on northern Europe to distribute the New World products and to supply manufactured goods. Spanish wine, wool, iron ore, and gold were exported, and in return Spain received woolen cloth, metal products, salt, and fish.

Attempts to start industries in Spain during the sixteenth century failed. The main obstacle was the inflation caused by the flow of precious metals into the country. Spanish prices were double those in northern Europe, and wages were almost double. This made Spanish goods too expensive to compete with products from northern Europe.

Some historians claim that the attitudes of the Spanish aristocrats also hurt their nation's economic growth. According to this view, nobles looked down on tradesmen and professional people. To have a place among the idle rich was the Spaniard's dream, for the upper class enjoyed large, secure estates and tax **exemptions**. A merchant or professional person who could gain some wealth tried to buy a title and a piece of land and join the aristocratic class. According to this view of Spanish history, the aristocratic outlook proved fatal to the creation of a strong business community. If that were true in Spain itself, it was not always true in Spanish America, where thousands of colonists went to better their lot. Again contrary to popular thought, a strong middle class developed in the Spanish colonies of America. From this class—which included Indians, mestizos, mulattos, and Negroes, as well as whites—came most of today's Latin American military leaders, poets, journalists, historians, physicians, businessmen, writers, government officials, and educators.

Even if inflation and prejudice against business had not hurt Spain's development, its political mistakes would have. Under Philip II, the country poured its best young men and a great deal of wealth into a series of wars to maintain Hapsburg leadership in Europe and to destroy Protestantism. Believing that a country should have only one religion, Roman Catholicism, Philip persecuted all other faiths. He tightly controlled commerce and industry and sent Spain's military strength against the Protestants and France. During Philip's reign, the Dutch threw off Spanish rule. Then another disaster struck Spain—the destruction of its "Invincible Armada" (fleet) in 1588 by the English, led by **Sir Francis Drake** and other ship captains. A later series of defeats at the hands of France sent Spain into complete decline.

Eventually, the mines of the New World were exhausted, no longer supplying the homeland with gold and silver. Gone was the wealth that had produced beautiful palaces and cathedrals. Castile, the richest area of Spain, declined because of heavy taxes, poor government, depopulation, and ruined industry. So Spain's economy stagnated, and its wealth and power ebbed away.

As the nation declined, so did its overseas empire. Holland and England took over the trade with the colonies, although Spain kept much of its empire until the early nineteenth century.

Catholicism Versus Protestantism

At the same time that European countries were exploring the rest of the world, they were also involved in conflicts at home which caused great trouble in Europe. Most of the monarchs wished to stop the bitter religious rivalry. They tried a number of different methods to accomplish this—**partition**, **compromise**, **suppression**, and **toleration**. We will see how each of these methods worked.

Partition. When Martin Luther defied the Roman Catholic Church and the Holy Roman Emperor Charles V in 1521, Charles vowed to stamp out Protestantism from Europe. His efforts to do so initially were hampered by other conflicts, namely his war with France and his defense of the Empire against the Turks. But war between Protestant realms and Catholics finally came to the Holy Roman Empire under Charles in 1546. At first, the imperial Catholic forces seemed to be winning; but the Protestants, whose power and influence had had time to grow during the twenty-five-year interim, managed to regroup when Maurice of Saxony, an ally of Charles, turned against him and Charles was forced to sign a peace agreement. The Peace of Augsburg (1555), which ended the fighting, provided that the ruler of each state in the Empire could determine the faith of his subjects. State borders served also as the borders between the rival faiths—the principle of partition.

The wars of religion came to France in 1562. Swiss Reformer **John Calvin** had been sending pastors to France since 1555. By 1562, at least 10 percent of the population was Protestant. This rapid growth, along with the conversion of many important nobles, frightened the Catholics. When **Henry II** died in 1559, he left the monarchy in a shambles. For a time, the queen, **Catherine de Médici**, managed to keep peace between the Catholics and **Huguenots** (French Protestants). She arranged a meeting to work out a compromise between the two faiths; but no agreement was possible; and in 1562 war broke out.

Gaspard Coligny (1519–1572) rose to the position of admiral of France. He became the political leader and protector of the French Huguenots, but was murdered in the St. Bartholomew's Day Massacre.

Religion was only one motive for the French civil wars. Many nobles and townspeople also fought to be free from royal control. As in all civil wars, great cruelty marked the fighting. Entire cities were wiped out; assassinations were frequent; many people became refugees. Royal power declined as province after province fell under the control of the great nobles.

Peace finally came to a war-weary France through the efforts of **Henry IV**. Converting from Calvinism to Catholicism, he received the loyalty of most French people. In 1598, he issued the **Edict of Nantes**, giving the Huguenots the right to occupy and fortify 200 towns for their protection. Private worship was allowed everywhere and public worship places for Protestants were officially designated, including certain noble estates. Here again was the principle of *partition*.

Compromise. Another method used to bring peace between rival religious groups was *compro-*

mise. A state worked out a settlement that would satisfy most of its people and then forced everyone else to submit to it. This happened with the Church of England or Anglican Church under **Elizabeth I**. Elizabeth's settlement was partly a product of her own personality. As the daughter of **Henry VIII** and his one-time mistress, **Anne Boleyn** (who was later executed by Henry, officially for adultery, but more likely for failure to give him a male heir), she grew up in an atmosphere of fear and anxiety. Although she would have preferred to be a Catholic, she could not rule England as a Catholic. Her strongest supporters were Protestant, and the Catholic Church regarded her as illegitimate and therefore unfit to reign.

Elizabeth sponsored a statement of faith for the Anglican Church. This statement was largely Protestant, with some points, such as the one on Holy Communion, deliberately vague. The church **liturgy** was like that of the Roman Catholic Church, except it was in English. The monarch was the "supreme governor" and "supreme defender" of the English church, which was administered by a group of bishops.

Although some clergymen refused to accept the settlement, most of the people were content with it. Certain devout Catholics, led by Jesuits, opposed the Anglican compromise. But in the long run, the Calvinist Protestants or **Puritans** were the most dissatisfied with the arrangements. Both of these groups were persecuted for their beliefs.

Suppression. Another method of handling religious conflict was *suppression*. A state chose one side in a dispute and then wiped out the other by murder or exile. The tactic worked in many parts of Europe, but Philip II of Spain made the greatest use of it. One of the most powerful rulers of Europe in his day, Philip worked tirelessly to

The Tours of Elizabeth

Queen Elizabeth I loved to be entertained by the important people of her realm. Each summer she spent about two months making a "royal progress" through her kingdom. Taking more than three hundred wagons on her trips, she would ride horseback or in an open litter so that her subjects could see her.

On one of these occasions in 1575, she stopped at Kenilworth Castle, the home of Robert Dudley, Earl of Leicester, one of her dearest friends. He spared no expense to make her visit pleasurable. For three weeks, he staged water shows, fireworks, displays, elaborate musicals, and dances. While the Queen might spend her evenings dancing or listening to music, the daylight hours would find her hunting deer in the castle's large parks and woods. An expert with the crossbow, Elizabeth loved to hunt. She also watched such activities as bearbaiting (chained bears fighting fierce dogs), acrobatics, and running the quintain (a game based upon medieval jousting).

While her poorer subjects ate simple food, the Queen enjoyed elaborate feasts in her travels. One such meal was served by 200 young men and included 300 different dishes. Elizabeth and her company could choose from beef, venison, fish, capon, pork, mutton, breads, and sauces.

The summer tours, which started early in her reign, ended only with the Queen's death at the age of seventy.

build his dynasty and to strengthen the Roman Catholic Church in his share of the old Holy Roman Empire.

The Escorial, the symbol of his reign, still stands today on a barren hillside some 25 miles northwest of Madrid. It was a most unusual palace because it did not have enough space for a king's court, yet it contained a monastery and a large church.

Philip viewed the Church as an agent of the government. He thought it should help him politically and financially. Like most rulers of his time, he saw any religion other than his own as a threat to his power.

Philip used a religious court, the **Inquisition** (or "Holy Office"), to try heretics. Of course, all Protestants were heretics. The court, originally established by Ferdinand and Isabella to root out certain subversive Jewish collaborators with Muslims who threatened Christian Spain and Europe, now ruthlessly hunted down the Protestants and urged them to renounce their faith. Those who refused were put in jail, or worse, tortured and killed. Soon the Protestant movement died out in Spain.

The king also had to deal with the Spanish **Moriscos**. In 1502, these Muslims had been given the choice of exile or conversion to Catholicism. Most had chosen conversion. They remained in Spain as a **subculture** with their own language, dress, and customs. Many Catholics suspected that the Moriscos were still Muslims at heart. In 1567, Philip outlawed Morisco practices and they revolted. The king stopped the rebellion and moved its survivors to remote parts of Spain. Later, they were sent out of the country.

Philip made the mistake of trying his suppressive policy in his possession in The Netherlands. To stop the spread of Calvinism in the Low Countries, Philip ordered strict enforcement of heresy laws. Out of this persecution came one of Protestantism's greatest creeds, the 1561 ***Belgic Confession of Faith***, written by a courageous, underground Reformed pastor-theologian, **Guido de Brès**, who died a martyr in 1567. The *Confession* was intended to show Philip that the Protestants were true followers of the Christian religion, and as such were willing to be loyal citizens of the government in all things lawful. However, the signers of the *Confession* vowed to "offer their backs to stripes, their tongues to knives, their mouths to gags, and their whole bodies to the fire" rather than deny the truth confessed in their creed. The goal of freedom of worship was not realized, and many of the dedicated Protestants did indeed suffer these horrors.

Guido de Brès and de la Grange visited by Countess de Reux in Doornik prison

St. Bartholomew's Day Massacre

One of the most gruesome episodes of persecution during the Reformation occurred in France on the festival day of St. Bartholomew. It was the year 1572, a time of growing political power for the Huguenots in this Roman Catholic country. Perhaps no one resented Protestant power more than Catherine de Médici, mother of King Charles IX. Though at first she tried to bring peace between Catholics and Protestants, she now felt personally threatened. Thus she consented to a plot to kill all the Huguenots.

At 2 a.m. on the appointed day, the bells of Paris began to ring—the signal to begin. Few Protestants escaped. One who did was the 13-year-old Maximilien de Béthune, later to become Duke of Sully and a noted minister under Henry IV.

Awakened by the bells, the young man began to dress while his tutor and valet went outside to see what was happening. He never saw either man again. A few minutes later his frightened landlord came with the news that Protestants could save their lives and property by converting to Catholicism and going immediately to Mass. The landlord was on his way to Mass then and begged Sully to come with him.

The young man decided instead to try to reach the College of Burgundy where he was a student. Donning his scholar's robe and taking the Catholic prayer book under his arm, he ventured out into the street. There a terrifying scene met his eyes. Soldiers rushed madly from house to house, breaking down doors and shouting, "Kill, kill the Huguenots!" Victims were dragged or fled shrieking into the streets, to be silenced by the sword.

Three times on that dangerous journey, the murderers stopped Sully and spared him only when they saw his prayer book. At last he made the gate of the school, only to face a greater peril. The guard refused to let him in. As Sully stood pleading with the man, both the number and fury of the soldiers seemed to increase about him. Finally, by means of a bribe Sully gained entrance, and the principal hid him in a closet for three days. At that time, the order came to halt the killing, and the young man was able to return to his home. However, before the bloodshed stopped, perhaps 10,000 men, women, and children lost their lives.

Based on ***Memoirs of Maximilien de Béthune Duke of Sully*** (Philadelphia: Edward Earle, 1817).

As if the religious suppression were not enough, Philip angered the nobles in the Low Country region (present-day northern France, Belgium, and The Netherlands) by excluding them from his government or by giving them minor parts. In 1576, the Protestants rioted—smashing the images, stained-glass windows, and other religious art in the Catholic churches. Philip promptly sent in an army. The Duke of Alva, Philip's commander, launched a campaign of terror against the Netherlanders, killing 100,000 of them in only six years. As the fighting continued, the Calvinists moved to the north, leaving the southern provinces to the Catholics. In 1579, ten southern provinces formed a league to defend Catholicism. By 1581, the seven northern provinces declared their independence from Spain.

The new state, called the United Provinces, chose William of Orange as its leader. William was nicknamed "the Silent" by some French diplomats. Actually, he was an **articulate**, friendly person. His determination, patience, tolerance, and belief in government by consent of the people kept alive the spirit of independence and served as a spark for democracy. Each of the seven provinces was fairly independent of the others. It took all of William's considerable tact to keep them working together.

Frustrated, Philip II offered a large reward to anyone who would kill William. In 1584, a young Catholic fanatic managed to assassinate the Dutch ruler. The revolt continued, however, under the leadership of William's son. Finally the Dutch got their independence through the **Treaty of Westphalia** (1648). Philip's suppression policy caused almost 80 years of war and cost Spain some of its richest provinces.

Toleration. William of Orange was one of the few people in sixteenth century Europe who favored *toleration*, the idea that the state should allow different religions to exist. Through his influence, freedom of conscience increased in The Netherlands. During the seventeenth century, the land became a refuge for the persecuted from all over Europe, including the English "Pilgrims" who eventually journeyed to America to begin the world's greatest experiment in freedom.

Toleration, a policy which seems so reasonable in the twentieth-first century, was thought to be a danger by many to Christian society. Toleration can indeed be misused by some to make room for humanistic secularization which in turn destroys both freedom and the possibility of toleration.

Northern European Protestant Exploration

Rulers in Northern Europe had listened eagerly to tales of gold and silver and spices. They laid plans to get in on the profits coming to Spain and Portugal. No one felt strong enough to challenge the two southern nations directly. Although France, Holland, and England sent explorers to the New World, these men stayed far north of the Spanish colonies there, hoping they could find a passage to the East by going around the north side of North America.

In spite of Spain and Portugal's head start at gaining an empire, the nations of Northern Europe had many advantages too. Northern nations had developed thriving capitalist economies, and their upper classes looked on business as a worthy vocation. Also, the inflation that sent Spanish wages and prices through the ceiling came more slowly to the north.

Holland Takes Over Trade with the Indies. The Dutch at first had little to complain about. Their

William of Orange, "the Silent," 1533–1584

position as one of the richest areas in the Spanish Empire gave them a share of the colonial trade. They reaped great profits supplying Spain and Portugal with manufactured goods and distributing colonial produce in Europe. However, when the Dutch revolted against Spain in the sixteenth century, they lost much of this business. Heavily dependent on the sea for trade, Holland sent ships directly to India. These voyages proved so successful that in 1602, the government and several private groups formed the Dutch East India Company, with a legal monopoly on trade with the Indies.

And where were the Portuguese when Dutch ships invaded their private trading area? By this time, Spain had taken over Portugal and was using both nations' fleets to protect routes to the

New World. Thus the Dutch found it an easy matter to drive Portugal out of the Indies.

Holland did not try to colonize the East but rather built forts and made treaties with local rulers to gain control of the trade. From their bases in the East Indies, they carried on a thriving commerce with China, Japan, and India. They did settle a few colonists at the Cape of Good Hope in Africa to man a supply station.

In the Western Hemisphere, the Dutch gained a small province, Suriname or Dutch Guyana, in South America and founded New Amsterdam (New York) on Manhattan Island in North America. The English explorer Henry Hudson, who sailed for Holland, found and claimed the

The largest Spanish fleet since the Armada put out to sea in 1639 in one last effort to subdue Holland. Dutch ships, though badly outnumbered, attacked the fleet and disabled or captured 70 out of the 77 galleons. This defeat hastened Spain's decline.

entire Hudson River valley for the Dutch. They started another outpost, Fort Orange (Albany), and gave out large estates to families such as the Roosevelts, who were destined to play a major role in later history.

In the seventeenth century, Holland became wealthy and powerful. Although a small land with few natural resources, by 1600 it had the world's largest merchant fleet, numbering 10,000 ships. Mass producing ships which were economical to operate, they were able to undercut the competition. Soon they were carrying most of the cargo between Spain, France, England, and the Baltic Sea. The English could not compete with Dutch merchant shipping until the eighteenth century.

At this time, Holland had a unique **republican** form of government. The seven Dutch provinces were joined in a loose federation. They had a national assembly, the States-General, composed of delegates from each provincial assembly. The provincial assemblies dated from the Middle Ages and represented the nobility and the towns. Each provincial assembly elected its own executive leader (*stadholder*).

The States-General handled foreign affairs and defense, which Calvinists saw as two of the few roles of a civil government. It usually chose as its executive (captain-general) the *stadholder* of the province of Holland, who was also leader of four other provinces. This complex arrangement often caused a crisis of authority. Much of the **Dutch Republic**'s history in the seventeenth century involved the struggle over provincial sovereignty versus a tight federal union.

Frederick Henry of Orange nearly succeeded in uniting the Dutch. He persuaded the assemblies of the five provinces of which he was *stadholder* to promise that his position would pass on to his

One key reason why the Netherlands achieved so much in the 17th century was due to its unswerving commitment to the Reformation. In this cartoon, the teachings of the Calvinist Gomarus outweigh the rags of the teachings of Jacob Hermandszoon or Arminius. Arminius led the Remonstrants who objected to the teachings of the Reformed Church. The Synod of Dordrecht (1618–19) was called to settle the controversy. This international meeting of Reformed teachers stressed the doctrines of unconditional predestination, total depravity, definite atonement, and the perseverance of the saints.

sons. He also behaved like a king in his handling of foreign affairs and in the court he kept at The Hague. But his alliance with Charles I of England brought his downfall. Charles was the fierce enemy of the Calvinist Puritans, who controlled the English Parliament and eventually overthrew the English monarchy in a revolution led by Oliver Cromwell. By 1653, The Netherlands, a Calvinist country, had gone back to its former status.

Like Spain and Portugal, Holland eventually began to slip from its place of economic power.

The Dutch East India Company, which operated out of such harbors as Enkhuizen on the Zuider Zee, imported products from the Orient to Europe.

The Netherlands in 1648

DUTCH REPUBLIC

SPANISH NETHERLANDS

Groningen

Zuider Zee

North Sea

Amsterdam

DUTCH REPUBLIC

The Hague

Utrecht

Rotterdam

Archbishopric of Cologne

Brügge

Antwerp

Ghent

GERMANY

Bishopric of Liége

Brussels

SPANISH NETHERLANDS

Liége

KINGDOM OF FRANCE

Luxembourg

Palatinate

Lorraine

Henry Hudson, English navigator and explorer who discovered the Hudson River and Hudson Bay

The British and French passed laws which hindered Dutch shipping. For example the **Navigation Acts** in England required that exports from English colonies be carried on English ships. A long series of wars, first with England (1652–1674) and then with France (1667–1713), also weakened Holland. In these wars, Holland lost its territory in North America to England.

There was yet another factor in the Dutch decline; they lacked the manpower and resources to maintain their rate of growth. Both the English and the French had larger populations and more abundant natural resources to support empire-building once they started.

English Explorations. Hoping to find a route to the East Indies, England's global explorations began in the late fifteenth century when **King Henry VII** sent **John Cabot** off into the North Atlantic. In 1497, five years after Columbus sailed to the New World, Cabot explored the coast of what is now the United States and claimed it for England. He could not find a pas-

sage to the East, but he did discover that the sea off Newfoundland teemed with fish. Compared to gold, silver, and spices, his find may seem unexciting; but in the meat-poor world of the sixteenth century, fish were a very important trade item. Also, the Newfoundland fishing fleets trained generations of Northern European mariners in ocean navigation.

Cod fishing did not satisfy those who wished to find spices, so the search for a passage to the Indies continued. When these attempts failed, both the English and French tried to trade with the Spanish colonies. Spain quickly put a stop to this, only to find its ships then falling prey to

English and French pirates. Two English buccaneer captains, **John Hawkins** and **Francis Drake**, became famous for their bold strikes, not only at Spanish ships but also against the rich settlements in the New World.

France Claims Canada and Louisiana. At the beginning of the sixteenth century, France explored the St. Lawrence River valley in North America, hoping to find the long-sought passage to the Indies. Early attempts at settlement there failed. Not until the seventeenth century did the French make a serious attempt to start colonies. They built the towns of Quebec (1608) and Montreal (1642) in Canada. Using the river system of North America, they explored much of the eastern part of the continent. In 1682, they laid claim to the entire Mississippi Basin, which they named Louisiana, after the French King Louis XIV.

In spite of great efforts, French colonial expansion made little progress. The settlements did not receive enough support because France was too busy with affairs in Europe. As late as 1690, there were only 20,000 Frenchmen in all of Canada.

Decline of the Ottoman Turks

It will be recalled that in 1556, the Holy Roman emperor, **Charles V**, weary of his responsibilities and the struggles of his time, abdicated the throne. The Hapsburg empire was split—the western share (Spain, Italy, the Low Countries, etc.) going to his son **Philip** and the eastern share (Austria, Germany, Bohemia, and Hungary) went to Charles' brother, **Ferdinand I**. Most of Hungary, at that time, was actually under occupation by the Turks, even though Ferdinand had inherited it as king as early as 1526.

The conquest of Hungary by the Ottoman Turks sent shivers through Christian Europe, for it looked at the time that the Turks might overrun the whole of the continent. In 1529, the sultan **Suleiman (the Magnificent)** laid siege on Vienna. That siege proved unsuccessful and the Turks were forced to retreat. Though several renewed threats of attack followed, the Ottoman force, in characteristic fashion for oriental despotic regimes, became riddled with internal strife and corruption. The sultans soon lost their vigor and seemed content to indulge themselves in the demoralizing pleasures of their harems. As a result, their armies and administrations became further corrupt.

A brief revival of Ottoman vitality occurred about 1683, and new invasions of Europe were launched. Vienna, under the able leadership of Polish King **John Sobrieski**, again stubbornly resisted and even turned the assault into an utter rout of the Mohammedans. The Ottoman

Empire steadily declined, although remnants of it existed as late as the early 20th century. The last sultan was overthrown by **Kemal Atatürk** in 1922 who established the modern Turkish nation.

Austria took new courage from its 1683 victory at Vienna. Under a gifted general, **Prince Eugene of Savoy**, who had earlier distinguished himself against the French forces of Louis XIV at the Rhine, the Turks were completely driven out of Hungary. Thus as France was gaining the ascendancy over the Hapsburgs in Western Europe, the Hapsburg Austrian empire was on the rise in the East.

The Thirty Years' War

War in Bohemia. As previously noted, for many years, Catholics had worn the crown of the Holy Roman Empire. Of the seven voting states which elected the emperors, the majority were usually Catholic. Then in 1618, the Protestants thought they had a chance to gain the throne.

Bohemia, a part of the modern Czech Republic, was one of the voting states in the empire. The nobles of Bohemia elected its kings, and for nearly a century they had chosen a Catholic Hapsburg. By the early seventeenth century, however, many Bohemians had become Protestant. (These Protestants were the descendants of the followers of John Hus, one of the earliest sparks of the Reformation. Hus had died a martyr in 1415, but a tiny remnant of his followers survived to become the *Unitas Fratrum* [Unity of the Brethren], the forerunner of the Moravian Church.) The Bohemian Protestants, numbering more than 200,000, feared the power of the Hapsburgs and the Catholic Church. Their fears

seemed confirmed when **Ferdinand II**, grandnephew of Charles V and an intolerant Catholic Hapsburg with rigid piety, was named king of Bohemia in 1617 and king of Hungary in 1618. Despite promises to the contrary and despite the terms of the Peace of Augsburg negotiated by his father (Ferdinand I, brother of Charles V), Ferdinand II began to persecute Protestants.

Before long, the Protestants decided they had had enough. A huge, angry crowd swarmed Hradschin Castle in the king's absence and threw two of his representatives out a window. Although they fell 50 feet, they landed on a pile of rubbish and were not seriously hurt.

Then the Bohemian representative assembly, the Estates, met to elect a new king. They chose a handsome young Calvinist prince, **Frederick, Elector Palatine** (Royal Elector) of the Rhine. In the Palatinate in 1619, Frederick arrived in Prague for his coronation. The Protestants were jubilant. Now they controlled four of the seven votes needed to elect the Holy Roman emperor. At last a Protestant would win.

But that was not to be. The mighty Hapsburg army, commanded by **Count Tilly**, attacked Bohemia. Frederick expected help from other Protestant nations, but it did not come. In November 1620, at the **Battle of White Mountain** near Prague, Count Tilly crushed Frederick's troops. Frederick ruled Bohemia for such a short time that he has gone down in history as the "Winter King." A further result of this defeat was the absorption of a part of the Palatinate by Bavaria in 1628.

After the Hapsburg victory, Jesuits arrived in the conquered land to force Catholicism on the people. Protestant lands, especially of the nobles, were seized and given to loyal Catholics. Ferdi-

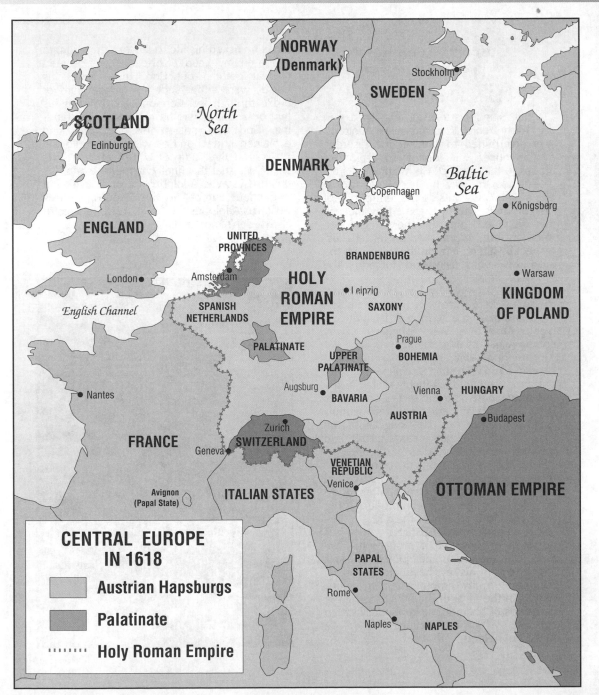

CENTRAL EUROPE IN 1618

- Austrian Hapsburgs
- Palatinate
- .... Holy Roman Empire

Heidelberg, Germany, was the capital of the Palatinate. This Reformed Protestant area was continually attacked by Roman Catholic forces. Many of the residents fled to the Netherlands, and from there came to North America to settle in Pennsylvania.

nand, who had been elected Holy Roman emperor in 1619, again became king of Bohemia.

Denmark Enters the War. The sweeping Catholic victory frightened other Protestant princes of Europe. They united behind **Christian IV** of Denmark and entered the war. Christian IV had built his power and wealth by controlling the entry to the Baltic Sea. Now, in addition to helping the Protestants, he wanted more territory for his dynasty.

Taking stock of the Protestant army, Emperor Ferdinand saw that he needed help. He struck a bargain with a strange, sinister **mercenary** soldier, **Albert von Wallenstein**. A man of boundless ambition, Wallenstein had gotten rich from the lands seized from the Bohemian Protestants. He agreed to furnish an army of 20,000 men at no cost to the empire. As he fought the Danes, he proved to be an excellent general. Christian withdrew from the war in defeat.

The Hapsburg tide had now come in. It looked as though German Protestants would be forced to convert to Catholicism. Then in 1629, Ferdinand ordered all lands which Protestants had taken since 1552 to be returned to the Catholics. The order was known as the **Edict of Restitution.** Not only were the Protestant princes upset, but now so were the Catholic rulers, who suspected that Ferdinand was using his edict as an excuse to gain more control over Germany. The Protestant princes feared Wallenstein and demanded that his army be dissolved. To ease their suspicions, Ferdinand dismissed Wallenstein and disbanded his army.

Sweden's Turn. If Ferdinand's order for conversion of all Protestant lands could have been fully enforced, it would have destroyed Protestantism in Germany. But the German Catholic princes hindered enforcement. The death blow to Ferdinand's dreams came when the Swedish king, Gustavus Adolphus, invaded Germany in 1630. A brilliant soldier, statesman, and devout Lutheran, Gustavus was one of the most competent rulers in early modern times. Before his invasion of Germany, he had defeated the Danes, the Russians, and the Poles. Called the "Lion of the North," he entered the war not only to save Protestantism but also to stay in control of the Baltic Sea.

Although the Thirty Years' War had started with a religious issue, the battle became a political contest. Part of the money to finance the Swedish forces came from the Catholic king of France, a longtime enemy of the Hapsburgs. With the best-trained army since the Roman legions, Gustavus defeated the Catholics near Leipzig.

Ferdinand had only one hope left—Wallenstein. The crafty general raised an army and met the Swedes in the **Battle of Lützen** (1632), also near Leipzig. Although the Protestants won, Gustavus

Gustavus Adolphus (1594–1632)
Lion of the North

During Sweden's invasion of Germany in the Thirty Years' War, Gustavus Adolphus was determined to prevent the disorder, disobedience, and looting so typical of armies in that conflict. He maintained strict discipline. One day he happened to see two stolen cows outside the tent of one of his corporals. Taking the man by the ear, the king led him to the executioner. Another time he punished an officer's disrespect by hitting him on the head with the flat of his sword, using such force that the sword broke.

Influenced deeply by his Lutheran faith, the king held prayers twice a day for his soldiers and offered a sermon at least once a week. Absentees were punished. Every company had its own chaplain.

In the king's view, rigorous training went hand in hand with strict discipline. Constant drill produced soldiers highly skilled in the use of weapons and the tactics of warfare. Before a battle, the army would sometimes stage a practice run. The king chose the most effective military ideas available and brilliantly refined and adapted them to his needs. But he also worked out new techniques, constantly experimenting to find the best method. His personal attention to the development of guns produced the most advanced artillery of the day.

So greatly was Gustavus Adolphus admired in Europe that professional soldiers from many countries joined his army. Few men in history have inspired such complete loyalty among their followers. Always in the thick of the fight, sharing the hardships of his men, he continually set an example. When fortifications had to be built, he helped with the digging. Many times he risked his life to spy out the strength of the enemy. Scornful of danger, he seemed to fear nothing but God. Three times his horses were either shot from under him or broke through ice. Cannon balls tore up his tent or landed where he had just been standing. God had spared his life, the king explained, and when God will it, he would die.

It was in the Battle of Lützen of the Thirty Years' War that this finally happened. After his death, Gustavus Adolphus became a legend throughout Europe. To the Swedes, he was Gustavus Adolphus the Great, most beloved of all Sweden's monarchs.

was killed in action. Wallenstein tried to grab political power for himself, but he was murdered by his own officers who were then generously rewarded by Ferdinand.

France Takes Center Stage. By all rights, the war should have ended at this point, but France stepped in and kept it going. Now the conflict lost nearly all of its religious nature and became chiefly a dynastic struggle. Because France had a better army and brilliant leadership, the tide soon turned in its favor. The Hapsburgs were so badly defeated that Spain, the center of Hapsburg power, sank to second-rate-power status in Western Europe. France now took its place as the leading European state.

The war was ended, but it had left Germany so exhausted that it took almost a century to recover. Most of the armies had lived off the land. The soldiers, who were usually mercenaries, had no pity on the civilians. Disease and famine aided the troops in their dread task, to such an extent that the population decreased drastically—from 15 million to less than 5 million.

The Thirty Years' War was an international conflict. By the time the fighting ended, most of the states of Europe had joined in—France, Spain, Sweden, Denmark, Bohemia, and the **principalities** of Germany. The treaties which concluded the war are considered the first modern international peace treaties.

Peace of Westphalia. The series of treaties which settled the war in 1648 is known as the **Peace of Westphalia**. The settlement was a victory for Protestantism and the German princes, a defeat for Catholicism and the Hapsburgs. Under the settlement, a prince could again choose the religion of his state from among Calvinism, Lutheranism, and Catholicism. One of the terms recognized the sovereignty of more than 300 princedoms, cities, and **bishoprics**. Another demanded that the emperor have the consent of the princes before he could pass laws, raise taxes, recruit soldiers, or make war or peace. Since these small units argued all the time, agreement on most issues was nearly impossible.

Other terms of the Peace of Westphalia recognized The Netherlands and Switzerland as independent states, clear victories for Calvinists, who had borne the brunt of the heaviest persecutions.

The Peace of Westphalia settled religious differences that had long troubled Europe. Catholics and Protestants realized that neither was strong enough to destroy the other. Therefore, they must learn to live together. With the treaty, the geographical boundaries of the Catholic and Protestant realms was largely fixed to where they are today.

At the same time, the Eastern Orthodox churches in Eastern Europe, Asia Minor, and the Balkans were undergoing severe oppression from the Turks. Despite the persecution, Orthodoxy grew, especially in Russia, where it became a powerful institution.

From Counter-Reformation to Absolutism

During the sixteenth century reign (1515–1547) of **Francis I**, France had become one of the great powers of Europe. At the same time, the long rivalry between the Hapsburgs and the French kings began. The Hapsburg family then ruled what is now Spain, Germany, Austria, Belgium, and The Netherlands. For more than two centuries, the struggle between these two ruling families was to shape European history.

Despite constant warfare, Francis strengthened the monarchy. Among the most significant steps in this process was the **Concordat of 1516**, in which **Pope Leo X** conceded most of the control of the Catholic Church in France to Francis. This was somewhat ironic, in that Francis had little real interest in or knowledge of theological matters, preferring rather humanistic learning, secular cultural refinements, and social merriment. Four years earlier (1512), a devout churchman, **Jacques Lefèvre**, had initiated the beginnings of a religious reformation movement based on his scriptural studies of the doctrine of *justification by faith,* the central issue raised by Luther in Germany in 1517. The reforms sought by Lefèvre and his supporters were opposed by the conservative theological faculty of the University of Paris, known as the **Sorbonne**. Catholic leaders pressured Francis into persecuting the reformers, something which he was reluctant to do but which he found necessary in order to maintain the support of the French church. When Francis was captured and imprisoned by Charles V during one of their wars, Francis' mother, the interim regent of the French throne, intensified the persecution. Among the reformers who suffered in this persecution was a young man named **John Calvin**, who was banished from France in 1534. Calvin, of course, was destined to shake the world in the years to come with his views and activities in Geneva.

The persecution of Protestants intensified under Francis' son **Henry II**. Despite the persecution, Calvinism grew in France. Dozens of Calvin's pastoral students secretly returned to France as missionaries and won many converts among the artisan class in the cities and among the nobility. This group of converts, known as the **Huguenots**, had grown large enough by 1559 to hold a national synod and adopt a confession of faith written by Calvin himself.

Catherine de Médici (1519–89), part of the famous Médici family of Florence, Italy, married into the royal family of France. She instigated the St. Bartholomew's Day Massacre out of fear of growing Huguenot political influence.

the throne. Henry IV sought to end the religious strife. He did so when he, on one hand, converted to Catholicism in 1593 and, on the other hand, issued the **Edict of Nantes** in 1598, granting limited religious freedom to the Huguenots. During his reign, France prospered domestically in many ways. At the same time, Henry kept a close eye on the international situation in Europe, cultivating friendships with independent states and other interests which were enemies of the hated Hapsburgs. In 1610 he went to war with the Austro-Spanish powers, but during preparations for the campaign, he was assassinated by a Catholic fanatic.

Henry was succeeded by his nine-year-old son **Louis XIII**. His youthfulness demanded a regency once again, and this role was filled by his mother, the Italian **Marie de Mèdici**, who lacked both the character and intelligence needed to succeed. Rivalries developed between the Italian nobles surrounding Marie and the court's French nobles, mostly Huguenots. The French nobles took up arms against the regent. Although they were eventually pacified with pensions and honors, they continued to hold out the threat of renewed religious wars.

Into this rivalry stepped one Armand Jean du Plessis, better known to history as the famous (or infamous) **Cardinal Richelieu**, a member of Marie's royal council. Richelieu, as the king's chief minister, became the true power in France. He proceeded to disseminate the Huguenot nobles' political power while paying lip service to Protestant religious rights. He cleverly consolidated and centralized the royal power (in fact, his own) by several means, including shelving the ancient popular assembly, the Estates-General, and ignoring the powers of the *parlements,* the system of law courts. Through Richelieu's actions, the French throne became answerable to

Armand-Jean Richelieu (1585–1642) was a bishop in the Roman Catholic Church in France. He was the chief architect of French absolutism, which implemented Catholic hierarchical views of power. He was as ambitious as he was ruthless in building a centralized government by destroying the influence of the Huguenots and the nobility.

no one but itself. His consolidation of power at home was matched by his skills in maneuvering France into a position of supremacy in Europe. He did this by supporting the Protestant German princes against the Catholic Hapsburgs during the Thirty Years' War. In the 1648 **Peace of Westphalia**, signed six years after Richelieu's death, France gained many advantages.

After Henry died an accidental death during wedding festivities for his daughter, he was succeeded respectively by three sons, who were sickly or otherwise weaklings. His widow, **Catherine de Médici**, exercised considerable power during this period and instituted a measure of religious freedom. Catherine attempted to mediate between two rival branches of the **Valois** royal family, the **Guises** (who were staunch Catholics) and the **Bourbons** (who had aligned themselves with the Reformation). This rivalry resulted in a period of ghastly civil strife with both religion and politics at its heart. When the last of Henry II's three sons, the effeminate **Henry III** was murdered, the first of the Bourbon kings, **Henry IV**, ascended to

France under Catholic Despotism

These factors laid the basis for the brilliant reign of **Louis XIV**, who came to the throne at age five upon the death of Louis XIII in 1643. Many practices begun by this monarch were widely imitated by other European rulers. France became the leading Roman Catholic power of the seventeenth century. (After considering Louis XIV, we will return to the colonial rivalries which occupied the French and English for almost a century.)

Louis XIV (1638–1715), the despot of France

The Sun King. During Louis XIV's youth, the government was controlled by Richelieu's successor as chief minister, **Cardinal Jules Mazarin**. Mazarin continued Richelieu's absolutist policies, and when he died, Louis did not appoint a suc-

cessor. Although it is historically unconfirmed that Louis XIV ever uttered the famous phrase attributed to him, "I am the state," this boast well describes the facts. Between 1661 and 1715, Louis *was* the government of France. All major government affairs were reported to councils that he controlled. He could jail people without trial simply through royal order. No group in France had power to challenge him. Louis was an **absolute** monarch.

The French monarchy expressed an ancient idea held by many people in the 1600s. They believed that the king ruled by **divine right**. In other words, God had chosen him to rule, and he was responsible to God alone for his actions. Since the ruler was thought to be God's agent on earth, the people had a duty to submit to him without question. This idea prevailed in France until the **French Revolution** in 1789. The "divine right" doctrine was vigorously debated and held by kings in England as well, but the so-called **Glorious Revolution** that brought **William and Mary** to power in 1688 put an effective end to the doctrine there.

Everything that Louis did was in keeping with his exalted view of the monarchy. He chose as his emblem the sun, the center of the universe. His subjects called him "The Sun King." People in other parts of Europe referred to him as the "Grand Monarch."

The Court. A great king must have a great palace, and **Versailles** was such a palace. It provided a magnificent setting for the court. Several thousand nobles lived in its splendid rooms and were waited on by 4,000 servants. The expense of all this was enormous. Since Louis loved ceremony and lavish display, court life revolved around an elaborate social calendar. The Sun King was the center of every activity. The nobles received only

The Palace at Versailles

minor parts or watched the pageantry from the sidelines.

A day at the court began when the king arose and ended when he retired for the night. These two events were public occasions with the leading nobles handing the king his clothes. All day long, the nobles served the king as he went from one activity to another. In addition to about 5,000 nobles who lived at Versailles, nearly 5,000 more lived nearby. They flitted from party to party, from receptions to the gambling tables, from the hunt to concerts, plays, and balls. Immorality at the court caused scandal after scandal. Flattery and hypocrisy were the keys to success, and the more sensitive people were depressed and bored. Louis seemed to want it that way. While the nobles were busy with petty court activities, his middle-class civil servants were taking away their power in the provinces. The nobles became useless social **parasites**.

Running the Government. While Louis personally controlled the government councils, he appointed 34 **intendants** who had the actual power of local government. He left the structure of local provincial rule intact, but he had control through his own middle-class **bureaucracy**. To head off any challenge to his power, he refused to call a meeting of the French representative assembly, the Estates-General.

Colbert. One of the few men that the king trusted with power was his finance minister, **Jean Baptiste Colbert**. A brilliant, hard-working administrator, Colbert was devoted to his king and country. He directed commerce, industry, agriculture, the colonies, art, and finance. He worked out a system for the country's finances and stopped much of the graft. Under his capable leadership, state income tripled. However, Louis's many wars and costly court made it impossible to balance the budget.

Colbert believed that the economic as well as the political affairs of the state should serve the king. He devised a policy to achieve this—**mercantilism**. It called for careful government regulation of the economy. Colbert believed that a hoard of gold and silver was necessary for a strong nation. Because France did not have precious metal mines, it would have to export more goods than it imported in order to increase gold and silver supplies. With this in mind, he encouraged industries with overseas trade. He also built a larger merchant fleet.

Colbert saw the need for colonies as sources of raw materials and as markets for finished goods. He expanded domestic trade by building better roads and canals and ending internal tariffs. While French business was encouraged to be as self-sufficient as possible, industries were given **subsidies** and required to produce high quality goods. Colbert wanted French products to command respect in other lands.

The finance minister served his king well, but his efforts to solve French financial problems failed. Besides the cost of constant warfare, the heavy regulation tended to discourage initiative and caused more economic problems—just as centrally regulated socialist systems of modern times have done.

But Louis and Colbert did bring about a great flowering of the arts, literature, and science in France. The French Academy polished French writing to a peak of perfection. Indeed, French replaced Latin as the leading language of Europe, and French culture became a model for much of the continent.

Religious Persecution. In spite of lessons which should have been learned from the religious wars, Louis would not tolerate non-Catholic religions. The religious rights of the Huguenots had been guaranteed by the Edict of Nantes in 1598. However, in 1679, Louis tried to force them to become Catholics. Louis destroyed most Protestant churches, limited their schools, and boarded troops in Protestant homes (ordering them to be as offensive as possible). At the same time, he offered tax exemptions and bonuses to Huguenots who converted to Catholicism. In 1685, Louis revoked the Edict of Nantes, the legal basis for Protestant rights. More than 200,000 Huguenots fled the country, taking their considerable skills to The Netherlands, Prussia, England, and America.

The Army. Louis sought further fame by his military adventures. He wished to enlarge France to what he considered her natural boundaries—the Rhine River and the Alps Mountains. The staggering cost of these wars tarnished his glory rather than increased it.

The French army had an exceptional leader named **Louvois**. He was responsible for the fine discipline and the brilliant use of artillery and engineering by Louis's forces. Louvois started using uniforms, bayonets, and the kind of organization found in modern warfare. In a complex system, he linked supply depots with barracks located at strategic places in France.

Louis's military victories made the rest of Europe fear and respect France, but these wars weakened the land internally. On his deathbed, Louis advised his great-grandson and heir to avoid further wars.

French Catholics tried to convert the natives of North America. Many French priests were tortured and killed by the tribesmen. However, a Jesuit named Father Marquette so succeeded in winning the Indians' confidence that he could travel among them merely by carrying a peace pipe. In 1673, on a government mission to find a route to the Pacific, Marquette discovered the Mississippi River.

English-French Conflict

England Settles the Atlantic Coast. More than 100 years passed between the time Cabot claimed the Atlantic coast of North America and the time the first English settlers arrived. But by the middle of the seventeenth century, the English had started a series of colonies in North America as well as on the islands of the West Indies. These

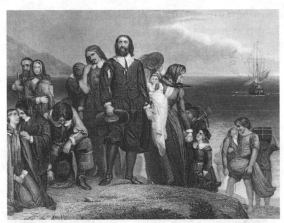

The Pilgrims first set foot on North America in 1620.

colonies differed from those of other countries in that the government did not found them. Religious groups settled North America, seeking freedom of worship. Other groups of people came in hopes of making a better living in the New World.

The English settlements also differed from one another. In Virginia and its neighbors arose a style of life and economy based on tobacco growing. To the north, the Puritans who settled New England engaged in fishing, trading, lumbering, and the fur trade. The most valuable of England's new colonies were the West Indies, where sugar plantations produced their rich crop. By the late 1600s, more than 300,000 English-speaking people lived in North America.

As the tide of English settlers swelled, more and more often they found themselves competing with the French for the same space. A string of French forts rose along the Mississippi River, cutting off westward movement of English pioneers.

Unlike the French colonies, English settlements allowed a degree of religious freedom and encouraged people to start private businesses. Also, the English colonies elected legislatures which were

First Winter at Plymouth

It was a raw December day when the Pilgrims arrived at Plymouth, the beginning of winter. They had not intended to land so far north, but it was too risky to travel farther in such weather. Unloading their supplies, they began to build. They worked in haste; however, it was already too late to protect themselves adequately from the fury of that first winter in the New World. William Bradford, elected governor of Plymouth for nearly thirty years, tells of the sufferings of those first months.

In two or three months time half of their company died, especially in January and February, being the depth of winter. Lacking houses and other comforts, infected with scurvy and other diseases, which this long voyage and harsh conditions had brought upon them, there died sometimes two or three of a day. Of some one hundred persons, scarce fifty remained. And of these in the time of most distress there were but six or seven sound persons, who, to their credit, spared no pains, night nor day, but with abundance of toil and hazard of their own health, fetched wood for the sick, made fires, prepared food, made their beds, washed their loathsome clothes, clothed and unclothed them. In a word, they did all the homely and necessary tasks for them which dainty and queasy stomachs cannot endure to hear named—and all this willingly and cheerfully, without any grudging in the least, showing herein their true love unto their friends and brethren. A rare example and worthy to be remembered... while they had health, yea, or any strength continuing, they held back nothing from any that had need of them. And I doubt not but their reward is with the Lord....

Adapted from William Bradford, *Bradford's History of Plymouth Plantation* (Boston: Wright & Potter, 1901).

usually at odds with the governor appointed by the crown. In the French colonies, governors appointed by the king ran affairs.

In addition to establishing their power in the New World, the English tried to take over the East Indies from the Dutch. When they failed in this attempt, they made greater efforts in the Orient and India. Soon England gained several major trading posts in India and stood toe to toe with France, which had posts there too. The East India Company, with a monopoly on trade from the Cape of Good Hope to the Straits of Magellan, was in charge of British trade with India. Through bribes and diplomacy and by taking advantage of weak native states, the company became the most powerful political force in the land during the eighteenth century.

The Second Hundred Years' War. These events set the stage for a duel between France and Britain—a duel for empire. This contest lasted almost a century. Each time the two nations clashed, fighting took place in Europe as well as overseas. Of course, the European phase involved a lot more than rivalry over colonies. Battles there aimed at keeping a balance of power among the strong nations. The overseas wars were fought over North America, India, and the control of world trade.

Although the first three wars settled some issues in Europe, they accomplished little in North America, where most of the overseas fighting took place. The British gained certain coastal areas such as Nova Scotia, but the question of who should control the Mississippi Valley remained unsettled. This was a key issue, for if the French held that area, English settlement would be limited to the Atlantic seaboard.

The final struggle, the **French and Indian War** or **Seven Years' War** (1756–1763), went badly for the British at first. Then under the leadership of **William Pitt the Elder**, English fortunes changed. He threw everything into the colonial war and paid Prussia to keep France busy fighting in Europe. A series of victories followed for the British, with the decisive one coming at the **Battle of Quebec** (1759). When Montreal fell in the following year, the French colonial empire in North America was finished.

In India, the Seven Years' War also ended in a British triumph. Several events led up to the war. **Joseph Dupleix**, the French leader, had trained Indians to fight with European methods. Using his army to help friendly native rulers, he had brought a series of states under French control. But France began to worry that Dupleix's tactics would lead to war and thus removed him. War came anyway in 1756. The French might have won, had it not been for **Robert Clive**, a British genius at empire-building. Using Dupleix's techniques, he formed alliances with a number of native princes. At the **Battle of Plassey** (1757), he defeated a large pro-French army and brought about their eventual surrender.

What factors finally enabled England to win its 100-year struggle with the French? For one thing, Britain put more effort into its overseas expansion. Then too, the British managed to stay out of many of the European wars. The French, on the other hand, were determined to keep their power in Europe and had less energy to spend in the colonial wars. Another explanation for the British victory was the fact that their North American colonies were more heavily settled than the French possessions. The French allowed only Roman Catholics to come to America, or they might have had many Huguenot settlers. Finally, British industrial and commercial development supplied them with a better fleet and superior technology.

The war was ended by the **Treaty of Paris** of 1763, an agreement which had global significance. The treaty gave England control of North America and India, setting the nation well on its

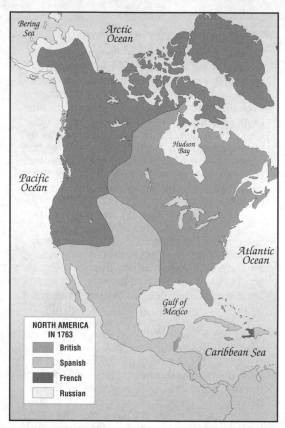

NORTH AMERICA
IN 1763

British
Spanish
French
Russian

way to world power. The great empire later built in the nineteenth century had its foundation in the victory over France in the Second Hundred Years' War.

Absolutism in Prussia

Prussia Takes the Absolutist Path. Rulers throughout Europe admired the absolute monarchy of Louis XIV and tried to copy it. No one met with more success than the **Hohenzollern Dynasty** in Prussia. This German state imported the techniques of Louis wholesale. Soon it had a

standing army and mercantilism, and its centralized government had reduced the nobles' power.

The parts of northeast Germany belonging to the Hohenzollerns, Brandenburg and East Prussia, did not seem very promising in the mid-seventeenth century. Much of the land was poor and sandy, and the Thirty Years' War had turned the area into a wasteland. Yet Prussia would later become the determining force in German history, the center around which the German nation would arise.

Frederick William, **the Great Elector**, began to rule during the troubled times of the Thirty Years' War. Foreign troops held most of the Hohenzollern lands then, but he managed to recover and even add to them at the Peace of Westphalia. To build a strong state, he relied on two institutions, the army and the bureaucracy. Despite the coming of peace, he continued to build a larger army. By the end of his reign, the Prussian army was one of the finest in Europe. It represented the ruler's power in tax collecting and police action in his far-flung territories.

The Prussian bureaucracy became one of the most efficient and highly centralized in the world. The nobles (*Junkers*) were forced out of government. Their places were taken by men under the ruler's direct control. A central Council of State under Frederick William's direction ran the entire bureaucracy. Middle-class civil servants were very important in the council.

Frederick William invited emigrants to settle in Prussia. When Louis XIV revoked the Edict of Nantes, thousands of Huguenots came, bringing many skills needed by the growing state.

Applying mercantilism to the Prussian economy, Frederick William set up high tariffs, limited imports, and gave subsidies to encourage industries. He also built roads and canals and developed an efficient postal service. The city of Berlin was rebuilt and made a place of beauty. By 1688, it had 30,000 residents (compared with 6,000 in 1640). Travelers were amazed at its development.

In another achievement, Frederick William entered the Polish-Swedish War and secured clear ownership of East Prussia. As Duke of Prussia, he became one of the crowned heads of Europe, rather than just another German prince.

A Military State. After Elector Frederick William's reign, his coarse, hard-working grandson, **Frederick William I**, continued building Prussia. The new king was a strange, miserly person with a violent temper. He hated lazy people. A sincere but misguided Protestant, he considered theaters "temples of Satan" and closed them all. Although he was only five feet, five inches tall, he admired tall people and built a palace guard of 3,000 giant soldiers, some as tall as eight feet.

Previously, armies had depended upon volunteers, mercenaries, or troops called up by **impressment** (forcing men into the military ser-

Strict Prussian military punishment.

vices). In 1732, the country set up a **draft system**. All adult males were subject to call, but in practice, most soldiers came from the poor classes. To keep discipline, the king handed out savage punishments for the smallest offenses.

In another important change, the king limited the officer corps to the landholders with nobility. This action won support for the crown. By 1724, most noble families had a son who was an army officer. Military leaders received many advantages, including a sound education, a high standard of living, and social prestige. History ascribes to Frederick William I the foundation of Prussian, and later German, **militarism**. A twentieth-century Nazi once wrote, "Frederick William I speaks through Adolf Hitler."

The king carried his military ideas over into the bureaucracy. He set up a general directory to keep watch on government workers. Special councils did the same in various parts of the domain. His control extended even to the local level where all self-government was ended. The king watched over every detail of government and severely punished laziness, corruption, deception, and waste.

The Prussian system of education was also controlled by the government and was designed to advance the cause of the state. This educational model was later adopted in the United States in the 1840s under the label of common or public schools. Government schools, by design, served the compelling interests of the secular state of Prussia, and also served the interests of those individuals in the U.S. who desired to transform their country into a secular socialistic state.

Religion did not escape his control. The king did not regard the Church as a place to preach the Gospel of Christ, but rather as a useful public institution. Its main purpose was to teach people the attitudes that would make them better sub-

Frederick the Great, 1712–1786

jects. (This attitude was also later reflected in Nazi Germany.) Though Frederick William I was a staunch Protestant, he allowed Roman Catholics religious freedom because he did not want them to leave Prussia.

Prussia Becomes a Great Power. Frederick II, also known as **Frederick the Great**, came next to the throne of Prussia. As a youth, Frederick had hated the austere life of the court. He wanted to paint, play the flute, and discuss philosophy. His father, Frederick William I, was determined to break the boy's spirit. The king burned his son's books, destroyed his flutes, and publicly beat him. At the age of 18, Frederick tried to run away, but he was caught and returned home. He was then forced to watch the execution of his best friend, who had helped him in the attempted escape. After serving a prison term, he accepted his father's plan for his life.

Frederick II became a cynical, bold, hard-working absolutist king. His father had built a large army but never used it much in battle. Frederick risked the Hohenzollern war machine several times to enlarge Prussia. Under his direction, the Hohenzollern Dynasty challenged the Austrian Hapsburgs for leadership in Central Europe.

While Prussian strength grew, Austria's declined. In a war in the early eighteenth century, Austria lost its southern Italian lands to Spain. When **Maria Theresa** came to the Austrian throne, she faced a difficult situation. Her father had tried to protect her by getting pledges from other European rulers to guarantee her territories. Although she was an able ruler, she did not have the military strength or the finances to wage war. Frederick II took advantage of the situation. He started a war with Austria in 1741 and seized its province of Silesia.

Now the stage was set for one of the most difficult conflicts Prussia ever faced, the Seven Years' War (1756–1763). Austria had made alliances with France and Russia in an effort to take back Silesia. Worried because these countries had Prussia surrounded, Frederick struck first. With considerable skill, he moved his armies on interior lines to face one enemy and then another. Despite his brilliance, he was on the verge of defeat three times. When the war finally ended, Prussia kept Silesia. However, Frederick's loss of half a million men seemed to teach him a lesson. During the rest of his reign, he worked to keep peace and to improve Prussia's domestic affairs.

As the architect of Prussian glory, Frederick the Great laid the groundwork for later German nationalism. According to Goethe, the great German poet, Frederick was "the polar star, who seemed to turn about himself Germany, Europe, nay the whole world."

From Feudalism to Absolutism in Russia

The czars of Russia found the idea of absolutism much to their liking, especially the first of the modern line of czars, **Peter the Great**. Before his time, Russia was of little importance in European affairs. But after 1700, with the decline of Sweden and Poland, Russia played a significant part. By the time of the Seven Years' War, it had become a European power.

Russia developed into nationhood over the eight centuries from its invasion by Scandinavians in the ninth century until Czar Peter. During this 800-year period, development of Russia as a nation occurred in three phases. The *first* was its discovery and "gathering" of itself as a people, unified by the Orthodox Church, with Kiev as its center. In its *second* phase, the national self-realization came as the Russians defended themselves against the Mongol invasions. The rise of Moscow as the seat of power represents Russia's *third* phase of development. As someone has observed, the actors of this historical drama comprised "a colorful cast—conquerors, idealists, strong-willed women, impostors and greedy rogues."

Russian Isolation. Several cultural and political details must be understood in order to appreciate Russia's role in modern history. During the Middle Ages—the earliest period for which a recorded history exists for Russia, it held a blend of Oriental and European peoples living in isolation from Western Europe. The native inhabitants were the pagan **Slavs**, peaceful, family-oriented tillers of the soil. Among the European peoples were the Scandinavian Vikings or **Varangians**, who moved down the Russian rivers from the Baltic to the Black Sea more than a thousand years ago, opening a trade route between Northern Europe and Byzantium. These peoples, first led by the legendary warrior-king, **Rurik** in 862, were democratic freemen who elected or deposed their kings at public meetings. Among these peoples were the Swedish East Vikings, also known as the **Ros** or **Rus**, from whom the name Russia eventually came. They introduced the first government with a ruler and laws at a capital called Kiev, which became the center of early Russian culture. It was here that the tenth-century Varangian leader **Vladimir, the Grand Prince of Kiev**, once a debauched and cruel pagan persecutor of Christians, Jews, and Muslims, decided to explore the three great religions and chose Christianity. He decreed, and sometimes forced, the baptism of all Kievans and put the nation on the path to Orthodoxy. By the turn of the millennium, Kievan culture flourished, but after Vladimir, the society fell into confusion. Under **Yaroslav the Wise**, the Russian ancestral city-state of Kiev reached its zenith. Beginning in 1036, Yaroslav codified the laws, built cathedrals, encouraged artisanship, and ended the threat of the savage **Pecheneg** nomads from the east. His grandson, **Vladimir Monomakh**, revived Kievan culture in the early twelfth century and led many successful campaigns against the next marauding threat from the east, the **Polovtsy**.

Mongol (also called Tatar, Tartar, or Turco-Mongol) invasions, led by the fierce, Asiatic warlord, Genghis Khan, overwhelmed the Kievan society in the thirteenth century and established nearly 250 years of Mongol dominion. Russian princes paid tributes to their new overlords from 1240 to 1480. The Mongol warriors, an aggressive force of cruel horse-riders, drove the Turkic tribes of the Asian steppes ahead of them as they descended upon the peaceful, cooperative, and unprepared Old Slavonic peasants of south and west Russia in the late Middle Ages. The con-

Worship in a Russian Orthodox Church emphasizes ceremonies and elaborate icons.

quered Russians were subjected to the despotism, greed, and paranoia that characterized the Mongol Golden Horde. The Mongol khans (princes) were not so much interested in establishing governments as they were in acquiring booty, which they needed to pay off their followers, who otherwise would have been inclined to join other warlords. As the Tartars intermarried with the Slavs, the Mongol traits of cruelty, greed, paranoia, and self-aggrandizement, along with a sense of world-conquering destiny, began to reshape the Russian character, and remained one of several key influences on the Russian mind into modern times.

Gradually, Russian refugees from Mongol rule settled in the western forest. Their main settlement became the town of Moscow, which in turn became the center of the kingdom of Muscovy. One of its rulers, **Ivan III (the Great)**, overthrew the Mongols and founded modern Russia. He imported Byzantine culture, Italian artists, and, most importantly, the full trappings of Eastern Orthodox religion.

The Russian Soul. Eventually, **Russian Orthodoxy**, a defective form of Christianity, became perhaps the greatest single factor shaping the Russian soul. Early Russian Orthodoxy had several features which are significant in this regard. It emphasized liturgy, formalism and mysticism. Worship of God was best accomplished through **icons**. Theologically, it put forth the false doctrine of the **deification** of man as the essence of salvation—by a mystical union with Christ. The great saints of Russian Orthodoxy were those who practiced a mystical life style. **St. Theodosius** epitomized this view of life. This sometimes led to the notion of willful submission (a kind of fatalistic nonresistance) to oppression or tyranny.

Another aspect of Orthodoxy, as exemplified in the famous monk, **St. Sergius of Radonezh**, was social and political involvement, usually in the form of church support for the reigning political power, whatever or whoever that might be. Orthodoxy taught that the czar had absolute authority in secular affairs, while the church had absolute authority in spiritual affairs. However, the two authorities were designed to undergird and support each other in their respective realms. This mutual supplementing would create the ideal Christian state over which church and state would share power.

Prominent in Russian religion, moreover, was the idea of the **"third Rome."** Churchmen taught that both the first Rome (the one in Italy, the seat of Western Catholicism) and Byzantium (the eastern seat of Greek Orthodoxy) had become corrupt. The fact that both cities and their ancient civilizations had been overrun was proof of God's judgment. Moscow, the center of Russian Orthodoxy, was now the "third Rome" and was commissioned by God to be the final repository of true Christianity. This vision of **Holy Russia** created a sense of world destiny and superiority among the Russians. The Soviet Communists of later days built their ideas of "world salvation" through Russia on this deep-seated aspect of the Russian soul.

Continued Isolation. Following Ivan the Great, further contact with the rest of Europe came during the reign of his grandson, **Ivan IV (the Terrible) (1547–1584)**. Ivan the Terrible was a bizarre and erratic person, given at times to horrific atrocities and at other times to rationality and culture. During his "good periods," he did much to advance culture and religion. Yet Russia remained almost untouched by the great developments that brought about modern civilization between 1400 and 1700. It had no large scale commerce, no middle class, no Renaissance nor Reformation, and took no part in the rise of modern science.

One of the features of this continuing isolation was widespread illiteracy, even among the clergy. Without scholarship, the "theological" disputes of churchmen centered mostly upon customs and liturgical traditions. Fierce debates occurred over what to modern Western minds appears to be

An example of Russian Orthodox architecture, St. Basil's in Moscow was part of the Kremlin, the center of power of the Russian Orthodox Church. Moscow was called the third Rome and took the place of Constantinople, after its fall.

trivial, such as whether the sign of the Cross was to be made with one, two, or three fingers.

Following Ivan the Terrible's death, the Russian Church began making moves to establish itself in a position of primacy among the churches of Eastern Orthodoxy, most of which were under Turkish domination at the time. As part of this effort, religious scholarship was increased and other reforms were undertaken. The work was done primarily by scholars from Kiev. Some in the church resisted their ideas, claiming they were tainted by detestable Western and Catholic ideas. But the scholars received the enthusiastic support of Patriarch Nikon, who imposed substantial changes upon the church. The pious, but somewhat weak-willed **Czar Alexis**, who ruled from 1645–1676, used his police to enforce these changes. (Alexis later deposed Nikon.)

Ivan the Terrible

Ivan IV was called "the Terrible" because of his total disregard for human life and his violent rages. He ordered Novgorod, Russia's second largest city, destroyed when he suspected that the citizens were guilty of treason. Another time he struck and killed his eldest son in a rage. And yet, at times, Ivan IV was completely normal and sensitive to the spiritual needs of his people.

He supported a plan to build churches in all communities so that people might hear the Gospel. But the churches he built were more than houses of worship; they were places where common people could learn to read and write. As people came to the local church on Sunday morning, the priests gave them lessons in basic skills. The Bible was taught in picture form, similar to Greek icons and frescoes. Thus even illiterate people could visualize God's message to man. Portions of the Bible were translated into the many languages spoken throughout the huge Russian empire.

But a group of devout, traditionalist churchmen known as the **Old Believers** rebelled against both church and czar, questioning, if the Russian Church were truly the "third Rome" and keeper of all truth, how Orthodoxy could be revised. A severe persecution of the Old Believers ensued, sending many into exile or dispersion. The greatest leader of the Old Believers was **Archpriest Avvakum**, who insisted on stringent personal piety and ritualistic purity. He challenged aspects of Russian life which he believed were pagan or revisionist. Avvakum was constantly tortured by the czar's officers and for 12 years was imprisoned in a hole in the ground. He was finally burned at the stake in Moscow in 1682.

The Old Believers concluded that the czar and his minions were the Antichrist. They came to believe that suicide was the most appropriate way to resist the Antichrist, and late in the seventeenth century, many, when approached by the imperial police, would gather themselves in their churches and set fire to the buildings. Tens of thousands died in this way.

The schism between the Old Believers and the revisionists was never healed. As a result, the Church was weakened and, under Czar Peter, Alexis' son, it was subjected to state power.

Siberia Falls to the Cossacks. Meanwhile, despite isolation from the West, Russian settlers did take part in exploration by pushing overland across Eurasia to the Pacific. Leading this drive to the east was a wild, violent people called the **Cossacks**. The Cossacks were not a distinct ethnic or racial group but a multi-ethnic group of peasant-soldiers consisting mostly of fugitive serfs and their descendents. In time, the term came to mean anyone who lived on the frontier, the steppe fringe of southern Russia. Runaway serfs from Poland and Russia escaped to this frontier where they lived by hunting, fishing, and plun-

dering in the same manner as the Mongols had. Something like pirates on land, Cossacks raided the czar's cities and killed his messengers. At other times, they hired on as border guards or soldiers for Moscow. In time, communities of free Cossacks developed, led by military commanders in the Dneiper and Don River valleys.

One of these leaders, Yermak, was hired by a merchant family, the Stroganovs, who owned a vast tract of land. This was an area with rich soil, iron, salt mines, and many fur-bearing animals. Some of the most valuable parts of the Stroganov lands stretched beyond the Ural Mountains into the Mongol state of Siberia. Yermak and his band drove deep into Mongol territory. The simple Mongol weapons (bows and lances) were no match for Yermak's cannons and firearms. When the Mongol capital of Sibir fell, the Russians applied its name, Siberia, to the entire area from the Ural Mountains to the Pacific Ocean.

The push to the east moved at an astonishing speed. By 1640, settlers reached Okhotsk on the Pacific coast. In a few short years, they had covered a distance one and one-half times greater than that between the Pacific and Atlantic coasts of the United States.

Driven by love of adventure and even more by a desire for furs, the Cossacks let nothing stop their advance to the Pacific. Sable, ermine, beaver, and other furs were extremely important in Russian trade and finance. In fact, the government acted as the chief fur dealer. As Russian rule spread in Siberia, the natives had to pay a tax in furs to the czar. Fur trappers' forts, looking like the timber block houses of the American frontier, sprang up across that vast land. Finally, Russia **annexed** Siberia, a highly profitable move for the nation. Later the czar made every province send a yearly quota of settlers to Siberia.

Others came to avoid military service, religious persecution, or serfdom. Serfdom existed in European Russia but not in Siberia. Although the Russians had made their way across Eurasia without meeting anyone powerful enough to stop them, they came to an abrupt halt at the border of the mighty Chinese (Manchurian) Empire on the south. The Russians were forced to go south to find food. They had traveled too far from Europe to get supplies from there and could not grow grain in cold Siberia. After several conflicts, the Chinese and Russians signed an agreement, the **Treaty of Nerchinsk** (1689), which fixed the border between the two countries.

On the home front, Russia went through a period of disorder beginning in 1604 called the "Time of Troubles." Civil war and foreign wars with the Poles, Swedes, and French threatened its destruction. During this period, Russia was officially ruled by a mentally retarded son of Ivan the Terrible, **Czar Fedor**. However, the real power was wielded by Fedor's brother-in-law, a ranking individual of Tartar descent, **Boris Godunov**. The legendary Godunov, later celebrated in several famous Russian literary or musical works, attempted to restore order during this chaotic period. When both Fedor and Godunov died, several pretenders to the throne arose and further political and social chaos ensued, along with drought and famine which left a million Russians dead. The disorganized nobility raised up a czar, but unrest continued. Cossacks led an assault on Moscow, while Poland and Sweden attempted to install czars of their own. Russia might have collapsed and perished had it not been for the Russian Orthodox Church. The church sent emissaries into the countryside calling the people to patriotism and renewed faith against the potential invasion of Catholics and Westerners. The people rallied a national army and stopped the Poles and Swedes from further challenge.

This nationalistic effort culminated when, in 1613, an assembly restored order by electing **Michael Romanov**, member of a respected family, as czar.

During the mid-seventeenth century, Russian law was codified, ostensibly to establish justice among all classes. However, the legal system actually worked more and more against the peasants, until serfdom was again deeply entrenched. As this was transpiring, several Cossack uprisings developed in the south. One result was the rise of separatistic and nationalistic sentiments among the Ukrainians (Little Russians) there.

The **Romanov Dynasty** ruled Russia from 1613 to 1917. Although the early Romanovs sought greater contact with the West, Russia remained an agricultural country with little commercial or city life. Its culture was so different from that of the West, and the location so far from the main stream of modernizing influence, that it did not become a modern state. However, like most Western nations, it did develop a strong monarchy that eventually opened Russia to the West and planted the seeds of its own demise.

Peter Admires Western Culture. The reign of **Peter I (the Great)** (1672–1725) marked a turning point in Russian history. Largely through his efforts, Russia became a world power. Peter, more than most absolutist rulers, put the welfare of his subjects last. A crude, savage, giant of a man, he was coarse in manners and speech and had a violent temper. He delighted in obscene, drunken orgies and in torturing his foes.

On the other hand, he brought boundless energy to his drive to make Russia great. To reach his goal, he sought closer contacts with the West so that Russians could absorb European ideas and technology. He was the first czar to travel abroad, visiting Prussia, Austria, Holland, and England.

In the spring of 1697, some 250 Russian officials, advisers, young nobles, and a husky sailor calling himself Peter Mikhailov set out from Moscow on a mission. The sailor was none other than Czar Peter himself, and the object of the trip was to learn from European civilization. Peter particularly wanted to study Western technology and felt that he would have more success if his teachers did not know he was ruler of Russia. Arriving in Holland, Peter and several companions obtained jobs as workmen at the East India Company shipyard. There they learned shipbuilding by helping build a frigate from start to finish. In Holland, Peter also studied anatomy, dentistry, and engraving. As the tour progressed, the czar also mastered gunnery in Germany and studied watchmaking, navigation, and coinage in England. While he traveled, he gathered models, plans, and specifications to use in improving Russian technology. Hundreds of craftsmen, technicians, naval men, engineers, and teachers were hired to work in Russia. When the Russians returned home, Peter launched a great technological and cultural revolution. Always in a hurry, he tried to achieve in a few decades what had taken Western Europe hundreds of years to accomplish.

On his trips, he studied shipbuilding, and he toured factories, hospitals, and public institutions. Often he would disguise himself and take a laboring job in order to learn a new skill.

Peter's love for the West led him to try to change the culture and attitudes of his people. He ordered them to wear Western clothing and shave off their beards, a sin in the eyes of the traditional Russian Church. He encouraged the use of tobacco, also viewed by many Russians as sinful. Women, who had been excluded from social life in the oriental fashion, now began to take a place in society. Peter encouraged education by starting schools and a printing industry and by demanding educated men for the civil service.

The most striking example of Western influence on Peter was his new capital city of St. Petersburg. Moscow was too set in its ways to suit him. In 1703, he decided to build a new city in the extreme northwestern corner of the land. It was as close as he could get to the West and still be in Russia. There in a bleak swamp, a new town arose at an immense cost in money and lives. St. Petersburg was not just another example of kingly splendor. Rather it was a "window on the West" through which Peter expected his subjects to look.

Peter's Army. After ruthlessly stamping out opposition in Russia, Peter began building the armed forces and reorganizing his administration. Using European models, he changed the basis for nobility from ancestry to state service. The new system made nobles highly dependent on the czar and encouraged more of them to become army officers.

To furnish money and men for war, he tried two major reforms—the poll tax and the draft. Because military costs were so great, often 80 percent of the budget, in 1719 he ordered a count of every male in the land except the clergy and nobility. Military costs were divided by the total number of males to determine the amount of the poll tax. To increase the size of his army, he set a quota for each village and town. Men between the ages of 20 and 25 were drafted for life. The army grew from 40,000 in 1700 to 200,000 in 1725. The troops used Western equipment and were trained to fight European style. However, the peasant soldiers' ignorance and fear of new ideas made Peter's goal of building a modern army hard to reach.

In addition to rebuilding the army, Peter created the Russian navy. He built shipyards, set aside forests for timber, and set up factories to produce navel supplies. By the end of his reign, he had more than 800 vessels on the Baltic Sea.

More Reforms. Peter also strengthened the nation's economy by making favorable trade agreements with other lands, building mills, and encouraging better farming methods. The Russian Orthodox Church opposed many of his reforms. Consequently, he left the office of the patriarch (the leader of the Church) vacant and made the Church subordinate to the government. The peasants also opposed Peter's changes. They revolted many times during his reign, and thousands fled to the thinly settled eastern frontier. Feared and hated by his subjects, Peter, as we have noted, seemed to some Russian Christians a match for the Bible's description of the Antichrist.

At War. Peter's "reforms" were necessary so that he could engage in a long series of wars. From 1695 to 1723, Russia was constantly at war, except for thirteen months. The goal of all this fighting? Warm water ports for Russia on the Baltic and Black Seas. Russia's only major port before the war, Archangel, lay on the White Sea, frozen over for ninth months of the year.

Peter's main enemies were the Swedes and the Turks. In 1700, Russia joined Poland and Denmark in the **Great Northern War** against Sweden, ruler of the Baltic Sea. Peter expected an easy victory. To his surprise, the young Swedish king, **Charles XII**, turned out to be a military genius. At the **Battle of Narva**, a force of 8,000 Swedes smashed a Russian army of 40,000. Peter rebuilt his shattered army and by 1707 faced Charles again. The Swedes invaded Russia, but this time Peter fell back before their advance and drew them deeper into the Russian plains. Like later invaders, Napoleon and Hitler, Charles met Russia's best ally, winter. Weakened by the frigid winter of 1708-09, the Swedes were defeated at the **Battle of Poltava**. As a result, Russia won much of the eastern coast of the Baltic Sea. Other campaigns took territory in southern Russia from the Turks and the western coast of the Caspian Sea from the Shah of Persia (Iran).

The Russians Claim Alaska. During the rest of the eighteenth century, Russians pushed eastward, this time across the **Bering Strait** into North America. Under Peter the Great, **Vitus Bering** was appointed to lead an expedition to explore Alaska. Attracted by the great number of sea otters, Russian fur traders followed the explorers. However, the Alaskan colonies had trouble getting supplies from Siberia. Their leader, **Alexander Baranov**, decided to send expeditions down the North American coast to start settlements which would provide food. In 1812, they founded Fort Ross, their southernmost settlement, on the Russian River near San Francisco. It was only a matter of time before Russian settlers began running into American settlers on the West Coast. Conflict between the two groups finally ended in 1867 with the sale of Alaska to the Americans for $7 million.

For your consideration

Questions

1. How have Spain and Portugal influenced the culture of Latin America?

2. How do you think you would have reacted to the Inquisition in Spain if you had been a Protestant there? How do you feel about people with different religious beliefs than yours?

3. What role does religion play in modern politics? Name some modern political conflicts related to religious questions.

4. Why did the Catholic king of France help Gustavus Adolphus fight the Catholics?

5. In the sixteenth and seventeenth centuries, religion and politics were often mixed. What is your position on the separation of church and state. Defend your opinion.

6. What factors influenced some of the European countries to fall from power in the sixteenth and seventeenth centuries?

7. Who would have been more likely to leave their home country for the New World—French Roman Catholics or English Puritans? Why?

8. What characteristics of Prussia were evident in Germany in later years?

9. What are the main factors that have influenced the Russian character?

10. What has been the historical relationship between the Russian Orthodox Church and the governments of Russia?

Projects

1. Do some research on the sea captain and pirate, Sir Francis Drake. Tell the class about one of the exciting adventures in his life.

2. Magellan and his crew faced incredible hardships on their voyage around the world. Use reference works to find out the details of this voyage and write a firsthand account of it from the viewpoint of one of the sailors.

3. If your community has a museum with colonial exhibits, visit the museum and make a list of items in the exhibit which were made in the colonies and another list of items imported by the colonists.

4. Many Americans criticized Secretary of State Seward's purchase of Alaska from Russia. Imagine you are a member of Congress assigned to find out if this was a bad investment. Check some reference books to determine the value of Alaskan resources and Alaska's strategic importance for U.S. security. Report to the class.

5. On some of the trips made by Peter the Great, he went in disguise and got a job in order to learn something valuable. Find out more about Peter's travels and report on them.

6. The mercantile system depends on the flow of imports and exports. What goods do you have or use at home or school which come from your home state or country? Which are imported?

Word List

circumnavigated	nationalities
plundered	domesticated
exemptions	suppression
partition	compromise
toleration	Spanish Inquisition
New Laws	inflation
republican	divine right
liturgy	subculture
articulate	mercenary
principalities	bishoprics
absolute	parasites
bureaucracy	mercantilism
subsidies	impressment
militarism	annexed
stadholder	icons
Black Legend	Third Rome

People and Groups

Vasco da Gama	Ferdinand Magellan
Huguenots	William the Silent
Philip II	William of Orange
Hapsburgs	Hohenzollerns
Louis XIV	Jean Baptiste Colbert
Louvois	John Cabot
Francis Drake	Vasco de Balboa
Bartholomew Diaz	Ferdinand & Isabella
Joseph Dupleix	Frederick William I
Maria Theresa	Gustavus Adolphus
Count Tilly	Albert von Wallenstein
Moriscos	Frederick of Bohemia
Varangians	Frederick the Great
Romanovs	Mongols (Tartars)
Cossacks	Ivan the Great
Ivan the Terrible	Peter the Great
Slavs	Archpriest Avvakum

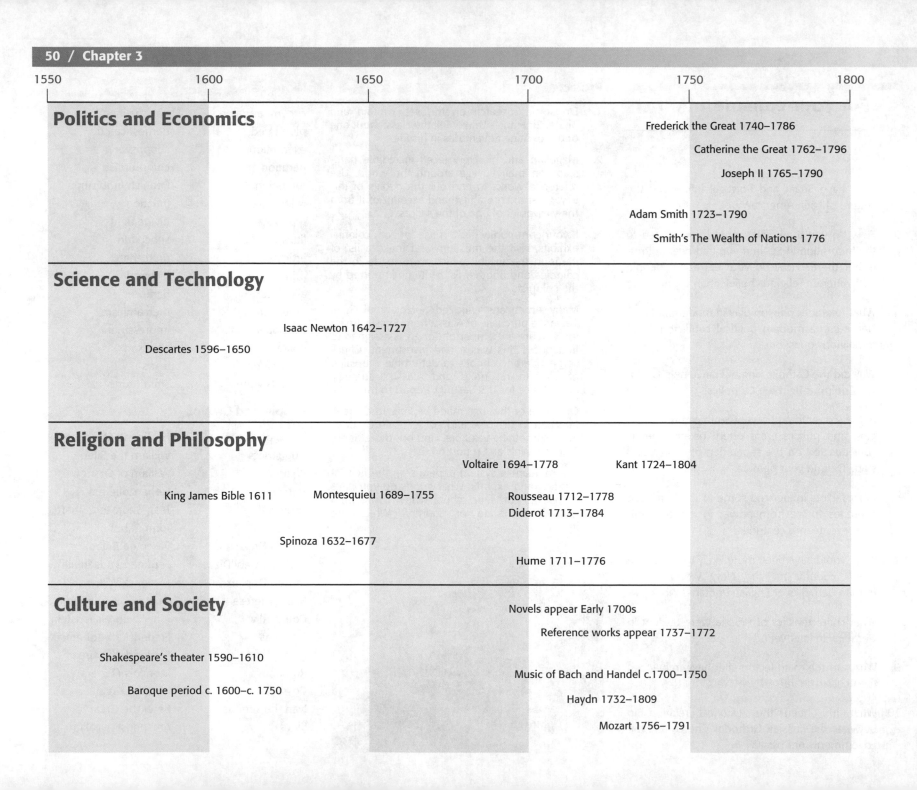

1550   1600   1650   1700   1750   1800

Politics and Economics

Frederick the Great 1740–1786

Catherine the Great 1762–1796

Joseph II 1765–1790

Adam Smith 1723–1790

Smith's The Wealth of Nations 1776

Science and Technology

Isaac Newton 1642–1727

Descartes 1596–1650

Religion and Philosophy

Voltaire 1694–1778   Kant 1724–1804

King James Bible 1611   Montesquieu 1689–1755   Rousseau 1712–1778

Diderot 1713–1784

Spinoza 1632–1677

Hume 1711–1776

Culture and Society

Novels appear Early 1700s

Reference works appear 1737–1772

Shakespeare's theater 1590–1610

Music of Bach and Handel c.1700–1750

Baroque period c. 1600–c. 1750

Haydn 1732–1809

Mozart 1756–1791

3

The Darkening of the Western Mind

The 18th Century has been called the *Age of Reason*, due to its belief in the innate power of the human intellect. It is a period that has also been called the *Enlightenment*, a term reflecting the belief of the key thinkers of the era that their new ideas would erase what they viewed as the intellectual darkness imposed upon the minds of men by Christian traditions and biblical authority. Because the philosophies of this period sought for absolute human freedom—to think and to act apart from God—the period ended in the atrocities of the French Revolution. Yet these ideas were not fully worked out at this time. The Reformation bore its cultural fruit during this period in the countries of the Reformation.

An era that takes its name and character from the world of ideas is difficult to pin to a specific timetable or marked historical events. In a sense, the Enlightenment had its proximate beginnings in the Renaissance. But because the Renaissance was really a revival of interest in the classical knowledge of the Greeks and Romans, it may be said that the Enlightenment had its distant roots in the ancient pagan world.

It has been argued that the Enlightenment also owes much to the Protestant Reformation. Perhaps there is some small truth in that argument in light of the fact that the Reformers 1) questioned accepted religious thinking, and 2) disrupted the unity of Western Christendom,

The frontispiece from Diderot's *Encyclopédie* epitomizes the Enlightenment. Personified as a Greek goddess, Truth, at the center is surrounded by Imagination (left) and Reason (right). Below them is Theology on her knees. Below them are the arts on the left and the sciences on the right.

thereby weakening the authority of the church as a societal institution. It cannot be truthfully said, however, that the Reformation contained the philosophical or religious seeds of the Enlightenment. The Reformation may have challenged cer-

tain aspects of earthly authority, but it was not anti-authoritarian *per se*. The focus on authority merely shifted from the earthly institution of the church back to the God of the Bible and Christ, the Head of the Church.

The Reformation doctrine of the *priesthood of all believers* is often cited as the spark of democracy and individualism in Western culture. This doctrine holds that men have direct access to God without the intervention of the church or the earthly ranks of the ordained priesthood. Some have seen this as an anti-authoritarian doctrine which substituted the power of the individual for the former authority of the church, and by implication, the authority of other would-be human power structures. Again, it may be true that this doctrine encouraged individual dignity and independence culturally. But individualism was not at the heart of the doctrine. The Reformers, in teaching that man may come directly to God by faith without the intervening works of ecclesiastical rites or allegiance to an earthly religious system, were not elevating or glorifying man. The Protestants, in discounting human mediation, sought to remind the world of the one true Mediator, Jesus Christ. Access to God comes through the Son of God Himself.

The Reformation was an attempt to restore biblical orthodoxy to religious faith and to present people with a Christ-centered worldview. The

Enlightenment was a conscious effort to move civilization in the opposite direction. While the key thinkers of the Enlightenment did not all agree on everything, they had one thing in common—a critical attitude toward orthodox beliefs of all kinds, but especially toward orthodox Christianity. They sought to destroy belief in the supernatural. If they acknowledged God at all, He was viewed as the "mechanic of the universe" who had constructed a marvelous material machine, built certain operating devices and laws into it, and then detached Himself from any interest in it. Man's opportunity and duty was to recognize his freedom from divine authority and from any earthly authority which claimed to act on God's behalf. If there was interest in discovering any truth about God, it would have to come through examination of the mechanism He created—the universe. God's plans, if He had any, would thus be revealed through science, rather than religion. Observation and experimentation, not revelation or religious dogma, were the new methods for discovery of truth.

We may say there were two main causes of the "Enlightenment." First, the continued influence of the Renaissance developed in countries and men that rejected the Reformation. In many cases they were part of the Roman Catholic developments in France. The Counter-Reformation movement of the French Jesuits had a powerful interest in using ancient skepticism and other means to counter the influence of Protestantism.

Secondly, in the countries of the Reformation, there was a weakening of the new generation as many of the battles and results of the Reformation were taken for granted. There rose up many men who apostatized from the faith of their fathers and sought to undermine it with sophisticated unbelief. There were those who had links to the humanism of Erasmus, that asserted the autonomous freedom of the human will. It was simply the next logical step to assert the freedom of the human mind. Thus we find the battle against the sovereignty of God taking on a new form.

French Unbelief and the "Enlightenment"

The leading lights of the Age of Enlightenment were a group of Frenchmen and their like-minded contemporaries elsewhere, known as *Philosophes* (philosophers). They admired reason and elevated it above all else, including faith in the Bible. Man's ability to think—along with his alleged innate capacity to do good—would be his best hope for salvation. Reason, good sense, and a humane regard for one's fellow men were the highest virtues. These virtues, furthermore, were considered to be put to their best use in the development of an ideal secular society and a political state that would be devoted entirely to the general welfare.

Some of the *Philosophes* acknowledged a god, although their view of God was not in line with the Bible. Such Frenchmen as **Montesquieu**, **Voltaire**, and **Rousseau**, were **deists**, believing that a god exists and created the universe with self-governing laws but that he left it to its own power and had no further relationship to it.

In England and elsewhere there were similar developments. The Englishman **Sir Isaac Newton**, was clearly a **theist** who believed in a Creator-Provident God but who may not have had a fully orthodox view of the Christian Gospel. The middle of the eighteenth century, however, ended in the skepticism of the Scotsman **David Hume**, who believed that we cannot know anything for certain. Still others, such as German **Baron d'Holbach**, advanced **atheism**. As the Enlightenment progressed, its philosophers drew out the destructive implications of a radical, humanistic and anti-Christian worldview. Professing to be wise, they became fools.

Montaigne. One man who developed the idea of doubt or skepticism was a Frenchman **Michel de Montaigne**. Educated in law, he spent his early years in politics. In 1568, he retired to his family castle near Bordeaux to think and write. Here he began his famous *Essays,* which he continually revised and expanded until his death in 1592.

During Montaigne's life, the works of some ancient Roman philosophers came to light. They argued that there was not enough proof to decide whether any knowledge was possible. Therefore, one ought to set aside the search for answers on all controversial questions until a better method of ascertaining the truth could be found. In the meantime, it was best to follow the old beliefs and practices. Montaigne adopted this position, wrote about it, and gained many followers. With such skepticism, his *Essays* comment on almost every important phase of human life and conduct. This era's skeptical attitude widened the gap between faith and reason, which continues in Western culture to this day.

While Montaigne questioned the scientific approach, he laid an important intellectual foundation for the Age of Reason by reviving the ideas of doubt and skepticism.

Other writers accepted the scientific approach. They tried to make science a new faith. From their pens came explanations of the latest discoveries and a mechanistic view of the universe even laymen could read and understand.

Fontenelle. Bernard de Fontenelle, another Frenchman, wrote one of the more interesting of these popular science treatments. *Conversations on the Plurality of the Worlds* (1686) explained the new science using a dialogue between the author and a fashionable lady. Visiting in her garden, for six evenings they discussed astronomy. Patiently he quieted her fears and doubts about an earth that moves. Finally she saw that the new view was better and remarked, "I value it (the universe) more since I know it resembles a Watch, and the whole of Nature the more plain and easy it is, to me it appears the more admirable."

Montesquieu. The French *Philosophe* with the most advanced political ideas was **Charles-Louis de Secondat, Baron de la Brède, et de Montesquieu** (1689-1755). Unlike some other *Philosophes*, he did not believe that all people are equal. He opposed absolute kings because they were inefficient and crushed liberty. In his writings, he also attacked slavery, religious persecution, censorship, the use of torture, and the abuses in the Roman Catholic Church.

In 1728, Montesquieu set out on a tour to discover for himself the conditions in other lands. Upon arriving in England, he was deeply impressed by the British government. After he returned to France, he spent many years writing his rambling masterpiece, *The Spirit of Laws* (1748). In the book, he stated that one man or a small group should not hold all the power of government. He urged France to follow England's example and divide government powers among three departments to safeguard liberty. In England, he thought, the executive, legislative, and judicial branches of government were separate, and each checked and balanced the power of the others.

Actually, Montesquieu misunderstood English government at the time. He did not see that Parliament was then supreme in the land. Nevertheless, his idea for dividing government power became the model for those who wanted to protect individual freedom. It had a great effect on the American Constitution in 1787.

The title of his great 1748 treatise referred to his notion that behind every form of government there is some vital motivating force or "spirit." To him, the spirit of a monarchy was "honor"—a sense of noble status and responsibility. Republics, Montesquieu found, were driven by a spirit of "virtue" or civil consciousness. Despotisms depended upon a spirit of "fear." In each case, when these supporting principles were weakened, the form of government with which they were identified was also weakened.

He also concluded that climate and other aspects of a state's physical environment helped to shape its government and people's response to government.

Whatever one might say about the logic expressed in *The Spirit of Laws*, its central thrust was the promotion of freedom. It was the separation of powers that best secured freedom, safety, and security for citizens, he believed, arguing that men can be free only if they feel secure and safe from harm. In his words:

> The political liberty of the subject is a tranquility of mind due to the assurance each person has of his safety. In order to have this liberty, it is [necessary] that government be so constituted that no man need be afraid of another.

For monarchies, political forces controlled by a working and reasonable aristocracy served as a necessary buffer between king and subjects. This last tenet was opposed by Voltaire, who believed that aristocrats were basically self-serving and therefore could not have the interests of the state at heart.

Montesquieu agreed with the traditional idea that *treasonable acts* may be punishable by law, even to death. But he opposed punishments for treasonable *thoughts* and *words*, unless the words were tied to actions.

Montesquieu rejected Locke's central theories concerning the "natural rights" of man and "social contract" as the basis of government. He held that there is no perfect form of government suitable for all people. Perhaps because he thus failed to provide his rationalistic age with simple logical solutions, his work was not as popular as some of the other political theorists of his day, especially Locke.

Voltaire. The most famous *Philosophe* was **Francois-Marie Arouet**, (1694–1778) who took the name **Voltaire**. As a young man, he offended a noble by some of his writings and was forced to take refuge in England. He admired the freedom there and became acquainted with the ideas of two of the foundational thinkers of the rationalistic movement, the scientist **Isaac Newton** (whom we shall consider later) and the political theorist-apologist **John Locke** (see below). Convinced that the world was a great machine run by natural laws, he spent the rest of his life teaching this **mechanistic, materialistic** and **deistic** view to others. Returning to France, he wrote essays, dramas, novels, and poetry. Because the content of his work was deemed a threat by the Roman Catholic Church, he had to live just across the border in Switzerland. Although he was the friend of aristocrats, princes, and kings, he sought what he viewed as **social justice** for other classes based on the laws of nature and nature's God.

Voltaire had a stinging wit and command of satire, and he used them most often to ridicule his-

Voltaire, 1694–1778

toric Christianity. He held that the only valuable elements of Christianity were those which agreed with the ancient classical philosophers; the rest of the Christian faith was nonsense. He ridiculed the Old Testament Hebrews as uncultured primitives with bad morals, and he ridiculed the early Christian Fathers as ignorant, bickering, power-mad myth-mongers. The Bible, in Voltaire's view, was a collection of dangerous absurdities and silly platitudes. He found theology "amusing" and revelatory of man's insanity. Among his most famous satiric statements is this: "If God did not exist, He would have to be invented." Another slogan, "Crush the infamous thing!" was aimed at the church and the *ancien régime* (old order).

While Voltaire believed in the necessity of monarchy, he argued that kings must rise above their personal interests and seek the good of the state and society as a whole. He did not oppose absolutism as such, but rather *arbitrary* absolutism. He was an advocate of civil liberties, including

freedom of speech and the press; but he felt these could best be accomplished by well-informed, humanely enlightened kings, rather than by popular assemblies.

He held a low view of the poor masses in society, however. To Voltaire and others of like mind, the lower classes were too stupid and morally inferior to have a voice in the governance of society. He held that the masses had to be controlled by fear. Religion and politics could be combined to effect the needed social control. Religion had a role in that endeavor, not because of any inherent truthfulness about it, but because of its *usefulness* as an instrument of hellfire fear. Both politics and religion were valuable, therefore, for their pragmatic benefits.

While the masses were largely unworthy individuals because of their ignorance, the middle classes had somewhat more value because they had learned to read and think. Thus education was highly prized because it made use of man's natural capacity to think, a capacity which had been subverted and enslaved by priests and other authorities.

Diderot. It is hard to say how widely the ideas of the *Philosophes* and other Enlightenment thinkers would have spread had it not been for one of their number by the name of Denis Diderot (1713–1784). Diderot compiled and published the new outlook in his monumental literary work known as the *Encyclopédie* (Classified Dictionary of Sciences, Arts, and Trades). This French work, which appeared in 28 volumes between 1751 and 1772, was more than a mere collection of facts. It declared that man could improve himself if he replaced faith with reason as his guiding principle. Such teaching threatened all established authority. The earlier volumes were banned. However, by the time the last one appeared,

opinion had changed, and the *Encyclopédie* could be openly distributed.

Diderot wanted to make useful knowledge widely available. He stated his ambitious purpose as follows: "Should all the libraries of the world be destroyed, this work alone would preserve everything essential so that human knowledge would not be impaired by the catastrophe."

He obtained articles from more than 130 experts and writers. A *Who's Who?* of eighteenth century talent, it included Voltaire, Rousseau, and the famous mathematician, Jean le Rond d'Alembert. A unique feature of the *Encyclopédie* was its 11 volumes of illustrations. The 3,000 pages of pictures had a tremendous impact. Many of them helped doctors and scientists. The industrial diagrams showed craftsmen step by step how to do everything from making rope to weaving lace. The work also subtly criticized current ideas and institutions. The article on the goddess Juno indirectly criticized the cult of the Virgin Mary. The article on salt called the taxes on necessities an injustice to the poor. The article on Geneva condemned the French government.

Rationalism: the Idolatry of Human Reason

Descartes. Although Frenchman **René Descartes** (1596–1650) is best known as a groundbreaker in the field of mathematics (as we will see in Chapter 6), he was also a rationalistic philosopher. In 1604 he studied at the Jesuit College of La Flèche. Descartes held that to arrive at truth, one must first doubt everything. Believing that man could be misled by the observation of his senses, he thought that the laws of mathematics provided a safeguard against confusion when

Descartes, the Father of Modern Rationalism

"I think, therefore, I am," wrote René Descartes, and with this statement he, in effect, opened the Age of Reason. Descartes hoped to end the constant disputes of philosophers by finding a certainty that all rational men would accept. In order to first rid his mind of all preconceived notions, he climbed into an alcove for a stove one cold winter day, determined to doubt everything that could be doubted. After a long period of thought, he realized that he could doubt everything except the fact that he was sitting there doubting, thinking. He felt that he had arrived at the first principle in his worldview—the very act of thinking proved his own existence.

Descartes hoped to arrive at truth and certainty about all things beginning from man's reason alone. To him, because mathematics and science came from God they are divine. His reasoning led to both pantheism and a denial of existence of the revealed message from God in the Bible. After Descartes, many thought that they could search for meaning in life through humanistic philosophy, rather than by faith in the eternal, revealed truth of the Bible.

coupled to man's reason. As doubt revealed false preconceptions and prejudices, these must be discarded. Only then could the construction of truth begin. The first positive step in the quest for truth was then to find some idea that could not be doubted, and Descartes landed on what to him was the absolutely certain truth that man is a rational being. This was the foundation of his faith, which has become known as Cartesian philosophy. Its basic tenet was his famous slogan, *cognito, ergo sum*—"I think, therefore I am." Beginning with one simple truth, man can work up, step by cautious step, to more complex facts. Although he conceded some areas of spiritual knowledge to be outside the reach of human reason, such as the knowledge of the existence of God, all other truths about the world were discoverable only by reasoning them out. Here the dualism of Descartes' thinking is evident, as well as his separation of the body from the mind.

Spinoza. The Dutch Jewish philosopher Baruch (or Benedict) Spinoza (1632–1677), like Descartes, relied upon mathematical deductions in his quest for truth. However, he sought to overcome the dualism in Cartesian thinking. To Spinoza, all of mind, matter, and time were of one substance, which he called God or Nature. In this way the autonomy of human reason was to be established by making it divine. But this philosophy is nothing but pantheism, and it contradicts the Christian truth that, while God is minutely involved in His creation, He is totally separate and distinct from it. Spinoza believed that evil exists only in the finite mind. When everything is considered in its infinite wholeness, evil dissipates. Man should therefore seek to adjust himself to an infinite order of things, surrendering his passions and submitting to the orderliness of an eternal perspective. It can be seen that Spinoza's intellectual mysticism had much in common with the ancient religions of

the Far East and the modern New Age movement.

British Empiricism and Naturalism

Hobbes. The leading political theorist at the midpoint of the 1600s was an Englishman, **Thomas Hobbes**. His major work, *Leviathan* (1651), argues that men are naturally self-seeking, vicious, and strife-prone. To avoid anarchy, men have historically agreed to set up government to maintain peace. To this government, they submit themselves *absolutely* in exchange for *protection*. The absolute sovereign, in addition to his obligation to provide security, is obliged to promote

Title page from Hobbes' *Leviathan*

truth, he argued, adding that if the sovereign fails in his obligations, the people have a right to revolt.

Locke. Hobbes' passionate defense of royal absolutism was dealt a blow when the English Parliament triumphed over the king in 1688. That event necessitated, if you will, the appearance of an apologist to defend the Glorious Revolution against the theories of Hobbes. **John Locke** (1632–1704), who had been in political exile in Holland since 1683, rose to the occasion. In his famous *Two Treatises on Government* (1689), he provided the justification for **constitutional monarchy**. He contradicted Hobbes by insisting that *goodness* is the natural state of things. He argued that all men are equal and independent by nature. The state, he held, was the result of a *mutual contract* among men guided by their desire to safeguard their natural rights of "life, liberty, and property." He agreed with Hobbes that when governments fail to meet their obligations (in Locke's case, their *contractual obligations with the people*), men have the right to overthrow the governments. Implicit in his theories of social contract was the idea of sovereignty of the people or **popular sovereignty**.

Locke's political and philosophical theories became a foundational part of the general faith of the Enlightenment. Underlying his theories was the notion that no authority exists beyond human will and reason. This was satisfactory to Locke because of his belief in the natural goodness of man.

In his *Essay Concerning Human Understanding*, he held that the mind of man is at birth a blank tablet upon which knowledge is inscribed through experience. For this reason, he is known as the founder of British **empiricism**. Because he exalted experience, he scoffed at the idea of miracles. So-called miraculous phenomena, he

John Locke, the founder of empiricism

insisted, are only natural occurrences that seem extraordinary because they lie outside man's understanding. As to the Christian religion, it could be reduced to the central fact that Jesus is the Messiah. Beyond that, most of what Christians believe is myth invented by superstitious or power-thirsty clergymen, he said. From Locke's rationalistic religious views, it was only one short hop to the "theology" of the deists—that the only proof of God's existence is in His works of nature.

Hume. Born into a Scottish Presbyterian family in 1711, **David Hume** had reasoned his way out of his religious faith before he ceased being a teenager. He began publishing his views while in his 20s, and his writings covered a wide variety of subjects, from population and economics to politics and religion. His opinions were daring, even for his freewheeling day. He challenged old doctrines and new ones alike. Hume disagreed with **Adam Smith**'s teaching that free economic exchange is the basis of wealth. He challenged

Locke's social contract theories, arguing that political institutions have anthropological roots.

His most controversial works, however, were on the subject of religion. In one work, an essay entitled "The Natural History of Religion," he argued that all religions grew out of the human emotions of *hope* and *fear*. To argue, in the 1700s, that religion had any sort of "natural" origins was indeed radical. In *Dialogues Concerning Natural Religion*, Hume ridiculed both Christian and deist views on the nature of truth. The book featured three speakers: a believer, a philosopher, and a skeptic. The philosopher argued that nature is so complex and marvelous that only a God of superior intelligence, not blind chance, could have produced it. The believer is shocked by such a "rational" explanation and points to the orthodox idea of revelation for his explanations. The skeptic is unconvinced by either, but challenges the philosopher's allegiance to reason. "What peculiar privilege has this little agitation of the brain called thought, that we must make it the model of the whole universe?" the skeptic asks.

Hume's contribution to the intellectual realm of his day was the idea of **skepticism** and doubt. In this, he did much to undermine the notion of **absolute truth** and opened the door to modern **relativism**, existentialism, and situational ethics. He insisted that man can be certain of nothing, except in the area of mathematics, where equations were said to be true all of the time without qualification. All other areas of knowledge depend on "facts," and facts are always open to interpretation, he said. *Probabilities* were the best men could depend upon in their search for truth.

Deism: The Religion of Rationalism

In the middle of the eighteenth century, however, French and German scholars began a process now known as **higher criticism**. This process was designed to analyze the Bible text from a literary and archaeological standpoint. As a result, some intellectuals began to discount the Bible as the revealed Word of God and a source of spiritual and historical truth. Rather, they saw it as merely a sourcebook of ancient religious information, some of which could be classified as myth.

Deism. Among these new thinkers were the **deists** and **rationalists**. They set out to build a religion based on reason rather than revelation. To show the rational basis for belief in God, deists pointed out the vastness of the universe, its beauty and order, as well as the perfection with which it functions. And in this universe, man has a place, drawing upon the resources of his world to meet his needs. Deists thought this order *proved* the existence of a Creator-God.

Further, rationalists saw human beings and their culture as basically good. According to Scripture, however, people are by nature sinful and have an inborn tendency to do wrong rather than right and thus they need salvation from outside themselves.

While the deist ideas opposed Christian teachings, the movement did not at first openly *attack* Christianity. Rather, it tried to change the church from within. Like earlier humanists, deists preferred things of this life to spiritual matters and tried to bring this emphasis into the church. As we will note later, this separation of spiritual and temporal things was a revival of the ancient Greek philosophy of **dualism**, which considered

William Hogarth's, *The Sleeping Congregation* (1728) illustrates the dead formalism and lifelessness of 18th century deistic religion.

the higher faculties of the mind to be separate from and entrapped by the physical world, including the body.

The chief spokesman for French Deism was **Voltaire**. The Catholic church in France had few able to defend the historic faith. Indeed, French Catholicism was so rigid that those who desired change had little hope. As Voltaire described the French situation, man's problems were superstition, intolerance, and persecution. Moreover, the priests exploited people.

The writings of Englishman **Edward Herbert** (1583–1648) offer a closer look at deism. A soldier, diplomat, and philosopher, Lord Herbert had written the first book on the subject. He opposed special revelation, saying it corrupted natural religion by introducing superstition. In Herbert's view, all religions have five ideas in common: (1) the existence of a supreme being, (2) the need to worship the supreme being, (3) the importance of virtue and piety for worship, (4) the necessity of repentance, and (5) the future life of rewards and punishments. Whenever human beings rely on reason, he felt, they recognize the truth of these ideas. He believed that deism was the teaching of the one true religion which existed before people were misled by priests and prophets of the various religions. He also taught that the rites and doctrines of institutional religion had caused the most savage persecution of humankind.

People began to wonder whether or not Christianity was supposed to be the religion for people throughout the world. There were millions of people who had never heard of Christ. Astronomers and other scientists also discussed the vastness of the universe, and they wondered how this fit into the Bible's teachings.

Witch Trials and Deism. A factor that was used by deism was the prevalence of witchcraft and witch trials during the seventeenth century. The devil's kingdom with its demons and human allies, witches, are always present when there is a resurgence of biblical truth in society. This Satan worship was not new, but reached back into the Middle Ages and reflected the corruption of the church at that time. At the witch's sabbath, devil worshippers made fun of Holy Communion, renounced baptism, and indulged in strange sexual practices. However, in the medieval Roman Catholic culture, superstition was widespread. The Reformation rejected the superstitious ideas of Roman Catholicism, but not a belief in the biblical teaching about Satan. After the Reformation many of these witches were put on trial and executed. Some witchcraft may have resulted from contact with slaves brought from Africa where witchcraft was dominant. However, the element of superstition was still alive in many people's minds.

Deism used this superstition to promote their own ends. They sought to use reason to disprove the supernatural. For example, in the Netherlands, Belthazar Bekker, a follower of Descartes and a pastor, wrote *The World Bewitched* (1691). This book attempted to prove on the basis of the philosophy of Descartes, that because there is no direct connection between man's body and mind, that an 'evil spirit' could have no influence on the bodies of men. The teachings of the Bible, he said, were simply adapted to the ignorance of the people of the times. An English judge dismissed one of the last witchcraft trials with the sarcastic remark that there was no law against a woman traveling between London and Oxford on a broomstick. As a result trials of witches declined during the eighteenth century, though this did not mean that Satan became inactive. In fact at this time the development of secret societies, many of which had occultic elements, was on the increase.

Atheism: the Denial of God

La Mettrie and D'Holbach. If Hume led the world into doubt about God and the existence of any divine source of absolute truth, two other men went further to deny God entirely. Although **atheism** was not a new concept, it gained new respectability through physician **Julien Offroy de la Mettrie** and scientist-author **Baron D'Holbach.** La Mettrie was willing to concede the possible existence of a Supreme Being, but he contended that this Being need not be worshipped nor considered for any purpose, especially not as a source of moral truth. La Mettrie

said man must be his own lawgiver, and human laws should be based on man's biological and psychological needs. He prescribed pleasure-seeking as a preventive medicine for pain. He died while indulging himself in a sumptuous meal hosted by one of his patients.

Holbach, born in the German Palatinate, was a resident of Paris. He enjoyed hosting dinner parties which often served as forums for radical ideas. By the 1760s, Holbach had settled upon an atheistic outlook, and he became a zealous apostle for this view. He churned out volumes of propaganda on atheism, some of which had to be printed and circulated clandestinely. His *System of Nature* argued that man is unhappy because he is ignorant of nature. This ignorance could be blamed on religion which is promoted by self-serving clergymen and rulers, he argued. Holbach said there simply *is no God*, but only nature. Man's moral principles must come from nature just as his physical aspects and emotions do. Thus no society can hope to be truly moral unless it is an atheistic one. Society, ideally, must be secular; and laws should be written and obeyed for practical reasons not religious ones, he said.

The Enlightenment Spawns Revolution

The "Enlightenment" was interested in more than just the discussion of these ideas. They had decided that since natural laws govern the physical universe, these laws must also form the basis for government and society. Acting on this belief, they applied reason to social life and traditions — especially to economics, religion, law, and government.

That Sovereignty is Inalienable

The first and most important deduction from the principles we have so far laid down is that the general will alone can direct the State according to the object for which it was instituted, i.e. the common good: for if the clashing of particular interests made the establishment of societies necessary, the agreement of these very interests made it possible. The common element in these different interests is what forms the social tie; and, were there no point of agreement between them all, no society could exist. It is solely on the basis of this common interest that every society should be governed.

I hold that Sovereignty, being nothing less than the exercise of the general will, can never be alienated, and that the Sovereign, who is no less than a collective being, cannot be represented except by himself: the power indeed may be transmitted, but not the will.

In reality, if it is not impossible for a particular will to agree on some point with the general will, it is at least impossible for the agreement to be lasting and constant; for the particular will tends, by its very nature, to partiality, while the general will tends to equality. It is even more impossible to have any guarantee of this agreement; for even if it should always exist, it would be the effect not of art, but of chance.

From Rousseau, *The Social Contract*, 1762

Rousseau. One of the most radical of the Enlightenment thinkers was **Jean-Jacques Rousseau** (1712–1778). Although he began as a loyal *Philosophe,* he took a radical departure from the general rationalistic outlook of the Enlightenment. The good qualities of people stem from emotion, he argued, and evil habits come from reason. Therefore, **intuition** and feelings are far better guides for action than philosophy and reason. In time, the **Romantic** movement grew out of Rousseau's ideas and replaced rationalism as the major outlook of Western civilization.

Born in a turbulent working-class section of Geneva, Switzerland, he ran away from his troubled home at the age of 16. He could never really feel a part of society. Rousseau's unhappy life probably shaped his view of the world. In his writings, he claimed that people in a natural, or primitive state are basically good. Civilization, however, corrupts them. He felt that the uncivilized man living in a forest or tropical island was a happier and better person than the average Frenchman. Free of the desire for wealth and progress, the primitive person treated his fellow man better. What caused humankind to backslide from this pure, primitive state was the ownership of private property. Rousseau's glowing depictions of the **"noble savage"**—one of the great clichés of the day often attributed to Rousseau but actually penned by John Dryden—found a foothold in Western humanism and can still be seen in modern anthropology and environmentalism.

In *The Social Contract* (1762), with its title borrowed from Locke's vision of government, Rousseau suggested a kind of government that would preserve as far as possible the natural equality of humans. In what amounted to a kind of social religion, he stated that all citizens, when they agree to form a government, lay down their individual wills for the general or common will. If individuals try to place their own interests above the general will, inequalities and injustice result. Those who try to do this must be *forced* to obey the general will of the social collective. He distinguished between the *"general will,"* in which each citizen acknowledges that the community's welfare coincides with his own, and the *"will of all,"* which he described as the mere amalgamation of all self-interested, private opinions. The general will could theoretically be the will of a minority, even a minority of one.

The perfect society, he argued, would be one in which the individual is both ruler and subject. The citizen can legitimately obey only those laws which he himself makes. He realized that this kind of society would be dependent upon a sense of responsibility. But Rousseau did not explain how to carry out his policies, nor did he seem to realize that forcing a person to behave according to the general will could lead to the most vicious form of tyranny. Nevertheless, these ideas became central doctrines of socialism and communism in later years.

Economic Revolution. In *economics*, the "Enlightenment" believed that people should be able to do as they wished without government control over their business activities. The French advocates of this view coined the term *laissez-faire* (hands off!) to describe their insistence on government noninterference with economic enterprise. Coming from France, whose economy was heavily weighted toward agriculture, these physiocrats, as they were called, saw the productive capacity of nature (land) as the chief source of wealth.

Adam Smith. The most famous advocate of *laissez faire* doctrine, however, was a Scotsman, Adam Smith (1723–1790). Smith, coming from a land where commercial enterprises and manufacturing were the main economic forces, disagreed with his French counterparts on what the primary source of wealth is. To Smith, people and their labor, more than land, were the key. He argued in his famous *An Inquiry into the Nature and Causes of the Wealth of Nations* (1776) that people, in their labors, are motivated by self-interest but this will serve the common good. An "invisible hand" somehow will reconcile the pursuit of self-interest with the maximum economic advantage of society as a whole. What did he mean by an "invisi-

Adam Smith

ble hand," and how would it control economic good? In *The Wealth of Nations,* he wrote:

As every individual, therefore, endeavours as much as he can both to employ his capital in the support of domestic industry, and so to direct that industry that its produce may be of the greatest value; every individual necessarily labours to render the annual revenue of the society as great as he can. He generally, indeed, neither intends to promote the public interest, nor knows how much he is promoting it. By preferring the support of domestic to that of foreign industry, he intends only his own security; and by directing that industry in such a manner as its produce may be of the greatest value, he intends only his own gain, and he is in this, as in many other cases, led by an *invisible hand* to promote an end which was not part of his intention. Nor is it always the worse for the society that it was no part of it. *By pursuing his own interest he frequently promotes that of the society more effectually than when he really intends to promote it.* I have never known much good done by those who affected to trade for the public good. It is an affectation, indeed, not very common among merchants, and very few words need be employed in dissuading them from it. *(Emphases added.)*

One plausible interpretation, in light of the spirit of the Enlightenment, is that Smith's "invisible hand" was merely a reference to the "laws of nature" which a deist-style God had built into the universe—in this case, the world of economics. According to this view, Smith was arguing that the laws of nature work in such a way that if enlightened individuals are free to use their labor and capital, they will naturally do what best promotes their own profit, and society will automatically gain by the overall increase in productivity.

Some present-day Christian analysts, especially those who find in Smith's writings useful messages against the common-good notions of welfare socialism, have argued, however, that Smith's "invisible hand" is really the hand of conscious "Providence." In this view, God is all the time working out everything to the good of those who are faithful to His moral and social laws. Such analysts see biblical justification for Smith's arguments of economic freedom, and they contend that if biblical economic laws and principles are allowed to be freely followed by individuals and corporations, the whole society will automatically prosper under God's blessing. These interpreters point to the following passage in Smith's *Theory of Moral Sentiments* as proof that Smith was not a deist:

> The administration of the great system of the universe… the care of the universal happiness of all rational and sensible beings, is the business of God and not of man. To man is allotted a much humbler department, but one much more suitable to the weakness of his powers, and to the narrowness of his comprehension; the care of his own happiness, of that of his family, his friends, his country…

The idea of God administering the affairs of His created universe certainly is contrary to the deist view. However, the passage above suggests that Smith saw God's care as being at work through "rational and sensible beings," and in such statements, Smith seems to fit within the Enlightenment framework.

Social Revolution. Enlightenment writers also wanted changes in *religious practice*, especially greater toleration. Often by this they meant toleration of their own unorthodox or heretical views, not necessarily toleration of historical religious truths. They argued that it is foolish to force a person to accept ideas opposed to his conscience. Faith is a matter of personal concern, over which society should have no control. By arguing for a private view of religion, they sought to keep it from influencing public or social policy. This idea can be seen in Thomas Jefferson's notion of the "separation of church and state." It is still a favorite ploy of liberals in our own day.

In the *Philosophes'* campaign for liberty, they attacked what they considered to be social injustices. Slavery, cruel treatment of the insane, and the torture of prisoners all came under attack. Voltaire led the way by getting personally involved in the case of a man named Jean Calas. Calas was a French Protestant (Huguenot) who had been accused of murdering his son, supposedly because the boy intended to convert to Catholicism. For this crime, the father was condemned, tortured, dismembered, and burned at the stake. At first, Voltaire found the incident to be a fine example of the folly of all religion. If Calas were guilty, it proved how hideously Protestant Christians could act. If Calas were innocent, it proved that the Catholic Church was guilty of murdering him. But as he examined the case more fully, he became enraged over the execution. Voltaire set out to clear the man's name. His efforts took three years. He raised funds for the poor Calas family, hired lawyers to look over the court record, interviewed people, and concluded that the son had been mentally disturbed and had committed suicide. Voltaire's persistent demands led the courts to declare Calas innocent and to dismiss the judges responsible for the case.

Most Enlightenment programs for a better society emphasized education. *Philosophes* assumed, contrary to what the Bible and historic Christian creeds teach, that people are by nature basically good. Being good, they are also rational and capable of being improved through education. By contrast, most people of that time thought that only the rich and wellborn could be educated. The *Philosophes* went on to claim that if natural laws were discovered and explained to people, they would follow these laws. People could then create a society where everyone would be happy. The attitudes of the *Philosophes* spread to other lands and influenced people like Benjamin Franklin and Thomas Jefferson.

The Enlightenment agenda also usually called for changes in government. Many Enlightenment political thinkers followed John Locke's idea that governments start when people form contracts with rulers to protect individual rights. Citizens may revolt against the government if it fails in its duty. Most *Philosophes* did not believe in democratic or representative government, however. They felt that nations could function best if controlled by an absolute, but enlightened ruler, aided by a group of educated men (the *elite*). These elite men, who supposedly understood society's needs better than society itself, would establish freedom of thought and promote educational and material progress—according to the reasonings of the elite, of course.

From 1750 to 1754, Voltaire was the writing teacher for Frederick the Great. Here Voltaire critiques one of Frederick's French poems. Frederick was among Europe's "enlightened" rulers.

'Enlightened' Monarchs Implement Humanism

Many eighteenth-century European rulers tried to live up to the expectations of the *Philosophes*. The most famous of these rulers were Frederick II (the Great) of Prussia, Joseph II of Austria, and Catherine II (the Great) of Russia. Believing that only strong leaders could force changes on those who were gaining from the old order, the *Philosophes* supported these absolute rulers. Because these "enlightened" monarchs were believed to be acting in the interests of their people, there was little danger that they would abuse their power, the elitist thinkers and philosopher-kings thought.

The German Aufklärung. The impact of the Enlightenment came later to Germany, because of the continuing influence of the Reformation, the conservative Holy Roman emperors, and the petty rulers who, for the most part, cared little for cultural refinements or radical ideas. After the Reformation, a type of intellectualism eventually became dominant in many Lutheran universities. While Pietism reacted to this, the German Enlightenment (*Aufklärung*) promoted rationalism and deism. The German Gottfried Wilhelm Leibnitz (1646–1716) brought rationalism to its culmination. His pupil Christian Wolff (1679–1759), professor at Halle and Marburg, popularized and spread rationalism. Rationalism became the dominant philosophy in Germany by the end of the eighteenth century. French Deism also began to impact German thought.

A number of German deists attacked the Christian faith. **Hermann Reimarus** defended natural religion and rejected miracles, saying that the biblical writers had made up the supernatural parts. The great miracle of revelation, according to Reimarus, is the world. In nature, one can find God, morality, and **immortality**. Another German, **Gotthold Lessing** (1729–1781), believed that all religions are equally valid and that the guidelines of the Bible are childish while those of reason are mature.

Frederick the Great. Frederick the Great of Prussia fully opened the doors to the Enlightenment in Germanic realms. He welcomed Voltaire to his palace and studied under him. It was Voltaire who first assigned the title "the Great" to Frederick II.

Frederick believed that the prince should live and rule only for the welfare of his people. To improve the lot of his subjects, he undertook great public-works projects, such as land reclamation and the construction of highways and canals.

He worked hard to develop manufacturing and to modernize the economy. He also undertook the project of reforming Prussian laws. In a state like Prussia, made up of many territories with quite different social and historical backgrounds and extending more than 500 miles, the laws varied greatly from place to place. Believing that natural laws applied universally, Frederick felt strongly that Prussia needed a uniform legal system. Although the task was not finished until after his death, it must be attributed to him. He also promoted religious toleration, statist education, and economic growth.

It may be remembered that Frederick, as a youth, had a strong predisposition for music and the other fine arts. While his father had hardened him into a tough military man and administrator—a character he resolutely maintained throughout his reign, he never lost his love for culture. Thus with the rise of the Enlightenment, Frederick reacted with enthusiasm to the new intellectual and cultural trends. While, Voltaire was a guest of the Prussian king, he influenced some of his cultural projects. Frederick himself wrote a great volume of poetry and historical literature, little of which was particularly distinguished, despite Voltaire's tutelage. Frederick also accepted the humanitarian inclinations of the Enlightenment agenda. He put an end to torture in criminal cases and reformed the civil courts. From Frederick's approach to rule came the phrase "benevolent despotism."

Catherine the Great. Russia had one of its most intelligent, progressive, and able rulers in Czarina Catherine II (1729–1796). But Catherine was not a Russian; her name was not even Catherine. She had changed it to make herself more acceptable to the Russian people. For the same purpose, she had converted from Protestantism to the Rus-

The Hermitage, the famous art museum in St. Petersburg, houses the collection begun by Catherine the Great.

Despite this situation, she tried to reduce Russian law to a system and bring the church more completely under government control. She studied the works of the *Philosophes* and invited several of them to visit Russia to explain their ideas. Catherine was especially influenced by Montesquieu. His idea that government should be suited to the physical needs of the country seemed to justify absolutism in Russia. The size of the land seemed to indicate that only this type of rule could be effective.

Catherine laid grand plans to remake Russian society. She would limit serfdom, educate the lower classes, abolish torture, and establish a jury system with peasants included as judges. But the nobles and bureaucrats did not understand her ideas and did not want to give up their privileges.

A realist, Catherine recognized the futility of trying to force reform. "Often it is better to inspire a reform than to enforce it," she wrote. Indeed, her position depended on the people she would have to oppose. Despite all her hopes for a more just society, under her reign serfdom actually increased and the rich gained even greater advantages.

sian Orthodox Church and studied Russian in secret during the evening hours.

From the time Catherine was invited to the Russian court to be considered as a bride for the heir to the throne, she had one grand ambition —to be empress of Russia. To that end, she was willing to leave her home in one of the small German states to marry the obnoxious future Czar Peter III, grandson of Peter the Great and his second wife, Catherine I. When he finally came to the throne, his rule lasted for only six months. He mismanaged the country so badly that the nobles removed him and gave the throne to Catherine, a promiscuous woman who had many illicit lovers

during her career. Her foreign policy was imperialistic, extending Russian influence into Poland, annexing the Crimea, warring against Turkey, and making Russia the dominant power in the Near East.

Catherine is usually classed with the enlightened rulers, although her real contribution to their cause was a subsidy for certain *Philosophes*. Critics often excused Catherine's shortcomings because Russia was a very backward land, and she had a shaky claim to the throne. Under these circumstances, she ruled only by agreement with the Russian nobility. It was impossible for her to try any truly enlightened reforms.

Joseph II. Although Frederick and Catherine followed many of the ideals of the Enlightenment, they did not have to sacrifice their own personal or political interests. This was not the case with Joseph II of Austria, who came to the eastern Hapsburg throne following the reign of his mother Empress Maria Theresa. He was considered, by the new thinkers of his day, a better example than Frederick of an "enlightened" ruler. With Joseph, modern thought finally entered the Hapsburg realm. Trying out the new ideas suddenly and completely, Joseph shocked his subjects into resistance, however. He abolished serfdom and made all classes subject to taxation. He canceled the special privileges of the Roman

Catholic Church and made Protestants and Jews equal with Catholics. He encouraged judicial reform and adopted more liberal economic policies.

Joseph's moves aroused strong opposition from all classes, particularly in Belgium and Hungary. The great differences among the people in his empire made it difficult to put his plans into practice. As opposition mounted, he used force to carry out his will. Police brutality soon angered even those who agreed with the new ways. As Joseph was dying, he asked that his reforms be canceled. His brother and successor, Leopold II, ended major parts of the enlightened program, hoping to restore order. He did retain the decrees that freed the peasantry and granted increased religious liberty to non-Catholics.

Despite the sincerity of the enlightened rulers, they met with little immediate success. Usually the clergy and the nobles opposed the reforms and persuaded the successors of enlightened rulers to restore the old order. The Enlightenment agenda would eventually have to depend upon violent revolution to accomplish its ends.

Evaluating the Enlightenment

The Revolt against Biblical Authority. Time has tested the validity of the *Philosophes'* belief in the goodness of man—that if given the proper environment and education, he would build a good society. On the immediate heels of their verbal ferment came bloody and oppressive revolutions. The problems of society have not disappeared. We still find injustice, prejudice, crime, greed, selfishness, political oppression, and war. In fact, the deeper the philosophics of the Enlightenment

have become ingrained in Western society, the more intense these social problems become.

Is man himself to blame rather than society or ignorance? The Enlightenment raised a basic question about the nature of man. Could he be his own worst enemy or have an inner bent toward self-interest and violence which outweighs all other influences? If so, then people will never build the good society of which they have dreamed through the unredeemed efforts of man alone. The truth of the matter is that the Enlightenment delusion that denied the total depravity of man was colossally wrong. The beliefs of the *Philosophes* in that regard amount to wishful thinking, and no amount of wishing will change natural man's heart of darkness. Only the redeeming work of Jesus Christ and the daily operation of the Holy Spirit can do that. *Man's only hope for a better world, therefore, is through the **sovereign work of God** through, first, the **evangelizing** efforts of the church, and, second, the **reforming** efforts of those whose hearts and behaviors have thus been changed and submitted to the Lordship of Christ.*

Christians who may agree that man's only hope for a righteous society is Jesus Christ remain divided on the question of how successful the church's efforts on earth will ultimately be. Some believe that earthly society will continue to get worse and worse and that when Christianity has been all but obliterated from the earth, Christ will return and snatch a final victory by closing out His church's evangelizing mission on earth and either taking the remnant to heaven or setting up an iron-fisted millennial rule on earth—or both. Others believe the opposite—namely that the church's effort will be more and more successful until the Kingdom of God is spread upon the earth "as the waters cover the sea," to use a biblical picture. When this effort reaches its

culmination, Christ will return to reap the great harvest His church has produced. Still others take a middle view. They understand the Bible to teach that both evil (the kingdom of Satan) and righteousness (the Kingdom of God) will gradually increase through human history until both have "ripened" in God's eyes. At that time, God will bring history to an end and continue His rule through Christ and His church in eternity.

In none of these scenarios does orthodox Christianity accept the idea of the perfectibility of man on the basis of human criteria, as the Enlightenment did. In orthodox Christian thought, the only sense in which man can be seen as "perfectible" is the spiritual sense—through progressive holiness (sanctification) under the power of the Holy Spirit during his earthly life and then his final glorification in eternity.

The Enlightenment planted several false and disastrous ideas into the soil of Western civilization, and we are still reaping the harvest. One was the idea of the equality of all religions. As Frederick the Great put it, "All religions are equal and good in so far as those who profess them are honest men, and if the Turks and pagans came and wanted to populate the country, we should be ready to build their mosques and temples." In addition to putting all religions on a par, that statement also reflected the idea that religion was under the providence of the state, and the state could therefore control it. The statement, in its reference to "honest men," also reflects a belief in an abstract, secular morality in which nonreligious virtues are assumed to exist. In this view, morality is not tied to the law of the one true God, the Lawgiver of the Bible. Morality and ethics are human inventions, and the standards of right and wrong and the standards of behavior may continual change as men's ideas change. There may also be any number of views of right and wrong at any given time in a pluralistic society. Again, this is a formula for moral chaos and all sorts of wrongdoing.

The Enlightenment elevated the "common good" or collective interest to a position of highest necessity. The government was placed in a position of power to enforce the common will. That made the political state the most significant and powerful force in society and all things, including religion, were supposed to serve the state. The state has since come to be seen as "God walking on earth," and is looked to for all provision, protection, and wisdom. These ideas eventually gave rise to the horrors of Nazi Germany and totalitarian communism and the spirit-crushing disabilities of Western welfare socialism.

The Enlightenment also hung its hopes for a utopian society upon education. In time, schools were no longer seen as centers for learning the true knowledge of God and His creation. Instead they became centers for social engineering and the creation of the new secular, socialistic man, who was to be individually free from traditional moral restraints and committed to the dream of global social unity.

The Enlightenment also revived the **dualism** of the ancient Greeks, the separation of spirit from matter, and body from mind. The Reformation had sought in its day to counter the Roman Catholic error of dualism and demonstrate the essential unity of man's nature. The Reformers saw that since God had created everything, everything was originally good, including man's soul and body. It was sin, not the body that was the problem. The way man could know any truth was not by beginning with either his mind or senses, but with revelation. Thus man could not simply know God by studying His handiwork, he must depend upon God to reveal Himself through His Word and Spirit. The Reformation-

era *Belgic Confession of Faith*, besides noting God's continued, intimate involvement in His creation, acknowledged both fountains of knowledge in its second article, entitled "By What Means God Is Made Known Unto Us."

> We know Him by two means: First, by the creation, preservation, and government of the universe; which is before our eyes as a most elegant book, wherein all creatures, great and small, are as so many characters leading us to see clearly the invisible things of God, even his everlasting power and divinity, as the apostle Paul says (Romans 1:20). All which things are sufficient to convince men and leave them without excuse. Second, He makes Himself more clearly and fully known to us by His holy and divine Word, that is to say, as far as is necessary for us to know in this life, to His glory and our salvation.

The twentieth-century popular Christian philosopher Francis Schaeffer well summarized the Enlightenment this way:

> The utopian dream of the Enlightenment can be summed up by five words: reason, nature, happiness, progress, and liberty. It was thoroughly secular in its thinking. The humanistic elements which had risen during the Renaissance came to flood tide in the Enlightenment. Here was man starting from himself absolutely. And if the humanistic elements of the Renaissance stand in sharp contrast to the Reformation, the Enlightenment was in total antithesis to it. The two stood for and were based upon absolutely different things in an absolute way, and they produced absolutely different results.

Jansenism and Roman Catholic Mysticism

During the 18th Century Roman Catholicism underwent a number of changes. The decades of brutal civil wars between Catholic and Protestant (Huguenot) forces ended. By the beginning of the seventeenth century, rebuilding began all over the country. A shrewd and clever government minister such as **Cardinal de Richelieu** helped cut the power of the nobles and destroyed the power of the Huguenots at the Siege of La Rochelle in 1626. With the influence of the Reformation quenched, the Catholic Church and the Jesuits continued their efforts at a counter-Reformation.

It was during this period that many new religious orders began. **Vincent de Paul** founded the **Lazarists** to promote Romanism in the rural areas. Grieved by the hopeless poverty of the common people, he also started the **Sisters of Charity**. These nuns tended the sick and the poor who lived in the slums of Paris.

Another priest, **Francis de Sales**, was the cofounder of a religious order for women. He became bishop of Geneva and exercised great power in bringing back many Swiss into the Catholic fold.

As the Jesuits became more and more powerful, there were those in the Roman Catholic Church that became critical of their methods. Among these was a group called the Jansenists.

Jansenism. A Dutch bishop named **Cornelius Otto Jansen** began teaching that the Jesuits had lost sight of the fact that a person can be saved only through God's love and grace. This love comes only to those whom God chooses. Jansen's view on **predestination** was similar to Augustine. Indeed, his enemies accused him and his followers of being "warmed-over Calvinists." The **Jansenists** insisted that they were not Protestants. Jansen himself published a book entitled, *The Doctrine of St. Augustine on the Health, the Sickness and the Cure of Human Nature* (1640).

The Jansenists said that Catholic Jesuit moral standards were too low. Jansenists also felt that the Jesuits put too much stress on free will—the idea that each person is free to choose or reject salvation and that God neither compels nor prevents this choice.

Soon Jansenism spread to France where it attracted many important people. The convent of Port-Royal became the leading center of the movement. Perhaps the doctrines of the Jansenists could have been overlooked. But their independent turn of mind and their preaching against deteriorating moral standards drew them into a struggle with the Jesuits and the French government. Besides urging purity and holy living among the clergy and people, they wished to reduce the secular power of the Catholic Church. Also they said the Jesuits granted pardon for sins too easily. Such laxness, they felt, encouraged immorality. Jansenists themselves led strict, **austere** lives and worshiped in simplicity.

A group of Jansenist clergy and laymen settled near Port-Royal. There they gave themselves to study and **contemplation**. One of their members, **Blaise Pascal** (1623–1662), had already gained fame as a scientist and philosopher. Pascal published a defense of Jansenism in his *Provincial Letters* (1656). In this book, Pascal claimed that the **Jesuits** undermined the Christian faith by teaching a morality based on what the average person does, rather than what people ought to do. Among other things, Jesuit morality held that *the end justifies the means.* Pascal's brilliant wit,

Blaise Pascal

together with his moral strength, struck a hard blow at the Jesuits.

His early death prevented him from publishing another book—one written to win others to Christ. The notes that he kept for the work were later published in 1670 with the title *Pensées.* A profound book, it argues for the existence of God from the act of faith. Based upon the idea of one's personal relationship with Jesus Christ, Pascal could say, "The heart has its reasons, which reason does not know." But his stress on faith apart from reason and the Bible led to a view that has been called fideism, that something is true because I believe it.

Finally Louis XIV became involved in the Jansenist dispute. The king was alarmed by the large number of important people who had joined the movement. Louis tried in vain to persuade two successive popes to denounce Jansenism. Finally, **Clement XI** condemned the group. In 1709, Louis sent the people living at Port-Royal away, later leveling the building to the ground.

Blaise Pascal

Twelve-year-old Blaise Pascal was sitting on the floor surrounded by diagrams of circles, triangles, angles, and parallel lines when his father found him. Asked what he was doing, the boy replied, "I am trying to prove that the three angles of a triangle add up to two right angles." Blaise's father was amazed and delighted. Completely on his own, his son had discovered a basic principle of geometry.

At the age of sixteen, Pascal added a new idea of his own to geometry, an idea now called Pascal's Theorem. At nineteen, he won fame for his invention of the first workable calculating machine. Five years later, he proved that vacuums exist and that air has weight. Before the age of thirty, he had already earned a place as one of the great thinkers of the West.

But then an event took place which radically changed Pascal's life. While reading the Gospel of John one day, he had a vision of Christ. Joy overcame him as he totally yielded himself to this wonderful Being. All the worldly fame and favor which were his seemed worthless, and he desired to have no other goal than to live only for God. He left his career and joined the Jansenist sect at the convent of Port-Royal. From that time on, Pascal devoted his talents to writing—supporting the Jansenist cause and refuting atheism.

Gifted with one of history's most brilliant minds and at the same time possessed of a fervent love for Christ, Pascal came to some interesting conclusions about the place of reason. In the search for truth, he said, reason was neutral. Evidence for the existence of God could never replace faith. "We come to know truth not only by reason, but still more so through our hearts; we shall never believe with a vigorous and unquestioning faith unless God touches our hearts; and we shall believe as soon as He does so.... What a vast difference there is between knowing God and loving Him!"

Quietism. By the end of the seventeenth century, there appeared a new form of mysticism. Like the Quakers, the **Quietists**, began teaching that a Christian could reach perfection only by becoming passive—he must abandon himself to God. **Miguel de Molinos**, a Spanish priest living in Italy, started the movement. Molinos set down guidelines which would lead a person to union with God. He condemned all outward religious observances and focused on an inward fellowship with God. The Jesuits succeeded in having him jailed. Nevertheless, Quietism spread to France.

The leading French Quietist was **Jeanne Marie Bouvier de la Motte Guyon** (1648–1717), a woman from an important family who went about teaching and winning many converts. She wrote numerous works on Quietism. Madame Guyon believed that a person should put everything else out of his mind and simply think about God until he lost all self-interest. She and other Quietists taught that this should be a Christian's main activity. **Bishop Jacques Bossuet**, who had been a tutor to the son of Louis XIV, warned her to stop such teaching. Others accused her of being mentally ill, but she went on preaching her ideas. Again and again she was arrested, and finally she was condemned by the pope and imprisoned in the infamous Bastille for seven years.

These conflicts in the Roman Catholic Church of France showed that the Jesuits gained the upper hand, and that the impact of true Christianity inside had become less and less. The stage was now set for a complete rejection of Christianity itself, which came violently in the form of the French Revolution.

Culture of the Reformation and Enlightenment

Literature. Some of the literature of the early seventeenth century has remained popular. Cervantes' satiric novel *Don Quixote* (1605) presents the adventures of the title character and his squire, Sancho Panza. The excitement of their difficulties and the realistic characters combine to make an enjoyable work. Readers understand the struggle between idealistic ambition to accomplish good and the humorous frailties of the main character.

The Age of Enlightenment was an age of ferment, but most of the ferment was in the world of words, rather than action. It was in the *writings* of the new-thinking philosophers that the world began to make monumental changes. Literature, therefore, can be said to be one of the most significant keys to the change in civilization which the Enlightenment sparked. The literature of England and France is the most significant, but one must also look to German literature of the period to get a full understanding of this aspect of culture during the Enlightenment period.

Drama and the Theater. The most outstanding developments in drama occurred in England, and the name of **William Shakespeare** comes to the fore. His plays were and still are extremely popular. His plots are set in many places and time periods. In *Richard III* and other historical plays, he examines kingship. The sin of rebelling against a monarch brought terrible results, but so did the failure of the king to do his duty. To Shakespeare, the past served as a warning to the present. Shakespeare wrote during the reigns of **Elizabeth I** and **James I** when everybody was interested in the royal succession and the monarchy. Even

William Shakespeare, 1564–1616

today, people enjoy plays which show the uses and abuses of political power.

Probably better known are his comedies and tragedies. The comedies provide pleasant entertainment. The plays use disguises, mistaken identity, and satire. *Much Ado About Nothing, A Midsummer-Night's Dream,* and *The Taming of the Shrew* show people trying to outwit each other in hilarious situations.

Shakespeare's tragedies are based on themes which are significant in all ages. Othello has to decide whether to trust his wife or his aide. King Lear finds that talking about love and loyalty is not the same as having love and loyalty. Guilt, honor, and responsibility are significant in *Macbeth* and *Hamlet*.

The theater in France featured the plays of **Corneille**, **Racine**, and **Moliere**. Their fine writing and elegance set a standard which affected other authors. Moliere's ability to show human failings with gentle cynicism still attracts viewers today.

Poetry. Besides plays, many poems were written. One outstanding English poet, who preceded the Enlightenment, was **John Donne** (1572–1631). A famous preacher in London, he wrote poems about his religious ideas and about love and life in general. Sometimes he used puns and unusual comparisons to express complicated thoughts. Most of this poems were written for his friends or his own enjoyment. They were not published in a book until after his death.

English poet **John Milton** (1608–1674) also belongs to the older order, although he was one of the giants of seventeenth century literature. Milton, a champion of the Puritan movement, was very much aware of the religious and political developments of his day. Himself the victim of personal tragedies, such as the loss of his son and his own eyesight, Milton wrote poems which reflected the Providence of God. His masterpiece, *Paradise Lost*, recounts the creation and fall of man in the Garden of Eden.

America had its early poets. In New England, people often wrote poems on particular occasions. **Anne Bradstreet** wrote about parts of her daily life, such as her husband going on a trip or her house burning down. **Edward Taylor** wrote meditations about the verses he read in the Bible.

The poet who perhaps best exemplifies the Age of Reason is the Englishman **Alexander Pope** (1688–1744), a nominal Catholic and ardent deist and rationalist. Pope was a witty critic of his age and often glorified his Enlightenment contemporaries. Famous for his "heroic couplets," Pope wrote of Isaac Newton, for example,

> Nature and Nature's Laws lay hid in Night:
> God said, "Let Newton be!" and all was Light.

In his famous *Essay on Man*, he exemplified the humanistic spirit of the Enlightenment when he wrote:

> Know then thyself, presume not God to scan;
> The proper study of Mankind is Man.

Pope believed it was the poet's duty to teach as well as entertain.

Poetry, which relies so much on emotions, did not fare especially well in Enlightenment France where logic and rationality were the highest virtues. Voltaire tried his hand at poetry, without significant success. He feigned to guide the would-be poet-ruler Frederick the Great, but nothing significant materialized there either. A legislator by the name of Boileau wrote a work in 1674 called *Art of Poetry* in which he examined the character of French poetry. The work demonstrated the considerable rigidity of poetry when it is influenced by the formalism of classical thinking.

Prose. The new thinking in Europe lent itself much more to prose than to poetry, and great volumes of prose—essays, novels, periodicals, and reference works—were turned out by Enlightenment writers, especially in the eighteenth century.

Periodicals such as *The Spectator* and *The Tattler*, made up of essays, became popular in England. *The Spectator* featured a number of fictitious

London Coffeehouses

As coffee made its debut in England in the 1600s, a number of coffeehouses opened up to serve the new beverage. Soon these establishments became meeting places for people to exchange news and gossip and discuss the issues of the day. Before the rise of the newspaper, Londoners dropped into a favorite coffeehouse daily to hear the latest news. When newspapers appeared, people still visited the coffeehouses to read the papers, and reporters even came to get information. Many men kept regular hours at their coffeehouses, so that their friends and clients knew where to find them. Eventually, each house developed a group of customers with similar work or interests. For example, Samuel Johnson and other writers often met at Will's.

In these centers of business, cultural, and political life, people freely discussed the faults of the government and society. Amazed that the authorities allowed such criticism, one foreign visitor called the coffeehouses and other public places the seats of English liberty. In fact, King Charles II became so nervous about this liberty that his government tried in vain to close them. Eventually, home delivery of mail, the growth of daily newspapers, and the establishment of private clubs succeeded where Charles failed.

In the following account, a visitor from Switzerland describes his first impressions of a London coffeehouse:

In London, there are a great number of coffeehouses, most of which, to tell the truth, are not over clean or well-furnished, owing to the quantity of people who resort to these places and because of the smoke, which would quickly destroy good furniture. Englishmen are great drinkers. In these coffeehouses you can partake of chocolate, tea, or coffee, and of all sorts of liquors, served hot; also in many places you can have wine, punch, or ale.... What attracts enormously in these coffeehouses are the gazettes and other public papers. All Englishmen are great newsmongers. Workmen habitually begin the day by going to coffeehouses in order to read the latest news. I have often seen shoeblacks and other persons of that class club together to purchase a farthing paper.... Some coffeehouses are a resort for learned scholars and for wits; others are the resort of dandies or politicians, or again of professional newsmongers.

From César de Sassure, *A Foreign View of England in the Reigns of George I and George II* (London: E.P. Dutton, 1902)

Ben Franklin discussing the latest publications with patrons outside his print shop in Philadelphia.

characters who formed a club and discussed philosophical issues in non-philosophical ways. They extolled the virtues of goodness of heart, family affections, kindness to women and children, decency in language, and restraint in wit. Most of the essays were written by **Joseph Addison**, who with **Richard Steele**, had first published *The Tattler*. Addison told his readers that his purpose was "to make their instruction agreeable, and their diversion useful. For which reasons I shall endeavour to enliven morality with wit, and to temper wit with morality." He said his aim was to bring philosophy "out of the closet and libraries, schools, and colleges, to dwell in clubs and assemblies, at tea-tables and in coffee-houses."

Addison was also a poet whose work sometimes reflected somewhat deist views. For example, Addison penned a famous hymn loosely based on Psalm 19, which is still beloved to many Christians today, in which he reflected the deist idea that God is best known through His creation:

Ben Franklin

A scientist, printer, inventor, writer, postmaster general, diplomat, philosopher, politician—not seven men but one—all in the person of Benjamin Franklin. He was one of America's most remarkable citizens.

Franklin's life brings to mind a series of dramatic pictures—of him flying a kite in a thunderstorm to prove that electricity and lightning were the same. It was his experiments with electricity which first made Franklin famous. A picture well known to Philadelphians was that of the reliable printer, publisher, and writer. In addition to the popular ***Almanack***, he published a successful newspaper and missed the honor of putting out America's first magazine by only three days.

Other pictures of Franklin show him streamlining the postal system as the new nation's first postmaster general; organizing Philadelphia's first volunteer fire department, first fire insurance company, first circulating library; helping found the Pennsylvania Hospital and the University of Pennsylvania; and working on inventions such as his bifocals, stove, and lightning rod. He was a member of the Royal Society of London for the Improvement of Natural Knowledge, an elite Enlightenment scientific organization.

Perhaps the most familiar image of Franklin is of the politician/diplomat—speaking in Britain's House of Commons as troubles worsened between England and its colonies, negotiating the alliance with France which tipped the balance in favor of the colonies in the War of Independence, and signing the Declaration of Independence and Constitution. Thus he attended the birth of the new nation at every step.

The Spacious Firmament on high
With all the blue Etherial Sky,
And spangled Heav'ns, a Shining Frame,
Their great Original proclaim:

Th' unwearied Sun, from Day to Day

Does his Creator's Power display,
And publishes to every Land
The Work of an Almighty Hand.

Europe did not have a monopoly on the periodical, of course. In America, the best known publisher of this type of literature was **Benjamin Franklin**. He worked on several newspapers, and is best known for his annual editions of *Poor Richard's Almanack*. Pamphleteering was also a popular form of literary endeavor, and Americans, especially just prior to their War of Independence, made prolific use of the **pamphlet** to express their views on all kinds of subjects. One of the most prolific pamphleteers was the vehemently anti-Christian, **Thomas Paine**, who was a strong advocate of Enlightenment thinking and sociopolitical revolution.

A series of 85 essays published in America in 1787 and 1788 under the name *The Federalist* must also be cited in this review of significant eighteenth-century literary works. Written by **Alexander Hamilton**, **James Madison**, and **John Jay**, *The Federalist Papers* explained and urged the adoption of the new **United States Constitution**, which was then before the states for consideration. These essays were widely published in newspapers and helped secure ratification of the historic document, which many believe reflected Enlightenment views of government (especially Montesquieu's) mixed with Puritan Christian values.

It was the **novel**, perhaps, that best captured the imaginations of seventeenth- and eighteenth-century readers. Novels based on the experience of a main character were widely read. Some characters traveled to far-off lands and had fabulous adventures; others had to cope with everyday situations. **Daniel Defoe**'s *Robinson Crusoe* (1719) and **Samuel Richardson**'s *Pamela: or, Virtue Rewarded*

(1740) are good examples. Each successful book was later imitated by other writers.

Some authors used stories to express their philosophical views. Flaws in society were pointed out by the English satirist **Jonathan Swift** in *Gulliver's Travels.* Far from an innocent children's story, Swift's book attacks mankind's pettiness, war, and vices.

In *Candide,* **Voltaire** satirizes people who have faith in God. "Let's eat some Jesuit," he wrote at one point in the novel. He suggests that people must be concerned with making their own decisions and fulfilling their own desires.

One of the most wildly popular novels of the period was Rousseau's *La Nouvelle Héloise* (1761), which went through 72 editions. Though its plot and style were not innovative, it aroused public interest because it reflected growing sentiments—feelings for nature, simple virtues, elementary passions, and pleasures.

Enlightenment **moralists** were fond of championing the rights of children. In *Emile,* Rousseau argued that children should be given great freedom to develop naturally. Other writers inspired people to make donations to foundling hospitals and promote education. The French social critic **Abbé de Saint-Pierre** called the new spirit of humanistic virtue *bienfaisance,* and the English novelist **Henry Fielding** called it "goodness of heart." Having destroyed traditional Christian morality, the *Philosophes* were eager to replace it with humanistic morality to ensure that their calls for freedom did not result in anarchy—which, in fact, did happen within a few years. The new thinkers refused to see themselves as the cause of the revolutionary violence and exploitation that grew in the wake of the Enlightenment, however. The problem was merely that the new ideas had not been fully accepted. **Diderot**, in his

play, *Le Fils Naturel* (1757), has one of his characters saying, "Certainly there are still barbarians; when won't there be? But the time of barbarism is past. The century has become enlightened. Reason has grown more refined and the nation's books are filled with its precepts. The books that inspire benevolence in men are practically the only ones read." History has shown what an idle vision that was, even as early as 1789, the beginning of the bloody French Revolution (which began four years after Diderot's death) and the Reign of Terror that began to unfold.

Reference Works. We have already mentioned one of the most monumental works of the Enlightenment, Diderot's *Encyclopédie.* Besides using his work as a compilation of facts and an instruction book of numerous skills, Diderot used the multi-volume work as a propaganda vehicle. His writings and those of others in it were intended to be weapons against ecclesiastical authority and the remaining semifeudal aspects of French society.

But there were other people besides the *Philosophes* who were interested in organizing knowledge in the eighteenth century. One of the outstanding achievements was **Samuel Johnson**'s *Dictionary of the English Language,* published in 1755. In this work Johnson attempted to standardize English. Some of his definitions seem humorous today, but his achievements in giving accepted spellings, meanings, and usage were overwhelming.

The first edition of the *Encyclopædia Britannica* was published in three volumes in 1768. Because people wanted to be able to learn about many different subjects, there were cross references from one topic to another.

In 1737 **Alexander Cruden** published a concordance to help people in their Bible study. In this

work, he tried to list all the Bible verse references where particular words are found. As an index of words, it helped people to study topics or characters mentioned in more than one place. *Cruden's Concordance* is still widely used today by Christians.

These dictionaries, encyclopedias, and concordances are good examples of the intellectual energy which was used in the eighteenth century. People knew that they needed tools to help arrange their ideas.

The Bible. One cannot leave a discussion of seventeenth-century literature without mention of the greatest achievement of all time in English literature—the **King James (Authorized) Version** of the **Bible**, published in 1611. That the name of this particular Stuart king should be associated with the grandest and most sacred work of English literature is what one biographer calls "a blasphemous joke." James was a wicked monarch whose life was full of dark plots and murderous intrigue. He persecuted the devout Puritans with a vengeance. He created censorious "High Commissions" while himself indulging in drunkenness and homosexuality. Yet the translation of the Bible which he commissioned is dedicated "to the most high and mighty prince James by the grace of God King of Great Britain, France, and Ireland, defender of the faith."

Acknowledging their debt to men like William Tyndale who had gone before, the translators of the Authorized Version created a masterpiece of elegant beauty and truth which has endured for nearly 400 years. The King James Version of the Bible has been revered among English-speaking peoples everywhere for the precision of its translation and majesty of its style. This Bible served as the fountain and foundation of religion, language, and law for English-American civilization during the centuries following its release.

In 1786, the Roman Catholic scholar, Alexander Geddes, said of the King James Version, "If accuracy and strictest attention to the letter of the text was supposed to constitute an excellent version, this is of all versions the most excellent." Later, even a caustic critic of the Christian faith, George Bernard Shaw, paid homage to the Authorized Version, saying, "The translation was extraordinarily well done because to the translators what they were translating was not merely a curious collection of ancient books written by different authors in different stages of culture, but the Word of God divinely revealed through His chosen and expressly inspired scribes. In this conviction they carried out their work with boundless reverence and care and achieved a beautifully artistic result."

Painting. Throughout the seventeenth and early eighteenth centuries, some Europeans adopted a new artistic style—the **baroque** (the word may come from the Italian *barocco*, a likely reference to the early seventeenth-century painter **Federigo Baroccio**).

The art they produced had an air of extravagance, of **grandeur**. This was particularly evident in the Roman Catholic artist, **Peter Paul Rubens**. Such Baroque artists, both painters and engravers, used elaborate theatrical effects to create a "larger-than-life" quality. They tried to give the viewer a feeling of boundless space so that the mind could grasp the infinite. Lines reached out from the front of the picture. Passageways led to the edge of the painting. Devices such as mirrors appeared in the painting itself. Space and light were essential. Three-dimensional perspective was a major feature. Among the most popular subjects were those drawn on themes from classical Greek and Roman myths.

By contrast many of the Dutch painters demonstrated a different approach. Being a Calvinistic

Rembrandt's *Night Watch* (1642) shows his dramatic use of light.

country it expressed more the outworking of the Reformation. We see evident in the work of men such as **Rembrandt van Rijn, Frans Hals, Jan van Goyen** an interest in all aspects of creation, not just religious subjects. They explored many different kinds of painting, events as well as the solid world of the middle class—town scenes, landscapes, animal pictures, and still lifes. They tried to capture the quiet, everyday world in a way that would appeal to wealthy people. Another type, portrait painting of individuals and groups of people, helps us to understand the vitality of the Dutch culture.

From a Christian perspective, the greatest painter of the seventeenth century was **Rembrandt**. That he was a child of the Reformation is unmistakable in his religious works. More importantly, his personal faith in Jesus Christ as Savior is evident. The depth of his personal conviction is clear, for example, in his great 1633 painting, *Raising of the Cross*, painted for Prince Frederick Henry of Orange. In the painting, several figures are erecting the Cross of Christ. Among them is a painter in a blue beret. It is a self-portrait of the artist himself, acknowledging that his own sins helped to nail Christ to the Cross.

In his other paintings, in true Reformation tradition, Rembrandt takes a realistic view of nature, neither glorifying it nor depreciating it. His people exhibit great depth yet remain down-to-earth. There was no illusion in his works, but there was an abundance of meaning. This was often conveyed through the dramatic use of light.

Architecture. The **rococo** style in painting and architecture, was related to baroque, but reflected more the views of the Counter-Reformation. It had a quality of opulence seen in golden cherubs, angels, sunbursts, curling vines, and intricately carved designs swirled around the walls and framed paintings on the ceilings. Statues in flowing marble robes and twisted columns added motion to the patterned walls. The mass of decorative detail overwhelmed the viewer, filling him with awe.

It seems that the Jesuits played a special role in the development of this style which was intended to be visually impressive. Ornate buildings began to dot Rome. To design the plaza in front of St. Peter's Basilica in Rome, the church chose the leading baroque architect, **Gian Lorenzo Bernini**. He ringed the plaza with two great semicircles of columns. Upon entering, the viewer was struck with the realization that before him lay the nerve center of a powerful religion.

Rococo architecture spread from Italy to every part of Europe, particularly in Catholic Austria and Bavaria. It was also used by the Jesuits in the building of churches in South America. Some Protestants were also building lavish churches. The French, with their usual flair for the artistic, created baroque structures which rivaled those in Italy. The practical French also designed more convenient room arrangements.

However, it was **Louis XIV** who raised French baroque architecture to its greatest heights. Louis

This Catholic Church in Saltzburg, Austria, is an example of the ornate rococo style of architecture.

determined to build a palace that would reflect the glory of France and the majesty of its king. Disliking Paris, he chose a site a few miles from town. There for more than 40 years, tens of thousands of workers labored to make Versailles the showplace of the world. Awesome, pompous, magnificent, the completed palace became the symbol of the baroque.

In Germany, many petty princes built smaller versions of Versailles. Monasteries, palaces, and entire towns, such as Salzburg, Austria, were built or rebuilt in the new style. Many villages in Bavaria still boast domed churches with beautiful baroque carvings and frescoes.

In England, the outstanding architect was **Sir Christopher Wren**, also a mathematician and astronomer. Following the Great Fire of London in 1666, he designed several dozen church buildings, including St. Paul's Cathedral. This magnificent structure, still prominent in the London skyline, has a dome which is 365 feet high.

Late in the eighteenth century there was a revival of purer, classical Greek and Roman styles. This classical style was particularly popular in America, as seen in the government buildings in the new capital city of Washington, including the Capitol and the Supreme Court building, the latter of which resembles a Greek temple. The classical revival in architecture paralleled the rise of the classical period in music.

Music. In the baroque period, music took a new form which enabled more people to enjoy it. During the medieval period, music had been largely **monophonic**, consisting of a single line of notes or single "voice." Examples of this type of music can be heard in Gregorian chant or the "plainsong." During the Renaissance, with composers such as **Giovanni Palestrina**, music became **polyphonic**. Polyphonic music had several lines of *melody*, all working in cooperation with one another. Members of the choir sang different melodies, weaving them together in a pattern of beauty. In baroque music, which continued the use of polyphonics, another ingredient was added—**harmonics**. Most baroque music has only *one melody*, with other voices or instruments supplying *harmony*. Harmony is an element of music which is not a line of independent melody but rather consists of tones which complement or complete the melody to make up a chord. Some baroque composers also made use a polyphonic device known as **counterpoint**, the use of two or more related but independent melodies woven into a single harmonic texture. **Rococo** music, which was a variation in the baroque style that began in the early eighteenth century, added trills, theme variations, and other embellishments to musical scores, in contrast to the baroque's tendency to establish a single emotional quality throughout a composition.

Christopher Wren

The man popularly regarded as the greatest of English architects was actually an astronomer, and he did not begin his architectural career until after the age of thirty. As a member of the Royal Society, Christopher Wren had done studies of blood transfusion, meteorology, and motion, as well as astronomy. It was in his capacity as a scientist that he was first asked to design a building. In the 1600s, work was not as highly specialized as it is today. In fact, only a few decades earlier, master craftsmen had designed most important buildings rather then men like Wren, who was not overly familiar with a hammer and chisel.

A trip to Paris in 1665 changed Wren's life. He went there an astronomer and returned an architect. Several famous architects were working in Paris at that time. Wren met with them and traveled about the area studying the new buildings and collecting architectural drawings. When he returned to London, he was full of new ideas.

The Great Fire of 1666 which destroyed the heart of London gave him the opportunity for which he was so remarkably prepared. Wren was appointed to a commission to draw up plans for rebuilding the city. Even more important, he received the task of redesigning St. Paul's Cathedral and more than fifty other churches. Despite the large number of structures, he managed to give them variety and interest. His graceful church spires and the dome of St. Paul's are his major contributions to architecture. In his work, Wren produced the English version of the baroque style.

Like poetry, music is a lyrical medium of expression. As such, it did not lend itself well to the new logical thinking of the Age of Reason. For the most part, therefore, the greatest music of the seventeenth and eighteenth centuries does not reflect Enlightenment ideas—there is little connection between it and the philosophical-political climate of the time. In fact, the true giants of the musical world during this period were clearly in the Reformation mold, "never suffering a moment's religious doubt," as one historian has put it. Most experts are agreed that the music of this period is of unparalleled greatness in all of human history.

The great baroque and rococo composers came primarily from Italy, Germany, France, Austria, Sweden, and England, with names such as **Antonio Vivaldi**, **Alessandro Scarlatti**, **Archangelo Corelli**, **Luigi Boccherini**, **Tomaso Albinoni**, **Claudio Monteverdi**, **Georg Philipp Telemann**, **Dietrich Buxtehude**, **Francois Couperin**, **Jean-Joseph Mouret**, **Johann Sebastian Bach**, **Johann Pachelbel**, **Jeremiah Clarke** and **George Frederic Handel**, to name just a few. Some of these men were extremely prolific; the luminary of the Italian baroque, Vivaldi, for example, composed several thousand complex musical works. These composers influenced one another, and they wrote compositions in numerous musical categories, including: sonatas, concertos, sinfonias, oratorios, and operas. The French, and other composers interested in French culture, frequently wrote music for such dance forms as the minuet, bouree, ballet, and gavotte.

Toward the end of the period, from the mid-eighteenth century, music entered another phase which has become known as the **classical** era. Its composers were primarily influenced by a style of music which developed in Vienna, Austria. These composers are therefore said to belong to the Vienna Classic School. They include **Franz Joseph Haydn**, **Wolfgang Amadeus Mozart**, **Ludwig van Beethoven**, and **Christoph Gluck**. Classical music, which carried over into the nineteenth century in the works of such composers as **Felix Mendelssohn**, is characterized by formal elegance, simplicity, proportion, order, and correctness, the virtues of the classic Greeks. Of the classical composers, Mozart and Gluck were most influenced by the Enlightenment; Haydn hardly at all, as he remained a pious and faithful Catholic working in an area of Europe that was less receptive to the new thinking. Beethoven began his musical work in the classical mold, but his later works (written in the midst of the nineteenth century's revolutionary and heroic military turmoil) reflected the events and ideals of the Romantic period and Napoleonic empire building.

During the span of the baroque-classical era, music also shifted from compositions and performances for the rich and famous in private and chamber concerts to music in new, large concert halls for public consumption. With that shift came a change in the financing of musical composition. At first, most composers wrote under commissions from nobles, kings, and other wealthy individuals. Later, they wrote on speculation and depended upon the payment of public audiences.

Musical Masters. Perhaps the greatest musical genius of the period was **Johann Sebastian Bach**, who was born in 1685 into a large and musical family. Bach himself was the father of 20 children, several of whom became masterful musicians in their own right. Bach lived most of his life as an organist and music master in various provincial towns and small, princely courts in Germany. He studied the music of other composers intensely and tried to incorporate all that he learned into his own music. He taught himself to play violin.

As choir director of the school and Church of St. Thomas in Leipzig, Bach was expected to compose and produce **cantatas**. These were choral works with choruses, solos, and other parts in

Johann Sebastian Bach, 1685–1750

cluded them with the notation, *S.D.G.*, meaning *Soli Deo Gloria* (to the glory of God alone). He was even known to inscribe some of his "secular" works with the notation, "in the name of Jesus." To him, all of life's activities were to be done in the name of Christ. With such ideas, he placed himself at the heart of the Reformation. But his faith also compelled him to a level of creativity marked by the highest standards of excellence. His music is astonishingly intricate and often of complex mathematical structure. His keyboard music reached new heights of precision tuning and tone. A century later, the composer Robert Schumann remarked, "Music owes as much to Bach as [the Christian] religion owes to its founder." Bach died in 1750.

George Frederic Handel was born in the same year and in the same German province of Saxony as Bach, but he later moved to England and remained there for the rest of his life. He too exhibited a firm faith in God, and his compositions include some of the greatest sacred music known to man. His glorious oratorio, *Messiah*, based on scriptural prophecies and teachings about Christ, is beloved by millions as one of the most masterful inspirational works of all time. Other oratorios, such as *Israel in Egypt* and *Saul*, also used biblical themes.

Yet Handel's musical environment was less that of the church (as in Bach's case) and more that of the English court and the public concert hall. He enjoyed writing huge-sounding compositions for large audiences, rather than intimate works for the elite. His *Firework Music*, for example, employs a full orchestra and 101 cannons. His English audiences adored him, perhaps because he drew many of his themes from folk music, country dances, nature, and street sounds. His *Water Music* was intended to be played on river barges floating down the Thames. Although born

Statue of Handel at his birthplace, Halle, Germany

in Germany, he was adopted by the English, who honored him as a national monument by burying him, at his death in 1759, in Westminster Abbey.

Franz Joseph Haydn (1732–1809) is sometimes called "the father of the symphony," since it was he, more than any other composer, who developed and set the style for large orchestra music. Though he was not the first to write symphonies, he composed 104 of his own, along with 83 string quartets, and many other works, including an oratorio masterpiece, *The Creation*, celebrating the divine origin of the world. His music was widely appreciated throughout Europe.

Haydn spent most of his humble and pious life composing under commissions from two wealthy Hungarian princes, Paul and Nicholas Esterházy. Though an Austrian, he spent many years in Hungary. Upon finally leaving Hungary, he wrote an interesting symphony which became known as the *Farewell Symphony*. In it one can sense his longing for Austria and yet his nostalgia for Hungary. As the symphony comes to a close, members of the orchestra leave the stage one by one until only one or two players remain to finish the closing bars.

dramatic form, usually centering around biblical events and the church year. Cantatas usually lasted about twenty-five minutes and were accompanied by the organ and an orchestra. A devout Lutheran, Bach also wrote two passions (musical presentations of Christ's death on the Cross) to be sung during Holy Week services.

Bach wrote both secular music and sacred music, both humorous and serious music; he used his compositions to entertain and to teach. He used both popular and aristocratic elements in his music. He is considered the master of two musical forms, the **toccata** and **fugue**. But in all cases he viewed his work as an act of faith and worship. His stated goal was always to write "well ordered music in the honor of God." Bach viewed God as the Great Creator-Craftsman of the universe and of the plan of salvation, and Bach's music was therefore always to be of the highest technical craftsmanship, as well as beautiful. He often began his compositions with the initials *J.J.*, meaning *Jesu Juva* (Jesus help); and he often con-

When he was in his sixties, Haydn paid two visits to London (1790 and 1794) and was amazed at the musical freedom enjoyed by composers writing, not for some prince, but for the public. "How sweet a little liberty tastes!" he wrote. "...though my mind is burdened with a multitude of tasks...the knowledge that I am no longer a hired servant repays me for all my trouble." His two oratorios, *The Creation* and *The Seasons*, grew out of this discovery of freedom and were addressed to the common man. Toward the end of his life, he was especially moved by correspondence from humble people who expressed gratitude for the pleasures his music had given to them in family and home settings.

In contrast to Haydn, one of his pupils, **Wolfgang Amadeus Mozart**, led a short and dizzying life. Mozart, under his father's guidance, began his musical career as a small child. By age six, he was giving harpsichord concerts. At age eight, he performed for Hapsburg Empress Maria Theresa. At 12, he composed his first opera. Whereas many child prodigies burn out before adulthood, Mozart's musical genius and skills became steadily better. During his short 35-year life span, he turned out hundreds of masterpieces, each as glorious as the next. His works are full of grace, grandeur, emotion, and precision. Haydn considered him the greatest composer ever. Other composers of the era viewed his music as nearly divine, a curiosity in light of the fact that Mozart often led a fairly profane life. He became interested in the philosophies of the Enlightenment and was a member of the **Freemason** movement. His mythical opera, *The Magic Flute*, portrays many occultic ideals of the Masonic order. At the same time, he remained a Catholic, and his religious inclinations are best seen in his last (unfinished) work, the deeply moving *Requiem*. It was a mysterious work commissioned by a wealthy patron unknown even to Mozart. The by-then sickly Mozart worked feverishly on it, seemingly in a state of depression, as though he knew it might be his own funeral composition. According to one modern (and dubious) legend, he was haunted in writing this work by the ghost of his domineering father, Leopold, whom he supposedly had not properly honored in death.

Although he had friends and contacts in high places, including the courts and church hierarchy of Austria, he never attracted much financial support. He quickly spent what he did earn, and he died a pauper. It was raining on the day of his death, so the few friends who attended his funeral went home before his body reached the graveyard. He was dumped into an unmarked grave, and to this day no one knows where he lies buried. In contrast to his ignoble end, his legacy of splendorous music could hardly be more illustrious.

Baroque **operas** proved to be stilted and fairly unpopular. Few are still performed. Mozart's more lighthearted approach to operas, often written in the vernacular German instead of the previously requisite Italian, gained more popular support for this musical genre. It was **Christoph Gluck**, a Bavarian, however, who really changed the world of opera. Gluck became weary of the artificiality of baroque opera, in which ornate musical passages were often force-fitted to inappropriate and superficial story lines and singers frequently would wail on for long stretches, stringing out a single word. Gluck determined to design operas in which story and music were more closely related and credible musical dramas could be unfolded. This he accomplished in several works, along with poet **Raniero de Calzabigi**, who wrote librettos (stories) for his operatic scores. Gluck and Calzabigi thus revolutionized opera, and the greater interest in this musical form made them rich and famous. Most of the popular operas of today come from a period following Gluck.

Instruments and Notation. Medieval music was often vocal music sung *a capella*—without instrumental accompaniment. That began to change during the Renaissance. During the baroque era, as musical instruments continued to develop, composers wrote many selections for instruments alone without any words. Important instruments at this time included the violin, which was just being developed; the trumpet, without the valves of today's style; and the harpsichord, which was soon replaced by a more versatile keyboard instrument, the piano. The piano was originally called the *piano-forte*, meaning "soft-loud." This name reflected the fact that the piano used a new mechanism for *striking* the strings, allowing for variation in intensity and volume, and therefore feeling. The harpsichord used a *plucking* mechanism which did not allow for such variation. Impressive pipe organs, drums, flutes, and other string and wind instruments were also used during this great musical period.

Another change which brought music out of elite circles was a new form of musical notation. Earlier scores depended upon a combination of notes and numbers which required some improvisation and special knowledge by musically literate professionals. The new form of music featured musical lines in which every note to be played or sung was written out, allowing average musicians to read and render the scores.

Many compositions were written for groups of three or four instruments. Full orchestras included about two dozen players. Music was used in the church and in homes of the well-to-do. Musicians often performed in theaters, before and after plays, and during intermissions.

For your consideration

Questions

1. How did most of the *Philosophes* feel about democracy or representative government? about the common man? about equality? Do you see any contradictions in these views?

2. Do you agree with Rousseau's views of reason and emotion? of primitive man? Why or why not? How did Rousseau differ from most of the other *Philosophes* on the value of technological progress?

3. Explain the religion of the deists? Why was this religious view compatible with the Enlightenment philosophies?

4. Compare and contrast the central ideas of the Reformation with those of the Enlightenment? Give your own evaluation of Enlightenment philosophy.

5. What is your favorite novel? Why do you like it? What topics are found in your favorite poems or songs?

6. Name some ways the music of Bach and Handel express Christian ideals. Considering factors other than words, tell whether Bach's music or contemporary Christian music better expresses a biblical worldview.

7. What is meant by the term "benevolent despot"? Discuss the theories and practices of the "enlightened" rulers you studied in this chapter.

8. Are men and human societies perfectible? Explain your answer.

Projects

1. Benjamin Franklin had skills as a writer, scientist, and politician among many others. Make a report about just one aspect of his life.

2. Many of Shakespeare's plays were performed at the Globe Theater. With a small group, describe this theater and tell how the public then felt about Shakespeare's plays. Assign parts and read or perform a portion of one of his plays.

3. Many phrases often quoted today such as "no man is an island" and "for whom the bell tolls" come from John Donne. Read some of his poems and meditations and make a list of phrases you recognize.

4. Find examples of baroque art and architecture to show to your class. Sources may include books, encyclopedias, and art magazines. Be prepared to explain the characteristics of baroque art.

5. Locate recordings of the various musical forms mentioned in this chapter—oratorios, cantatas, chant, polyphonic religious music, symphonies, opera, etc. Give a demonstration to your class by playing the selections you have found.

6. Write a mock letter to one of the *Philosophes,* commenting on his views and expressing your own views.

Word List

skepticism	mechanistic
natural laws	Jansenism
intuition	satire
meditations	concordance
grandeur	monophonic
polyphonic	harmonics
oratorio	cantata
passions	dualism
atheism	popular sovereignty
materialistic	theist
satiric	empiricism
absolute truth	relativism
pantheism	*laissez faire*
"invisible hand"	baroque
rococo	counterpoint
classical music	Parliament

People and Groups

Philosophes	Michel de Montaigne
Thomas Hobbes	René Descartes
John Locke	Voltaire
David Hume	Montesquieu
Rousseau	Baron d'Holbach
Adam Smith	Blaise Pascal
Baruch Spinoza	Denis Diderot
Frederick II	Catherine II
Joseph II	Deists
William Shakespeare	John Milton
John Donne	Alexander Pope
Benjamin Franklin	Joseph Addison
Samuel Johnson	Jonathan Swift
J.S. Bach	G.F. Handel
Wolfgang A. Mozart	Franz Joseph Haydn
Rembrandt van Rijn	Peter Paul Rubens
Christopher Wren	Christoph Gluck

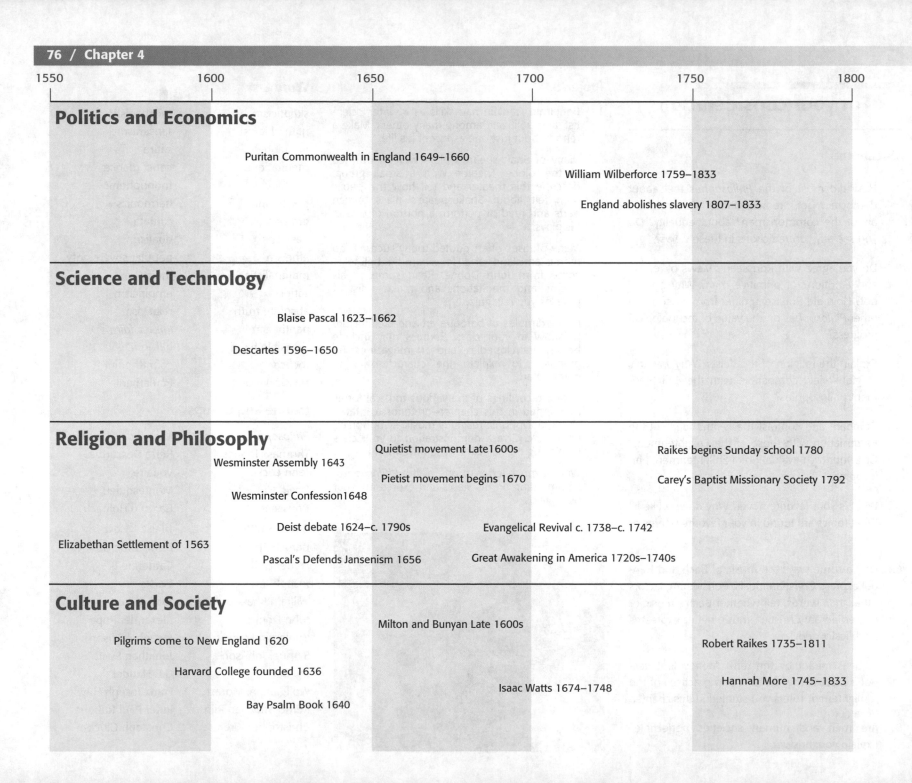

1550   1600   1650   1700   1750   1800

Politics and Economics

Puritan Commonwealth in England 1649–1660

William Wilberforce 1759–1833

England abolishes slavery 1807–1833

Science and Technology

Blaise Pascal 1623–1662

Descartes 1596–1650

Religion and Philosophy

Quietist movement Late1600s

Raikes begins Sunday school 1780

Wesminster Assembly 1643

Pietist movement begins 1670

Carey's Baptist Missionary Society 1792

Wesminster Confession1648

Deist debate 1624–c. 1790s

Evangelical Revival c. 1738–c. 1742

Elizabethan Settlement of 1563

Pascal's Defends Jansenism 1656

Great Awakening in America 1720s–1740s

Culture and Society

Milton and Bunyan Late 1600s

Pilgrims come to New England 1620

Robert Raikes 1735–1811

Harvard College founded 1636

Isaac Watts 1674–1748

Hannah More 1745–1833

Bay Psalm Book 1640

Puritanism and the Great Awakening

Even as Western European society was affected by the apostasy of the 'Enlightenment,' so it also experienced a revival in Christian thought and expression in the 18th Century. In the last chapter, we traced the developments in humanistic philosophy, as deistic and atheistic thinkers sought to move Europe away from traditional Christian viewpoints into a secular and socialistic outlook. Throughout the seventeenth and eighteenth centuries, furthermore, Protestantism continued to change and develop. Among the developments was the organization of Protestantism into various groups, what we now call denominations. Some groups emphasized holy living and a vital personal faith while individual leaders focused on one point of doctrine or another. Others emphasized the Kingdom of God as a vital force within earthly society, and they sought to bring their faith into public affairs, societal concerns, and culture. Still others felt that the authorized, state churches had not gone far enough in practicing the ideas of the Reformation. Eventually, much of the original fire of the Reformation began to die down. While some abandoned the faith for humanism, God brought many in Protestant countries to true faith through a series of revivals or awakenings that swept Europe and America. While the Enlightenment had gained much influence, Christianity continued to have a powerful effect on Western culture, as the Awakenings transformed the political, social and industrial landscape.

The Puritans

Religious changes in England resulted primarily from the influences of the **Puritans**. The Tudor monarchs—Henry VII, Edward VI, and Elizabeth I—had shaped the English Reformation. But the "reformation" of the English church was more political than spiritual, more institutional than doctrinal. During persecution under the Catholic monarch, **"Bloody Mary" Tudor**, many Protestants fled to Geneva where they were exposed to the teachings of **John Calvin**. They returned to England when **Elizabeth I** succeeded Mary to the English throne. Fired up by what they learned in Geneva, the returnees, now part of the same Calvinist movement that had earlier brought sweeping changes to the church in France, the Low Countries, and Scotland, wished to purify the English church, believing that too many Roman Catholic practices and beliefs had been kept in the new English Protestant church—the Anglican Church. They were not satisfied with the accommodations made by Elizabeth in an agreement known as the **Elizabethan Settlement of 1563**. Many faiths added practices to their worship which were not specifically

The Westminster Assembly meeting in London from 1643 to 1649 was made up of leading Puritan theologians.

taught in the Scriptures. Calvinists and later Puritans tried to avoid this. Also they wanted a godly pastor in every parish, elected by the people and ordained by fellow pastors, not by the bishop or the state. Every pastor was to have equal standing, unlike the episcopal system of the Anglicans. Each pastor would faithfully proclaim the Word of God, administer the **sacraments**, and oversee the discipline of immoral or wayward church members.

> Puritanism did not cause its adherents to hold views radically different from their countrymen's but rather to see things in a subtly different light, sometimes dissimilar in kind..., sometimes in intensity.... But put all the subtle differences together and the man stands out as a Puritan.... For the Puritan was not quite like other people. Probing endlessly the implications of Christian doctrine to himself and to his society, he tried to force both to act accordingly.
>
> Alden T. Vaughan, **The Puritan Tradition in America, 1620-1730,** (Columbia, S.C.: University of South Carolina Press, 1972)

Puritan beliefs. Among the main points of religion stressed by the Puritans were God's law, which convicts us of sin, and His grace, which enables us to keep God's law. This was nothing new to Protestant theology. It was just that the Puritans gained new understanding of how to apply doctrine *to the believer's life*. To a Puritan, conversion meant a complete change in his life and attitudes. The believer was expected to live in a sober and disciplined fashion. Many have criticized the Puritan life-style to the point that "puritanical" has become a modern synonym for dour, joyless prudishness. The truth is, life was a joyful, well-rounded, satisfying experience for the Puritans. As they put it: "Man's chief end is to glorify God and to enjoy Him forever." They found joy in worship and in a life of duty to God. This can

Cotton Mather (1663–1728) a Puritan leader in New England was one of many outstanding Puritan pastors. He wrote a history of New England in **Magnalia Christi Americana** (1702).

be seen in a prayer by the Puritan leader, **Cotton Mather:**

> Grant me thy gracious assistance, O my God, that in this my undertaking I may be kept from every false way: but that sincerely aiming at thy glory in my undertaking, I may find my labours made acceptable and profitable unto thy churches and serviceable unto the interests of thy gospel; so let my God think upon me for good; and spare me according to the greatness of thy mercy in the blessed Jesus.

As this prayer implies, the Puritan exercised his faith in all his daily activities. He saw work as a way to serve God. The Middle Ages had applied the term "religious" only to full-time church activity. But to the Puritan, any **vocation**—whether it be merchant, lawyer, pastor, or homemaker—was a divine calling. All honorable callings had dignity and spiritual implications.

One student of Puritan doctrine has said that "Puritanism was the whole movement that began in the sixteenth century to exhort men to prepare for a miracle of grace and ended by asserting the presence of the Holy Spirit in every individual." Puritans all agreed that the Church of England was wrong on this point, and they held that the error was on the subject of "the new birth."

> They insist that the natural man cannot grow in grace; he has to be reborn. They explain the rebirth as a vivid personal experience in which the individual soul encounters the wrath and redemptive love of God. It is an experience for which the church may prepare a man, and after which it may claim to guide him, but which in its essential nature is beyond the church's control (Alan Simpson. *Puritanism in Old and New England*).

For the Puritan, to be "born again" meant two things—to be spiritually *regenerated* and to live a *sanctified* life. It meant to have a new character that was marked by a sense of accountability to God and His law. This character found expression in a life of self-examination in the light of God's law, self-denial in the face of one's sinfulness, and self-discipline under the guidance of the Holy Spirit. In this way, Puritan *theological doctrine* gave rise to a unique *worldview*. This doctrinally based worldview is visible in the statement of a twentieth-century theologian, J. Gresham Machen, who followed in the Puritan tradition:

> The Christian cannot be satisfied as long as any human activity is either opposed to Christianity or out of all connection with Christianity. Christianity must pervade not merely all nations, but also all of human thought. The Christian, therefore, cannot be indifferent to any branch of earnest endeavor. It must all be brought into *some* relation to the gospel. It must be studied either in order to be demonstrated as false, or else in order to be made useful in advancing the Kingdom of God. The

Kingdom must be advanced not merely extensively, but also intensively. The Church must seek to conquer not merely every man for Christ, but also the whole of man.

This idea naturally produced a new and unique view of society and government, which the Puritans called a *holy commonwealth*. The Puritans did not believe in religious liberty in the sense that anyone should be allowed to believe whatever he wishes and to act any way his conscience will allow him to act. They preached liberty of conscience, but by that they meant that every man must be given the right to believe the truth as expressed in the Word of God and to act in obedience to that belief. They did not believe men had a right to act contrary to the Word of God. In the early seventeenth century, the American Puritan leader **John Cotton** argued that both liberty and government authority depend upon a clear understanding of biblical truth. If one's behavior depends upon one's spiritual condition, then it makes a difference what one believes and what society as a whole accepts as truth. Cotton held that whenever there is a change in a society's belief system, one can expect a change in the tangible aspects of liberty among the people and change in the exercise of authority among rulers. The nineteenth century Dutch statesman Abraham Kuyper, who also followed the Puritan vision, reflected this idea when he wrote of his desire to govern The Netherlands as prime minister according to God's law:

One desire has been the ruling passion of my life. One high motive has acted like a spur upon my mind and soul. And sooner than that I should seek escape from the sacred necessity that is laid upon me, let the breath of life fail me. It is this: that in spite of all worldly opposition, God's holy ordinances shall be established again in the home, in the school and in the State for the good of the people; to carve as it were into the conscience of the

John Owen (1616–1683) was one of the leading Congregational Puritans. He was appointed in 1652 by Oliver Cromwell to be vice-chancellor of Oxford University.

nation the ordinances of the Lord, to which Bible and Creation bear witness, until the nation pays homage again to God.

Some critics have suggested that there were inherent "tensions" or internal "dilemmas" within Puritan thought which eventually led to its demise. The writer Edmund Morgan, in his work, *The Puritan Dilemma* (1958), described it this way:

Puritanism required that a man devote his life to seeking salvation, but told him he was helpless to do anything but evil. Puritanism required that he rest his whole hope in Christ but taught him that Christ would utterly reject him unless before he was born God had foreordained his salvation. Puritanism required that man refrain from sin but told him he would sin anyhow. Puritanism required that he reform the world in the image

of God's holy kingdom but taught him that the evil of the world was incurable and inevitable. Puritanism required that he work to the best of his ability at whatever task was set before him and partake of the good things that God had filled the world with, but told him he must enjoy his work and his pleasures only, as it were, absentmindedly, with his attention fixed on God.

The Puritans themselves, when challenged about such alleged tensions in their beliefs, denied there were any dilemmas. To them the doctrine of the sovereignty of an Almighty God resolved any such conflicts. Man, even regenerated man, is indeed finite and sinful; but God remains in control of human events and, in His grace, works all things to His glory, they believed. As one recent writer, Terrill Irwin Elniff, explained it: "The Puritan worldview would maintain that these dilemmas are not inherently contradictory, but rather that each horn of the dilemma is simply there as a limited aspect of reality and ultimately resolved only in the sovereignty of God."

The Puritan Movement. The Puritans began as reformers within the Church of England. They did not initially see themselves as political revolutionaries or as the originators of a new church. Although genuine Puritans were never a majority in England, their ideas became more and more influential—among all classes of people, from nobles and the landed gentry to intellectuals to businessmen and tradesmen. Soon their influence outstripped their actual numbers, especially when they began to speak out on public issues such as the power struggle between Parliament and the English monarchs.

During the struggle against the Stuart rulers in the early seventeenth century, Puritans gained a majority in the English Parliament. Deeply convicted that God is sovereign over human affairs, the Puritans were not afraid to question the

Thomas Watson (1646–1689) was a Presbyterian Puritan who studied at Emmanuel College. He was rejected by the Anglican establishment in 1662. His *Body of Divinity*, containing sermons on the Westminster Catechism, is still in print.

power of the king. Their opposition led to the defeat and execution of Charles I, but they were not able to agree on the form that the new government should take. The variety of political and social solutions they offered left their leader, **Oliver Cromwell**, no choice but to set up a military dictatorship. These events are discussed more fully in chapter 5.

Persecution. Neither before the Holy Commonwealth under Cromwell nor after it did the Church of England have any room for Puritan piety. In addition to cruel punishments by **Archbishop William Laud**, authorities found many ways to deal with the Puritan problem. They did not permit Puritans to publish their views, speak out in church, or hold meetings apart from the regular Anglican services. Some Puritans, called **Separatists**, left the Anglican Church in order to set up their own congregations; and worship services were often held in secret. Several leaders of

these churches were hanged and many members were jailed. But each Puritan knew that he would have to pay a high price to follow his beliefs, perhaps even give up his life. During the brief period of Puritan rule in England, the persecution subsided. Under Cromwell's regime and with his support, the Separatist movement became known as Congregationalism. In 1643, an assembly of Presbyterian Puritans, Congregationalists, and Episcopalians met at Westminster and adopted a statement of faith known as the *Westminster Confession of Faith*. This historic confession was the last of the great Reformation creeds and was used along with two catechisms adopted by the Westminster Assembly, the *Larger Catechism* and the *Shorter Catechism*. By 1648, Parliament had accepted these documents as the official creed of the churches. (The *Confession* was also adopted by the General Assembly of Scotland.) Thus the official work of reforming the Church of England into the Calvinistic mold was completed the same year (1648) as the Thirty Years' War ended with the Peace of Westphalia on the European Continent. An assembly of Congregationalists met shortly after Cromwell's death in 1658. This assembly at Savoy Palace in London adopted a *Declaration of Faith and Order Owned and Practised in the Congregational Churches* (the Savoy Declaration) and endorsed the *Westminster Confession*. After the restoration of Charles II to the English throne in 1660, however, Puritans again met intense persecution, and many of their achievements were reversed. The movement eventually lost much of its force in England.

Radical Groups

However, there were other movements in England that went beyond the Puritan biblical

Matthew Henry (1662–1714), a Presbyterian Puritan, wrote a seven volume *Commentary on the Bible*, which is still quite popular today.

vision. A number of radical dissenting sects developed, each seeking to fulfill its particular vision of the Kingdom of God. Some of them fall broadly under the label of Puritan, and some do not. A group called the **Levellers** wanted political democracy with the right to vote for all males, freedom of religion, and equality before the law. Another group, the **Diggers**, believed that because the earth was God's creation, it was common property. They were arrested for planting crops on the common land (something like a public park) at St. George's Hill, Surrey, in 1649. The second coming of Christ and the establishment of His Kingdom inspired the Diggers as well as many other Englishmen. The most radical of all were the **Fifth Monarchy Men**. They taught that a completely new form of government should be established in England. Christian believers, joining together in assemblies under the control of Jesus Christ, would run the country.

Another of the radical dissenter groups, which sought to undermined the Puritan stress on the Bible, was the **Society of Friends** or **Quakers**. Founded by George Fox, they taught that the new age of the Spirit would come when people would be guided by God's **inner light** (rather than by the Bible) into religious and moral truth. In this they were similar to the Enlightenment thinkers. But they were mystical in practice, members of the group would sit in silence during their meetings and wait for the Spirit of God to descend upon them. From time to time, someone might rise to speak. Often the presence of the "inner light" led to shaking and quaking, hence the name Quakers. In their plain meeting houses, they worshiped without minister, sacraments, or liturgy. Quakers led simple lives, opposing war and enduring great persecution from society and the church. Crowds attacked Fox constantly. But the Quakers promoted the idea of toleration of all religions. One Quaker, William Penn, established the colony of Pennsylvania, which became the home of a wide variety of mystical sects and persecuted Protestants.

New England Puritans

While Puritanism was being persecuted in England, many Puritans sought for a new beginning and founded settlements with reformed churches in New England. This movement began with the English Separatist group called the Pilgrims at Plymouth, Massachusetts, in 1620. Under leaders such as **John Winthrop** and **John Cotton** in the early 1600s, Puritans developed the Congregational Church. Members had to

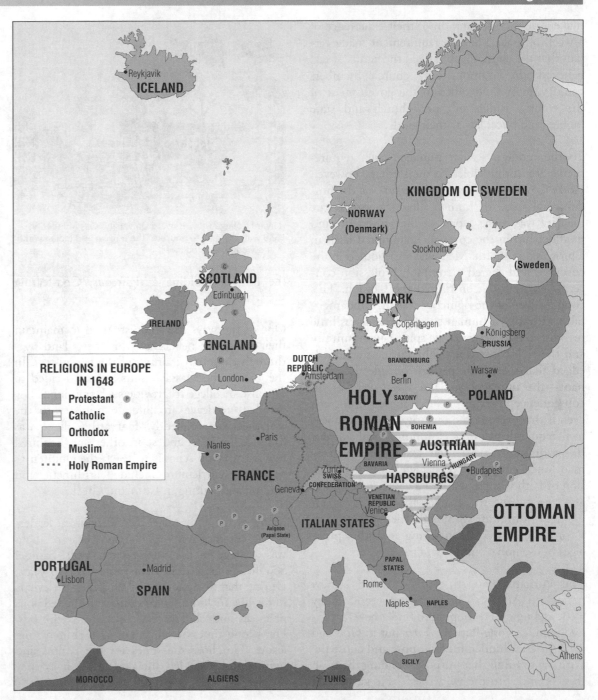

RELIGIONS IN EUROPE IN 1648

- Protestant ⓟ
- Catholic ⓒ
- Orthodox
- Muslim
- ---- Holy Roman Empire

make a public "declaration of their experience of a work of grace." Such a requirement made certain that the church would be in the hands of real believers. In addition, only church members could vote or hold office in the government of the colony. Rulers of both church and state looked to biblical law as their guide.

To the modern secular pluralist, such requirements are unthinkable. To the Puritan, however, God's Covenant of Grace with man was the fundamental issue of human life. A person's true identity was to be a part of that covenant, and membership in the covenant manifested itself in a profession of faith. Men who were joined in the covenant and shared a common profession concerning the truth constituted the Church. This congregation of the righteous was the fundamental institution of human society. There was little real distinction between the spiritual community and the civil community. The Puritans acknowledged that there were persons outside the covenant—the unregenerate, but these were of no consequence in terms of the operation of society, even if they were in the majority. Their duty was to live quiet lives in the community and support the community with their taxes. Divine grace made one a covenant-keeper. The genuine profession of faith was the mark of a covenant member and the means to separate the true covenant member from those who might merely feign faith in order to participate in voting and other privileges of the holy commonwealth.

The Puritans who struggled to build a new nation on America's shores had a vision. They went as a new Israel hoping to find a new "promised land." As one Puritan writer put it, God had kept America hidden for a purpose and chose the Puritans to fulfill that purpose. Sending them on this "errand into the wilderness," He gave them

Harvard College (now Harvard University) was founded in 1636 with the goal to educate "the English and Indian youth in knowledge and godliness."

the task of building a righteous, God-fearing society.

One of the ways the colonists tried to maintain their religious beliefs in this new land was through thorough training of their ministers. In the 1630s, the Massachusetts settlers decided to establish a college to provide such training. They dreaded "to leave an illiterate ministry to the churches"; consequently, **Harvard College** was founded in 1636 and soon other laws required towns to set up schools to teach the children as well. The curriculum included arithmetic and reading and writing in Latin and Greek!

Many of the early religious and political leaders of the colonies went to Harvard. One of them was a judge in the Salem witch trials, Samuel Sewall. He kept a diary for more than 50 years. During that time, he recorded many of the events in his life, including information on the religious practices and church services in Massachusetts. For a long time, Sewall served as a church song leader. He chose the tunes for the psalms and hymns and then led the congregation as they sang.

Printed sermons were apparently very popular reading material. After people heard a sermon, they wanted a copy to read for themselves. Sometimes they also got together to discuss the sermons. A lot of other religious writing was also printed in the colonies. The first book printed was the *Bay Psalm Book* in 1640. The psalms in this volume were carefully translated from Hebrew into **metrical** English verses so they could be sung.

The first Bible printed in America was finished in 1663. It was a translation into the Algonquian language done by **John Eliot**. He preached to the Indians for nearly 40 years. Several towns for "praying Indians" who had become Christians were founded in Massachusetts.

Puritan Literature. Both in England and America, Puritans contributed to the literature of their day. Besides the printed sermons, they wrote theological works, pamphlets about controversial topics, and other books designed to instruct or exhort. These materials had a wide circulation.

Samuel Williard (1640–1707), epitomized early New England Puritanism. He served as president of Harvard college in 1700, and his *Compleat Body of Divinity* (1726) on the Westminster Catechism was one of the first studies of theology in America.

The world remembers John Bunyan as the author of the most popular book in the English language after the Bible—*The Pilgrim's Progress*.

Two of the literary giants of the seventeenth century, **John Bunyan** and **John Milton**, were Puritans.

Arrested in 1660 for preaching outside the established church, Bunyan spent several years in prison. There in his cell he wrote several works, including his literary masterpiece, *The Pilgrim's Progress*, published in 1678. This book has established him as one of the most influential religious writers of all time. With vivid imagination, he traces the journey of a man named Christian from the City of Destruction to the Celestial City. Bunyan's story likens the spiritual journey every Christian takes through life to a physical journey beset with many dangers and adventures. This tale actually describes the author's own spiritual life.

John Milton's two immortal works, *Paradise Lost* (1667) and *Paradise Regained* (1671), deal with the fall and redemption of humanity. Considered by some as the greatest poem in the English language, *Paradise Lost* was written in a time of great personal tragedy for Milton. Two of his children and his first and second wives had died. Then by 1652, he became totally blind. Finally when Charles II came to the throne, the poet also lost his government position and his income. Yet he was able to rise above his troubles.

Another notable work which had previously come from Milton's pen was a defense of freedom of the press, the *Areopagitica* (1644). In it he protested the strict government **censorship** of the time and explained the reasons why people should be allowed to publish their opinions without interference.

Although not strictly a Puritan work, **John Foxe**'s *The Book of Martyrs* played a key role in the development of Puritanism. Foxe had fled England during the persecutions by Bloody Mary. While in exile, he began work on a history of Christian martyrs and included stories of many devout Protestants who had been persecuted, tortured, and martyred under Mary. These stories praised the lives and commitment of faithful men and women who dared to sacrifice their lives for the Kingdom of God. The Puritans strongly identified with those in Foxe's book, and *The Book of Martyrs* was extremely influential in the development of the Puritan identity as the new Israel, covenanted with God and destined to establish His Kingdom upon earth.

Puritan Architecture and Music. Dissenting churches had relatively plain buildings for worship. On the walls, there were often Bible verses, the Ten Commandments, the Apostles' Creed, and the Lord's Prayer. The pulpits were placed centrally, not only allowing the people to see and hear clearly but also demonstrating the centrality of the Word of God in Puritan worship.

A portrait of John Milton. While Bunyan wrote in the language of the common man, Milton's works show the author's extensive education.

Music was very important. In cathedrals, most of the singing was done by the choir, but in some churches the whole congregation participated. Some groups sang only the Psalms, while others used other parts of Scripture as well. People also began to compose their own sacred songs. Some of these set forth what God was like and what Christ had done. Some expressed the writer's feelings about God and His greatness.

One well-known writer of hymns was **Isaac Watts** (1674–1748). Watts served as a preacher for a congregation in London for many years. As a young man, he began to imitate the Psalms and to compose hymns. He wrote hundreds of songs, many of which are still quite popular. "Joy to the World" is one of the most familiar Christmas carols. His praises to God are found in "I Sing the Almighty Power of God" and "O God Our Help in Ages Past." "Jesus Shall Reign," "Alas! and Did My Saviour Bleed?" "Am I a Soldier of the Cross?" and "When I Survey the Wondrous Cross" are also found in many hymnbooks.

In summary, the Puritans shaped much of English and early American society. They deeply influenced the religious, social, literary, and intellectual life of the English-speaking world. However, few religious groups have more sharply divided scholars than the Puritans have. Some feel Puritanism is a great blessing and fundamental to understanding modern Western civilization, especially Americanism. Others strongly resent the movement and despise its legacy of bringing biblical faith to bear upon the whole of life.

Lutheran and Moravian Pietism

The Peace of Westphalia that ended the Thirty Years' War allowed each ruler in Germany to choose the faith of his subjects. However, he had only three options—Catholicism, Lutheranism, or Calvinism. In each German state, the church was dependent upon the ruler. The prince was above the discipline of the church and answered to God alone. The state treated pastors as employees and regarded the church as a tool for teaching such attitudes as integrity, loyalty, and obedience. Because Lutheranism had stressed faith and not works, and the Bible more than the Holy Spirit, eventually a kind of formalism became common. In the churches, the vital faith of the Reformation seemed to have hardened into formulas and unsanctified living. Even some of

Pilgrim's Progress

Son of a tinker from the lower class, John Bunyan received little schooling and as a youth led a wild life. His conversion a few years later affected him so deeply that he made the Bible his entire education and studied it constantly. To it he owes the force and charm of his own writing.

In this excerpt from his great allegorical book, **The Pilgrim's Progress**, Christian has just become aware that his soul is in danger of perishing and has set out for the Heavenly City. Very soon he meets the devil, Apollyon, who rules the City of Destruction:

By now, in this Valley of humiliation, poor Christian was hard put to it; for he had gone but a little way, before he espied a foul fiend coming over the field to meet him; his name is Apollyon. Then did Christian begin to be afraid, and to cast in his mind whether to go back or to stand his ground. But he considered again that he had no armor for his back; and therefore thought that to turn the back to him might give him the greater advantage with ease to pierce him with his darts. Therefore he resolved to venture and stand his ground; for, thought he, had I no more in mine eye than the saving of my life, it would be the best way to stand.

So he went on, and Apollyon met him. Now the monster was hideous to behold; he was clothed with scales, like a fish (and they are his pride), he had wings like a dragon, feet like a bear, and out of his belly came fire and smoke, and his mouth was as the mouth of a lion. When he was come up to Christian, he beheld him with a disdainful countenance and thus began to question him.

Apol. Whence come you? and whither are you bound?

Chr. I am come from the City of Destruction, which is the place of all evil, and am going to the City of Zion.

Apol. By this I perceive thou art one of my subjects, for all that country is mine, and I am the prince and god of it. How is it, then, that thou hast run away from thy king? Were it not that I hope thou mayest do me more service, I would strike thee now, at one blow, to the ground.

Chr. I was born, indeed, in your dominions, but your service was hard, and your wages such as a man could not live on, "for the wages of sin is death" (Romans 6:23); therefore, when I was come to years, I did as other considerate persons do, look out, if, perhaps, I might mend myself.

From John Bunyan, **The Pilgrim's Progress** (New York: C. Scribner's Sons, 1918).

the clergy led immoral lives. But a number of Calvinistic churches were active in Germany from Switzerland to Holland along the Rhine River. These churches stressed the importance of piety and godliness sharing much with the English Puritans through Dutch Calvinism.

Spener. Not everyone was happy with the decline in the Lutheran churches. Among these was a Lutheran pastor in Frankfurt, **Philipp Jakob Spener**, who was born in Alsace and studied in Strasbourg along the Rhine, where Calvin had taught a hundred years earlier. He traveled to Geneva and other parts of Switzerland and Germany where he came into contact with Reformed

Theology and German-Dutch Puritanism. In 1675 he set forth his attempt to wed Puritanism to Lutheranism in his book *Pia Desideria* (Pious Desires). He gathered into his home a group of people wanting a deeper Christian life. They discussed sermons, prayer, the Bible, and various Christian books. For many of these people, this was the beginning of a warm, personal faith. Thus began the **Pietist Movement**.

Reacting to Lutheran orthodoxy which stressed correct doctrine more than good behavior and involvement in temporal affairs over private devotion, the Pietists expressed their salvation by doing good works, which put them at odds with

August H. Francke, 1663–1727

Luther's emphasis on faith as the heart of salvation. The Pietists showed a great concern for the ordinary spiritual needs of people more than for intellectualism and theology. In the Pietist view, religion was something that had to be felt inwardly, something highly personal. Though adopting strict moral standards, they had at the same time a strong sense of God's love and the forgiveness possible through Christ. To Spener, Christianity was *life* more than *knowledge*. This was an overreaction.

Spener's book soon became well known throughout Germany. In it, he made suggestions for bringing the church back to a living faith. People needed to study the Scriptures in order to grow spiritually, he said. He encouraged the formation of small groups within churches for the purpose of Bible study and prayer. He taught that laymen must be more involved in religious work within the church. Christians ought to begin *doing* what the Bible says instead of just *talking* about it. When Christians debate theology, they should show a spirit of love so that others can be won to

Jesus Christ. Seminaries should help ministers to become true moral and spiritual leaders. Like the Puritans, Pietists opposed worldly amusements such as theater-going, dancing, and card-playing and favored moderation in dress, eating, and drinking.

Spener met strong opposition, making his pastorates in Frankfurt and Dresden difficult. He worked more happily in Berlin until he died in 1705.

Francke. Spener spread his ideas through publications, letters, and personal contact. Before long, they reached a professor at the University of Leipzig named **August H. Francke**. After becoming a Pietist, Francke started a Bible study among the graduate students of the university. When a new university was founded at Halle, Spener secured a position there for him. Soon Halle became the international center of Lutheran Pietism. Gifted with limitless energy, boundless enthusiasm, great organizational ability, and a flair for what later ages would call public relations, Francke built an amazing complex. It included an orphanage, boarding schools, a Latin school, a publishing house, a pharmacy, and a Bible institute.

In addition to all these activities, Francke was the most important member of the Halle theological faculty for many years. He inspired many of his students to serve God as foreign missionaries. Some went to America and did much to establish the Lutheran Church there. In New England, the Puritan minister Cotton Mather wrote of the Pietists, "The world begins to feel a warmth from the fire of God, which thus flames in the heart of Germany, beginning to extend into every region."

However, opposition grew. In 1695, the University of Wittenberg, Luther's old base, condemned

283 theses of Spener as **heretical**. Despite such problems, the movement became popular in other parts of Germany, especially Württemberg, as well as Scandinavia.

Zinzendorf and the Moravians. In 1727, a German nobleman, **Nikolaus Ludwig von Zinzendorf**, resigned from a promising career in government to serve God in the Pietist movement. A godson of Spener and a former student of Francke, Count Zinzendorf had allowed a group of refugees to settle on his estate near Dresden. The settlers were part of what was left of John Hus's persecuted following, which had become known as the Moravian Church. Under the leadership of Zinzendorf, they founded a village called Herrnhut. There the Moravians followed some of the ancient practices of the apostles—foot washing, love feasts, the kiss of peace, and the casting of lots to make decisions. Life at Herrnhut was almost **monastic**. While people worked in the kitchens and gardens, they sang joyful hymns or musicians played sacred music on their instruments. Child-care centers reared the children and to some extent members made their personal belongings available to the whole community.

Zinzendorf felt that he could be both a Pietist and a Lutheran. However, the Moravians did not want to be a part of the Lutheran Church. Zinzendorf accepted their difference of views and showed a tolerance toward other creeds. The antidoctrinal element in Moravian Pietism was so strong that it became a kind of precursor to the ecumenical movement. Zinzendorf worked out a plan for the reunion of the Protestant, Roman Catholic, and Eastern Orthodox churches. He was also interested in some rather strange doctrines and mystical practices.

The state authorities accused Zinzendorf of heresy in 1734, but he was not condemned. By then,

Nikolaus Ludwig von Zinzendorf, 1700–1760

Herrnhut had become a haven for Protestant refugees from all over Germany. In 1736, the Austrians complained to the state of Saxony, where Zinzendorf lived, that he was persuading their subjects to leave Austria for Herrnhut. As a result, he was banished from his homeland. For eleven years, he traveled widely, including North America where, in 1741, he sought to unite all the different Christian groups in Pennsylvania.

Even before his exile, the count had been interested in preaching the gospel in faraway places. In 1730, while attending the coronation of the king of Denmark, he had met natives of Greenland and the West Indies. Returning to Herrnhut full of zeal, he inspired the Moravians to send missionaries to these islands, to Georgia in the American colonies, and to Central America. Through their zeal, the Moravians launched a missionary effort, but little of this movement now remains in these places.

Summary. Pietism has become a vital force in world history, shaping the future course of a large part of the Christian Church. This movement brought new spiritual life to many people in Germany and influenced the Lutheran Church there. From Germany to England came the Moravian message and way of life. A young Anglican minister, **John Wesley**, walked into a Moravian mission on London's Aldersgate Street one day and reached the turning point in his life. Moravian missionaries and other Pietists fleeing persecution brought their faith to America. Rescue missions among the poor and the Sunday school movement are among the legacies of Pietism. Many Pietists, such as Paul Gerhardt, wrote many hymns which churches still sing today. These include "Jesus, Thy Blood and Righteousness" and "Jesus, Still Lead On."

The Lutheran Pietist desire for holy living, Bible study, and missions was similar to the Anglican **Evangelical movement**, where it has done much to encourage human compassion and decency in modern society.

Critics of Pietism charge, however, that its emphasis on the personal nature of religion led too many Christians to abandon culture, allowing non-Christian and humanistic philosophies to capture the minds and imaginations of people everywhere. According to these critics, the gains which the Reformation had made in extending the principles of the Kingdom of God into societal life and culture were undone by the Pietists' tendency to withdraw into spiritual havens within the church. Furthermore, as the Calvinist theologian B.B. Warfield argued, the Pietists' view of holy living and good works was not fully in accord with the biblical doctrine of grace. Many Pietists viewed the acquisition and growth of faith as human efforts and taught that Christians must zealously work to acquire more faith, pray more, live more victoriously, and withdraw more and more from the sinful world. Pious human effort thus became a remedy for sinfulness, contrary to the Reformation's biblical view that God's grace is the only remedy. The strong contrast they drew between faith and life, doctrine and practice, became a negative influence on the church for years to come.

The Evangelical Awakening in England

Religious life in England had reached a low point in the early 1700s. A visitor declared, "There is no such thing as religion there and the subject, if mentioned in society, excites nothing but laughter." Moral standards had given way. Workers and

In the early 1700s, England was probably the most drunken nation in the world. This engraving by William Hogarth is called *Beer Street* (1751).

George Whitefield

other poor people suffered cruelly, but few Englishmen seemed to care. The lower classes were ignorant, depraved, and drunken. Politics was corrupt. Harsh laws had people executed for petty crimes such as stealing a fish. In these hard times, many people turned to drink for comfort. Churches were poorly attended and public worship was a lifeless **formality**. For sermons, ministers often gave general moral talks that seldom included the Gospel of Christ.

The few faithful Christians had little influence. The greatest need for the church's services came at its weakest moment. By the middle of the century, a transformation in agriculture and industry began to change English life. Farmers were forced from their land to the new towns around factories and mines. The new settlements had no schools or churches. Into this dire situation, God himself raised up a number of evangelists and revivals to bring an Awakening to Britain and North America.

George Whitefield. It was the outstanding English preacher, **George Whitefield** (1714–1770), who linked the separate revivals into what has become known as the **Great Awakening**. Reared in poverty at Gloucester, he attended Oxford University and became a friend of John and Charles Wesley in the 'Holy Club.' In 1735, he was converted and began his preaching ministry. He made seven visits to the English colonies. After returning in 1738 from his first visit to Georgia, he made his initial contact with Howell Harris and the Welsh revival. He also began open-air preaching in Bristol. Whitefield was qualified for the task. He had a loud, clear voice and spoke with dramatic force. His preaching moved thousands to think about God. During one of his tours to America (1740–1741), he preached to more than 20,000 people at one time on the Boston Common. He traveled throughout the colonies, preaching to Congregationalists, Anglicans, Presbyterians, Reformed, Methodists, Baptists, Lutherans, and Quakers. In 1741 he preached all over England and made many trips to Scotland, taking part in the famous Cambuslang revival. Other evangelists followed his example and preached wherever they could get an audience. Among these was John Wesley.

The Wesleys. **John** and **Charles Wesley** were two of the nineteen children born to an Anglican pastor, **Samuel Wesley**, and his wife, **Susanna** (eight of the children died in infancy). At age six, John was plucked from a fire which destroyed the parsonage of the rough country parish at Epworth. John's rescue from the fire left a lasting impression upon him, and he often referred to himself as a "firebrand plucked out of the burning." Mrs. Wesley, a remarkable woman and mother, made sure that the family studied the Bible and had regular times for prayer.

The Wesley brothers attended Oxford University, where they excelled academically. John was ordained an Anglican deacon and priest. Charles started a religious club, which John later joined and led, upon his return to Oxford after assisting his aging father for a time in the Epworth parish. Their group of about 25 students met for Bible study, communion, and fasting. Because of their strict rules (or methods) of piety, other students called them "The Holy Club," "Bible Moths," and "Methodists." The name **Methodist** stuck and later became the title for the Wesleys' movement.

When the leader of the American colony of Georgia, **Count James Edward Oglethorpe**, issued a call for missionaries, John responded. He had thought of replacing his father at Epworth when Samuel Wesley died in 1735, but Susanna encouraged John and Charles to respond to the call to America. Determined to serve God, John

John Wesley preaching in London

worked nearly three years as a missionary in America. He worked with Moravians in Georgia and was challenged by them with questions about whether His relationship with Christ as Savior was a personal one. Such questions troubled him. Although he and Charles worked vigorously, their efforts met with little success. Charles fell ill and returned within about a year. John became discouraged and also returned to England.

On the boat to America, he had met a group of Moravians. During a fearful storm, they alone remained calm, firmly trusting in God. Their assurance of salvation had touched Wesley deeply. He longed for that certainty himself. For ten years, he had fought against sin and tried to live according to the law of God. But his efforts left him unsatisfied, he said.

Back in London, he worshiped with the Moravians for a time. One night at their prayer meeting on Aldersgate Street, John had what he viewed as a remarkable spiritual experience, similar to one Charles had had a few nights earlier. As he later recalled, "About a quarter before nine, as I was listening to Luther's description of the change which God works in the heart through faith in Christ, I felt my heart strangely warmed. I felt I did trust in Christ, Christ alone for salvation; and an assurance was given me, that he had taken away my sins, even mine, and saved me from the law of sin and death."

From this, Wesley concluded that conversion was supposed to be an instantaneous experience, preceded by a long struggle. He believed that if a conversion were genuine, a person should be able to pinpoint the time, date, and place.

Immediately after his "conversion," he went to Germany to visit with Zinzendorf and his colony. Although the Moravians had done much to

Anti-Methodist Riot in Cork

change his life, he was not entirely satisfied with their religious practice. Wesley, a religious activist, found the Moravians a bit too meditative and mystical. Returning to England, Wesley had a burning desire to share his experience with the needy people about him. Already one of his Oxford friends, **George Whitefield**, was preaching in the open-air to miners in the fields near Bristol with powerful results. Whitefield exhorted Wesley to join him in these labors. As an Anglican pastor, Wesley did not think this was proper. He struggled with his conscience for a time, but by 1739, he too was preaching in the fields. Thus began an amazing ministry.

Reaction. Some listeners reacted violently to Wesley's sermons. When he spoke to miners, sailors, and factory workers about their sins, they frequently attacked him. Yet his absolute fearlessness and complete trust in God carried him through situations that would have frightened the bravest person. He even seemed to thrive on trouble.

Notice how he describes one encounter in his Journal:

(Some said) "No, no! knock his brains out; down with him, kill him at once."

Others said, "Nay, but we will hear him first."

I began asking, "What evil have I done? Which of you all have I wronged in word or deed?" And continued speaking for above a quarter of an hour, till my voice suddenly failed:

Then the floods began to lift up their voice again; many crying out, "Bring him away! Bring him away!

During the last half-century of Wesley's life, he preached more than 40,000 sermons and journeyed more than 250,000 miles, mostly on horseback. He traveled throughout the British Isles as well as to Holland and Germany. For fifty years, he preached across the length and breadth of England, gathering converts into new and existing religious "societies." Converts were expected to convert others. In contrast to Whitefield, Wesley was more of an organizer. He issued Methodist society membership tickets to converts. These tickets were renewed quarterly, a method he used to ensure that only genuine converts were members. Classes were organized within the societies, and members were required to pay a penny a week. These contributions raised large sums for continuation of the new evangelical work. Many lay preachers were used in the ministry. Wesley wrote materials to help train the lay ministers. Methodist preachers, including, for a time, Charles Wesley (along with his wealthy wife), rode horseback circuits from place to place. At John Wesley's death, there were more than 125,000 Methodists with 1,500 preachers. Good organization, fervent preaching, warm fellowship, personal conversion, and hearty hymn-singing made the Methodists a powerful force both in England and America.

John's brother, Charles, became the "sweet singer of Methodism." He wrote hundreds of hymns,

Methodist circuit riders such as Francis Asbury (1745–1816) spread the Gospel and Methodism in the American frontier.

including "Jesus, Lover of My Soul," "Love Divine, All Loves Excelling," "O for a Thousand Tongues to Sing," and "Christ the Lord is Risen Today."

Wesley's Methods and Teachings. John Wesley's long ministry broke many established Anglican traditions. For one thing, preaching in the open air was a novelty. But to Wesley, who was often denied access to established churches, it was the only way to answer his burning desire to see souls of the unchurched saved. The idea of preaching to the unchurched was itself new to religious practice in England. Wesley also had no reservations about invading established parishes of other clergymen to reach the unsaved. They often criticized him for this, but he countered that "the world is my parish." Well-paid ministers in established churches had neglected their flocks, preferring instead to enjoy the good life with the gentry. They would leave the church work to poorly paid vicars. Wesley felt his methods helped to overcome that neglect. Wesley's use of unordained preachers also was a ground-breaking practice. He adopted this practice reluctantly, but

the need to reach starving souls and the lack of ordained clergy committed to the task overpowered his reluctance.

Theologically, Wesley was in many ways within the orthodox Protestant tradition, but in others he held to views which were not common to the Reformation. He continued much of the Anglican views that accepted the **freewill** view of salvation known as **Arminianism**—that a person's salvation depends upon man's free choice to repent and accept Christ as Savior. But he added the idea that Christ has made it possible for all men to believe if they will only make a decision. He bitterly denounced his fellow evangelist Whitefield's teaching of the **Calvinist** view of **divine election** and **predestination** as part of God's plan of salvation. Because of this, it seems, he made many important decisions by casting lots.

Wesley shared many of the concerns of Pietism in fighting against gross sins, especially drunkenness and gambling. But he developed a new teaching called Perfectionism, in which he said that a Christian can become totally free from practicing sin in this life. While he never claimed to have attained this, some latter Methodists developed the holiness movement which eventually led to Pentecostalism.

The Anglican Evangelicals

While many of the converts in the Awakening were from among the ranks of the unchurched, other thousands in the nation's existing churches also found a renewed faith. Many of the clergy became better pastors within their own churches.

Within the Church of England, the evangelical revival helped the group known as **Evangelicals**. Many were Calvinists who stressed conversion, strict morals, simple worship, and a life of service to others such as William Romaine, James Hervey, Henry Venn, and Augustus Toplady.

One of this group, **John Newton**, had lived a wild and wicked life of utter disregard for God, had been a captain of a slave ship, and a slave himself. He was converted and became a minister in 1758. Like Whitefield and Toplady he was a strong Calvinist. Newton wrote a number of letters to encourage people from all walks of life on how to live and think as a Christian. Many of these were published, such as the popular *Cardiphonia* (Voice of the Heart). An outstanding preacher, he preached a series of sermons on the texts from Handel's *Messiah*. He also wrote such popular hymns as "Amazing Grace," "How Sweet the Name of Jesus Sounds," and "Glorious Things of Thee Are Spoken." His autobiography,

John Newton, the converted sea captain, became a leading Calvinistic Anglican evangelical. Through his many letters he gave wise counsel to a wide range of Christians.

Out of the Depths, is a Christian classic. In his last will and testament, he wrote:

> I commit my soul to my gracious God and Saviour, who mercifully spared and preserved me, when I was an apostate, a blasphemer, and an infidel, and delivered me from that state of misery on the coast of Africa into which my obstinate wickedness had plunged me; and Who has been pleased to admit me, though most unworthy, to preach His glorious gospel. I rely with humble confidence upon the atonement, and mediation of the Lord Jesus Christ, God and Man, which I have often proposed to others, as the only foundation whereupon a sinner can build his hope, trusting that He will guard and guide me through the uncertain remainder of my life, and that he will then admit me into His presence in His heavenly kingdom.

Having been captain of a slave ship, Newton knew the evils of slavery well. He became a strong influence on one of his friends that helped abolish the slave trade in England.

This man was **William Wilberforce**, who served as a member of Parliament. Fellow Evangelicals active in public life persuaded him to lead the fight in Parliament to abolish the slave trade. A letter from John Wesley, written shortly before Wesley's death, also urged him to take up this cause. Wilberforce worked against the trade in slaves for 20 years before he met success in 1807. The complete abolition of slavery in the British Empire in 1833 came about just after he died. It is noteworthy that this great Christian's efforts resulted in abolition of slavery without the bloodshed which transpired in the American Civil War. The American abolitionist movement had resulted from revolutionary agitation by humanistic clergymen influenced by Enlightenment and Romantic philosophies.

Hannah More was an Evangelical leader in education at the turn of the century. A patron of the Sunday school movement, she wrote many religious tracts for mass distribution. The upper classes and even people in the court read some of these. Her writings, and particularly Wilberforce's, helped improve the morals of the upper classes. Cockfighting died out, and "dirty book" stores closed for lack of customers.

A more famous advocate of Sunday schools in the late 1700s was the Gloucester newspaper publisher, **Robert Raikes**. A man with great concern for children, he organized schools to give religious and moral training to poor youngsters. The schools met on the only day when the children did not work. Students learned to read the Bible and often received lessons in arithmetic as well.

The Sunday school was a significant step in the development of popular education. Before this time, only charity schools took poor students. But they could not handle the vast numbers who wanted to come. Most received no schooling. By the time Raikes died, 31 years after the first school was opened, approximately a half-million poor students were attending Sunday schools. These schools aroused an awareness of the need for education, but it was several decades before the state began to believe that it held the responsibility for education.

Effects of the Revival. The Evangelical revival stirred people in the Baptist, Congregational, and Presbyterian churches also. **John Howard**, a sheriff and concerned Christian, tried to change the terrible conditions in English prisons. Other Christians joined together in attempts to stop gambling, dueling, child labor, drunkenness, and pornography. Many gave food and clothing to the needy and medical care to the sick. During this time, Christians also provided legal aid for the poor and housing for widows and orphans.

The Evangelical revival changed the course of history in England. Some historians say that the revival saved England from a violent upheaval like the French Revolution. Social reform, the desire to win the lost to Christ, provided a work-ethic for industrialization and missionary concern that gave the English the motivation and ability to assume world leadership during the nineteenth century.

The Great Awakening in North America

By 1700 the thirteen English colonies in North America had reached a low ebb in culture and religion. There were churches in every colony, but the original faith of the Puritans was in decline. In New England there was less concern about true Christian belief than when the first settlers had come. On the frontier, the difficulties of daily life often brought out the worst in people. In the cities some of the ideas of the Enlightenment were beginning to have an impact.

Revival Starts. The American revival was originally independent of the English Awakening. Nevertheless, God would eventually combine these various movements. In 1720, a man named **Theodore Frelinghuysen** (1691–1747) came to America to pastor a Dutch Reformed Church in New Jersey. Having undergone spiritual renewal himself, he was concerned by the spiritual deadness of many in the churches there. Born at Lingen in East Friesland near the German-Dutch border, Frelinghuysen imbibed the Dutch/German Reformed Puritanism that stressed the centrality of regeneration as a work of the Holy Spirit that gives men the ability to believe. His fervent preaching stirred the whole area of the

The Old Tennent Church

Jonathan Edwards, 1703–1758

this building, the elder Tennent trained his sons and a number of other young men for the ministry. His **Log College** courses included Latin, Greek, Hebrew, logic, and theology. In all his teaching, the father stirred his students with evangelical fervor. When Gilbert began preaching, his message also reflected the evangelical spirit. Keeping the outer forms of religion did not make one a Christian, Gilbert Tennent told his congregations. One must be personally surrendered to Christ and allow his whole life to be changed. Many New Jersey Presbyterians were converted. Despite the opposition Tennent received from officials and governing bodies of his own denomination, he preached a sermon on the danger of an unconverted ministry. Reports of his "awakening" sermons that warned parishioners of their need to run to Jesus Christ for shelter from the coming wrath of God upon sinners, spread quickly.

Various ministers repeatedly sought to hinder his work and discredit his ministry. Threatened by Tennent's powerful preaching and the zealous response it elicited, the Philadelphia Synod of the Presbyterian Church in 1738 forbade ordained ministers of other presbyteries to preach in vacant pulpits without first seeking permission from the presbytery that church was in.

As Tennent's influence grew and awakening preachers were added to the Presbyterian roles, more exclusionary rules were added to the Philadelphia Synod's church directory; and as Tennent's vision for the church expanded, the synod's narrowed. The Philadelphia Synod absorbed the authority of local presbyteries to examine and ordain ministers and erected committees of its own for the task. Ministers were tested with the utmost scrutiny on correctness of doctrine although their own personal faith and practice were left unexamined. By 1741, the denomina-

Raritan Valley, near New Brunswick and Princeton.

Encouraged by what he saw happening in the Dutch Reformed churches, a nearby Presbyterian minister, **Gilbert Tennent** (1703–1764), began evangelistic preaching. When Tennent compared the success Frelinghuysen knew among several Dutch congregations in New Jersey's Raritan Valley to his own feeble ministry, he was grieved, but not at the Dutch preacher's success. Instead, he records, "I was exceedingly grieved that I had done too little for God." It was not too long afterwards that Tennent began preaching the whole counsel of God to "awaken" his congregation.

Tennent was one of four sons of **William Tennent**, a teacher who had built a log schoolhouse on a corner of his property in Pennsylvania. In

tion forbade lay members from attending revival services, whether in Presbyterian churches or not, under the threat of church discipline.

Tennent welcomed George Whitefield and secured pulpits for him when he visited America even though the Presbyterian minister didn't share Whitefield's views on church government nor his zeal for evangelical cooperation. And although Whitefield had already amassed followings the New Brunswick pastor would never know, Tennent did his best to pave a level highway for Whitefield in the colonial church, realizing the cause was Christ's and not his or Whitefield's. In 1740–1741 he accompanied Whitefield on an evangelistic tour through the colonies.

Jonathan Edwards. In 1734, a revival broke out in New England. One of the most brilliant scholars America has produced, **Jonathan Edwards**, was pastor of the Congregational Church in Northampton. Edwards had a profound faith in God. Preaching clearly and with great **conviction**, he had been preaching a series of sermons on Justification by faith and had described the results of sin and the horrors of hell. Many of his listeners wept and hundreds placed their faith in Jesus Christ. The same thing happened again when the revival reached its peak in 1740. In Northampton, virtually every person came under conviction. During the first year of the revival there, three hundred persons were converted.

Edwards was surprised at the response to his preaching. He could only explain it as the work of God. He did try to analyze the revival in works such as *Some Thoughts Concerning the Present Revival of Religion in New England* and *A Treatise Concerning Religious Affections*. These books discuss both helpful and harmful aspects of the awakening.

The problem of keeping what his church had gained in the revival troubled Edwards. He saw that the unconverted members had a bad influence on the others. However, preventing the unconverted from taking Holy Communion did not work. This attempt caused such a furor among the foolish congregation that Edwards was forced from his church in 1750. After preaching at Stockbridge to the Housatonic Indians he became president of **Princeton College** in 1758.

Within a few years, after the revival in Northampton began, similar revivals occurred at various locations throughout New England. By 1740, mass conversions were being recorded throughout the region. Between 25,000 and 50,000 new Christians were added to the

Sinners in the Hands of an Angry God (Excerpt)

Are there not many here who have lived long in the world, and are not to this day born again? and so are aliens from the commonwealth of Israel, and have done nothing ever since they have lived, but treasure up wrath against the day of wrath? Oh, Sirs, your case, in an especial manner, is extremely dangerous. Your guilt and hardness of heart is extremely great. Do not you see how generally persons of your years are passed over and left, in the present remarkable and wonderful dispensation of God's mercy? You had need to consider yourselves, and awake thoroughly out of sleep. You cannot bear the fierceness and wrath of the infinite God.—And you, young men and young women, will you neglect this precious season which you now enjoy, when so many others of your age are renouncing all youthful vanities, and flocking to Christ? You especially have now an extraordinary opportunity; but if you neglect it, it will soon be with you as with those persons who spent all the precious days of youth in sin, and are now come to such a dreadful pass in blindness and hardness.— And you, children, who are unconverted, do not you know that you are going down to hell, to bear the dreadful wrath of that God, who is now angry with you every day and every night? Will you be content to be the children of the devil, when so many other children in the land are converted, and are become the holy and happy children of the King of kings?

And let every one that is yet out of Christ, and hanging over the pit of hell, whether they be old men and women, or middle aged, or young people, or little children, now hearken to the loud calls of God's word and providence. This acceptable year of the Lord, a day of such great favour to some, will doubtless be a day of as remarkable vengeance to others. Men's hearts harden, and their guilt increases apace, at such a day as this, if they neglect their souls; and never was there so great danger of such persons being given up to hardness of heart and blindness of mind. God seems now to be hastily gathering in his elect in all parts of the land; and probably the greater part of adult persons that ever shall be saved, will be brought in now in a little time, and that it will be as it was on the great outpouring of the Spirit upon the Jews in the apostles' days, the election will obtain, and the rest will be blinded. If this should be the case with you, you will eternally curse this day, and will curse the day that ever you was born, to see such a season of the pouring out of God's Spirit, and will wish that you had died and gone to hell before you had seen it. Now undoubtedly it is, as it was in the days of John the Baptist, the axe is in an extraordinary manner laid at the root of the trees, that every tree which brings not forth good fruit, may be hewn down, and cast into the fire.

Therefore, let every one that is out of Christ now awake and fly from the wrath to come. The wrath of Almighty God is now undoubtedly hanging over a great part of this congregation. Let every one fly out of Sodom: "Haste and escape for your lives, look not behind you, escape to the mountain, lest you be consumed."

—Jonathan Edwards

churches in a region whose total population was then about 300,000. The revival that swept New England vastly changed the moral and religious climate there.

When Edwards preached his famous sermon, "Sinners in the Hands of an Angry God," he had to stop on several occasions to await silence as his listeners' loud weeping was drowning out his voice.

Results of the Great Awakening. Where God is at work in a powerful and dramatic way, opposition spurred by the Evil One is not far behind. Christ faced continual opposition from those that should have welcomed Him, as did Paul when he preached Christ among those who should have been best prepared to receive Him.

Critics of the Awakening did not like the excitement and emotional displays at the meetings.

Sometimes people in the audience went into convulsions, laughed hysterically, screamed, or had visions and trances. A few of the preachers even encouraged these activities. Also, many who took part in the revival had harsh words for those who would not join in the meetings.

Despite its faults, the Great Awakening did much to shape the future nation. It resulted in the founding of many churches and saw a great number of the population become converts to Christ. Rank and file church members took their faith more seriously. Much of the concern for the needs of people and practical righteousness appeared in the Awakening. As in England, many social and moral changes resulted.

In addition, the Awakening made a great contribution to education. Aroused Christians realized the importance of literacy for the spread of the Gospel. While training for missions and ministry were seen as essential, the need for general knowledge and godly wisdom among the populace was also seen as a key to the growth of the emerging nation. Previously, the churches had to have men trained in England. But now the desire was to have independent schools. Among the many colleges started because of the revival, the best known are **Princeton**, **Rutgers**, **Brown**, and **Dartmouth**.

The concern for evangelical Christian freedom contributed to the United States Constitution. Modern-day Americans who enjoy First Amendment freedoms—of religion, press, speech, and assembly—have benefited from people who were set free from the slavery of sin during the Great Awakening. Their zeal for ecclesiastical and educational independence led to a desire for political freedom as well. Thus the Great Awakening shaped American thought and life on the eve of the struggle for independence and the westward push across the continent.

Many years later, President Calvin Coolidge recognized the connection between the Great Awakening and the creation of the United States as a free, prosperous, and independent nation:

> The American Revolution was preceded by the great religious revival of the middle of the eighteenth century, which had its effect both in England and in the colonies. When the common people turned to the reading of the Bible, …when they were stirred by a great revival, …the way was prepared…. It was because religion gave the people a new importance and a new glory that they demanded a new freedom and a new government. We cannot in our generation reject the cause and retain the result.
>
> If the institutions they adopted are to survive, if the governments which they founded are to endure, it will be because the people continue to have similar religious beliefs. It is idle to discuss freedom and equality on any other basis. It is useless to expect substantial reforms from any other motive.

Sadly, there were many false conversions during the Great Awakening which diminished it influence. And a defective type of revivalism was promoted by some. This happened because the faith of some was merely emotional and lacked depth. In any event, by the end of the eighteenth century, a **Second Great Awakening** swept the growing American nation and helped keep the United States from straying off its foundation of righteousness and allowed it to continue its remarkable development.

Princeton Theological Seminary was founded in 1812 near Princeton College by Ashbel Green and Archibald Alexander. Ashbel Green (1762–1848), pastored a Presbyterian church in Philadelphia made up of converts from the Great Awakening.

The Rise of Protestant Missions

Out of the revivals grew the modern missionary movement. Puritanism and the evangelical revival were powerful influences on the development of the Protestant missionary effort. The Reformation itself was a great missionary work, the mission field being Central and Western Europe, areas which, although not heathen, were grossly ignorant of the true gospel. It was not until Europe was truly evangelized that the true light would shine out to other parts of the world.

In the Reformation period Gustavus Vasa, King of Sweden, sent a missionary to Lapland. In 1620 the King of Denmark urged the chaplains of Danish settlements in India to preach the gospel to the Hindus. Gustavus Adolphus also had plans for missions which his godly chancellor Oxenstierna tried to carry out after the king's death in 1632. He sent **John Campanius** to work among the Indians along America's Delaware River and had Luther's small Catechism translated into the Indians' language. In 1721 **Hans Egede**, a Norwegian pastor, went to the Eskimos. Later, when Zinzendorf was visiting the Norwegian court, he met two Eskimos whom Egede had baptized. The result was the sending of Moravian missionaries to Greenland.

The New World. Among the Reformed we find that Calvin hoped to promote gospel work in Brazil. But the Puritans were the first Reformed Protestants to actually establish mission works. The voyagers in the *Mayflower* were ambitious to reach their Indian neighbors with the gospel. **Robert Cushman**, one of their number, was set apart to promote the conversion of the Indians. Oliver Cromwell, had a keen interest in mission-

John Eliot, the Apostle to the North American Indians

ary work, especially because the Indians of North America were the first heathens to become British subjects. **John Eliot**, a New England Puritan, is considered the apostle to the Indians, and did much to spread the gospel among them in the New World. Later **David Brainerd**, a graduate of Yale College, and a friend of Jonathan Edwards carried on a missionary work among Indians in eastern Pennsylvania. Even Edwards himself was involved in preaching to the Indians.

As the frontier moved westward, so did the work of missions in North America. In the 1830s, Methodist and Presbyterian missionaries went to the Oregon Territory to bring the gospel to the Indians. **Jason Lee** was appointed as a missionary

to Oregon by the Methodist Church in 1833 and preached his first sermon at Ft. Vancouver in September 1834. The American Board of Foreign Missions sent Presbyterians **Henry Spalding** and medical missionary **Dr. Marcus Whitman**, and their families, to Oregon in 1836, where they founded a mission in Walla Walla. Although the Whitmans were later killed by Indians in 1847, the work of all of these missionaries greatly aided the settlement of the Oregon Territory.

As Spain's colonies in South America began to gain their independence, a brief opportunity for Protestant missions arose. Taking advantage of that opportunity was **James Thomson** of Scotland. He arrived in Argentina in 1818 to help develop the education system in that country. Using the Bible as an important part of his curriculum, he was invited to work in Argentina, Chile, Peru, and Columbia. Thomson was even able to establish a national Bible society in Columbia. Regrettably, his efforts were not followed up and the Catholic clergy was able to undo much of what he had accomplished.

English Baptist missionaries were active in Jamaica. **William Knibb** was the best known of these missionaries, arriving on the island in 1824 and remaining there until his death in 1845—except for trips to England on behalf of the Baptist mission. He was a tireless advocate of the blacks on Jamaica, and worked to secure land for them after they gained freedom from slavery.

India. Much of the momentum of Protestant missions is traced to the a group of Calvinistic Baptist ministers in Northamptonshire, England. In 1792 they founded the Particular (Calvinistic) Baptist Missionary Society. **William Carey**, who had already published a pamphlet urging Christians to use all the means at their disposal in missionary effort, became the first of the new Society's missionaries. His motto was, 'Expect great things from God; attempt great things for God'. Carey went to Calcutta, India, in 1793 but had to settle further inland because of opposition by the British East India Company. He was especially gifted in languages. Carey was able to translate the Bible, various portions of the Scriptures, tracts, and Christian books in about forty different Indian languages or dialects.

Another English missionary who was highly skilled in language work was **Henry Martyn**. In 1805, Martyn left England for India as a chaplain with the British East India Company. Not only did he work among Europeans and natives in India, but he also labored with the Muslims in Persia. Martyn spent much of his time translating the Bible into Hindustani (Urdu) and Persian.

Long before the arrival of William Carey, however, German Pietists had been active in south India. **Bartholomaeus Ziegenbalg** arrived at the Danish settlement of Tranquebar in 1706, where he translated the New Testament and part of the Old Testament into the Tamil language. The greatest missionary of this movement was **Christian Schwartz**, who labored in India from 1750 until his death in 1798. Schwartz gained the trust of both the British and Indians to such an extent that he held important political positions with both, while never forgetting his primary calling as a missionary.

Burma. **Adoniram Judson**, from Massachusetts, was one of the most devoted of missionaries from America. In 1812 he and his wife sailed for India, sent by the American Board of Foreign Missions. It was in Burma that he accomplished his greatest work. He mastered the Burmese language without undue difficulty, but six years passed before he baptized the first convert. Because England was at war with Burma he suffered almost incredible hardships. But as his work met with success and he has become known as 'the apostle of Burma'.

South Africa. A Dutch Reformed minister by the name of **John van der Kemp** laid the foundation for the Christianization of South Africa. **Robert Moffat** followed in his steps, when Britain gained possession of the Cape Province which had been taken from the Dutch during the Napoleonic wars. As a missionary he worked with the London Missionary Society.

Pacific Islands. The nineteenth century saw the beginning of efforts to reach out to the islands of the Pacific with the gospel. The voyages of exploration of Captain James Cook, the settlement of

William Carey's translation work in India

New South Wales or Australia as a convict station, and the acquisition by England of New Zealand, contributed to Christian interest in the South Seas. One of the pioneer missionaries to the South Pacific islands was **John Geddes**, a Scottish Presbyterian from Nova Scotia. He sailed to the Pacific in 1847 and founded the mission to the New Hebrides Islands. He labored with great difficulty on the island of Aneityum for many years but God blessed his work. After his death in 1872, a memorial was placed in the church where he worked. It stated that "When he landed in 1848 there were no Christians here, and when he left in 1872 there were no heathen."

The gospel was first brought to Australia by evangelical Anglicans. Anglican chaplain **Richard Johnson** came to Australia with the first fleet in 1787 and opened the first church building in Sydney in 1793. The second chaplain to arrive in Australia was **Samuel Marsden**, who also went on to New Zealand. Marsden begin the first Christian mission to the Maoris and conducted the first Christian worship in New Zealand.

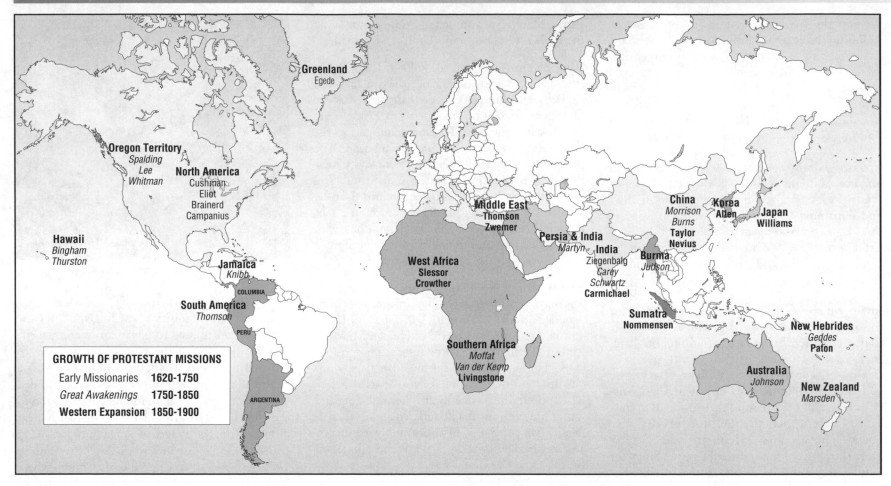

GROWTH OF PROTESTANT MISSIONS

Early Missionaries	1620-1750
Great Awakenings	1750-1850
Western Expansion	1850-1900

American Congregationalists missionaries went to Hawaii in 1820. Seven families, led by **Hiram Bingham** and **Asa Thurston** arrived on the islands to preach the gospel. God blessed the mission to such an extent that the most serious problems faced by the missionaries were with Western traders and sailors, not with the islanders. Within fifty years, the work had progressed so well that Hawaiians were sending out their own missionaries and the American Board felt able to close the mission work.

China. By the beginning of the nineteenth century, China had been closed to any Christian influence for almost 200 years, ever since the Ming Dynasty had expelled the Jesuit missionaries in the seventeenth century. However, China could not remain closed forever. **Robert Morrison** from England arrived in China as early as 1807 and accomplished a remarkable work as the pioneer of Protestant missions. He became the chief European expert on the difficult Chinese language. With the help of a few others, he translated the entire Bible into Chinese. Morrison was

diligent in the work of the gospel but seven years passed after his entry into China before he was able to baptize the first convert. **William Chalmers Burns** of Scotland labored in China from 1846–1868. He spent much time studying the Chinese language and adopted Chinese dress, but endured years of labor with few outward signs of success. However, he laid the foundation for later English Presbyterian mission work in China.

For your consideration

Questions

1. What is the danger of interpreting the Bible according to one's preconceived worldview or according to current scientific belief? Why does science have limits? Why does reason have limits?

2. Do you agree with the Puritan belief that one's faith affects his whole life-style? Why or why not?

3. How have Quaker attitudes influenced modern society? How have Puritan ideas influenced modern society?

4. What reasons might a government have for censorship of the press?

5. How did the gospel reach the Indians of North America? How are religious beliefs spread from one country to another today?

6. What is your opinion about the proper relationship between church and state? Do you agree, for example, with the policies of the German princes during the period following the Thirty Years' War?

7. What social concerns in your country or region could be addressed by Christians? How should religious activities be affected by social conditions?

8. Is it possible to be a church member or church leader without being a real Christian? How does this hurt the church?

9. Do church members acting in the name of Christianity always demonstrate the Christian viewpoint? Give examples.

Projects

1. Find out what kinds of religious persecution are taking place in our present world. Write a report or create a work of art to express your feelings about martyrs.

2. If you live in an area where it is possible, visit an old church building, such as a Puritan meeting house in New England. How does the architecture differ from modern church buildings? Do you see any connections to varying modern and historical beliefs in these differences in architecture?

3. Find and examine a "Psalter." Join with your class or family in singing some of the Psalms.

4. Organize a panel discussion on social concerns met by religious groups today. If you are not part of a class, prepare an individual report. You might include rescue missions, crisis telephone hot lines, day-care centers, adoption agencies, etc.

5. Do further research on the Great Awakenings of the 1700s. Prepare a report on how these Evangelical revivals impacted England, North America, and beyond.

6. Because of religious persecution in this period, the lives of many religious leaders were filled with danger. Choose a leader and read his or her biography. Tell the person's story in a report.

Word List

sacraments	vocation
"inner light"	metrical
censorship	Great Awakenings
"born again"	heretical
casting of lots	monastic
formality	conviction
Covenant of Grace	Westminster Confession
Herrnhut	freewill
Arminianism	divine election
predestination	'Holy Club'
Pietism	Holy Commonwealth

People and Groups

Puritans	Quakers
Cotton Mather	John Cotton
Separatists	Levellers
Fifth Monarchy Men	Diggers
William Laud	Oliver Cromwell
John Winthrop	John Eliot
John Bunyan	John Milton
John Foxe	Isaac Watts
"Bloody Mary" Tudor	Westminster Assembly
David Brainerd	Count Oglethorpe
Moravians	John Newton
Pietists	William Carey
William Penn	Hannah More
Philipp Jakob Spener	Theodore Frelinghuysen
August H. Francke	Henry Martyn
Count von Zinzendorf	Samuel Marsden
John Wesley	George Whitefield
Charles Wesley	Adoniram Judson
Methodists	John Newton
Evangelicals	William Wilberforce
Jonathan Edwards	Gilbert Tennent
Robert Moffat	Barth. Ziegenbalg
Captain James Cook	Hiram Bingham
John Geddie	Robert Morrison
Dr. Marcus Whitman	William Chalmers Burns
John van der Kemp	King Gustavus Vasa

1550   1600   1650   1700   1750   1800

Politics and Economics

American War for Independence 1775–1783

Reign of James II begins 1685

Turgot & Necker attempt
economic reforms Mid- to Late–1700s

Charles I beheaded and
Commonwealth begins 1649

French Revolution begins 1789

France becomes a republic 1792

English monarchy restored
with Charles II 1660

Reign of Napoleon 1799–1815

Reign of James I begins 1603

Glorious Revolution in England 1688

Congress of Vienna 1814–1815

Science and Technology

Religion and Philosophy

Great Awakening in America 1720s–1740s

Religious freedom guaranteed by the U.S. Bill of Rights 1791

Churches Disestablished in America—Late 1700s

King James Version of the Bible 1611

Toleration Act in England 1689

Cavalier Parliament persecutes
Dissenters and Catholics 1661–1665

Robespierre makes deist cult of the
Supreme Being the religion of France 1794

Puritans attempt church reform in England 1641

Civil Constitution of the Clergy in France 1790

Culture and Society

In 1689 John Locke publishes
Two Treatises of Government

In 1794–1795 Thomas Paine publishes
The Age of Reason

Secular lifestyle returns to England and
House of Stuart Restored 1660

Republican Independence and the French Revolution

A great change in political thought developed in the seventeenth and eighteenth centuries. The older forms of government centering around monarchs or conquerors began to give way to new ideas. These ideas flowed from two sources; the Reformation and the "Enlightenment." In the countries where the "Enlightenment" was dominant, violence, bloodshed, and turmoil ushered in a revolution. In the countries where the Reformation was dominant, despotism was replaced by means of reformation. This chapter describes the changes that took place in Britain, America, and France. It would be beneficial to establish a definition of the term **revolution** and **reformation**, since the developments in these three countries had different motivations and results. A **revolution** is motivated by a desire for autonomous freedom from God's authority as expressed in biblical revelation. It results in a violent overthrow of a government based on a radical humanistic reordering of the whole social order apart from God's law. This was the essential characteristic of the **French Revolution**. A political **reformation** or war for independence is motivated by a biblical view of liberty to serve God according to His Word. This results in a rejection of all forms of political tyranny, wherein man exalts himself above the law of God. This is characteristic of the **Glorious Revolution** in England and the **American War for Independence**. While revolution seeks for freedom it brings a worse form of tyranny. A political reformation based upon biblical truth is the only foundation of true freedom. Thus the French Revolution brought destruction and chaos, while the Puritan political reformations brought true liberty and peace.

Patrick Henry (1736–1799) made his famous speech, "Give me liberty or give me death" before the Virginia House of Burgesses in 1775, a few weeks before the outbreak of the American War for Independence. Henry was a descendent of French Huguenots.

Puritan Struggle Against English Absolutism

Most of the Tudors who had ruled England in the sixteenth century had been popular. **Henry VIII** and **Elizabeth I** compelled the nobles to obey them, reorganized the government, and restructured the church. But in most of their activities, they worked closely with the Parliament. In the seventeenth century, the ideas of **constitutionalism** and **limited monarchy** were further developed. Constitutionalism is a system of government in which the ruling powers are limited by enforceable rules of law and are restrained by various checks and balances so that basic human rights are guaranteed. In a limited monarchy, the king is subject to the law of the land, not above it.

James I. When the last Tudor, Elizabeth I, died childless in 1603, her nearest male relative was **King James VI** of Scotland, son of **Mary Stuart** (Mary Queen of Scots, the antagonist of Protestant Reformer John Knox). James Stuart came to England's throne as **James I**, the first monarch of England's **House of Stuart**. Although he was a highly educated and knowledgeable man, James was a personally distasteful individual—weak, unwise, vain, and cowardly. Furthermore, he had a lot to learn about English affairs. The English

King James I, 1566–1625

people looked on him as a foreigner, and he seemed to do everything conceivable to lose the loyalty of Englishmen. Not satisfied with the great powers the Tudors had amassed, James tried to bring to England the absolutist idea of the divine right of kings, a theory which did not fit English political custom, considering its constitutional bent ever since the **Magna Carta** (1215). The Tudors were, in practice, absolutists; but they had always publicly given lip service, at least, to the constitutional arrangement and to Parliament. James sought to establish absolutism on the sure foundation of divine-right doctrine. He made it clear that he saw himself as above the law.

Parliament. Parliament did not accept the divine right theory but believed instead in the historic rights of Englishmen. These rights guaranteed one's control over his own person and property. Neither of these rights could be taken away without consent of the individual involved, either directly or indirectly, through one's representatives in Parliament. Parliament and the courts of common law checked the king's power and protected the people's rights.

Although Parliament was not really democratic during the seventeenth century, it was a powerful body. Rich town merchants and the leading country families were represented in the House of Commons.

Puritans. The conflict between king and Parliament reached a crucial stage when the Puritan party took over the House of Commons. A reformist group within the Church of England, the Puritans demanded simpler church services and a more fully Protestant theology. Since James I was from Calvinistic Scotland, they thought he might grant their demands. Having come from Scotland, however, James had witnessed the fact that Calvinists had wrested the church from the power of the crown. He assumed, erroneously, that the English Puritans were identical to the Scottish Presbyterians. When he arrived in England, the reform-minded Anglican Puritans took him a petition with signatures of about a thousand reformist clergymen, hence its name, the **Millenary Petition**. The petition asked him to stop the use of the sign of the Cross in baptism and of the ring in marriage, as well as the wearing of certain **vestments**. The petition also asked that clergymen be allowed to marry and that abuses in the church be stopped.

To the Puritans, religious images and the priests' rich vestments were obstacles to direct communion with God. These objects, and the pomp and show which accompanied them, attracted too much attention and tended to exalt the priests. In the Scriptures, Puritans found no such gulf between the clergy and lay people. Both should work together as equals, but with different functions.

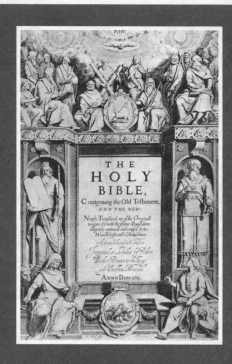

The King James Version

William Tyndale was first to translate the Bible into English from the original Greek and Hebrew. He completed the New Testament but was martyred before he could finish the Old Testament. Miles Coverdale translated the rest from Latin and German versions. Their combined work was published as Matthew's Bible in 1537. In 1560 the Geneva Bible appeared, translated by Puritan exiles in Geneva, Switzerland. This version became the household Bible of the Puritans. But its Calvinistic notes irritated James I and he sought to overcome its influence. In 1611, fifty-four Anglican scholars produced the Authorized or King James Version. Three major revisions have been made in recent times. In 1979 the New King James Bible appeared, which sought to maintain the original translation with updated words.

James agreed to meet with the Puritans, but granted only one of their requests—for a new revision of the Bible. A group of scholars produced the King James Version, which appeared in 1611 (see Chapter 3). He gruffly rejected their other requests and ordered that any clergy who failed to follow the Anglican liturgy, as set forth in the *Book of Common Prayer*, should be removed from his office. He liberalized policies toward Catholics but was forced to retreat under pressure from Protestants. An angry group of Catholic conspirators, under a man named **Guy Fawkes**, planned to blow up the Parliament building, but the plot was foiled.

The Puritans in Parliament continued their arguments with James. They wanted him to aid his son in law, **Frederick of the Palatinate**, the "Winter King" of Bohemia, and the Protestant side in the Thirty Years' War. They also wanted James to marry his son **Charles** to a Protestant princess. They lost on both counts. James delayed sending aid to Frederick. When he finally did act, he was severely defeated. As to Charles, he was pledged to and married **Henrietta Maria**, the Catholic daughter of Louis XIII of France.

Charles I. When Charles followed James on England's throne as **Charles I**, religious strife increased. Charles appointed **William Laud** Archbishop of Canterbury (chief bishop of the Church of England). Laud had orders to make all Anglicans use the same liturgy even if it meant driving the Puritans from the church. He felt that every Anglican had to follow the same outer form of worship. It was a matter of supreme importance to him that the communion table be placed at the east side of the church building and that all should bow at the name of Jesus. Heavy punishments were given to those who did not conform. At this time, the Puritans were moving increasingly toward a more strictly Calvinistic theology

Of God, Of Man, Of the Divell.

This satirical cartoon contrasts a Puritan minister (left) holding a Bible with two Anglican bishops who are holding the ***Book of Common Prayer*** (center) and a book of superstition (right).

and worldview. This theology included a strict view of the Sabbath. They were thus shocked and angered when Laud issued a **Declaration of Sports**, authorizing and encouraging games on Sunday. These measures drove the remaining Puritan ministers from the Anglican Church and further estranged the Puritan clergy and laymen from the national establishment.

In time, the Absolutist and High Church parties joined forces to oppose the Puritan and Parliamentary interests, and this alignment seriously split the English realm. Charles continued to pursue his despotism, encouraged by his chief civil adviser, **Thomas Wentworth**. Wentworth, a more intelligent man than either Charles or Laud, believed that an enlightened king could govern better than a disorganized parliament. So he sought to make the crown more efficient and large-minded, even while encouraging Charles to act boldly in all things. He was not entirely successful in his pursuits.

Meanwhile, Charles further eroded his support when, in 1637, he attempted to impose the Anglican forms of ceremonial worship upon the Scottish Presbyterian churches. The Scotsmen adamantly refused to comply and signed a solemn National Covenant pledging the utmost resistance. Charles sent an army to attack rebellious Scotland, but his army was disorganized and ill-financed. It was defeated by the resolute **Scottish Covenanters**.

Money Matters. Financial as well as religious problems divided the monarchy from the Parliament. The House of Commons collected part of the money needed by the English kings. This was done through enactment of a lifetime authorization called **Tonnage and Poundage**, which parliaments traditionally gave to all new monarchs upon their ascension to the throne. But when Charles became king, Parliament declined to make the grant. Like his father, Charles challenged Parliament and tried to raise money on his own, through his officials. He forced wealthy men to make loans to him. He taxed residents of seaports to support the fleet. People who built houses in towns that hundreds of years before had been part of the royal forest had to pay a forest fine. The people, especially the merchant class which had a strong representation in Parliament, hated these taxes, which were based on old laws which had not been enforced for many years.

The Rights of Englishmen. In addition to religion and taxes, the third major argument took place over the issue of rights. Lawmakers wanted the right to free speech in Parliament. Other Englishmen felt they had the right to freedom from forced loans and imprisonment without trial. Because he needed money, Charles I caved in to Parliament and signed the **Petition of Right** in 1628. This document protected Englishmen from unfair taxes and illegal imprisonment, as well as other royal abuses.

The Puritan Political Reformation

The Long Parliament. Because of his constant quarrels with Parliament over religion, money, and civil rights, Charles I tried to rule England without Parliament between 1629 and 1640. Before it was dismissed, however, Parliament declared that anyone supporting movements of the church toward "popery" and anyone paying unauthorized Tonnage and Poundage to the crown was an enemy of the English people. By 1640, Charles's need for money was so great (including his need for revenue for wars against France and Spain and revenge against Scotland) that he was forced to again call the assembly in 1640. Parliament, instead of aiding Charles, immediately began reminding him of national ills. He again dismissed it, an act which led this session to be called the **Short Parliament**. Charles again attacked the Scots and was again humiliated. Late in 1640, he summoned Parliament once more, knowing he would be at its mercy. Once in session, Parliament refused to adjourn. For twenty years, the body remained formally in session, earning the title, the **Long Parliament**. It had Charles firmly in its grip and effectively took the government of England into its own hands. It ordered both Laud and Wentworth arrested. They were both eventually executed.

Ignoring his requests for money, Parliament made a number of demands. It wanted the special courts such as the **Star Chamber** and **High Commission**, used by the king to try his opponents, abolished and Puritan political prisoners

released. The **Triennial Act** was passed, requiring the king to call Parliament into session at least every three years. Parliament required that the existing session could not be adjourned without its consent. Also, taxation would require Parliament's permission. The king agreed to all these measures.

By 1641, the Puritan members of Parliament felt the time had come to reform church government and practices. At this point, a split began to emerge within Parliament, as some of the more traditional Anglicans resisted the Puritan reform proposals. As the split in the House of Commons widened, Charles gained new courage to challenge Parliament's rule. He personally led an armed invasion of the House in an attempt to arrest five of the most radical leaders. This failed, but the attempt angered Parliament enough to seek control of the army. Aware of the danger, Charles fled London, one of the Puritan strongholds, and called upon his loyal subjects to help him defeat Parliament.

England's Civil Wars. Those who followed the king, the **Royalists** or **Cavaliers**, were generally young nobles. Farmers and farm laborers made up the rank and file of the king's army. The Parliamentary troops, called **Roundheads** because they had shaved their hair to distinguish themselves from the long-and-curly-haired Cavaliers, were older and mostly from the merchant class. Fighting as common soldiers for Parliament were city dwellers and **artisans**. The center of Parliamentary power was London, whereas the royal headquarters was at Oxford. Because the navy was on the side of Parliament, Charles was prevented from getting help from France and Holland.

At first the war went in favor of the king. By late 1643, Charles threatened London. To meet his advance, Parliament introduced the **New Model**

Oliver Cromwell is one of history's puzzling figures. He refused to become king; however, as Lord Protector he had to govern England with a heavy hand. While he encouraged religious liberty, he could not keep order without limiting freedom in general.

Army. A Puritan force, it was highly disciplined and commanded by capable leaders such as **Oliver Cromwell**. In a series of brilliant victories in 1644 and 1645, the New Model Army crushed the Royalists. Charles, fighting in the north, had to surrender to the Scots who had entered the war on Parliament's side.

Charles, however, negotiated with the Scots, knowing that a rift had developed within the English Parliament between members who favored a Presbyterian form of church government for England and members of a group known as Independents (Congregationalists). The Independents favored religious tolerance—for all Protestant practices but not for Catholic practices. Though in a minority, the Independents had the support of the increasingly powerful Cromwell. The Scots, angered by the anti-Presbyterian moves by the Congregationalists in Parliament, conspired with the king, and a second civil war broke out in the summer of 1648. Cromwell and his skillful lieutenants quickly crushed the uprising and seized Charles. In December 1648, the victorious army laid siege to the Parliament building and excluded the 143 Presbyterian members from Commons. The remaining sixty members, known as the **Rump Parliament**, claimed to be the true government of England. The Rump redefined the nation's treason laws and a special **High Court of Justice** found Charles guilty of violating them. He was publicly beheaded on January 30, 1649, on a scaffold erected in front of his Whitehall palace.

It was an event that shocked the world. Never before had a king been executed as a result of votes and actions by representatives of the people he governed. Most Englishmen were also shocked. While they disliked Charles's policies, they did not necessarily want their king executed

The execution of Charles I was a public affair, as were most executions. However, women were usually executed privately behind the walls of the Tower of London.

or the monarchy ended. The historical government of England was ended.

Cromwell's Commonwealth. In place of the monarch, a Protestant **republic** called the **Commonwealth** appeared. The House of Commons and a Council of State which it elected ran the government. Cromwell dissolved the House of Lords. The real authority remained with the army under Cromwell, however. According to a plan of the Independents, he placed the church under the control of county committees who also ran the local governments. In a move to weaken opposition, the new government took Royalist lands and turned them over to **speculators**, merchants, lawyers, army officers, and lesser nobles. Many of these new landowners were able to keep their property after the Commonwealth ended.

The new government had its share of troubles from radicals in England and revolts in Scotland and Ireland. Earlier in the seventeenth century, the English had angered the Irish by trying to convert them to Protestantism. In addition, English kings, particularly James I, had settled Protestant colonists in Northern Ireland on land (the Ulster district) taken from Irish Catholic rebels. Rebellion had broken out in 1641, but neither Parliament nor the king could spare the troops to put it down.

After the execution of Charles I, the Irish and Scottish proclaimed his son, **Charles II**, as their king. This was too much for Cromwell. With the heir to the English throne a next-door neighbor, the Commonwealth would be in constant danger. So in 1649, Cromwell first led an army into Ireland and defeated the rebels in savage fighting. Thousands of rebels were then forced to give up their land to English and Scottish settlers. These events added to a centuries-old legacy of hatred and bitterness among the Irish that has not yet disappeared.

Cromwell dissolves the Long Parliament.

Having defeated the Irish, Cromwell marched against the Scots and scattered their army. When Charles led a second attack against Cromwell in 1651 at Worcester, the Puritan warrior won the greatest victory of his life. Charles eventually escaped to the continent.

While the army took care of Ireland and Scotland, Parliament argued over what direction the new government should take. In 1653, Cromwell led troops into the House of Commons and dissolved the body. Later in the same year, he called a new Parliament of inexperienced but godly men (often termed "Barebone's Parliament" because one of its members was named Praise-God Barebone). But this inept group wanted radical changes not favored by the army. Consequently, the new assembly was also dismissed.

The leaders of the army then drew up a new constitution providing for an executive, the **Lord Protector**, who ruled with a single-house Parliament, the legislative body, from which all Stuart partisans were banned. This **Instrument of Government** was the first written constitution in

England. But the new assembly elected under this agreement could not work with the Lord Protector, Cromwell, and tried to revise the Instrument of Government. Lacking support from the people, Cromwell again put England under military rule to keep order in the country. In 1657, he called a second Parliament, which worked more smoothly with him. It created a second house to replace the old House of Lords and tried to make Cromwell king. Cromwell rejected the offer of kingship because such a title was repugnant to many in his republican army. The new Parliament met a second time and tried to limit the executive powers. Cromwell dismissed it in 1658. It became apparent that Cromwell's rule depended upon the army and was, in fact, a military dictatorship.

Cromwell died in 1658. His son Richard tried to carry on the government, but he lost control of the army and was forced to resign. The military leadership encouraged a recall of the Long Parliament as the nation deteriorated into anarchy.

Well meaning in his effort to establish a biblical model for government in England, Cromwell was never able to overcome the long-standing religious tensions in England. By the end of his life, he realized that the Commonwealth had never been able to establish a definitive governing principle for the nation.

Restoration of the Stuart Kings. Charles II, who had been in exile on the continent, sent word that he was willing to accept Parliamentary government. Reassured, the assembly invited him to take the throne. He accepted and left to Parliament the problems of **amnesty** for his opponents, the restoration of the Church of England, and rival claims to **confiscated** lands. All the acts passed by Parliament between 1642 and 1660 were held to be **null and void**. Legally, the previ-

The Diary of Samuel Pepys

With the Restoration came a violent reaction to the strict Puritan life-style of the Commonwealth. Theaters and other places of amusement began to flourish again. Card-playing, tea parties, and balls filled social calendars. As both men and women fussed over their appearance, frills, ribbons, and bizarre hairdos came into style. The court of Charles II was marked by cynicism, wit, brilliance, and looseness. Society in general adopted a shallow, carefree attitude.

Samuel Pepys, a high official of the navy, either observed or took part in many of the events of the time. He jotted everything down in his diary—gossip about public figures, his reactions to the latest play, his domestic squabbles, his opinions on current issues, his attention to daily trifles—all told with great relish. Because Pepys never intended his diary for any eyes but his own, it is quite frank. He uniquely captures the flavor of life in the Restoration period.

Pepys watched the parade celebrating the coronation of Charles II. Afterwards the young man described what he had seen.

(April, 1661)

22nd. Up early and made myself as fine as I could, and put on my velvet coat, the first day that I put it on, though made half a year ago. And being ready, …went to Mr. Young's, the flag-maker, in Cornehill; and there we had a good room to ourselves, with wine and good cake, and saw the show very well. In which it is impossible to relate the glory of this day, expressed in the clothes of them that rode, and their horses and horse-clothes, among others, my Lord Sandwich's Embroidery and diamond were ordinary among them. The Knights of the Bath was a brave sight of itself.... Remarkable were the two men that represent the two Dukes of Normandy and Aquitane. The Bishops came next after Barons.... My Lord Monk rode bare after the King, and led in his hand a spare horse, as Master of the Horse [Cavalry]. The King, in a most rich embroidered suit and cloak, looked most noble.... The streets all gravelled, and the houses hung with carpets before them, made a brave show, and the ladies out of the windows…

In 1665, the bubonic plague broke out in London, the worst occurrence since the Black Death of the fourteenth century. Many people in the 1600s believed that the disease was spread through the smell of the victim.

(June, 1665)

7th. This day, much against my will, I did in Drury Lane see two or three houses marked with a red cross upon the doors, and "Lord have mercy upon us" written there; which was a sad sight to me, being the first of the kind that… I ever saw. I began to worry about myself and my smell, so that I was forced to buy some roll-tobacco to smell and chew, which took away the apprehension.

Adapted from *The Diary of Samuel Pepys*, Henry B. Wheatley, ed. (New York: G.E. Groscup, 1892).

ous 18 years were treated as if they had never occurred.

In actual fact, however, no society can turn back the clock; and seventeenth-century England was no exception. A monarch had been executed by due process of law. During the last days of the king's life, the House of Commons had declared that the people, under God, held all just power.

The English people could not forget the death of the king nor the reason for it. Despite the **Restoration** of the monarchy, they remembered that organized opposition had brought down a monarch in the name of the people. The kings of England could never again behave in an absolutist fashion without facing the same kind of opposition that had cost Charles I his life.

The Glorious Revolution

A Limited Monarch. The restored Stuart kings, **Charles II**, who ruled from 1660 to 1685, and his brother, **James II**, who ruled from 1685-1688, could not undo the reforms of the Puritan Reformation. However, the settlement of 1660 made little attempt to deal with the specific issues that had caused the revolution. The relationship between the crown and Parliament was not spelled out. But all acts that had passed the Parliament between 1640 and 1642 and that had received Charles I's approval were held to be valid. That made absolute monarchy impossible in England for these laws clearly limited the king's power to levy taxes and control the courts. They also required that Parliament be summoned at least every three years.

The Restoration happened because the landed aristocracy and the upper-middle-class city merchants joined together out of a mutual desire to protect their property. After the death of Cromwell in 1658, the breakdown of law and order had frightened them. They later disagreed about issues relating to agriculture or business interests, but they continued to defend property.

The Restoration was welcomed, as well, by many in the population who disliked the austere lifestyle imposed upon them during the Puritan Commonwealth. Theaters reopened; dancing again became fashionable; and the country returned to a life of gaiety and profligacy so well modeled by their licentious "Merry Monarch," Charles II. One historian has written that Charles "though endowed with a good deal of natural sagacity, had little mental energy and not the faintest particle of that rectitude which we define as character. His pleasures went before everything else." To the Puritans, including the great poet **John Milton**, the Restoration was a grievous thing, a "paradise lost."

Religious Problems Continue. Even though the political settlement of 1660 avoided basic issues, it was somewhat successful. The religious settlement was not. An election in 1661 returned a Parliament that was staunchly Anglican and, at first, Royalist. Called the **Cavalier Parliament**, this body passed a series of harsh measures between 1661 and 1665 against Roman Catholics and **Dissenters**—the latter name applying to all such groups as Presbyterians, Puritans, Baptists, and Quakers. Persecution of violators was vicious. According to the new laws, only members of the Church of England could serve in local or national government. The legislation also forced Dissenting ministers out of their pulpits in the Anglican Church and made it almost impossible for them to start their own independent congregations. Charles opposed many of these acts, not because of sympathy for Dissenters, but rather because of his secret and increasingly strong inclinations toward Catholicism. His brother James, then duke of York, was a Roman Catholic and was forced to resign his office of Lord High Admiral as a result of the new religion laws, the chief of which was known as the **Test Act**.

By the 1670s, Charles, who had been raised in Louis XIV's France and came to enjoy the French court's decadent but exhilarating life-style, had begun to follow a pro-French foreign policy. In a 1670 treaty with Louis XIV, in which Louis promised Charles an annual grant of money to join him as an ally against the Dutch, Charles promised to openly profess Catholicism when the right moment might come. The alliance with Louis, an absolute Catholic monarch, frightened the English, including the staunchly Anglican Cavalier Parliament. Could this be the first move in an attempt to bring back Roman Catholicism, pope and all? The Stuarts tried unsuccessfully to ease these fears by marrying James's oldest daughter Mary to the Calvinist Dutch ruler, William III, the sturdy stadholder who had just rebuffed Louis's military aggressions. In 1678, an adventurer of questionable reputation, Titus Oates, started false rumors of a Catholic plot to murder King Charles, massacre Protestants, and aid in a French invasion of Ireland. A wave of anti-Catholic hysteria swept England.

Anti-Catholic feeling also grew in the Parliament, which by now did not trust Charles II and did not like the prospect of a Catholic, James, becoming the next king (Charles had no heir). Between 1679 and 1681, three Parliaments tried to exclude James from **succession** to the throne. They might have passed such a bill except for the opposition of the House of Lords. After dissolving the last of these Parliaments, Charles ruled illegally for four years without the assembly.

In 1682, the king moved against the opposition. Its leader, the **Earl of Shaftesbury**, was accused of treason. Although a jury acquitted him, he had to flee to Holland. Charles seemed to have the upper hand, but only because he had the support of the conservative, Anglican landowners who feared a repeat of the Puritan regime. These gentlemen believed in obedience to the monarch as taught by the Church of England. Their enemies called them **Tories**, after Irish Catholic bandits who preyed on Protestants. Against the king, there arose a new party branded by the Tories as **Whigs**, after "whiggamore" (i.e., *whiggamaire*) a cry used by Scottish Covenanter **guerrilla fighters** to urge on their horses. This division of Parliament, namely its opposing political parties, was of historic significance. To this day, these two parties continue to contend against each other in

William III (1650–1702), the Prince of the House of Orange, became King of England, Scotland, and Ireland in 1689.

Mary II (1662–1694) ruled jointly with William III during the golden age of England and Holland.

British politics under the names **Conservative** (Tories) and **Liberal** (Whigs).

A Bloodless Coup. James II followed his brother Charles on the throne in 1685. He immediately angered Parliament by insisting that Catholics be appointed to public office. When the assembly refused to support such action, he adjourned it. Then he named Catholics to positions in the government, army, navy, universities, and even the Church of England. In 1687, he suspended all laws which kept Dissenters and Roman Catholics out of the government. To Parliament, all of this meant one thing—the Catholic absolutism of Louis XIV was sweeping across the English Channel.

Such a threat required drastic action. The English were doubly alarmed when news came that a son had been born to James. By rights, this son would be the legitimate heir, taking precedence over his

daughters **Mary** and **Anne**. In 1688, the Whigs and Tories put aside their differences and joined to offer the throne to William III of Holland and Mary, James's Protestant daughter. William landed in England with a small force and moved slowly to London. James fled to France. Without firing a shot, a dynasty had fallen and a revolution had taken place. **William and Mary** agreed to become the joint rulers of the land. Thus came the **Glorious** or **Bloodless Revolution**.

Parliament passed a **Bill of Rights** and a **Toleration Act** (1689) which guaranteed civil rights, the supreme power of Parliament, and freedom of worship for all except **Unitarians**, **Roman Catholics**, and **Jews**. The Toleration Act stated that only Anglicans could serve in the higher posts of the government and army, but even this restriction could be lifted by special permission. Compared to the religious laws of most other

European countries, such as France, even limited toleration was a great step forward in the history of freedom of religion and other human rights.

Twentieth-century historian Ferdinand Schevill has critiqued the significance of the Glorious Revolution in these words:

> ...[T]he Revolution of 1688 had secured the victory in the long civil struggle in England to Protestantism and the parliament. It was without doubt a triumph for the English people, but it was not in any present-day sense a democratic triumph. If henceforth the parliament was the decisive factor in the government, let us not fail to observe that, composed of an hereditary House of Lords and a House of Commons elected by various groups of free-holders, the parliament was exclusively representative of the propertied classes. Therefore, while the Revolution displaced the royal with a parliamentary regime, its socio-economic significance lies in its vesting political control in the landed gentry and the great merchants of the towns. For almost a century and a half, until the Reform Bill of 1832, England was governed by an unusually successful combination of an aristocracy of birth and an oligarchy of wealth.

As we have seen in an earlier study, English Enlightenment writer **John Locke** gave the English people the means to justify their new political invention—**parliamentary government**. His *Two Treatises of Government* (1689) argued that government is a contract between a ruler and the citizens. If a ruler breaks the agreement by denying the people's natural rights of life, liberty, and property, revolution is justified. The most effective form of government is representative, he also claimed.

In one of the ironies of history, Locke's defense of the revolution of 1688 was later used by the American colonists in 1776 when they revolted against the British. As one writer has stated: "The

Hush-a-bye Baby

At the birth of a son to James II, the English lost patience with their ruler. They were willing to wait for James to die, but now another Roman Catholic king would follow him. This was too much for Protestant England to bear; hence the negotiations with William and Mary began.

During this time of unrest a new nursery rhyme appeared. "Hush-a-bye Baby" was actually a political poem directed against James II and his newborn baby. The "treetop" referred to the dangerous position of the baby. The "wind" was blowing from Europe, bringing William and Mary to England. When the "bough broke," poor King James II and his family would tumble from their high political position. Just before William and Mary arrived, everyone was singing this seemingly harmless song as an act of defiance against the hated king.

Declaration of Independence is John Locke reduced to a few dramatic statements."

William III reigned until he died in 1702 (Mary died in 1694) and was succeeded by **Queen Anne**, Mary's sister, who ruled from 1702 to 1714. Under the 1701 **Act of Succession**, James II's Catholic heirs were passed over in favor of Anne, and she was to be followed by **George I** of Hanover, grandson of Protestant **Frederick of the Palatinate** (the Bohemian "Winter King") and **Elizabeth**, daughter of James I. George I was thus the first of England's royal **House of Hanover**, which also included his successors, **George II** and **George III**, the latter of whom was monarch when the American War for Independence broke out.

British-French Rivalry

When William III came to the English throne, he immediately became embroiled in war. He successfully beat back another Irish rebellion when the Irish Catholics rallied behind the deposed Catholic James II. James fled again to France.

In 1688, Louis XIV became involved in his war of aggression in Europe known as the **War of the Palatinate**. William entered and helped win the war against France, in part to protect his native Netherlands but also to secure a position of power for his new realm of England. His alliance with the Dutch laid a foundation for future maritime and colonial policies which eventually allowed England to rise to a position of world greatness a century later.

During the reign of George I, England, under the administration of Whig statesman **Robert Walpole**, saw an advance of mercantilism, favoring the middle-class merchants and the landed class who had organized under the Whig Party to control Parliament. Walpole's policies led to an extension of English international trade and expansion in the New World. This expansion put England into further conflict with contemporary European rivals France and Spain, the other two main colonial powers in the New World. The rivalry in North America was particularly intense between England and France. Before the opening of the eighteenth century, these two powers began to clash over American colonial claims.

By mid-century, the conflict had become full-blown war, the **French and Indian War**, part of what was known in Europe as the **Seven Years' War** (1756-1763). While there were European issues as stake, the war was primarily over whether North America and India would become

the colonial prizes of England or France. Unfortunately for France, its interests were being advanced by one of its weakest and most corrupt kings ever, the despicable **Louis XV**, heir of the Sun King. We will learn more about Louis XV later in this chapter as we examine the events leading to the French Revolution. In the meantime, however, it should be noted that the reign of Louis saw the revival of the French nobles as a primary focus of power in France. These corrupt nobles were not as skillful as the merchant class had been under Louis XIV in furthering France's economic interests at home and abroad. Due in part to this ineptness, England was able to gain the ascendancy in the colonial contests.

When the French and Indian War began, England too was disorganized. But a particularly able leader arose in the person of **William Pitt**, who became British secretary of state in 1757 and for four years was virtually the one-man government of George II's England. His strengthening of British sea power weakened France and its effort to supply its North American colonial fighters. Under Pitt's leadership, British forces on the ground in North America were able to reverse earlier problems and defeat the French-Indian alliance. Britain also defeated France in their conflicts in India. Before the end of the war, Pitt had wanted to widen the conflict by assaulting the interests of Bourbon-ruled Spain, which had entered the war near its close out of support for Bourbon France and out of fear of British expansion in the New World. But he was undermined by a new minister of George III (who came to power in 1760). Pitt was forced to resign, but England was unable to avoid engaging Spain anyway and proved successful, both in the Caribbean and Asia.

In the **Peace of Paris** (1763), Britain accomplished virtually every goal it had in fighting the war. It now ruled India, Canada, and the Atlantic seaboard colonies. Its next major task was to organize its new empire, but its first attempt to do so led to disaster.

The American War for Independence

When peace came after the Seven Years' War, the English decided that the American colonies should make a greater contribution to the expense of the government. This last phase of the English-French struggle vastly increased Britain's national debt. The new territories acquired from the French brought increased administrative costs. On the western frontier, a large military force was needed because of the Indian threat. English landlords and merchants objected violently to higher taxes for any of these purposes. It seemed logical that the colonies should pay. At the same time, however, Britain wanted to slow down the rate of western settlement so it could be more carefully controlled. The colonists were not happy with these changes.

Unfortunately, the economic changes which the British wished to make would affect the colonists' political freedom. In the colonial assemblies, the people, through their elected representatives, were able to have their way because the assemblies had the power to levy taxes. If British authorities, namely the Parliament in which Americans had no representation, could raise money directly from America, the colonists and their representatives would be powerless. Furthermore, the *Americans were used to self-government and were determined to keep it*. As events were to prove, they were even willing to lay down their lives for it. It is this history of covenantal and representative self-government, established in the early Puritan and Covenanter colonies, which leads us to conclude that their eventual war was not essentially a revolution but an armed conservative insurrection to maintain an established order. It was a war for independence, not for revolutionary political change.

Since many colonial leaders believed in the Enlightenment teaching of free trade, the new British laws made them angry. For example, the Stamp Act of 1765, which levied a tax on every printed paper and legal document, came at a time of depression. Because no American representa-

The Boston Massacre, March 5, 1770

tives sat in Parliament, some colonists felt this was taxation without representation. They decided to **boycott** English goods. Before long, the boycott and problems in collecting the money forced Britain to repeal the hated tax.

As soon as this crisis passed, some duties called the **Townshend Acts** were levied on tea, glass, paper, and other goods. Protests broke out in Boston, and five colonists were killed by British troops. In 1770, all the duties were repealed except those on tea. Still not satisfied, some colonists dressed as Indians one night, boarded a ship loaded with tea, and dumped its cargo into Boston Harbor. The "Boston Tea Party" failed to amuse the king, who closed Boston's port and changed the constitution of Massachusetts. Along with these attempts to tighten economic control over the colonies, the crown increased its judicial and political power.

The Role of Religion. Much debate has occurred over the years as to the role of religion and contemporary philosophy in the American revolt.

There can be little doubt that Puritanism, the religion of the early settlers and the rationale for their very arrival on American shores, left a lasting legacy which carried on into the late eighteenth century birth of the nation. Puritanism emphasized principles which can be seen in the American political development—voluntary association, limits on power, a necessity for civic involvement by the saints, and a careful delineation of the realms of the church and state. The heart of the Puritan system was the idea of covenant, initiated by God and concerned both with individual salvation and the creation of a people (or society). Puritanism also emphasized the rule of fundamental laws that harmonized with the Bible.

The Great Awakening also had an impact on the creation of the American ideal and identity. The Awakening preachers taught that men are depraved sinners, and can be saved only by the work of the Holy Spirit uniting them to Christ. This essentially Puritan and Reformed teaching challenged not only the formalism of the Anglican Church, but also its view of authority, that the monarch is the head of the church. As England attempted to promote imperialistic control, the Awakening revived the Puritans' stress upon Christian freedom. Moreover, the Puritan understanding of sin and depravity fostered the idea of limiting the power of government. The way was now clear for the political ideas that had been developed by Scottish Convenanters and French Huguenots. These ideas included the rejection of a hierarchical view of political authority in favor of a representative government under law, which is a constitutional republic.

Secular philosophies were also present in the formative American vision. One was the Enlightenment idea of radical libertarianism. According to this belief, *power* is evil and corrupting, and must be limited and restrained in every way compatible with social order. Related to this was the idea that *privilege*, an artificial and man-made endowment, is an impediment to mankind's hope for fulfillment. These ideas were deeply ingrained in Whiggism—the prevailing political philosophy of the day. As one analyst has summarized it:

> The historian of religion would stress three interrelated intellectual strands that gave the pattern to the new national consciousness; [1] the new emphasis on evangelical Calvinism (the prevalent religious commitment of the people), stressing the individual's direct, personal, experiential relationship to God; [2] the general acceptance of the deistic theory of inalienable rights and contractual self-government; and [3] the resurgence of the radical Whig ideology with its fear of hierarchical tyranny (the united despotism of church and state)...*(William McLoughlin).*

This political cartoon appeared in London after Boston harbor was closed by Parliament. It showed how ineffective the closure was because of the assistance Boston received from the other colonies, illustrated by the people in the boat.

Drafting of the Declaration of Independence by Franklin, Jefferson, Adams, Livingston, and Sherman

What stand did colonial churches take on the "revolutionary" ferment? For the most part, they favored resistance to the English. Most of the Presbyterians, Congregationalists, and Baptists actively supported the colonies' moves toward independence. The Anglicans (Episcopalians) in New England remained loyal to England, but in the South they opposed the British. In the Middle Colonies, the Episcopalians were evenly divided. Episcopal clergymen were often in a dilemma, since part of their ordination vow included support for the king of England as the head of their church. Nevertheless, two-thirds of the signers of the **Declaration of Independence** were Episcopalians.

Methodists were also in a difficult position. John Wesley took the English side, with the result that active American patriots were skeptical of the Methodists' commitment to the colonial cause. Quakers and Moravians, being conscientious objectors to war, did only what little they could to give moral support to their fellow colonists.

In 1774, Protestant resistance increased when the British **Quebec Act** gave broad power to the Roman Catholic Church in Quebec. (The act also closed off immigration from New York, Pennsylvania, and Virginia into the Ohio Territory.)

There was one Presbyterian clergyman, however, who was seen at the time as the chief spiritual (and perhaps political) architect of the American revolt. His name was **John Witherspoon**, the president of Princeton College and the only clergyman to sign the Declaration of Independence. He was an heir of the Scottish Covenanter movement of 1648, in which Christian men covenanted to protect religious and civil liberty. Walpole once observed, "Cousin America has run off with a Presbyterian parson." An English peace emissary, **Adam Ferguson**, wrote at one point:

> We have 1,200 miles of territory occupied by 300,000 people of which there are about 150,000 with Johnny Witherspoon at their head, against us—and the rest for us. I am not sure that if proper measures were taken but we should reduce Johnny Witherspoon to the small support of Franklin, Adams, and two or three more of the most abandoned villains in the world, but I tremble at the thought of their cunning and determination against us.

Witherspoon did not see the colonists' actions as treasonous or as motivated by selfish economic concerns. He and his followers did not see their actions as "revolution" but as necessary for the preservation of a godly order which America had originally been destined to establish. For Witherspoon, freedom of conscience and therefore freedom to worship was bound up with the notion of political or civil freedom. In one of his many

John Witherspoon (1723–1794), born in Scotland, was a descendant of John Knox. As a Presbyterian pastor he was president of Princeton College, and a member of the Continental Congress.

political sermons, this one in 1776, he said, for example:

> So far as we have hitherto proceeded, I am satisfied that the confederacy of the colonies has not been the effect of pride, resentment, or sedition, but of the deep and general conviction that our civil and religious liberties, and consequently in a great measure the temporal and eternal happiness of us and our posterity, depended on the issue [of God's moral government]. The knowledge of God and his truths have from the beginning of the world been chiefly, if not entirely confined to those parts of the earth where some degree of liberty and political justice were to be seen, and great were the difficulties with which they had to struggle, from the imperfections of human society, and the unjust decisions of usurped authori-

ties. There is not a single instance in history, in which civil liberty was lost, and religious liberty preserved entire. If therefore we yield up our temporal property, we at the same time deliver the conscience into bondage.

Witherspoon preached numerous sermons along such themes, and inculcated his Calvinist political theology into his Princeton students, many of whom became core individuals in the American drive for liberty and independence. Among his students were a future American president and vice president, nine cabinet officers, 21 U.S. senators, 39 U.S. representatives, three Supreme Court justices, 12 state governors, six members of the Continental Congress, 33 judges, and 13 college presidents in eight states.

In summary, an examination of the writings and speeches of the Founding Fathers leads to the general conclusion that Puritan Christianity, Enlightenment philosophies, and Whig political ideology were thoroughly mixed through one another to form the original guiding principles of the new nation. As one commentator, Mark Noll, has put it, "Witherspoon, [Cotton] Mather, and many other believers in the colonies could merge Whiggery and Christianity so effortlessly since both seemed to be grounded in the character and laws of God and to point in only one direction where the conflict with Great Britain was concerned."

Before leaving the issue of religion in the American revolution, we must consider the subject of **disestablishment**. An "established" church is one which is officially declared the legally recognized church of a given state. In lands with established churches, all citizens are expected to belong to that church and support it with their taxes, whether participating in its worship or not. In early America, there were a number of established churches. In the colonies of New Hampshire,

First Dutch Reformed Church, New Brunswick, New Jersey, in the area where the Great Awakening began in America.

Massachusetts, and Connecticut, the Congregationalist Church was the established church. The Episcopal Church was established in New York, Maryland, Virginia, North Carolina, South Carolina, and Georgia. In the other four colonies (Rhode Island, New Jersey, Delaware, and Pennsylvania), there was no established church, probably due to the fact that a majority of the population were Baptists or Quakers, who believed strongly in the separation of church and state. Establishment policies made it difficult for other faiths, such as Presbyterians, Lutherans, and the Reformed, because ministers of established churches were the only ones authorized to perform various religious rites.

Disestablishment became a major issue as the new nation was constituting itself. Baptists, sup-ported by other dissenting bodies, led the fight for complete religious freedom, which was eventually successful as this idea became embodied in the Constitution. The First Amendment's religious disestablishment clause was intended to prevent the *national* government ("*Congress* shall make no law....") from showing favoritism for any one church and to prevent the *national* government from imposing any single established church upon any state. It was never intended, however, to preclude the free exercise of religion in public life, as late-twentieth-century interpreters came to hold. The vast majority of the Founding Fathers, from Calvinist John Witherspoon to Whig John Adams, viewed religion—to them "religion" meant Christianity—as an absolute necessity for a virtuous government and society. Adams expressed a fear of the disasters that would arise if "the government of nations may fall into the hands of men who teach the most disconsolate of all creeds, that men are but fireflies and that this all is without a father."

In a proclamation on March 23, 1798, when the United States was experiencing hostilities from France, Adams, then president, reiterated a view commonly held earlier by colonial leaders:

> As the safety and prosperity of nations ultimately and essentially depend on the protection and the blessing of Almighty God, and the national acknowledgment of this truth is not only an indispensable duty which the people owe to Him, but a duty whose natural influence is favorable to the promotion of that morality and piety without which social happiness can not exist nor the blessings of a free government be enjoyed; and as this duty, at all times incumbent, is so especially in seasons of difficulty or of danger, when existing or threatening calamities, the just judgments of God against prevalent iniquity, are a loud call to repentance and reformation; and as the United States of America are at present placed in a hazardous and afflictive situation... — under these considerations it has appeared to me that the duty of imploring the mercy and benediction of Heaven on our country demands at this time a special attention from its inhabitants.

When they were eventually disestablished, the churches in America not only disconnected themselves institutionally from the civil state, but most also separated from their European church counterparts and set up their own organizational structures. This occurred during the period roughly surrounding the War of Independence. John Wesley ordained **Thomas Coke** as superintendent of the Methodist Societies in America. He was joined in 1784 by **Bishop Francis Asbury**. A group of Episcopal clergymen sent **Samuel Seabury, Jr.** to England to be consecrated bishop. The English Church refused, so he went to Scotland to obtain his office. In 1785, a general convention created the Protestant Episcopal Church in the United States. The Reformed churches broke ties with the Classis of Amsterdam. The German Reformed group became the Reformed Church in the United States. The Dutch Reformed Church took the name the Reformed Church in America. The Roman Catholic Church received its first American leader, **John Carroll**, in 1784 (he became bishop in 1789). Baltimore became the first Roman see in the United States. Baptists, Presbyterians, and Quakers formed their own national organizations. The numerous, but highly independent, Congregationalists refused to organize themselves beyond local levels, somewhat handicapping their growth.

The American War. In September 1774, the **First Continental Congress** met in Philadelphia and challenged the English Parliament's right to control the colonies. Shortly before a second meeting of the Congress, a colonial force met the British

The British had hoped to capture colonial arms and ammunition at Lexington and Concord; however, Paul Revere warned the colonists. A small force was ready for the Redcoats when they came to confiscate the weapons.

ers and the New England merchants, opposed the rebellion. As punishment, Loyalists lost their citizenship and property and had to pay fines. The sale of Loyalist holdings made landowners of many more Americans.

At first the colonists fought alone. They bottled up the British in Boston and tried to conquer Canada. Though taking Boston, they lost Canada. By 1776, English forces landed at New York and began a drive to divide the colonies. In 1777, however, with the defeat and surrender of England's General Burgoyne at Saratoga, the British plan was frustrated. Moreover, this victory encouraged the French to enter the war on the American side. French arms and troops were to prove decisive. Later the Dutch and Spanish likewise declared war on Britain.

The character of **George Washington** was also crucial to the American cause. He was the unanimous choice of the colonial representatives to

army at Lexington Green and Concord Bridge (April 19, 1775). There a farmer fired "the shot heard round the world"—after the British had shot and killed some of the patriots. The war had begun.

To the colonists, their rights as free people were at stake in the struggle. Rather than a bunch of hotheaded radicals, initially they were conservatives, merely trying to keep the liberties they possessed. But as the war progressed, its nature changed. Veering off in new democratic directions, the colonists declared their independence on July 4, 1776. In the Declaration they stated an old English Puritan idea—that people did not have to submit to Parliament if its laws were unjust. Further, the Declaration took the Enlightenment

and Puritan belief in equality and made it a cornerstone of the American nation. "All men are created equal," the colonists proclaimed. Finally, the Declaration listed the unfair acts of the king, hoping to win allies as well as world sympathy.

The war was partly a civil war and partly another eighteenth-century European colonial war. Pitting colonist against colonist, the conflict drove some 80,000 Loyalists (people who supported the king) out of the colonies. Many Loyalists remained, but they kept silent about their beliefs. It has been estimated that 20 percent of the colonists were active Patriots, 15 percent were Loyalists, and the remaining 65 percent were indifferent. In general, the established, well-to-do people, with the exception of the Virginia plant-

George Washington, 1732–1799

lead the army, so much did they admire and trust him. A sober, responsible Virginian, he came out early for independence.

In the face of impossible circumstances, Washington's integrity and determination kept the Continental Army together. Never numbering more than 20,000, the army fell to 5,000 men during the winter of 1776–1777. England had more than 30,000 troops in America in 1776 and almost won the war. However, with French aid and Washington's leadership, the fighting began to turn in the colonists' favor. A sizable French army and a French fleet enabled Washington to force Britain's surrender at Yorktown in 1781. In the **Treaty of Paris** (1783), Britain recognized the independence of the colonies.

Putting Together a Government. Long before the surrender, the Patriots had busied themselves with forming a government for the new nation. When the conflict started, they had set up legislative bodies, often based on the existing colonial

The Americans were victorious over British forces at the Battle of Saratoga in 1777. This victory proved to be a turning point in the American War for Independence.

assemblies. They also adopted written constitutions. These new documents included a **Bill of Rights** and required that a man own property in order to vote. However, considering the widespread ownership of property, nearly every free man voted from the beginning.

The new states worked toward social as well as political change. They broadened opportunities for land ownership by repealing several laws. Before the war, these laws had maintained a rich, landed upper class by requiring an estate to be passed on to the oldest son or to be sold within the family. Religious tests for officeholders were ended.

At the same time that the states were writing constitutions, the **Second Continental Congress** was creating a government for the federation of states. The plan of union, called the **Articles of Confederation**, did not go into effect until 1781. It provided for a Congress with the power to conduct war, carry on foreign affairs, and handle money matters, but not to regulate trade, levy taxes, or borrow money. There was no president or national courts under the confederation. Disputes between the states were settled by a complicated system of **arbitration**. Keeping their independence, the states sent delegates to Congress; however, each state delegation had only one vote.

The lack of cohesiveness of the new nation under the Articles of Confederation worried the wealthy classes. Because these people felt the need for a stronger central government, a **Constitutional Convention** was called in Philadelphia in 1787. Out of the meeting came the **American Constitution**. The document created a federal republic with certain powers given to the central government and all others reserved to the states. While the states had less independence than under the confederation, still they were more than mere

Independence Hall in Philadelphia was where the Constitutional Convention was held in 1787.

subdivisions of the central bureaucracy. The Constitution also provided for a separation of powers within the national government—the legislative, executive, and judicial branches—with checks and balances on each.

Conclusion. The American War for Independence has had a profound effect upon other peoples. During the late eighteenth century, some Europeans pointed to the republic in America as proof that Enlightenment ideas could be put into practice. The United States seemed to demonstrate that it was possible for a people to set up a government based on the rights of the individual. Others have seen that Puritan ideals, such as the rule of law and covenant and the dignity of the individual under God, found expression in the American system.

At the time the movement for independence began, each of the colonies, by reason of its history and its nature, was a Christian mini-society. The idea of a secular state was largely foreign to the thinking of the early Founders. The war for independence was designed to perpetuate the historic Christian order which the first settlers had sought to establish, an order which some colonists felt was being threatened by certain tyrannies emanating from the motherland. Along the road, meanwhile, the new thinking of the Enlightenment had become popular in some circles; and several of the American Founders or agitators—notably **Thomas Jefferson** and **Thomas Paine**—were clearly influenced by some of these philosophies. By the time George Washington left the presidency, the French Revolution—the triumph of radical, humanistic, secular political ideals and the brutal violence and theft which accompanied these—had occurred, and some of

Thomas Jefferson, 1743–1826

James Madison (1751–1836), studied under Witherspoon at Princeton College. He was the primary author of the United States Constitution, and served as the fourth president.

these ideas had begun to creep into American institutions. Washington subtly warned the nation to avoid the Enlightenment ideals. In his Farewell Address in 1796, Washington said:

> Let it simply be asked, Where is the security for property, for reputation, for life, if the sense of religious obligation desert the oaths, which are the instruments of investigation in courts of justice? And let us with caution indulge the supposition that morality can be maintained without religion. Whatever may be conceded to the influence of refined education on minds of peculiar structure, reason and experience both forbid us to expect, that national morality can prevail in exclusion of religious principle.

More than one hundred years earlier, the Puritans had settled in America, convinced that inequality and unjust government did not have to be accepted as a way of life. In 1776, the Patriots declared these views to the world. While neither the Puritans nor the Patriots originally had in mind framing a new and independent nation, it is to the credit of the Patriots that when all other

Abigail Adams

President John Adams had the blessing of being married to one of the most outstanding women in colonial America. In 1774, as a rising young lawyer, he went to Philadelphia for the First Continental Congress. For the next ten years, his service with the government kept John and Abigail apart except for short periods of time. To Abigail fell the task of educating their five children and managing their farm and John's business affairs. She supervised hired help and tenants, and occasionally improved their holdings by purchasing additional property. Later her grandson observed that her wisdom and skill may have saved the family from the financial disaster which overtook many men in public service then. Though these achievements may seem ordinary today, in colonial days few women were prepared to handle so much responsibility.

Abigail's opinions were as unique as her capabilities. When most women of her day concerned themselves only with domestic affairs, she formed conclusions about many of the social and political problems of the time. In lengthy and lively correspondence, she and her husband exchanged views.

"I long to hear that you have declared an independency," she wrote him, early supporting separation from Britain. In another letter, she questioned slaveholders' devotion to liberty since they deprived their fellow creatures of liberty. Despite her neighbors' disapproval, she sent a black servant boy to evening school. Insisting that all people should have equal rights regardless of color or sex, she repeatedly expressed concern in her letters about the unequal educational opportunities for women and the problem of women's rights.

While John and Abigail usually held similar views, she sometimes adopted a position before he did. This gifted woman in so many ways was truly a full partner in her husband's career.

alternatives seemed to dissolve, they had the imagination to do it. With no model before them, they created the means though which some of mankind's most cherished dreams and ideals could be fulfilled.

Was the American "revolution" a Christian outcry, or was it an Enlightenment movement? Both views have been held and argued strenuously during the course of the nation's history. The most accurate answer is probably that it was a little of both, with the balance tipping toward a Christian interpretation. The Christian (Calvinist/Puritan) rationale was expressed cogently in a Huguenot work widely read at the time, called *Vindiciae Contra Tyrranos*.

> *Vindiciae Contra Tyrranos* held, among other things, to these doctrines: First, any ruler who commands anything contrary to the law of God thereby forfeits his realm. Second, Rebellion is refusal to obey God, for we ought to obey God rather than man. To obey the ruler when he commands what is against God's law is thus truly rebellion. Third, since God's law is the fundamental law and the only true source of law, and neither king nor subject is exempt from it, war is sometimes required in order to defend God's law against the ruler. A fourth tenet also characterized this position: legal rebellion required the leadership of lesser magistrates to oppose, *in the name of the law,* the royal dissolution or contempt of law. All these doctrines were basic to the colonial cause (R.J. Rushdoony, *This Independent Republic*).

The Enlightenment view was most vigorously presented by **Thomas Paine** in such pamphlets as *Common Sense* and *The American Crisis*. Paine and others who shared his views argued for pure, unchecked democracy. He held that political power for the people could be gained only by the violent overthrow of the existing order. He urged the colonists to stop trying to convince Britain of their views and to *demand* independence by

whatever means were necessary. Paine later discredited himself among most Americans (with the possible exemption of Jefferson) by writing other works, principally *The Age of Reason*, which were virulently anti-Christian, blasphemous, and contemptuous of the rule of law.

In summary, the "Witherspoons" had their motive—a godly, covenantal order; the "Paines" had their motive—a secular, man-centered order. But both shared a common hope for an outcome —freedom to live out their convictions. The history of the United States has often been marked by the tensions that perhaps were inevitable in a system where opposing worldviews have had the freedom to compete. The battle for the minds and hearts of Americans continues; and the American political system was designed to ensure that the battleground remains even. That does not mean, however, that it was designed to ensure that neither side would ever win.

Decline of the Old Regime in France

The revolutionary changes that came to England in the seventeenth century were a great help to the middle class. Its merchants and lesser nobles who supported Parliament gained for themselves both civil and religious freedoms. However, for their counterparts in France during these same years, the story was quite different. Throughout most of continental Europe, there existed a social and political system known to history as the *ancien régime*, French for *Old Regime*. A relic of feudalism, this system was directed by absolutist kings and by privileged classes who enjoyed special status and wealth at the expense of the masses.

Versailles, the Orangery

Government Suffers from Neglect. Louis XIV's absolutist government demanded the leadership of a hard-working, intelligent person. Unfortunately, **Louis XV**, who followed Louis XIV, was lazy and selfish. He devoted much of his time to immoral women and hunting. Although this was not unusual for an eighteenth-century king, the absolute ruler of a great state could not afford to waste so much time. Louis XV was always an adolescent trying to do a man's job. His long reign, from 1715 to 1774, saw a substantial deterioration of French society. Near the end of his reign, he began to see trouble on the horizon and is reputed to have remarked: "Things will hold together until my death." His mistress, **Madame de Pompadour**, then responded with her famous line: "After us the deluge."

Louis XVI, the 20-year-old grandson of Louis XV, came to the throne next. He was a well-meaning, shy, kind, moral person. He spent his time with his family and his hobby was that of a locksmith. In reality quite slow-witted, he did not have the ability to carry out the duties of an absolute monarch. He nevertheless had a modest will to be of benefit to his people. By this time, the opinions of the *Philosophes* had penetrated Versailles, and Louis seemed to want to play the part of an enlightened despot, as some other European monarchs were. His 18-year-old wife, **Marie Antoinette**, daughter of Hapsburg **Empress Maria Theresa** of Austria, was an entirely different sort of person. Bright, charming, frivolous, and haughty, she held more power over her husband than any mistress had held over Louis XV. The French hated her for her foreign birth, extravagance, and unwise meddling in matters of state.

The machinery of government of seventeenth-century France continued in use throughout the Old Regime. Ruling without a national assembly, the absolute monarchs of the seventeenth and eighteenth century in France controlled the press and the courts. They could spend tax money as they pleased. Their powers were checked somewhat by the difficulty of controlling the government ministers, councils, and intendants who were supposed to carry out their will. Also the court, custom, and corruption limited royal power. The kings had no prime minister to coordinate the work of government. If the monarch did not manage affairs of state, there was no one else to do it. Since Richelieu, the day-to-day administration of the government of France had largely been in the hands of middle-class civil servants. Under Louis XV's neglect, this hitherto faithful class fell into corruption and disorganization, although it seemed to continue to hold influence in foreign affairs, particularly on the North American question.

Holding the strongest legal check on royal power was the *Parlement of Paris* and the provincial *parlements*. These were the highest courts in France. Only with their approval could the king's decrees become binding on the courts of the land. Thus the *parlements* had a legislative function. But because the judges were noblemen who had been promoted by the king from the middle class, they

The Revocation of the Edict of Nantes, 1685

"On 18 October 1685, Louis [XIV] signed the Revocation of the Edict of Nantes. By perpetual and irrevocable decree the fundamental and irrevocable edict was pronounced null and void. Huguenot places of worship were to be demolished, religious gatherings of any kind were forbidden to the "pretended" Reformed religion, all ministers unwilling to embrace the Roman Catholic religion were to leave the kingdom within fifteen days or as an alternative to take the degree, Doctor of Laws; Calvinistic schools and seminaries were forbidden, all children were to be baptized by the curé of the parish, and Protestant exiles had to return within four months or forfeit their property to the state. None of the "pretended" Reformed subjects could take away from the kingdom or territories any of their property or possessions under penalty of the galleys for men, and confiscation and imprisonment for women. Forbidding the exercise of any religion other than that of the king's choice was the extreme conclusion of a philosophy which stressed the divine right of kings conjoined by *cujus region ejus religio*.

Consequences of the Revocation of the Edict of Nantes echo across history. A massive dispersion followed the recall. French Protestants took flight to England, Ireland, Holland, Belgium, Germany, Scandinavia, Switzerland, Russia, Austria, [South] Africa, North and South America. The Elector of Brandenburg openly welcomed the newcomers; pressure from the English public made Catholic James II issue a Brief (1686) taking the French refugees under his protection and ordering a general collection to be made throughout his kingdom. Poole in **Huguenots of the Dispersion** estimates that the number settling in England, Ireland and America, was about eighty thousand. The social occupations of those who made up the exodus included teachers, philosophers, craftsmen, artists, weavers, farmers, stone workers, merchants, sailors, gunsmiths, iron workers, sculptors, writers, architects, bankers, lawyers, industrial leaders, soldiers; namely, intellectuals and the industrious middle class. Such a loss to France was gain to other nations. As controller-general of finances Jean Baptiste Colbert had so often predicted, the economic development of France suffered disastrously.

Realizing that many were taking flight, Louis ordered the borders closed and patrolled; ships were stopped and searched; all magistrates were ordered to report suspicious movements by any Protestants. Instructions were sent to the intendants to be especially easy with Protestant bankers and manufacturers in order to retain them. Nevertheless, approximately one-tenth (200,000) escaped, according to Professor Salmon; others estimate that it was from 500,000 to 800,000. No one really knows for sure.

…Pastor Jean Claude was forcibly escorted to the frontier by the king's footmen. From exile in Holland he wrote his scathing report to the world concerning religious persecution in France. The book was banned in France and French ambassadors tried to suppress it at foreign courts to prevent its widespread publication…. His own words powerfully cry out:

…But above all we protest against that impious and abominable position, which is nowadays made the general rule in France, by which religion is made to depend on the pleasure and despotick power of a mortal prince, and perseverance in the faith branded with the names of rebellion and treason, which is to make a man a god, and tends to the introducing and authorizing of atheism and idolatry."

Janet Gray, **The French Huguenots**: **Anatomy of Courage**, Grand Rapids, Baker Book House, 1981, pp. 243–246

Those with Huguenot ancestry in the United States include George Washington, John Quincy Adams, John Tyler, Patrick Henry, Paul Revere, Alexander Hamilton, John Jay, and John C. Fremont. Among Protestant leaders in England and the United States were Augustus Toplady, William Romaine, Charles Spurgeon, John L. Girardeau, Robert L. Dabney (d'Aubigne) and others.

Louis XVI, 1754–1793

were likely to defend noble privileges. Also the king could appear in person and force the *Parlement of Paris* to accept his order. So even the strongest legal check on royal power was not very effective.

The Three Estates. Under the Old Regime, people fell socially into three **estates** (classes): the clergy, the nobility, and everyone else. The first two estates included about 2 percent of the population, but they owned most of the country's wealth. People from these classes held the highest offices in the government and church and paid almost no taxes. But within each estate were vast differences in income and status.

The major church officials of the First Estate, such as bishops and abbots, came from the nobility. Often unqualified, they neglected their spiritual duties. On the other hand, the parish priests, generally from the lower classes, worked with the people but received little income. The ranking clergy owned vast tracts of tax-exempt land, from which they collected rents. They also collected taxes (called tithes) from their landed parishioners. As for the Second Estate, the most important and usually the wealthiest nobles lived at Versailles, while their agents squeezed the peasants for all the taxes they could get. While they were technically required to pay some direct and indirect taxes, many managed to avoid them by reason of their influence. Many in this excessively wealthy class held army, navy, and church posts. But many nobles who remained in the provinces were not rich. In fact, the economic line between poor nobles and peasants was often very thin.

The Third Estate included everyone not of the clergy or nobility. Some 20 million peasants and 4 million artisans and middle-class people, out of a total French population of 24.5 million, made up this estate. Upper middle-class townsmen (*bourgeoisie*) in this group were increasing in wealth and numbers. These merchants, bankers, lawyers, shopkeepers, physicians, and professors were the most progressive and ambitious citizens in the country. They resented the social advantages of the nobility and the fact that their own sons could not get good positions in the army, the church, and the bureaucracy. Now well-to-do, they wanted the political power and social standing that should go with their wealth. Their demands for reform grew louder and louder. Coupled with the ferment-causing *circumstances* of middle class was the new *philosophical* ferment of the Enlightenment, most of which came from this very class, with the aid of a few liberal-minded members of the nobility, such as Montesquieu and Mirabeau. This combination of material and intellectual factors stirred the middle-class to lead the way toward radical restructure (*i.e.,* revolution) of French society. These factors in part distinguish the French Revolution from the American War for Independence, which was essentially a conservative action to preserve the early covenantal order which had been established in the colonies.

Perhaps one of the key factors that paved the way for revolution, was the long term persecution of the Huguenots. As a result of the bigotry and opposition to the Reformation on the part of its rulers, France was deprived of the leavening influence of the gospel. It had no Puritans or Great Awakening to create the political climate for true liberty as was evident in North America. The hierarchical despotism promoted by the Jesuits and Richelieu resulted in an absolutism that went hand in hand with a destruction of the power of the Huguenots. When Louis XIV revoked the Edict of Nantes in 1685, making Calvinism illegal, thousands of Huguenot families fled the country in a mass exodus. With these champions of Christian liberty out of the way, it was just a matter of time until tyranny was answered by anarchy.

At the bottom of the lowest estate were the peasants. Eighty percent of the French people made a living by working the soil. Although some peasants owned their land, most were **sharecroppers**. Despite the fact that serfdom had disappeared, many annoying feudal practices continued. For example, peasants could not keep the lords' pigeons from feeding in their fields nor kill game animals, even when these ate their crops. In addition, the peasants paid the highest taxes.

At its best, the French tax system was unjust and inefficient. Not only did the crown collect taxes in a confused manner, but it also mismanaged the money. In the total absence of budgeting or planning, no one knew how much the government owed or the amount of its income. France's credit was so poor that it had to pay 20 percent interest to borrow money. At the same time, England paid only 4 percent interest on its debts. By 1789, the payment on the French debt was equal to half of its income.

Taxes fell haphazardly on the Third Estate—an income tax, a poll tax, a property tax, and tolls on goods moved from one province to another. In addition they were forced to work on roads several days a year without compensation. Many taxes were collected by farmers-general who bought the right of collection and made a profit on it. A tax collected in this fashion was the salt tax. Each family was forced to buy a certain amount of salt each year, and the price varied from district to district depending on the whim of the tax farmer.

In some areas, these taxes took as much as 60 percent of a peasant's income. Living in small stone or mud huts, the poorest peasants worked from sunrise until dark. Most owned only one outfit of clothes and ate only soup and bread. Rarely could they afford meat.

Despite the poverty of its peasants, France was still the richest country in Europe in terms of overall wealth and resources. Yet it could not collect enough money to meet government expenses. A series of wars in the eighteenth century strained the French treasury to the breaking point. It was the cost of aiding the Americans in their war against the British that increased the debt to an unbearable level. The resulting financial crisis contributed to the outbreak of the **French Revolution**.

The French Revolution

With the success of the American "Revolution," the heady whiff of liberty and equality wafting across the Atlantic was too much for Frenchmen to bear—even though "equality," a favorite Enlightenment theme, was never a major issue in the American upheaval. Some of the French, like many Europeans, saw the American experience as proof that Enlightenment ideas were not mere pipe dreams. A number of deist Americans, such as **Thomas Paine**, **Thomas Jefferson**, and **Benjamin Franklin**, had spent time in France discussing their vision of the situation in America. Moreover, a number of high-ranking French military leaders, principally the **Marquis de Lafayette**, had helped the Americans gain more freedom than they themselves enjoyed. The French participation in the American war created an enormous debt for France, and this debt added to the financial crisis which was already skidding the French state toward bankruptcy.

Economic Reforms Attempted. Louis XVI began his reign with some wise moves. These included the dismissal of a large body of ministers inherited from the dissolute court of Louis XV and the appointment of an excellent administrator, the physiocrat economist and statesman, **Anne Robert Jacques Turgot**, as controller general. Turgot devised a practical plan to solve the nation's financial problems. Included in his sweeping proposals were the cancellation of tax privileges enjoyed by those at the top of the feudal order, an end to industrial monopolies by the guilds, and wholesale abandonment of the intense mercantilist-style regulation of commerce. The proposal may well have worked had Turgot been able to implement them. In 1776, however, he was dismissed when the privileged groups which stood

to lose under the reforms persuaded the weak-willed Louis to replace him. The *Philosophes* were heartsick at the dismissal of Turgot, whose program had epitomized their views. Voltaire wrote: "The dismissal of this great man crushes me.... Since that fatal day, I have not followed anything, I have not asked anyone for anything, and I am waiting patiently for someone to cut our throats."

A young banker, **Jacques Necker**, was given the task of trying to stave off economic collapse. He tried some stopgap measures but soon was forced by the continuing crisis to adopt Turgot's draconian, free-market plans. The privileged clergy, nobles, the royal court, and wealthy middle-class interests in the *Parlement of Paris* combined to challenge Necker, actually taking up arms against him in 1781 and persuading the king to dismiss him. Since Necker's program had been popular among the masses, agitation arose from their ranks. The Third Estate began to recall from the dim past an institution known as the **Estates-General**, which they romantically believed had once been a kind of representative body. Clamor arose for the recalling of the old institution.

Meanwhile, Louis entrusted one hapless man after another with the financial crisis, all to no avail. France's international credit rating plummeted further and the country was unable to secure loans. The *Parlement of Paris* declined again and again to register new royal tax edicts, and by mid-1788, the government became paralyzed and unable to avoid bankruptcy. The king, in desperation, reinstated Necker and issued a call for a meeting of the Estates-General to be held in May, 1789.

The Estates-General. The Estates-General historically had consisted of three houses—one representing the clergy (first estate), another the nobles (second estate) and a third the merchants/commoners (the third estate). If the body were again so constituted, it was clear that the privileged first and second estates would control everything the assembly would do by a 2 to 1 margin. Necker thus arranged for the third house to have twice as many delegates in the new assembly. Historically, each house had one vote. If that were the case again, double membership within one house would not solve the two-houses-against-one problem. A solution would have been to arrange for the three estates to meet en masse in the new Estates-General, balancing the power between the upper and lower classes. But Necker failed to specify how the houses were to organize themselves, and neither he nor the king proposed a legislative agenda. When the meeting opened in 1789, a complete deadlock arose immediately. Sustained by aroused public outcry, the commoners decided to go ahead on their own. They boldly organized themselves as a self-contained National Assembly.

The outraged nobles, along with two brothers of the king, convinced Louis XVI to send troops to blockade the hall where the Assembly planned to meet. Undaunted, the commoner delegates met on a nearby tennis court and vowed to continue in session until they could complete a new constitution for the nation. It was a frank act of revolution and defiance. The king flinched. On June 27, 1789, Louis ordered the two other estates to join the commoners in a new combined institution. The monarchy was for all practical purposes broken on that fateful day, as the government slipped into the hands of the conjoined National Assembly.

Political Parties Form. Interestingly, the commoners in the group received support for their agenda from a significant number of liberal nobles and clergymen in the other two estates. This coalition gave the reformist movement a working majority. It did not, however, give the

Mirabeau, 1749–1791

majority any significant governing wisdom. The Assembly was totally inexperienced in the task of governing, and spent much of its initial time debating the latest philosophical and political trends. This trendiness led to the emergence of something like political parties, as the most skillful men began to gather about themselves delegates of like mind. Among the best of these was **Marie Joseph Paul Yves Roch Gilbert du Motier, the Marquis de Lafayette.** The popular and moderate young nobleman espoused the cause of freedom and sympathized with the people, rallying the liberal wing of the nobles about him.

The **Abbé Emmanuel Joseph Sieyès**, a liberal priest, gathered about himself representatives of the philosophical realm. To him, government was a mechanical contrivance which would operate properly if intelligently planned, engineered, and administered.

The most fanatically democratic extremists in the Assembly began to gather around a young street-wise lawyer, **Maximilien Robespierre**, whose abject infamy and villainy would soon become the scourge of one of history's most sordid epochs. Robespierre was a strong devotee of the writings of the radical, romantic philosopher **Rousseau.**

Towering over the whole Assembly was a nobleman by the name of **Honoré Gabriel Riquetti, Count of Mirabeau.** Though wild and scandalous in his youth, Mirabeau became an eloquent leader in the Assembly of a campaign for a constitutional monarchy. Mirabeau saw that an effective government could not be fashioned by a congress of philosophers. He concluded that the government would have to become truly representative of all the vital national interests, including the masses. Perhaps regrettably, he was never able to develop a consensus around his views, and the Assembly bogged down. It set aside all affairs other than its primary task: to deliberate upon and design a new constitution.

The Rise of the Mob. Sadly, deliberation was not the desire of the throngs in the city streets of Paris or in the countryside. Revolutionary fever had been growing steadily and was reaching a boiling point. With the monarchy and its government in moral and financial collapse, government services also collapsed, adding to the confusion and chaos. Mobs began to roam about, falling upon and murdering royal officials. In the face of this, the king and Assembly failed to unite to devise solutions, but viewed each other with mutual suspicion. In early July 1789, a party from the court, led by one of the king's brothers, persuaded the king to reassert his authority. The king, always easy to persuade, dispatched soldiers into the streets of Paris in a would-be show of strength intended as a prelude to dismissing Necker and other popular ministers as well as dissolving the Assembly.

The Taking of the Bastille

At the sight of the royal troops, excited crowds of workers and craftsmen, led by shopkeepers and managers of small industries, surged into the Paris streets. Seizing whatever weapons they could find in local **arsenals**, the mob stormed an old royal fortress, lately used as a prison, the infamous **Bastille**. It was July 14, 1789, the date now usually assigned as the official outbreak of the **French Revolution**. The Bastille had become more than a prison; it was the *symbol of tyranny* in the eyes of the mobs. Into this fortress, hundreds of enemies of the nobility and the crown had disappeared, on the strength of *lettres de cachet* (letters with the royal seal). With these documents, the crown and its friends could dispatch any enemy without proof of any actual wrongdoing. When the Bastille fell, the fiery imaginations of the people rose; and all over the world the news roused visions of the dawn of a utopian new era of citizen power.

Fall of the Bastille

As special envoy and American minister to France, Thomas Jefferson witnessed the beginnings of the French Revolution. Leaders of the Revolution and European diplomats at Louis's court gave him first hand information on events as they occurred. At the time of the storming of the Bastille, the American statesman happened to be staying in the home of Monsieur de Corny, spokesman for the people's deputation to the prison. Here is Jefferson's account of what took place.

M. de Corny, and five others, were then sent to ask arms of M. de Launay, Governor of the Bastille. They found a great crowd of people already before the place, and they immediately planted a flag of truce, which was answered by a like flag hoisted on the parapet. The deputation asked the people to fall back a little, advanced themselves to make their demand of the Governor, and in that instant, gunfire from the Bastille killed the four people nearest to the deputies. The deputies retired....

On the retirement of the deputies, the people rushed forward, and almost in an instant, were in possession of a fortification of infinite strength, defended by one hundred men, which in other times had stood several regular sieges, and had never been taken. How they forced their entrance has never been explained. They took all the arms, freed the prisoners, and such of the garrison as were not killed in the first moment of fury; took the Governor and Lieutenant Governor to the Place de Grève (the place of public execution), cut off their heads, and sent them through the city, in triumph, to the Palais royal.

Adapted from **Thomas Jefferson: Writings,** Merrill Peterson, ed. (New York: The Library of America, 1984, p. 90).

The street violence frightened the most malevolent of the aristocrats who suddenly realized their hopes of squelching reform were not going to be easily realized. Large numbers of them fled the country, many "settling" near the border in Germany, from where they continued to conspire on ways to restore the old order. For his part, Louis XVI decided to make gestures toward the people. He paid a formal visit to Paris and expressed approval over the recent activities. His expressions were joyfully received, since most Frenchmen still had a heart for their ancient monarchical traditions. Among the steps he applauded was the creation of a new municipal government in Paris and the establishment of a new National Guard, led by the popular Lafayette and pledged to maintain the peace. When trouble again broke out in October, following dark rumors about new aristocratic plots, a huge mob trekked to Versailles to seize the king; but Lafayette managed to defuse the situation, except for a demand that the king transfer his residence to Paris. Louis agreed to do so. On October 6, the rioters escorted the royal family to the capital, dancing and singing along the way. They referred to the family as "the baker, the baker's wife, and the baker's son," perhaps in response to an alleged but likely unuttered comment by Marie Antoinette. When told the people had no bread (bad harvests had produced a bread famine), she was reputed to have said: "Then let them eat cake." In fact, according to some reports, she had orga-

Lettres de Cachet

Under the Old Regime, the king would often give or sell letters of cachet to his favorites. These letters ordered the arrest and imprisonment of a person without a trial. The king's friends sometimes used these letters to get rid of their enemies. In this manner many people disappeared, never to be heard of again. They did not know who had had them arrested or why. When the Bastille was stormed, a great many of the prisoners who were released fell into this category.

nized soup kitchens for the poor. In any event, the monarchs were now, in effect, Lafayette's prisoners, though that probably was not his original intention.

Centers of Radicalism and Propaganda. The surging unrest in the streets during this time was to a large extent the consequence of an unprecedented epidemic of radical agitation by demagogues roaming the cities and countryside. Floods of pamphlets and newspapers inundated the citizens with fanatical exhortations against the old order. Public opinion was also influenced by the formation of numerous political clubs which met in coffeehouses and seemingly everywhere else. Two clubs, the **Cordeliers** and the **Jacobins**, rose to prominence. Among the leaders of the lower-element Cordeliers were rabid extremists such as leftist Assemblyman and lawyer **Georges Jacques Danton** and physician-scientist **Jean Paul Marat**. The Jacobins recruited members from among the upper levels of the *bourgeoisie*. Before long, this club also became radicalized and leaders such as Lafayette, Sieyès, and Mirabeau were overshadowed by more radical men like Robespierre, who skillfully manipulated the club into a countrywide mass vehicle of agitation.

Chaos and Reform Widen. Aware of this growing insurgence, the National Assembly moved to enact reforms. The nobles and clergy, on August 4, 1789, renounced the privileges of their respective estates in the name of revolutionary equality. But still confronting the body was the disastrous national financial situation. In a truly revolutionary move on November 2, the Assembly voted to confiscate the vast properties of the church. These properties were to be used as collateral for the issuance of a massive new supply of paper money, known as *assignats*. With this new cash,

Hall of the Jacobins in Paris. A network of Jacobin clubs were formed throughout France which promoted radical socialism.

the government proceeded to meet its most pressing obligations.

But the headiness that comes with printing bundles of paper money soon seized the day, and new infusions of unbacked cash followed, setting off a tremendous inflation.

With the loss of their income-producing properties, the clergy needed another source of support. The Assembly responded to this need by nationalizing the Roman Catholic Church. In July 1790, it enacted the **Civil Constitution of the Clergy** and began paying the salaries of the priests. The creation of an indigenous French church under the control of the government, naturally, was not greeted with pleasure by **Pope Pius VI**. He promptly excommunicated all clergymen who took the new oath prescribed by the Assembly. Most of the clergymen bolted from the new arrangement and remained loyal to the ancient church. These were then deposed from their pulpits, parishes, and positions, adding a serious religious disturbance to the spreading general disorder.

The National Assembly went still further. In another sweeping act, it wiped out the entire old administrative structure of intendancies, which had long run the nation. In its place, a new political and administrative division of the country was drawn up. France was divided into eighty-three departments (counties), a structure which remains mostly intact today. Offices in these divisions became elective, rather than appointive.

In perhaps its most substantive act, the National Assembly completed its prime objective, the development of a constitution. The basic framework was first set forth in the famous **Declaration of the Rights of Man and of Citizens**. The document was patterned after the English Bill of Rights of 1689 and the American Bill of Rights which had recently been appended to the United States Constitution. In this new French Declaration, the heart of the old order, the divine right of kings, was swept away and sovereignty was vested in the people, to whom government officials at all levels were to be accountable. The Declaration embodied most of the ideas of the Enlightenment. It declared the natural rights of man—liberty, property, security, and resistance to oppression—sacred and inalienable. It called for freedom of expression, outlawed **arbitrary** arrest, and guaranteed the rights of accused persons.

In the spring of 1791, the new constitution was completed, creating a limited monarchy and establishing a thorough decentralization of power. A new **unicameral** legislature was to be created, with members to be elected only by "active citizens," which effectively meant property owners. It was clearly a middle-class power ploy, and again reflected the views of the *Philosophes*.

Mirabeau was the leading advocate of the new limited monarchy, but in April 1791 he died, predicting that the well-deliberated reform efforts would soon collapse and be washed away in a bloodbath.

Louis XVI found the new constitution highly distasteful, and secretly arranged for himself and his family to flee France. On the night of June 20, 1791, as the disguised royal family approached the border, a suspicious young radical detected them and galloped to the next station where an alarm was sounded. Excited villagers in the area rolled out of bed and poured into the streets, halting further progress by the royal carriage. News of the attempted flight somewhat frightened the moderates, who feared what might become of France without at least a figurehead monarch. But the radicals back in Paris saw an opportunity. Danton, Robespierre and their respective clubs portrayed the flight as **abdication** and publicly proclaimed that France was a **Republic**. A serious split arose between the moderate, monarchist democrats and the hothead radicals. The moderates were still in the majority in the Assembly and accepted a conciliatory explanation from the king. They welcomed him back into office. In return, Louis agreed to accept the new constitution.

The new **Legislative Assembly** created by the constitution met the day after the National Assembly adjourned, October 1, 1791. All of the 745 members were new, however, and had little idea how to govern. The Legislative Assembly quickly divided into party factions. The **Feuillants**, a minority, supported the new constitution. The **Girondists**, another minority element, favored replacing the constitution and creating a republic. The majority, at first torn between the two ideas, soon fell under the spell of Girondist oratory, and almost from the beginning the Assembly became dedicated to ending the monarchy.

Oath of the Tennis Court, by Jacques-Louis David. Members of the National Assembly swore to establish a constitution based on a purely humanistic theory of rights. On August 26, 1789, they issued ***The Declaration of the Rights of Man and of Citizens***.

By this time, exiled aristocrats had managed to stir Austria and Prussia into preparing to make war on France. Austria was ruled by **Leopold II**, brother of Marie Antoinette. Learning of this, the Girondists sought to preempt attack by declaring war on Austria in 1792. Austria was joined by Prussia. The French were quickly defeated in the Austrian Netherlands (Belgium) and the allies next invaded France.

With these events, the wrath of the republicans in Paris waxed hot, and they charged the government with treason for failing to defend the nation. The king was named as the author of the new calamities and accused of conspiring with the foreign despots to overthrow the Revolution. The mob again arose and stormed the king's residence. Mercenary Royal Swiss Guards were the only troops that remained loyal to the king, and they put up a gallant fight as Louis slipped away to seek shelter in the halls of the Legislative Assembly. The Swiss Guards were massacred. The Assembly voted to depose the king from office, and order the election of a new National Convention to write a new constitution. The government was now in the hands of the Assembly and a committee of ministers it appointed.

But the capital was in reality in the hands of fanatics who continued to agitate in the streets.

Supporters of the Revolution

On August 10, 1792, the municipal government was overthrown. The fiercely determined radicals, Robespierre, Danton, and Marat, led the victors. Danton rose to the top and can fairly be seen as the self-appointed national dictator at this stage. He sought to consolidate his power by issuing a frenzied call to rebuff the invasion of the fatherland. The entire male population was drafted for military service and weapons production entered high gear. Amazingly, in light of the national disorder and chaos, the defensive action, full of revolutionary zeal, proved successful. In a few weeks, the Austrians and Prussians were driven from French soil.

At about the same time, a series of hideous crimes were committed in Paris. As a result of the spread of terror in Paris, thousands of citizens suspected of supporting the king, had been arrested and imprisoned. In September 1792, terrorist mobs swarmed through the prisons and massacred the inmates. The bloody business went on without a single effort to stop it. Paris was nearing absolute anarchy.

The new National Convention called to draft a new constitution met on September 21, 1792, and for three years thereafter. The convention was divided between the Girondists and the more radical element, which became known as the **Mountain**, because delegates sat on high tiers in the hall. The radicals were led by Danton, Robespierre, and Marat. The Girondists, mostly "enlightened" idealists with utopian dreams for a new society, denounced the violence of the radicals, especially the September massacres. Between the two groups were the majority of delegates, the potential swing group known as the **Plain**. The Girondists called for an investigation of the massacres, hoping to prove the leaders of the Mountain culpable.

The King is Tried and Executed. In December, the Convention summoned citizen **Louis Capet**, as the deposed king was now called, to appear and give answer to the body, now sitting as a court. The Mountain men, with a threatening mob to back them up, won enough of the Plain

Execution of Louis XVI at the Place de la Révolution.

to their side, and citizen Capet was condemned. On January 21, 1793, Louis XVI was beheaded on a monstrous new instrument of death, the **guillotine**.

All of Europe was shocked and scandalized. The despotic states formed a massive coalition intending to come against Revolutionary France. The coalition included virtually all the powers of Europe—England, Austria, Prussia, Spain, Holland, Piedmont; France was surrounded.

The Girondists wanted domestic order restored as a matter of primary importance. The Mountain insisted on a massive response to the new foreign threat and was willing to jeopardize new individual liberties to do so. But there was little time to debate the differences. The rash Mountain leaders called on the mob to invade the Convention, and the pressure resulted in the ouster and arrest of thirty-one leading Girondists.

The Reign of Terror. The Mountain extremists were now virtually without restraint, and this party decided to establish itself as the power with which to be reckoned. It did so by adopting a policy of **mass public terror**. This new phase of the Revolution has become known to history as the **Reign of Terror**. It began in earnest on June 2, 1793. To execute their will, the leaders established a council with the ironic name of the **Committee of Public Safety**. Its most conspicuous member was Robespierre, the hero of the mob and the Jacobin "intellectuals." He managed to discredit and eliminate Danton and Marat, and became the undisputed master of the domestic scene. (Other leaders of the extremist element prosecuted the war against the European coalition and won amazing victories which, it must be conceded, saved France from foreign conquest.) Beside the Committee, the other main instrument of the Terror was the **Revolutionary Tribunal**, a "kangaroo" court which "tried" the cases of

Mirabeau, Robespierre, and the Guillotine

the enemies of the Revolution, who soon numbered in the thousands. Mere accusations were tantamount to verdicts of guilt; the trials were ghastly shams; and the convicted were speedily carted to the guillotine. Among the victims was Queen Marie Antoinette, in October. Her 15-year-old daughter was released in 1795, but her son, later recognized as Louis XVII, died as a result of inhuman treatment by his jailors. Twenty-one Girondist leaders, and one of their patrons, a **Madame Roland**, also were beheaded shortly after the queen died. The duke of Orléans, head of a branch of the House of Bourbon sought to save himself by joining the Jacobins and taking the pathetic name of Citizen Equality (Egalité). He became a delegate to the Convention and was among those voting for the death of King Louis XVI. It was his last act; he was accused of complicity with the Girondists and executed.

In the countryside, the Reign of Terror eventually generated a hostile reaction. Anti-revolutionary uprisings occurred in at least two cities. One was Lyons, which was nearly destroyed in punishment. A pillar was erected and inscribed: "Lyons waged war with liberty; Lyons is no more." Another was Toulon, a seaport, which was subjugated under the skillful leadership of a young artillery officer from Corsica, who had earlier

come to France (which he hated) as a military cadet. His name was **Napoleon Bonaparte**. Insurgents in Vendée were also crushed. A deputy of the Terror, named **Carrier**, was dispatched into the western part of the country and launched horrors which made the Paris crimes look petty.

The excesses of the Reign of Terror began to be its own undoing. The prosecutors of the Terror began to turn upon one another. The most radical wing, the **Hébertists**, launched a vicious, atheistic war against Christianity and invented a new religion they called the Cult of Reason, which they forced upon the city of Paris and some 2,000 other towns, closing all Catholic places of worship. The churches were renamed "Temples of Reason." At a festival at the Notre Dame Cathedral, an actress replaced the Virgin Mary and was hailed as the "goddess of the French people." France was dubbed the "Republic of Virtue," and ancient republican Rome became its model. Even fashion was altered: women wore loose, Romanesque robes, sandals, and flowing, natural hairdos. Architecture was simplified; the press and theater were turned into instruments of propaganda.

Robespierre became alarmed at the influence of the Hébertists, denounced them before the Revolutionary Tribunal; and they were executed. Danton was next to be done in (on April 5, 1794), after he began to suggest that the Terror had served its purpose. This was treason to Robespierre. By that spring, Robespierre seemingly had no rivals; except perhaps his own madness. This became more and more evident, as on May 7 he forced the Convention to impose his own eccentric brand of deistic faith—akin to that of Rousseau's—upon the nation. Of all his actions, he took this new excursion into theology most seriously, calling for a paganish festival for the new national faith, over which he presided as high

Jacques-Louis David's ***The Death of Marat*** (1793), shows the assassination of a leader of the French Revolution in his bathtub. The French Revolution was the immediate result of the exaltation of human reason, but it ended in bloodshed.

priest of the Supreme Being. On the heels of the festival, the Revolutionary Tribunal quadrupled its condemnations; and no person, however zealous for the Revolution he might have once been, was exempt from the guillotine. In June and July of 1794, the Reign of Terror reached its height, or rather its depth, of unspeakable depravity. To the Terrorists, the Revolution was a greater event than the birth of Christ. Its leaders therefore replaced the historic Christian calendar and proclaimed September 21, 1792, the day the monarchy ended, as the first day of Year 1 of a new epoch in history. Months were renamed, and a new metric system of measure was instituted.

Finally, the Reign of Terror entered the Convention itself. When it became apparent that death could come to any member at any time, the constant fear overcame the delegates. Robespierre's opponents, members of his own party, turned against him. On the date of Thermidor 9 (July 27, 1794), he was condemned by the Convention and executed on the following day, along with twenty other of his henchmen. His bloody head, with jaw gaping open in seeming horror at his own monstrosity, was held aloft before the screaming crowd.

The Reign of Terror, always cloaked in the rhetoric of Virtue by Robespierre, had ended— with as many as 40,000 murdered victims after all was done. More than two-thirds of them had been peasants, artisans, and workers. The popular notion that the aristocracy bore the brunt of the Terror is thus clearly a myth. Shortly before her execution, Madame Roland summed up the bitter irony by facing a statue of the goddess Liberty and crying: "O Liberty, Liberty, what crimes are committed in thy name!"

Conclusion. The French Revolution was a historic horror of monstrous proportions, committed in the name of "Liberty, Equality, Fraternity." Yet its "virtues" have been hailed by the disenchanted and power-mad of many generations since. It was the triumph of humanism and became the model for all socialistic revolutions in modern history. Its tools were envy, hatred, bloodthirstiness, disinformation, lying, propaganda, the subversion of language, the use of foreign militarism as a diversion and imperialistic device, and even, sometimes, the use of democratic forms. Its imitators' names are well known—Lenin, Stalin, Trotsky, Hitler, Mao, Castro—and somewhat lesser known—John Brown, Francisco Villa, Ché Guevara, Patrice Lumumba, Nicholae Ceauçescu, Nelson Mandela, Pol Pot, Ho Chi Minh, Eldridge Cleaver, Bernadette Devlin, Yassar Arafat.

On an even more fundamental level, the French Revolution represented the birth of the cult of the common man and raw democracy, in which the will of the people is god—and thus the fountain of all virtue. In this cult, the tools are not *always* violence and bloodshed, but may include such seemingly benign instruments as education and religion. Yet the goal is the same: the unrestrained elevation of autonomous man, individually or collectively, in substitution for a divinely-ordained order.

Very Social by Thomas Nast, depicts the gruesome side of revolution. First conspirator, "After we have killed all Kings and Rulers, we shall be sovereign." Second conspirator, "And then we shall kill each other, what sport."

The Napoleonic Reaction

The fall of Robespierre marked a major change in French attitudes. Luxuries and amusements that had been banned now reappeared. Knee breeches, the former dress of aristocrats, came back into style; and women, forsaking the severe classical look, began to wear luxurious and revealing clothes.

The new conservative mood might even have led to another monarchy had not middle-class politicians drawn up a new constitution, which was completed by the Convention in 1795. This document, the third since 1791, put heavy stress upon property ownership for participation in government. The voters chose electors, who in turn selected legislators and other officials. Only 20,000 men were qualified to be electors. Because a group of five directors led the legislature, the government was called the **Directory**.

Napoleon's Star Rises. Monarchists, whose numbers were again on the rise as a reaction to the Terror, did not like the new constitution and the republican regime it established. In 1795, thousands of them rose in revolt. The government turned its defense over to **Napoleon Bonaparte**, the young artillery general who happened to be in Paris at the time. He ordered his cannon to fire into the rebels. Their ranks broke, and the rioters retreated, leaving behind their wounded and dead.

The man who saved the Directory was destined to play a major role in world history. Born on the island of Corsica, he was one of five sons of a poor but noble Italian family. Shortly before his birth, Corsica had been annexed by France, so he was born a French subject. At the age of 10, he

Napoleon Bonaparte, 1769–1821

was sent to military school. Because morale was rather low at the school and the studies were boring, Napoleon busied himself learning mathematics and reading Roman history. In 1784, he entered the military academy in Paris, where he mastered the use of artillery. His ability won him a post in the army in 1785. While on garrison duty, he read the *Philosophes* and became a convinced republican. During the Revolution, he joined one of the Jacobin clubs.

Had it not been for the ferment of the times, Napoleon might never have had his chance for fame. When most of the nobles fled France, they left many openings in the officer corps of the army. Therefore, a bright young man like Bonaparte could rise rapidly. In 1795, a grateful Directory rewarded him for breaking the Paris

mob. The government approved his plan to conquer Italy and put him in charge of the project. Moving south, he defeated the Austrians who occupied the area, and France took control. Suddenly Napoleon was the hero of all France. Rather than satisfying the general, however, all the attention and admiration seemed to fan the flames of his ambition.

Next he was placed in charge of an army that was supposed to invade England. However, the English fleet in the Atlantic remained the world's strongest navy and posed an obstacle to a direct assault on Britain. Napoleon proposed, instead, that England be attacked indirectly by a campaign against Egypt. England did not own Egypt at the time; it was a province of the Ottoman Empire. But Napoleon felt controlling Egypt would be essential in eventually taking India, the great British outpost in the East. The assault on Egypt proved to be a failure, however, as the famous **Admiral Horatio Nelson** destroyed the French fleet in the **Battle of the Nile** (1798) and a plague broke out among the troops. Napoleon continued to press a land war, but his army was trapped. He eventually deserted the remnant of his besieged army and stole his way back to France, where he was welcomed as a hero, probably because things had gone badly for France at home and in Europe during his absence. He was still remembered for his Italian victories.

Directory Overthrown by Napoleon. As mentioned, several European powers had again attacked France and this time seemed to be winning. As people grew unhappy with the Directory's handling of the war, Napoleon recognized his chance to be something more than a great general. With the help of two other leaders and the army, he overthrew the Directory. In its place, the victors established the **Consulate**, with Napoleon as First Consul. Then he led his forces

against the attacking countries, defeating Austria, forcing Russia out of the war, and making a truce with Britain. For the first time in ten years, France was at peace. And it now dominated Europe.

Even before these victories, the First Consul ordered a new constitution to be drafted. While Napoleon embraced the general ideals of the Revolution—the end of privilege and the establishment of equality before the law, he also saw the need for strict order in society if France were to rebuild from the ashes left by the hot Revolutionary flames. The new constitution did not contain guarantees of the rights of the citizen or of freedom of speech and the press. Under the new system, the voters chose a series of electors who made the political decisions. Even though the new constitution undid some individual free-

Napoleon gained control of France through a *coup d'état*, when he sent his soldiers into the Hall of the Assembly.

doms, it was approved by a vote of 3,011,107 to 1,567. The French thus received for a time the most honest and effective government in their history.

Napoleon, though having had no previous experience with government, learned quickly and concentrated reconstruction efforts in all the major areas of need in France: the economy, the administration, religion, education, and the code of laws.

In the economic realm, he ended the use of worthless and inflationary paper money and returned France to an honest monetary system based on gold and silver. He saw to the creation of a central bank, called the **Bank of France**. The government launched various public works, creating a better system of transportation and communications. The tax system was revised, and a national budget program was adopted. All of these measures helped business to recover and returned a measure of material prosperity to France.

Napoleon retained the administrative divisions (departments) which had been created when the Revolutionary democrats sought to decentralize power. But under Napoleon, the departments were all administered by **prefects** *appointed by Napoleon and directly controlled by him*, with military precision (Napoleon's passion and highest trait). The government of France was thereby again completely centralized.

As may be recalled, the National Assembly's establishment of a national church had created a religious schism. The new church was a failure, as the people remained loyal to traditional Catholicism. Napoleon sought to come to terms with the Roman Church. Being a pragmatist, he had several reasons for desiring better relations with the Catholics. First, though his personal faith was a

vague collection of deistic opinions, he believed that France was basically Catholic and that making peace with the church would help him achieve his plans. Then he felt that people needed the authority of religion to be happy. In an agreement with the papacy known as the **Concordat** (1801), he recognized Roman Catholicism and promised state pay for the clergy. The church gave up its claim to recently confiscated properties. Church officials were to be appointed by the state with the consent of the pope.

Attached to the agreement without papal consent, however, was a statement that Napoleon could act as he thought best for the advancement of France. The pope protested this statement, but in vain. In 1804, **Pius VII** assisted at Napoleon's coronation, but later he refused to cooperate on other matters. The argument between the two ended with Napoleon excommunicated and the pope looking out through the bars of a French prison.

Napoleon also laid out a new national educational system with three levels: primary, secondary, and university. Although the final two phases were worked out, primary education never

Pope Pius VII, 1740–1823

moved beyond the planning stage. Napoleon used the upper educational programs, which were under the administration of the University of France, to instill into France's educated people a devotion to his own system of autocracy.

Another of Napoleon's achievements was a new code of laws. One of the goals of the Enlightenment had been a more rational legal system. When the **Code Napoléon** was completed, it was a consistent, clear set of laws that applied in a fair way to the secular, middle-class social order of the early nineteenth century. The Napoleonic Code was roughly based on the codification of Roman law by the Emperor Justinian in the sixth century, the last previous effort made in Europe to organize the law systematically. To the old code were added contemporary provisions recognizing some of the equalitarian and humanitarian principles of the late Revolution. Napoleon's wars introduced his law to many other nations in Europe, and most Latin American countries adopted it as well.

From First Consul to Emperor. With the help of an efficient, harsh secret police, Napoleon kept the French state under his thumb. Acts against

Napoleon's Coronation

Pope Pius VII came all the way from Rome to honor Napoleon by crowning him emperor. When the ceremony opened in the beautiful cathedral of Notre Dame, Napoleon and his wife Josephine knelt before the pope. Then everyone gasped in amazement as Napoleon rose to his feet, took the crown from the pope, and placed it upon his own head. He then took his wife's crown and crowned her also. By this act, the emperor declared that he owed his crown to no one but had gained it through his own merits.

the state were severely punished, the press censored, and freedom of speech restricted. In 1804, a grand ceremony in Notre Dame Cathedral made official what already existed in fact. With France's high officials looking on, **Napoleon I** was crowned **hereditary emperor** by the very country that had shed so much blood to get rid of monarchs. Again Napoleon had asked the people to vote on his move. They approved, 3,572,329 to 2,569.

Despite his great domestic success, Napoleon was not satisfied. He had read too much Roman history and won too many victories. Why should his glorious reign stop at the French border? He would carve out a European empire greater than that of the Romans.

However, just across the English Channel the British were planning roadblocks for Napoleon's path to glory. Fearful of French strength on the Continent, Britain persuaded the Austrians, Russians, and Swedes to join in an attack on France in 1805. After defeating an Austrian army, Napoleon led his soldiers into Vienna and set up headquarters at Schönbrunn, the Hapsburg palace. In the meantime, he collected a fleet to invade England. However, the British under Lord Nelson's command destroyed the French fleet off Cape Trafalgar. This loss shattered Napoleon's hopes of taking England. Nelson's victory established British naval supremacy for the next century.

Napoleon's plans for England thwarted, the emperor met and defeated the combined Austrian and Russian forces in 1805. Only Prussia remained, and in 1806, Napoleon and **Frederick William III** clashed. The Prussian military machine was a traditional apparatus, steeped in the slow, methodical approaches of defensive war; the French army was a more modern, offensive unit, filled with revolutionary fervor and capacity

for swiftness. Prussia was soon overrun as well. Russia next made peace with Napoleon, in 1807; and **Czar Alexander**, who was given a free hand against Sweden and Turkey, agreed to join the emperor in his effort against Britain. By 1812, Napoleon ruled most of Europe west of Russia. People began to look on him as another Alexander the Great. He seemed invincible. The German composer, **Ludwig van Beethoven**, typified the attitude of many by celebrating Napoleon's greatness with his heroic Third Symphony (*Eroica*). However, after Napoleon proclaimed himself Emperor of France, Beethoven angrily removed his dedication to Napoleon on the autograph score of his *Eroica* Symphony.

Napoleon next proceeded to reorganize Europe according to his wishes. He put members of his family on the thrones of the various states. Holland was ruled by his brother **Louis**, Spain by **Joseph**, Westphalia (a new realm consisting of western German provinces and some taken from Prussia) by **Jerome**, Tuscany by his sister **Maria**, and Naples by **Caroline**. Napoleon also announced that the Holy Roman Empire no longer existed. Much of south and central Germany he would organize into the **Confederation of the Rhine**, with himself as protector (dictator).

Though clearly a monarch, Napoleon always portrayed himself as a "son of the Revolution," and everywhere he conquered he brought the central ideals of the French Revolution. The primary effect of this was to once and for all eliminate feudalism from Europe, a step which endeared him to the common people, who saw him as a liberator. This fundamental change in the social order was particularly marked in Germany, whose map Napoleon permanently altered.

Only Britain stood in Napoleon's way to even greater conquests. It was impossible to invade the island because of the British navy. Consequently,

Napoleon worked out a plan to shut the British out of European trade. This plan, called the **Continental System**, would ruin British business and create mass unemployment, forcing the land to sue for peace, or so Napoleon hoped. In 1806, Napoleon ordered states controlled by or allied with France to stop importing British goods. Britain responded in 1807 by demanding that neutral vessels trading at continental ports stop at British ports first. Its navy was to enforce the order. England hoped that neutral ships would

Napoleon's Ideas

Legend has created a heroic image of Emperor Napoleon; however, in real life the emperor was not so noble. The following statements by him reveal something of his true character.

Love is the occupation of the idle man, the distraction of the warrior, the stumbling block of the sovereign.

Education and history, these are the great enemies of true religion.

When a king is said to be a kind man, the reign is a failure.

Women are mere machines to make children.

I like only those people who are useful to me, and only so long as they are useful.

The main thing is one's self.... Isn't it true, Gourgaud, that it's a lucky thing to be selfish, unfeeling? If you were, you wouldn't worry about the fate of your mother or your sister, would you?

A legislator must know how to take advantage of even the defects of those he wants to govern.

H.A.L. Fisher, *Napoleon* (New York: H. Holt & Co., 1913). Gaspard Gourgaud, *Talks of Napoleon at St. Helena with General Baron Gourgaud*, (Chicago: A.C. McClurg, 1903). Comte de Las Casas, *Memorial de Ste-Helene*, (London: H. Colburn, 1823).

Fontainebleau, Napoleon's residence in France

carry its goods to the Continent. Countering the British move, Napoleon threatened to confiscate any neutral ship that stopped at British ports. American merchants were caught in the middle of this economic war, and eventually the United States was forced into the **War of 1812** against the British.

By 1812, Napoleon ruled absolutely in an enlarged France, which now extended into Germany and Italy. This greater France was surrounded by dependencies with subjected rulers or family members who exercised power at Napoleon's direction.

The Empire Falters. But the Continental System backfired on Napoleon. It hurt certain of the conquered European states so much that they rebelled against it. Portugal and Spain would not enforce the system, so French troops had to move in. In Spain, which Napoleon had lately given to

brother Joseph, the emperor confronted a new phenomenon—**nationalism**. As he had conquered other European states, the defeated rulers ceded him the rights of conqueror. The Spaniards, however, with their own government now gone, united as a national people and revolted. A nationalistic uprising was new to Napoleon. So was the rebels' approach to warfare. Lacking an organized state army, the Spaniards formed small bands and conducted **guerrilla warfare**, a method for which the French army was unprepared. Furthermore, the British, under **Arthur Wellesley, duke of Wellington**, supported the Spanish and Portuguese resistance. From 1808 until 1814, Napoleon's forces fought a costly struggle which severely drained the emperor's resources. He finally had to pull out.

Encouraged by these events, the Austrians began fighting France again. Austria called upon the German states for help. Prussia, being occupied by French troops, could not help. Other German realms in the Confederation of the Rhine were so subservient to Napoleon that their princes disallowed the spread of the Austrian call to arms. Austria was defeated by Napoleon for a fourth time. But the economic pinch of the Continental System continued to create cracks in Napoleon's empire. He even had to depose his own brother Louis from the throne in Holland over issues related to the carrying of English goods. The same issue, this time with the Vatican state under suspicion, resulted in the imprisonment of the pope at Fontainebleau (near Paris) and confiscation of the pope's territory.

To boost his fortunes, Napoleon divorced his wife **Josephine**, who had failed to give him an heir, and married the young Hapsburg archduchess, **Marie Louise**, daughter of Austrian **Emperor Francis**. His new bride presented him with an

heir a year later, in 1811, giving Napoleon assurance that his new dynasty would continue.

In 1811, the cooperation between Czar Alexander and Napoleon began breaking down, as the Russian leader also declined further enforcement of the Continental System. Napoleon made plans to invade Russia. In doing so, he amassed the greatest military effort Europe had ever seen, with more than 600,000 soldiers.

The Grand Army advanced far into the Russian territory, but the Russians avoided pitched battles, drawing the French deeper and deeper into the eastern frontier. By September 1812, Moscow had fallen. The day after the French took the city, a fire set by the Russians destroyed three-quarters of it. With winter approaching and supplies running low, Napoleon had to withdraw. Russian troops savagely attacked the fleeing French columns, and the retreat turned into a rout. When the army finally escaped from Russia, only 100,000 ragged and starving men remained.

Encouraged by Napoleon's defeat, his old enemies joined against him once again. At the Battle of Leipzig (1813), the Allies defeated Napoleon and forced him to flee back to France. Following him there and joined by England, which had just driven France from Spain, the Allies forced him to abdicate his throne. He was then exiled to the **Island of Elba** in 1814. The Allies occupied France and installed **Louis XVIII**, brother of the king who had been guillotined in 1793. Louis was instructed to implement the ideals of the French Revolution, and France's borders were restored to their revolutionary-era lines.

The victors met in Vienna in 1814–1815 in a congress, known as the **Congress of Vienna**, to consider the reconstruction of the rest of Europe. While they were yet meeting, a startling event occurred. Napoleon managed to escape from

Elba, and on March 1, 1815, he landed on the coast of France. Peasants and soldiers rallied under his banner once more as the rallying cry, *"Vive l'empereur!"* again rang through the land. Louis XVIII fled the country. The *bourgeoisie*, unhappy with the burden of Napoleonic war and despotic government, remained cool.

Napoleon, now facing a stronger and united Europe and the realization that his empire had collapsed, managed to rule only a little longer. The period of restoration became known as the **Hundred Days**.

The Allies meeting in Vienna resolved swiftly to once again invade France. Wellington was already entrenched in Belgium at the head of a force composed of Dutch, English, and German troops. The Prussians marched to join him there. Because Belgium was close, Napoleon decided to meet this European army there first. The battle ensued at **Waterloo**. In a single day, Napoleon was squeezed by his enemies and defeated. His army was annihilated by sundown. Napoleon fled to Paris and abdicated a second time. He planned to escape to America, but was taken aboard a British ship, carried to England and then, in accordance with a verdict against him, exiled to the remote and hostile mid-Atlantic island of **St. Helena**. After six years in embittered isolation, he died (1821).

In Paris, meanwhile, Louis XVIII had been restored. France was heavily fined for allowing Napoleon back, and the country was ordered to restore art treasures the emperor had pilfered from throughout Europe.

Napoleon's Legacy. Napoleon's career was over, but he left a legacy which continued to influence the modern world. His conquests did more to spread **nationalism** in Europe than anything else. Patriotism and the love of one's own country

The Battle of Waterloo, in Belgium, where Napoleon met his downfall in 1815

became more important than loyalty to a particular ruler. National boundaries were adjusted in the peace treaties following the Napoleonic Wars. Throughout Europe, people began to consider themselves as citizens of a country, not only subjects of a sovereign.

Patriotism came to have a universal appeal. Germans, for example, who had lived in small states that had hated each other for centuries, fought side by side as Germans at the Battle of Leipzig. Napoleon's foes rallied their countrymen to overthrow him by the appeal, "We must save our nation."

Bonaparte also fixed upon France a legend of glory that has influenced French politics ever since. French people remembered the fame of the Grand Empire long after they forgot its cost in human life and wealth. On the other hand,

because Napoleon consistently tried to identify himself with the Revolution, the inevitable reaction against him tended to repudiate some of the revolutionary ideals. Napoleon taught **authoritarian** rulers who have followed him the basics of dictatorship: propaganda, secret police, the use of elections to gain support, state use of education and religion to **indoctrinate** people, and the value of foreign wars to distract citizens from their loss of freedom. Again, in some of these respects, Napoleon was advancing lessons learned in the French Revolution, and it is possible to say that later authoritarian systems such as **Fascism** had roots in the radical demagogic-terrorist system of the Revolution.

For your consideration

Questions

1. How are our political leaders limited by law?

2. Why is the power of taxation so important?

3. Describe the historical (mid-17th century) background to the current struggles in Northern Ireland.

4. Are there restrictions on free religious exercise in your state, province, or country? If so, give examples.

5. Do you agree that all men are created equal? Explain why or why not.

6. Explain differences and similarities between the French Revolution and the American War for Independence. Why did the French Revolution deteriorate into chaos and terror? Why, do you think, this did not happen in America?

7. Contrast Enlightenment and Puritan views of revolution.

8. Does human "greatness" sometimes depend upon circumstances? Point out some circumstances that helped Napoleon to fame.

9. Are patriotism and nationalism positive virtues? Can they have negative aspects? Explain.

10. Describe some differences between the government of the United States under the Articles of Confederation and that under the U.S. Constitution.

Projects

1. Do some research on the abuses of the rights of Englishmen by Charles I, by the nobles, by the courts, and by the Church of England. Present your findings in a report.

2. Give an oral or written report presenting your personal evaluation of the Puritan Commonwealth and Oliver Cromwell. Add to your presentation opinions that you think the following individuals might have had about this movement: members of the House of Lords and the House of Commons, a Royalist, a Roman Catholic in Northern Ireland, a middle-class merchant, an Anglican priest, a Puritan housewife, and an army officer.

3. The Puritans had a strong influence on the development of representative democracy. Using your text and other sources, write an essay or make a chart of the Puritan ideas and practices which have contributed to representative democracy.

4. Draw a map of one of the military campaigns during the American War for Independence.

5. Listen to recordings of national anthems and patriotic songs, such as: "La Marseillaise," "God Save the Queen," "My Country 'Tis of Thee," "Star-Spangled Banner," "O Canada," "Yankee Doodle," "God Bless America," "America the Beautiful," etc. Discuss the words.

Word List

limited monarchy	vestments
Bastille	artisans
speculators	amnesty
confiscated	null and void
succession	guerrilla warfare
boycott	confederation
arbitration	estates
sharecroppers	arsenals
arbitrary	fraternity
guillotine	authoritarian
hereditary emperor	indoctrinate
Tonnage & Poundage	republic
disestablishment	Whiggism
bourgeoisie	abdication
nationalism	Consulate
prefects	Fascism

People and Groups

James I	James II
Charles I	Charles II
William Laud	Thomas Wentworth
Cavaliers	Roundheads
Oliver Cromwell	Dissenters
Long Parliament	Rump Parliament
William and Mary	House of Stuart
House of Hanover	Robert Walpole
William Pitt	Patrick Henry
John Witherspoon	George Washington
Thomas Jefferson	Thomas Paine
Louis XV	Louis XVI
Marie Antoinette	Lafayette
Anne R.J. Turgot	Jacques Necker
Max. Robespierre	George Danton
Horatio Nelson	Arthur Wellesley

1550   1600   1650   1700   1750   1800

Politics and Economics

American War for Independence 1775–1783

Puritan Commonwealth
begins in England 1649

Glorious Revolution in England 1688

French Revolution begins 1789

Reign of Napoleon 1799–1815

Science and Technology

Newton's Principia published 1687

Copernicus publishes his discoveries 1543
Vesalius's writes book on anatomy 1543
Brahe builds observatory 1576

Royal Society of London founded 1662
French Academy of Science founded 1666

Kepler completes laws of planetary motion 1619
Harvey's book on blood circulation 1628
Galileo attacks traditional astronomy 1632

Foundations laid in chemistry,
botany, zoology c. 1660–c. 1710

Religion and Philosophy

Great Awakening in America 1720s–1740s

King James Version of the Bible 1611

Religious freedom guaranteed by U.S. Bill of Rights 1791

Puritans attempt church reform in England 1641

Culture and Society

In 1689 John Locke publishes
Two Treatises of Government

Voltaire 1694–1778

Rousseau 1712–1778

Baroque period in the arts c. 1600–c. 1750

6

Protestantism and the Rise of Modern Science

It is remarkable that the rise of modern science occurred following the Reformation in Western Europe. While there were many factors involved in its development, it seems that Protestantism was one of the key factors that provided the environment that made this possible. Prior to this time the Roman Catholic/Greek worldview prevailed, which combined materialism and mysticism. With the Reformation stress on the sovereignty of God over all things, including every aspect of creation, men were able to explore God's world with a confidence that God created it in an orderly fashion.

Science and its application—industry and technology—have changed man's life dramatically since the Reformation. Science and technology as they flourished in the West helped Europe and America to have dominion over the world. For these reasons, one cannot understand world history without knowing something about the rise of modern science in the so-called **Scientific Revolution**. Amazingly, most of the knowledge the world has gained through scientific study has come into being since the sixteenth century, when men had newly rediscovered the Word of God. The Bible pointed them to, among other things, God's handiwork. Men of science began to have a great curiosity about the way in which God created the world, and how they might learn from His works.

The Royal Greenwich Observatory in England, founded in 1675

The *roots* of science, of course, go deep into history—to ancient Mesopotamia, Egypt, Greece, and medieval Islam. Yet the West, after the Reformation, made unique contributions that led to the rise of modern science. It was in the West that science became part of society in general, rather then solely the realm of intellectuals. Here the scientist and craftsman worked together, urging one another on. The development of modern science in the context of a society influenced by the gospel of the Reformation would lead to unheard-of progress in the industrial results that followed. While there were other factors involved in the rise of modern science, it was the faith of the Reformation that was pivotal. Says R. Hooykaas,

> The confrontation of Greco/Roman culture with biblical religion engendered, after centuries of tension, a new science. This science preserved the indispensable parts of the ancient heritage (mathematics, logic, methods of observation and experimentation), but was directed by different social and methodological conceptions, largely stemming from a biblical worldview. Metaphorically speaking, whereas the bodily ingredients of science may have been Greek, its vitamins and hormones were biblical. (R. Hooykaas, *Religion and the Rise of Modern Science* [Grand Rapids: Eerdmans, 1972], pp. 161–162)

Yet because there was a mixture of Christian and non-Christian elements, it is necessary to develop discernment between true and false science. Abraham Kuyper wrote that because of the new birth there are two kinds of people in this world, Christian and non-Christians. And because Christians live by the Word of God they have a different set of beliefs or presuppositions than the non-Christian. This leads to, as Kuyper said, two kinds of science;

> …because they have different starting points; and because of the difference in their nature they apply themselves differently to this work, and view things in a different way. Because they themselves are differently constituted, they see a corresponding difference in the constitution of all things. They are not at work, therefore, on different parts of the same house, but each builds a house of his own. (Abraham Kuyper, *Principles of Sacred Theology* [Grand Rapids: Baker Book House, 1980], p. 155)

We should therefore not speak of science as a neutral idea, but distinguish between true and false science. This explains why we believe in Christian education as a distinct task.

Science is said to be based on objective methods. But in fact, science, like every area of human thought and endeavor, is affected by man's sin and finiteness. We need to be aware that people in the 17th and 18th century as well as today appeal to science to give their goals the respectability of supposed objectivity while they have hidden ideological, philosophical, or religious agendas.

Science, being the activity of man, is subject to the Bible, not vice versa. For the Christian, it is not valid to draw a distinction between faith and perception, between the Bible and science. Because the Bible is true and because God created the world, Christianity gives a true picture of how things in the world truly exist. Therefore, one must begin with the Bible in order to truly understand creation. Christianity, being true and objective, is the only platform from which scientific inquiry can reliably be launched. False ideologies lead to false understandings of the world, and scientific inquiry conducted from a false premises will lead to false conclusions. There are no such things as "bare facts" or "brute facts" because all "facts" are created by God and must be understood as having been interpreted by Him before man encounters them. Scientific facts therefore must be viewed as having a prior God-given *meaning*. Each fact of the universe must be understood in the context of the whole of biblical truth. Only as we relate each fact of creation to what God reveals in the Bible can we have any coherent understanding of the world.

It is ultimately impossible to approach science from a position of religious neutrality. Modern non-Christian or secular science has, in fact, begun to see itself as a religious creed and the source for understanding moral right and wrong.

Dr. Jacob Bronowski has said that "science is to get rid of angels, blue fairies with red noses and other agents whose intervention would reduce the explanation of physical events to other than physical terms." This statement suggests that science must be *atheistic* in its approach to the physical world. God, who is presumably one of Bronowski's "other agents," cannot be seen as a Creator or Intervener in the universe. Anthropologist Edmund Leach has gone even further to suggest that science itself is the new god. He has described the modern scientific understanding this way:

> There can be no source for…moral judgment except the scientist himself. In traditional religion, morality was held to derive from God, but God was only credited with the authority to establish and enforce moral rules because He was also credited with supernatural powers of creation and destruction. These powers have now been usurped by man, and he must take on the moral responsibility that goes with them.

Such statements indicate that atheistic science is not a religiously neutral enterprise, as some less honest secular scientists claim. The fact is science is not, cannot, and should not be neutral. There is not one but two kinds of science. A true Christian approach to science will have an understanding of the Creator and His word at its foundation. Although neutrality is impossible, it is not correct to say that objectivity is impossible. Objectivity is seeing things as they really are. And it is only by submitting to God in His word that we can find true objectivity. For God stands above all things and communicates to us those fundamental principles that enable us to be objective. In fact it is this very view of the universe that provided the most significant impetus for modern scientific inquiry that began in the sixteenth and seventeenth centuries. By reasoning from biblical truth, some of the new scientists were enabled to see creation in a new light. In so doing, they were able to overcome prevailing myths—from both false religious and philosophical presuppositions.

We should not think that scientific knowledge provides us with all the answers to life. It is limited and is only one of the parts of human knowledge; it is not **absolute**. It is not unchanging, divinely revealed, and perfect. Science is knowledge which man acquires about the created universe through **observations** and **experiments** which can be formulated into **general principles or theories** (some principles of which may be found in Scripture). This process for acquiring such knowledge is called the **scientific method**. But all human activities should be performed out of a heart of faith, according to God's word and unto His glory. The use of the scientific method is merely one of the tools for fulfilling the basic commandment which God gave to mankind in the Garden of Eden: *"Be fruitful, and multiply, and replenish the earth, and subdue it: and have dominion over the fish of the sea, and over the fowl of the air, and over every living thing that moveth upon the earth"* (Gen. 1:28b).

The Medieval Synthesis

Christianity plus Greek Philosophy. Before the birth of modern science, the medieval view of the world began to change. The medieval view came from a blend of ancient pagan beliefs and church teachings, often false teachings. One of the ancient philosophers, Aristotle, had tried to give an orderly account of every detail about man and nature. He explained events in nature by suggesting purposes for them. For example, earth is the proper home for heavier objects and the sky the home of light elements. A heavy body falls to earth because it is its nature to do so. Fire and air move upwards because it is their nature to rise. Each seeks its proper home. Also, he held that everything in nature tends toward perfection. Mankind can think of perfection, but all other beings fall short of that goal.

Of course, Aristotle's system contained many other details. It was a pagan system that claimed to explain everything, and some key medieval thinkers believed it. With all reality accounted for, medieval people who accepted Aristotle's explanations uncritically saw no need to investigate or to have dominion over nature.

Yet, Christianity was the dominant influence in medieval Europe. People believed God had made the earth for them. He sent the rain and the sunshine. He loved and cared for them. Some of these people saw the present life only as a time to prepare for heaven. The most important knowledge was the plan of salvation as presented by the Roman Catholic Church. All truth and all experience had to help people understand their eternal destiny. In its isolation, medieval Europe had only slight knowledge of other cultures. Agriculture served as the basis for the economy, with little trade going on at first. People saw their rulers as appointed by God. Medieval society looked on the universe as unchanging, designed to fulfill God's purpose.

This does not mean that the Middle Ages was an entirely static period, as humanist scholars of the Renaissance and later periods attempted to show. Some who understood the world as God's domain also saw man's responsibility as God's steward over the world. They founded schools and medical facilities and developed mechanisms to help men with their labors. Technology was constantly improving. During this period,

Thomas Aquinas, the great systematizer of medieval Roman Catholicism combined the Greek philosophy represented by Aristotle (on the left) with biblical faith represented by the apostle John (on the right).

numerous key inventions arose, including the crank, the watermill, the windmill, the plough, the horse collar, and horseshoe. Christianity had taken the ancient Greek scientific tools of logic, mathematics, and reasoning into the biblical conception of Creation and led mankind out of the bondage of Greek metaphysics, which had a basic contempt for the material world. Christianity thus, provided the "vitamins indispensable for a healthy growth" of science.

By the 13th century, the faith of medieval man was again being challenged by the writings of

Aristotle and other ancient Greeks, which were pouring into Europe. Aristotle's doctrines began to undermine the church's explanation of things. The secular, humanistic scholar **Peter Abelard** taught students to question everything. A group of thinkers, known as the **Scholastics**, developed a system of disputation which also questioned and debated all aspects of knowledge and placed great emphasis on the trustworthiness of human reason to solve all mysteries.

In the midst of this environment of compromise between pagan classicism and Christianity, the Dominican monk **Thomas Aquinas** began to distinguish himself as the church's leading scholar and defender of the faith. However, Aquinas himself used reason and Aristotelian logic to reach his conclusions, which he argued proved the existence of God behind all facets of knowledge. He refuted some of Aristotle's points and sought to reconcile other points to Christianity. He accepted Aristotle's premise, for example, that every effect has a cause and every cause a prior cause. Aquinas said that preceding causes could thus be traced logically back through a hierarchy of causes to a First Cause or Prime Mover—God. He also accepted Aristotle's teaching that the goal of life is to ascertain truth, and Aquinas held that knowledge could be acquired through free acts of the God-given human mind, which he thought had not been affected by the fall into sin.

This approach touched off a furor from those who saw it as a challenge to the idea of divine revelation as the only ground of truth. Aquinas' methods and doctrines soon entered deeply into Christian thought and challenged the 800-year-old positions of St. Augustine—that knowledge comes by divine revelation and that purity of heart is foundational to the clarity of mind. Augustine had taught that man's mind was fallen and affected by sin, and this view had been dom-

inant in the Western church. Because of his view that God is sovereign in both creation and redemption, he promoted a unified view of the world. For him the conflict was not between spirit and matter, but between sin and grace, between the City of God and the City of Man.

Aquinas introduced a basic dualism between nature and grace. Grace is the area of the supernatural. Nature is the area of the natural. In the area of grace God is sovereign. In the area of nature, man and the world are free. Thus man and nature are not to be transformed by God's grace but merely supplemented with it, like icing on a cake. In fact, Aquinas believed that grace was a substance that was lost in the fall and is given back in the sacraments. This dualism became the foundation of his view of the world.

Astronomy Develops. Among the sciences, **astronomy** first challenged the medieval Thomistic outlook. Only in this field had enough data been gathered to apply the new scientific method. Many ancient cultures believed in astrology—the idea that the stars influence human affairs. In order to cast someone's horoscope, the astrologer had to know the position of the stars and planets on the person's birthday. Many medieval kings and important leaders ordered astrologers to keep records of **planetary** movements. This information was combined with ancient Greek theories of the universe.

Basic to these theories was the belief that nature consisted of heat, cold, moistness, and dryness. These combined to form the four elements which the Greeks thought made up the world. Heat and dryness made **fire**; heat and moistness produced **air**; cold and moistness combined into **water**; and cold and dryness made **earth**. The world stood still at the center of nine hollow spheres that rotated about it daily (the **geocentric** theory). These spheres were made of a mysterious, crystal-

clear substance, far purer than anything on Earth. Fixed in each of the first seven spheres was a heavenly body. These included the Moon, Mercury, Venus, the Sun, Mars, Jupiter, and Saturn. The eighth sphere contained the stars. These bodies moved about Earth but did not change position with respect to one another. Finally, the outermost ring, called the "first mover," made the other eight spheres move. Beyond it was heaven.

Distance within this system, although great, was not so vast as our modern view of the universe. One medieval writer stated that if a person could travel 40 miles or more a day, he could not reach the sphere of the fixed stars in 8,000 years. (By this calculation the sphere of the stars would be just beyond 116.8 million miles. The nearest star, except for the Sun, is actually 25 trillion miles away. Light emitted from this star, Alpha Centauri, takes 4.3 years to reach Earth.) Many early

Medieval Astronomer

astronomers did believe that all power and movement came from God, but the celestial spheres were also believed to influence events on Earth. For example, Saturn made people sad and brought disaster; Mars produced wars; Venus encouraged love; and Jupiter brought prosperity.

The Sun constantly lighted the entire universe. Night was the cone-shaped shadow cast by the earth. Since the Sun moved while the Earth stood still, night was thought to be a long black finger revolving like the hand of a clock. Space was neither dark nor silent. When people looked up at the night sky, they looked *through* darkness but not *at* darkness. And if one were properly in tune, he could hear every planet in motion in its proper sphere, making harmony and sound. Most scholars did not think of Earth as flat, but as a globe. They did believe that some rather strange creatures lived here, since zoology was not too advanced at the time.

The medieval conclusion about the world system (which we refer to as the **medieval synthesis**) was very satisfying for most people. Anyone could plainly see the heavenly bodies moving in a circular path around the Earth. The Earth seemed to stand still in the midst of all this movement. Christian theology was made to fit the medieval view of the universe. **Dante**'s great epic poem, the *Divine Comedy*, described the universe in geocentric terms and located heaven and hell in it. As the center of the universe, Earth made a proper home for man, the crown of God's Creation. Also it was to the Earth that Jesus Christ, God's Son, came to suffer and die for man's redemption.

Ptolemy. Astronomers, however, had trouble with this system. The planets did not move as they should. Already in the second century A.D., an Egyptian named **Claudius Ptolemy** had tried to revise the geocentric system. To account for the way the planets moved, he had said that the

Earth was not quite in the center. He also had said that the heavenly bodies moved in small circles whose centers, in turn, moved in larger circles around the Earth.

The Muslims translated Ptolemy's book, the *Almagest*, and brought it to the West during the twelfth century. Although his description of planetary motion was helpful, Western scholars found errors in it. At first they thought this might be due to faulty translation from the Greek. But even when they checked the book in the original language, they could not make his theory fit their observations.

This diagram of the Aristotelian/Ptolemaic or Thomistic view of the universe shows the earth as the center, with the sun and planets revolving around it.

The Cosmological Discovery of Copernicus

Copernicus. The year 1543 marks the beginning of the Scientific Revolution. It was then that **Nicholaus Copernicus** published his book, *The Revolutions of the Heavenly Bodies*. In the next century and a half, man's view of the universe changed totally. The medieval method of reasoning was replaced by the scientific approach.

Copernicus was born in Poland in 1473. After studying liberal arts, church law, and medicine, he was appointed to a cathedral in East Prussia. There he spent his life practicing medicine, studying astronomy, and managing church property. A person of many interests, he had a good understanding of economics and Greek. (At that time, few men in northeastern Europe knew Greek.)

In 1514, the pope asked him to help correct the calendar. He refused because he felt that the movements of the Sun and Moon had not been studied enough. People knew that the calendar was in error, but they did not know how to correct it. The more astronomers studied the skies, the clearer it became that Ptolemy's system had serious flaws.

To allow for these problems, someone suggested that the spheres within which the planets and stars operated did not center on the Earth. Finally, the number of spheres was increased to eighty. But still the theory did not fit observed facts.

The Sun at the Center. This problem fascinated Copernicus. He remembered that an ancient astronomer, **Aristarchus**, had argued the Earth and other planets revolved around the Sun (the

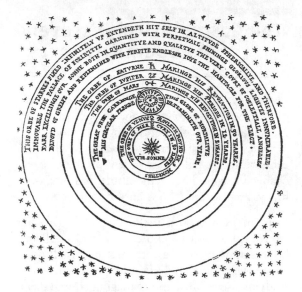

Copernicus described his theory of the universe by likening the sun to a monarch on his throne, ruling the planets that circled about it. His view of the arrangement of the heavens is known as the heliocentric (sun-centered) theory.

heliocentric theory). Aristarchus also thought that the Earth revolved daily on its axis. Copernicus decided to make mathematical calculations based on these ideas to see if they might come closer to the facts. He kept the idea of the planets moving in small circles as these orbits rotated around the Earth. Although his results were not much more correct than those based on geocentric ideas, they attracted much attention.

The idea of the Sun at the center of the solar system shocked most Europeans. **Martin Luther** scornfully remarked, "This fool wishes to reverse the entire science of astronomy; but sacred Scripture tells us that Joshua commanded the Sun to stand still and not the Earth."

Scientists also picked apart the new theory. How could the Earth revolve on its axis without causing a constant wind, they asked. Because the

Earth's atmosphere revolved at the same speed and in the same direction, replied Copernicus. The scientists had another problem—if the earth moved around the Sun, then the stars would change positions in the skies. But as everyone knew, they did not. Copernicus answered that the Earth could move in an orbit around the Sun without causing the stars to seem to change positions. The distance traveled by the Earth was so small compared to the distance to the stars that the actual change in position could not be measured.

The greatest problem for Copernicus dealt with gravity and motion. Aristotle's idea on motion fit the geocentric theory, but not the new heliocentric system. Also, since the professors of science and philosophy in the universities believed Aristotle, they were unlikely to accept the new theory. The new **cosmological** system demanded that a person deny his senses. Anyone with two good eyes could see that the Sun moved around the Earth. It is not surprising that it took a century of debate before the Copernican system won the day.

Copernicus was a man of devout faith. His observations led him to marvel at the handiwork of God in Creation. In his view, the vast universe was "wrought for us by a supremely good and orderly Creator."

"So great is this divine work of the Great and Noble Creator!" he once remarked.

Scientific Method. The new outlook led to a three-sided debate about the proper scientific method:

- Followers of Aristotle defended the medieval synthesis. They made little use of mathematics and experiments. Instead, they analyzed scientific problems by logical arguments from a few basic premises. (A premise is a fact either proved or assumed to be true.)

- A second group, led by scientists such as Tycho Brahe and Francis Bacon, favored the inductive method. They believed that the scientist should gather data from experiments and observations. On the basis of this data (the particulars), he could make a **hypothesis** which could then be tested by himself or others. Eventually, it should be possible for scientists to arrive at **conclusions**.

- A third scientific approach was the mathematical *deductive method*. This point of view was very much dependent on the ideas of **Plato**. He had believed that the important details of the universe could be explained by mathematical proofs. Under his influence, mathematics became more important than experiments in Greek science. Copernicus, **Johannes Kepler**, and **Galileo** were all interested in the mathematical deductive approach to nature. Under a deductive system, one draws a conclusion about a particular thing on the basis of a general principle or given universal premise. To Platonists, mathematics provided the overall general truth, from which one could deduce ideas about nature.

Tycho Brahe. Because the inductive method was a new approach, it should be considered more closely. One of its supporters, **Tycho Brahe**, came from the high nobility of Denmark. Through the **patronage** of **King Frederick II** in 1576, he built a fantastic castle observatory on an island off the coast of Denmark. Called **Uraniborg** (the Castle of Heaven), it became a center of science and learning for all Europe. The observatory was the first advanced research institute and served as a model well into the twentieth century.

Brahe developed some of the ideas of Copernicus through careful observation. He designed enormous measuring instruments so that he could gain the highest possible accuracy. Unlike Copernicus, who studied ancient astronomers and

Tycho Brahe at his observatory on the island of Hven (1587)

worked with mathematics, Brahe spent his time searching the heavens.

Brahe worked out a theory of the universe in which the Earth stood still at the center with the Sun and Moon revolving around it. However, he had the five then-known planets revolving around the Sun. His theory appealed to many. It kept much of the Copernican system without the troublesome idea of an orbiting, rotating Earth.

Brahe also observed a new comet in 1577 which caused him to reject the idea of crystal-like spheres. He was the first person since the ancient Greeks to make major improvements in the way astronomers did their work. He gained greater accuracy than any astronomer before him.

Francis Bacon. The other leading advocate of inductive science was an English lawyer, states-

man, and philosopher—**Francis Bacon** (1561–1626). He urged scientists to forsake Aristotelian thought. In this, he reflected the ideas of an earlier thinker by the same name, the thirteenth century Oxford scientist, **Roger Bacon**, who had encouraged firsthand experimentation with the world rather than merely poring over the works of antiquity in search of truth. To progress in science one should observe and experiment, Francis Bacon said, restating Roger Bacon's outline of the basic idea of the modern scientific method. The latter Bacon observed, "For as all works do shew forth the power and skill of the workman… so it is of the works of God; which do shew the omnipotency and wisdom of the maker." Francis Bacon did not see the need for making hypotheses the basis for scientific investigation. Nor did he understand the importance of mathematics.

Bacon's main contribution was as a scientific theorist, rather than a practical experimenter. His writings were laced with moralizations and principles to which he felt men needed to be guided for correct scientific procedures. Bacon felt that scientists of the past had wasted too much energy in gathering isolated bits and pieces of information, without developing sound scientific theories to go with these data. He said true scientists must go to nature for raw material and to learn nature's lessons, but these then must be harnessed into workable methods. Furthermore, he urged scientists to use their knowledge to give men happier and more productive lives. "The true and lawful goal of the sciences is none other than this: that human life be endowed with new discoveries and power," he said. This concept led society to think in terms of material progress, an idea that has played a major role since the nineteenth century.

Francis Bacon attacked the scholasticism of Aristotle and Aquinas, believing that nature should be understood by inductive reasoning. In his book **Novum Organum**, he developed a new scientific method, and sought to rebuild all knowledge on the new plan. The ship, displayed on the title page, represents human knowledge going beyond the limits of the mediaeval thinking, with a limitless optimism.

The Struggle for Change

Despite Luther's disparaging remarks about the views of Copernicus, a number of Lutherans took the lead in promoting his ideas. In 1539 one of Melanchthon's students, Georg Rheticus, a professor of mathematics at Wittenberg, visited Copernicus, and became convinced that he was right. He published a report of his findings which led the way for acceptance of these ideas among Lutheran Protestantism. In fact, the Lutheran theologian Osiander wrote a preface to the first edition of Copernicus work, *De Revolutionibus Orbium Coelestium* (1543). Other teachers such as Caspar Cruciger and Erasmus Reinhold, both colleagues of Luther came to support it. But it was Johannes Kepler who championed it.

Johannes Kepler. A quarrel with the Danish court interrupted Tycho Brahe's work and forced him to take employment with the Holy Roman emperor. Moving his equipment and materials from Uraniborg, he spent his last years at the alchemical-astrological institute in Prague. Lamentably, he died before completing his theories. However, his brilliant helper, **Johannes (John) Kepler** (1571–1630), carried on his projects.

As a German Lutheran professor of astronomy, Kepler served **Emperor Rudolf II** for a time. Although he was somewhat inclined toward mysticism, Kepler believed strongly that the universe was created by God and followed divinely constructed mathematical principles in its operation. He believed that God guided him in his studies. In *The Harmonies of the World* (1619), he offered this soaring hymn of praise to God:

> Thou Who dost by the light of nature promote in us the desire for the light of grace, that by its means Thou mayest transport us into the light of glory, I give thanks to Thee, O Lord Creator, Who has delighted me with Thy makings and in the works of Thy hands have I exulted…. [T]o the men who are going to need these demonstrations, I have made manifest the glory of Thy works, as much of its infinity as the narrows of my intellect could apprehend… Great is our Lord and great His virtue and of His wisdom there is no number: praise Him, ye heavens, praise Him, ye sun, moon, and planets; use every sense for perceiving, every tongue for declaring your Creator. Praise Him, ye celestial harmonies; praise Him, ye judges of the harmonies uncovered…and thou my soul, praise the Lord thy

Kepler demonstrated the elliptical orbits of planets in his book *New Astronomy* (1609).

Creator, as long as I shall be: for out of Him and through Him and in Him are all things…. To Him be praise, honor, and glory, world without end. Amen.

Kepler tried to find some way to make Copernicus's ideas and Brahe's observations fit together. Brahe had kept more complete records of planetary movements than anyone else. As Kepler studied these records, he made a great discovery. A planet did not move in a circle about the Sun, but rather in an **ellipse**. This fact became Kepler's **First Law of Planetary Motion**. His **Second Law** had to do with the fact that a planet does not move at the same speed all the time, as had been supposed. Instead it moves faster as it nears the Sun and slower as it goes away. All observations seemed to fit these laws. The small circles and the off-center spheres of earlier theories were no

longer needed. The circle no longer served as the basis of cosmic movement. Still Kepler was not satisfied. He searched for a principle of order that would explain planetary movement. In 1619, after years of study, he announced his **Third Law**. It stated, in mathematical formula, that the time it takes any planet to revolve around the Sun depends on its distance from the Sun.

Kepler's laws have stood the test of time. In fact, physicists have found that his ideas describe the movement of atomic particles around nuclei. His influence extended far beyond astronomy and physics. His use of mathematics established it as the basis for expressing the laws of physical science. Above all, he began the search for a single law, which could be expressed mathematically, to explain the motion of the universe.

Kepler continued to ponder the problem of why the planets move. He read a book by an English physician, **William Gilbert**, who, after experimenting with magnets and compasses, had decided that the center of the Earth was a huge magnet. His theory led Kepler to think that a magnetic force from the Sun drove planets in their own orbits. It was an interesting explanation for planetary motion, but it was wrong. Before scientists could find the right answer, they needed to know more about motion. The great Italian scientist, **Galileo Galilei** (1564–1642), filled in this knowledge gap.

Galileo Galilei. Only a small group of scholars knew of the new discoveries, for Copernicus and Kepler wrote in Latin. In fact, most of the books written in Europe before 1620 were in Latin. Only a few people could read them. Even this tiny group, trained by the church or in the new Latin schools, would have had trouble following the mathematics of Copernicus and Kepler. It was the fate of Galileo to make the new astronomy clear to a much larger audience, and upon

Ahead of His Times

Johannes Kepler was a man ahead of his times. He predicted human space flight and resolved to have sky maps ready for this purpose. His book, *The Dream*, is considered by some to be the first example of modern science fiction. In a time of religious wars and hatred, he believed in tolerance of others' beliefs.

Kepler contributed greatly to the Scientific Revolution. He found better ways to use mathematics in problem-solving, designed a valveless water pump, suggested that air has weight, and most important, laid the foundation for modern astronomy with his laws of planetary motion. Yet Kepler did not take all the credit for these achievements, as shown in this excerpt from a biography of the scientist.

"With refreshed spirit, Johannes took up again the old Nemesis of Mars's orbit. He plunged into fresh calculations....

"He solved the orbit of Mars—not after eight days as he boasted, but after six years. Yet he solved it all the same. He showed that Mars traveled in an elliptical orbit with the sun as one of the focus points.

"After a little while he proved the other planets traveled in elliptical orbits as well. In the other cases, however, the orbits differed only slightly from perfect circles. It would have been difficult to discover the true nature of their orbits.

"'Was it chance that I began on Mars?' Johannes wondered. No other planet would have led him to the truth. 'No, it was the hand of God that guided me to work on the very planet best able to reveal the secret.'"

From John Tiner, *Johannes Kepler* (Milford, Mich.: Mott Media, 1977)

his head fell the wrath of the Roman Catholic hierarchy. While Protestantism was receptive to Copernicus, Roman Catholicism became a powerful opponent.

Galileo was born in Pisa in 1564 of a noble family. After teaching mathematics at the universities of Pisa and Padua, he took a position at the court of the **Duke of Tuscany, Cosimo II de' Medici**. Galileo had a great ability to work on a problem and come to the right answer without doing actual experiments. (Contrary to legend, he never dropped light and heavy weights from the Leaning Tower of Pisa.)

Galileo did not fully trust observation. He felt that a person should not depend on his senses, but rather upon rational understanding of the laws of the universe as demonstrated through mathematical models and formulas. Because he believed that mathematics held the key to the universe, he felt that the Copernican system was right. Mass and motion were the twin concepts that explained nature to man. Both were to be expressed with geometry. As he put it:

> Philosophy is written in the great book which ever lies before our eyes—I mean the universe—but we cannot understand it if we do not first learn the language and grasp the symbols in which it is written. The book is written in the mathematical language, and the symbols are triangles, circles, and other geometrical figures, without whose help it is impossible to comprehend a single word of it.

Galileo learned of the developments in lens grinding made in The Netherlands. With this knowledge, he built the first telescope. Turning it upon the heavens, he discovered Jupiter's four moons. He studied Earth's Moon and found it was made of the same substance as the Earth. It had no light of its own. He discovered moving spots on the Sun, showing that it turned on its axis. These details, which he presented in a book, could not be accounted for by Ptolemy's theory.

Now, thanks to the telescope, Galileo found the evidence that the planets move around the Sun.

The pope denounced the Copernican theory as, "false and in all points antithetical to Holy Scripture." Galileo was charged with heresy and taken into custody by the papal authorities. Here, Galileo stands before the Court of Inquisition in 1633.

Nor were the heavenly bodies made of a crystal-like substance, pure and perfect. The Sun had spots; the Moon had craters; and the planets seemed to be made of the same thing as the Earth. Nature must be the same in the heavens as it is on Earth, concluded Galileo. Therefore, whatever makes things move on the Earth must also cause heavenly bodies to move.

Galileo put aside Aristotle's idea of motion and the church's teaching that angels continued to guide heavenly objects. Through experiments he showed that moving objects on Earth obey mathematical laws. The same is true in the heavens, he claimed.

In 1632, he published his *Dialogue Concerning the Two Chief Systems of the World, the Ptolemaic and the Copernican*. Written in Italian, rather than Latin, the book criticized current Thomistic (Thomas Aquinas) astronomy. Galileo used dialogue in such a way that it made the medieval astronomy and its supporters look stupid. Although Galileo had powerful friends, his dialogues greatly upset many Roman Catholic theologians and leading Jesuit scholars. He was brought before their **Inquisition** and forced to deny his beliefs. His book was banned, and he spent the rest of his life under house arrest.

While some Roman Catholic churchmen felt Galileo was making mathematical law, rather than God, responsible for universal motion, the existence of mathematical law did not rule out God. That was how Galileo himself saw it. To him, these laws "brought clear testimony of a Lawgiver." In 1610, he wrote to a friend at court, "I give thanks to God, who has been pleased to make me the first observer of marvellous things unrevealed to bygone ages." Galileo found the human mind to be God's finest creation and an instrument for comprehending all of God's other creative works.

The Roman Catholic church could have accepted mathematical law as a description of the way God worked, but its commitment to the scholasticism of Aquinas prohibited this. The Roman Catholics were committed to their views on the basis of human tradition. This traditionalism led them to maintain the old Aristotelian/Ptolemaic view. But this dependence on human tradition can swing both ways. While the older humanism had the upper hand in Romanism of the seventeenth century, by the twentieth century the Jesuit Pierre Teilhard de Chardin advocated the synthesis of the evolutionary hypothesis with Christian theology. Roman Catholic thought has always sought to make Christianity a supplement to humanism.

René Descartes. One seventeenth century thinker who developed the non-Christian view of

science was **René Descartes** (1596–1650). Trained by the Jesuits in France, he was both the father of Rationalism and a mathematician. He sought in mathematics a model for man and the whole universe. His famous *Discourse on Method* (1637) revealed his rationalistic faith. The **Cartesian Method** saw a universe of objects independent of God, capable of being studied with an independent mind. He did not see God as the foundation of the universe or existence, but rather he saw man's reason as that foundation. He conceived of the universe as a great machine ruled by mathematical laws. In place of the formulation, "God created me, therefore I am," Descartes uttered his famous, "I think, therefore I am." In addition to his humanistic philosophical work, he conducted much empirical research. He is considered the father of analytical geometry, although he was not the first to consider the links between algebra and geometry. He contended that mathematics was the one discipline capable of expressing scientific ideas with full clarity.

The Synthesis of Isaac Newton

Copernicus, Kepler, and Galileo each discovered new knowledge about the universe. They directed their efforts at challenging the classical Thomistic outlook. It remained for one man of genius to pull together, or synthesize, all the strands of the new science. **Isaac Newton** (1642–1727) discovered the basic laws of nature explaining the motion of the entire universe, what we call the area of physics.

Born the same year Galileo died, he was the son of an English farmer, Newton would have followed his father's profession. However, as a young

Peter Ramus and the Puritans

Peter Ramus (1515–1572) was a leading opponent in France of the Aristotelianism of Aquinas. His thesis was "Whatever is affirmed from Aristotle is contrived." In 1561 he was converted to Protestantism but was killed in the massacre of St. Bartholomew's Day in 1571. His stress upon a practical approach to logic and the importance of knowledge from experience appealed to the English Puritans. He defined logic as a tool of demonstration rather than an abstract idea. His writings were particularly studied at Cambridge University in England and Harvard College in New England. The University of Cambridge became a center of Ramism in the 16th century when William Temple, Dudley Fenner, and George Downham lectured on Ramism. John Milton was deeply influenced by this philosophy as well, and published a book on it. In Germany, at the Reformed University of Herborn, the Ramist Johann Heinrich Alsted (1599–1638) wrote his *Encyclopedia Septem Tomis Distincta* (1630), which attempted an encyclopedia of all areas of thought from a Christian point of view. This work was very influential in New England and was endorsed by Cotton Mather as the best guide to all the sciences. The practical and experimental bent of English and American Puritanism provided the cultural basis for English speaking countries to lead the way in both scientific discovery and industrial innovation.

man, he showed an extraordinary interest in science. He enrolled at Cambridge University in 1661, where at the age of 27 he became professor of mathematics. Cambridge was the center of Puritan thought, having stressed the experimental method. The influence of Bacon as well as the philosophy of Peter Ramus, a Huguenot, had laid the groundwork for the stress upon inductive experiment. This Protestant environment was very favorable for scientific development.

An Eccentric Genius. Born in obscurity, Newton rose to fame as a genius of the highest order. In his time, his views of the universe became accepted in Europe as the final word. He was nearly worshipped by some. The Enlightenment English poet, Alexander Pope, penned a witty famous line suggesting that Newton was God's first creation. The German Gottfried Leibnitz wrote, "Taking mathematics from the beginning of the world to the time when Newton lived, what he did was much the better half."

Newton's genius had an **eccentric** twist. He could put his studies aside for years. But when he picked them up again, he could so lose himself in thought that he would wander toward his college dining hall, become distracted, and then return to work unaware that he had not yet eaten. He had to be forced to finish his task. When rivals claimed to have solved scientific problems before him, or when friends, such as **Edmund Halley**, encouraged him to finish his book, only then would Newton finally go back to work. Once Halley discovered that Newton had worked out precise calculations and had mislaid them while others were frantically trying to do what he had forgotten.

The story about an apple hitting Newton on the head, causing him to develop his theory of gravity, likely is not true. But it shows how legends tend to grow around famous people. Even Newton, the careful scientist, indulged in fancy at times. In some of his unpublished studies are wild speculations, but his published work contained only hypotheses which can be proved. One wonders how he could combine imagination and accuracy in the right amounts for his major work. Yet this proud, eccentric, suspicious man produced a picture of the physical universe accepted for generations. His worldview remains scientific truth for most people today. Scientists still consider it correct for all but the very small and the very fast **phenomena** in nature.

Law of Gravity and Laws of Motion. Newton did nearly all of his work in astronomy. In 1665 and 1666, the plague forced him to leave Cambridge for his home. There he tried a series of mathematical experiments with motion. He brought together Kepler's ideas of planetary movement and Galileo's view of motion on Earth. The result was the **universal law of gravity.** Newton showed that the same force, gravity, causes planets to stay in their heavenly orbits and objects to fall to the ground on Earth. All parts of the universe—stars, Moon, Sun, and planets— obey the same law of gravity.

His proof for the new theory depended on demonstrating that the Moon moves toward the Earth at the same rate as a body falling to Earth, 16 feet per second. (Even though the Moon moves toward the Earth, it never falls into the

Newton's work in astronomy won such acclaim that it has overshadowed his other achievements. Through his many experiments with light he was one of the founders of modern optical science.

Earth because its momentum carries it on past.) Because correct figures to work out his proof were not available for several years, he did not publish his findings until 1687.

The *Principia*, as the book is called, demonstrated the law of gravity in relation to the planets. Newton also defined **force, momentum**, and **inertia** with exact mathematics. Furthermore, the book showed that the pull of the Moon and the Sun causes tides on Earth, that the Earth and other planets are flattened at their poles, and that the path of comets can be traced because they are under the Sun's influence. His **Three Laws of Motion** were:

◆ A body will continue to be in a state of rest or of uniform velocity unless acted upon by an external force.

◆ The acceleration produced in a body of mass is in direct proportion to the force applied.

◆ Whenever two bodies experience an interaction, the force of the first body on the second is equal and opposite to the force of the second body on the first.

Scientific Methods and Tools. Newton established the methods of much of modern science. *First,* he insisted on experimental observation. He was suspicious of general ideas and felt that, whenever possible, they should be tested by experiments. He was wary of "hypotheses," by which he meant metaphysical imaginings untested by experiment. *Second,* he believed in simplicity. When several valid explanations for a phenomenon exist, one should accept the simplest. A *third* method was his great use of mathematics. The universal law of gravity is a mathematical formula—the product of the masses and the square of the distance between them. Using experimental observation and mathematics together has proven highly successful for science.

Newton could use mathematics to a greater extent than scientists before him because of the progress made during the seventeenth century. In 1600, Roman numerals were still commonly used. Modern symbols for multiplication, division, and addition did not yet exist. By 1700, a virtual explosion of mathematical knowledge had changed all this. One after another, decimals, logarithms, analytical geometry, and the laws of probability came into use. Arabic numerals and the base-10 decimal system came to Europe by way of Muslim scholars from Hindu India, as did positional notation, the number zero, and negative numbers.

To arrive at the law of gravity, Newton created a new mathematical tool—calculus. (It was also developed independently by Leibnitz.) Nearly every philosopher or thinker had to be a mathematician. One seventeenth-century writer explained that any book—whether on theology, history, philosophy, or physics—would be better if its author knew mathematics.

Not everyone accepted Newton's work right away. But he did not experience the same sort of opposition that Galileo had faced. Between 1633 and 1687, most educated people had accepted the heliocentric theory and the mathematical description of the universe. However, the followers of Descartes refused to believe Newton's ideas. Descartes used methods of geometry to solve problems in other branches of learning. Descartes' followers believed that the world was a machine with a physical, material cause for planetary movement. Because Newton had only offered them a mysterious force, gravity, they did not accept his synthesis until well into the eighteenth century.

Other scholars found that Newton had replaced God with nature. Some said that a belief in gravity made the universe into a cold, heartless machine. The universal law of gravity, many realized, answered only part of the question. It explained *how* the universe worked, not *why*.

Despite these criticisms, Newton's ideas were accepted. His laws were universal, applying to the heavens above and the earth below. It amazed and delighted people. Voltaire wrote that Newton had taught men to "examine, weigh, calculate and measure, but never to conjecture.... He saw, and made people see; but he didn't put his fancies in place of truth." For 25 years, Newton presided over that select body, **The Royal Society of London for Improving Natural Knowledge**.

Newton was always ready to defend his theories against critics, but he was the first to admit that he did not always *understand* what his observations and proofs told him were true.

Historian Peter Gay has evaluated Newton's impact in this way:

These two consequences of Newton's work—confidence in the scientific method and modesty about man's capacity to know—appear at first to be contradictory. But they do come together, and it is precisely where they join that the energy for the Enlightenment arose. Newtonian thought meant, first of all, that only patient and skeptical inquiry could produce reliable results. The vaulting philosophical systems of the 17th Century metaphysicians, and the improbable tales of saints and miracle- workers, were equally suspect and equally useless.

Second, Newtonian thought meant that the scientific method could, with care, be applied to nonscientific disciplines—to theology, history, morals, politics. Third, Newtonian thought meant that men did not have to concern themselves with airy fantasies about first causes, but could instead concentrate their intellectual energies on practical problems, on improving man's lot in this world. This is how

the *Philosophes* understood Bacon: thinking, they said, must bear useful fruit; talk must be to some practical purpose.

Newton would have been deeply shocked by some of the conclusions the *Philosophes* reached using his scientific method. He would have despised the deists, who turned God into a master mechanic, and would have been outraged by the atheists, who denied Him altogether.

In the third edition of his *Principia*, Newton explained that the true source of the beautiful and orderly system of the universe was the "counsel and dominion of an intelligent and powerful Being" who governs all things, not as the "Soul of the World, but as Lord over all." He continued with words which, in effect, deny that God was anything like the deists' mechanical deity or the naturalistic, pantheistic god of Rousseau:

The Supreme God is a Being eternal, infinite, absolutely perfect.... And from his true dominion it follows that the true God is a living, intelligent, and powerful Being; and, from his other perfections, that he is supreme, or most perfect. He is eternal and infinite, omnipotent and omniscient; that is his duration reaches from eternity to eternity; his presence from infinity to infinity; he governs all things, and knows all things that are or can be done.... We know him only by his most wise and excellent contrivances of things [*in this statement, Newton was not reflecting orthodox Christianity, which also speaks of revelation as the key source of knowledge about God—GJM*], and final causes; we admire him for his perfections; but we reverence and adore him on account of his dominion: for we adore him as his servants; and a god without dominion, providence, and final causes, is nothing else but Fate and Nature.

Nevertheless, Newton may have unwittingly helped promote the secularization of natural science by his belief in the neutrality of human reason and perception. In combining the inductive method of Bacon with the mathematical method his system did not clearly stress the providence of God in maintaining the universe and the laws by which He governs it. God was needed more as an explanation of the origin of things than for its present order. According to R. E. D. Clarke, Newton was an Anglican, but held to an Arian view of Christ, which denied his deity and stressed his created human nature. This was an essential part of Deism. Because we find both biblical and unbiblical ideas in his thinking, the Christian needs to show discernment in evaluating his ideas.

When Newton died he was buried with full honors in Westminster Abbey. He had made his countrymen proud to be English.

The Transformation of Medicine

Ancient Authorities. While some men explored astronomy and physics, others probed the mysteries of the human body, of chemistry, and of biology. According to ancient theories, the body was made up of blood, phlegm, black bile, and yellow bile. These, it was thought, corresponded to the four qualities of the universe—heat, cold, dryness, and moistness—and must be in balance for a person to have good health. The proper treatment for any illness was bloodletting (drawing blood from the patient).

Galen, Hippocrates, and Aristotle—ancient Greek physicians or thinkers—taught a simple view of the human body. Galen, for example, thought that one kind of blood flowed through the liver and the veins to the body, while another kind flowed from the heart through the arteries.

Although he was right about the flow of blood, he did not know that the heart pumped it or that the blood comes back to the heart.

It is strange that Galen's views were not questioned sooner. Renaissance surgeons practiced **dissection** (cutting a body into its separate parts for study). Apparently their respect for Greek ideas was so great that when they found something that disagreed with the ancient master, they assumed that they were wrong. Presuppositions can indeed be powerful.

Anatomy. What the study of anatomy needed was careful observation and an open mind. Renaissance artists and scholars brought both to the field. Painters studied human anatomy carefully so that they might show the smallest details correctly. Some of them, such as **Leonardo da Vinci**, even dissected human bodies. They made careful drawings of what they saw. Later, they published their findings so that scholars could study them.

As they read more of the classical medical texts discovered during the Renaissance, European scholars found that the ancients had disagreed with one another. That gave sixteenth century scholars the courage to challenge Galen, as Copernicus had challenged Ptolemy on astronomy. **Andreas Vesalius**, a professor at the University of Padua, was the first to contribute important new knowledge to anatomy.

Even as a schoolboy, Vesalius showed great curiosity about the structure of the body. He dissected bodies of mice, rats, dogs, and cats. At the university, he studied with some of the best doctors of his time. But Vesalius was disappointed to learn that everything his teachers knew came from Galen's ideas. They had done little or no dissection to gain firsthand knowledge.

Andreas Vesalius, 1514–1564

Vesalius began looking in cemeteries for skeletons to study. Once he took a corpse down from the gallows in the middle of the night in order to examine it. He did many dissections. In 1543, he published a book with illustrations correctly showing human veins and arteries. Occasionally, he disagreed with Galen's facts, but on the whole he did not challenge the ancient writer's theory. Vesalius made dissection a necessary part of the study of anatomy. He brought the inductive method to the field, much as astronomers had brought a new approach to their study.

William Harvey, an English physician, took the most important step toward a modern view of anatomy. By experiments with living animals, he discovered how the blood circulates. In 1628, he published a book which explained that the heart pumped blood through the arteries. Then the blood returned through the veins. However, he was never able to find out how the blood got from the arteries to the veins.

In 1660, an Italian, **Marcello Malpighi**, discovered the capillaries with his microscope. He saw that they connected the arteries and the veins—thus supplying the missing link in Harvey's system. A Dutch lens grinder, **Anton van Leeuwenhoek**, confirmed Malpighi's findings and also discovered the corpuscles in blood. This find was the final link proving the modern view of the circulation of the blood. Leeuwenhoek had finally laid to rest the medieval notion about the four elements that make up the body.

For the most part, these men only collected and observed data. They did not form theories to account for their discoveries. Perhaps in many fields of science, it would be impossible to find laws that apply in the same general way that the universal laws of gravity apply to astronomy and physics.

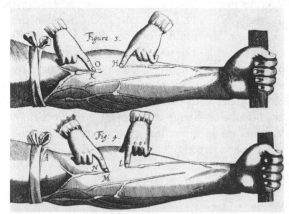

In this illustration from his book, ***Movement of the Heart and Blood***, William Harvey showed that blood passes through valves of the veins in the arm in only one direction.

Doctors. However, one man did try to find a universal law of disease. **Benjamin Rush**, an early American medical scientist, became professor of medicine at the University of Pennsylvania in 1792. He taught a single and consistent system of medicine based on the idea that there was only one disease.

'Wretched Beasties'

Probably no other dry-goods dealer in seventeenth-century Holland spent his evenings the way Anton van Leeuwenhoek did. Night after night, he ground tiny glass lenses and then peered through them at everything he could find. The eye of an ox, the brain of a fly, the hair of a sheep, the muscle fiber of a whale, the scales of his own skin—all suddenly appeared unbelievably complex and awesome beneath his lens. In time Leeuwenhoek was making the best lenses in the world and through them viewing a world no man had ever seen before.

One day he placed a drop of water beneath his microscope and gasped in amazement at what he saw. Little animals were swimming about, animals a thousand times smaller than one could see with the naked eye. He had discovered microscopic life. Leeuwenhoek then found out that these "wretched beasties," as he called them even lived in his own mouth.

Because Leeuwenhoek was uneducated, he had little knowledge of science or of the significance of his findings. They might have gone unnoticed had it not been for a fellow townsman who was a corresponding member of England's Royal Society. That learned group heard of the Dutchman's discoveries and were so impressed that they made him a member, an honor usually given only to scholars and geniuses. Though far from brilliant, Leeuwenhoek showed what one can achieve through the exercise of unlimited curiosity, patience, and determination.

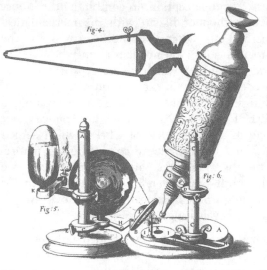

This early microscope belonged to Robert Hooke, who was in charge of experimental work for London's Royal Society.

As he told his students: "I have formerly said that there was but one fever in the world. Be not startled, Gentlemen; follow me and I will say that there is but one disease in the world. The cause of disease is irregular, convulsive, or wrong action in the system affected."

He prescribed the same treatment doctors had used since medieval times—bloodletting and enemas. These would reduce the convulsive action by a process of exhaustion. During his lifetime, the world hailed him as the Newton of medicine. However, thirty years after his death, it called him a fool.

Regrettably, the medical world did not make use of the excellent work of Harvey and Vesalius. Of course, certain outstanding doctors tried to treat disease in a more scientific way. One of these, **Sanctorius**, was a friend of Galileo. Sanctorius invented medical instruments, such as the fever thermometer, to measure the symptoms of disease. He designed scales to weigh people because he was convinced that weight affected health.

Another creative doctor was Englishman **Thomas Sydenham**, who lived in the middle 1600s. He assumed that there were many diseases and described the symptoms, causes, and course of various ills. He analyzed fevers, gout, hysteria, and measles. Dr. Sydenham prescribed rest, care, and beer for his patients. Why these? Well, why not? The doctor had noticed that the poor, who did not receive medical care, used these remedies and they often survived; whereas the rich, who got medical attention, usually died. However, Dr. Sydenham did make a lasting contribution to the practice of medicine. He pioneered in the use of drugs such as laudanum and quinine.

One can see that not much came of all the anatomical and medical research. Not until the nineteenth century discovery of bacteria's role in causing disease did medical practice really

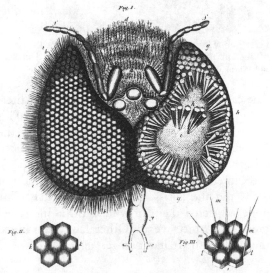

Jan Swammerdam, a Dutch naturalist, was possibly the greatest comparative anatomist of the 17th century. His *Bible of Nature* included a study of the anatomy of the honeybee.

improve. Before that time, it was common for women and infants to die in childbirth. Epidemics broke out frequently.

Chemistry. Aristotle's physics taught that the world was made up of earth, air, fire, and water. However, one ancient writer named **Democritus** had a different idea. He thought that all substances were composed of tiny, solid atoms (corpuscles). Things did not look alike because the atoms were joined together differently in each object or being.

In the middle 1600s, **Robert Boyle** began to think that Democritus was right. His experiments on the **composition** of matter overturned the medieval view. Democritus had believed that atoms joined by chance, but Boyle and other seventeenth-century scientists felt that atoms acted according to certain mechanical laws. Since atoms occupied space and moved, they should be subject to law and mathematical description. Boyle also performed many valuable experiments with air and water. He is considered the father of modern chemistry. As a committed Christian, Boyle believed that science was God's "second book" of revelation, revealing His wisdom and glory.

Botany and Zoology. In botany and zoology, the Englishman **John Ray** laid the foundation of the modern sciences. He did not perform experiments, but he did classify thousands of plants and animals. His thorough, careful observations filled an impressive series of volumes published between 1686 and 1710. In them he described and classified plants, animals, fishes, and insects. His books gave the most complete and best-arranged survey of living nature ever to appear. Ray believed in technological progress. He also believed in a mechanical universe under divine guidance. When he applied these views to life science, he helped to end much of the myth and

A Great Surgeon

One of the outstanding surgeons of the sixteenth century, Ambroise Paré, contributed as much to the development of surgery as Vesalius did to anatomy. After he retired in Paris, many of the important people of France became his patients, including four monarchs. In the excerpt below, he describes how, as a young army doctor, he learned to dress gunshot wounds.

The soldiers within the castle, seeing our men come on them with great fury, did all they could to defend themselves, and killed and wounded many of our soldiers with pikes, guns and stones, whereby the surgeons had all their work cut out for them. Now I was at this time a new soldier; I had not yet seen gunshot wounds at the first dressing. I had read in Jean de Vigo, *Of Wounds in General*, that wounds made by firearms are poisoned by the gunpowder, and for their cure he bids you cauterize them with oil of elders, scalding hot, mixed with an antidote. And to make no mistake, before I would use this oil, knowing that it was to bring great pain to the patient, I asked first what the other surgeons did for the first dressing; which was to put the oil, boiling well, into the wounds; wherefore I took courage to do as they did. At last my oil ran short, and I was compelled, instead of it, to apply a mixture of egg yolk, oil of roses and turpentine. In the night I could not sleep, fearing I should find the wounded to whom I had not applied the oil, dead from the poison of their wounds; which made me rise very early to visit them; where, beyond expectation, I found that those to whom I had applied my mixture had little pain and their wounds without inflammation or swelling, having rested fairly well that night. The others, to whom the boiling oil was applied, I found feverish, with great pain, and swelling about the edges of their wounds. Then I resolved never more to burn thus cruelly poor men with gunshot wounds.

Adapted from Stephen Paget, *Ambroise Paré and His Times* (New York: G.P. Putnam's Sons, 1897)

mystery of that study. Ray laid the foundation for the Swedish taxonomist **Carolus Linnaeus**, who developed the modern system of classification.

Society and the New Science

Why did the flowering of science take place in the West and not elsewhere? To a large extent, the scientific drive must be attributed to Christianity, both directly and indirectly. For devout Christian scholars, the study of Scripture provided a sharp contrast to the writings of classical pagan thinkers. These Christian scholars developed an interest in probing God's Creation in search of truth in order to glorify Him better. We have seen some of their worshipful reactions earlier in this chapter. Others who were predisposed to reject biblical answers studied nature in search of discoveries which they hoped would overturn traditional interpretations by the Roman Catholic Church, many of which were indeed imaginative, erroneous, and superstitious. In this way, they hoped to discredit spiritual authority and advance the autonomy of mankind. In the end, however, it was the men of science equipped with a godly worldview who made the crucial discoveries, while men dedicated to ancient views continued to arrive at false conclusions.

There were also social reasons why scientific thinking spread faster in Europe. Many cultures rejected those who studied nature. In the Orient, religious beliefs included the view that the material world was evil or insignificant. Oriental man's goal was to rise above the material world and enter the higher world of spiritual light. By contrast, during the Scientific Revolution, an appreciation of science spread among Europe's educated upper class. Generally, those who

Van Kessel, in his *Still Life* (1618), shows the new interest in God's creation by Protestants in the Netherlands. Many Dutch paintings in the 17th century show a great attention to the details of creation. This reflects the Calvinistic idea that God, in His infinite wisdom, made every creature for His own purpose, and therefore each has a special value among His works.

accepted the new approach were leaders in public and private life. Some opposition to science did arise even among the **elite**. Some Catholic universities remained strongholds of medieval thought until the end of the seventeenth century. A few schools, like Padua, were exceptions.

Scientific Organizations. Because of the attitude of some universities, scientists were forced to form organizations to support their work. At first, they met in private homes to discuss their problems and wrote to those who lived too far away to attend. Later societies and academies were started.

The earliest academy was not scientific but literary and met in Florence in 1433 and 1443. This group studied the Italian language. Using the Florentine academy as a model, scientists started other academies in Naples (1560), Rome (1603), and Florence (1657). But these groups could not withstand the anti-scientific spirit in Italy. The pope suspected them of witchcraft. None lasted more than thirty years. Other lands continued the work of the Italian pioneers.

In London, a number of scholars interested in Francis Bacon's work began meeting together in 1645. Called the **Philosophical College**, they did experiments and held scientific discussions. Most of the members of the college were Puritans, whose view of the world as the Kingdom of God spurred them to investigate the creation. In 1662, they were instrumental in forming The Royal Society of London for Improving Natural Knowledge. Prominent early members of the Royal Society included **Isaac Newton**, architect **Christopher Wren**, physics pioneer **Robert Hooke**, and chemist **Robert Boyle**.

Government Support. Kings and governments became interested in the new discoveries. They founded and financed scientific societies and laboratories. Some rulers appointed court scientists and mathematicians. The **Royal Observatory** was begun at Greenwich, England, in 1675. **Jean Baptiste Colbert** (see chapter 2) directed the founding of the **French Academy of Science** in 1666. Its members received salaries from King Louis XIV and grants to cover research expenses. Members could do personal research or work on group projects suggested by Colbert. These included such ambitious tasks as drawing an accurate map of France. Taking decades to complete, the map required much surveying and the cooperation of **cartographers**, astronomers, and mathematicians. The French published a scientific journal and founded a royal observatory. The **English Royal Society** also published a scientific journal. These journals enabled scholars to exchange information far more effectively than by writing letters.

By the end of the seventeenth century scientific societies had appeared in most parts of Europe. **Peter the Great** was responsible for starting one in St. Petersburg. Even in Eastern Europe, science was becoming important.

Impact of the Societies. These societies did not solve all the problems or reach all the goals set for them. But they encouraged discoveries and gathered and spread information through lectures and publications. They organized the application of scientific research. In so doing, they prepared the way for new manufacturing techniques that brought the Industrial Revolution.

Many society members were professional scientists supported by patrons. Others were physicians, clergymen, and country gentlemen who dabbled at science in their spare time. Their presence lent an amateurish quality to the scientific discussion. However, knowledge was not as specialized as it is today, and experiments then did not require complex equipment. Many creative laymen, working only a few hours a week, made important discoveries. They and the societies to which they belonged did much to make science popular in Europe.

Contribution of the Craftsmen. But science could never have made its great gains without the cooperation between scholars and craftsmen. The instrument maker, the laboratory worker, and the scholar who formed theories from the data depended on one another. Metalworkers and other mechanics made Tycho Brahe's instruments. He used them with great skill, and Kepler interpreted the data.

The research "institute" that Brahe founded on his island off the Danish coast included carpenters, glass blowers, metalworkers, and other skilled craftsmen. During the seventeenth century, such craftsmen made a host of devices for experimentation and observation. There were pumps to take the air from a cylinder, globes of metal, glass tubes for thermometers and barometers, balance scales to measure weight, clocks to record time, and lenses for telescopes and microscopes. The work of these craftsmen enabled scientists to make their discoveries.

Dr. Pieter Paaw performs an anatomy lesson at the University of Leiden (1616). Students from all over Europe came to this Protestant university to study medicine. Hermannus Boerhaave (1668–1738) became the leading teacher of medicine in his day, and a fellow of the Royal Society of London. His students helped create schools of medicine in London and Edinburgh.

Impact of Science. If society helped science, science also helped society. Science showed people the need to be precise and accurate. Geographers, economists, and military writers worked more carefully. Property owners, tax collectors, and diplomats were aided by the more accurate maps produced. Statistics were applied to economics and other social institutions. Dutch businessmen

Science—the Latest Fad

Awed and impressed by the new science, eighteenth-century society took an almost fanatic interest in the steady progression of scientific discoveries. In London coffee-houses and Paris salons, people exchanged news about the latest findings. It became fashionable to decorate one's home or study with scientific apparatus and to adopt a scientific hobby. The Marquise de Pompadour, mistress of Louis XV of France, gave her spare hours to astronomy; Ben Franklin experimented with electricity; Samuel Johnson with chemistry; and England's George III with botany. Public scientific demonstrations and lectures drew large crowds. The center of merriment at gala parties might be an enthusiastic group rubbing iron rods and giving one another electric shocks.

Even in that masculine world, women entered heartily into the science craze, and some made scientific contributions. English writer Oliver Goldsmith commented on his visit to France, "I have seen as bright a circle of beauties at the chemical lectures of Rouelle as gracing the court of Versailles." The noted astronomer, William Hershel, taught his sister to keep records for him. In time, she became an astronomer in her own right, winning a number of honors. A Paris socialite named de Coigny was an amateur anatomist. The Marquise du Châtelet, Voltaire's mistress, wrote an essay on the nature of fire which the Academy of Science printed. More notably, she translated Newton's *Principia* into French, a task which required advanced knowledge of astronomy, gravitation, and mathematics. All this amateur activity, on the part of both women and men, contributed much to the advancement of science in its early days.

eries of the 17th century paved the way for the industrial transformation of the 18th century, particularly in England. The Protestant Reformation had extensive cultural results. Among these were a new understanding of the universe in such a way that man was now equipped to better subdue it for the glory of God.

Yet we should not forget that there were non-Christian ideas at work in this time. When the technical application of scientific detail affected everyone's daily living, some people began to feel that reality could only be carefully measured and described by numbers and experimentation. Others knew that the material world should be measured and understood without losing sight of the spiritual and intellectual world, which is also real, although it cannot be measured quantitatively. Science is one of many tools of knowledge; it is not a savior.

The scientist, the student of science, and the beneficiary of science would do well to remember that the findings of science are not absolute truth, even though nature is the Creation of an absolute and perfect God. Technology, being an endeavor of finite human hands, cannot solve all human problems or meet all human needs. Science, being an endeavor of finite human minds, can never reveal everything about reality. Reality also includes other forms of knowledge as well as things which the human mind does not yet understand and can never know. Reality also includes intangible things, matters of the heart and spirit which may or may not be affected by the material world. Scientists must also remember that nature itself bears the effects of God's curse against sin.

It is good to remember further that the so-called *laws of science* are descriptions by man of how the creation works. It would be better to replace the term *laws of science* with the *laws of Creation*.

A Theatre of the Marvels of Nature (1719), an early museum of natural history put together by Levinus Vincent, a Dutch collector and writer.

These divine laws mankind probably will never be able to plumb to their depths, since to know them exhaustively would require mankind to have the mind of God. Mankind, at best, can look into nature as though he were seeing "through a glass, darkly" (I Cor. 13:12). One day, redeemed Christian men and women who have been translated into their glorified eternal existence will no doubt understand God's creation more fully. In the meantime, science and technology should never be used by men in vain attempts to exceed their bounds as creatures and "play God" (Gen. 11:1-9).

used statistics to develop life insurance. Many European cities began to number houses rather than merely naming blocks. The scientific discov-

For your consideration

Questions

1. Discuss the relationship between science and religion—both false and true religion.

2. What is the difference between astrology and astronomy? Which follows scientific principles?

3. Discuss Aristotelian, inductive, and deductive reasoning. Describe the differences in these approaches to science.

4. Science is often seen as the way to material prosperity and the key to progress. Do you see any problems with this view? Discuss the relationship between science and technology.

5. Name some basic scientific equipment used in the sixteenth and seventeenth centuries. Name and describe the uses of any pieces of scientific equipment you have used.

6. Why does the text use the word totalitarian to describe the grip of science on the modern minds? Support your answer.

7. Evaluate the impact of Newton's discoveries about gravity, in his day and in modern times. How is gravity overcome? Under what conditions does it cease to have effect?

8. How do people today feel about researchers' use of animals, humans (including unborn humans) for dissection or experimentation? How do you feel about it?

9. How has science affected your life?

Projects

1. Draw or construct a model of the solar system according to Copernican theory.

2. The astronomers during this time knew of five planets (besides Earth). Name them and find out when they were discovered.

3. Do some research to find out about some of the experiments conducted by scientists mentioned in this chapter.

4. Take a field trip to a planetarium or science museum. Prepare for your trip by making a list of questions for which you would like to find answers.

5. Do some research on how Newton's three laws of motion apply to various modern technologies, such as space travel. Report on your findings.

6. Do some research on various modern approaches to medicine, including traditional medicine, naturopathy, homeopathy, oriental practices, osteopathy, and chiropractic. Present a report.

7. Write a report expanding the material in the text concerning Galileo's conflicts with the church. Discuss whether the conflict could have been avoided, and if so, why and how.

8. Most of the early pioneers in scientific development were men. Select the name of a woman who made early contributions to science. Give a report explaining why men led and what contribution the woman you selected made to science.

Word List

absolute	observations
experiments	scientific method
astronomy	astrology
planetary	geocentric
synthesis	heliocentric
cosmological	inductive method
patronage	deductive method
hypothesis	ellipse
armillary sphere	mysticism
totalitarian	eccentric
phenomena	inertia
dissection	composition
elite	cartographers
Cartesian Method	force
momentum	anatomy

People and Groups

Peter Abelard	Scholastics
Thomas Aquinas	Claudius Ptolemy
Nicholaus Copernicus	Aristarchus
Aristotle	Plato
Tycho Brahe	Johannes Kepler
Galileo Galilei	Roger Bacon
William Gilbert	Francis Bacon
René Descartes	Isaac Newton
Edmund Halley	Galen
Leonardo da Vinci	Hippocrates
Andreas Vesalius	Marcello Malpighi
A. van Leeuwenhoek	Benjamin Rush
Sanctorius	Thomas Sydenham
Democritus	Robert Boyle
John Ray	Robert Hooke
Philosophical College	Ambroise Paré
William Harvey	St. Augustine
Royal Society of London for Improving Natural Knowledge	

Tulipa globosa serotina aureo lote punctata.   *Tulipa globosa serotina cinnabrio colore.*

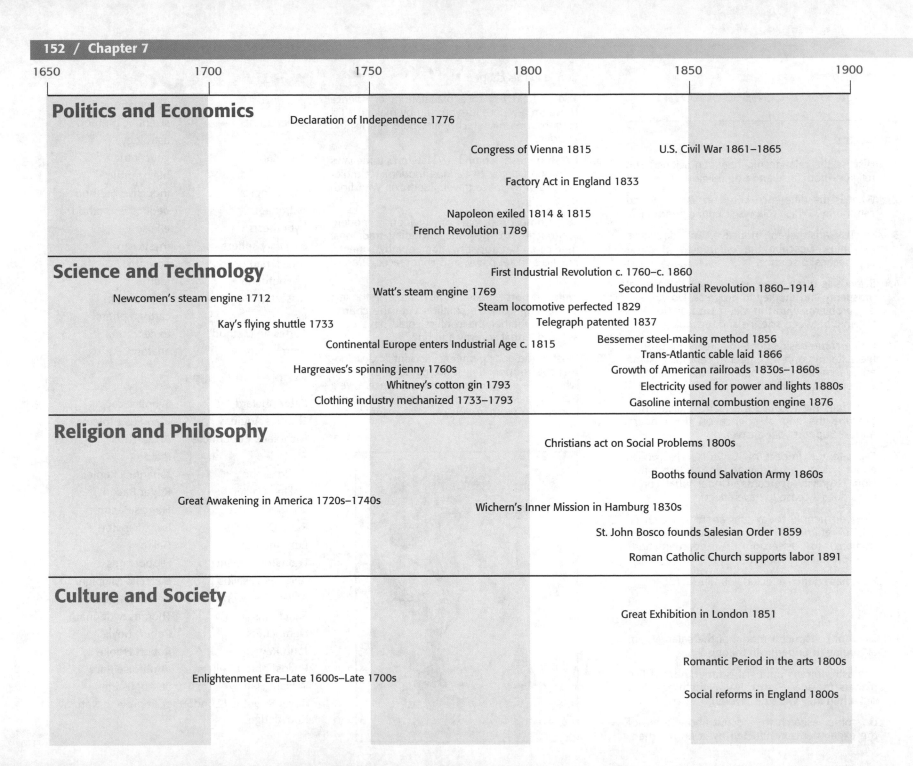

1650   1700   1750   1800   1850   1900

Politics and Economics

Declaration of Independence 1776

Congress of Vienna 1815   U.S. Civil War 1861–1865

Factory Act in England 1833

Napoleon exiled 1814 & 1815

French Revolution 1789

Science and Technology

First Industrial Revolution c. 1760–c. 1860

Newcomen's steam engine 1712   Watt's steam engine 1769   Second Industrial Revolution 1860–1914

Steam locomotive perfected 1829

Kay's flying shuttle 1733   Telegraph patented 1837

Continental Europe enters Industrial Age c. 1815   Bessemer steel-making method 1856

Trans-Atlantic cable laid 1866

Hargreaves's spinning jenny 1760s   Growth of American railroads 1830s–1860s

Whitney's cotton gin 1793   Electricity used for power and lights 1880s

Clothing industry mechanized 1733–1793   Gasoline internal combustion engine 1876

Religion and Philosophy

Christians act on Social Problems 1800s

Booths found Salvation Army 1860s

Great Awakening in America 1720s–1740s   Wichern's Inner Mission in Hamburg 1830s

St. John Bosco founds Salesian Order 1859

Roman Catholic Church supports labor 1891

Culture and Society

Great Exhibition in London 1851

Romantic Period in the arts 1800s

Enlightenment Era–Late 1600s–Late 1700s

Social reforms in England 1800s

Protestantism Spawns Industrial Progress

In the wake of the scientific discoveries of the 17th and 18th centuries, the Protestant West, especially Britain and the United States, led the world in an unprecedented level of industrial development. It was, to borrow the title of a Charles Dickens novel written during the period, an epoch of "Great Expectations." What had begun with a rediscovery of the word of God in the Reformation had been revived in the evangelical Great Awakenings in the 18th century. This had produced in England and the United States a people with a desire to be not only politically but economically free. This was manifest in a new spirit of innovation and entrepreneurialism.

For centuries prior to the scientific and technological revolution, daily life for the common man in Western Europe moved at the same sedate pace. Changes came slowly and seemed scarcely noticeable. The vast majority of people worked on farms or in small workshops in the town. Using simple tools, they tilled the soil and made by hand all the goods that people wanted. Energy to run the mills, pumps, spinning wheels, looms, forges, and plows of the time came from human and animal muscle. Levers, pulleys, moving water, and wind added force. As in ancient times, the products of these labors were often exchanged for other products. Only gradually did money come to be used in trade. The workmen, tradesmen, farmers—the vast majority of people—enjoyed few of the comforts we take for granted

In the 18th and 19th centuries the towns and cities of England and the United States were transformed by industrial enterprise.

today. Life for them was a day-to-day struggle for survival.

Then in the century between 1760 and 1860, the period of the evangelical awakenings, all this changed. The way the majority of people made their living, where they lived, and how they lived changed greatly. A person born in 1800 saw his

world altered more in his lifetime than it had been in the previous thousand years. So swift and so radical was this transformation that historians consider it a revolution—the **Industrial Revolution**. When the **Industrial Age** came, it ended the Roman Catholic medieval way of life permanently and laid the foundation for modern society. In many respects, the Industrial Revolution should be termed more precisely as the "Industrial Reformation."

Factors Leading to Industrial Reformation

England leads the way. The British forged ahead of other European nations in this industrial development. Geographically, Britain had a great advantage. No point on the island was more than 70 miles from the sea and excellent harbors existed on every coast. Because distances were short and few natural barriers stood in the way, canals and railroads could be built quickly and profitably. Rich deposits of coal, iron ore, and other minerals abounded, and the upper reaches of many rivers provided water power. Even the damp climate favored the making of cotton cloth, since the thread did not become brittle and break when woven by machines.

The **Commercial Reformation** of the previous two centuries had given the British the tools to make use of these natural advantages. Britain had built the largest merchant fleet in the world. It traded not only with the colonial empire in the New World, but also with the Baltic area, with the Turkish lands in the Mediterranean, with Africa, India, China, and with Spanish and Portuguese America. As a result, a large amount of investment capital built up in Britain. At the same time, an excellent banking system made it possible to channel unused funds into industry. The British experimented with more advanced forms of business organization, most notably the joint-stock company, or corporation, as it is called today. Trading in **securities** was a well-established practice from the beginning of the London Stock Exchange in 1698.

Financiers, Bankers and Stockbrokers

A spirit of inventiveness grew out of this expanding trade. In the 200 years before the Industrial Reformation, the techniques of smelting ores and making brass had greatly improved. Someone discovered that coke (coal baked at a high temperature to drive out gas and tar) could be used to produce iron. Coke became a cheap substitute for charcoal (made from wood). The demand for charcoal had been so high that several countries of Western Europe faced **deforestation**. Technological advances also took place in the cloth, glass-blowing, woodworking, brass-kettle, and clock-making industries. Inventions useful to scientific researchers, such as the thermometer and air pump, appeared in this period. Vastly improved clocks made it easier for seafarers to get their bearings.

Enclosure Acts and the End of Feudalism. British agriculture also saw many changes. Experiments with fertilizer, new crops, and crop rotation increased yields. Larger sheep and cows also increased the amount of available meat.

Greatest efficiency was obtained when landowners could make these improvements on large farms. In order to increase the size of their holdings, they had Parliament pass **Enclosure Acts**. These acts allowed them to fence in lands which had once been available to all the people of a village.

As time passed, improvements in agriculture made it possible for fewer workers to produce all the food needed by the whole population. Many ex-farmers became wage earners, working for landlords on farms or spinning and weaving cloth in their own cottages for town merchants. Some moved to factory towns seeking employment.

Mechanization of agriculture and other aspects of industrialization brought the ancient order of feudalism into disarray. Serfdom was being abolished. In England and France, feudalism was gone by the end of the 1700s. By the middle of the 19th century, it was largely a thing of the past in Europe and Russia. Unable to make a living on the land, the peasants (former serfs) were drawn to the towns and to the burgeoning new industries in search of a living. All across Europe—from England to Russia—rural residents poured into the new industrial centers, where their new freedom from toil on the land turned too often into freedom to starve. The old feudal order, despite its oppressiveness, had at least given the peasant class a fixed place in the social order and a source of provision in time of need. Now on their own and often without the education or social skills to order their own existence in an urban setting, many poor men floundered.

Other Factors. At the same time, Parliament repealed older laws allowing special monopolies and interference with trade. Businessmen were pretty well left to do as they pleased with their property. The landed upper class encouraged the pursuit of wealth, and new wealth provided funds

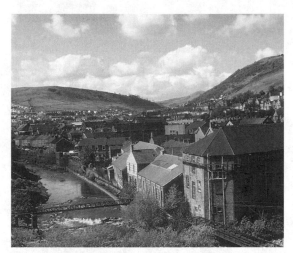

A view of the Rhondda Valley, north of Cardiff, the capital of Wales. Deeply influenced by the Evangelical Awakening, Wales supplied many of the raw materials and labor to contribute to the new industry of England.

for investment in business enterprises, thus creating jobs and income for additional workers. Increased wealth also enabled people to move up the social scale. Once an aristocracy of birth, the British nobility was becoming an aristocracy of wealth.

There was another factor which gave Britain an edge toward industrial progress. The great eighteenth-century wars and the French Revolution had sapped the strength of France, Britain's rival for mastery of the oceans. Although still fairly wealthy, France lacked the good system of tax collection and public finance that Britain had. Also, political corruption and a lavish court wasted French money. Because of its location, France had to keep a large army as well as navy, which further strained the national budget.

In 1750, France's foreign trade had been 25 percent larger than Britain's. Only a few years later, the loss of French territories in the Western Hemisphere and India to Britain had reversed their positions. British merchants now had larger

amounts of capital to invest in productive enterprises at home. These industries made more and cheaper goods for the new markets opening up in India and Spanish America.

The Effect of the Evangelical Awakening. England had the advantage of a strong Puritan heritage, which exalted work, profit, progress, and productivity. The Calvinistic "work ethic" frowned upon idleness and saw work as an act of obedience toward a provident God. Puritanism was also future-oriented, a fact which led to interest in long-term progress and long-term economic growth. With its emphasis on covenantalism, Puritanism encouraged the notion of full productivity from every member of the family. It also championed freedom and self-government, thus helping to overcome stifling government regulation of economic activity and the demoralizing influence of slavery. These Christian values were revived in the Evangelical Awakening in the days of Whitefield and Wesley. The influence of the Christian faith turned many from a life of carelessness, sloth, and drunkenness to a life of diligence and discipline. The practical bent of Puritanism, combined with the Evangelical Awakening, became a powerful influence that provided the unique social conditions that joined scientific innovation with industrial entrepreneurialism. Thus the economic life of England was eventually changed by the principles of the Reformation. Of course, these ideals were not always upheld, as greed, hunger for power, and sinful self-interest sometimes overpowered them. Though not every person was motivated by a living faith in Christ, the Puritan work ethic had become an entrenched force in the mind of Englishmen. Regrettably, some eventually lost the Puritan vision of work's godly purpose.

Shipped from such ports as New Orleans, the United States became one of England's suppliers of cotton which played a key role in the development of the new industry.

England Leads Industrial Reformation

A growing demand for textiles triggered the Industrial Reformation. At first, the British wore only woolen clothing. But then linen, silk, and, above all, cotton came on the market. Cotton goods from Asia, such as muslin and calico, so flooded England in the seventeenth century that the woolen cloth industry persuaded the government to ban the import of cotton cloth. Because cotton goods were cheaper and more comfortable than wool, the market for them continued to grow in Europe and Africa. British cotton manufacturers felt the pressure to increase output.

New Inventions. At the time, workers produced the cloth in their own homes. Merchants owned the raw materials and the equipment needed to spin, weave, and dye the cloth. They placed these items in the cottages of the peasants they employed and paid them wages. We call this method of producing goods the **domestic system** or **cottage industry**.

Recognizing the almost unlimited potential of the home market, clothmakers around Manchester and elsewhere in Lancashire (northern England) began experimenting with new processes. **John Kay** made the first breakthrough with his **flying shuttle** (1733), which sped up the weaving of cloth. Now looms could use thread faster than spinners could produce it. Prizes were offered for the invention of spinning machines.

In the 1760s, **James Hargreaves** invented the **spinning jenny** (named after his wife). This machine enabled a single worker to spin eight threads of yarn at once. In a few years, the machine was improved to turn out a thousand threads. As a result, hand-operated home spinning wheels all but disappeared.

At about the same time, Richard Arkwright invented a water frame, which used water power to run machines. Samuel Crompton combined the water frame and spinning jenny. Spinners

The mechanization of the cotton industry was accomplished by such inventions as the spinning jenny.

now far outproduced the weavers. The balance was again restored through the power loom invented by Edmund Cartwright. This loom could weave ten times as much cloth as a hand loom. So through the process of balance and imbalance, textile production became mechanized. An invention in one area necessitated an invention in another.

Raw Materials. These improvements in cloth manufacture put heavy pressure on producers of raw cotton. In 1793, an American, **Eli Whitney**, came up with a simple device to remove the seeds from cotton fibers—the cotton gin. This invention caused the **plantation culture** in the American South to expand rapidly. Before long, the Southern economy came to depend on the English Industrial Revolution.

Prior to that time, most cotton had come from the West Indies. The United States then became the chief supplier of this raw material. By 1830, three-quarters of the British cotton was grown on slave plantations of the Southern states. Plantations sprang up in the Gulf states and Mississippi Valley. The British textile industry made American slavery profitable.

Raw cotton imported into Britain increased 500 percent between 1790 and 1820. During the same period, cotton manufacturing became the leading industry and made up almost half of the country's exports.

Mechanization in this industry set the pattern for others. By producing large quantities of goods at a steadily lowering cost, cloth merchants broke free from dependence on the existing demand. They created their own market. And they showed businessmen that investing in manufacturing could bring profits. The textile industry demonstrated how to use abundant resources, labor, and new inventions. Thus it stimulated investment in

Eli Whitney (1765–1825), transformed the processing of cotton with the cotton gin.

more costly, risky, and complex forms of industrialization.

Coal, Iron, and Steam. Cloth making could not have been mechanized without developments in the coal and iron industries. By 1712, **Thomas Newcomen** had made a simple steam engine which pumped water out of coal mines. This enabled deeper mining. Coal production increased. At the same time coke came into use in smelting iron ore.

The importance of this is obvious. Harnessing heat energy reduced man's dependence on animal, water, and wind power. Coal, and later oil and gas, became the world's main energy sources. Because the West possessed and used these resources, it dominated the world until the last quarter of the twentieth century.

Thomas Newcomen invented the first practical piston steam engine in the early 1700s. James Watt's engine was a transformation of the Newcomen design.

A Scottish instrument maker named **James Watt** and his business partner, Matthew Boulton, greatly refined the steam engine. It could then run the machines in textile mills. It took vast sup-

plies of coal to heat the steam boilers of these engines and large amounts of iron to build the new engines and machines. In order to meet this need, the coal and iron industries expanded. Along came the puddling process for removing impurities in iron. At the same time, foundries began using Watt steam engines to run bellows, hammers, and rolling and splitting equipment. These changes caused a rapid increase in output. By 1800, Britain produced more coal and iron than the rest of the world put together.

Transportation. The textile, mining, and metal industries grew at such a remarkable pace that Britain's roads and waterways could not handle all the traffic. By 1830, some 2,500 miles of canals were dug for transport of bulky shipments of coal and iron ore. Many of the canals linked the new industrial centers with seaports. Upon them came the **steamboat**, first on the rivers, then the oceans. The first successful paddle-wheel steamboat (1807) was the work of an American, **Robert Fulton**. Gradually, great merchant ships furled their sails and turned over their business to ironclad, propeller-driven newcomers. Roads,

Robert Fulton, 1765–1815

which often turned into impassable mire, were improved too, using the **macadam** technique. Made with crushed stone and hand surfaced, these roads could be used in any type of weather.

The most important means of transportation, the **railroad**, was used first in the mines for carrying

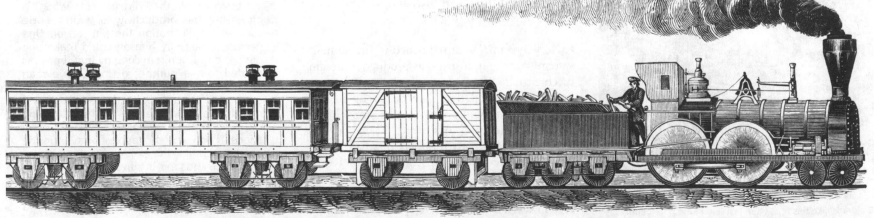

The First Industrial Reformation was powered by the steam engine. In 1804, Richard Trevithic of England built the first steam locomotive.

coal. Horses pulled wagons with flanged wheels over the iron rails. In the 1820s, steam engines were placed in moving vehicles called **locomotives**. **George Stephenson** perfected a locomotive named the *Rocket* in 1829. It had a fearfully high top speed—29 miles per hour (with a 13-ton load). He was hired to build the first major commercial railway, a 31-mile stretch of track linking Liverpool and Manchester.

This touched off a flurry of construction. By 1843, 1,900 miles of track crisscrossed Britain. Because railroads could transport passengers and freight faster and cheaper than roads and canals, trains soon came to dominate long-distance traffic. They also consumed a major part of the coal and iron output, thus increasing pressure on these industries to expand.

Communications. Along with transportation, major developments occurred in the field of communications. A key factor in this development

Railroads, like this one, were first laid in the nineteenth century and made the Industrial Reformation possible in Europe.

Samuel F. B. Morse, 1791–1872

was electricity, which was first put to practical use when **Samuel Morse** in America and **Charles Wheatley** in England simulateously patented the **telegraph** in 1837. Within a few years, telegraph wires stretched across nations. By 1866 a cable was laid across the Atlantic ocean. Communication between the United States and England was now instantaneous. In 1876, **Alexander Graham Bell** invented the **telephone**, and it's use became almost universal overnight.

Factory System. What happened to the domestic system (cottage industries) as production became mechanized? The cost and size of the new machines required that they be set up in large buildings, usually in towns. Workers now had to go where the machines were. These factories could absorb the vast numbers of small farmers driven off their lands by enclosures and other changes in agriculture. Women and children also joined the labor force in textile mills. The **factory system** was a key feature of the Industrial Revolution.

The nature of work was different in the factories. Each worker did only a portion of a task, not the whole process. In this **division of labor**, the motions were simple and easily learned, and skilled workers like master spinners or weavers were no longer needed.

Something else important happened during this period. As displaced farmers and small craftsmen flocked to the towns for jobs, some parts of the country lost much of their populations. By contrast, cities such as Manchester, Birmingham, Sheffield, Leeds, Newcastle, and Glasgow mushroomed in size.

World Leader. By 1815, (as Napoleon's career was ending on the Continent and Americans were beginning their great westward expansion) Britain was the industrial leader of the world. The British controlled the manufacture of textiles and tools. Their navy and their merchant ships enabled them to send their products everywhere. British banks and other financial institutions exercised worldwide influence.

Division of Labor

The noted economist Adam Smith pointed out in ***The Wealth of Nations*** (1776) the importance of the division of labor in increasing the productivity of workers. He used as an illustration the pin maker. One person working by himself could make one pin per day. But pin making by that time was divided into a number of tasks. One man drew out the wire, another straightened it, a third cut it, a fourth pointed it, a fifth ground it at the time for receiving the head. Making the head required two or three distinct operations. Then came the tasks of putting on the head, whitening the pin, and putting it into the paper. Thus the business of making a pin was divided into about 18 distinct operations. A small firm with ten men and the necessary machinery could make about 48,000 pins a day.

Spread of Industrial Development

Obstacles. European businessmen who wanted to begin their own industrialization during the latter part of the eighteenth century met with problems. Endless wars ravaged the Continent and revolutions swept over France. In this unsure economic climate, people would not make investments. Workers were not moving to the cities. At the same time, British merchants had captured much of the Continental market. Their lead in technology and investment capital seemed impossible to overtake.

Europe was divided into many states, especially in Germany and Italy. Political barriers hindered travel on the rivers and slowed the building of canals. The sorry condition of roads throughout Europe made land transportation slow, hard, and costly. Customs duties and tolls obstructed both foreign and internal trade. As these fees were a main source of income for the governments, states did not want to give them up.

Before 1815, the guilds were still strong. These craftsmen opposed the factory system and other new forms of business. Then too, West European peasants had better title to their lands than their English counterparts, while east of the Rhine, serfdom still prevailed in most areas. In either case, few farmers moved from the land to the towns. Those who did make money from commerce preferred to invest in land or in secure, small-scale, family-owned ventures.

Progress. Only after 1815, with the post-Napoleonic peace, did the picture begin to change on the Continent. Certain regions underwent an "Industrial Reformation" of their own. In The Netherlands (especially Belgium), France, and

Cyrus McCormick (1809–1884) transformed agriculture with his invention of the reaper in Virginia in 1831. With a two-man crew, this machine could cut as much grain in a day as 4 or 5 men with cradles or 12 to 16 men with reaping hooks could cut. Moving to Chicago, he built a large factor to manufacture this invention. Being a Presbyterian, he used much of his wealth to promote Christian institutions.

Prussia, populations grew rapidly. Farm workers began drifting into the cities in search of work. Large deposits of coal and iron ore fueled industrialization. Napoleon's improved administrative systems also helped business wherever the emperor had imposed them.

Governments spurred the economy by subsidizing inventions, sponsoring industrial shows, chartering banks, building railroads, and giving tariff protection. Tariffs protected domestic goods by making foreign goods higher priced. British industrialists invested heavily in Continental railroads and business firms. Europeans copied British machines and skills and hired British engineers, managers, and skilled workers for their young industries.

However, Europe's "Industrial Reformation" rode to success mostly on the railroads. The Belgians, French, and various German states built railroad networks linking producers and markets. Rapid industrial growth followed. Railroads also united countries, such as France and Prussia, as never before.

Before long, Europeans were developing their own techniques and industrial complexes. In Germany, the **Krupp** steel and armament works became the world's largest maker of arms. Belgium took the lead in overall industrialization. France and Germany developed important iron and coal industries. By the middle of the nineteenth century, other nations of Europe had small-scale industries too.

The United States. "Industrial Reformation" also jumped the Atlantic to the United States. Eli Whitney, the inventor of the cotton gin, contributed the crucial idea of **interchangeable parts**. These were made to careful specifications in large quantities by special machines. Then they were assembled into the final product. In the 1790s, he applied this process to making the first 20 cotton gins. Then he used it in filling a government order for 10,000 muskets. **Samuel Slater** set up the first successful American factory. To protect British industry, Parliament had barred skilled mechanics from leaving the country. It also forbade the export of machinery or plans. Slater, who had been a supervisor in a Manchester mill, came to America illegally.

The textile industry gradually developed in the New England states. In 1814, a new model factory opened in Waltham, Massachusetts. It carried out all the cotton-making operations under one roof.

As the American West opened up, it became a great new market. American businesses grew rapidly and their profits were plowed back into new plants and machinery. To supply this market, the country needed better transportation. By 1830, nearly 200 steamboats churned up the Western rivers. State governments borrowed heavily to build more than 3,300 miles of canals. Also, railroad construction started in the 1830s. Within ten years, the United States was the world leader in track mileage. By 1860, British capital and iron had provided the means for laying 30,000 miles of track.

In the same year, the United States took third place among the industrial nations of the world. After the Civil War came the great boom that pushed it into first place. By the end of the century, Germany and the United States had surged ahead of Britain and France to become the world's industrial giants.

By the early 1900s, Italy, Austria-Hungary, Russia, Sweden, Canada, and Australia had joined the ranks of industrialized countries. Japan was the first of the non-Western countries to experience the Industrial Revolution. The newcomers learned from the British experience. Thus their factories were newer and more efficient. Britain gradually fell behind as its industrial facilities became more and more outdated.

Expansion of Industrial Development

After the end of the Civil War in the United States (1865) and the Franco-Prussian War in Europe (1871), there was a gigantic new surge of industrial growth. Such enormous changes took place that this period has been called the **Second Industrial Revolution**, although no clean break occurred between the earlier industrialization and the new wave. Coal and iron production, railroad construction, and **urbanization** remained key features of the new growth. Yet the emphasis in production shifted. New areas of economic life opened up.

Just what did happen in the Second Industrial Revolution that distinguishes it from the original industrial surge? The *scale* of industrial production increased and output became more *varied* as many more countries entered the Industrial Age. At the same time, the *applications* of new scientific knowledge created important new industries.

Steel. An improvement in the iron industry had a profound impact on industrial developments. This was the creation of steel. Steel is made by adding carbon and small amounts of other metals to iron, thus making it stronger and more workable. In 1856, an English scientist, **Henry Bessemer**, came up with the idea of blowing air through molten iron to remove impurities. Further advances in the making of steel followed. The **Siemens-Martin** open-hearth process allowed the use of scrap iron and low-grade ore. The electric furnace was adopted in countries which lacked coal.

Bessemer's mammoth converters blew air through molten pig iron, thus burning out the carbon. For the first time, it was possible to make steel in large quantities.

Steel is a versatile metal, far stronger than wrought iron. It quickly replaced iron in railroads, steam engines, cables, and heavy machines. With steel, larger and lighter steamships could be built. Steel made the automobile possible. It was the basic metal in the new inventions that replaced hand labor—the sewing machine, circular saw, and rotary printing press, among others.

Steel transformed the office with the introduction of the typewriter and the tabulating machine. This metal also changed the basic form of city building. Steel beams and girders and concrete reinforced with steel replaced wood, brick, and stone. Skyscrapers with riveted steel frames now appeared on the American skyline.

Energy. Along with new equipment came new sources of power—electricity and oil. Electricity transformed communications by means of the telegraph, telephone, phonograph, motion picture, and radio. Messages that took days or weeks to deliver in 1800 could now be sent in minutes or seconds.

Thomas Alva Edison, 1847–1931

The new electric lights brightened homes and businesses. By 1914, electricity began to be used for heating and for running home appliances such as refrigerators and washing machines. The electric motor appeared everywhere—in factories, city-street railways, subway systems, even in giant locomotives. In 1914, electricity provided more than half the power used in British industry and an even larger amount in Germany. A.E.G. (General Electric), a German firm which made motors, generators, and other electrical goods, became the largest single industrial firm in Europe.

In 1876, an invention came along that placed the means of fast personal transportation in the common man's garage—the gasoline **internal combustion engine**. This engine ushered in the age of the automobile. Petroleum became one of the world's fastest growing industries. But the steam engine, refined and improved, remained the major power source. In the 1880s, steam turbines began to propel ships and generate electricity.

Mass Production. The Second Industrial Revolution also brought a great change in the way goods were made—the change to mass production. In 1908, Henry Ford installed an assembly line in his Detroit automobile plant. Drawing on the principle of interchangeable parts, he used an endless conveyor belt. Workers assembled each car as it passed along the line, doing the same simple task over and over again. Many industries adopted this technique and saw their costs drop dramatically.

Automation. Automatic machinery such as the photoelectric cell took over jobs like opening doors, inspecting tin cans, and counting sheets of paper. Huge cranes moved loads that before took the efforts of dozens of workers. Machines were even invented to run other machines and to carry out manufacturing processes.

Research. Industry looked to science for further help. Most large firms had laboratories or research divisions. There scientists worked on

The final operations on the Ford Motor Company's first assembly line took place outside the building where workers lowered the auto body onto the chassis.

inventions that the company could use or market. Many of the discoveries of the time came from these laboratories. In the first "Industrial Reformation" most had come from the mind of an inventor working by himself.

New chemical industries put special emphasis on research. Their laboratories added many products to housewives' shopping carts and workers' supply rooms. From one substance they could often derive a number of products. Coal tar, for example, turned out to be a source of dyes, medicines, perfumes, artificial food flavors, and high explosive elements.

The Germans took the lead in chemicals with the discovery and production of synthetic dyes. They followed up with fertilizers, celluloid, lacquers, photographic plates and films, and fabrics like rayon. Another product of research, high explosives, enabled countries to build great tunnels through the Alps and spectacular canals like the Suez and Panama. From chemistry came cheap paper and photographic equipment. These spurred the growth of the mass communications industry. Improvements in canning increased the year-round supply of fruits and vegetables, upgrading the diets of rich and poor alike. Chemical firms turned out a dazzling array of new medical drugs. X-rays, effective anesthetics, and vaccines insured better health and longer lives for people in the West.

The Second Industrial Revolution or "Reformation" transformed much of Europe, North America, Australia, and Japan into modern industrial states. The quality or standard of living for their people rose to unheard of heights. Between them and preindustrial peoples grew an ever-widening gulf as the twentieth century progressed.

New Forms of Business Organization

Capitalism in one form or another has been a factor of human life throughout history. In its most basic definition, **capital** is merely "savings." In this most basic sense, anyone who accumulates savings is a "capitalist." Capitalism, as a system, comes into its second level of development when an individual saver or group of savers put their accumulated funds to work in a commercial or industrial enterprise.

Commercial Capitalism. In this second stage of capitalism, which first flowered during the Reformation era, craftsmen worked in their homes or small shops producing goods for sale and exchange. We call this **commercial capitalism**. The merchant capitalists controlled economic life, and governments depended on them for money. In turn, the governments passed laws helpful to business.

For the most part, businesses continued to be owned by one person or by partners. They expanded by reinvesting profits, not selling stock to the public. The owners generally took an active part in management of the business. Individual savings were pooled in merchant companies or banks to finance sometimes risky and sometimes distant undertakings.

Industrial Capitalism. As business and industrial enterprises intensified, Europe entered a third stage of capitalistic development. In the beginning, the new coal, iron, textile, and other early industries were still small-scale. Money still came from the sale of goods; profit was the difference between the selling price and total cost of production. The profits were plowed back into the business. If a businessman needed extra funds to buy raw materials or new machinery, he would get a short-term bank loan.

However, as the industrial era progressed, the pattern began to change and the third stage of capitalism came into flower, **industrial capitalism**. The expanding factory system steadily boosted production and lowered the price of goods. New roads, canals, and railroads brought the cheaper goods to the very doors of small, family-owned firms or partnerships. The small businesses could not compete. Industrial production and distribution had to be carried out by larger firms. They were more efficient and could operate at lower rates of profit. In this stage, large industry began to heavily dominate economic life.

Finance Capitalism. Because of scandals, joint-stock companies had been outlawed in many countries prior to the nineteenth century. In 1825, Britain did away with its law against these companies. Other countries followed suit. Joint-stock companies, or corporations, offered a chance for investment at low risk. In the event of bankruptcy, the stockholder could not lose any more money than the amount he had paid for his stock, regardless of the company's debts. The managers, like the workers, were just employees and could not be held personally responsible for losses. That encouraged investment by common people as well as by capitalists. The wealth and savings of the entire country were put to work.

This investment system was the fourth stage of development, **finance capitalism**, although some scholars see it as an integral facet of the third stage, industrial capitalism.

> By means of the investment system industry and commerce draw the capital they require to function not only from the opulent few but also from members of such professions as law and medicine, from clerks and other members of the so-called white collar class, and even from the better-paid workers. All these groups command savings, possibly small, certainly not large in amount, from which they desire a return either in the form of interest on bonds or dividends on certificates of ownership called shares.
>
> Nonetheless, the relatively broad role of the general public in the latest phase of capitalism must not induce us to close our eyes to the fact that the control of the invested sums that keep the wheels of industry and commerce turning was taken over by a picked body of bankers and managers in immediate charge of the various business undertakings. Here is perhaps the most characteristic feature of the Age of Industrial Capitalism: the money supplied by the many was employed by the few often enough to advance their own selfish interest and with little or no regard for the many small and widely scattered shareholders, constituting the body of legal owners (Ferdinand Schevill).

As this writer notes, the key person here was the banker—the one who handled money, credit, and stock. It was his job to find and build up investment funds. The bankers, in fact, controlled the corporation since they supplied the money to keep it alive.

The large manufacturing firms, public utilities, department stores, insurance companies, and banks nearly all started as or changed into joint-stock corporations. Industrialists and bankers formed a tight alliance.

The actual owners of a corporation, the many thousands of small stockholders, had little to say about how it was run. Certain kinds of stock entitled the owners to vote on corporation decisions. Other kinds did not. Banks, insurance companies, or other financial institutions held most of the voting stock.

The proxy was another means for controlling a business. The **proxy** notice, which went to stockholders, gave management's suggestion as to how to vote. Many stockholders knew little about the corporation. They were willing to vote the managers' choice. Thus the large financial backers, or financiers, could place their own people on the board of directors. Since the board chose the management, the financiers could keep a tight rein on the business.

A third way that financiers might control a business was through a **holding company**. They would create a company that did not really produce anything. Instead the company owned the stock of several other firms. It managed these other firms for a fee and received dividends on their stock.

Laissez-faire. A basic shift also occurred in the very nature of capitalism. The first "Industrial Reformation" operated mainly on the basis of a free-market economy. Here the government does very little to regulate business. It follows a policy of *laissez-faire* (hands off!), as outlined by the French *Philosophes,* and of **free trade**, as outlined by Adam Smith (see Chapter 3).

These were the *economic* components of a broader *political* philosophy of unchecked freedom which had arisen in Western Europe: **liberalism**. (We shall explore this philosophy in

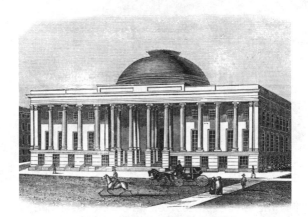

Third Merchants' Exchange, Wall Street, New York City

greater detail in chapter 9.) Political economists, in Britain particularly, studied their field by supposedly using the new scientific method and claimed to discover that economic affairs are governed by "natural laws" just as the physical world is. These economists, known as members of the **"classical" school** of economics, became the inspiration and apologists for the rising industrialist middle class. Workingmen were to understand that their situation was not the result of malicious attitudes by the masters of industry but the inevitable outcome of immutable laws of nature.

The new industrialists wanted to be left alone. They thought that the government should pass laws only to protect property, keep order, and provide justice with respect to contracts and debts. Education and charity were personal matters and should be left to individuals, families, churches, and voluntary organizations. These views generally reflect the teachings of the Bible with regard to the duties and limits of civil government, and this approach contributed to the material progress experienced by nations which followed biblical principles of economics. As

noted earlier, however, these libertarian ideals were not always matched by a sense of moral responsibility and became a license for exploitation. Neglected was the second half of the equation—man's moral duty to do justly and love mercy. Enlightenment philosophers had instilled in many the idea of unqualified individualism, along with the idea that the universe was a mechanism with a social order governed by natural laws and the idea that the lower-class masses were insignificant. These philosophies deeply influenced the rising capitalist class, which hoped to overthrow the centuries-old economic order in Europe, **mercantilism**, under which absolutist governments closely regulated economic production and distribution as protectors of the people. Historian Samuel C. Burchell notes:

> Having finally gained the right to operate without government control, entrepreneurs were loath to give up any part of that freedom. When there were fluctuations in the economy, they argued that such events were unavoidable, the result of "Natural Laws." Thus there was a Natural Law of Supply and Demand, a Natural Law of Diminishing Returns, an Iron Law of Wages, which made labor a commodity like any other commodity, subject to the fluctuations of supply and demand. The owners of capital believed that these laws were immutable and that if they were permitted to function without restrictions they would eventually lead to the greatest good for the greatest number. In practice, they led to great profits for a very few and to great misery for countless others. Mistaking freedom from control for license to do as they pleased, capitalists indulged in practices that took no account at all of the worker's right to a living wage and decent working conditions.

> Inevitably this large, and largely neglected working class came to be one of the gravest and most persistent problems of the Age of Progress.

Free-market philosophy also disapproved of protective tariffs or other barriers to free trade, such as concerted action by working people or specialized interests. In 1846, Britain repealed the protective tariff on grain and adopted a free-trade policy. France did likewise in 1860. Some other countries followed suit.

To make the free-market system work, Britain went on the **gold standard**. The value of British money was pegged to a specific weight in gold. Most other industrial countries did this as well. By the 1870s, a person holding the money of any country could exchange it for gold; a person with gold could exchange it for any money. All currencies had a fixed value and were readily exchangeable. *This arrangement, too, reflected a biblical principle of honest money; and it was another major contributor to the economic success of the period.*

However, some new industrial nations did not fully accept the idea of *laissez-faire*. Prussia and the United States set up protective tariffs in the earliest stages of their industrialization. In the 1870s and 1880s, more and more countries introduced or raised tariffs to protect their infant industries. Tariffs were usually designed to level the field among countries whose internal economic conditions otherwise put them at a disadvantage against competing countries.

By the early 1900s, Britain stood almost alone as the citadel of free trade. Through the global financial system centered in London, the British were able to dominate the economic order. They produced so efficiently that they did not need protection. In fact, Britain had a surplus of capital for investment in other parts of the world. Railways in the United States and South America were built mainly with British money.

Business Protects Itself. Large firms found ways to protect themselves against changes in the business cycle. Some brought under their control the whole production process, from obtaining raw materials to marketing the finished product. This

The House of Krupp

One of the world's most famous industrial works belonged to the Krupp family in Germany. Beginning in 1811 as a struggling steel mill with four hired men, it grew to a firm with 20,000 workers by the turn of the century. Expansion became possible when Alfred Krupp introduced the steam engine into his factory. Then he invented the steel gun, cast-steel axles, the seamless railway tie, and the breech-loading rifle. Since Krupp owned ore deposits, coal mines, steel mills, shipyards, and finishing plants, he controlled the entire process of producing steel and manufacturing finished products. The Krupp works became the symbol of German industrial efficiency.

Prussia's fortunes became entwined with those of the Krupp works when Alfred perfected the method of casting steel cannon. These weapons helped Prussia defeat Austria in 1866 and France in 1870, and gave the Krupp family control of Germany's arms industry.

When World War I broke out, the Krupps supplied German troops and contributed a new and mighty weapon, the giant cannons which shelled Paris and other cities from more than 70 miles away. After the war, the Allies forbade the company to make arms, an order which it disobeyed. Throwing their support to Hitler, the Krupps helped him rearm Germany for a second assault on Europe.

As World War II progressed, the Krupps seized property in occupied countries and used concentration camp inmates as slave labor in their factories. For these and other offenses, the Nuremberg trial judges sent Alfried Krupp, the current head of the firm, to prison. In the late 1960s, control of the Krupp empire passed to stockholders as the company became a corporation.

worked especially well in the steel industry. **Andrew Carnegie** in the United States and the **Krupp** works in Germany owned coal and iron mines, produced raw iron, made it into steel, stamped and shaped the final product, and manufactured it into ships and railway or military equipment. This type of business structure is called **vertical integration**.

Other firms engaged in **horizontal integration**. Two or more firms producing at the same level would work together to reduce competition, fix prices, and protect markets. This joint effort took several forms—**trusts**, **mergers**, and **cartels**. The trust combined firms under one head, such as **John D. Rockefeller**'s Standard Oil Company. A trust differed from a merger in that the companies in the trust usually kept their own identity. A corporation that was merged with another did not.

A cartel fixed prices and assigned each member firm a percentage of the market. The various members remained independent. Cartels were especially common in Germany. There they helped to promote world trade by keeping prices very high at home and by selling at a loss abroad. Often cartels were international. For example, the steel rail cartel had members in Germany, France, Britain, and the United States.

Labor. While business found its own forms of protection, the working people were sometimes at the mercy of the system and **business cycles**. In hard times, some employers cut wages and fired workers. In good times, they hired new workers and offered higher pay. Some factory owners set long hours and made harsh rules for their employees. There were instances of workers, even children, laboring up to 20 hours or more a day for wages that could not keep body and soul together. Because workers usually outnumbered jobs, they found it necessary to accept low pay

Cornelius Vanderbilt (1794–1877), was an American transportation tycoon. He began in business with ferries and steamboats, and went on to build a great railroad empire. By the time of his death, his New York Central System connected New York City with the major cities of the Middle West. He used some of his wealth to assist Christian educational institutions.

and poor working conditions. Labor unions were banned due in part to the fear that they might encourage revolutions such as in France.

What could workers do in the face of the unlimited power of industrial giants? One person was helpless in dealing with a great corporation. Legal or not, working people formed unions. In their early days, unions were mutual self-help groups. But gradually they pressed for the right of **collective bargaining**. If all the workers joined together, they could deal with management on a more or less equal basis. Unions mainly wanted better wages and fringe benefits. Their chief weapon was the **strike**, in which employees stopped work until their demands were met or a compromise

made. Unions became legal only after a long, bitter struggle.

The workers also had a political weapon in their arsenal, the labor or **socialist** parties. In almost every European country, working-class leaders worked with a labor party to pass laws helpful to labor. These political parties were run largely by middle-class intellectuals who were able to accrue power to themselves by acting as representatives of the working class. If the parties could not achieve their demands through law, they tried to overthrow the government. In some cases, revolution aimed at shifting the power base was the primary objective; and the appearance of working through law was merely a preliminary step or pretext. They believed that a government which opposed change was merely a tool of big business.

In the United States, organized labor did not form a political party. Instead, unions followed the lead of **Samuel Gompers**, head of the **Ameri-**

Samuel Gompers (1850–1924), American Labor Leader

can Federation of Labor (AFL). He agreed to support the party whose program came closest to what labor wanted.

<hr />

The Impact of Industrial Reformation

Standard of Living Rises. As the Industrial Reformation progressed, the workers' lot slowly improved. Labor's new productivity lowered the price for manufactured goods, and increased profits for businessmen meant overall improvement in economic conditions. Eventually, lower-class people were able to buy a wide range of items unthinkable in the past. Real wages (the actual purchasing power of wages) rose greatly. The average Englishman in 1913 could buy four times as much as the worker in 1801. The consumption of foods like milk and meat rose dramatically during the century.

Although all classes gained from the rising standard of living, the upper classes benefited most. Poor people still lived in inadequate housing, while the middle class had nicer homes and furnishings; and the wealthy could afford several houses for different seasons of the year. Again, this was nothing new. The poor were content with simple pleasures, while the middle and upper classes enjoyed cultural activities and travel. In short, though industrialization remarkably raised the standard of living of the Western world, the gap between rich and poor narrowed only somewhat. The lower classes came to resent this more and more as time went on and as socialist propagandists and agitators advanced the ideas of class struggle and envy.

Improvements in Health. The scientific and technological revolutions were accompanied by a significant increase in population in the advanced counties. Between 1750 and 1850, the population of Great Britain and Ireland tripled, from 10 million to 30 million. Germany increased from 25 million to 70 million people between 1815 and 1914. The total estimated population of Europe rose from 190 million in 1800 to 460 million in 1914.

This significantly altered the relationship between Europe and the rest of the world. In 1750, about 19 percent of the world's people lived in Europe. By 1900, it was 25 percent. If one added to this the Europeans who had come to live in the Americas, the ratio passed 30 percent.

What caused this jump in population? Birth rates remained about the same as before industrialization. So obviously people were living longer. Hospital care had improved. Cities adopted public health measures, built sewage systems, and provided safe water supplies. Vaccines and antiseptics controlled killer diseases such as smallpox, cholera, typhus, and bubonic plague. New mater-

By 1859 a drainage system was under construction in London, which contributed much to improve the city's health.

nity and infant hospitals helped many more children to survive.

British agriculture played a part also. Total food supplies increased dramatically. Better transportation brought food from distant areas. More people had an adequate and varied diet. Even the working classes could get milk and citrus fruits. Some diseases like scurvy, caused by nutritional deficits, vanished. Warmer housing and better clothing reduced deaths from respiratory problems.

Europe Dominates the World. The Industrial Reformation enabled Europe to dominate the whole non-Western world. Areas already under Western political control became Westernized culturally. Thousands of emigrants boarded the new steamships and trains for eastern Russia, the South Pacific, and southern Africa. They brought with them the culture of their mother countries. Industrialization gave them the tools—railroads, repeating rifles, and plows—to conquer the peoples there and tame the wilderness. Europe became so powerful that its economic and cultural influence seeped through China, Iran, and Turkey. But in Africa, India, and Southeast Asia, Europe took complete control. Chapter 10 describes this process in more detail.

The New Middle Class. The Industrial Reformation also created a new social order. The new industrialists, financiers, and owners of factories, mines, railroads, and shipping lines joined with the middle-class merchants, bankers, and lawyers to form the new middle class. Because of their wealth, they could either challenge the power of the landed aristocracy or join with it to govern the nation.

By the end of the nineteenth century, the middle class could be somewhat distinguished as upper and lower. The great bankers and captains of

The Protestant work ethic was crucial in the development of industry in England and the United States. Here workers are involved in the manufacture of metal castings.

industry lived in wealth and luxury. They invested heavily in business and had a strong influence in the governments of industrial countries. They became, in effect, the new aristocracy, especially in the United States. The lower middle class—small shopkeepers, factory owners, middle management people, professionals, and civil servants—lived more simply but yet comfortably. They jealously guarded their social status against threats from above and below.

Prior to the Industrial Reformation, townspeople made up only a small part of the working class. Most workers toiled on farms either as serfs, tenant farmers, or day laborers, but owned no property. Only as large numbers of workers came to the cities did the working class gain a sense of identity. Their marketable resource was labor.

The growth of industrial cities like London, illustrated here by Gustave Doré, were filled with activity and had to deal with a new problem, traffic congestion.

When they grew conscious of their numerical strength, they formed labor unions and political groups. Through these groups, some fought real exploitation and some sought power to satisfy their feelings of envy and resentment.

Urbanization. The same factors which enabled population increases led to the growth of cities. Before the industrial era, cities had depended solely on the amount of food that could be grown nearby. This limitation no longer existed. The end of epidemics removed another limitation. In

addition to pure water and sanitary sewers, cities soon provided garbage collection, better housing, public transportation, fire-fighting and police forces, and street lighting. All of these made urban living more pleasant and safe and resulted from the general economic growth brought about by free enterprise.

Manufacturing plants clustered in the cities, attracting more and more workers. Service industries sprang up to meet the needs of the city dwellers and at the same time provided more jobs. Small farmers continued to move to the cities for work and better pay. So did immigrants from abroad—the Irish in Britain, the Polish in Germany, and Europeans of all kinds in the United States.

For many, city life was attractive. They could escape from the lonely rural life, customs that never seemed to change, humdrum toil, and the uncertainties of farming. City shops had a greater array of goods. The city offered cultural life, spectator sports, and a chance for an education.

The era also saw international migrations unprecedented in history. Potato famines in Ireland during the 1840s caused the Irish to leave the country in droves. Anti-Semitic campaigns in Poland led Jews to flee that country in large numbers during the 1880s. Some 25 million Europeans left for America, Australia, and other parts of the world between 1871 and the early 1900s, when World War I finally slowed the migration phenomenon.

Plight of the Workers. Industrialization, perhaps because it occurred so rapidly that social policies had not yet been constructed to deal with it, at first caused suffering for great numbers of people. Cities grew so quickly that governments were overwhelmed. They could not supply the services people needed or enforce building codes. Drab

slums sprang up everywhere. Often housing was in short supply and people were packed into buildings from attic to cellar. Frequently an entire family lived in a single room. Cases were reported of 50-60 persons sharing a single living space. Tenements hurriedly constructed with the poorest of materials and workmanship became "dark, foul-smelling warrens of humanity," as one writer has described them. Another writer, the English scholar G. M. Young, put it this way:

> The imagination can hardly apprehend the horror in which thousands of families...were born, dragged out their ghastly lives, and died: the drinking water brown with faecal particles; the corpses kept unburied for a fortnight in a festering London August; mortified limbs quivering with maggots; courts where not a weed would grow, and sleeping-dens afloat with sewage.

Political corruption strained the city budget and added to the misery of the poor. Factory smoke stained the buildings and dirtied the air and streets. There were no sewers. The sewage simply

Fleeing from various forms of despotism, famine, persecution, and poverty, many Europeans immigrated to the United States in search of work and opportunity. The industrial development of such countries provided benefits to the whole world.

ran down the streets. Malnutrition and epidemics swept the neighborhoods, but the poor did not have money for doctors or nourishing foods. Skilled workers in particular suffered as machines took over their jobs. They either did not work at all or took jobs alongside unskilled workers in factories. Of course, their income dropped greatly.

Because the tasks were simple and repetitive, even children could do them. Many employers preferred to hire women and children since they would work for lower wages than men. People, even children, worked sometimes an average of 14 to 16 hours per day. Unsafe equipment caused many injuries. There was no unemployment pay

Often in a state of disrepair, ugly, and depressing, the homes of the poor contained only the bare necessities of life. Industrial development combined with Christian charity would improve the lives of the poor and handicapped. Illustrated here is Dudley Street, London, by Gustave Doré.

for those who had lost their jobs. United States slave owners used to argue that their Negroes were better treated than "wage slaves" in northern factories. The Southerners may have been right. For most workers, work was drudgery. It had no meaning. Life had no meaning. Broken homes, alcoholism, and crime abounded.

On the other hand, the workers' lot before the Industrial Reformation had usually been just as bad. Low wages, hard work for women and children, and unemployment were nothing new to farmers or small-town craftsmen. These conditions had prevailed in Europe for centuries. Rural housing was wretched, and farm workers found they could earn higher wages in the factories in town. Factory rules might seem inhumane, but the shops in rural villages had not been ideal places to work either.

Christian Charity and Concern for the Poor

This era provided great economic freedom for many who were innovative and hard-working. But as profits increased there were some persons who ignored the moral precepts of the Bible which teaches that we should practice charity, justice, and righteousness toward one's fellow man. This lack of responsibility perpetuated terrible suffering among many of the poor, during the early days of the era. Lacking moral sensibilities themselves, many of the poor fell into crime and other forms of degradation. But eventually, the Christian values at work in England and America enabled the benefits of industrialism to benefit even to the poorest people through works of charity. There were others who sought for a different answer, socialism, and in the years that fol-

lowed there would be a conflict between the Christian approach and a materialistic view that sought salvation through state control of the economy.

Novelists like **Charles Dickens** wrote about the terrible conditions in the slums of London. In Russia, the writer **Feodor Dostoyevsky** also saw industrialism as a threat to human dignity, as did **Victor Hugo** in France. Through reading their works, many people became aware of the plight of the poor for the first time. Some intellectuals and members of the old aristocracy particularly were appalled at the abuses of industrialism. They demanded changes. The problem of the poor, says Burchell,

> ...was attacked with equal concern by coldly practical politicians and by warmhearted humanitarians, by conservative governments and by liberal-minded men of affairs. For some the spur was moral indignation, for others it was the threat of revolution....

> Most of these pressures for reform of all kinds came from above, from within the ruling class. They brought about the changes that might otherwise have been a long time in coming, and relieved some of the worst causes of the workers' desperation. But in the long run the most effective pressures came from below, from within the ranks of the workers themselves.

Royal commissions and select committees of Parliament were constantly conducting investigations into alleged abuses. "Blue books" and "white papers," as reports of findings were often called, were continually being issued. The political parties split on the issue, often along confusing lines, with the conservative Tories usually taking the side of labor and the liberal Whigs aligning themselves with capital.

Workers and the Industrial Revolution

What did life hold for teenagers from working class homes during the "Industrial Reformation?" Hard work, and that was about all. Because a father usually could not make enough money to support his family, all the children had to go to work when they reached the age of six or seven. In 1842, Lord Ashley chaired a parliamentary committee which looked into the conditions of the workers. The committee's report contained the following statement by a 17-year-old girl, whom they described as ignorant, filthy, and ragged.

My father has been dead about a year; my mother is living and has ten children, five lads and five lassies; the oldest is about thirty; the youngest is four; three lassies work in the mill; all the lads work in the mines; one lives at home and does nothing...

All my sisters have been mine workers, but three went to the mill. Alice went because her legs swelled from working in cold water when she was hot. I never went to day-school; I go to Sunday-school, but I cannot read or write. I go to the mine at five o'clock in the morning and come out at five in the evening; I get my breakfast of porridge and milk first; I take my dinner with me, a cake, and eat it as I work; I do not stop or rest any time during the day; I get nothing else until I get home, and then have potatoes and meat, but do not get meat every day. I work in the clothes I have now got on, trousers and ragged jacket....

I move the carts of coal from the face of the seam to the bottom of the shaft, a mile and more under ground and back; they weigh 300 pounds; I push eleven carts a day; I wear a belt and chain to get the carts out; sometimes the miners beat me, if I am not quick enough; sometimes they pull me about; I am the only girl in the mine; there are about twenty boys and fifteen men....

Adapted from the *Ashley Report* (1842).

Child labor in a textile mill.

Factory owners were also divided concerning reforms. Not all of them fit the stereotype of reactionary, intransigent men who were insensitive to workers. Many were leaders in the campaign for improvement. In 1850, **Sir Titus Salt**, a textile industrialist, built a model factory town, known as Saltaire, in the countryside, with good houses, schools, churches, parks, and backyards. **W.H. Lever**, founder of Lever Brothers, built Port Sunlight in 1888, a factory town with gardens and houses equipped with indoor plumbing.

Even Prince Albert showed concern. He personally designed a low-cost, four-family, brick apartment dwelling with indoor plumbing, three bedrooms, a kitchen and parlor for working families. He proposed a low rent of three shillings a week. Alas, only one model was ever built—for display at the Great Exhibition.

British trade unions such as the **Amalgamated Society of Engineers (ASE)**, formed in 1851, and the **Miners' National Association (MNA)** were the workers' instrument of reform.

Elizabeth Fry at Newgate

Misery was commonplace in early nineteenth century England, but the wretchedness in its prisons surpassed belief. In the famous Newgate prison, about 300 women and children were crowded into two cells and two wards. Why were the children in prison? Chiefly because their mothers committed crimes and no relatives were willing to care for them.

Newgate, in all its ugliness and filth, was a terrible place in which to grow up. The women cooked, got drunk from the prison tap, and took part in frequent, violent brawls. A few mentally disturbed inmates actually attacked visitors to the ward.

It was to this fearful place that a gentle Quaker woman named Elizabeth Fry requested entrance in 1813. Prison officials insisted that it was too dangerous. But Mrs. Fry had determination and important friends. At length her prayers and efforts were rewarded, and she became a regular visitor to Newgate, where she won the confidence of the women prisoners.

Mrs. Fry saw to it that Newgate had a school for its children. Its inmates were provided with new cloths and work to keep them usually occupied. They were classified according to the nature of their crimes and had female supervision. Many were converted as Mrs. Fry read to them from the Bible or counseled them. In time, the whole atmosphere in the women's prison changed. The brawls and violence gave way to order, and the dirt to cleanliness.

Through Elizabeth Fry's work, attitudes toward prison reform began to change. Soon she received invitations to speak in other parts of England and even abroad. Prisons in many parts of the world adopted her methods. Because of Mrs. Fry and others like her, prisons have become more humane.

Protestants Works of Charity. But it was for Christians to provide a great answer to the problems of the time. Stressing biblical charity, they gave clothes, food, and medical care to those in need. They built hospitals, orphanages and other institutions to help the poor. Christians worked for new laws to improve working and living conditions and to do away with certain abuses in society.

In Britain, the reform movement arose directly out of the Evangelical and Methodist revivals. Thousands of people were brought into the churches and embraced teachings about helping those in need. We have noted in an earlier chapter how **Robert Raikes** and others formed Sunday schools to help educate the poor. One of the most tireless Christian workers on behalf of the poor was **George Mueller** of Bristol, who formed orphanages and homes for juvenile delinquents. His projects became known as examples of Christian work depending heavily on faith for provision. Mueller once described the motivation for service that arose within him after his conversion (1825) and then his "full surrender of the heart" in 1829:

> The love of money was gone, the love of place was gone, the love of position was gone, the love of worldly pleasures and engagements was gone. God, God, God alone became my portion. I found my all in Him; I wanted nothing else. And by the grace of God this has remained, and has made me a happy man, an exceedingly happy man, and it led me to care only about the things of God.

Great preachers of the period offered the gospel of Christ as the highest hope, and in some cases, thousands flocked to hear this encouraging message. Among the greatest of these preachers was the Calvinistic Baptist **Charles Haddon Spurgeon**, whose London Metropolitan Tabernacle attracted crowds of more than 5,000 at a time.

The Metropolitan Tabernacle in London

But Spurgeon and the church, believing that faith without works is dead, were involved in supporting the Stockwell Orphanage, which was founded in 1867. A Mr. Gough visited the orphanage and said of Spurgeon,

> I have seen Mr. Spurgeon hold by his power sixty-five hundred persons in a breathless interest. I know him as a great man, universally esteemed and beloved; but, as he sat by the bedside of a dying pauper child, whom his beneficence had rescued, he was, to me, a greater and grander man than when swaying the multitude at his will. (Richard Cook, *The Wit and Wisdom of Charles Spurgeon* [Baltimore: R. H. Woodward, 1892], p. 173.)

Other inspiration came from men like Thomas Chalmers, who labored in Glasgow, Scotland, and the Congregationalist minister and romantic-era writer **George MacDonald** (1824–1905). In one of his essays, for example, he wrote of one's duty to his neighbor, which, he said, was anyone with whom one comes into contact:

> He with whom I have any transactions, any human dealings whatever. Not the man only with whom I dine; not the friend only with whom I share my thoughts; not the man only whom my compassion would lift from some slough; but the man who makes my clothes; the man who prints my book; the man who drives me in his cab; the man who begs from me in the street, to whom, it may be, for brotherhood's sake, I must not give; yea, even the man who condescends to me.
>
> With all and each there is a chance of doing the part of a neighbour, if in no other way yet by speaking truly, acting justly, and thinking kindly. Even those deeds will help to that love which is born of righteousness. All true action clears the springs of right feeling, and lets their waters rise and flow. A man must not choose his neighbour; he must take the neighbour that God sends him. In him, whoever he be, lies, hidden or revealed, a beautiful brother. The neighbour is just the man who is next to you at the moment, the man with whom any business has brought you in contact
>
> Thus will love spread and spread in wider and stronger pulses till the whole human race will be to the man sacredly lovely. Drink-debased, vice-defeatured, pride-puffed, wealth-bollen, vanity-smeared, they will yet be brothers, yet be sisters, yet be God-born neighbours.

Of highest concern to some socially concerned Christians was the factory system and its use of child labor. They launched an attack on this system, hoping to arouse public opinion. So successful were their efforts that one Christian member of Parliament, **Michael Sadler**, put before that body a factory reform bill. His friends circulated a large petition to gain support and testified at parliamentary committee hearings. Those opposed to the bill fought hard and Sadler lost his seat, but the **Factory Act** of 1833 passed. It banned labor by children under the age of nine, set a limit on the working hours of those younger than eighteen, and called for inspectors to oversee enforcement. This law, and others that followed, were only necessary because private industry would not clean up its own "house."

After Sadler, another member of Parliament led the reform movement. An Evangelical, **Anthony Ashley Cooper** (1801–1885) served in government for well over 50 years. Elected first to the House of Commons, he moved to the House of Lords when he became the **7th Earl of Shaftesbury.** During all those years, he labored unceasingly to help the poor and oppressed.

Lord Shaftesbury, also known as Lord Ashley, was a descendent of the 1st Earl of Shaftesbury, who had helped restore Charles II to the English throne, and the 3rd Earl of Shaftesbury, a Enlightenment moralist and pupil of John Locke. The nineteenth-century Shaftesbury helped reform the treatment of the mentally ill, restrict the labor of women and children, and limit the working hours in factories and mines, outlaw the use of boys as chimney sweeps, provide a basic education for slum children, create better urban housing, and further public health in London. He served on countless boards and committees of charitable organizations, regularly went to factories and slums to see conditions firsthand, and repeatedly gave money out of his own pocket to needy persons and charities.

Shaftesbury wanted Britain to be a tool which God could use to carry out His purpose in the world. All of the politician's concerns were rooted in his religious faith, and he expressed this faith in everything he did, whether political, social, or religious.

While Shaftesbury worked to bring reform through law, another man, **William Booth**, a Methodist evangelist, wanted the church to take a more active role. However, he found mostly apathy among church people. The respectable church in England was too aloof, he felt. It had

The early Salvation Army ministered to the needs of the poor and the immigrants in the slum sections of cities in America and England.

cut itself off from the spiritual and physical needs of the masses. So Booth and his wife **Catherine** founded the **Salvation Army** in the 1860s. The Salvation Army not only preached the Gospel to the poor, but also provided food, clothing, and shelter. They gave local aid to people in trouble, cared for released prisoners, and fought against the white slave trade (selling women into prostitution).

In his famous book, *In Darkest England and the Way Out* (1890), General Booth exposed the misery of the slums. He suggested that for many, life in Britain was no better than in the African jungle. He denounced the church's neglect and set out a scheme for reordering society that foreshadowed the future welfare state.

Religiously motived reform was not limited to England. In Germany, Pastor **Johann H. Wichern** started working among slum children in Hamburg in the 1830s. His work grew into what was called the **Inner Mission**. Later becoming a vital part of the Lutheran Church, it brought back those who had strayed from the church and strengthened the weak and sick. Within 20 years,

Catherine Booth

Catherine Mumford Booth cofounded the Salvation Army with her husband, General William Booth. Although physically frail, she was an untiring worker—visiting the homes of people in need, bathing sick mothers and babies, stopping to talk to drunkards on the streets, rescuing fallen women, and holding small services in cottages for her neighbors.

In 1860, William was preaching to an audience of 1,000 in Bethesda Chapel. Just as he made his final remarks, Catherine felt compelled by God to speak. Past rows of startled listeners she walked to the podium and whispered to her husband. William then sat down.

Catherine told the audience that she had felt for years God wanted to use her to speak, but that she had never been able to before that day. Thus began her public ministry at a time when women did not speak in public, nor even write except under a man's name. But Catherine could speak so effectively that she often substituted for her husband, or they would hold simultaneous lectures in order to reach more people. The father of Dr. Randall Davidson, chaplain to the Archbishop of Canterbury, once remarked, "If ever I am charged with a crime, don't bother to engage any of the great lawyers to defend me. Get that woman!"

Partly due to Catherine's influence, female officers in the Salvation Army had equal rights with males and could even hold the highest positions in the organization. William declared, "The best men in my Army are the women." Throughout Catherine's life she was the human force that energized the Salvation Army to do battle for God against poverty, drunkenness, and social injustice, first in London and then around the world.

Some of the above information was based on Sallie Cheshem, *Born to Battle* (Chicago: Rand McNally, 1965), pp. 33–34, 83.

In 1870, the children's ward of the Presbyterian Hospital in Philadelphia was founded by Presbyterian Christians.

the Inner Mission had grown into a group of city missions which cared for the sick and mentally retarded and helped ex-convicts.

In the middle 1800s, dozens of churches opened missions, homes, and schools for poor people in the cities. Home mission, tract, and **temperance** groups saw organized evil in the slums. In the following decades, many important social service agencies grew out of these groups. Among them were the Young Men's Christian Association (YMCA), Volunteers of America, Florence Crittenton homes, Baptist Home Mission Society, and a host of rescue missions, settlement houses, and halfway houses for recovering alcoholics and ex-convicts.

Christians were also concerned about the medical needs of society. Christian denominations were very active in the building of hospitals, particularly in the United States. The **Red Cross Society** was formed under the efforts of Jean Henri Dunant, from Geneva, Switzerland who had been converted in the Réveil, or European Awakening.

Having witnessed the great suffering after the Battle of Solferino in 1859, sought to arouse the interest of European governments in a treaty that would provide neutrality and protection for the care of the wounded in war. In 1864 the first Red Cross treaty was signed. In compliment to Switzerland, the Red Cross took its symbol from the Swiss flag. The first use of the emblem was made during the Civil War in the United States.

The Rise of Socialism

Some people did not follow the biblical teachings that encouraged charity as the solution for social needs. Instead, they believed that the whole political and economic basis for society should be overturned and that the government should solve poverty by taxation. Known as **socialists**, they came mainly from the conscience-striken middle class. They wrote about their ideas, and a few tried to form working-class organizations. At the time, it seemed that people paid little attention to them, but by the twentieth century, their beliefs came to dominate political thinking. A factory owner, utopian-socialist **Robert Owen**, had risen from the working class himself and made his New Lanark cotton mills models of reformist thinking. He was a pioneer and experimenter in socialist-style public education, labor relations, and cooperative (communist) communities. Two Germans living in England were to have a greater influence, **Friedrich Engels** and **Karl Marx**. Engels, while an agent of his father's textile business in Manchester, England came into contact with Marx who was in exile due to the failure of the revolutions in Germany. Together they wrote the *Communist Manifesto*.

Agricultural work was transformed by new inventions in the United States and England.

For your consideration

Questions

1. What adjustments would farm families have to make when they moved to town?

2. Why did the Industrial Reformation take hold first in England?

3. How did Germany's lead in armament production affect the future course of world history?

4. In what three ways was the Second Industrial Reformation different from the initial industrialization surge?

5. How might a craftsman in the 1700s have felt about the quality of the product he made? How might an assembly line worker in the 1900s have felt about the quality of the products his company produced? Do you think mass production always lowers the quality of goods? Explain.

6. Trace the development of capitalism through its various stages from the Renaissance through the Industrial Age.

7. What are some of the benefits of technology? What are some of the dangers?

8. What is the proper relationship between business and government? Should these two institutions try help each other? If so, how?

9. Is socialism or capitalism more in keeping with biblical economic principles? Support your answer.

Projects

1. Interview a person over 60 years old and another person over 80. Make a list of the major changes they have seen. Find out how they felt about the changes. List discoveries and inventions that came in your great-grandparents' lifetime; your grandparents' lifetime; your parents'; your own.

2. Imagine someone gave you $2,000. List ways you might use the money as a capital investment.

3. If you are mechanical, you might like to work on an invention of your own. Or you might find a particularly clever invention and explain its operation to your class or family.

4. Make a collection of pictures of the inventions or discoveries of the First and Second Industrial Reformations. These could be clipped from magazines or photocopied from illustrations in books.

5. Set up a simple assembly line with some classmates, friends, or family members. Assemble a simple project, such as a birdhouse, bird feeder, or bookend. Have each participant perform only one of the tasks involved in the process.

6. Read a novel or story by Charles Dickens, such as *Nicholas Nickleby, Oliver Twist, Hard Times, A Christmas Carol, Bleak House, Little Dorrit,* or *Great Expectations.* Give a report.

Evangelical Lutheran St. John's Orphan Home for Boys, Sulphur Springs, near Buffalo, N.Y.

Word List

securities	deforestation
domestic system	plantation culture
division of labor	urbanization
internal combustion	factory system
proxy	*laissez-faire*
industrial capitalism	commercial capitalism
finance capitalism	cartels
vertical integration	Industrial Reformation
horizontal integration	gold standard
exploitation	temperance
steam engine	socialism
Enclosure Acts	spinning jenny
cotton gin	macadam
interchangeable parts	steel
capital	capitalism
holding company	trusts
business cycles	collective bargaining

People and Groups

Prince Albert	John Kay
James Hargreaves	Richard Arkwright
Samuel Crompton	Eli Whitney
Thomas Newcomen	James Watt
Robert Fulton	George Stephenson
Samuel Morse	Charles Wheatley
Alex. Graham Bell	Krupp family
Henry Bessemer	Henry Ford
Andrew Carnegie	Samuel Gompers
Charles Dickens	AFL, ASE, MNA
Feodor Dostoevsky	Elizabeth Fry
Victor Hugo	George Mueller
Robert Owen	Charles H. Spurgeon
Michael Sadler	Johann H. Wichern
Anthony A. Cooper	George MacDonald
Wm/Catherine Booth	Samuel Slater

1750   1800   1850   1900   1950   2000

Politics and Economics

Socialists control
German Parliament 1912

U.S Civil War 1861–1865

World War I begins 1914

Russian Revolution 1917

Communist Manifesto 1849

In 1867 Marx publishes
Das Kapital

Science and Technology

First Industiral Revolution 1760—1860

Second Industrial Revolution 1860—1914

Theodor Schwann discovers
biological facts 1800s

Einstein's theory of relativity 1905

"Science" of psychology established c. 1870

Roentgen and Curies study
radioactivity—Early 1900s

Freud's psychological theories c. 1900

Darwin's theory of evolution 1859–1871

Religion and Philosophy

Social Gospel expounded–Late 1800s

U.S. Prayer Meeting Revival 1857–58

Liberation theology develops 1800s

Doctrine of Immaculate Conception 1854

Welsh Revival 1904–1905

Papal infallibility decree 1870

Roman Catholic Church supports labor 1891

Culture and Society

Gladstone sets up state education 1870

Age of great novelists–Late 1700s–Late 1800s

Nietzsche's writings–Late 1800s

Romantic period in the arts 1700s—1850

Spencer outlines Social Darwinism 1862–1896

Child labor regulated in England 1833

8

Evolutionary Optimism and Romanticism

As the nineteenth century wore on, Western Europe reaped many benefits from the Protestant Reformation, the Great Awakening, and their cultural results in the new science and industry. There was a measure of political peace over much of Western Europe. It was a time of moderate prosperity for many. Infant death rates fell sharply and life expectancy increased. At the same time productivity rose as technology advanced, enabling many families to improve their standard of living. Shorter working hours meant leisure time for amusements and even for travel. More people could enjoy cultural activities. Sadly, however, the period saw a deterioration of the historic, Protestant Christian worldview.

In 1851, a Great Exhibition was staged in London under the sponsorship of Prince Albert, husband of England's Queen Victoria. The exhibition was a dazzling display of England's material progress during the past century. It also reflected a new kind of faith which had arisen among men during that period—faith in "Progress" itself, or as Prince Albert saw it, belief in history's advance toward "the realization of the unity of mankind." The philosophy of Progressivism held simply that any change from old to new is always a change for the good. This Age of Progress or **optimism**, as it has been called, was a period in which apostate man assumed new faith in himself—in his supposed ability to achieve nearly anything to which he set his mind. Instead

The World's Columbian Exposition of 1893 in Chicago was one of the largest displays of industry in the 19th century.

of giving thanks to God for the blessings of prosperity, they gave glory to themselves.

This optimism, being humanistic, proved to be a severely flawed faith. What began in the French Revolution with the presumption of man's sup-

posed inalienable right to the "pursuit of happiness" ended in the darkness of grief, alienation, and a realization that this supposed law of nature was nothing more than a man-made idea. Proclaiming himself to be wise without God, humanistic man became a fool, believing himself to be a descendent of animals. The new pseudo-science of evolution became one of the key concepts behind a humanistic view of progress. Man and society were seen as progressing from a primitive to an advanced state of civilization.

This optimistic humanism attacked Christianity as being a part of man's early development. The philosophy of **Darwinism** was soon joined to a moral **relativism**, **materialism**, and theological **liberalism**. While rationalism and deism had been rejected because they reduced man to a mere part in a machine, new ideas were developed that taught that human emotion and national history go beyond reason. This was expressed in Idealism and Romanticism.

Many other countries appeared eager to enjoy the prosperity of England and the United States, which was an outworking of biblical faith. Men the world over came to see material advancement as something to be envied. Among these were socialists and Communists who, while envying this prosperity, sought to destroy it with their new ideas of collectivism and redistribution of wealth. Social democracy made gains in many countries as people thought that man could better himself through the government. Tax-paid, universal public education developed in many countries and became a key tool of the humanists and socialists to create a secular culture. The era ended in shocking disillusionment, however, as the world plunged into war—the likes and extent of which history had never before seen.

Yet by God's grace, a remnant of the faithful Church rose to minister as a witness to the world. Determined Christian leaders battled hard for the historic faith, both in specifically religious endeavors and in the political, social, and cultural realms. As a result, the contrasts between the Christian worldview and the humanistic worldview became more and more prominent.

The Secularization of Western Science

Never had faith in science been so great. Because industrialization and inventions affected people's everyday lives, the scientific took on an almost magical quality. Through the **mass media**, the public learned of the latest discoveries and opinions of scientists. Going beyond improvement of working conditions and living standards, a new humanistic view of science had a profound impact on man's view of himself and his place in the universe, not to mention man's view of God.

Innovative developments in physics, biology, and psychology began to call into question the scientific worldview of the eighteenth century. Newton's magnificent law of gravity, the idea of an orderly, harmonious, and predictable world, came under attack. So did the belief in the timeless, unchanging quality of nature and human existence.

In the early nineteenth century, major breakthroughs occurred in chemistry and physics. The new discoveries paved the way for what has been called the Second Industrial Revolution. Scientists learned that matter was made of atoms which then combined into molecules to form compounds. New chemical compounds were created in laboratories and then put to industrial use.

Biology. In the 1800s, **Theodor Schwann** made one of the most important biological finds. He showed that all living beings are made up of cells and that most cells grow by dividing and multiplying. Later other scientists learned that all cells have a substance which they called **protoplasm**.

Through study of the microscopic world, **Louis**

Louis Pasteur, 1822–1895

Pasteur and **Robert Koch** learned that germs cause disease. This enabled medical scientists to attack a host of age-old enemies—rabies, cholera, diphtheria, tuberculosis, bubonic plague, and yellow fever. Moreover, anesthesia and new antiseptic techniques made surgery safe for the first time. The discovery of vitamins enabled doctors to cure diseases such as scurvy, rickets, and beriberi.

However, a great controversy opened in the field of biology—evolution. Theories of **organic evolution**, the idea that living beings changed and developed, were not new. In 1809, **Jean de Lamarck** had said that these changes came through "inherited acquired characteristics." For example, giraffes developed long necks by reaching for leaves on tall trees, and ducks developed webbed feet by trying to swim. Body changes were said to then be passed on to their offspring. Over a long period of time, a new species developed. Another field of study also contributed to the discussion. Geologists had concluded from studies of fossils that the earth was far older than had been thought and had undergone many great upheavals. Beside this, the German philosopher,

Georg Hegel saw all of reality as a self-unfolding of the Idea of Reason through a series of revolutions.

The Evolutionary Worldview of Darwinism

Charles Darwin (1809-1882) sought to develop a scientific argument for the theory which he said explained how organic development had taken place. As a young naturalist, he spent five years on a British survey ship in the Southern Hemisphere. During that time, he acquired a vast collection of fossils and made notes on the life forms he saw. After another 20 years of research, he published his famous *On the Origin of Species by Means of Natural Selection, or the Preservation of Favored Races in the Struggle for Life* in 1859. It is curious that one year earlier, Darwin had received a paper from another Englishman, **Alfred Russel Wallace** which clearly set forth a theory of evolution nearly identical to the one Darwin advanced in *Origin of Species*. Darwin applied his theory to humans in his highly controversial *The Descent of Man* (1871), arguing that the human race sprang from some apelike ancestor.

Darwin said that every species produces more offspring than the environment can support, a popular notion still advanced by population control advocates. The offspring then struggle to survive, competing with one another for food, shelter, and the chance to reproduce. In this struggle, some individuals have unexplained characteristics or **variations** that give them a slight advantage. They have stronger muscles, longer horns, sharper claws, better body color, or sharper eyesight than their brothers and sisters. These variations enable them to win in the com-

Charles Darwin, 1809–1882

petition and thus reproduce themselves. This is the "survival of the fittest." The unfit are weeded out and the winners pass on their superior qualities to their offspring. Over a long period of time, the species will change greatly. Which offspring will have the variations enabling them to survive? Nature makes that choice—in other words, there is "natural selection."

Darwin's theory assumed that chance caused the variations. It did not deal with the basic question of where life on earth came from. None of Darwin's followers have yet come up with an explanation for that foundational question. Further, Darwin's theory said that all life was interrelated and subject to the same laws of development. Darwin thought that living beings gradually developed by the single process of evolution from simple to more complex forms. This process of

change would continue in the future. Scientists have since learned that variations within species work to accomplish the opposite of what Darwin argued. The "fittest" are not the ones most likely to survive and new creatures do not develop from variations in earlier ones but rather these variations tend to help conserve species.

At the heart of Darwin's scientific beliefs was a false theory in geology which had been advanced by **Sir Charles Lyell** (1797–1875)—the theory of **uniformitarianism**. Darwin took along a copy of Lyell's *Principles of Geology* when he went on his famous voyage to the South Seas aboard the H.M.S. *Beagle*. According to Lyell's theory, the present is the key to understanding the past. What men observe now in nature explains how nature operated in the past because the operations of nature have always been the same. This theory ran counter to the historic Christian position that the past—God's creative activity as revealed in the Bible—is the key to understanding the present world. Darwin was an acknowledged agnostic and was highly critical of the Bible. He also admitted that he was a poor scholar and lacked a basic scientific tool, skill in mathematics.

The second half of the title of Darwin's 1859 masterwork … *the Preservation of Favored Races in the Struggle for Life* reveals a dark side to Darwin's popular theories. His arguments gave new impetus to the "kill or be killed" instinct in fallen man and, when applied to social developments, it led directly to the racial superiority policies of **Adolf Hitler** and the class conflict horrors born in the theories of **Karl Marx**. The ideas of these men have resulted in the worst mass murders in all of history, including the holocausts of Nazi Germany, the massacres of **Joseph Stalin** and other Communists, and mass abortion in the middle and late twentieth century.

Evolutionists believe that the lowest and earliest form of life was the protozoa, which then developed the more complex forms through random mutations. Evolutionists disagree over the exact positions of some of the species.

Biologists following Darwin refined his hypothesis. They dropped the idea that acquired changes in body structure (such as a giraffe's stretched neck) could be passed on to offspring. **Hugo De Vries** set forth the **mutation** hypothesis in 1901. He thought that evolution came not from variations but from mutations (radical genetic changes). These were said to have enabled the favored beings to survive and could be passed on to the offspring. If enough mutations took place, within a short time a new species might develop.

Even though the theory of organic evolution came to be widely accepted as scientific fact, many questions remained. What caused the variations and mutations? Mutations could be produced artificially in laboratories by using chemicals or radiation, but how did these changes occur naturally? What guided the process of natural selection? Could it really be pure chance or were other forces at work? Did species simply age just as human beings do? How could we account for the "missing links" in the evolutionary chain? Do these gaps place the whole theory in doubt?

Responses to Darwinism. Darwin's books touched off a bitter controversy, quickly earning him the title, the "most dangerous man in England." Many scientists widely rejected Darwin's ideas. Among those who did were the eminent geologist **Jean-Louis Agassiz** of Harvard, the leading specialist of his time on fossil fish; **William Whewell**, a professor of science at Cambridge University; **Sir John Herschel**, a great English astronomer, mathematician, chemist, and physicist, who called Darwin's theories the "law of higgledy-piggeldy"; biologist **Philip Gosse**; mathematician-geologist **Adam Sedgwick**, who was Darwin's teacher; anatomist **Sir Richard Owen**; entomologist **Andrew Murray**; and the great physicists **Lord Kelvin** and **James Clerk Maxwell**. Sedgwick called Darwin's ideas "rank materialism" and charged that their only purpose was to "make us independent of a Creator." Professor **George F. Wright** of Oberlin College called Darwinism "one-tenth bad science and nine-tenths bad philosophy." French scientists and publishers adamantly disputed Darwin.

In America, many scientists and Christian theologians were also highly critical of Darwin. For example, **Charles Hodge** (1797–1878) wrote in his book *What is Darwinism?*, which was published in 1874, that:

> The conclusion of the whole matter is that the denial of design in nature is virtually the denial of God. Mr. Darwin's theory does deny all design in nature, therefore, his theory is virtually atheistical; his theory, not he himself. He believes in a Creator. But when that Creator; millions on millions of ages ago, did something—called matter and a living germ into existence—and then abandoned the universe to itself to be controlled by chance and necessity, without any purpose on his part as to the result, or any intervention or guidance, then He is virtually consigned, so far as we are concerned to non-existence … What is Darwinism? It is Atheism.

In this cartoon by Thomas Nast, the Gorilla complains to Mr. Bergh, president of the Society of Prevention of Cruelty to Animals that, "That man wants to claim my pedigree. He says he is one of my descendents." Mr. Bergh replies, "Now, Mr. Darwin, how could you insult him so."

But eventually liberal theologians and socialists found the philosophy behind Darwin's theories much to their liking. Darwinism also received a major boost from American botanist **Asa Gray**, who tried to convince scientists that Darwinism could be reconciled with the Bible. Sadly some men who were associated with orthodox Protestantism followed this line of thinking, such as James McCosh, A. A. Hodge (the son of Charles Hodge), and James Woodrow (the uncle of President Woodrow Wilson). This type of thinking has been called *theistic evolution*. Many of these men also accepted the idea of the great lengths of time needed for evolution and thought that they could prove that the days of Genesis were not 24 hour days but long ages of time. In this they rejected the idea that God created all things directly and promoted a kind of Deism.

Although few serious scientists accept Darwin's discredited original theories any more, the general theory of evolution remains the primary approach to science in American public education today, largely because the only alternative is to accept God as Creator, a doctrine which also means God must be accepted as Lord and Master of the universe and mankind. This is a fact which modern secular man is not willing to accept. Science, in its insistent hope of salvaging Darwin's philosophies, has too frequently departed from true science to pursue theoretical positions. Even a staunch admirer of Darwin, the mid-twentieth-century historian Ferdinand Schevill, acknowledged that Darwinism is as much religion as science, and perhaps questionable as science. Yet its character may explain why it has such widespread acceptance. Says Schevill:

> There is something beautifully unifying and inclusive about the evolutionary theory. Bred in the hard realm of science and having a solemn scientific air, it yet brings to many people something of the expansive feeling of religion.

By all such it is welcomed as a new hope, a credible modern pantheism. We should not fail to note, however, that to the strict scientist it is still what it was to Darwin—a useful hypothesis and nothing more. That means that, admitting the evidence in favor of an evolutionary development of animate nature to be overwhelming, the method by which the development takes place and which Darwin assumed to be 'natural selection' is still subject to redefinition.

Developments in Physics

Meanwhile a number of changes were taking place in other fields of science. Earlier Scientists had thought that heat, light, magnetism, and electricity were all weightless substances that flowed in and out of material substances. But a Scottish physicist **James Clerk Maxwell** (1831–1879) discovered that energy existed apart from matter and could be changed from one form into another—electricity into heat or magnetism into electricity. Maxwell was raised as a Bible-believing Scottish Presbyterian, and became a dedicated Christian who loved the Puritans. He was a strong opponent of Darwinism and wrote refutations of Pierre Simon Marquis de Laplace, and Herbert Spencer. His life demonstrated that it was Christian faith which led to true scientific discoveries that improved society and culture. His discovery that light, electricity, radioactivity, and other kinds of energy were part of the electromagnetic spectrum led to a new understanding of the structure of matter and many inventions. Einstein called his contribution, "the most profound and most fruitful that physics has experienced since the time of Newton."

Maxwell's Prayer

While some scientists followed the new materialistic view of the universe which left no room for God, others continued the development of true science out of a Christian worldview. James Clerk Maxwell was one such notable Christian scientist. Below is a quote from one of his prayers.

"Almighty God, who hast created man in Thine own image, and made him a living soul that he might seek after Thee, and have dominion over Thy creatures, teach us to study the works of Thy hands, that we may subdue the earth to our use, and strengthen our reason for Thy service; and so to receive Thy blessed word, that we may believe on Him who Thou hast sent, to give us the knowledge of salvation and the remission of our sins. All which we ask in the name of the same Jesus Christ, our Lord."

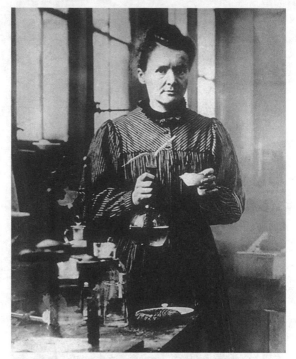

Marie Curie, 1867–1934

Another Christian scientist, William Thompson or Lord Kelvin (1824–1907) discovered the new laws of **thermodynamics**—creating the branch of science dealing with the transfer of heat and the interrelationships of heat energy—spelled out what science had learned about energy. He formulated the first and second laws of thermodynamics. The *first law of thermodynamics* stated that energy can be changed from one form into another but cannot be created or destroyed. The *second law of thermodynamics* stated that while the total energy in the universe is constant, the amount of energy we can use for work is steadily running down. His discovery of these laws flatly contradicts the evolutionary hypothesis that matter increases in order over time. Lord Kelvin's Christian faith led him to oppose uniformitarianism and Darwinism.

Marie Curie

In the late 1800s, scientists knew that uranium was radioactive, but they did not understand why. Marie Currie, a young scientist in Paris, became interested in radioactivity and began to study it. She examined every known substance to see if any others were radioactive. Her work convinced her that an unknown element caused the strange radioactive rays. Aided by her husband Pierre, she began to search for a new element.

For four years, Marie and Pierre labored in the cold, damp shed which had been given to them for a laboratory. They boiled pitchblende in a big pot, stirring it with an enormous iron bar. In the excerpt below, their daughter Eve tells of the climax of all these efforts.

Marie continued to treat, kilogram by kilogram, the tons of pitchblende residue which were sent her on several occasions from St. Joachimsthal. With her terrible patience, she was able to be, every day for four years, a physicist, a chemist, a specialized worker, an engineer and a laboring man all at once. Thanks to her brain and muscle, the old tables in the shed held more and more concentrated products—products more and more rich in radium. Mme. Curie was approaching the end: she no longer stood in the courtyard, enveloped in bitter smoke, to watch the heavy basins of material in fusion. She was now at the stage of purification and of the "fractional crystallization" of strongly radioactive solutions. But the poverty of her haphazard equipment hindered her work more than ever. It was now that she needed a spotlessly clean workroom and apparatus perfectly protected against cold, heat and dirt. In this shed, open to every wind, iron and coal dust afloat which, to Marie's despair, mixed itself into the products purified with so much care. Her heart sometimes constricted before these little daily accidents, which took so much of her time and her strength.

Pierre was so tired of the interminable struggle that he would have been quite ready to abandon it. Of course, he did not dream of dropping the study of radium and of radioactivity. But he would willingly have renounced, for the time being, the special operation of preparing pure radium....

He counted without his wife's character. Marie wanted to isolate radium and she would isolate it. She scorned fatigue and difficulties, and even the gaps in her own knowledge which complicated her task. After all, she was only a very young scientist: she still had not the certainty and great culture Pierre had acquired by twenty years' work, and sometimes she stumbled across phenomena or methods of calculation about which she knew very little, and for which she had to make hasty studies…

In 1902, forty-five months after the day on which the Curies announced the probable existence of radium, Marie finally carried off the victory in this war of attrition: she succeeded in preparing a decigram of pure radium, and made a first determination of the atomic weight of the new substance, which was 225.

The incredulous chemists—of whom there were still a few—could only bow before the facts, before the superhuman obstinacy of a woman.

Radium officially existed.

Excerpted from Eve Curie, *Madame Curie: A Biography*, translated by Vincent Sheean, Copyright 1937 by Doubleday & Co. Reprinted by permission of the publishers.

These discoveries led to the re-examination the very nature of matter and energy. By the early 1900s, scientists such as **Wilhelm Roentgen** and **Pierre and Marie Curie** were studying radioactivity. They found that atoms were not bits of solid matter but highly complex structures. Atoms of the radioactive elements released energy as the elements decayed. **Max Planck** showed in 1901 that atoms did not give off energy in a steady stream but in bundles, each called a **quantum**.

Niels Bohr and others found that the atom was almost like a tiny solar system. At the center, or nucleus, were one or more protons. Around them

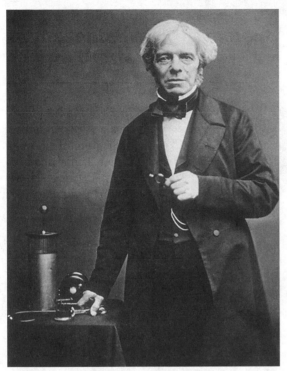
Michael Faraday, 1791–1867

revolved a number of electrons. Working from this idea, **Ernest Rutherford** bombarded a nitrogen atom to reduce its electrons and change it into a hydrogen atom. He had proved it possible to change one form of matter into another.

Michael Faraday (1791–1867) rose from being a bookbinder to one of the most prominent scientists of the 19th century. He labored in the areas of physics, chemistry and electricity. He discovered chemicals, enunciated the laws of electrolysis, and built the first generator and electric motor. His discoveries made the electrical world of today possible. As a Christian, Faraday sought to apply his faith to his life and work. During the Crimean War he was asked to develop poison gas but firmly declined the request.

Since the old understanding of the physical world had been undermined by these and other discoveries, a new explanation was needed, some scientists believed. It took the greatest scientific genius of modern times to offer that explanation. That genius was the physicist **Albert Einstein**, born in 1879. His theory of **relativity** in the early 1900s did away with the Newtonian view of absolute space, time, and motion. He also disproved the idea of a substance called **ether** filling the space of the universe. People had believed that all motion could be measured against ether, just as a car's speed could be measured in terms of the distance traveled on a road. Instead, space, time, and motion are all relative to the observer and his own movement in space, Einstein argued. The observer moves because he stands on a moving planet. There is no fixed point anywhere in the universe against which to measure time or the speed of a moving object, Einstein's **theory of relativity** posited. This theory had major implications for religion and philosophy, as we shall see later in this chapter. While his theory is true in regard to finite man, Einstein did not consider the fact that God is outside of time and space. God is not subject to relativity, but remains absolute and infinite. The God of the Bible alone provides those who believe in Him with an absolute point of reference in the universe for truth and morality.

As to the physical world, though, Einstein held that people live in a four-dimensional world. To the three dimensions of space (length, breadth, and height), Einstein added another one, time. Furthermore, he said, the universe is **finite** (limited). Matter does not go on forever, but curves back on itself. This made the universe a gigantic sphere.

Einstein then argued that the size of a body depends on its motion. A body traveling at a high speed is shorter than one moving at low speed.

Painless Surgery

Anesthetics have been in use for only about 150 years. Medical patients through all the preceding centuries knew physical pain to be one of mankind's fiercest enemies. In the following excerpt, an eyewitness describes the first use of anesthesia in an operation in 1846. Dr. William Morton, discoverer of the effects of ether, administered the anesthetic to the patient.

The day arrived; the time appointed was noted on the dial, when the patient was led into the operating-room, and Dr. Warren [and] a board of the most eminent surgeons in the State [Massachusetts] were gathered around the sufferer. All is ready—the stillness oppressive. It had been announced that a test of some preparation was to be made, for which the astonishing claim had been made, that it would render the person operated upon free from pain. Those present were incredulous, and as Dr. Morton had not arrived at the time appointed, and fifteen minutes had passed, Dr. Warren said, with significant meaning:

"I presume he is otherwise engaged."

This was followed with a derisive laugh, and Dr. Warren grasped his knife and was about to proceed with the operation; at that moment Dr. Morton entered a side door, when Dr. Warren turned to him, and in a strong voice said:

"Well, Sir, your patient is ready."

In a few minutes he was ready for the surgeon's knife, when Dr. Morton said:

"Your patient is ready, Sir."

The operation was for a congenital tumor on the left side of the neck, extending along the jaw to the maxillary gland and into the mouth, embracing the margin of the tongue. The operation was successful; and when the patient recovered he declared he had suffered no pain.

Dr. Warren then turned to those present and said:

"Gentlemen, this is no humbug."

The conquest of pain had been achieved.

From Washington Ayer, *Occidental Medical Times,* March 1896.

He also said that mass can be changed into energy or energy into mass. This principle later enabled scientists to tap the vast energy sources within the atom itself and make the atomic bomb, as well as electrical power for peaceful use.

The Social Impact of Darwinism

New Social Sciences. August Comte, born in 1798, founded the science of **sociology**. He observed society and collected facts hoping to find the laws which make it work apart from Biblical truth. At about the same time, the study of **anthropology** began to analyze human types and to investigate so-called prehistoric and primitive cultures and social institutions. **Psychology**, the study of the workings of the human mind and behavior, became a separate science around 1870.

At the turn of the twentieth century, psychology broke up into a number of rival schools of thought. One school, **behaviorism**, held that there was no such thing as mind, consciousness, or free will. People were physical beings only. The behaviorists explained all human behavior as physical responses to the environment.

Another important school of thought had already started with **Sigmund Freud**, a Jewish doctor in Vienna. He thought that the causes of nervous problems lay in the unconscious mind, which he said has the most important influence on the adult's actions. People are chiefly self-centered, driven by the basic urges of power, sex, and self-preservation, Freud taught. However, civilized society demands that these urges be curbed. The healthy person, as he matures, learns to direct these energies into channels which society approves. Those who fail to learn this, repress or

Sigmund Freud, 1856–1939

drive these feelings deep into the subconscious, where they may be forgotten. Yet the repressed thoughts and wishes trouble the personality with pain, physical symptoms, fears, **obsessions**, and lapses of memory, Freud held.

His treatment method, called **psychoanalysis**, requires long periods of questioning by the doctor. Dreams are interpreted and the patient's subconscious actions are studied. Eventually, the patient becomes aware of what has caused his problems. This is supposed to result in a cure. By arguing that large areas of human behavior lie outside conscious control, Freud and his followers claimed that the subconscious mind directs a person's actions more than his conscious thought or his will. Therefore, they suggested, people are not really rational beings. Further implications were that people were therefore not responsible

or culpable beings and that, as such, they could not reasonably be held accountable for their sins.

Social Darwinism. The impact of the secularization of science and the new pseudo-sciences upon Western moral and religious values went far beyond the findings and theories of scientists. The outgrowth of Darwin's theory was **Social Darwinism**, the application of the idea of organic evolution to society. The best-known advocate of Social Darwinism was **Herbert Spencer**, a popular writer born in 1820, who maintained that biological evolution caused social change.

Spencer saw evolution as a universal law which applied not only to living things but also to sociology, economics, and government. Conflict was good and necessary for human progress. Competition among people, business firms, and nations would eventually result in the "survival of the fittest," a term he coined. The "unfit" should not survive. Governments must not interfere in social or economic areas or help the weak survive.

Herbert Spencer, 1820–1903

However, if individuals wanted to help the weak (the poor and oppressed), they could. Such charity showed that they had evolved to a higher, more noble level.

Social Darwinism downgraded humans to the purely material level. Man no longer had value as a creation of God, but only as an object of use or uselessness to society. If a person was considered useful to society, he had value. If not, he was disposable. The nature of human society was not a cooperation for the benefit of all, but instead vicious competition. The successful person was the most "fit" regardless of how he gained success. Power became the highest goal and the determiner of both success and fitness. If survival was the only thing that mattered, then, according to Social Darwinism, there was no higher standard to judge their actions. The upper and middle classes deserved to be rich because they were "more fit" than the lazy, shiftless poor, claimed the Social Darwinists. In the same manner, "nature" determined that big businesses would take over smaller ones. Certain "superior" races should rule over "inferior" races—whites over blacks, Germans over Slavs, Gentiles over Jews. Using the biological theory of evolution, one could justify the rule of the strong over the weak in all aspects of life. The most fanatic advocate of Social Darwinism turned out to be Adolf Hitler, who made competition between nations and races the cornerstone of his political program.

A German philosopher and writer named **Friedrich Wilhelm Nietzsche** carried Social Darwinism to its logical end. He believed that natural selection should be allowed to operate freely in society. The constant weeding out of the unfit would one day produce a race of "supermen." These noble beings with moral courage and strength of character would rule the masses.

Friedrich Nietzsche, 1844–1900

Those who perished in the struggle were moral weaklings and cowards.

Nietzsche took upon himself to announce that *God was dead*. Thus man must go it alone and make his own rules for living. But the weak try to hinder the strong by inventing religion—Christianity, Judaism, and oriental cults—which glorify "slave virtues," Nietzsche contended. The qualities these religious weaklings prize—humility, patience, hope, love, acceptance, brotherly kindness, concern for the weak, and self-denial—are vices, not virtues. Nietzsche argued that these qualities help the unfit to survive and pour their "bad blood" into the human race.

The ancient pagan German virtues—bravery, strength, love of danger, loyalty, honor, intelligence, and cunning—were much better. He defined good as "all that increases in man the feeling of power" and bad as "all that comes from weakness." In this new paganism, violence and struggle would lead to a better world, destroying

the values of Christianity and Western civilization. Carried to the extreme, Nietzsche's ideas produced the horrors of the Nazi death camps of World War II and the terrors on the streets in modern cities.

Nietzsche's views also contributed to the twentieth-century feeling that life is empty and meaningless. Some thinkers assume that life ends in the nothingness of death—a philosophy known as **nihilism**. Thus one set of moral values is just as good as another. This lack of purpose in life has

The Impact of Relativism

According to the Christian philosopher Francis A. Schaeffer, Western society was at one time guided by absolute principles—things that are ultimate or final and to which there are no exceptions—that were rooted in Christianity. Because of the impact of modern science and thought, people have largely given these up, but human nature still desires absolutes. One that is especially popular today is the "51-percent vote."

In the days of a more Christian culture, a lone individual with the Bible could judge and warn society, regardless of the majority vote, because there was an absolute by which to judge. There was an absolute for both morals and law. But to the extent that the Christian consensus is gone, this absolute is gone as a social force. Let us remember that on the basis of the absoluteness of the 51-percent vote, Hitler was perfectly entitled to do as he wished if he had the popular support. On this basis, law and morals become a matter of averages. And on this basis, if the majority vote supported it, it would become "right" to kill the old, the incurably ill, the insane—and other groups could be declared nonpersons. No voice could be raised against it.

From Francis A. Schaeffer, *How Should We Then Live?* (Old Tappan, N.J.: Revell, 1976), pp. 223-4.

driven many of them to suicide, inner withdrawal, despair, frustration, or violence.

Moral Relativism. The new secular materialistic "science," with its stress on ceaseless change and physical relativity (see earlier on Einstein), fanned the flames of **relativism**. As an idea, relativism had been around for some time. Even in the eighteenth century, some philosophers had begun to question whether final truth exists. According to this view, what is right or wrong and good or bad is not absolute but varies depending on the person, circumstances, or society. Something is wrong only if the individual or society thinks it is wrong. Because what one thinks varies with time and place, what is wrong or right will vary.

Relativism had a devastating impact on personal and social morality. If man's grasp of truth is relative, who could finally say what truth is or what is right and wrong? This left every man and nation to decide for themselves. The Russian novelist **Feodor Dostoyevsky** struck at the heart of the matter in *The Brothers Karamazov* (1879): "If God does not exist, then everything is permitted."

Materialism. A further impact of the new "science" was **materialism**. The German zoologist, **Ernst Haeckel**, declared bluntly that nothing spiritual existed, that the universe was made up of matter alone. There was no basic difference between living and nonliving matter except that the living was more complex. According to Haeckel, life itself was only physical, not spiritual. The human mind differed only in degree from the minds of lower animals. Memory, imagination, the senses, and thinking were merely functions of matter.

The behaviorists in the field of psychology adopted the materialist view. They saw man as merely a physical being shaped by environment or economic forces, without a spiritual nature. In

New Lanark

Idealist and builder of socialist utopias, Robert Owen founded his most successful model community at New Lanark, Scotland. After taking control of what he called a "wretched community," he went about creating a good environment for his mill workers. He shortened the work day, banned the use of cruelty, built decent employee housing, cleaned and paved the streets, and started a store where workers would not be cheated by shopkeepers. He handled the problems of drunkenness, dishonesty, and absenteeism with a system of fines and rewards. His other efforts aimed at developing in the villagers a sense of community and social responsibility.

To the children of the community Owen, an atheist, gave special attention. Realizing that the task of building a new society would be more easily accomplished by teaching children proper habits than by trying to change adult habits, he built the first grammar and nursery schools in the country. In these schools, he put into practice what were then unique theories of education: children should enjoy learning; education should be relevant to the child; discipline should be achieved through kindness rather than punishment.

New Lanark became a showplace of progressive ideas, drawing visitors from all over Europe. More prosperous than many of their competitors, Owen's mills disproved the argument that reform would lead to bankruptcy. While New Lanark did not become the vanguard of a new social order for the whole world as its founder expected, many of his ideas on education and social action have greatly influenced modern society.

Owen, like many modern humanist and secular educators, believed that man could be changed from evil to good by giving him a good education and by improving his life conditions. He said in his autobiography that the New Lanark experiment was "to ascertain, in fact, whether replacing evil conditions by good, man might not be relieved from evil, and transformed into an intelligent, rational, and good being;—whether the misery in which man had been and was surrounded, from his birth to his death, could be changed into a life of goodness and happiness, by surrounding him through life with good and superior conditions only."

their view religion and morality were only by-products of physical development. However, materialists' arguments were undermined by Einstein's discovery that matter can be changed into energy. This means that matter is not the only reality—a fact which true religion has always known—and thus the whole basis for materialism crumbles.

Moral relativism and materialism left a value vacuum in Western society. In this vacuum, Nazi and communist doctrines took root and flourished. Such an outcome was quite logical. If there is no right, then the only alternative is might, imposed by governments or revolutionary groups. The results of an atheistic, man-centered system of values, enforced by human beings claiming total power were the purges of **Stalin**, the Cultural Revolution of **Mao Tse-tung**, and numerous other bloodbaths and reigns of terror in Asia and Africa.

Economic Idealism

As the nineteenth century progressed, an ideology that steadily grew in importance was **socialism**. Its followers took their basic ideas from the Enlightenment and the French Revolution, as well as from Darwinism. They felt it was wrong that owners of property and wealth could direct all the labors of society for what socialists supposed was merely their own personal profit. Thus the way to a just social and economic order was to eliminate **capitalism**.

Socialists called for some form of collective or governmental ownership of what they labeled "the means of production"—land, machines, factories, transportation systems, and banks. They rejected competition as too wasteful and harmful, preferring rather some system of cooperative labor or even communal living (members would own all property in common). They emphasized a fairer distribution of goods instead of just increasing the level of production.

The early socialists believed that people could build a better society through rational thought and action. They saw human nature as the product of environment, and said that the evil in people could be changed to good by creating a new environment or society. This new order would promote the well-being of all its members instead of providing profits for the few and misery for the others.

Some socialists tried to set up model communities. Among them was **Robert Owen** (see the insert above). They experimented with schemes for redoing society and new types of productive enterprises. To be sure, they were ignored by all but their disciples and had little influence. They deceived themselves by thinking that once man's social environment and institutions were improved, all evil and suffering would vanish. In fact, the greatest socialist of all, **Karl Marx** (1818-1883), saw through this and ridiculed it as **utopianism**. He said that any attempt to establish socialism before conditions were ripe would surely fail. He claimed his approach was "scientific" because it followed supposed universal laws of social interaction.

European socialism matured in the last third of the century, thanks to the work of two towering personalities, Marx and **Friedrich Engels**. Both were bourgeois (middle-class) Germans.

Marx, a Jew, earned a doctor's degree in philosophy but went into journalism because his radical political views kept him from obtaining a university teaching post. Even this was too much for the

Marx-Engels Statue in former East Berlin

Prussian authorities. They closed his newspaper and forced him to leave Germany. Meanwhile, the young Engels went to Manchester, England, to manage a textile mill owned by his father. After gaining a superficial knowledge of the conditions of the English working classes, he wrote an anticapitalist book.

Marx and Engels Join Forces. The two young men met in 1844 and formed a lifelong friendship. Together, they wrote a pamphlet entitled the *Communist Manifesto*, an outline of action for small radical groups.

When revolution broke out in Germany in 1848 (see next chapter), they returned home and tried to direct it along socialist lines. They published a radical newspaper for the laboring classes and worked with a group called the **Communist League**. With the collapse of the revolt in 1849, both went back to England. Engels picked up his business career, earning money to help support his friend.

Georg Wilhelm Friedrich Hegel, 1770–1831

Marx spent his time developing the details of his theory and working in the British Museum library on a massive book on economics. Entitled *Das Kapital*, the first volume appeared in 1867. After his death, his disciples compiled two more volumes from his notes. Marx also wrote some important smaller books and a great many letters to other socialists, trying to start a working-class movement.

The Ideas Behind Communism. Marx borrowed heavily from earlier thinkers, combining their ideas into a new system. Chief among these was the German philosopher **Georg Wilhelm Friedrich Hegel** (1770–1831). Hegel advanced an idealism which was a reaction to the rationalism of Enlightenment philosophy, especially that of Kant. He had adopted new ideas of **romanticism** that God and nature were one, and he was impressed by the new "science" of evolution, by which God and man lost their fixed and absolute character and came to be seen in relativistic terms. Hegel developed a comprehensive new system with a new Absolute—an ever-changing world soul which is discovered through a process known as **dialectics**, by which one concept (**thesis**) is always challenged by an opposite concept (**antithesis**) and the two concepts form a new conception (**synthesis**). The universe is therefore in a perpetual state of flux and self-creation. Hegel applied this system to all aspects of life, including history, politics, and religion. His system was extremely complex, and included the concept of self-contained existence which he referred to as Spirit and identified as Freedom. All men are incarnations of Spirit and are absolutely free. Man can, in effect, make himself god. Collective man, the State, is god walking on earth. As he put it, "the State is the Divine Idea as it exists on earth" and "the universal spiritual life, to which individuals by birth sustain a relation of confidence and habit, and in which they have their existence and reality."

Marx adapted the dialectic idea to materialist thought, and one of the basic ideas that emerged from his writings is the "materialist view of history" or **dialectical materialism**. He insisted that his system was scientific because it followed inevitable historical "laws" by which workers would triumph in the end.

Like the behaviorists, Marx thought that the chief causes of change were economic factors, the material conditions of life. Men do not create society on the basis of ideas, but in response to basic economic situations and physical needs. The way goods are produced and exchanged is actually the foundation of society.

According to Marx, such things as technology, inventions, natural resources, and property ownership determine the nature of a society. They determine its social relationships, political structure, laws, moral values, and religious beliefs. For example, medieval society was noted for feudalism, chivalry, and Roman Catholicism because it was based on agriculture carried on by noble landowners and serf labor.

Changes come in a society through the process Marx called dialectical materialism. He saw all history as a process of development through time. Change comes out of a clash of opposites (Hegel's dialectic). Out of the current state of affairs (the thesis) would arise an opposite state of affairs (the antithesis). The clash between these two would result in a compromise. This joining of the two produces a better state of affairs (the synthesis). Before long, the synthesis becomes the new thesis; an antithesis grows out of it, and a new and still better synthesis results. This upward evolutionary process continues to repeat itself until a state of perfection is reached.

Marx said that the outstanding feature of history is a struggle between classes. Production involves two classes—the exploiter and the exploited, the ruler and the oppressed, the capitalist and the worker. An economic system naturally expands and production techniques change. This results in the rise of a new class which is most deeply involved in production and which in time challenges the old ruling class. This challenge takes place in a dialectic fashion. The old ruling class is the thesis, the emerging new class the antithesis. A new system (the synthesis) develops, having the best features of both classes. This process of historical evolution will continue until all classes have "freed" themselves. "Communism" or the "classless society" is the result.

Throughout history, class struggles have taken place, Marx said. In Rome's slave society, the plebeians challenged the patricians. In modern times, the rich, commercial, bourgeois class attacked the feudal ruling class. But as the bourgeois class developed strength, its antithesis, the *proletariat*, or working class, came into existence. The *proletariat* then challenged the *bourgeoisie* and brought about a new synthesis.

Marx devoted much of his writing to the growth of the *proletariat* and the moral decline of the *bourgeoisie*. He defined the *bourgeoisie* as the owners of capital. The *proletariat* are wage earners who possess nothing but their hands. The workers give a product its value by their labor, yet the owner of capital does not return the full value of the product to them in wages. Instead, he keeps back as much as he can as "profits." The worker does not get a fair return for his labor. Marx called profit "surplus value" and argued that this proves that capitalism is "organized theft."

Marx said that tensions would build within the capitalist system because more and more capital would come into the hands of fewer and fewer people. Many of the *bourgeoisie* would "sink" into the *proletariat*. As the working class grew, so would its distress. Factories would close down, causing unemployment. Depressions would occur, living standards would drop, and the situation would become intolerable. Before long, a permanent class war would set in between the *bourgeoisie* and the *proletariat*. Workers would view the existing system of law, government, morality, and religion as bourgeois weapons to keep the masses down.

Finally, the *proletariat* would seize power from the *bourgeoisie* in a revolution and set up a "dictatorship," with the state (Hegel's collective god) as its agent. Private property would begin to disappear. The state would eventually disappear also—replaced by voluntary groups. They would be in charge of production and provide for social needs. The wage system would no longer exist.

Each person would work according to his abilities and be paid according to his needs.

Flaws in the Theory. Socialist parties sprang up in industrial nations during the last three decades of the nineteenth century and became quite influential. In 1912, the Socialists had the largest party in Germany's parliament. There were, however, some basic flaws in Marx's thinking. He would probably be forgotten today if his theory had not been rescued and transformed by a Russian malcontent named **Vladimir Lenin**.

Marx overrated the influence of economic conditions. Ideas usually move people to action more than material factors and class interests. Religion and patriotism undoubtedly have a stronger hold on people. It is significant that **Marxism** tended to have the greatest impact on intellectuals and workers who had lost their religious faith. Stressing selfless devotion to the higher cause of class struggle, Marxism took on the form of a religion. But it was hard to convince workers to give their loyalty to the world *proletariat* instead of to their own nation. When the showdown came in World War I, most socialist leaders supported their countries even if it meant shooting fellow workers on the enemy side.

Despite Marx's claims to being scientific, his concept that society evolves upward defies the scientific principle of **entropy.** That principle says that when things follow their natural course, they deteriorate rather than develop into higher and better forms.

Marx did not fully understand capitalism either. His idea of surplus value ignored other factors which made wealth. The total number of capitalists actually increased rather than decreased as he had predicted. Most important, capitalism did not break down but grew stronger. The living standard of workers rose steadily under capital-

This cartoon by Thomas Nast reveals Communism's animosity toward the biblical view of the family. It is represented here as the Destroyer of all, who says, "Home ties are nothing. Family ties are nothing. Everything that is—is nothing."

ism. Newly organized labor unions put pressure on employers for better wages and working conditions, and profits made it possible for employers to provide those things.

When working people gained the right to vote, they formed political parties which worked for their goals. These goals included government ownership of railroads and public utilities, restrictions on monopolies, minimum wage laws, factory regulation, limits on working hours, and social insurance to cover sickness, accidents, and old age. In short, by using the power of the government and the state, workers were able to force a redistribution of wealth. While Marx had complained about the alleged "organized theft" of capitalists, his followers, by giving the democratic state or a dictatorship the power to redistribute wealth, were in effect establishing the concept of "legalized theft."

Marx, actually, did not like to see workers dealing with employers and achieving their demands through legislation. This was the most dangerous threat to his preferred method—revolution—because it made workers content with capitalism. His fears were confirmed in the 1880s and 1890s when the socialist movement split into two factions.

One faction (the revisionists) wanted to change Marxian theories to bring them into line with the realities of the times. They argued that workers could reach their goals by nonviolent, gradual reform, through ballots instead of bullets. Violent class conflict was not always necessary. Capitalism could be changed to meet workers' demands. Among the groups adopting this approach toward socialism was the **Fabian Society** in England which taught that education, democratic means, and long-term patience would usher in a socialist society through natural processes rather than pre-emptive revolutions.

The other faction (the orthodox) did not want any changes in Marxist doctrine. The revolution must come; a dictatorship of the *proletariat* is necessary to destroy capitalism. The bourgeois national state must be replaced by the international *proletariat*. By 1914, however, this viewpoint lost out in most parties, except in Russia.

Anarchists. There were even more radical movements in Europe at this time, but they did not have the support that Marxism did. So-called **anarchists** demanded the end of all governments based upon force or coercion. They wanted the state to be replaced by a collective order based on consent of the people. Although most anarchists were peaceful, a few believed that violence and assassination of political leaders were the only ways to bring down the state. Prominent people murdered by them included the American President **William McKinley**, the king of Italy, the president of France, and the empress of Austria.

On May 4, 1886, anarchists in Chicago, Illinois, were largely responsible for a riot in **Haymarket Square** that grew out of workers' demonstration for an eight-hour working day. Police attempted to disperse the gathering of about 1,500 protesters when a bomb exploded, killing eleven people and injuring more than a hundred others. A trial convicted eight anarchist leaders, and four of them were hanged. Opponents of the labor movement often cited the incident to discredit the declining Knights of Labor organization, the forerunner of the major labor unions in America.

The Rise of Theological Liberalism and Cults

German Idealism. Hume's skepticism spread a sense of futility throughout eighteenth century philosophy and natural science. The rationalism and empiricism of that period were replaced by a new humanistic philosophy in the 19th Century—Idealism. Men such as Kant, Fichte, Schelling, and Hegel sought for truth in the irrational and saw nature and history as the unfolding of God. **Immanuel Kant** (1724-1804) was educated in Lutheran Pietism, and became a professor at the Prussian University of Königsberg. In works such as the *Critique of Pure Reason* (1781), he said that science and reason cannot prove the existence of God, moral law, and immortality. Science, he believed, while describing the physical world, cannot provide a guide for morality. However, human experiences such as *awareness of beauty, conscience,* and *religious feeling* are so real they cannot be doubted even though science cannot explain them. These instincts are given by God for the purpose of teaching people good and evil. They force humans to choose between right and wrong, he said.

In effect, in the area of the these intangible qualities (*noumena*), Kant turned reason on the rationalists and used their own logic to defeat them. After his insistence that science is limited and that we cannot find moral truths in the same way we find scientific facts, the eighteenth century deist debate subsided.

Kant thus sought to disentangle science (physics) from philosophy (metaphysics). He said that the world of appearances—the **phenomenal** world, as he called it—was the realm of science. Science's task was to describe this world through general laws. The other world—which he called **noumenal**—is the proper realm of philosophy, he said. Science should not concern itself with the unseen "realities" behind the appearances. One of the results of this view was to separate science from any theological restraints or influences.

Kant, influenced by Hume, held that it is impossible to know either of these worlds as a matter of certainty. In this he contributed to the growing sense of hopelessness. Although material phenomena cannot ultimately be known to exist, they do serve as raw material from which sensations are formed. Objects themselves do not exist, but our mind's perceptions of them create their existence. Thus material reality exists only as the mind conceives it. The other world—of unseen things—also may not really exist and cannot ultimately be known. However, a kind of reality can be assigned to this world as well by something called 'faith.' This humanistic faith, rather than knowledge, allows one to accept the three great problems of metaphysics—God, the will, and immortality, he said.

Kant taught that human reason is the final authority for *conduct*. For Kant, moral conduct (ethics) must be based on a sense of duty to do what the mind has decided is right. No action based on a fixed absolute or standard can be considered moral. Kant described two kinds of commands: *the hypothetical imperative* and *the categorical imperative*. The hypothetical imperative dictates a course of action needed to reach a given end identified by the mind. The categorical imperative dictates a course of action to be followed because of its righteousness and necessity. Kant's formulation of the categorical imperative is a gross distortion of the Golden Rule: "Act as if the maxim (rule) of your action were to become through your will a general (or universal) natural law." This meant that the individual mind can make up its own rules of conduct, but the individual should try to construct rules for himself that everybody could safely live by. Kant's ethic has gradually become a part of modern thinking and helps to explain the modern experience, foreshadowed in the Bible, of every man doing what is "right in his own eyes." Touted as a formula for freedom, it has become a formula for social chaos.

Kant was anything but Christian in his outlook. It is true that orthodox Christianity teaches that man cannot find God or moral truth scientifically, nor prove the existence of God or the truth of His Word by factual evidences. Kant argued something akin to this. But his claim that man comes to God and moral truth by way of blind faith based on intuitive human experiences is contrary to biblical doctrine. The Bible teaches that man can know God only by divine revelation and grace. Faith is an instrument given by God which allows man to see, understand, and apply the gifts of grace—revelation, the atonement of Christ, and a holy life of righteousness—to himself. Kant's *categorical imperative* is a human moral construct; God's ordinances are divine imperatives handed down from Heaven to condemn sinners, to show men their need for divine help, and to be guides of behavior for those enabled by God's grace to please Him.

Liberalism. In agreement with Kant, some theologians moved away from Enlightenment rationalism. Liberal theologians began to emphasize the importance of experience and feeling as the heart of religion. Thinkers **Friedrich Schleiermacher** and **Albrecht Ritschl** were in the forefront of this movement. Schleiermacher believed that the central foundation of Christianity—the existence of God—was meaningless. The only meaningful idea of God was one that was a projection of human feelings, he held. As he put it, "ideas and principles are all foreign to religion.... If ideas and principles are anything, they must belong to knowledge which is a different department of life from religion." Schleiermacher thus outlined a fragmented view of man's life, and separated religion from other aspects of life. In contrast, as Spanish Christian scholar David Estrada Herrero has put it, the biblical view of man holds that

> the human faculties are so closely interwoven that they all partake of the experience of faith, and they are all participants in the effects of God's revelation. The mind, the heart, and the will come to form an indissoluble unity.

As evolutionary thought became the spirit of the age, the church was profoundly affected. At first, the church, grounded in the belief in a Creator God, resisted evolution and its many implications. Soon, however, Protestantism began to waver and make adjustments to the new thinking. Protestantism became susceptible to this

Friedrich Schleiermacher (1768–1834), the Father of Theological Liberalism

when those raised in Protestant homes did not embrace their parent's faith. Adjustment to the ideas of the evolutionists was also aided in the nineteenth century by the development of the critical approach to the Bible. The new critics espoused a view of the Bible that discounted the idea of divine inspiration and portrayed it as an eclectic collection of merely human writings which had been altered and edited over the centuries. Though laced with much moral guidance, the Scriptures were not to be seen as infallible, inerrant, absolute revelation from God. This view opened the door wide to the Scriptures being adapted to the new evolutionary thought.

The orthodox interpretation of God's revelation of truth in the Bible was no longer accepted. The Bible was seen as a book of human authorship only, with various writers and editors combining their ideas. Supernatural elements were considered myths by people who believed that scientific reasons for how things work were always necessary. Besides denying biblical miracles and prophecies, many also rejected the scientific and historic accuracy of the Bible. Since they accepted evolution as the explanation of man's origin, they no longer believed in the fall of man or the need of redemption by Christ. They tended to see Jesus not as God in the flesh, but merely as a good man. By imitating His example, other humans could reproduce the life-style and ethics of Jesus.

Schleiermacher's views were followed by the mediating theology in Germany, which sought to steer a middle course between rationalism and evangelicalism. J. A. W. Neader, the converted Jew became a leading church historian in Berlin. Others such as Karl Ullmann, Isaac Dorner, August Tholuck, Lange, Nitzsch, Twesten, and Richard Rothe continued the effort to replace biblical authority with human experience and feeling. This movement ultimately undermined the confessions of the Reformation and replaced revelation with symbolism.

In the United States these views were propagated by John Nevin and especially Philip Schaff (1819–1893), a German who had studied at Tübingen and Berlin, eventually became a professor at Union Theological Seminary. Combining the mediating theology with the liturgical interests of the Anglo-Catholic movement they created the Mercersburg theology, a precursor to 20th century ecumenicism. At Union Theological Seminary in New York City the ideas of Isaac Dorner became popularized by Charles Briggs (1841–1913), who led the attack on the inerrancy of the Bible in favor of German criticism. Union Seminary became one of the centers of liberalism in the United States.

But in Denmark, a reaction to the mediating theology of Bishop Hans L. Martensen appeared in the thinker **Søren Aabye Kierkegaard** (1813–1855), who emphasized faith as something that is

Søren Aabye Kierkegaard, 1813-1855

above and beyond reason. He called for an absolute commitment to faith as an antidote to despair and pessimism. He held that to avoid these negative consequences, people must optimistically seek meaning in life without trying to rationally understand it. He proposed a "leap of faith" to do this. Kierkegaard described reason (pessimism, despair) as a "lower story" totally isolated from the "upper story" of non-reason ("faith," optimism), with an impassable gulf between them. In the lower story, man is valueless—a meaningless machine. Meaning can only be found in the upper story of "faith" and experience, not in rationalistic statements or propositions of truth. Kierkegaard's ideas led to a secular and religious philosophy known as **existentialism**, in which experience is the ultimate good and the only thing which can be of value.

The Social Gospel. Emphasizing social action rather than belief as a means of following Jesus, some American Protestants initiated a movement

known as the **"social gospel"** in the late 1800s. In an attempt to deal with the mounting problems of industrialization and urbanization, they aimed to change society to meet Christian standards. A main spokesman of the Social Gospel, **Walter Rauschenbusch**, had developed his views while he was the pastor of an immigrant German Baptist church in a section of New York's slums called "Hell's Kitchen." He believed that winning people to Christ would provide the power to change society. The church existed to create the Kingdom of God which would transform all aspects of life. He once wrote:

> The social gospel is the old message of salvation, but enlarged and intensified. The individualistic gospel has taught us to see the sinfulness of every human heart and has inspired us with faith in the willingness and power of God to save every soul that comes to him. But it has not given us an adequate understanding of the sinfulness of the social order and its share in the sins of all individuals within it.... The social gospel seeks to bring men under repentance for their collective sins and to create a more sensitive and more modern conscience.

Another leader, **Washington Gladden**, often called the "father" of the Social Gospel, believed that society could be made Christian if people loved their neighbors as themselves. Gladden was the pastor of a Congregational Church in Columbus, Ohio, which included both employers and laborers. He expressed alarm at what he saw as a growing conflict between these two classes. He preached a number of sermons on labor problems and appealed to the teachings of Jesus for principles which he said would produce harmony in society. The church could set up the Kingdom of God on earth, he taught, not through force or an economic program, but by inspiring people with a love for justice and spirit of service. He is famous for a hymn that begins:

O Master, let me walk with Thee
In lowly paths of service free;
Tell me Thy secret; help me bear
The strain of toil, the fret of care.

Gladden called for cooperative or government operation of railroads, mines, and public service industries, although he did not call for the abolishment of all private property as the socialists did.

Earlier in England, the "social gospel" movement was led by a group of Christian Socialists, including theologian **J.F.D. Maurice**, novelist **Charles Kingsley**, and lawyer **Malcolm Ludlow**. Between 1848 and 1854, these and other churchmen attacked the idea of *laissez-faire* capitalism. Maurice argued that competition is not an economic law of the universe and should be replaced by the true law—that man is made to live in cooperative community and universal brotherhood. They considered socialism as a further development of Christian ideals for human harmony.

The movement made little headway in England, but its ideas gained a stronger foothold as they were carried over to America. Social Gospel teachers built their theology on the fact that sin is a corporate problem not an individual one, and that salvation, therefore, must deal with social structures and institutions. They said that Christians must work toward the reform of the social order so that civilization may be saved. According to these theologians, the chief collective sin of mankind was capitalism. They said that man could not be truly saved—God's Kingdom could not be established—until the capitalist system were overthrown, but they disagreed on how that should happen.

As this movement gained great influence in America, many seminaries changed their teaching to accommodate the social gospel ideas. In 1908, the Federal Council of Churches of Christ in America was established and wrote a *Social Creed of the Churches*, calling for occupational safety improvements for workers, minimum wage laws, old-age pensions, and rights of arbitration for worker disputes. Yet in all this, the church more and more lost sight of its primary biblical mission—the preaching of the pure gospel of salvation through faith.

The social gospel ethic survived in liberal churches into the twentieth century. Later in the century, the Christian Reconstruction Movement stressed social reconstruction, but looked to Old Testament law as the means to accomplish social reordering. The founder of this movement, **Rousas J. Rushdoony**, repudiated the social gospel when he wrote:

> The social gospel is… a denial of canon law. It sees a one undivided realm, the state, as the true order of God and man. The state is given the overall jurisdiction and sovereignty over church, school, family, business, farming, and all things else which belongs only to God. The essential function of the social gospel is to render all things unto Caesar and nothing to God.

> True canon law is the application of the canon or rule of Scripture to the problems of life. (Rushdoony, R.J., *The Foundations of Social Order* [Philadelphia: Presbyterian and Reformed Publishing, 1968], pp. 134–135)

Rise of Cults. The growing unbelief of the nineteenth century and the undercutting of historic Christian doctrines set the stage for the introduction of a number of religious cults which even more seriously departed from biblical teachings. Strangely, a number of them originated in west-central New York State.

In September 1827, **Joseph Smith** of Palmyra, New York, claimed to have received from an angel named **Moroni** a set of golden plates which contained new scriptures, telling of Christ's appearance to ancient tribes in South America, who were remnants of God's Chosen People. Smith and his followers established the Church of Jesus Christ of Latter-day Saints or **Mormons** in 1830, led by Twelve Apostles, including Brigham Young. The church was centered in Kirtland, Ohio until 1837, when community opposition forced it to move to Missouri and then to Nauvoo, Illinois. Violent persecution prompted Young to lead a band of Mormons to the Valley of the Great Salt Lake in Utah, where they set up a society which flourishes today.

Another unorthodox sect which arose around 1831 was known as the **Millerites** or **Adventists**. Their leader, farmer and lay minister **William Miller** (1792–1899), used certain passages in the biblical books of Daniel and Revelation to calculate what he said was the exact date of Christ's return to earth, March 21, 1843. The figures were revised when that date came and went. By 1846, a group split off from the Millerites over the issue of the Jewish Sabbath and certain interpretations of Daniel. The leader of the **Seventh-day Adventist** splitter group was **Mrs. Ellen White**, whose writings set forth an austere system encompassing generous giving, abstention from alcohol and tobacco, and a comprehensive program of health and evangelistic practices.

The **Spiritualist** movement began in Hydesville, New York. It was led by **Andrew Jackson Davis**, organizer of the Children's Progressive Lyceum. He joined with sisters **Margaret and Kate Fox** in the holding of seances, during which they claimed to make contact with the spirit world. Their gatherings grew famous and claimed two million followers by 1855. A national organization was formed in 1893, but numbers have dwindled in the present day.

In 1866, **Mary Baker Eddy**, after recovering almost instantly from a serious injury, applied her studies in the relationship of mind and spirit to outline a new "scientific system of divine healing." Her religious movement became known as **Christian Science**, which described God as a "Principle of all harmonious Mind-action." Her book, *Science and Health with Key to the Scriptures*, became the textbook of Christian Science, which was established as a church in Boston in 1879. The Boston "Mother Church" was called the First Church of Christ, Scientist, but was neither Christian nor scientific.

In 1872, **Charles Taze Russell** began to attract large crowds when he also preached on the second coming of Christ. The **Russellites** (also known as **Millennial Dawnists** and **International Bible Students**) were formally organized in Pitts-

William Miller stirred up a prophetic enthusiasm by predicting from elaborate calculations that the end of the world would come in 1843. In England, Edward Irving also gained a following by predicting the end between 1835 to 1901.

burgh into what later (1931) became known as **Jehovah's Witnesses**. They formed the **Watchtower Bible and Tract Society, Inc.** in 1939. Witnesses are required to donate large amounts of volunteer time spreading their faith door-to-door and in the streets. They refuse to salute national flags or bear arms, on grounds that government is a tyranny in league with Satan. Satan's other main allies are the teachings of traditional Christian churches and the oppressions of business. The Russellites denied the deity and resurrection of Christ, as well as the Trinity. They taught a second possibility of salvation during a future millennium, and they believed in the annihilation of the wicked. They, like the Mormons, adopted many of the teachings from an ancient heresy known as **Gnosticism**.

Modern Roman Catholicism. While liberal 'Protestantism' had adapted themselves rather readily to new scientific thinking and modern philosophies, the Roman Catholic Church remained much the same during the first three-quarters of the nineteenth century. This is perhaps explained in the fact that Catholicism had always had a fixed body of doctrine and a highly formalized ecclesiastical structure with a powerful, single figure at the top defining the church's positions. Throughout Europe, Catholicism had resisted change, since much of the change challenged the church's historic dominance in European life. This resistance to change remained in force during the nineteenth century. It was reinforced by a new nationalist fervor in Italy which resulted in movements toward unification of that long-segmented peninsula. Unifications usually resulted in the loss of the Vatican's property holdings and power, and change of all kinds came to be seen as the general characteristic of modern times.

Pope Pius IX, whose long reign spanned more than a quarter of the century (1846-78), led the

Vatican City

resistance to modernism, including theological modernism and liberalism. As many intellectuals were rejecting the faith and statesmen were distrusting the clergy, the new scientific and philosophical ideas alarmed the church. In 1864, Pius IX issued a wide-ranging encyclical against modernism, to which he attached a now famous *Syllabus of Errors*. The *Syllabus* denounced everything from freethinking scientists and religious tolerance to lay marriage, lay education, and opposition to the temporal power of the church. The faithful saw this as a heroic attempt to stem the tide of unbelief engulfing Europe.

Pius IX sought to consolidate this resistance by calling the first ecumenical council of the Roman Catholic Church in 300 years. The so-called First Vatican Council of 1870 reaffirmed the supreme authority of the pope on earth over the church. It took a further remarkable step by declaring that when the pope speaks ***ex cathedra*** (in his official position as pastor and teacher) and defines "a doctrine regarding faith and morals," he is **infalli-**

ble. Since his right was claimed in a very narrow sense, it did not apply to the usual papal decrees. It was, however, widely misunderstood, and some Catholics even broke with Rome while secular leaders became uneasy about the papal claim to universal power.

Most of the common people in Catholicism remained pious and faithful while devotion to the Virgin Mary increased. In 1854, the pope proclaimed the dogma that the Virgin Mary had been born free from sin. This doctrine is called the **Immaculate Conception**. A girl named **Bernadette** reported visions of Mary in Lourdes, France, in 1858, causing Catholics from all over the world to make pilgrimages to the town.

The Roman Catholic Church also reacted to the problems of industrialization. **Giovanni (St. John) Bosco**, an Italian priest, assisted poor boys in the rapidly growing Italian city of Turin. He founded the **Salesian Order** (named after Francis de Sales) in 1859, which started orphanages, schools, and workshops. In time, this order extended Don Bosco's program of social work around the world. The priests and religious orders labored in the industrial cities of Western Europe and in the United States.

The papacy moved from a position of opposition to compromise with respect to socialism. **Pius IX** initially labeled socialism as an error and would have nothing to do with modern developments. He believed that true religion was being threatened by the new worship of materialism. When Pius IX died, **Leo XIII** (1878–1903) succeeded him. In 1891, Leo issued his encyclical (papal letter to all bishops) supporting the socialists' claim that capitalism exploits the poor. Leo saw no reason to take issue with states that did not conform to traditional church views, and he held that political forms were irrelevant. In this way, Roman Catholicism began to fall in step with the

progressive, secularizing spirit of the times. Leo placed the Catholic church firmly on the side of labor and socialism.

The encyclical declared that private property is a natural right but must be used justly. Capitalism deserved much of the blame for keeping the working class in poverty, it said. The employer must not overwork his employees or deny them just wages. It is the state's duty to see that workers are properly housed, clothed, and fed. Laws should be passed to prevent strikes by removing the causes of labor-management conflict.

Leo condemned **materialism** but claimed that much in socialism was Christian in principle. Catholics could, if they wished, form socialist parties and labor unions of their own. This cut the church's tie to capitalism and permitted the establishment of Catholic socialist parties. Catholic trade unions, such as those in Germany, also resulted. It is not surprising that the European countries that were predominantly Roman Catholic became socialistic in the twentieth century and some have been swayed by Marxist thought.

The Witness and Works of Evangelical Christianity

Historic Protestant Orthodoxy. Despite new theological trends, many people still retained their belief in the historic Christian faith. Missionaries went around the world to tell others the Christian message of salvation (see chapter 10), while Christians discussed in chapter 7 showed their concern for finding solutions to social problems.

Political Influence. In Britain, public life was seen as a good way for people to express their

Christian faith. The outstanding prime minister, **William Ewart Gladstone**, set up the British educational system in 1870 and helped efforts to gain the secret ballot and extend voting rights. Other men identified with mainstream churches served the cause of the workers—**John Wilson**, union leader and member of Parliament, and **James Keir Hardie**, chief founder of the British Labour Party.

The American **William Jennings Bryan** was a brilliant spokesman for social justice and world peace. Three times a candidate for president and a tireless critic of both Darwinism and Social Darwinism, Bryan was an outstanding evangelical Protestant. He was a champion of farmers and working people, and gathered much Populist support during his campaign for the Democratic

A brilliant politician and natural orator, Gladstone helped bring about many vital reforms in England. It was during his term of office that urban workers received the right to vote.

candidate for president in 1896. He was a strong supporter of the Bible and was eloquent in his attacks on the evils of liquor.

Le Réveil in Europe. The awakenings of the 18th Century eventually found their way to Europe after the days of Napoleon. Le Réveil, as it was called, spread through Switzerland, France and the Netherlands reviving the faith of the Reformation and forming new churches and institutions. It began when the Scottish Calvinistic evangelist, **Robert Haldane** (1764–1842), traveled through France and Switzerland to preach the gospel in 1816. At Geneva he found many theological students ignorant of the great teachings of the Reformation. His lectures on Paul's Epistle to the Romans led to the conversion of César Malan, François Gaussen and Jean Henri Merle d'Aubigné

César Malan (1787–1864), originally under the influence of Voltaire and Rousseau, became a powerful preacher after his conversion, preaching throughout France and other parts of Europe. Along with Frédéric and Adolphe Monod they brought about a new Protestant influence in France leading to the founding of the Free Church Movement.

François Gaussen (1790–1863) helped found the Evangelical Society of Geneva with d'Aubigné in 1831 and a Reformed Evangelical theological school a few years latter. Of his many writings, his *Theopneustia* (1840) set forth the verbal inspiration of the Bible against the bitter attacks of rationalists. **Jean Henri Merle d'Aubigné** (1794–1872) went on to study church history in Germany and preach there and in Brussels. Upon his return to Geneva he joined Gaussen in the teaching at the new seminary. His *History of the Reformation of the Sixteenth Century* (1863–1878) in eight volumes became a classic, and set forth a Christian view of history.

Jean Henri Merle d'Aubigné

In the Netherlands, the Réveil had powerful intellectual results for the defense of the faith and provided a clear biblical answer to the apostasy of modern humanism. The poet, scholar, and historian **Willem Bilderdijk** (1756–1831), a strong Calvinist and patriot of the House of Orange, inspired a number of students at Leiden to provide both a protest and alternative to the ideas of the Enlightenment. Among these was **Isaac da Costa** (1798–1860), a Jewish convert, who exposed the liberalism of his day in a scathing critique, *A Warning Against the Spirit of the Age* (1823). It became a manifesto of the anti-revolutionary sentiments of the Réveil. Among the students at Leiden who came under this teaching were H. P. Scholte, Anthony Brummelkamp, Simon Van Velzen, A. C. Van Raalte who separated from the established church and founded the free Christian Reformed Churches. But it was **Guillaume Groen van Prinsterer** (1801–1876)

who carried the ideas of the Réveil to a culmination in his lectures exposing the French Revolution, entitled *Unbelief and Revolution* (1847). He provided a powerful biblical analysis not only of the Revolutionary spirit but provided the basis of a Christian view of history and philosophy. He went on to found a political movement, the Christian Historical or Anti-Revolutionary Party, and served as a member of parliament. He also became deeply involved in the promotion of separate Christian schools, not controlled by the state. But he only laid the foundations.

It was the pastor, theologian, and newspaper editor, **Abraham Kuyper** (1837–1920), who took up the work of Groen van Prinsterer in the Anti-Revolutionary Party, becoming himself a member of the parliament, and gained national influence when he served as a highly effective prime minister. A staunch Calvinist, he founded the Free University of Amsterdam, where he was assisted by the great theologian and scholar **Herman Bavinck** (1854–1921) in promoting the Bible as the unconditional basis for a whole structure of human knowledge in every facet of life. In 1897, noting the twenty-fifth anniversary of his editorship of *De Standaard* newspaper, he wrote:

> One desire has been the ruling passion of my life. One high motive has acted like a spur upon my mind and soul. And sooner than that I should seek escape from the sacred necessity that is laid upon me, let the breath of life fail me. It is this: That in spite of all worldly opposition, God's holy ordinances shall be established again in the home, in the school and in the State for the good of the people; to carve as it were into the conscience of the nation the ordinances of the Lord, to which Bible and Creation bear witness, until the nation pays homage again to God.

Few men of public affairs have had such a godly vision, but Kuyper worked tirelessly accomplish-

Abraham Kuyper

ing almost superhuman achievements with that motivation.

In 1898, Kuyper journeyed to the United States and delivered a series of lectures on Calvinism at Princeton Theological Seminary. In these lectures, Kuyper set forth what has been called "a classic expression of a vigorous and visionary stream of the Reformed faith"—a "life-system of comprehensive and far-reaching effect" with implications for religion, politics, science, art, and the future. Among other things, he said that the civil government, by its very nature, lacks the "data of judgment" for pronouncements or actions on spiritual matters and therefore must never infringe on the sovereignty of the church. "If the government rests with the plurality of persons, the Church which yesterday was counted the false one, is today considered the true one, according to the decision of the vote; and thus all continuity of state-administration and church-position is lost," he said. "Hence it is that the Calvinists have always struggled so proudly for the liberty, that is to say, for the sovereignty, of the Church, within her own sphere, in distinction from the Lutheran theologians."

Thomas Chalmers and the Disruption. While there had been decline and revival in Scotland during the eighteenth century, a powerful change in national life was introduced by **Thomas Chalmers** (1780–1847), theological teacher, preacher, social reformer, mathematician, and ecclesiastical statesman. He entered St. Andrews University when he was just twelve years old. Upon graduation he was a part-time teacher in mathematics while he began his first pastorate. Converted in 1811, his preaching was transformed and he began publishing for the *Christian Instructor* against the influence of the Moderates, who had compromised biblical truth for humanistic ideas. When in 1815 he began preaching in Glasgow, many flocked to hear his evangelical Calvinistic sermons. Deeply concerned about the social needs of the working man and the poor in Glasgow, he instituted a number of works for the needy, as well as Day and Sunday schools for children. His great success in following biblical patterns made his evangelical faith a force to be reckoned with. In 1823 he turned to the teaching of philosophy at St. Andrews and Edinburgh. He became the leader of the evangelical Calvinistic movement in the Established church and led a third of the church into the Disruption of 1843 which brought the Free Church of Scotland into existence. The implications of this movement for Scottish leadership in Christian missions and industrial innovation was far-reaching, not only in Scotland itself, but through its influence on American Christianity.

Preaching and Evangelism. For many members of the middle class, churchgoing in the United States was the respectable thing to do. However, numbers of the indifferent pew-warmers were stirred to a more vital faith in Jesus Christ by several notable preachers.

A shoe clerk named **Dwight L. Moody** (1837–1899) grew so concerned for non-Christians in Chicago that he became an evangelist. Although never a polished speaker, his campaigns in Britain and the United States drew large crowds and met with great success. Originally a Unitarian, he was converted to Christ and became a Congregationalist. Later, he began missionary work in Chicago. His Sunday school in North Market Hall

Moody is shown here preaching in the Agricultural Hall in London. This was the largest building ever used during his campaigns.

became the Illinois Street Church in 1863 and then the Chicago Avenue Church and still later the famous Moody Memorial Church. In company with the singer and hymn composer **Ira Sankey**, Moody launched his famous revival meetings. In addition to preaching, Dwight L. Moody started two schools, Northfield Seminary for Young Women and Mount Hermon School for Boys. In 1889, he also began a school for training Christian workers which is now known as the Moody Bible Institute. Sunday school children gave "five cents a brick" to help construct the first building on the campus of the Moody Bible Institute. Today this school is one of the largest evangelical training centers in the United States.

A sometimes associate of Moody, **Cyrus I. Scofield** (1843–1921), began his career as a lawyer of questionable repute and abandoned his first wife and family before linking up with some leaders of the Plymouth Brethern, followers of **John Darby**, who was advancing the revival of an old doctrine (Chiliasm) concerning the end times of the world. Scofield was commissioned to study the doctrine in England, and the result was a famous series of biblical notes detailing a theological system known as **premillennial dispensationalism**. This system divided history into segments during which God was said to have operated in different ways among men. It taught that Christ would one day return to earth, remove the faithful, and then set up a thousand-year reign upon earth, ruling the world with an iron hand from His throne in Jerusalem, after which a final battle between good and evil would ensue before the world comes to an end.

Preaching a more orthodox Christianity was the eloquent London preacher, **Charles Haddon Spurgeon**, who gained fame for his powerful and direct preaching style. Thousands were con-

Charles Haddon Spurgeon, 1834–1892

verted, and his church grew to more than 6,000 members. His sermons, published weekly, had worldwide impact; his devotional readings are still beloved by many. A descendent of Huguenots, he was a passionate champion of Protestant (Calvinist-Baptist) orthodoxy. Spurgeon was also an outspoken opponent of Catholicism, which he usually referred to as "popery."

Romantic Idealism in the Arts

At the same time that scientific and philosophic thought was changing, artists were seeking to implement idealism and romanticism in their work. The nineteenth century saw three succeeding (sometimes overlapping) trends in artistic expression. In the early years of the century, there

was a lingering element of the **classicism** of the eighteenth century. Classicism reflected a belief in a rationalistic order, strict form, submission to law, and strong self-discipline—the virtues of the Greeks and Romans. During the middle years, the bulk of the period, **romanticism** characterized philosophy and art. Romanticism despised the order and rationality of classicism in favor of freedom and subjectivity, even to the acceptance of disorder. As the century drew to a close, the artistic trend was toward **realism** and subjective **impressionism**, which were further reactions to both classicism and romanticism. These movements sought to give artistic expression of the scientific spirit, to view things as they are. Observation and portrayal followed exact lines and could not neglect details. The political parallel to classicism was conservatism; to romanticism, liberalism; and to realism, materialistic social democracy.

The **romantics**, who occupied center stage for most of the nineteenth century, felt that the eighteenth century emphasis on reason was misplaced. The pursuit of bare facts ignored the "spiritual" and emotional side of human nature, they thought. Whereas in historic Christian thinking, man's heart, mind, body, and soul are a unified whole, to the romantics, man's heart and feelings were primary. Thus romanticism was a reaction to both the Enlightenment and the Reformation. In a sense, however, it was not so much a reaction to the Enlightenment as an attempt to move *beyond* the limits of reason to find autonomous freedom. To the romantics, reason was not sufficient to fully explore the traditional metaphysical categories of god, the human soul, and the forces of the universe.

A foundational idea in romanticism, as advanced earlier by Rousseau, was the goodness of man. While earlier philosophies such as Renaissance humanism and Enlightenment thought had believed in the essential goodness of man, Romanticism made man himself the source of this goodness. This notion of *inherent* or *natural* goodness was an entirely new view of mankind and the world, and it was epitomized in the idea of "the noble savage." Primitive man is by nature good; civilization corrupts him. The same could be said about "nature." It too was said to be good in and of itself until civilization corrupts it.

Chiefly a trend in literature and the other arts, romanticism valued feeling, imagination, emotion, sentiment, and mystery. The romantic understanding of the term *feeling* went deeper than "emotion" to the ideas of *inner consciousness* and the *experience of ultimate being*, even the irrational elements of existence. Enlightenment writers emphasized the qualities people had in common. Romantics were interested in the individual personality and the differences among people, including nationality.

Most eighteenth-century artists, musicians, and thinkers had tried to analyze and structure everything. Romantics liked the spontaneous and unpredictable. The *deists* had stressed city life, mathematics and the culture of the intellectual middle class, the circle in which they moved. Romantics adored the pastoral life and nature. They were more concerned with the people as such, including the rural and urban lower classes. As a result, they were among the early supporters of the French Revolution, although they were later disillusioned by the results which quickly developed. They also encouraged such revolutionary political changes as the extension of voting rights.

The romantics had a sentimental, dreamy love for the past, especially the Middle Ages. It was an escape from the heartless, industrial civilization which they saw emerging. They viewed the medieval world as a society which had given people security and a sense of belonging. There the poor were content with their place in life. The noble lords saw their duty to protect those dependent upon them, and heroic deeds were part of the way of life. It was an age of "faith," vastly different from the cold reason and doubt of the Enlightenment.

But the "faith" of the romantics was still a faith in man. In some ways, it was a faith in art itself. One of the unique things about romantic artistic expression was its in-depth discussion of the role and function of art in civilized life. Artists debated whether art was to amuse, teach, or inspire. Was it a means of escape from a disagreeable world into a dream world of loveliness, or was it a means to give an existing culture, whatever its nature, its best expression? For many the answer was that the artist is the prophet of the new age. Abraham Kuyper saw this danger when he warned against the "Antithesis between Symbolism and Revelation." When the artist was seen to replace the prophets of Scripture we begin to hear one of the popular slogans of the day: "Art for art's sake."

As the century continued, many Victorian writers and other artists expressed their confident optimism for their contemporary world. (The period was named "Victorian" in England after Queen Victoria.) Although they realized that problems existed, they were convinced that solutions were possible. They felt that progress made in the scientific, industrial, and political areas of life would be spread throughout the British empire and around the globe. Their enthusiasm for this progress could be seen in the **Great Exhibition** of 1851 sponsored by Prince Albert. Millions of people visited the exhibits housed in the Crystal Palace.

People aimed to understand the world and its history as well as individual human beings. *For some, the writer replaced the religious leader as the one who could interpret the meaning of life and who could provide encouragement for moral action.*

As magazines and inexpensive books became more available, creative literature was read by a wider audience. Some critics wondered about the effect that a lower-class audience would have on the artistic level of the country. This is a concern which has continued into twentieth-century evaluations of television and the movies, the new "literary" forms.

Although every country within the western realm had elements of the romantic style within their cultures, this form of expression is perhaps best seen in English and American literature, French painting, and Germanic and Russian music.

Romantic Poetry. Romantic poets expressed feelings of enthusiasm or extreme sadness, along with insights into the causes of joy and pain. **William Wordsworth** described poetry as "emotion recollected in tranquility." Poets tried to capture and describe a particular moment in time. They tried to show how an event had made the observer feel.

Victorian writers such as **Matthew Arnold** communicated man's loneliness in a world where he no longer believes in God. Others struggled to reconcile scientific thought with religious beliefs. Still others, such as **Robert Browning**, used dramatic monologues to show characters and their psychological motivations.

Poets such as **Dante Gabriel Rossetti** aimed at pictorial simplicity and truth in their work. Some of their Victorian opponents felt that their poems were too sensuous.

Of all English poets of the romantic era, Wordsworth (1770–1850) perhaps best exemplified the thinking of the period. He believed that nature and country life were the best sources of subject matter for poetry. Many of his works exude the romantic's quest for salvation in communication with nature. In *The World Is Too Much with Us*, for example, Wordsworth passionately disavows civilization in favor of intercourse with natural beauty, even if becoming a pagan is the price.

> The world is too much with us; late and soon,
> Getting and spending, we lay waste our powers:
> Little we see in Nature that is ours;
> We have given our hearts away, a sordid boon!
> This Sea that bares her bosom to the moon;
> The winds that will be howling at all hours,
> And are up-gathered now like sleeping flowers;
>
> For this, for everything, we are out of tune;
> It moves us not.—Great God! I'd rather be
> A Pagan suckled by a creed outworn;
> So might I, standing on this pleasant lea,
> Have glimpses that would make me less forlorn;
> Have sight of Proteus rising from the sea;
> Or hear old Triton blow his wreathèd horn.

In *Ode: Intimations of Immortality from Recollections of Early Childhood*, Wordsworth speaks of a mystical cycle of life in which man and nature share a common soul stemming from a kind of pantheistic god. This soul civilization tends to imprison until by the end of earthly life, much of this uncommon inner light fades away into the common light of mundane life. Verse V of this work says, in part:

> Our birth is but a sleep and a forgetting:
> The Soul that rises with us, our life's Star,
> Hath had elsewhere its setting, And cometh from afar:
> Not in entire forgetfulness,
> And not in utter nakedness,
> But trailing clouds of glory do we come
> From God, who is our home:
> Heaven lies about us in our infancy!
> Shades of the prison-house begin to close
> Upon the growing boy,
> But he beholds the light, and whence it flows,
> He sees it in his joy;

The Crystal Palace

On May 1, 1851, the Great Exhibition opened in a glittering hall known as the Crystal Palace in London's Hyde Park. The first "world's fair" in history, it brought together under one roof 15,000 displays of machinery, manufactured goods, raw materials, curiosities, and art objects from all over the world. The building itself was one of the first prefabricated structures ever made. It contained one million square feet of glass fitted into a forest of 5,000 wood and iron columns and girders. It covered 19 acres of ground, stood 108 feet high, and contained 300,000 glass panes.

Taking the theme of "Progress," the exhibition aimed at displaying the "works of industry of all nations." According to Prince Albert, who inspired the fair, it would give a true picture of the progress made by the whole of mankind to that point. So the latest technology held the place of honor—the telegraph cable which would be laid across the English Channel in a few months, great locomotives, noisy presses, and steam hammers.

Victorian humor found expression in a few of the displays, such as the alarm bedstead. When it was time to get up, the bed threw its occupants into a tub of cold water. Also on display were exotic and artistic exhibits featuring carved ivory furniture from India, the spectacular Koh-i-noor diamond, elegant French porcelain, Chinese jade, and a Tunisian bazaar.

Because the admission charge was low enough for the common people to attend, the management feared riots. Actually, the crowds were quite orderly. By the time the exhibition ended, six million people had gazed at its wonders. More than any other event of the time, the fair at the Crystal Palace symbolized British leadership in the Industrial Revolution and the optimism of the times.

The Youth, who daily farther from the east
Must travel, still is Nature's priest,
And by the vision splendid
Is on his way attended;
At length Man perceives it die away,
And fade into the light of common day.

Themes of sensuous escapism can be found in **Samuel Taylor Coleridge**'s *Kubla Khan,* **Edward Fitzgerald**'s *Rubáiyát of Omar Kyayyám of Naishápúr,* **Percy Bysshe Shelley**'s *Ozymandias,* and **John Keats**' *Ode to a Nightingale.*

Other major figures of English romantic poetry were **George Gordon, Lord Byron; William Cullen Bryant; Elizabeth Barrett Browning; Alfred Lord Tennyson; Emily Dickinson; Christina Rossetti;** and **Robert Burns.**

In America, the lusty **Walt Whitman** thundered about man's unity with the land and celebrated man's quest to become master of his own fate.

Alfred Lord Tennyson, 1809–1892

Henry Wadsworth Longfellow, Edgar Allen Poe, and **Ralph Waldo Emerson,** among others, also celebrated romantic themes.

For the romantic poets, their new worldview was a fresh beginning for humanity, the dawn of a new era for the soul of the world. Shelley expressed it as a kind of reincarnation—the beginning of *The World's Great Age,* towering over the wrecks of history's earlier religions and enterprises:

The world's great age begins anew,
The golden years return,
The earth doth like a snake renew
Her winter weeds outworn:
Heaven smiles, and faiths and empires gleam,
Like wrecks of a dissolving dream.

The world is weary of the past,
Oh, might it die or rest at last!

The New Novels and Drama. Many famous novels were written during the romantic period. Indeed, the nineteenth century may well be called the age of the novel. **Sir Walter Scott,** whose narrative epic poem *Ivanhoe* reflects the romantic fascination with the Middle Ages, pioneered in writing historical fiction. **Charles Dickens** is best known for his social critiques against the dark side of the Industrial Revolution. Dickens was a romantic in terms of his strong sentimentality, but he fits within the realist category with his bleak depiction of poverty.

Nineteenth-century novels traced relationships between characters and events. Characters were developed more fully than in earlier novels. Authors often published their books in monthly magazines, a chapter at a time. This fact accounts for the great length and some of the repetition in fiction during this period.

Two important French novelists were **Honoré de Balzac** and **Victor Hugo.** Their massive works provide insight into a wide range of social classes and individuals. **William Makepeace Thackeray**'s *Vanity Fair,* which took its title from the allegorical place of worldliness in John Bunyan's *Pilgrim's Progress,* is one of many English novels which describe society with gentle satire. **Charlotte Bronte**'s *Jane Eyre* and particularly **Emily Bronte**'s *Wuthering Heights* follow motivations of characters from one generation to another, in a more rural English setting.

Russians such as **Leo Tolstoy** and **Feodor Dostoyevsky** narrated the sorrows and joys of their characters clearly and perceptively. They showed a world in which people and their actions matter.

In France, the novelist **Gustave Flaubert** plunged daringly into **realist** themes. His *Madam Bovary* (1857) was a story of the escapades of a housewife and a stinging study of a society which Flaubert depicted as stifling her. Flaubert was sued by the French government for committing an "outrage against public morals and religion."

The Norwegian dramatist **Henrik Ibsen** used realist techniques to depict natural characters in conflict with social custom and traditional environments. He has become known as the "father" of the modern drama. His dramatic poem *Peer Gynt* was used by fellow Norwegian romantic composer **Edvard Grieg** in two musical suites by the same name.

Realism was fairly short-lived in the world of literature. It was soon replaced by **naturalism,** just as realism was replaced by **impressionism** in painting. Naturalist writers sought to observe the world with scientific detachment, without giving moral guidance. Heredity and environment guided men as God or the gods had once done. Among the writers following the naturalistic school were England's **Thomas Hardy** and America's **Theodore Dreiser.** Characters were shaped by forces over which they had no control—their own inherited characteristics, society as a whole, tragic circumstances, and natural disasters. The ideas of Darwin and Marx had filtered throughout intellectual society.

Another artistic trend which surfaced late in the century was **symbolism**. It began in poetry (with Frenchman **Stéphane Mallarmé**) but soon spread to the novel, drama, music (**Claude Debussy, Richard Wagner**), and **post-impressionist** painting (see later section in this chapter). The symbolists sought to depict "spiritual reality" through imagery rather than to reproduce visible and tangible reality. By use of the imagination, they sought to achieve "total experience." This led them to seek out the unknown and exotic, and in so doing they hoped their art could "transcend life." Needless to say, this art form became increasingly difficult for common people to understand. Frequently, the symbolists fell into decadence, despair, and morbidity. French symbolist poet **Paul Verlaine** attempted to murder his friend and fellow decadent-symbolist, **Arthur Rimbaud**. This experience sobered him and drove Verlaine back to the Catholic faith for a time, but he ended his life in continual abject drunkenness. Rimbaud, who stopped writing by age 19, wandered the world and spent some time in the Ethiopian court. Symbolism influenced the work of such notables poets and novelists as **T.S. Eliot** (who later became a Christian), **James Joyce, Gertrude Stein**, and **Marcel Proust**.

The novel was also developed in American literature. Novelists included **Nathaniel Hawthorne, Herman Melville, Harriet Beecher Stowe**, and **Mark Twain**. These authors wrote books based on life in America, showing the bad as well as the good aspects of society. Hypocrisy, cruelty, humor, and loyalty were among their themes. Because the United States was such a young country, some Europeans felt that American art

was not of a high enough quality to be taken seriously. These attitudes began to be overcome by writers such as **Washington Irving, Longfellow**, and **James Fenimore Cooper**. Later, the realist **Henry James** wrote novels exploring the relationships between Europeans and Americans. In many types of philosophy and art, the United States still follows the lead of Europe, even today.

German Literature. A genius of German literary culture was the poet, dramatist, novelist (and scientist) **Johann Wolfgang von Goethe** (1749–1832). His broad range of interests and discussions caused him to be widely read, quoted, and admired. Although much of his work extends into the Romantic period, his talents bloomed early and allowed him to dominate the Germany cultural scene in the eighteenth century. A student of law at Leipzig and Strasbourg, he was attracted to mysticism and occult philosophy. He believed in individual freedom, but his calls for freedom were more personal (that is, for himself) than social. He had little sympathy for the revolutionary ideas imbedded in the political ideas of the English and French Enlightenment. He 'respected' the historical role of Christianity, but he considered himself "decidedly non-Christian." He was essentially a pagan, in the mold of the sensual Greeks. He held a pantheistic view of God and worshiped the wonders of nature. He found the doctrine of original sin repugnant and became furious when Kant, late in life, wrote that man was hampered by "radical evil"; he charged that Kant had "slobbered on his philosophical cloak." He believed in the need to perfect oneself through experience, he also bowed to fate, which he regarded as a "demonic" force that could overpower reason.

Romanticism in Music. Musical art in the nineteenth century also had many romantic elements. Lyric quality as well as strong, driving emotions

Beethoven Becomes Deaf

Beethoven's friends and associates never knew what kind of mood he would be in. One day he sent a letter to a lesser-known musician telling him, "Do not come to me any more. You are a false fellow." The next day, he sent another letter to the same man, "Good friend Nazerl," it read, "you are an honorable fellow, and I see you were right. So come this afternoon to me." This behavior was typical of Beethoven. To him, most other men were inferior, incapable of understanding his own heroic visions. The feelings of these lesser men mattered so little to Beethoven that he seldom hid his contempt for them.

Then in 1798, the great musician began to experience a whistling and buzzing in his ears. He had to be very close to the orchestra in order to hear the high tones. When the realization came that he might actually lose his hearing, he became enraged. In a letter regarding his estate, he recorded his inner feelings.

…I was compelled early to isolate myself, to live in loneliness… it was impossible for me to say to men speak louder, shout, for I am deaf. Ah how could I possibly admit an infirmity in the one sense which should have been more perfect in me than in others, a sense which I once possessed in highest perfection, a perfection such as few surely in my profession enjoy… I must live like an exile, if I approach near to people a hot temper seizes upon me, a fear that I may be subjected to the danger of letting my condition be observed….

As his illness progressed, Beethoven's pride and strength at last collapsed. His defiance dissolved into resignation. It was at this point that he made the great discovery, that the deafness did not lessen his creative energy. He could still hear the music in his mind; he could still compose. Beethoven went on to write his masterpiece, the Ninth Symphony, after he was totally deaf.

Ludwig van Beethoven, 1770–1827

contributed to the appeal of this music. Another important factor was **nationalism**. Some composers used folk tunes and dances or historical episodes as a source of ideas. Listeners felt **nostalgia** for the past and could identify with the music. Some pieces also expressed desires for the present, such as the liberation of one country from another.

Works by the late-eighteenth- and nineteenth-century European composers form the basic repertory of serious music played around the world. Symphonies by **Ludwig van Beethoven** (German), **Franz Schubert** (Austrian), **Johannes Brahms** (German-Austrian), and **Pëtr Ilyich Tschaikovsky** (Russian) are showcases of emotion, pathos, romantic ideals, and/or nationalistic pride. Orchestras increased in size, so these composers could strive for ever more impressive effects. Beethoven's music, born in the classical tradition and later infused with the romanticism of his day, formed the foundation for nearly all of Europe's music during the nineteenth century.

Lyrical melodies were prominent in the works of **Schubert**, **Carl Maria von Weber** (German), **Robert Schumann** (German), **Frédéric Chopin** (Polish-French), and **Franz Liszt** (Hungarian). Sonatas and concertos featuring one particular instrument such as violin or piano continued to be popular. Some composers blended two forms of art as they wrote songs using the poetry of great writers such as **Goethe** and **Friedrich von Schiller**. Schiller's *Ode to Joy* was used by Beethoven in his soaring Ninth Symphony. Others used a painting, a rural scene, or a literary work as a source of ideas for their music. These compositions helped the listener to see and feel as well as hear what was being played.

Operas combined dramatic flair with both vocal and instrumental music. Musicians throughout Europe wrote operatic works. Important composers of operas were **Georges Bizet** (French) and **Giuseppe Verdi** (Italian). **Richard Wagner**'s (1813–1883) operas used German heroes and mythology to express his pagan philosophy of life, in which he insisted that feeling rather than reason was the source of power. He was involved in the 1849 revolution in Germany, and was at one time an admirer of Nietzsche. He believed that musical art should create "a total experience." His operas underscored a variety of arts— drama, dance, painting, architecture, and, above all, full-bodied music. Wagner enlarged the brass and woodwind sections of orchestras, giving his music a tremendous volume of sound and a deep range of tone. His music was greatly admired by the Nazis in the 20th century.

There were a number of composers, however, that represented a more Christian attitude. **Johannes Brahms** was one of the few composers whose genius was recognized in his lifetime. Walter Niemann, in his biography of the composer, stated, "The fact that Brahms began his creative activity with the German folk song and closed with the Bible reveals better than anything else the true religious creed of this great man of the people." **Felix Mendelssohn** (1809–1847) was from a Jewish family that had converted to Protestantism. He was responsible for a revival of the music of Bach and wrote some great works himself such as *Elijah* (1846), the greatest oratorio since Handel's *Messiah*.

Johannes Brahms, 1833–1897

From Romantic to Impressionist Painting. Nineteenth-century artists followed several different styles. There was a strong contrast between the French and English schools. France led the way towards a secular perspective, while English art represented more of a Christian worldview.

Sir David Wilkie (1785–1841), the son of a Scottish minister adapted the Dutch genre painting to Britain and became quite influential on artists throughout the country who represented the Christian values of home, family, and work. This group of artists included William Mulready and the Norwich school. Their art appealed greatly to the new middle class who became their patrons. One of the most popular and therefore wealthiest artists was **Sir Edwin Landseer**, who traveled throughout Europe producing country scenes and portraits of children and pets, expressing the ideals of domestic happiness. This approach was also represented in Switzerland by **Albert Anker** (1831–1910), in the Netherlands by **Cornelis Jetses** and in Sweden by **Carl Larsson** (1853–1919). The trend toward romanticism was evident in the English landscape artists **John Martin** (1789–1854) painted dramatic pictures of biblical events while **J. M. W. Turner** often portrayed nature in stormy settings.

By the middle of the century the **Pre-Raphaelite Brotherhood** was formed by the Italian immigrant Dante Gabriel Rossetti, William Holman Hunt, Everett Millais and Edward Burne-Jones, which was inspired by the Anglo-Catholic or Tractarian movement and the German Nazarener. They attempted to return to pre-Reformation Europe and a revive Gothic and Catholic ideals. Hunt painted images of Jesus that became very popular. They painted moody subjects with intense colors. Their influence in England led away from a Christian perspective and degenerated into a morbid type of sensuality.

In the early part of the century in France, classical art forms gave way to popular romantic themes and styles. Among the neoclassical artists was the Frenchman **Jacques Louis David**, who spanned the eighteenth and nineteenth centuries. He participated in the French Revolution and became dictator of the arts, managing propaganda for such events as the Feast of Reason. He allegorized the actions of the Revolution by painting scenes depicting historical events, some from ancient times and others which were more contemporary. French romanticism was evident in the works of **Ferdinand Victor Eugène Delacroix**, who used brilliant color to capture the importance of events he painted.

Historian S.C. Burchell describes romantic-era artists in this way:

> When they did not paint portraits, stags and landscapes, they painted Classical nudes or nymphs and Renaissance angels, sometimes combining lascivious suggestion with moral sermonizing, often telling stories drawn from history, religion and ancient mythology.

> The success of such works reveals some of the criteria that guided the average person's taste in art around the middle of the 19th Century. He generally wished to be told a story, to be diverted and to receive a little moral instruction. The art that satisfied these demands relied on the imitation of a remote past. It did not deal with the life that people saw around

Cornelis Jetses, *Springtime in the Field*

them, nor delve into social problems; it did not demand that the viewer inquire into the unfamiliar; it conveyed no universal message, and it encouraged sentimentality.

In short, romantic art was escapist and irrelevant to real life. It exalted the irrational, the strange, and the mysterious as it revolted against the rationalism of the 18th century.

Certain elitists tended to dictate "correctness" of artistic expression. The artistic elitism, driven by men in love with tradition, was primarily centered in the **Salon des Beaux-Arts** of Paris. These men generally held the fate of would-be artists in their hands; thus those seeking success sought to please the artistic bent of the academies. Many artists in France, now critically acclaimed as masters, lived and worked in great poverty when they bucked the strictures of the art-world's elite. In 1863 alone, the **Salon des Beaux-Arts** rejected 3,000 of the 5,000 works submitted for its annual exhibition, an action which the press called a "massacre."

The most innovative styles to gain a prominent place in French art during the nineteenth century were **realism**, *art nouveau*, and **impressionism**. Realism emerged in the 1850s in France. The term does not signify that artists sought mere photographic accuracy; rather, the term was applied to attempts to portray its subject material in a matter of fact way. The first painter to employ this approach was **Gustave Courbet** from Ornans in eastern France. He was critical of the romantic goal of escapism and argued that the artist's own experience must be revealed in his work. "Show me an angel, and I will paint one," he once said. Despite appreciative responses from the popular Delacroix, Courbet and his realism were at first scorned. French realism was not able to incorporate anything beyond mere factuality and experience.

By the 1890s, another art form, *art nouveau* (new art), arose in Europe and swept the cultured West as a popular craze. (It was called *Jugendstil* in Germany and *Modernismo* in Spain). Art nouveau was characterized by swirling, ornamental lines and natural forms and dealt with symbolic, exotic, or decadent themes. Part of the Romantic infatuation with the irrational it idealized the organic idea which was so popular in Darwinism and Idealistic philosophy. It was used in architectural decoration, home furnishings, women's fashion, jewelry, and glassware. It was evident in the work of the Austrian **Gustav Klimt** as well as the Norwegian **Edvard Munch** and the English graphic artist **Aubrey Beardsley**. The designer **Louis Comfort Tiffany** (famous for his glass

Claude Monet, *Garden* (1900)

lamps) was one of its practitioners in the United States.

Impressionism was somewhat more subtle than realism. It's method involved capturing isolated moments in time and paint them with splashes of light to convey the artist's impressions. It reflected the radical empiricism of the French philosophy of positivism represented by Auguste Comte. Comte taught that all genuine knowledge is based on sense experience and can only be advanced by means of observation. The impressionists painted their subjective perceptions of reality rather than reality itself. Some impressionists also employed satire, ridicule, and insulting devices in their art. For example, **Edouard Manet** shocked gallery visitors with his *Déjeuner sur l'herbe*, depicting a nude woman picnicking with two bourgeois men in frock coats. **Emperor Napoleon III** complained that the painting was an "offense against modesty." While the three figures in the painting were inspired by a design in a painting by Raphael depicting three river gods, Manet sought to make a satire on the so-called bourgeois respectability.

Art Nouveau illustration by A. Cossard

By 1874, a group of impressionist innovators who had been repeatedly rejected by the Salon assembled an exhibition on their own. Among them were **Pierre Auguste Renoir**, **Camille Pissarro**, **Alfred Sisley**, and **Claude Monet**. It was a painting by Monet, *Impression: Sunrise,* that led a critic to coin the term "impressionist." Monet disliked the term and preferred the term "instantaneity," reflecting his goal to capture the fleeting "moment in time" in fields and in ordinary life at bathing parties, picnics, dance halls, theaters, or cafés. Light was an essential ingredient because of its fleeting nature and changing perception in the eye. Short brush strokes breaking up the color continuum helped to achieve the "instantaneity" effect. Monet was so insistent on capturing the transitory moment that he once painted the same haystack 15 times in changing light conditions as the day passed. It was said that he even found himself studying the changing tones of his wife's face as she lay dying. Unlike the realists, Monet and his impressionist group attempted to avoid moral suggestions and sociological comment in their paintings.

From Optimism to Pessimism. Artists throughout most of the nineteenth century both reflected and led the general feeling of confidence of their contemporaries. They believed that increasing knowledge and technological ability would solve the human problems which still existed. Some believed that life still had meaning, and they produced art that was both worthwhile and entertaining for the intended audience. But others, especially those who departed from the Christian faith and worldview (increasingly as the century wore on), fell into despair and meaninglessness. Among the most vivid examples of these latter artists were nonconformist "bohemians" **Vincent van Gogh**, **Paul Gauguin**, and **Paul Cézanne**. These men are considered **post-impressionists** or **symbolists,** a reaction to the visual reductionism

Vincent Van Gogh, *Wheatfield* (1890)

of impressionism. After frequent fits of insanity, Van Gogh, a clergyman's son and one-time theological student, committed suicide in 1890. In the late twentieth century, when society reflected much of Van Gogh's personal torture, his works fetched record prices in the tens of millions of dollars at art sales.

As colonial missionaries were streaming to the tropics to bring the Christian gospel to the heathen, Gauguin retreated to primitive peoples in search of universal truths from them. He found no answers, but used his art to pose unanswered questions. One masterpiece painted in Tahiti was titled *Whence Do We Come? What Are We? Where Are We Going?* The art of Gauguin and his followers aimed at a synthesis between realizing absolute freedom in art while seeking to retain the realism of the previous generation. It was an unstable equilibrium between a wrong view of

human freedom and false view of nature. Shortly before his death, he told the younger generation to strive for a freedom apart from any restraint,

> So what was necessary, without bypassing all the efforts already made and all the research, even scientific research, was to think in terms of complete liberation: to break windows even at the risk of cutting one's finger. From now on the next generation is independent and free from any fetters: it is up to them to try to resolve the whole problem... Before an easel a painter is no slave, neither of the past, nor of the present, neither of nature, nor of his neighbor. He is himself, himself again, always himself. (Quoted by H. R. Rookmaaker, *Modern Art and the Death of a Culture* [London: Inter-Varsity Press, 1973], pp. 91–92.)

For your consideration

Questions

1. What important developments made people in the late nineteenth century so optimistic?

2. How do people today feel about science?

3. What are some things you hope science accomplishes in your lifetime?

4. Discuss the flaws in the theory of evolution.

5. What kinds of influences do you think affect your behavior?

6. Name some ways Social Darwinism has been manifested in 20th century society.

7. Give a written critique of moral "relativism."

8. What are the most important values of the majority of people in the country in which you live?

9. How do you view the past? Is there an earlier period of history which especially attracts you? Why?

10. Who are the pacesetters in today's literature, music, and art? What is their view of life?

11. Was Victorian optimism justified? Why or why not?

12. Name some ways Christians today show concern for people with social problems.

13. How does materialism affect your goals?

Projects

1. Write a biographical sketch on one of the following: Marie or Pierre Curie, Albert Einstein, Louis Pasteur, Louis Agassiz, William Jennings Bryan, or Charles H. Spurgeon.

2. Do some research on the different approaches of Freudian psychoanalysis and behaviorist psychology. Explain how each might deal with a women who is troubled with deep anxiety but does not know why.

3. For one week, keep a log of television commercials which are particularly materialistic.

4. Find out some of the current goals and objectives of one of the political parties in your country. Analyze how these goals might be compatible with either socialism or a Christian worldview.

5. Listen to some recordings or attend a concert of classical, romantic, impressionist, and modern music. Which composer do you enjoy most? Why?

6. If possible, visit a museum to look at some nineteenth-century paintings.

7. Start a collection of art nouveau posters, illustrations, prints, or other pieces of art.

8. Read some romantic-era poetry. Look for examples of a) escapism, b) adoration of nature.

9. Read a nineteenth-century novel.

Photo of The Water Garden, Giverny, France, from which Monet painted.

Word List

mass media	romanticism
relativism	materialism
liberalism	Darwinism
nihilism	Social Darwinism
thermodynamics	Communism
quantum	relativism
ether	theory of relativity
finite	variations/mutations
material uniformity	psychology
socialism	psychoanalysis
capitalism	behaviorism
utopianism	dialectics
dialectical materialism	thesis
anarchists	antithesis
Marxism	synthesis
entropy	existentialism
dispensationalism	realism
premillennialism	impressionism
Social Gospel	classicism
orthodoxy	*art nouveau*
ex cathedra	nostalgia

People and Groups

Pierre & Marie Curie	Max Planck
Niels Bohr	Albert Einstein
Theodor Schwann	Louis Pasteur
Charles Darwin	Sigmund Freud
Karl Marx	Friedrich Engels
Friedrich Nietzsche	Georg W. F. Hegel
Søren Kierkegaard	Joseph Smith
Mary Baker Eddy	Charles T. Russell
William Gladstone	William J. Bryan
Abraham Kuyper	Dwight L. Moody
Charles H. Spurgeon	William Wordsworth
Ludwig von Beethoven	Vincent van Gogh
Claude Monet	Pablo Picasso

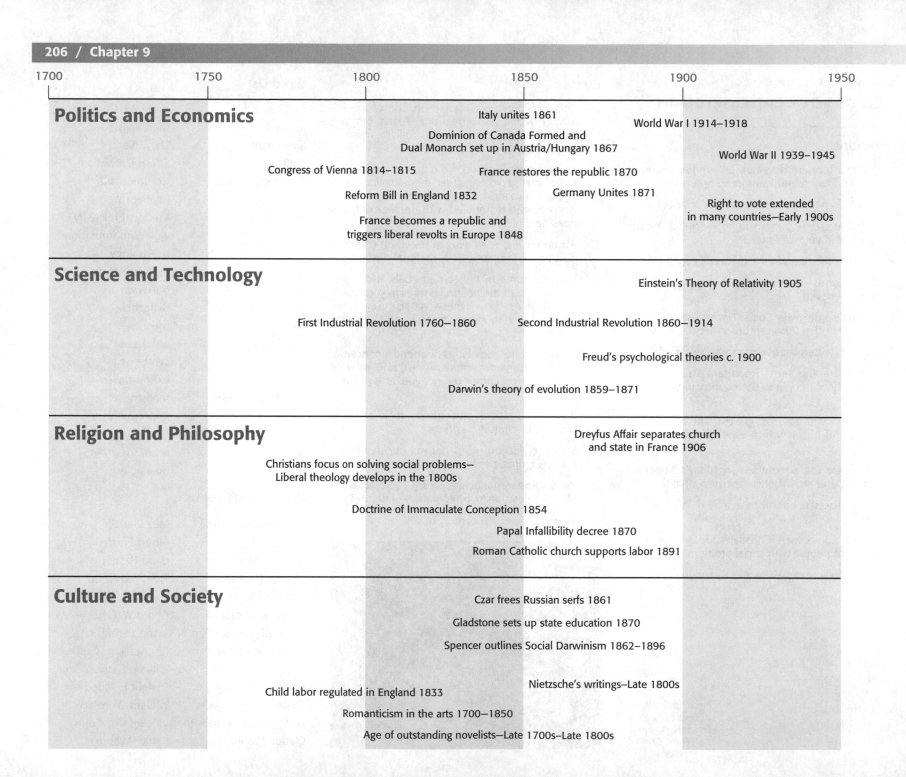

1700 — 1750 — 1800 — 1850 — 1900 — 1950

Politics and Economics

Italy unites 1861

World War I 1914–1918

Dominion of Canada Formed and
Dual Monarch set up in Austria/Hungary 1867

Congress of Vienna 1814–1815

World War II 1939–1945

France restores the republic 1870

Reform Bill in England 1832

Germany Unites 1871

Right to vote extended
in many countries—Early 1900s

France becomes a republic and
triggers liberal revolts in Europe 1848

Science and Technology

Einstein's Theory of Relativity 1905

First Industrial Revolution 1760–1860

Second Industrial Revolution 1860–1914

Freud's psychological theories c. 1900

Darwin's theory of evolution 1859–1871

Religion and Philosophy

Dreyfus Affair separates church
and state in France 1906

Christians focus on solving social problems—
Liberal theology develops in the 1800s

Doctrine of Immaculate Conception 1854

Papal Infallibility decree 1870

Roman Catholic church supports labor 1891

Culture and Society

Czar frees Russian serfs 1861

Gladstone sets up state education 1870

Spencer outlines Social Darwinism 1862–1896

Nietzsche's writings—Late 1800s

Child labor regulated in England 1833

Romanticism in the arts 1700–1850

Age of outstanding novelists—Late 1700s–Late 1800s

9

The Spread of Democratic Nationalism

The English Puritan Reformation and American War of Independence dealt a death blow to despotism and the Roman idea of the divine right of kings. But the French Revolution popularized the idea of 'Liberty, Fraternity and Equality.' As the influence of Protestant Christianity waned in various places, the idea of complete equality based upon the idea of the *Declaration of the Rights of Man and of the Citizens* and the views of Rousseau gained momentum. Not deterred by the atrocities of the French experiment, others sought to implement the same ideology in the name of democracy. The development of democratic governments was an important factor that enables us to understand the political developments in the nineteenth and twentieth centuries.

It is important here to define two terms: *democracy* and *republic*. A **democracy** is a system of rule based on popular *consensus*. A **republic** is a system of rule by *governors* chosen by the people as their representatives—rulers who have a proven record of superior ability, moral character, integrity, wisdom, righteousness, and other godly leadership traits. In a republic, these representatives exercise their best judgment and wisdom for the sake of the people who have chosen them to rule. In a democracy, decisions as to what is right and wrong are made on the basis of popular mood or dominant opinion, which are easily influenced and changed by special interest groups or by powerful and persuasive communicators.

As one Christian social analyst has recently put it:

> Democracies operate on the presupposition that if the issues are presented to the people, they will make wise choices and properly set the course for the nation's direction....There are two substantial problems with assuming

that the truth lies in "the people."

First, the concept of the numerical majority's ability to *discern* truth rests on the idea that truth itself is confirmed by sheer majority numbers rather than by informed, reliable witnesses or an objective God. Pure democracy is

This cartoon caricaturies the various European nations at the end of the 19th Century.

a simple case of "might (majority numbers) makes right." This is a highly suspect concept as human history proves over and over again. The second concern we Christians have is that Scripture proclaims man's universal fallenness and that stacking up numbers of fallen individuals' opinions does nothing but prove man's pride and folly to believe that numbers equate with either truth or objectivity…

A republic presupposes that the best an informed citizen can do is to elect good rulers whose rulership has already been evidenced in both their personal and career lives. Rulership skill is at the heart of the republic, not the ability of [influential communicators] to persuade the masses with slogans and simple partial-truths. (Dennis Peacocke, *The Bottom Line*)

Aligned with the idea of democracy was the spirit of **nationalism**. It arose as part of the Hegelian view of history. Instead of individual autonomy which motivated the French Revolution, Romanticism viewed the collective society as autonomous from God's revealed law. Tradition or national character was seen as an ultimate standard. The limits of human freedom were not to be defined by God's law but by the individual's membership in a higher human community. Romanticism enthroned the national community as the only true individual. Individuals do not exist, instead there are Frenchmen, Germans, Englishmen, etc. Their identity arises, not out of being created by God, but being "organically" evolved out of a specific people. The history of each nation was seen as the unfolding of God's consciousness or "geist." The driving force behind cultural and political activity was seen as a mysterious "national spirit" or "volksgeist" that could not be altered as it carried each citizen along to a national fate. The spirit of the people was idolized (centralized) in its political government, which became the source of law and moral

standards. Instead of the Bible, the nation became a kind of humanistic god, to which one was to sacrifice all. H. Henry Meeter says,

> It glorifies the State as the highest expression of all that is great and mighty in the individual man. The State becomes the apotheosis, the exaltation, of the individual ego. Each nation consequently considers its type of culture better than any other. There is then no peaceful living next to the other nations with a distinct culture; but each considers itself and its own culture the best, and regards its own highest destiny and calling to be to strive to be king of the universe. It has no higher ambition than to foist its own peculiar culture upon other nations, either by peaceful means or by war. (H. Henry Meeter, *The Basic Ideas of Calvinism* [Grand Rapids: Baker, 1956], p. 179)

The Political Order in 1815

Napoleon Bonaparte met defeat in 1814 at the hands of the combined forces of Europe. Now the victors wanted to make sure that France would not rise again. The four allied powers—Austria, Britain, Prussia, and Russia—agreed to get rid of Napoleon by exiling him to the Italian island of Elba. Then the allies placed the brother of the executed last French king on the throne. The new king took the name of **Louis XVIII**, but he was not a monarch in the tradition of France's former kings. Louis XVIII granted a "constitutional charter" which observed most of the changes of the past 25 years. Under the charter, the French people kept their freedom of speech, press, and religion.

The allies made a lenient agreement with the new king. They did not want to undermine his position or trigger resentments that might rouse the French to war again. France lost its holdings in Italy, Germany, and Belgium, which reduced the country to its boundaries of 1792. No financial **reparations** were required. In other words, France did not have to pay for war damage to other nations. Nor did the defeated country have to give up the art treasures Napoleon had looted from museums around Europe. Finally, the allies agreed to hold a conference in Vienna to settle all remaining questions.

Congress of Vienna. The Congress of Vienna, which ran from September 1814 to June 1815, was not really a congress at all. Although representatives of almost all European states (including six kings) attended, they never met as a whole to make the major decisions. The only occasions at which a majority of the delegates gathered were ceremonies, balls, receptions, tournaments, and parties. The Austrian government arranged these affairs to keep the visitors busy. In behind-the-scenes small committee meetings, the big decisions were made. The allies controlled the meetings, but they allowed France to enter the inner circle which made up the "Great Powers." To provide the lesser powers with something to do and ease their suspicions, there were a number of special committees dealing with minor matters.

The Congress of Vienna

Klemens von Metternich, 1773–1850

Able statesmen represented the Great Powers. The commanding personality was **Prince Klemens von Metternich**, the Austrian foreign minister. He had shifted his country's support away from Napoleon and insured the French defeat. Vain, self-centered, but a brilliant diplomat, Metternich realized that Austria's security depended on a stable, peaceful Europe.

The British foreign minister, **Viscount Robert Stewart Castlereagh**, like Metternich, was one of the ablest diplomats of the century. He was shy, reserved, and misunderstood at home (he later committed suicide in a fit of depression). But he helped to hold the others together when they began bickering. Castlereagh was firmly committed to mutual security and **balance of power** in Europe.

Rather than bringing diplomatic skills to the conference, **Czar Alexander I** of Russia brought his personal problems. Mentally unstable, he was haunted by guilt at gaining the throne as a result of his father's murder. No one could guess what he would do next. Posing alternately as the terror and savior of Europe, Alexander indulged in frenzies of reform and religious mysticism.

Never absent when important matters were being decided was that master of **intrigue** and political survival, **Talleyrand** (Charles Maurice de Talleyrand-Périgord, 1754-1838) of France. For a quarter century, he had always known just when to switch sides. He started out as a bishop during the French monarchy. Then he served as a diplomat under the revolutionary government and Napoleon. After betraying Napoleon, he played a leading part in convincing the allies to accept Louis XVIII. His last position was ambassador to London under **Louis Philippe**, whose reign we will examine shortly. Because Talleyrand knew that France's welfare depended on recognizing the interests of other powers and fostering good relations with them, he was acceptable to Metternich and Castlereagh.

Results of the Congress. The Congress restored most of the lands and thrones to the princes and kings who had been defeated by Napoleon. In France, Spain, Naples, and the **Papal States**, the former rulers took their places again. But many other German and Italian princelings did not regain their thrones.

Also, the Congress gave territory to the nations which had fought Napoleon. By these grants, the Congress tried to strengthen countries on France's borders in order to prevent future French expansion. A second principle guided the Congress in passing out rewards. Uppermost in Metternich's mind was the need to restore the balance of power in Europe. Prussia and Austria were to have equal strength. Russia should not become too strong. Great Britain did not take any lands on the continent, and France was not divided.

Possibly the most important aspect of the power balance was the alliance system that came from the Congress. In March 1814, Castlereagh had persuaded the other three allies to join with Britain in a twenty-year **Quadruple Alliance** against

France. Each would provide 150,000 soldiers to enforce whatever peace terms were reached.

Napoleon Strikes Again. Just as the last details fell into place in Vienna, word arrived that Napoleon had made a comeback. France was already in a state of unrest. Some Frenchmen had been seeking revenge for the Reign of Terror during the Revolution, and their actions turned the people against Louis XVIII. Taking advantage of the turmoil, Napoleon, who had escaped exile, forced the king to flee in panic, announced the reestablishment of the empire, and sought to regain power.

However, the allies quickly raised an army and met Napoleon's troops at Waterloo in Belgium. Again the forces of Europe defeated Napoleon. He was exiled a second time, to St. Helena, a lonely island in the South Atlantic. He died there six years later.

On November 20, 1815, a new, harsher peace treaty was concluded. France had to give up valuable land in the north, pay reparations and support an **army of occupation** for not more than five years.

Peace Returns to Europe. The settlement of 1815 was a great diplomatic achievement. Reasonable enough to be accepted by the defeated country, it ended two centuries of colonial rivalry between Britain and France. For the time being, it smoothed over the competition between Austria and Prussia to dominate German territory. The Europe rebuilt by the Congress of Vienna remained stable and at peace for at least 40 years. No general conflict occurred again until 1914. The peacemakers reached their goal of restoring the system of sovereign states existing in a balance of power with one another.

However, the delegates did not come to terms with the new *political ideas* of the times. **Liberal-**ism, **nationalism**, and **democracy** would eventually challenge and undo the Vienna system. In some cases, the changes were ideological and gradual; in others the tool of change was again **revolution**. One expert on the subject of revolution, Harold J. Berman of Harvard University, notes that the modern history of the West has been marked by periodic violent upheavals, in which "the preexisting system of political, legal, economic, religious, cultural, and other social relations, institutions, beliefs, values, and goals has been overthrown and replaced by a new one."

There is by no means a perfect symmetry in these periods of great historical change; yet there are certain patterns or regularities. Each has marked a fundamental change, a rapid change, a violent change, a lasting change, in the social system as a whole.

Each has sought legitimacy in a fundamental law, a remote past, an apocalyptic future.

Each took more than one generation to establish roots.

Each eventually produced a new system of law, which embodied some of the major purposes of the revolution, and which changed the Western legal tradition, but which ultimately remained within that tradition.

These upheavals were not, on the one hand, coups d'état or rebellions, or, on the other hand, long series of incremental changes that were accommodated within the existing system. They were fundamental transformations that were accomplished relatively rapidly and with great struggle and passion.

(From *Law and Revolution*, pp. 19-20)

The Quest for Social Order

In the period after Napoleon, many people had second thoughts about the Enlightenment and the French Revolution. Metternich believed that the only stable form of government was a hereditary monarchy as in the dynastic states. He did not oppose change as such, but he felt it must be carefully controlled. The great lesson learned from the era just ended was the danger of acting on theory only. Metternich feared the "revolutionary virus" which could topple thrones and unleash a new round of destruction. The alliance system created at Vienna was designed to prevent such a threat.

During this period, often called the "**Restoration,**" monarchs and nobles worked together. Both groups tried to regain privileges and property lost in the revolutions. Nearly everywhere, and especially in Britain and France, the monarchs and nobles joined to resist the rising *bourgeoisie*. Of course, the middle classes tried to keep the gains of the revolutions and increase their political power.

Catholic resurgence. Another feature of the Restoration, especially in France, was a return to religious faith. Many educated people, who turned from organized religion during the Enlightenment, now came back to the church. Catholic nobles had seen the simultaneous attack on the monarchy, aristocracy, and churches during the Revolution. They concluded the three belonged together. Monarchs too saw the church as a supporting pillar of the social order. As a result, a noteworthy Catholic resurgence took place after 1815.

This, alas, did little good for religion. In people's minds, it forged a link between the church and the Establishment. This image would bring an attack upon the church later in the century. Then, too, some who returned to the church seemed more attracted to the outward trappings of religion, such as Gothic buildings and colorful rituals, than to the real faith.

Among the best known defenders of Catholicism was **Joseph de Maistre**, born in 1754. A Frenchman who lived in exile, he blamed the skepticism of people like Voltaire for the French Revolution. Catholic Christianity is the foundation of society, de Maistre argued. All sovereignty comes from God and rests in the monarch. Because of this, the king's power cannot be limited by his subjects. Religion teaches people to obey the king and accept the natural inequalities in society. Many people adopted these beliefs.

The Enlightenment Rejected. A noted British orator and statesman, **Edmund Burke** (1729–1797), gave one the strongest arguments against rationalism. He questioned the entire basis of the French Revolution and attacked the use of reason to justify "natural rights." Writer Robert Nagle has noted that Burke supported the American War for Independence for the same reason he opposed the French Revolution—"he felt that traditional and legal rights were being trampled on by the state," a position that illustrates why Burke has been considered one of the fathers of **conservatism.**

Burke said that both society and government are products of a long historical development and must be respected. Changes in either must be made gradually. The institutions and customs that have come to us from the past have lasting value. If people suddenly discard or change these institutions simply on the basis of ideas about what a better society should be like, the very survival of civilization is threatened. As Burke put it,

Edmund Burke (left) opposed radical revolutions as well as unjust kings. Changes should come through channels of law by men who understand changing conditions, he said.

people who do not look backward to their ancestry will not look forward to their posterity.

Humanistic Forces Bring Change

Liberalism develops. Europe's return to an older, more stable social order did not go unchallenged. Resistance came from a varied group of people lumped together under the term **liberals**. Most of them came from the middle class—manufacturers, bankers, merchants, lawyers, professors, and journalists. High school and university students and younger army officers often joined the liberal ranks. They all shared a common goal—*change in the present order*. They did not believe that a political system should be kept simply because it had lasted a long time.

Classic liberals, who today would be called "libertarians," drew from the ideas of the Enlightenment and French Revolution. They placed *a high value on reason and mankind's ability to build a better world*. The chief end of government was to uphold the liberty and safety of all citizens. Government was subject to higher or natural law which required it to guarantee the "rights of man" or "civil liberties." These included freedom from imprisonment without trial and freedom of assembly, speech, and press.

The best kind of government to a liberal was a parliamentary or representative one that worked through discussion and legislation. The administration, including the king, should be law-abiding and responsible to the parliament. Except in England, liberals demanded that all those rights and responsibilities be spelled out in a written constitution.

In the early nineteenth century, **Jeremy Bentham** gave an interesting twist to liberalism. He felt that every idea and institution should be put to the test of "utility" (usefulness). Did this idea or institution contribute to the "greatest good of the greatest number" of people? Any ideas (or government) that failed to meet this test should be rejected regardless of its age. Bentham's views are called **utilitarianism**.

He further taught that the interest of the community was simply the sum of the interest of the individuals who made it up. The motives of individuals were purely selfish. Everyone sought pleasure and avoided pain. Since each one knew what was best for himself, society should give its members complete freedom to follow their own self-interest. Still, everyone would respect the rights of his neighbors because he would suffer revenge if he did not.

This was the belief underlying *laissez-faire*, better defined as **economic liberalism**. British liberalism differed from that on the Continent in that Britain adopted a *laissez-faire* policy. Economic liberals applied the belief in individual freedom to economics. Everyone was free to use his property for his own best interests. The state must in no way interfere with the economy but only act as a policeman, keeping order and protecting property.

These liberals said that natural laws governed the economic realm and one dared not tamper with unchangeable rules such as the law of supply and demand without bringing disaster. Another law concerned population and its increase in proportion to the amount of food available. This so-called law was advanced by **Thomas Robert Malthus** and remains a favorite of population-control advocates—including those favoring abortion, sterilization, and euthanasia—in our day. Malthus held that population always increases faster than food supply and therefore population must be checked by famine, war, disease, or abstention from having children—espe-

Thomas Malthus, 1766–1834

cially by those who cannot support a family. He said poor workers who failed to observe this absolute law had only themselves to blame if they died of starvation.

Freedom of contract was very important to the liberals. Every worker could bargain with his employer about wages and working hours. No laws or labor unions should interfere in this process. Liberals also wanted free competition. This kept prices down, weeded out inefficient producers, and enabled maximum production to meet public demand. There should be no monopolies, price-fixing deals, or protective tariffs. Free international trade would benefit everyone in the long run.

On the Continent, liberalism took a somewhat different form. In many places, liberals wanted freedom from foreign control and freedom for the nation. In central, eastern, and southern Europe, liberals also demanded constitutions and representative government, concepts previously unknown in these regions.

Early nineteenth-century liberals seldom sought one-man, one-vote **popular sovereignty**. They believed that only property owners should vote. They did believe, however, in equality before the law. That is to say, the poorest person would be on the same legal footing as a noble. *But the liberals were not democrats.*

There were radical democrats in Britain and Western Europe who went beyond the liberals in their demands. One group in England, the **Chartists**, wanted a far-reaching reform of Parliament. In France, Italy, and Germany, some radical democrats, mainly students and intellectuals, sought to establish something like the French Republic of 1793. They bitterly opposed all forms of monarchy and the Roman Catholic Church, which they felt propped up the present order.

Their political objectives were most clearly expressed by the various socialist parties which sprang up across Europe in the latter part of the century. Most of these were called "social democratic" parties. Socialists insisted that the people should control the economic system along with the government. They demanded equality in the social and economic realm as well as the political. (A fuller discussion of socialist philosophy was included in chapter 8.)

Nationalism develops. In the first half of the nineteenth century, liberals and nationalists often worked together. Both groups believed that the people should be sovereign. This belief was the most important link between the two. Also, both groups opposed the status quo and bitterly resented the Vienna settlement. A well-known nationalist of the time, Italian **Giuseppe Mazzini**, explained that one could be loyal to his nation and to humanity at the same time. When each

Giuseppe Mazzini, 1805–1872

state had won its right to a national existence, the states would then form a higher community of nations. In 1831, he formed the **Brotherhood of Young Italy**, and began to advocate the idea of a united republic for the Italian people. Among his followers was a young man named **Giuseppe Garibaldi**, who would later play an important role in Italian national unification. Mazzini envisioned a **nation-state** as "the totality of citizens speaking the same language, associated together with equal political and civil rights in the common aim of bringing the forces of society...progressively to greater perfection." In such statements, Mazzini proved himself to be both a romantic and a democrat.

In Germany, the philosopher **Johann von Herder**, declared that each people sharing a common language had a unique "spirit" or "genius." This had to be developed in its own way if it were to be real. The German national culture had to rise from the life of the people, not from copying foreign customs. What followed in Germany was a movement to explore the nation's past—its history, folklore, law, and language development. Some other nations followed their lead.

In the 1820s, intellectuals and idealistic students joined numerous nationalistic movements. Many of them were centered in secret societies committed to agitation for revolution. In Italy, there was the group called the **Carboni**. In Spain, Masonic lodges were a hotbed of nationalistic fervor. There were also the National Patriotic Society in Poland, and groups of liberals in Germany often formed as reading clubs. Various nationalistic leaders from the Continent, meeting in London, issued a manifesto which epitomized the passionate idealism of the movement:

> Everywhere Royalty denies national life... Revolution alone can resolve the vital question of the nationalities, which superficial intelligences continue to misunderstand, but which we know to be the organization of Europe. It alone can give the baptism of humanity to those races who claim to be associated in common work and to whom the sign of their nationality is denied; it alone can regenerate Italy to a third life, and say to Hungary and Poland 'Exist!' It alone can unite Spain and Portugal into an Iberian Republic; create a young Scandinavia; give a material existence to Illyria (Albania and vicinity); organize Greece; extend Switzerland to the dimensions of an Alpine Confederacy, and group in a free fraternity and make an oriental Switzerland of Servia (Serbia), Roumania (Romania), Bulgaria and Bosnia.

At first, nationalism stressed brotherhood and cooperation among the nations rather than rivalry. However, after 1848, it grew more and more aggressive and warlike, seeking power and glory. It took three forms: either the overthrow of a foreign ruler, the replacement of a monarch by popular government, or the unification of independent states. In Western Europe, it helped bind together existing states. In Eastern Europe, it forced the breakup of the old multinational empires and led eventually to World War I.

New Revolutions and Reaction, 1815–1850

Keeping the Lid on Revolution. The Restoration was a time of reaction almost everywhere in Europe. In Britain, the government was controlled by the landed aristocracy. It banned workers' protests against the high price of bread and used force against radicals. The Bourbon kings of France, **Louis XVIII** and his brother and successor **Charles X**, allowed aristocrats and clergymen to gain power at the expense of the middle class.

A number of Russian army officers who had been exposed to liberal ideas started secret societies to work for a constitutional monarchy or even a republic in Russia. When **Alexander I** died in 1825, they staged demonstrations which were quickly and brutally crushed. The new czar, **Nicholas I**, was even more of a tyrant (*more on this later*).

Efforts were made in the Austrian lands to stamp out all nationalism and liberalism. In Germany, Metternich managed to have new laws passed banning student political groups, placing government supervisors in the universities, and putting the press under strict censorship. In Italy, the restored rulers, mostly Metternich's puppets, refused to allow constitutions or legislative assemblies. Secret underground groups which worked for more liberal regimes were hunted down and wiped out whenever possible.

The statesmen had agreed at Vienna to meet regularly to deal with mutual problems. In 1818, France was allowed to become a full-fledged member of the club. The Quadruple Alliance became the **Quintuple Alliance**. Then a serious rift opened in their ranks. Austria, Prussia, and Russia agreed to take joint action to put down revolutions in any European state. Britain and France opposed the decision.

Despite strong protests, the **Holy Alliance** (Austria, Prussia, and Russia) became the policeman of Europe. They sent an army to Naples to restore the king to his throne. In 1822, they persuaded France to send troops to help Spain's King **Ferdinand VII**, who had been forced by liberals to respect a constitution.

The Revolutionary Spirit Continues. Despite all the efforts of absolute monarchs, the revolutionary spirit did not die. It only waited like a sleeping volcano for the right moment to erupt. One such moment came in 1821 when Greece tried to gain freedom from Ottoman Turkey. The movement won wide support from the romantic liberals of Western Europe, including the handsome English adventurer-poet, **George Gordon**, **Lord Byron**, who died in 1824 while working in Greece for its independence. The liberals compared modern Greeks with ancient Athenians fighting tyranny. Finally, France, Britain, and Russia helped bring about Greek independence in 1830. Unlike Britain and France, Russia was motivated not by a sympathy for liberalism, but rather by a desire to control the entrance to the Black Sea.

France's liberals grew angry as Charles X placed limits on their power. In July of 1830, they joined with certain capitalists to overthrow his regime with the help of republican workers and students in Paris. Liberals wanted a more reliable king, not a republic. **Louis Philippe**, a cousin of Charles X, agreed to serve as "king of the French people" and was nicknamed the "Citizen King."

Lord Byron, 1788–1824

His regime actually meant little change, for still only the wealthy could take part in politics. With rapid industrial growth, the working and lower middle classes expanded greatly in numbers. Their dislike for Louis Philippe promised future trouble for France.

Discontented people in other countries quickly followed the French example in their revolt against Charles. The Belgians threw off Dutch rule and set up a constitutional monarchy. The Holy Alliance powers wanted to help the Dutch, but the French and British would not allow it. Liberal revolts also swept Spain, Portugal, Italy, Switzerland, and Germany. In Poland, the nationalists declared their freedom from Russian rule, but Czar Nicholas I crushed their uprising. They appealed in vain to the West for help. Poland and its constitution disappeared, and the land became part of the Russian Empire. Thousands of Poles were exiled to Siberia and others fled to the West.

Unrest also mounted in Britain. A number of liberal laws had moved England toward free trade and more civil liberties. However, attempts to make Parliament more representative had failed. Finally, the Liberal (Whig) Party forced through the Reform Bill of 1832. The bill reassigned seats in the House of Commons and increased the number of voters. The new industrial middle class now shared political power with the landed aristocracy without having to stage a revolution.

Europe had made some progress in the direction of more freedom, but unrest plagued the international scene. It was divided into two camps—a liberal West and a reactionary East. Moreover, the West was trying to cope with the problems of industrialism. Its material advance rested on the backs of a hard-pressed working class. Still, many hoped that industrial society would better the lives of all. They looked for the day when liberals and nationalists would achieve their goals.

The Volcano Erupts. This optimism lay behind the most universal upheaval in Europe to that time. In 1848, Europe virtually exploded with revolutions. France triggered the event by ousting Louis Philippe and setting up a republic. Quickly the "virus of revolution" spread across the Continent. The whole Metternich system collapsed. In March, revolutionaries seized power in Vienna and Berlin and forced the monarchs to grant constitutions. Metternich went into exile, while liberals called a meeting in Frankfurt to draft a constitution for a unified Germany.

Nationalistic movements sprang up throughout the Austrian territories. The Hungarians, led by the inflammatory **Louis Kossuth**, declared their independence. The Czechs demanded self-government and freedom from German control. Revolts raged throughout Italy as that country tried to throw off its Austrian rulers.

Only two areas were free of uprisings—Britain, where the reform of 1832 and the prospect of further freedoms kept tensions down, and Russia, where rulers kept the lid on so tightly that nothing happened there.

But the enthusiasm of the spring of 1848 died quickly. In June, a bitter class war broke out in France between the wealthy property owners and the impoverished workers. This first revolt of the "have-nots" against the "haves" was crushed within a few days. Fearing another worker revolt, the French turned for leadership to **Louis Napoleon Bonaparte**, the nephew of the great emperor. Austrian armed forces put down revolts in Prague, northern Italy, Vienna, and Hungary. The Frankfurt Parliament could not persuade the Prussian king to accept the all-German crown, and it simply disbanded. After a few more efforts

Rising food prices and unemployment led to the 1848 revolts in France and Germany.

in 1849, liberals and nationalists in central Europe and Italy fled into exile or gave up politics altogether.

The failure of 1848 had grim results. Dreams of setting up liberal or democratic states through humane or peaceful means had shattered. People regarded these goals as mere romantic idealism, and the agents of change became more realistic. Whether ideas were "right" no longer mattered; they had to be "workable." Political or social change would not come through utopian dreams but by hardheaded action. The chief heirs of the new realism (also known as *Realpolitik*) were Prussian leader **Otto von Bismarck** and communist theorizer **Karl Marx**. Other realists were **Count Camillo Benso di Cavour** in Italy, **Francis Deák** in Hungary, and **Louis Adolphe Thiers** in France.

A Revolutionary Remembers

As a student in Bonn, Germany, Carl Schurz took part in the 1848 revolts. After much bloodshed, particularly in the city of Berlin, King Frederick William squelched the revolution. Its leaders, including Schurz, fled the country. Schurz went to America. While holding several important United States government posts, he worked to end political corruption there and championed the rights of minorities. In this excerpt, he tells of his student revolutionary days:

One morning, toward the end of February, 1848, I sat quietly in my attic-chamber, working hard at my tragedy of "Ulrich von Hutten," when suddenly a friend rushed breathless into the room, exclaiming: "What, you sitting here! Do you not know what has happened?"

"No, what?"

"The French have driven away Louis Philippe and proclaimed the republic."

I threw down my pen—and that was the end of "Ulrich von Hutten." I never touched the manuscript again. We tore down the stairs, into the street, to the market-square, the accustomed meeting-place for all the student societies after the midday dinner. Although it was still forenoon, the market was already crowded with young men talking excitedly.... Since the French had driven away Louis Philippe and proclaimed the republic, something of course must happen here, too. Some of the students had brought their rapiers along, as if it were necessary at once to make an attack or to defend themselves.... We wandered about in numerous bands—to the "Kneipe," where our restlessness, however, would not suffer us long to stay; then to other pleasure resorts, where we fell into conversation with all manner of strangers, to find in them the same confused, astonished, and expectant state of mind; then back to the market-square, to see what might be going on there; then again somewhere else, without aim and end.... In these conversations, excited as they were, certain ideas and catchwords worked themselves to the surface, which expressed more or less the feelings of the people.

Now had arrived in Germany the day for the establishment of "German Unity," and the founding of a great, powerful national German Empire. First in line the convocation of a national parliament. Then the demands for civil rights and liberties, free speech, free press, the right of free assembly, equality before the law, a freely elected representation of the people with legislative power.... Like many of my friends, I felt that the great opportunity had arrived for giving the German people liberty and to the German fatherland unity and greatness, and that it was now the first duty of every German to sacrifice everything for this sacred object. We were profoundly, solemnly in earnest.

Adapted from Carl Schurz, ***The Reminiscences of Carl Schurz,*** (New York: Doubleday & Co., 1919)

The Development of Modern Nation-States

The last half of the nineteenth century saw two parallel trends in politics—the continuing growth of nation-states and representative government. Before 1850, there were two important nation-states in Europe—Great Britain and France, and a few smaller ones—Spain, Portugal, Denmark, Switzerland, and The Netherlands.

Another typical situation occurred in Italy or Germany, both of which contained many small independent states, all with a single ethnic identity. A third pattern was the large (**multinational**) empire made up of a variety of peoples. Austria and Russia were typical examples.

After 1850, political leaders became more and more interested in setting up nation-states. A **nation-state** is defined as *a political unit where government authority reflects the will of citizens who feel they belong together as members of a community in a certain geographical area.* This sense of identity is often accompanied by the idea that other people are foreign.

The development of nation-states had two aspects. The existing smaller states had to unite into a larger one either by peaceful means or, more likely, through force. Then closer ties had to be forged between rulers and people. Forming representative governments and giving the vote to nearly all (male) citizens created these ties. To be successful, a nation-state also had to have some sort of constitution.

The 1848 revolutions had as their chief goal the formation of nation-states. However, it became clear that the Holy Alliance would have to be smashed first. In 1849, Russia helped Austria

Florence Nightingale

With light flickering from her lamp, she picked her way among the miles of hospital cots. Wounded soldiers kissed her shadow as she passed, and little wonder. Florence Nightingale had brought order out of chaos, comfort and hope in place of the ghastly conditions in the Crimean hospital.

Hospital was hardly an appropriate term for the ramshackle barracks which housed the Crimean War's casualties. Perched on top of large sewers, with no ventilation, filthy, understaffed, lacking even the most basic supplies, and filled to four times its capacity, the hospital was primarily a place to die. Florence and her staff of 38 nurses cleaned away the dirt, prepared nutritious food, and organized a laundry to wash clothing and bedding.

Florence herself had to cut through incredible snarls of red tape to get needed supplies and to improve patient care. With money she had collected in England, she provided what she could not obtain from the army. A complete transformation took place at the hospital, and before long she was placed in charge of all the hospitals in the area.

When the war ended and Florence returned to England, she was honored by both Queen Victoria and Parliament. However, all the acclaim made her feel uncomfortable. She believed that she had simply answered the call of God upon her life. "Christ is the author of our profession," she said of nursing.

Florence made nursing a respectable career for women and set new standards for cleanliness and comfort in hospital care. In addition to the hundreds of soldiers in an obscure European war who owed their lives to her, the lives of countless soldiers and civilians since then have been saved due to the safer and better medical care resulting from her dedication and vision.

crush the Hungarian revolt. Shortly afterwards, the two powers forced the Prussian king to give up a scheme to unify Germany.

A conflict in the remote Black Sea region in 1854 suddenly made the revolutionary goals possible by breaking up the Alliance. The conflict had its roots in the weakness the Ottoman Turks had shown in the Greek independence movement. Russia believed this weakness was an opportunity for it to gain control of strategic Constantinople at the entrance to the Black Sea. The czar began negotiations with Britain to carve up the Ottoman Empire, but Britain became wary when all plans seemed to give Russia control of Constantinople. Britain preferred to have weak Ottomans rather than powerful Russians in charge of that strategic spot. Britain signed a pact with the Ottoman sultan, and they were joined by France's Louis Napoleon, now called **Emperor Napoleon III**, in waging war against Russia. Louis, who fought mostly for the glory, told his people that he was actually protecting western Catholic interests against Eastern Orthodox interests (led by Russia). The Eastern Orthodox and Latin Catholic interests had frequently quarreled in the Near East under a grant by the sultan allowing certain worship privileges by Christians in the Holy Places of Palestine. In this two-year Black Sea conflict, known as the **Crimean War** (1854–1856), members of the Holy Alliance turned against one another. The Alliance fell apart. Now the way was opened for the unification of Italy and Germany.

Italy Unites. The most advanced Italian state politically and economically was Sardinia-Piedmont. It was a constitutional monarchy under **King Victor Emmanuel II** of the Italian House of Savoy. In 1852, **Count Camillo di Cavour**, a western-style liberal, became his prime minister. A tough-minded realist, Cavour set out to

This monument was dedicated to Victor Emmanuel II and erected in Rome between 1885–1911.

strengthen his country though a wide range of reforms. He also sought allies to help drive Austria out of northern Italy.

As his first move, he made his country a model of economic progress and good government. Next he entered the Crimean War in a deliberate attempt to gain international recognition. Finally, he persuaded the ambitious French ruler, Napoleon III, to help him fight Austria. This brief war in 1859 enabled Cavour to annex Lombardy, an Austrian province in northern Italy.

A tidal wave of revolutions then swept the smaller states in northern Italy as they threw out their Austrian-controlled rulers. The states voted to unite with Sardinia.

Meanwhile, a bold patriot, **Giuseppe Garibaldi**, led a small force against the Kingdom of the Two Sicilies in southern Italy. Stirred by Garibaldi's words and deeds, thousands of local patriots joined his army. The bravery of this man, his fervent love for Italy, his fiery spirit, drew men like a magnet. They were willing to lay down their lives for him. As Burchell describes it,

> On the night of May 5, 1860, Garibaldi's romantic band of volunteers, The Thousand, sailed from Genoa armed with little more than

Giuseppe Garibaldi, 1807–1882

a fervent belief in freedom (but with Cavour's secret approval). When they landed in Sicily, they were greeted at first with suspicion. The Sicilians were less interested in a united Italy or nationalism then they were in satisfying such simple wants as the abolition of the salt tax, a reduction in the price of bread and a chance to work. Soon, however, their desire to overthrow their corrupt government merged with the romantic nationalism of Garibaldi. Peasants came on foot and on horseback, armed with a variety of weapons: pitchforks and blunderbusses, pruning hooks and ancient cutlasses. In the streets of Palermo women, children and priests joined in building the barricades. In the battle that followed, Palermo was liberated from Bourbon oppression, and Garibaldi moved on to seize the city of Naples.

Garibaldi's army overthrew the king in short order, and the people voted to join a united Italy. In 1861, the new nation of Italy came into being. Within the following decade, Venice was acquired from Austria, Rome was taken over from the unwilling pope, and the Italian borders rounded out.

German States Unite. France had tried to keep Germany weak and divided for a long time, but by the early nineteenth century many Germans were unhappy with division. In 1848, liberals tried in vain to unite the separate states by peaceful means—the Frankfurt Assembly. More and more, people who were committed to unification began thinking in terms of power.

Although the old states and the German Confederation had been restored by the post-Napoleonic Vienna Settlement, Prussia was far ahead of the others. It had taken the lead in forming the German Customs Union (a kind of common market). The Union provided economic unity and helped bring industrial expansion. New telegraph and railroad lines drew the various parts of Germany closer together. Nationalistic liberals came to feel that Prussia, with its economic base and large army, was the one state that could unite Germany.

After 1850, Prussia had a parliament. In spite of the king's efforts to rig the voting in favor of the nobles, the wealthy commercial and industrial middle class controlled the lower house of the legislature. Many were liberals who wanted the parliament to have power over government spending. For 200 years, the army had been the domain of the nobles (Junkers). Neither the king nor the Junkers would stand for interference in the army by people's representatives. In 1862, a serious crisis arose. The parliament refused to vote funds for increasing the size of the army.

At this point, **Otto von Bismarck** was brought in as prime minister to solve the problem. He was a Junker, well-educated, and firmly committed to the Prussian monarchy. He regarded Prussia rather than "Germany" as his fatherland. In fact, he looked upon a union of all German-speaking peoples as a threat to Prussia. Such a union would reduce its power in dealing with Catholic Austria and the south German states.

Bismarck handled the parliament by simply collecting taxes and enlarging the army without budget approval. The liberals objected, but he ignored the constitution. Prussia's power was far more important, he declared.

Bismarck launched a series of short wars—against Denmark, Austria, and France. His victories enabled him to expand Prussia and replace the German Confederation with a new confederation under Prussian control. Soon he drew the south German states into the new German Empire (**First Reich**).

It was a federation of monarchies with the member states retaining their identity and self-government. Yet the ministers were responsible to the

Otto von Bismarck, 1815–1898

Iron and Blood

A fellow Prussian once described Otto von Bismarck as containing "within himself the university student, the Junker, the guard lieutenant, the diplomat, the despot, the revolutionary; all that set off by a sort of ironic fantasy which makes him an artist—almost a poet.... He is a true Prussian." Explaining what he meant by a true Prussian, the observer stated that Prussian policy tended to ignore ideas, feelings, and traditions. It was the policy of the free hand, ready to play all possible games. Bismarck followed this policy so expertly that he has often been called an opportunist.

While the statesman could shift rapidly from one course of action to another, he would not budge an inch with regard to his goals. Known as the "Iron Chancellor," he knew what he wanted and his determination to get it never wavered. He sought to strengthen the power of the king because he believed that the king represented autocratic and military rule in Prussia. "I believe that I am obeying God when I serve the king," he declared.

Bismarck also wanted to unite Germany under Prussian leadership, a goal which he felt could be achieved only through war. He expressed this view in one of his famous speeches, given in 1862:

Prussia must concentrate and maintain its power for the favorable moment which has already slipped by several times. Prussia's boundaries... are not favorable to a healthy state life. The great questions of time will not be resolved by speeches and majority decisions—that was the great mistake of 1848 and 1849 —but by iron and blood.

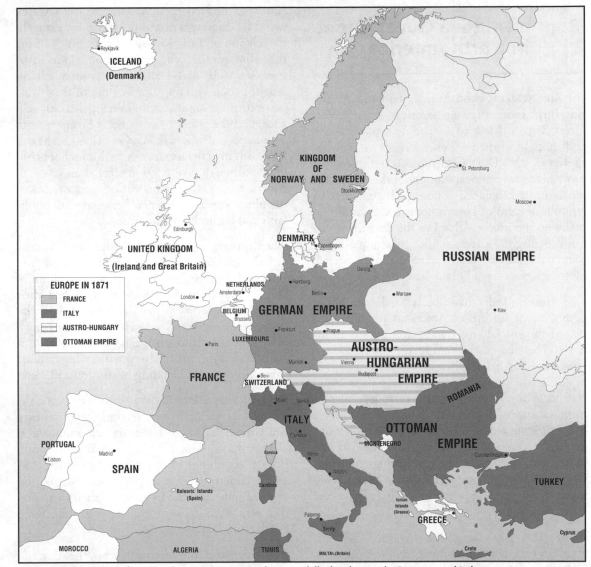

Compare this map with the map of Europe in 1815, noting especially the changes in Germany and Italy.

emperor (**kaiser**, German for "Caesar"), not to the legislature. The emperor, who was at the same time the Prussian king, had full control over foreign and military policy.

The new Germany was a nation-state but not one based on popular support as in Italy.

Whereas Sardinia-Piedmont merged its identity into the Italian kingdom, Prussia remained distinct as a state and controlled the empire. Cavour transferred his loyalty to Italy; Bismarck never removed his from Prussia. The German Empire was really nothing more than the expansion of Prussia through power politics. However, it quickly received the support of German nationalists.

Representative Government in North America

The American republic. At first, the United States was little more than an overseas extension of Great Britain. Most of its people spoke English and thought of themselves as British or Scottish. However, the U.S. Constitution reflected the most advanced political thought of the time—the separation and balance of powers. It guaranteed a republican form of government to the states that made up the union. Added to the document was a Bill of Rights, a remarkable and unique list of the civil liberties that each citizen possessed. However, not even all males had the right to vote.

The stress on individual liberty made republican democracy a feature of American politics. This played a crucial role in helping Americans develop a sense of national identity. The idea of representative federal democracy also aided in building the kind of government that could transform this scattered group of independently minded states into a real nation-state. But in order to achieve this, the leaders of the new country had to deal with two problems. The first had to do with the several million immigrants from Great Britain, Ireland, and Germany. The other involved the holding of the union together as the crisis over slavery worsened.

During the early years of the republic, "civil religion" and the common schools made Americans, including the immigrants, aware of nationality. **Civil religion** is a term describing a kind of faith which most members of society held and which was used by political leaders for their own purposes. Many Americans believed that they were chosen by God to show to all people the marvelous virtues of freedom and self-government.

America, the "redeemer nation," would save the world by creating a new order based on evangelical religion and democratic institutions. During the nineteenth century, sermons, literature, speeches, and, above all, the common schools taught people certain values. Some of these were patriotism, morality, self-government, self-reliance, and the ethics of evangelical Protestantism. The famous *McGuffey's Readers* helped build this civil faith in generations of American school children. Although civil religion created an image of America as a Christian nation, many church members saw a difference between this public faith and biblical Christianity.

The immigrants became "Americanized" as they quickly picked up the national customs and English language. Yet they could keep some of the old ways too. Often they established their own churches, newspapers, and social organizations. The old and new citizens shaped each other's values, although the basic American attitudes stayed the same. A new nationality resulted from this constant blending of cultures and ideas.

Struggle over States Rights. At the same time the nation was tearing in two. In the North, industry was growing rapidly. Factory owners and workers wanted tariff protection against British goods. But the South had close economic ties with Britain. Southerners lived largely from their cotton exports and had little industry of their own, and thus wanted to import the cheaper manufactured goods from Britain.

As the demand for raw cotton grew, the slave and plantation system sank deeper roots into American soil. Free workers could not compete with unpaid labor, so immigrants settled largely in the Northern states. Southern society became somewhat inbred and remained largely agricultural. It was more committed than the North to traditional values.

The cotton and tobacco economy of the Southern states rested on the back of slave labor.

Elsewhere in the world, slave labor was passing away. The British Empire abolished slavery in 1833, and the French colonists followed suit in 1848. Serfdom in Eastern Europe disappeared between 1807 and 1861.

In the United States religious social reformers, who seldom were orthodox Christians, followed the lead of some of their British counterparts in fighting slavery. Among the leaders of the antislavery movement in the 1830s and 1840s were people like the pacifist and moralist **William Lloyd Garrison**, who was part of a group that included liberal clergymen and secretly supported the terrorist activities of the fiery abolitionist, **John Brown**. Garrison was also a controversial advocate of women's rights, as were fellow abolitionists and feminists **Sarah** and **Angelina Grimké**. They urged compassion toward sinning and suffering men and argued that God would judge America for the sin of slavery.

By mid-century, slavery was a hot political issue in America. Some Northerners felt it violated the American ideals of liberty and democracy. Many Southerners resented the attempts by Northern

Abraham Lincoln, 1809–1865

Although General Lee did not surrender until 1865, the decisive battle of the Civil War was fought at Gettysburg in 1863.

Robert E. Lee (1807–1870) was the Confederate Army's most famous general.

businessmen and politicians to morally chastise their use of slave labor. After all, it was often Northern businessmen who profited from selling the slaves to the Southerners in the first place. The South's attitude toward intrusions upon its value system was not unlike the nationalism felt by many peoples in Europe.

It was fundamentally a clash between two "nationalisms" that caused the Civil War, not slavery alone. Southern whites had developed their own way of life. In their view, Northerners were hostile, foreign outsiders and the South was a distinct nation. Because most immigrants settled in the North, Southerners had also become a numerical minority in the United States.

In 1860, the election of **Abraham Lincoln,** as President of the United States, more or less sealed the doom of the Southern way of life. His Republican Party platform, calling for high tar-

iffs, supporting economic development on a nationwide scale, and expressing opposition to slavery, was strongly opposed by Southern leaders. Most Southern states withdrew from the union to form the Confederate States of America. The war that resulted was as bloody as any in the nineteenth century. The use of modern weapons, vast armies, railroads, and the total industrial output of the warring powers hinted at what lay ahead in World War I.

With the Northern victory, the United States became a true nation-state, rather than the federation of independent states which many of the Founding Fathers had envisioned. Lincoln's program and the Civil War fundamentally altered the character of the nation: what had originally been "*these* United States of America" became known as "*The* United States of America." The Fourteenth Amendment said the states could not deprive any person of life, liberty, or property without due process of law. What "due process" meant would be determined by the central government. The federal authority gave slaves their freedom and voting rights and tried to force liberalism and democratic equality upon the South. In the post-Civil War years, economic power shifted from small business to nationwide enterprises. Political power made a parallel shift from the states to the central government—a process which continued to plague the nation through the twentieth century.

Canada Becomes a Nation-State. Canada had a mixture of French and English-speaking settlers, but the French resented being in the British Empire. In 1791, British authorities created two provinces, a French Lower Canada in the St. Lawrence Valley and an English Upper Canada in the Great Lakes Region. Britain gave them the same form of government as there had been in the thirteen colonies before the American War of Independence. This seemed to work for awhile. The Canadians even developed a measure of national feeling during the War of 1812.

However, constant tension among the old British settlers, new immigrants, and the French finally came to a head. In 1837, an unsuccessful uprising took place. A new colonial governor-general, **Lord Durham, John George Lambton**, came out to deal with the problem. He wrote a famous report in 1839 that laid the basis for the later formation of the **British Commonwealth of Nations**. He said that the French attempt to separate from Canada must be discouraged. All Canadians needed to have a common sense of patriotism. To achieve this, the two provinces should be joined into one. Railroads and canals ought to be built. Responsible self-government similar to that in Great Britain should be granted.

Booker T. Washington
1856–1915

Conditions did not change quickly for blacks. Civil laws, custom, and lack of education held most of them back. Despite these tremendous obstacles, some black people made outstanding contributions. Booker T. Washington, foremost African-American educator of his day, succeeded because he was conscientious, determined, and willing to work hard to reach his goals.

As a youth, Washington had one all-consuming desire—to attend college. Taking a position as a houseboy, he began saving all he could. Most houseboys lasted with his employer, Mrs. Ruffner, for only a few weeks, for she was strict and demanding. Washington worked for Mrs. Ruffner for about a year and a half, earning her complete trust. Then he decided it was time to pursue his dream of a college education.

With the pitifully few dollars he had been able to save, he set out for Hampton Normal, a black agricultural school in Virginia. Hitchhiking most of the 500 miles, he stretched his money out by sleeping under boardwalks and skipping meals. Finally, after spending many days without a bath, a decent meal, or a change of clothes, he arrived at Hampton. He had 50 cents left in his pocket.

The head teacher looked at him doubtfully as he begged to be admitted. At length, she told him to go sweep the next room. Washington put everything he had learned at Mrs. Ruffner's to work, dusting four times, moving every piece of furniture, and cleaning every closet. When he finished, the head teacher could not find a speck of dirt in the room. She signed him up as a student. According to Washington, no one entering Harvard or Yale had more satisfaction in passing his college entrance exam.

The **Durham Report**, officially known as the *Report on the Affairs of British North America*, went into effect in the 1840s, but the high rate of British immigration angered the French. Gradually, Canadians concluded the answer lay in a federation. The French and English areas would each handle their own affairs but be joined in a larger organization. So the **Dominion of Canada**, with a strong central government, came into being in 1867. A transcontinental railroad (completed in 1885) helped to link the far-flung territories.

Canada was the first example of liberty being granted within a European colonial empire without war or revolution. The new nation gradually gained independence in politics, economics, and military affairs. Canada developed its own sense of national identity, distinct from both the mother country and its neighbor to the south. Britain later gave dominion status to its other colonies with large European populations. These were Australia (1901), New Zealand (1907), and South Africa (1910). Eventually British colonies peopled by non-Europeans would also adopt dominion status.

The Canadian capitol is in Ottawa

Representative Government in Western Europe

Great Britain. When Victoria ascended the throne in 1837, a staid, placid era settled down upon the English. This period of orderly self-government, which bears the Queen's name, lasted for 64 years. Citizens devoted their energies to becoming prosperous, so much so that the period became known as the Age of Optimism or the Age of Progress (see chapter 8). But the beginning of the twentieth century brought social and economic unrest.

One problem concerned the right to vote. Earlier, the Reform Acts of 1867 and 1884 had given the vote to three-fourths of the adult males in Britain. For the first time, men could vote even if they did not own property. But the remaining males and British women demanded the vote also. Other groups wanted a secret ballot and salaries for members of the House of Commons. Working-class people could not afford to serve in the legislature at their own expense. By 1918, all of these demands had been met by a responsive British government.

Another development led Britain closer to democracy. The Cabinet had been established in the eighteenth century. Gradually it became the highest organ of government. A committee chosen by the majority party in the House of Commons, the Cabinet exercises authority in the name of the crown (king or queen). It determines questions of general policy, writes legislation, and decides which bills should be considered by the Parliament. It is responsible to the majority of Commons. Thus, if it is defeated on a key issue, it must either resign or dissolve Parliament and

Thomas Nast's cartoon depicts Universal Suffrage. In England and America, women were the last to gain the right to vote.

call a new election. If it resigns, a new Cabinet is chosen.

A third movement toward democracy occurred in the House of Lords. The power of this body had gradually eroded. First, the Cabinet became responsible only to the Commons. Then, in the early nineteenth century, the lower house gained full control over finances. The House of Lords could veto all other legislation, but the king might create new **peers** (lords) to force through a measure. Then in 1909, a political crisis arose. Lords refused to accept the budget of the Liberal Party Cabinet. That proved to be a mistake for the Lords. A bill was then passed which took away the Lords' veto power. They could delay a bill for a maximum of two years but not stop its

passage. However, the Lords' loss was democracy's gain, for British lords inherited or were appointed to their seats. Members of the Commons were elected.

Both the Liberal and Conservative parties (also know as the Whig and Tory parties after 1850) worked for social reform. Many new laws improved the quality of life for middle- and working-class people alike. But neither party could find a satisfactory answer to the Irish question, one of the worst minority problems in Europe. Ireland had been taken into the United Kingdom of Great Britain in 1801. Irish representatives sat in Parliament for Ireland, but this was not enough. The Irish felt exploited by British **absentee landlords** and the Protestant church.

After years of violence in Ireland and wrangling in Parliament, "home rule" was granted. But it was withdrawn again during World War I. A civil war broke out. Finally, in 1922, the island was divided. The south obtained dominion status and the north remained a part of the United Kingdom.

The Political Situation in France. Conditions in France were much more turbulent. **Louis Napoleon Bonaparte** had been elected president of the republic in 1848. However, by 1852, he had overthrown the constitutional regime and made himself **Emperor Napoleon III**. A skillful politician, he was the first modern dictator.

He appealed to the masses with spectacular performances at court and great building projects—new boulevards, parks, and sewers for Paris. He promised to improve the economy and restore national greatness if they would follow him and forget that they had lost democratic government. Through a liberal banking and free-trade policy, Napoleon III provided a good climate for business expansion. The workers gained higher wages and the right to form trade unions. Some social legislation improved their lot.

Unhappily for Napoleon III, costly mistakes in foreign policy proved his undoing. Defeated by Prussia in 1870 in battles that saw the loss of 104,000 Frenchmen, he was taken prisoner and sent into exile. When news of the emperor's capture hit Paris on September 4, a mob stormed the Chamber of Deputies and forced the lawmakers to declare France a republic again—the country's third. **General Louis Trochu** was named president by demand of the shouting crowd. By September 20, the Prussians had nearly encircled Paris, but for four months the siege was unsuccessful. Inside the city, Parisians resorted to ingenuity to create the weapons they needed. Among other things, they constructed hot-gas balloons

Emperor Napoleon III, 1808–1873

which drifted out of the city at night. Couriers in this way helped to organize relief troops outside the German lines. After 193 days, Bismarck and the French authorities signed a tentative truce allowing the French to organize a new government which would have the responsibility to decide whether or not to continue the war. The new government proved to be heavily conservative—mostly monarchists, headed by the right-wing historian **Adolphe Thiers**. Paris radicals were outraged at the thought that peace would be made with the Germans and republican rule would end. In peace talks, Thiers agreed to give up the conquered territories of Alsace and Lorraine along with a one-billion-dollar indemnity. Thiers also agreed to allow German troops to march through Paris in a victory procession and occupy the city until the treaty was ratified. The occupation lasted only two days, and Parisians afterwards scrubbed the streets to erase the shame. The conservative government attempted to control the radicals; but the attempt failed, and Thiers fled to Versailles.

On March 26, 1871, the people of Paris, fearing an approaching famine and anarchy across the country, seized the city and held it for 62 days. Their leaders formed a radical new council, called the **Paris Commune**, and mobs turned to violence much as they had done during the French Revolution. The Commune leadership almost instantly was marked by dissension and quarrels. They debated matters seemingly unrelated to the crisis; for example, they spent hours trying to decide whether to take religion out of schools. **Karl Marx**, who was said to have inspired the revolt, first expressed surprise at it but later supported it, wondering why more revolutionary steps such as seizure of the treasury of the Bank of France were not taken. The Commune flag was inscribed: "Social Revolution, Equality, Justice"; and the mobs demanded: "Freedom or Death."

The authorities outside Paris, forming an alliance with the Prussians, responded with death—a bloodbath that caused the Seine to run red. Bismarck, fearing that the revolution might spread to Germany's socialists, released 400,000 French army regulars which had been held as prisoners of war. They joined Thiers' government troops. Inside Paris, the Commune began losing support from the people, many of whom went into hiding rather than join the republican National Guard. On May 21, Thiers' troops entered the city and a bloody seven-day battle ensued. Thousands of Parisians were killed, including many women and children. The **Communards** committed atrocities of their own, including the murder of the archbishop of Paris and four other priests. By the time the bloodletting was over, 25,000 people had died—ten times more than had died during the fifteen-month Reign of Terror of the 1789 Revolution. Some 38,000 Communards were imprisoned and tried, including two notorious women, the poetess-revolutionary **Louise Michel** and the cigar-smoking gunboat operator **Hortense David**. During four years of trials, 25,000 were freed, 7,500 sent into exile, 5,000 fined or imprisoned, and 23 were shot.

In 1875, the National Assembly narrowly passed a series of laws creating the institutions of the "Third Republic." The people were too divided to adopt a written constitution, and they settled for this stopgap measure.

Unlike Britain, which enjoyed a two-party system, France had a host of parties. No party could ever obtain a majority. They had to form a **coalition** (a grouping of two or more parties) to provide the majority that would choose a government. The upper classes, Roman Catholic clergy, and army officers did not like the new order. However, because all male citizens could vote, republican parties were able to hang on to power. Eventually, they brought stability to France, but not before a serious threat to the new republic arose—two scandals of intrigue.

In 1889, a general with the backing of monarchists and clerics, **Georges Boulanger**, plotted to lead a war of revenge on the Germans. He pranced through the streets of Paris on a black war-horse (an act which has given him historical remembrance as "the man on horseback") and threatened to "throw the rascals out" of the republican Chamber of Deputies, which had been rocked by some financial scandals. But Boulanger soon lost courage for his project, fled to Belgium, and committed suicide. Yet his nationalist reactionary movement, known as **Boulangism**, lingered in French society—foreshadowing the evil of fascism.

Five years later a much more serious crisis arose. In 1894, **Captain Alfred Dreyfus**, a republican Jewish army officer, was sentenced to life imprisonment for selling military secrets to Germany. Soon the evidence against him turned out to be forged, the plot of fellow officers who were monarchists and Catholics. However, the army was unwilling to admit the mistake and reopen the case.

The issue quickly split the nation. The anti-Dreyfus group felt it was unpatriotic to question the army. They hoped to weaken the republic. On the side of Dreyfus were the republicans, socialists, and several important writers, particularly the novelist **Emile Zola**. They wanted justice, and they wanted disgrace for their political enemies too. In 1899, the case was finally reopened. Dreyfus was pardoned and in 1906 cleared of all guilt. He was restored to his army rank and the worst of the plotters were dismissed from service. The affair, with its revelation of anti-republican sentiment in the army, unsettled Frenchmen but ultimately strengthened the republic.

A decisive defeat for those who wanted a monarchy, the **Dreyfus Affair** also brought a final break between church and state in France. Conditions in the country had been leading up to this break for a long time. Many in the Third Republic opposed the Roman Catholic Church. The leaders were not atheists; they merely feared that the church would use its influence to undermine the republic. Also, the papacy in the 1870s had believed that the church had a higher authority than state governments. Nationalists did not intend to let some outside person dictate to France.

In the 1880s, France had expelled the Jesuits and made divorce legal. To reduce church influence in education, the government had required state **certification** of teachers and religious teaching orders. Other laws had made primary education in state schools free and had required children to have an elementary education. The intent had been to tempt parents to send their children to free public schools where they would escape church influence. (The same strategy was later used in the United States by socialists who designed the American public school system.) After further tensions between the Vatican and the French state, the government decided to stop choosing and paying clergy. In 1905, a full legal separation of church and state was implemented in France.

Elsewhere in Europe. Representative government became the norm. During the half-century before World War I, all male citizens gained the right to vote in Switzerland, Belgium, The Netherlands, Spain, and Portugal. Norway and Denmark even gave voting rights to women.

Italy gave workers the vote in 1912. But this did not solve the nation's problems—political unrest, economic underdevelopment in the south, and the ongoing quarrel with the Roman Catholic Church. **Pope Pius IX** was bitterly hostile to the Italian kingdom because it had "stolen" his property (Rome) in 1870. Even though the state offered him a generous payment, he withdrew into his palace and posed as "the prisoner of the Vatican," hoping for rescue by Catholics elsewhere. He urged Italian Catholics not to take part in the government or even vote. Liberal leaders responded with antichurch laws.

The Decline of Absolutist Empires

How did empires fare in the day of liberalism and nationalism? Great empires occupied Eastern Europe, having little in common except that each ruled more than one nationality. Germany and Russia were vigorous, growing empires moving toward becoming nation-states. Austria-Hungary, a multinational state, was decaying rapidly. All three had some type of absolutist regime and were under pressure to change.

Germany. In Germany, the Prussian monarchy with its army and aristocracy had matters firmly under control. They bought off the rising upper-middle class with protective tariffs and freedom to do as it wished in business affairs. In reality, Bismarck had designed the government to insure Prussian control and his own personal power.

Yet Germany was a constitutional monarchy and **Wilhelm I**, who was pushed by Bismarck to accept the title of German emperor (kaiser) at Versailles in 1871 during the siege of Paris, did not have absolute power. The upper house of the German parliament, controlled by the aristocracy, represented the 25 states and could block any laws it did not want. The lower house, elected by the people, had power over the budget and lawmaking. Its members could not introduce bills, and government ministers were not responsible to it. However, the **chancellor** (prime minister) still had to work with the political party coalitions to get laws passed. The states took care of education, justice, police, and enforcement of federal laws.

Unification brought a rising tide of nationalism. Writers glorified the history of Prussia and German achievements, past and present. The first challenge to the new order came from the Catholic Church. While Bismarck was trying to draw all German groups under the new state's power, the papacy insisted on ultimate loyalty from all Catholics. Since they had their own political party and most southern Germans who opposed unification were Catholics, Bismarck decided to put a damper on church power.

In 1871, he launched a campaign to restrict its worship, education, and political influence. The effort only increased sympathy for the church,

and after 1878 he backed off. He found that he needed the Catholic party's support for his legislation.

Germany had another important problem—the growing strength of socialism. Bismarck tried to break the working-class party with his anti-socialist laws. He hoped to win the workers over by offering them social security. It didn't work. In 1890, the Kaiser fired Bismarck. After that, expressions of nationalism became more noisy and uncertain; and the Socialist Party multiplied wildly. By 1912, it had the largest block of seats in the parliament. But it did not change its basic policy of simply opposing the regime rather than facing the great difficulty of getting a program of its own considered.

Russia. Czarist Russia had one of Europe's most backward regimes. Rigid police control, the army, and censorship kept the people in subjection. Western ideas that the king and subjects have mutual obligations, or that people have rights and can expect justice from the ruler, were unknown there.

Most of the people lived in a legalized bondage that went beyond European serfdom. They could be bought and sold and used in other work besides agriculture. The aristocrats ruled over their local areas with little interference from the central government. But by the mid-nineteenth century, serfdom was no longer economically desirable. Two-thirds of the privately owned serfs were mortgaged as security for loans. The quality of their work was so poor that farm output was small.

Russia also had its intellectuals—a small group of people who spent much time reading, writing, and debating with one another. They hoped that Russia would achieve its supposed destiny of leading the world to the creation of a better soci-

Russian serfs' hut in the late 19th century

ety. Some wanted Russia to imitate the West. Others said Russia was different from the West, and to copy the materialistic and faithless West would destroy Russia's unique destiny or mission. Finding the aristocracy unwilling to move in any direction, many turned to revolution and terrorism. This only invited the czar to tighten his grip on the country.

Russia's defeat in the Crimean War showed the bankruptcy of the antiliberal, autocratic czarist regime of **Nicholas I** (1825–1855). **Alexander II**, the more liberal czar who came to power in 1856 during the war, recognized that he either had to set the serfs free or face a revolution. Some of the nobles even felt that ending serfdom would greatly increase grain production and help Russia economically. On March 1, 1861, the czar, in a famous **Emancipation Manifesto**, declared all serfs legally free and gave their villages about half the land the serfs had worked. The government paid the nobles for the land. The peasants in turn were to make payments to the state for the next forty-nine years. Liberals around the world were jubilant, not recognizing for another generation the deceptive character of the manifesto.

The end of serfdom did not end the serf's problems nor did it make him a freeholder. He still could not move about without permission. Land payments and taxes put many serfs deeply in debt. And they still had to work the landowners' remaining plots—often the best land—for wages. These conditions failed to satisfy the "land hunger" of Russia's peasants, who had, in effect, become serfs of the state rather than landlords. Unrest increased among them.

Alexander made a number of other reforms, which gave the liberals and intellectuals hope that a national parliament might be established. It was not. Alexander, perhaps sensing that his record level of reform had gone far enough, reverted to a more autocratic approach, angering the intellectuals who felt the czar was trying to strengthen his regime. A younger generation of intellectuals actually began to lose interest in the liberal ideology and turned to newer ideas—nihilism and anarchy. The champion of anarchy was **Mikhail Bakunin**, who was forced to flee into exile where he tried unsuccessfully to ally himself with Marx and Engels, who considered him too radical. Still the nihilists and anarchists had a substantial influence on Russian society between 1850 and 1875. From this social disturbance there emerged groups of terrorists who grew impatient with nonviolent means for ending the autocracy. The government unleashed its secret-police forces against them. Often operating outside the law and without moral restraint, the police rounded up thousands of terrorists and marched them into inhumane concentration camps in Siberia. Meanwhile, terrorists made several attempts on Alexander II's life and finally succeeded in assassinating him on March 13, 1881, with a bomb tossed under his carriage as he was driving through St. Petersburg.

Alexander II, 1818–1881

He was succeeded by his son, **Alexander III**, a huge, stern despot who ruled even more rigidly than his predecessors. The new czar conducted violent **pogroms**, or massacres, against the Jews, causing a large number to emigrate to America and some to Palestine. (These pogroms have been commemorated in the bittersweet twentieth-century musical play and film *Fiddler on the Roof*.)

Alexander II and Alexander III both encouraged industrialization of Russia. However, the farmers carried the burdens. They were hit with higher taxes to help repay the foreign loans that provided capital for the industrialization. Also, high protective tariffs drove up the price of manufactured goods. Angry farmers formed or joined the underground terrorist groups. Dissatisfied urban middle-class and working-class people also turned to political action.

During Alexander II's reign, Russia again clashed with the Ottoman Turks when Christian Serbs in the Balkan provinces of Herzegovina and Bosnia rose up against the sultan because of increased taxes. Two sympathetic and already liberated Serb states, Serbia and Montenegro, took up the cause of their brothers in Bosnia-Herzegovina, and declared war on the Turks. Christian European powers tried to pressure the sultan to reform his policies in the Balkans, but he resisted. Russia again took upon itself the role of defender of Christendom in the Balkans, and its armies invaded first Romania and then, after several months of resistance at Plevna, the entire Balkan Peninsula, until they reached Constantinople. **Sultan Abdul-Hamid II** sued for peace.

Austria and Great Britain became highly concerned at this development, envisioning Russia in control of the Dardanelles, the connection inland from the Aegean Sea through the Sea of Marmora and the Bosporus Strait to the Black Sea. Austria and Britain also feared Russian control of a vast Balkan territory called "Big Bulgaria." Hinting at war with Russia over the issue, Austria and Great Britain convinced the czar to submit the treaty to a **Congress of Berlin** called for that purpose in 1878. Bismarck managed to get the treaty revised according to terms sought by Austria and Britain. Russia gave up most of Romania but was given other territories as compensation, including part of Armenia. Austria was given administration of Bosnia-Herzegovina. Britain received Cyprus from the Turks. "Big Bulgaria" was partitioned.

The **Treaty of Berlin** had given some limited new life to the collapsing Ottoman Empire by diminishing the Russian threat against it. At the same time, however, the Christian nations of the Balkans gained new freedom and independence from their Muslim and Russian masters and thus strengthened the region's historic identity. Bulgaria particularly gained new strength and expanded its territory. Alexander III of Russia was outraged at this move. Serbia was so upset it declared war on Bulgaria but was repulsed. Austria mediated a peace.

While the five new Christian states—Greece, Serbia, Montenegro, Romania, and Bulgaria—had a common enemy in the Turks, they were not by any means endeared to one another. Ancient ethnic rivalries persisted, a fact which again tossed the region into brutal turmoil in the 1990s following the breakup of Communist regimes in the Balkans.

Meanwhile, Russia had troubles in the Far East, where it had been attempting to expand. In 1905, Russia suffered a stunning defeat by Japan, which had been upset with Russia's advance in Asia. An outbreak of revolutionary violence back in the Russian homeland followed. **Czar Nicholas II** (1894–1917), who succeeded his father Alexander III, was forced to change the aristocracy into a constitutional monarchy. This satisfied the liberals and divided the revolutionary opposition. The more radical socialists lost out. But the elected assembly, the **Duma**, did not succeed in checking czarist power because Nicholas soon disbanded it. Discontent seethed again in Russia, and the eventual result was the world-changing Communist Revolution of 1917, which we shall take up in chapter 11.

The Austrian Empire. The Hapsburg Empire bounced back from the temporary setbacks of 1848–1849, but events in the 1860s changed it profoundly. With the loss of its footholds in Italy and Germany, Austria lost considerable power. One group within its borders, the Hungarians, had been unwilling members of the empire for many years. Now they became bold enough to demand equal footing with the Austrians.

In 1867, the two groups agreed to set up the **Dual Monarch**y, an utterly unique political invention. The empire of Austria in the west and

Saltzburg, Austria

the kingdom of Hungary in the east were equal, each with its own constitution and parliament. The official language of Austria was German, and of Hungary, Magyar. In domestic affairs, each functioned as an independent nation. They were joined within one border with common ministries for finance, foreign affairs, and war. The Hapsburg ruler permanently occupied both thrones.

Still both states contained many ethnic groups. Included in Austria were Germans, Czechs, Poles, Ruthenians (Ukrainians), Slovenes, and a few Italians. Within Hungary were Hungarians, Germans, Slovaks, Serbs, Croats, and Romanians.

Austria's province of Bohemia developed many industries—glass, porcelain, textiles, and heavy machinery. Some of their products became world famous. Hungary, dominated by great landowners, depended mainly on agriculture. A large, poverty-stricken peasant population worked small plots or labored on big estates. Many

drifted into the cities to find work, but industrial growth was slow.

Although shaken by economic, social, and racial problems, Austria became fairly prosperous. Vienna, capital of the empire, was an international city. People from all over poured into this lively intellectual and cultural center, where the popular musical **Strauss** family dominated the social scene for the bulk of the century. But as the various nationalities rubbed shoulders with one another, tensions rose between Germans and Slavs. Some citizens came to hate the Jews, many of whom had risen to important places in business, professional, and cultural life.

By 1907, Austria had given the right to vote to all males. In Hungary, only a quarter of the males could vote. By thus limiting the right to vote, the landowning class in Hungary was able to stay in power. The Hungarian refusal to consider the interests of its minorities outraged its neighbors. An explosive situation developed which would one day plunge the whole world into disaster. It was a Serbian nationalist who, in 1914, fired a fatal shot at an Austro-Hungarian archduke to spark World War I.

Throughout the nineteenth century, the map of Europe kept changing, sometimes to reflect decisions made in treaties and sometimes to reflect new political developments. As the next century began, some unrest remained even after those changes. This unhappiness led shortly to the Great War.

For Your Consideration

Questions

1. What does the term "balance of power" mean? How do modern countries try to maintain a balance of power among themselves?

2. What characteristics are good for a political negotiator to have?

3. What is the most important function of a national government?

4. Are revolutions ever justified? Under what conditions?

5. Give your evaluation of utilitarianism. Does it influence today's values? If so, explain some examples.

6. Why is nationalism such a powerful force? Discuss some modern examples of the exercise of nationalistic spirit.

7. Is representative democracy or direct democracy more active in the United States today? Discuss.

8. How is Canada affected by the United States?

9. Do you see any parallels in today's world to the political policies of Louis Napoleon? Discuss.

10. From your knowledge of Russian history, explain why the Russian people have historically had less freedom than those in many other places.

11. What should be the basis for the right to vote—sex, age, poll tax, property ownership, other qualifications? Discuss.

Projects

1. Use an historical atlas to trace the boundaries of France, Spain, Russia, Austria, and Italy after the Congress of Vienna.

2. In Canada, French and English-speaking peoples are still struggling with the idea of nationalism. Use some periodicals to compile a report on the current situation.

3. Put together a newscast script commenting on events during the 1848 revolutions.

4. Evaluate the role of American labor unions 100 years ago and today.

5. Many people emigrated from Europe and other parts of the world to the United States. Perhaps a near relative or friend of yours came to America or some other new country as an immigrant or refugee. If possible, interview this person. What do you think motivated people to come here? What are some problems which immigrants faced? Is it all right for some immigrant groups to refuse to accept the customs and language of their new country? Discuss whether immigrants entering a country illegally should be entitled to any of the privileges of citizenship.

6. During the reign of Queen Victoria, public education became widespread. Do some research to find out what schools were like in either England or America during that time. Discuss your beliefs about whether education should be under the control of civil government.

Words List

reparations	balance of power
intrigue	Papal States
army of occupation	censorship
utilitarianism	popular sovereignty
multinational	First Reich
dominion	kaiser
peers	absentee landlords
coalition	certification
chancellor	pogroms
liberalism	revolution
republicanism	economic liberalism
democracy	nation-state
nationalism	*Realpolitik*
conservatism	Duma
patriotism	constitutional monarchy
conservatism	civil religion
coalition	indemnity

People and Groups

Congress of Vienna	Adolphe Thiers
Prince von Metternich	Louis Kossuth
Viscount Castlereagh	Florence Nightingale
Talleyrand	Victor Emmanuel II
Louis Philippe	Abraham Lincoln
Quadruple Alliance	Lord Durham
Quintuple Alliance	Gen. Louis Trochu
Joseph de Maistre	Communards
Edmund Burke	Louise Michel
Jeremy Bentham	Hortense David
Thomas Malthus	Georges Boulanger
Chartists	Capt. Alfred Dreyfus
Junkers	Paris Commune
Giuseppe Mazzini	Emile Zola
Giuseppe Garibaldi	Kaiser Wilhelm I
Johann von Herder	Czar Alexander I
Lord Byron	Czar Alexander II
(Louis) Napoleon III	Czar Alexander III
Otto von Bismarck	Czar Nicholas I
Camillo di Cavour	Czar Nicholas II
Francis Deák	Mikhail Bakunin

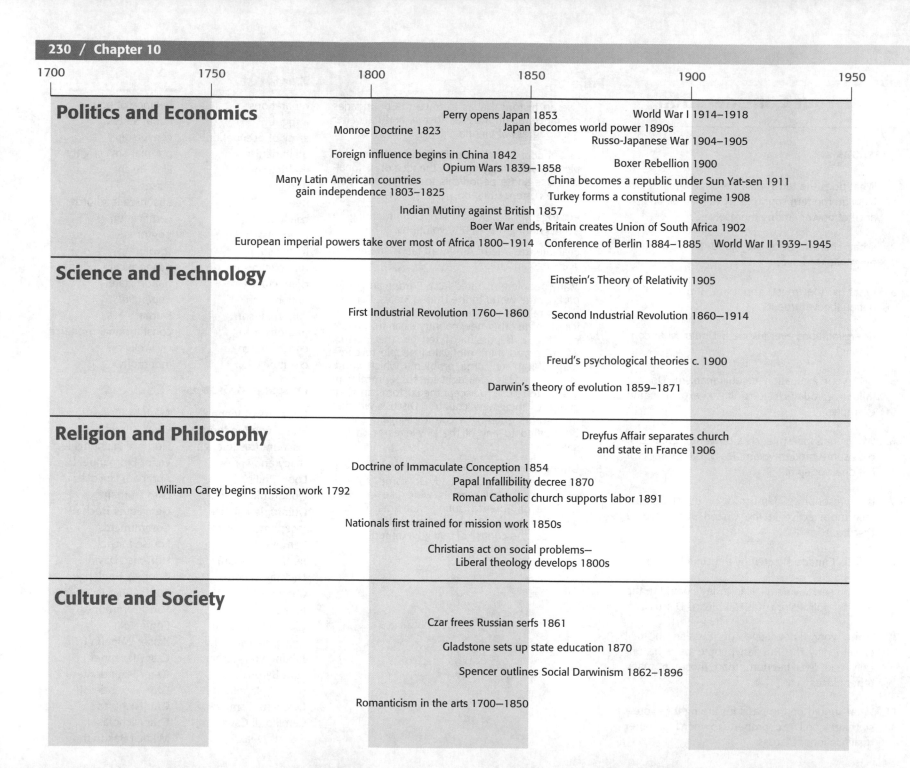

1700   1750   1800   1850   1900   1950

Politics and Economics

Perry opens Japan 1853

World War I 1914–1918

Monroe Doctrine 1823

Japan becomes world power 1890s

Russo-Japanese War 1904–1905

Foreign influence begins in China 1842

Boxer Rebellion 1900

Opium Wars 1839–1858

Many Latin American countries
gain independence 1803–1825

China becomes a republic under Sun Yat-sen 1911

Turkey forms a constitutional regime 1908

Indian Mutiny against British 1857

Boer War ends, Britain creates Union of South Africa 1902

European imperial powers take over most of Africa 1800–1914   Conference of Berlin 1884–1885   World War II 1939–1945

Science and Technology

Einstein's Theory of Relativity 1905

First Industrial Revolution 1760–1860

Second Industrial Revolution 1860–1914

Freud's psychological theories c. 1900

Darwin's theory of evolution 1859–1871

Religion and Philosophy

Dreyfus Affair separates church
and state in France 1906

Doctrine of Immaculate Conception 1854

Papal Infallibility decree 1870

William Carey begins mission work 1792

Roman Catholic church supports labor 1891

Nationals first trained for mission work 1850s

Christians act on social problems—
Liberal theology develops 1800s

Culture and Society

Czar frees Russian serfs 1861

Gladstone sets up state education 1870

Spencer outlines Social Darwinism 1862–1896

Romanticism in the arts 1700–1850

10

The Advance of European Imperialism

At the same time that democratic and socialist ideas were making gains in European and North American countries, these nations were also using new advances in technology and industry to spread their influence. Of course, Europeans motivated by economic and religious considerations had begun their travels several centuries earlier. As time went on, large numbers of settlers moved to the Americas, but elsewhere most of the Europeans were traders, missionaries, and military personnel.

In the nineteenth century, Western countries came to dominate the rest of the world. This phenomenon is often called **imperialism**. The term refers simply to "empire building," that is, the extension of political or economic rule of one state, nation, or people over another in territory outside the borders of the home country. Statesmen were anxious for their own countries to acquire "unclaimed" lands overseas before rivals could do so. When colonies protested against rule by foreigners, the Europeans acted to protect their own interests.

Western military skills and weapons helped tip the balance of power. The Industrial Revolution gave Europeans gunboats, artillery, and repeating rifles, plus the railroad and telegraph. Modern medicine and hygiene enabled soldiers to survive the tropics and other unfamiliar environments. Even the democratic nation-state played a part,

This cartoon shows the British Lion with some of its colonies.

in that European governments which engaged in imperialist ventures could count on their people's support. While all of these advantages allowed Europeans to extend their power and influence, Europeans also brought these advantages to their colonies, thus providing them with new technology; better health; greater knowledge; and advanced governmental, economic, and cultural systems. The greatest benefit, however, was the extension of the West's Christian influence.

By 1914, most of the world had come under Western political control. Large areas were Westernized as European settlers occupied the lands, destroyed or swept aside some native peoples, and set up Western political, economic, cultural, and religious institutions. This occurred in Australia, New Zealand, Siberia, and partially in South

Africa. Almost all of Africa, a large part of Asia, and the Pacific islands became European colonial possessions.

Imperialism often exploited the colonies, but it also brought basic social and economic progress to them. European civilization, shaped by the industrial and political revolutions, transformed the conquered areas. At the same time, missionaries were spreading Christian teachings throughout non-Western civilizations. Because these developments—political expansion and missionary effort—were contemporaneous, some people have misunderstood the relationship between them. The expansion of Christianity was not a tool of Western governments, but it was rather the outgrowth of conviction that all peoples needed to hear the message of Christianity. Sometimes missionaries had to oppose the procedures of their governments, although there were other occasions when they worked together.

Western capital and technology joined with the colonies' manpower, raw materials, and market potential. The fantastic increase in industrial and agricultural output which resulted built a strong global economy. Before long, non-Western peoples acquired the humanistic ideas of Europe—nationalism, liberalism, democracy, and socialism—and challenged Western control. Imperialism gave the West political control of the world, but at the same time the seeds of its own destruction. Often, because Western Christianity was weakening under liberalism and modernism, it was unable to compete with humanistic ideas in the colonial world.

Challenges to Early Imperialism

In North and South America, the native cultures had already been significantly changed by the arrival of the Europeans. Many pagan Indian tribes were destroyed or absorbed. Thus at the beginning of the nineteenth century, these two continents were more closely tied to Europe than the rest of the world. French, Spanish, and Portuguese colonies reflected many elements of their parent cultures, as did the English colonies and the newly independent United States of America.

Revolts in Latin America. Resentment had been growing in Latin America for decades, as Spanish

This Peruvian family is an example of the large Indian population found in some parts of Latin America. During the revolts against Spain, the poor and oppressed Indians often gave their loyalty to whichever side promised them the most.

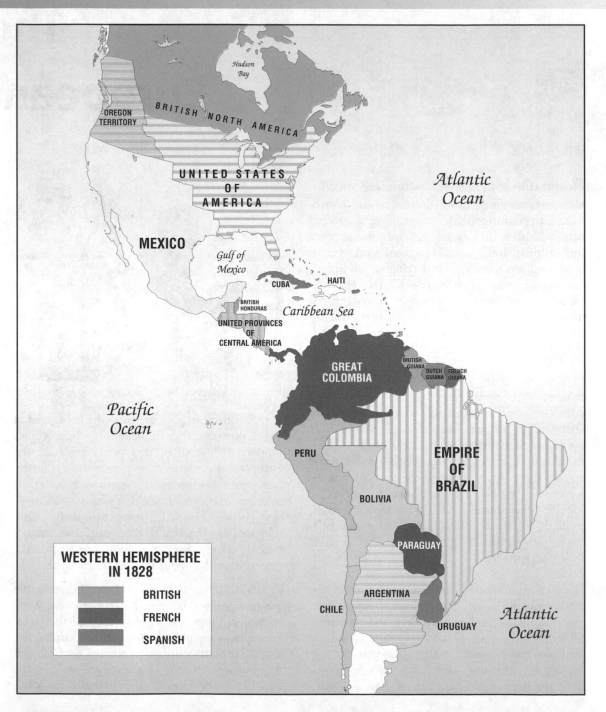

WESTERN HEMISPHERE IN 1828

BRITISH
FRENCH
SPANISH

mercantilism had enriched Spain at the expense of the colonies. In addition, persons of European descent born in the colonies (the **Creoles**) were excluded from holding high office in both the government and the church. These positions were reserved for Spanish-born aristocrats. In this already touchy situation, the American War for Independence and French Revolution fanned the fires of discontent.

Toussaint L'Ouverture, a black slave, launched a revolt against French rule in Haiti. The first to use guerrilla warfare, his straggling force of poorly equipped men used hit-and-run tactics. Within ten years, they controlled the island. **Napoleon I** was determined to regain it, but in 1803, the French force was wiped out by yellow fever and Haiti kept its independence.

During Napoleon's rule, Latin America was cut off from Spain and Portugal and was left to fend for itself. The colonies had to solve their own political and economic problems. Moving into the vacuum, Britain took over Spain's profitable trade with the area.

Meanwhile, wealthy Creoles took the lead in cutting Latin American ties with Spain. Between 1810 and 1825, **Simón Bolívar, José de San Martín**, and **Bernardo O'Higgins** liberated Spanish-speaking South America. Others worked for the same goal in Mexico, Central America, and Brazil. The help Britain gave to Latin Americans was probably as decisive as French aid had been to the North Americans 40 years earlier.

Monroe Doctrine. Since British exports to Latin America had increased 2,000 percent during the Napoleonic era, Britain tried to block any effort by Spain to regain control. The British foreign minister asked the United States (which had already recognized the new republics) to join him in a stand against Spain. Suspicious of British motives, **President James Monroe** decided to go it alone. He announced to Congress in December 1823 that Europe could no longer form colonies or meddle in the affairs of independent states in the Western Hemisphere. The **Monroe Doctrine** declared that any attempt by a foreign power to establish its influence in the Western Hemisphere would be considered to be an act of aggression against the United States and would be met with appropriate resistance from the United States. Of course, Britain had the sea power to enforce or violate the Monroe Doctrine, but because the doctrine potentially weakened Spain's control on Latin America, this American policy suited Britain's interests. In the years since it was first formulated, the Monroe Doctrine has become an integral part of fundamental American law and has governed U.S. foreign policy toward Latin America ever since.

The Rivalry of Imperialistic Nations

With the "no trespassing" sign of the Monroe Doctrine on the Western Hemisphere, Europe turned its attention eastward. The older imperial powers were still very active, and new nations joined their ranks. Spain and Portugal clung to some fragments of empires built two or three hundred years earlier. Belgium, Italy, and Germany joined in the scramble for Africa, and Russia expanded its Asiatic borders. Germany acquired territory in the Pacific, and even a modernized Japan adopted imperialistic policies similar to Europe's. Britain and France continued their rivalry, more through peaceful competition than violent conflict. The United States pushed its borders to the Pacific, under a philosophy and policy known as **Manifest Destiny**, a term first used in 1845 in a magazine editorial supporting annexation of Texas. This nationalistic philosophy, which was prevalent for much of the nineteenth century in America, held that it was not only inevitable but divinely ordained that the United States expand its territory and influence. After extending itself to the West Coast, the United States took over some islands in the Caribbean and Pacific.

With commerce as its main interest, Britain took strategic points—the Cape of Good Hope (Africa), and Singapore (Southeast Asia). Here ships could be sheltered, supplied, and sent out to defend the sea-lanes against enemies. India also seemed to offer great potential for trade, while large numbers of British settlers found new homes in Canada, South Africa, Australia, and New Zealand.

British imperialism at mid-century took the form of "informal" empire building instead of territorial annexation. Above all, Britain wanted overseas trade and preferred not to take political control abroad. However, if it became necessary to use force to keep the lines of commerce open, the British would do so. As Foreign Minister **Henry Palmerston** declared in 1841: "It is the business of the Government to open and to secure the roads for the merchant."

Algeria. French colonial activity was more political. France wanted to reclaim a place on the world scene, recover its national prestige, and turn attention away from troubles at home. Algiers, in North Africa, fell to the French in 1830. A long, drawn-out effort to take over all of Algeria followed. Beginning in the 1830s, France increased its influence in Egypt and Syria in several ways; finally this resulted in building the Suez Canal. The canal, which linked the Mediterranean Sea with the Indian Ocean through the Red Sea, provided a shipping route from Europe to the Far East, a short alternative to the long trip around the southern cape of Africa. Britain grew alarmed at this threat to its "lifeline" to India.

India. India was the centerpiece of the nineteenth century British Empire. In the 1850s, Britain put down a serious rebellion and then took full charge of Indian affairs as a step to better administration. Previously, control had been left to the British East India Company, with the government supervising it from London and supplying armed assistance. Instead of conquering all of India, Britain had seized strategic areas forming a ring around the country, along with some sections of the interior. Then treaties were made with the rulers of several hundred native states. These guaranteed the rulers' rights and possessions but turned over control of their external affairs to the British.

China. After securing India's turbulent frontiers by means of a long series of wars, the British turned toward Indonesia and China. They landed in Singapore in 1819 and then Malaya. Meanwhile, the British East India Company had a highly profitable trade in opium and tea with China. The Chinese government was justifiably upset by the amount of opium coming in and confiscated large amounts of the drug. Angered, Britain declared war in 1839. The Chinese soon discovered they were no match for British military technology.

The humiliating **Treaty of Nanking** (1842) marked the end of the **First Opium War** and the beginning of foreign rule in China. The country had to open five more ports to foreign traders, turn over the island of Hong Kong to Britain, pay for British losses, give up the power to set its own tariff rates, and exempt foreigners from Chinese law. France and the United States gained similar rights from the Chinese. In the **Second Opium War** (1856-1858), Britain and France

José de San Martín

Many have become famous by acquiring positions of power. An Argentinean revolutionist named José de San Martín achieved fame by giving up a place of power. Of course, San Martín's was noted for other things as well. He was an excellent general, maintaining one of the most disciplined and best-trained armies on the continent. With these troops, he liberated several South American countries from Spain.

After Argentina declared its independence, Spanish troops in Chile threatened to invade the country. To head off an attack, San Martín decided to take his army across the Andes Mountains into Chile. He divided his men into several groups and sent each through a different mountain pass, hoping to confuse the Spanish.

Up rocky slopes and across slippery ledges, the army picked its way. It endured hailstorms, subzero weather, and air so thin men and animals sickened from lack of oxygen. Cannon and heavy equipment were swung across chasms and up steep slopes on cables. Many pack animals slipped off the trails or died of exhaustion. But most of the men made it. Napoleon's crossing of the Alps at 8,500 feet was considered a great feat. But San Martín crossed the Andes at heights of 12,000 to 15,000 feet, through even rougher terrain.

The general's plan worked. He defeated the Spanish, and the joyous Chileans hailed him as a hero. They offered him the leadership of the country, but he refused. Then they showered him with gifts of money, which he also refused or gave to charity. To San Martín, only one thing mattered, the liberation of all South America.

Peru was next on the general's agenda. There another revolutionary, Simón Bolívar, was already leading forces against the Spanish. By working together, the two armies could probably free Peru. San Martín and Bolívar met on July 25, 1822, to discuss the matter.

Unlike San Martín, Bolívar loved the limelight and desired the wealth and power it could bring him. He was a politician as well as a soldier, while San Martín was chiefly a military man. When the two men met, they could not agree on what kind of government should be set up after independence. But one thing became clear to the Argentinean: the combined armies could not follow two leaders, and Bolívar would never share his power. There were only two alternatives—civil war between the forces of the two revolutionaries or potential independence for Peru under one of the leaders. San Martín turned his army over to Bolívar and sailed for Europe and retirement.

Bolívar went on to victory over the Spanish and became the leader of an independent Peru. But San Martín won a place in the hearts of Latin Americans, an honor given to only a few leaders.

worked together to crush the Chinese and, in the **Treaty of Tien-tsín** (1858), gained still more control. At the same time, the bloody **Tai-ping Rebellion**, a peasant-based movement, swept over China. It almost unseated the tottering **Manchu (Ch'ing) Dynasty**. Only with Western help did the government stay in power. Westerners preferred to deal with a weak, established government rather than with an aggressive, revolutionary one.

Japan. For many years, Japan had kept foreigners out and avoided any trade with the West. In 1853, **Commodore Matthew Perry** sailed an American fleet into a Japanese port. The big gunboats convinced the Japanese that they would have to trade with the United States. Several years later, the United States persuaded the Japanese to yield peacefully to demands for more commerce and diplomatic relations. After two small clashes in the early 1860s, it seemed that Japan would be opened to foreign rule like China.

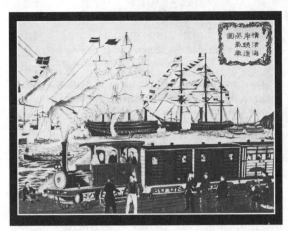

On Commodore Perry's second trip to Japan, he brought this miniature railroad to impress the Japanese.

Russian Expansion. Not only the West had designs on this part of the world. Around 1850, the Russians acquired pieces of central and east Asia. Worried about these gains in desert areas near India, the British kept them at a distance by threats and **diplomacy**. Russia also seized territory from China along the Pacific Coast and founded the new port of Vladivostok. This huge country's desire for warm-water ports was intense. As master of the seas, Britain did its best to keep such ports away from the Russians by shoring up the decaying Ottoman and Persian empires and making a friend of Japan.

Ottoman Empire. At this point, the Ottoman Empire was a complex mixture. Straddling three continents (Asia, Africa, and Europe), it contained Christians, Jews, and Muslims and lacked a sense of national identity.

During the second half of the seventeenth century, the Turks had launched a military offensive in Europe. At first they won several victories, but then a crucial defeat in 1697 forced them to give up some territory. Europe, freed from the threat of Turkish power, faced a new problem—what was

to be done with the Ottoman Empire? Should it be divided among Western nations? If so, which powers would get what? The issue affected world politics until the breakup of the Ottoman Empire in 1918, and the eventual outcome continued to affect Middle Eastern international affairs through the end of the twentieth century.

By the nineteenth century, European powers were chipping away at Ottoman holdings. Serbia, Montenegro, and Romania gained independence; and a self-governing Bulgaria was created. Cyprus was handed over to Britain, and Austria-Hungary annexed Bosnia. Egypt drifted out of the Ottoman **orbit** and was later taken over by Britain. France carved out its large North African empire from Ottoman territory.

Sultan Abdul-Hamid II, who ruled from 1876 to 1909, tried to hold his empire together by stamping out any form of nationalism or desire for a constitution. He also opened Turkey to large-scale European investment. But some reform-minded army leaders realized that Turkey could not survive much longer. In 1908, these "**Young Turks**" forced Abdul-Hamid to form a constitutional regime. When conservatives staged a counterrevolution in the following years, the Young Turks ousted the sultan and replaced him with one they could control.

They attempted to strengthen, centralize, and modernize the Ottoman Empire but it was too late. Between 1911 and 1913, Italy seized Libya; Albania obtained its independence; and two short wars left Turkey with only a small portion of its once-great empire in Europe. Even the Arab population grew unhappy with the Turks' policies. However, they did not think seriously about independence until later.

Though the Ottoman Empire eventually came to a close, the influence of the Turks and their Mus-

The Ottoman Imperial family is buried in Muradiue, Turkey.

lim religion lingered. Religious differences were a major factor, for example, in bitter ethnic strife between Muslim Albanians and Orthodox Serbs in the Serbian province of Kosovo in the 1970s and 1980s and an even more bitter series of "ethic cleansing" wars involving Orthodox Serbia, religiously divided Bosnia, and Catholic Croatia in the 1990s. These conflicts burst into violence and atrocities shortly after the collapse of totalitarian communism regimes which had held a tight unifying lid on the area between the end World War II and the 1990s.

Early European Imperialism in Africa

By the mid-nineteenth century, Europeans had founded settlements on Africa's Mediterranean coast and southern tip. As to the central and eastern sections of the continent, only a few traders, missionaries, and explorers braved the unknown.

During the Napoleonic era, the British took over the Dutch Cape Settlement (South Africa). A century of fighting followed, involving black populations, the British, and the **Boers** (as the original Dutch-speaking settlers were called). The independent, slaveholding Boer farmers resented the liberal outlook of the British. Though they did not seriously resist the abolition of slavery, they bitterly resented the British attitude which considered the Boers little better than "white savages" not far separated from the black natives.

When Britain abolished slavery in the Cape in 1834, the Boers fled northward in what became known as the **Great Trek** (1835-36). They collided with the expanding **Bantu** peoples, especially the **Zulus**, and formed the Republic of Natal. In 1843, the British took over Natal, and the Boers pushed deeper into the interior. There they formed the new republics of Transvaal and the Orange Free State.

The West Coast of Africa was, by far, the most important market region. Forts and trading posts dotted the shoreline. Coastal states like Dahomey (Benin) had grown powerful as suppliers of slaves. The Vienna Settlement of 1815 had declared an end to the slave trade and a British naval squadron tried to enforce this. However,

These African women are grinding grain in a Touarek village.

slavery did not stop until demand in the Americas fell off and steam vessels joined the British fleet. The squadron operated out of Sierra Leone, one of the three colonies set up to receive freed black slaves. The captives from seized ships settled there, and it became the leading edge of British advance in Africa.

New products—peanuts and palm oil—entered the list of items wanted by the West. Local French and British merchants began exercising political authority on their own. Gradually they pulled their governments into African affairs. In 1860, Prime Minister Palmerston declared that "trade ought not to be enforced by cannon balls, but on the other hand trade cannot flourish without security, and that security may often be unattainable without the exhibition of military force." With that excuse, the British took over the Danish and Dutch forts along the Gold Coast and grabbed Lagos (in Nigeria) for good measure. The French also began carving out an empire on the West Coast and in the interior. They claimed to be protecting their trade.

The Scramble for Africa. Belgian **King Leopold II** touched off another rush to Africa. A sort of royal robber baron, he wrote to a friend in 1877 that he did not want "to allow the opportunity to slip by of obtaining for ourselves a piece of this magnificent African cake." In 1878, Leopold and the adventurous New York journalist **Henry M. Stanley** (famous for his coverage of frontier Marshal James "Wild Bill" Hickok and for his "discovery" of the supposedly missing Scottish missionary Dr. David Livingstone in 1871) set up a private company. Stanley returned to the heart of Africa and made "treaties" with some 500 chiefs who handed over their tribal lands to the company. Other enterprising types also were claiming large portions of the interior for France, Portugal, and Germany.

Meanwhile, France moved into Tunis in North Africa, and Egypt came under British control, giving England a presence in the newly strategic Suez Canal area. An army of occupation and a British "adviser" compelled the Egyptian ruler to make reforms. Then the British picked up where they had left off in South Africa, defeating the Zulus but finally giving up on the Boer republics (for the time being).

Competition became so intense that German Chancellor **Bismarck** called an international **Conference of Berlin** (1884-1885) to sort out the problems. The **Berlin Agreement** of 1885 provided for free trade in the center of Africa, the end of slavery, and a way to claim new territory by "effective occupation." It also recognized Leopold's personal holdings as the Congo Free State. He was declared the Congo's sovereign

Henry M. Stanley, 1841–1904

ruler, but there were no formal ties to Belgium. Leopold and his subordinates exploited the Congo in brutal fashion. For example, they cut off the fingers of people who failed to do satisfactory work. Stanley, who worked behind the scenes as Leopold's agent while journalistically portraying him to the world as a benefactor of black Africans, later claimed not to have been aware of Leopold's atrocities, which he termed "moral malaria." In 1908, world opinion forced the Belgian government to take over the Congo from Leopold.

The result of the Berlin pact was a new rush to carve up the continent. The French swarmed over West Africa, and the British took over vast areas in Central and East Africa. The Italians also claimed areas of East Africa. Although America officially had little to do with the partitioning of Africa, Stanley's activities (he was an official U.S. delegate to the Conference of Berlin) indicates some America connection. Only Abyssinia (Ethiopia) successfully held back the European tide. The able **Emperor Menelik II** overwhelmingly defeated the Italians in 1896.

Another center of African resistance was the Sudan region of the upper Nile, where the British were held off until 1898. But the eventual African defeat brought the British face to face with a small French force which was also trying to lay claim to the area. English-French colonial rivalry had finally reached a climax. Although it led dangerously close to war, the crises was resolved by diplomacy.

The last serious problem in the scramble for Africa began in 1886. The discovery of gold in the Transvaal whetted the appetite of **Cecil Rhodes**, the British premier of the Cape Colony, for more land. Already a rich man because of his diamond mines, he saw this as a chance for greater wealth. Also he had a heroic vision of a

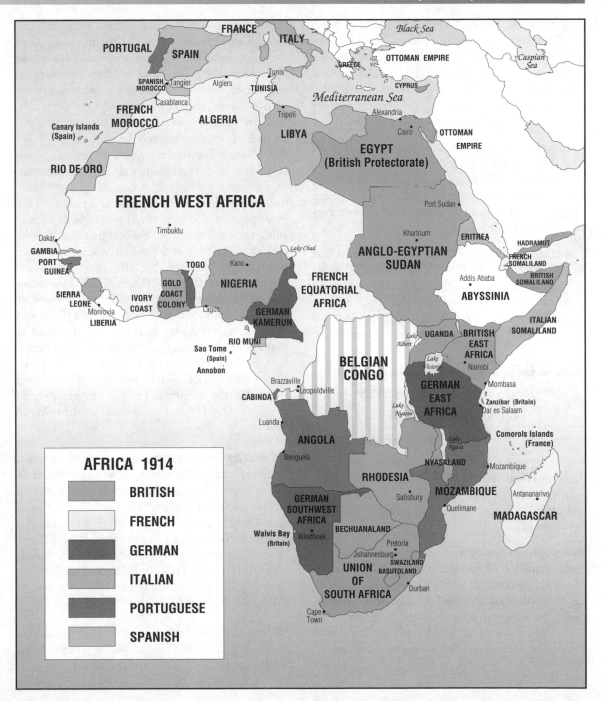

AFRICA 1914

BRITISH
FRENCH
GERMAN
ITALIAN
PORTUGUESE
SPANISH

mighty British empire in Africa, stretching from the Cape to Cairo. But the Boer republics lay in the way. Rhodes's attempts to outmaneuver or overthrow them failed. Finally, in the bloody **Boer War** (1899–1902), Britain conquered the Dutch-speaking territories and later brought them into a new Union of South Africa.

Meanwhile, France took over the large island of Madagascar. In 1914, the only independent states in Africa were Abyssinia (Ethiopia) and Liberia. But for all intents, Liberia, another of the states designed to receive freed slaves, was a **protectorate** of the United States.

The scramble for the Pacific was less intense but just as determined. The Dutch extended their rule over Indonesia; the Germans occupied northeastern New Guinea; and the British, French, Germans, and Americans parceled out thousands of Pacific islands among themselves.

Causes and Results of Imperialism

Western countries felt compelled to carve out these overseas empires. Current philosophies, political and economic ambitions, and religious zeal all contributed to the extension of Western domination.

Philosophical Motives. The nineteenth century enthusiasm for progress encouraged countries to expand their control. Social Darwinism *(see chapter 8)* convinced the leaders that real progress could be achieved only as the strong overcame the weak. Westerners could increase their own political importance and power by adding to their colonial possessions. But political power was, in the context of the time, merely a facet of

the European nations' understanding of the concept of sovereignty. Over the many centuries of their development, European states had come to see themselves as free and independent peoples concerned—as growing organisms naturally would—with their own development, growth, and strength. Empire building was seemingly a natural component of such development. Smaller states were somewhat restricted by their available resources, and their imperialism was therefore limited or nonexistent. It can be said therefore that imperialism was primarily the policy of the **great powers** who were physically capable of pursuing their self-interests. Since the pursuit of self-interest usually creates conflict when more than one power competes for the same goals, the imperialism of the great powers often resulted in war. Most professed an interest in peace, and they therefore employed diplomacy as far as it would carry them; but the last resort of war in pursuit of national-growth interests frequently was necessary, in the eyes of the heads of the various foreign offices. The global rivalries of the great powers finally culminated in the first great world conflict, World War I, and continued in World War II.

A Civilizing Mission. The optimism felt in much of Europe caused others to view imperialism in loftier terms. They felt that the white races had an obligation to bring their civilization and knowledge to backward peoples. As British writer **Rudyard Kipling** said, it was the "White Man's burden" to serve the needs of the "lesser breeds without the law." The "civilizing mission," as the French called it, was the right and duty given to Europeans by history and history's God.

Imperialism assumed the qualitative superiority of Western culture. This thinking ranged from totally **racist** to highly **humanitarian** views. It would be wrong, however, to deny the genuine

Rudyard Kipling, 1865–1936

idealism of many who went abroad. They really wanted to help those they felt were "less-favored." Often people left their homes and security to spend long, lonely years in uncomfortable tropic climates filled with many dangers. They were able to bear the hardships because they believed they were helping humanity. By bringing advanced ideas of justice and by combating such evils as slavery and intertribal warfare, they were able to do much good. These colonists overcame pagan superstitions, and they helped counteract the causes of disease and famine.

Western Culture. Early in the century, the English gave much thought to bringing the benefits of their civilization to India. The brilliant historian **Thomas B. Macaulay** wrote that the English language must be the language of

The Ganges River, Varanasi, India

An African Viewpoint

The white man considered Western ways to be logical and superior, but the African native often had a differing opinion. In the following excerpt, an African chief describes his contacts with the white man:

I was chief in my father's place then, and even though I remembered what had happened to my father, I offered to help the white man. They accepted my help, and for many months they ate my food. Then more and more white men came, and their villages grew. They brought some of their own food with them, yet they needed more of ours than we could spare. They did not do their own work but they asked us to supply men and women to do their work for them. I refused, because our people had work enough to do to keep their own fields cultivated and their own roofs thatched without working for foreigners. The white men said that in that case we would have to supply them with more food. They did not ask, they demanded, as though it was their land. I told them that it was my land, and my father's, and his father's before him, and that if they wanted to stay as my guests they were welcome to use the land to make their own plantations —there was room enough for all—but they would have to do their cutting and planting themselves. They said they had come to help us, but all they did was to send out men with guns whenever any of us reported any fighting among our neighbors. It was a good thing to stop the fighting, and we had all agreed. But when their men with guns started forcing us to work it was a bad thing. I took my family and my village and we all moved away deep into the forest and lived like savages until we could build another plantation.

The chief of the white men came to our village himself and called all the people together. He told them that I was no longer chief, that Masoudi was. People were astounded, because to them this was a heresy, and they expected the white man to be struck dead. But I stepped forward and said that the white man's head was turned by the sun and he did not understand that Masoudi could never be chief. However, Masoudi was like white men, so let him call himself chief, and let him take on all the foolishness of trying to deal with them. I told my people that I wanted nothing to do with the white man, and I did not want to be responsible to the ancestors for polluting the soil of our fathers by following the white man's ways. I gladly gave up being chief in the eyes of the white man, but to them, my people, I would remain as I had always been.

This pleased the village, and I think it even pleased Masoudi, who also knew that he could never really be chief. But the white men caught me and told one of their soldiers, an Azande, to beat me. For this I have never forgiven them. They could have beat me for themselves, for they had proved themselves stronger with their guns, and it would have been no disgrace. But to have me beaten by one of those savages from the north is a shame I shall never forget. Even our enemies we treat like men, not like children.

After Masoudi became chief I had nothing to do with the white men for some time. I thought that if I left them alone they would leave me and my people alone, and for a while it was so. Masoudi saw to it that cotton was planted, and that there were extra plantains to feed the road gangs, and he told some men to work on the roads. They asked me if they should do these things, and I told them that these things were nothing to me—they were white men's matters and Masoudi was the white man's chief. If they did not obey, then the white man would simply send in his foreign soldiers with whips and guns and lock them up in cages, like animals.

Excerpted from **The Lonely African,** copyright © 1962 by Colin M. Turnbull, pp. 76-77. Reprinted by permission of Simon & Schuster, a Division of Gulf & Western Corporation.

instruction in India because it was far superior to the Hindus' language and civilization. A civil servant in India at the time, Macaulay thought that Britain should direct the education of the more ignorant nations. He hoped to create an elite who would help the colonial effort. This select group would be "Indian in blood and color, but English in taste, in opinions, in morals, and in intellect." What he and others may not have foreseen was that their elite would later lead the revolt against colonialism.

During the following decades, the British set up a system of national education. Secondary schools and colleges used English, while elementary schools taught the masses in the local languages. This created a Hindu upper class familiar with Western culture and political thought.

Despite the desire of Europeans to bestow the benefits of their culture upon non-Westerners, they continued to maintain the differences between white and dark-skinned people. **Nationals** (native peoples) could work in the colonies, but they did not exercise any authority.

Following the mutiny in 1857, the British decided to share more power with the Indians. The mutiny, sparked by the **sepoys** (Indian soldiers within the British military units), brought together many who had a gripe against the British—landowners, dethroned rulers, and radical religious groups. After the rebellion was put down, a highly structured bureaucracy ran the country. Whites still held the high offices, but Indians in lower positions dealt with the masses. The **rajahs** and **maharajahs** continued to rule over their states. However, they looked to Queen Victoria as the ultimate sovereign and to British advisers who kept local policy in line with Britain's interests.

Britain devised another scheme, "indirect rule," for northern Nigeria. They used Nigerians as much as possible, keeping the number of white administrators to a bare minimum. Some of the other colonial powers also adopted this idea in the early 1900s. The size of the administrative task and the lack of European personnel required it.

Political and Economic Factors. Political balance in Europe was well-maintained following the 1815 settlement in Vienna. As the years passed, countries that wanted to increase their national glory looked to non-Western lands. Especially in the latter part of the century, the drive for overseas colonies intensified. Patriotism was increased by impressive achievements around the world.

Economic rather than political considerations have been emphasized by some historians as the dominant motivating factor in imperialism. Marxist thought usually focuses on the ways in which wealthier nations exploited the others by acquiring raw materials cheaply and selling unneeded manufactured products to the colonies. Sometimes Western capitalists are seen as investing their capital abroad so they would not have to pay higher wages to European workers.

Of course, the Industrial Revolution did affect economic patterns. As Western nations became more industrialized, they looked to their colonies to supply foodstuffs and raw materials for the world market. However, a country did not have to control another land to get its raw materials. In fact, the independent countries of the Western Hemisphere, along with Australia and New Zealand, were the major suppliers of Europe's raw materials.

Manufactured products not consumed in Europe went, for the most part, to developed areas, not to colonies. The British sold more goods to thinly populated Australia than to overcrowded India. In spite of protective tariffs, Western industrial countries traded mainly with one another, not with their overseas empires. Thus it cannot be said, as some have alleged, that colonialism was exclusively or primarily intended to create controlled markets for Europeans.

European banks did provide the capital for construction of railroads, ports, canals, mines, and plantations. The railroad networks and better facilities for merchant shipping increased the capacity for rapid transportation of both the natural resources and the finished products to markets throughout the world. Furthermore, investors devoted a large percentage of their funds to countries which were already developed.

Obviously, a desire for financial profit was one of the several motives which encouraged business ventures around the globe. But as an economic enterprise, imperialism was not immediately profitable for the governments involved. The income from the colonies generally did not cover the cost of the conquest and administration. For Germany and France, the total value of trade with their empires did not equal the expenses involved. Tax money from the home countries paid for administrative costs, public works, and troops to keep order in the colonies.

Global Economy. People around the world began to be part of a more unified economic system. Hired by colonial administrations, trading firms, and service industries, workers began to participate in the world economy rather than to provide food and products for their own local needs. Populations began to increase as advances in agriculture and medicine dramatically lowered the number of deaths from **malnutrition** and disease. High infant **mortality rates** were especially affected.

But non-Western producers were at the mercy of the world market. While European manufacturers had formed cartels to regulate output and prices and keep profits coming in, prices for agricultural and mine products were uncontrollable. Overproduction abroad or decreased demand in the West dropped prices sharply, with disastrous effects. An economic depression in the West not only lowered prices, but also cut back employment opportunities for people elsewhere. Dissatisfaction with this economic dependence would ultimately be one of many factors leading to twentieth-century freedom movements.

The Missionary Movement and Imperialism

The Great Commission was yet another motive which caused Westerners to move out into the rest of the world. In 1789, Christianity could almost have been described as a white man's religion. European missionaries of earlier centuries had had little success in establishing long-lasting churches. Yet today, Christianity is a world religion, found on every continent, with followers from every tribe and race. Indeed in the late twentieth century the Church was growing faster in non-Western countries than in the West itself. What caused this spectacular change?

As we have already seen in chapter four, the revivals in Europe and North America provided a great impetus to world missions. As Christians became more concerned about the unconverted at home, they in turn became more interested in seeing the lost won for Christ around the world. Missionary societies were formed and began to send missionaries like William Carey and William Chalmers Burns to foreign lands in ever increasing numbers.

The eyes of more and more Christians were opened to the worldwide need by these early missionary efforts. As Europeans and Americans increased their exploration and trade, they became more aware of the indigenous peoples of other lands. Because of their desire to share their religious beliefs with these inhabitants, more denominations and groups of Christians founded missionary societies in various countries.

The Missionaries. Missionaries gave up careers, families, and comforts in their homelands. Many pioneered in areas where no white person had ever gone, risking their health and often their

David Livingstone, 1813–1873

lives. Before the days of modern medicine, tropical diseases were often fatal. Headhunters and cannibals martyred many missionaries. Several parts of Africa became missionary graveyards, for few who went there ever returned.

One of the best known was **David Livingstone**, who explored southern Africa and tried to end the slave trade. **Hudson Taylor** founded the **China Inland Mission**, depending on God alone to supply his needs. And there were many others—**John Paton** went to the New Hebrides Islands, **Dr. Horace Allen** to Korea, **Amy Carmichael** to India, **Ludwig Nommensen** to Sumatra (Indonesia), **Mary Slessor** to Calabar (Nigeria), and **Samuel Zwemer** and **Dr. W. M. Thomson** to the Islamic world. Their stories and those of other brave envoys fill an exciting chapter in the history of the Christian Church.

Many of the early missionaries were lay people, often craftsmen or tradesmen. They had little or no university education and probably would not have been accepted into full-time church work at home. After the mission organizations became aware of the need to prepare workers better, they set up programs for this purpose. By 1850, they also saw the importance of training nationals.

Sometimes the nationals recognized this need first. In the early 1800s, an African teenager named **Samuel Ajayi Crowther** was rescued from a slave ship. Later he became a Christian and studied to be a teacher. Crowther convinced the Anglican **Church Missionary Society** that the Africans themselves had to evangelize the interior of the continent. In 1857, he led a completely African-staffed mission to the Niger region. There he started many churches and elementary schools, two high schools, and a college. The Anglican Church recognized Crowther's outstanding work by making him a bishop in 1864. He was the first black man to hold that position.

Relations with Government. The relationship between imperialist powers and missionaries was often complex. Missionary work was frequently viewed with suspicion. The British East India Company was so hostile to **William Carey**, that he had to work in an area claimed by Denmark. Likewise, British authorities banned missionaries from some Muslim-ruled areas in northern Nigeria. They feared that Christian evangelism would upset the delicate political situation there.

Concurrently, Western expansion did help open up much of the world to missionary efforts. For example, the results of the Opium Wars enabled missionaries to go into the interior of China, while Commodore Perry's expedition to Japan made it possible for missionaries to enter Japan. Perry even allowed an American Congregationalist missionary named **Samuel Williams** to accompany him to Japan.

Missionaries occasionally did look to the colonial powers for help. Sometimes they asked that a territory be annexed so that it could be opened to mission efforts. Because they feared that the Portuguese would bring both slavery and Catholicism, Scottish missionaries urged the British to set up a protectorate in Nyasaland (Malawi) to head off a possible Portuguese takeover. Missionaries sought government help in fighting the slave trade, in both West and East Africa. In China, they asked for protection against hostile groups of radicals. (For further information see the map on the "Growth of Protestant Missions" at the end of chapter 4.)

Impact of Missionary Work. As a result of missionary efforts, many people did accept the good news of salvation provided by the death and resurrection of Jesus. Later, believers joined together in churches. There was greater success in areas where people practiced pagan tribal religions such as animism than where there was a broader-based, better-organized religion such as Islam. As a result, some missionaries saw many converts, while others struggled for a lifetime with only limited results.

The greatest success of the gospel in the non-Western world has been in Korea. Dr. Allen, a Presbyterian medical missionary, arrived in 1884, and was soon followed by other Presbyterian and Methodist missionaries. The success of the mission effort was due, in large part, to the use of "**The Nevius Method**" by the Presbyterian missionaries in Korea. This plan, developed by **John L Nevius**—a Presbyterian missionary to China, emphasized five principles: personal evangelism, self-propagation, self-government, self-support, and systematic Bible study. These principles have led to the development of a large, active, and self-

John Livingston Nevius, 1829–1893

sufficient church in Korea that is now sending out its own missionaries.

Like other Westerners, the missionaries brought technology as well as the gospel to foreign lands. By training nationals to raise products for trade on the world market, they promoted economic development. A cocoa-growing project in the Gold Coast (Ghana) and a cotton program in Nigeria are good examples. The scientific and scholarly work of people like David Livingstone gave the world important geographic knowledge, paving the way for economic development.

An especially important gift of the missionaries was education. They taught people to read and write so they could understand the Bible. They established elementary and secondary schools and were also involved in the founding of several higher-level institutions such as the University of Calcutta. Even girls, who were often neglected or thought to be unimportant, received schooling.

In some places missionaries had to reduce languages to writing before they could translate the Bible and other books.

Literacy and education opened to nationals the literature and political ideas of the West. As a result of this broader awareness, a great many Third World leaders of the twentieth century were those who had been educated in mission schools.

Missionaries demonstrated their compassion for those who were suffering. They brought modern medicine which partially or totally conquered the age-old diseases that had wiped out millions of people. Many doctors and nurses ministered to both the spiritual and physical needs of the people. Christian workers also pushed for an end to such cruel native practices as slavery, human sacrifice, and **caste** systems.

Protestants led the way in nineteenth century missions. But Roman Catholics gradually increased their efforts as well. A number of new orders worked alongside the older Catholic mission organization, the **Propaganda** (founded in 1622). Although Protestant and Catholic missions did not work together, the Protestants themselves did help each other a great deal.

Cooperation in the foreign missionary enterprise laid the foundation for today's **ecumenical** movement. The first great worldwide meeting of churches was a missionary conference in Edinburgh, Scotland, in 1910. This encouraged people who wanted to unite the churches of the world to redouble their efforts. These Christians hoped for a day when the church would practice true unity and the kingdom of God would come to earth. Sadly, many in the ecumenical movement were more eager for unity than for truth.

In this cartoon, Benjamin Disraeli and Queen Victoria are embarking on the dangerous waters of imperialism.

Responses to Imperialism

Non-Westerners could respond in various ways to the West. They could withdraw—cut off all contacts with the foreigners and continue their traditional beliefs and practices. Or they could adapt—take on the Western ways that would help them to counter the undesirable effects of the foreign culture. Others attempted to resist and reject Western ways by force or other means.

Withdrawal. Attempts to reject imperialism and remain isolated in an ancient non-Western culture were usually unsuccessful. In a world which had improved means of communication and alternate modes of transportation at its disposal, complete isolation was impossible. One attempt to get rid of foreign intervention was the **Indian Mutiny** mentioned earlier. The fighting was bitter with many casualties, but it did not have a chance against superior British power.

China also tried to maintain its earlier isolation from the rest of the world, but the Manchu dynasty grew steadily weaker. Still the Confucian scholar-bureaucrats who ruled the country scorned anything Western. In the 1860s, they

"Great White Ma"

Battle cries rang from the African village. One of its men had been murdered and his blood cried out for revenge. Suddenly into the confusion of men preparing for war strode a small white woman. "Don't behave like fools," she shouted. Finally making herself heard, she quieted the warriors down. Then she hurried to the chief of the offending village, a man she had once nursed through an illness. He agreed to a meeting of the two villages. There they resolved the problem peacefully. Who was this woman who could stop a war in a part of Africa where violence and hatred had long ruled?

Mary Slessor was born in Scotland in 1848. Training for her future work in Africa began not in school but at home where her alcoholic father sometimes drove her into the darkened streets. At age 11, she had to go to work in a factory to support the family. These unhappy experiences gave Mary a deep sympathy for suffering people. In Nigeria, she would find many who desperately needed a touch of kindness.

While still in her 20s, Mary moved in to her mud hut on the Calabar Mission Field to begin her work. At the edge of the village, mangrove forests stretched off into the distance, endless miles of disease-ridden swamps, wild animals, snakes, heat and humidity, and savage peoples. Many Africans practiced witchcraft, belonged to secret societies, and drank heavily. Some of the customs were cruel, such as abandoning twin babies to die in the forest. Nigerians thought that twins brought evil.

Mary started churches and schools. She nursed the sick, dressing the most loathsome sores and giving medicine. She rescued twins and raised them herself. Her efforts to develop trade between villages lifted people out of poverty. The home for girls she started gave young women an opportunity to learn crafts. Mary raised the status of women in the area. Through the gospel she preached, thousands of lives were transformed, set free from fear and cruelty. Her unceasing labors and love for the Africans, practical deeds they could see, won their hearts. Something they could not see, the help of a powerful, prayer-answering God, won their respect. Their name for her was "Great White Ma."

How could a woman alone face the constant dangers, hardships, and loneliness of such a life? Mary wrote, "My life is one long daily, hourly record of answered prayer. For physical health, for mental overstrain, for guidance given marvelously, for errors and dangers averted, for enmity to gospel subdued, for food provided at the exact hour needed, for everything that goes to make up life and my poor service...."

reluctantly adopted a "self-strengthening" program. They would take the West's technology but not its ideas and institutions. This philosophy failed because Western science could only undermine, not strengthen, Confucian culture.

China's economy came increasingly under Western control. Monetary loans and economic agreements gave Western powers financial interest in Chinese affairs. Western gunboats patrolled the Yangtze River and coastal ports. The European settlement in Shanghai functioned as an independent city-state, since Chinese laws did not apply there.

The ultimate disgrace came with China's defeat by Japan (1894–1895). China had to surrender Formosa (now Taiwan) to Japan and recognize the independence of Korea, which Japan later annexed. Also extracted from the helpless Chinese empire were naval bases and **spheres of influence** for France, Britain, Germany, Russia, and Japan. These spheres were areas in China where an outside country had the sole right to carry on economic activities. The United States, concerned that China would soon be carved up into various European commercial protectorates, sought to protect its own trade interests by advocating Secretary of State **John Hay**'s "Open Door Policy" regarding China.

In 1898, the 27-year-old emperor, **Kuang Hsu**, was persuaded to launch a program known as the **Hundred Days of Reform**. It would have moved China well down the road to Westernization. But groups of conservative Chinese, with the aid of Kuang Hsu's aunt, the **Empress Dowager Tz'u Hsi**, blocked the program by starting anti-foreign movements. One of these conservative groups, the **Boxers**, declared war on all foreigners in 1900. The rebellion was a bloody conflict which resulted in the massacres of thousands of Christians as the Boxers marched northward toward Peking (now Beijing), which they entered in June 1900. Some 1,000 foreigners and 3,000 Chinese Christians were besieged in the Legation Quarter for 55 frightful days. A seven-nation expeditionary force quickly formed to rescue the Western diplomats whom the Boxers had besieged in Peking. Humiliating peace terms were once again imposed on China because of the **Boxer Rebellion**. The humiliation of the Manchus in the eyes of the Chinese and popular belief that reform would be impossible under the crafty old empress soon led to the demise of the dynasty.

Modernization. Meanwhile, Japan took a different course. The situation at first resembled China's—with treaty ports, Western settlements exempt from Japanese law, and much internal strife. But the response to the West there was modernization. The Japanese built up capital to develop industry. They opened schools to train people for service in government and business. They built rail and communication networks, along with port and shipping facilities.

These reforms came during the rule of **Emperor Meiji (Mutsuhito)**, 1867–1912). The offices of the shogun and the emperor were combined and the governmental structure improved. The Japa-

Japanese in traditional dress at Kyoto.

nese adopted a new legal code and constitution which reflected Western ideas. They restructured their army and navy according to European practice. Japan soon boasted a national postal system and compulsory public education which almost ended illiteracy. Heavy emphasis was placed on industry and export trade.

The Japanese did not simply copy everything Western. They chose only those things that added to the country's power—science, technology, arms, and political and legal organization. They kept their own culture, moral and family values, and religion. Thus, while Japan has never been a Christian nation, it has reaped many of the fruits of Christianity through its adoption of the best of Western developments and has in that way matched much of the West's success in the world.

Japan took its place as a world power in the 1890s. First, it persuaded the Western powers to cancel unfavorable treaties. Then the Japanese formed a military alliance with Britain in 1902. Modernized Japan showed its newly gained muscle in defeating China in 1895 and Russia ten years later. Russia and Japan quarreled over Manchuria and finally declared war upon each other.

Poorly supplied, Russia could not meet the challenge, and its rickety fleet was sunk by the new Japanese navy. At that moment, the American president, **Theodore Roosevelt**, stepped in. He arranged a peace settlement before the Russians could resupply their troops and attack an exhausted Japan.

The **Russo-Japanese War** (1904–1905) had enormous significance for world history. The Japanese had shown how to resist Westernization by adapting. A small Asiatic country had defeated a major European nation using the very tools of Western power. Asians took hope. Revolts in Persia, Turkey, and, above all, China reflected the new mood. In 1911, Dr. Sun Yat-sen finally overthrew China's Manchu dynasty, set up a republic, and tried a bitterly opposed program of modernization. Dr. Sun had been educated in Christian schools in Honolulu, Hong Kong, and elsewhere. He practiced medicine for awhile, but soon became more interested in political revolution. After numerous unsuccessful revolts led by Sun, a national revolution broke out when a bomb at a revolutionary facility accidentally exploded. Nervous Manchu officials rounded up known revolutionaries, an act which sparked the national revolution and the end of the Manchus. Further developments in China are discussed in chapters 13 and 14.

Continuing unrest in India and Indonesia, as well as all-Islamic movements in Egypt and North Africa, also showed the new approach to resistance by adaptation. This trend has been maintained throughout the twentieth century as Western and non-Western countries have been involved in military, economic, political, and philosophical confrontations with each other.

For your consideration

Questions

1. What have been some of the basic elements of economic progress?

2. How should missionaries relate to the government in their host country?

3. Why does a revolution in one area often encourage another somewhere else?

4. How do modern countries try to extend their influence?

5. Why did Britain need overseas trade?

6. Are there any circumstances in which one country should impose its desires on another? What aspects of civilization should be shared with all peoples?

7. What factors aided the disintegration of the Ottoman Empire?

8. Evaluate the actions of Leopold II in the Congo? What do you think Stanley meant by calling them "moral malaria"?

9. What are Africa's major exports today?

10. Do you consider Western culture superior? Discuss. How do you feel about the rights of strong nations over weaker ones?

11. Why has English become the second language of so much of the world?

12. Should everyone have access to the same kind of education? Why or why not?

13. What imported foods do you eat?

Projects

1. Do some research and then present a series of oral or written reports on one or more of the leaders of Latin American independence — Toussaint L'Ouverture, Simón Bolívar, José de San Martín, Bernardo O'Higgins, Emiliano Zapata, Francisco "Pancho" Villa, or others.

2. Find out about the problems involved in constructing the Suez and Panama canals. How have these canals changed world shipping patterns?

3. Debate or discuss in a report the morality of the British opium trade with China.

4. Write a biographical sketch of one of the missionaries mentioned in this chapter or some other pioneering missionary of your acquaintance. Try to find out his or her motives and feelings, successes and failures, and rewards and sacrifices.

5. Research the current status of Hong Kong and write a brief report.

6. Put together an "end of the decade" news report on the major events of the 1850s—the Indian Mutiny, the Second Opium War, Perry's contacts with Japan, and other events.

7. Christian missionary work has changed a great deal since its beginning. Do some research on modern missions—techniques, goals, results. What world trends affect missions today?

Word List

imperialism	great powers
animism	idealism
diplomacy	racist
orbit	Opium Wars
protectorate	spheres of influence
humanitarian	ecumenical
nationals	caste
malnutrition	Open Door Policy
mortality rates	Manifest Destiny
literacy	Monroe Doctrine
Indian Mutiny	British East India Co.
Berlin Conference	Vienna Settlement 1815
Nevius Plan	Boxer Rebellion

People and Groups

rajahs	Thomas Macaulay
maharajahs	Mary Slessor
sepoys	John Paton
creoles	William Carey
Toussaint L'Ouverture	China Inland Mission
Simón Bolívar	Dr. Horace Allen
José de San Martín	Hudson Taylor
Bernardo O'Higgins	Dr. W.M. Thomson
James Monroe	Samuel Williams
Theodore Roosevelt	Amy Carmichael
Matthew Perry	Ludwig Nommensen
Manchu Dynasty	Samuel Zwemer
Ottoman Turks	Samuel A. Crowther
Abdul-Hamid II	Sun Yat-sen
Young Turks	John Hay
Boers	Kuang Hsu
Bantu peoples	Tz'u Hsi
Zulu tribe	Henry J.T. Palmerston
Leopold II	Meiji (Mutsuhito)
Henry M. Stanley	The Propaganda
David Livingstone	John Nevius
Menelik II	Rudyard Kipling
Cecil Rhodes	Church Missionary Soc.

1900	1910	1920	1930	1940	1950

Politics and Economics

World War I 1914–1918   Hitler appointed German chancellor 1933

Communist Revolution in Russia 1917

Great Depression 1930s

Mussolini comes to power in Italy 1922

Atatürk forms Turkish Republic 1923

World War II 1939–1945

Stalin takes control in Russia
after death of Lenin 1924

Science and Technology

First tanks, war planes, submarines,   Einstein writes to President Roosevelt
and poison gas used in warfare 1914–1918   advocating research on the atomic bomb 1939

Religion and Philosophy

Churchmen divide over Naziism 1930s

Stalin persecutes Christians in Russia 1920s–1950s

Culture and Society

Much social legislation passed 1918–1930s

Persecution of Jews by the Nazis 1933–1945

11 The Collapse of Humanistic Optimism: World War I

Europeans greeted the new century with tremendous optimism. For many it meant progress in technology and science and the triumph of democracy. A few talked of ushering in the Kingdom of God. Everything seemed to herald a new and glorious dawn—empires extending into distant lands, diseases conquered at last, production increasing at a fantastic rate.

Yet with all this came warnings that all was not right. In many countries there were strikes and riots. Some writers did not share the general optimism. Novelists and playwrights such as **Henrik Ibsen** and **Thomas Mann** wrote of middle-class people as shallow and hypocritical. Many wondered what man was really like. **Karl Marx** saw him as the result of economics; **Charles Darwin** saw him as the effect of the survival of the fittest; and **Sigmund Freud** saw him as the product of repressed sexual drives.

In a few short years, World War I would bring much of the optimism of the 'Age of Progress' crashing into disillusionment.

Origins of the Great War

The Great War had numerous immediate causes, as we shall see shortly. But there were also some historical factors that made it possible:

u Europe had become a body of competitive sovereign states each with its own interests and a belief in the independent right to pursue them.

u An overactive sense of nationalism with a disposition toward hatred and violent rivalry.

u Imperialism with an associated export of capital which needed military protection.

u A massive and competitive build up of armaments.

u The division of Europe into two hostile alliances.

All of these factors combined to generate an additional, overarching factor: the undermining of centuries of goodwill produced by the civilizing institutions of the West—the Christian religion, the arts, science, commerce, etc. In their place, the above factors generated fear, suspicion, and hatred. This psychological factor is a major explanation for the violence that broke out in 1914.

We now explore in detail several of the historical causes before turning to an examination of immediate events and crises leading to the war.

Militarism. Few people in 1914 really wanted war, but most assumed it was inevitable. Europe had become an armed camp. All the nations had some form of military training. When one country increased the size of its standing army, the others quickly followed suit. Military spending

Edvard Munch, *The Cry*, 1895

mounted as each armed its forces with the most advanced weapons.

Germany's decision in 1898 to create a navy equal to Britain's triggered a frantic shipbuilding effort in both countries. A "battleship gap" developed. The Germans claimed they needed a navy

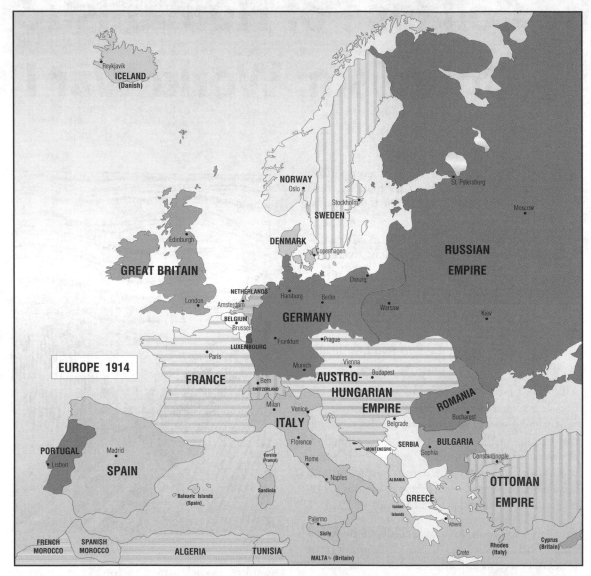

EUROPE 1914

books and pamphlets fanned nationalist flames. Writers glorified war and portrayed rival nations with emotion-charged words.

French anger smoldered over the loss of Alsace-Lorraine to Germany in 1871. This made any real peace between the two neighbors impossible. In Germany, however, propaganda groups said that their country needed even more power and territory. The people believed that the world did not appreciate them and their achievements.

The East bred a more troublesome nationalism. Russia promoted the idea that East European Slavs were one great family. The most powerful Slavic state (Russia) should be the guide and protector of its little brothers. The Slavic peoples in Serbia and Bulgaria should look to Russia for any needed help. However, Serbia dreamed of uniting all the south Slavic peoples into one state. Since most of these peoples lived within the boundaries of Austria-Hungary, Serbia constantly stirred up discontent among them and intrigued against the Dual Monarchy.

Alliances. Then a system of alliances, originally intended to keep peace, backfired. Germany in 1879 made an alliance with Austria-Hungary designed to protect Germany from France and Austria-Hungary from Russia. The **Triple Alliance** was formed in 1882, when Italy, incensed at France over actions in mutually coveted Tunis, joined Germany and Austria-Hungary in their mutual defense pact. (Romania joined in 1883; Italy later withdrew from that alliance; both eventually entered World War I on the Allied side.) Russia and France then formed the **Franco-Russian Duel Entente** (*entente* means "a friendly understanding or agreement) in 1890. Britain composed its differences with France and by 1904 formed the **Franco-British Entente Cordiale**. Britain made an alliance with Japan in 1902 and sought unsuccessfully to ally itself with

to protect their colonies and their foreign trade. What they really wanted was to show how powerful they were. Britain counted on its mastery of the seas to survive. It depended heavily on its Empire and imported much of its food. The British believed that Germany planned to challenge

them economically. Aggressive German businessmen competed in what had been British markets worldwide.

Nationalism. Another factor paved the way for World War I. Cheap, popular newspapers, known for "yellow journalism," and mass market

Germany as a check against the Russians. Britain had been wary of Russia because of the latter's Asian expansion, but Russia's defeat in the Russo-Japanese War (1904-1905) relieved some of Britain's concerns. Having been rebuffed by Germany, Britain grew closer to France, which was already on friendly terms with Russia. The French cabinet worked to bring Russia and Britain together. They did resolve most of their differences by 1907 and proceeded to, among other things, divide independent but "backward" Muslim Persia between themselves. Although it was never a formal treaty, the ensuing Russian-British-French **Triple Entente** (1907) became the foundation for the eventual **Allied Powers** against the Triple Alliance (called the **Central Powers** during the war) as the First World War broke out.

Europe was thus after 1907 divided into two major camps—the Triple Alliance and the Triple Entente—through which the countries committed themselves to help their partners in time of war.

The War to End all Wars

The Prewar Crises. The historical background for the Great War may perhaps be traced from the **Franco-German War** of 1870-71, which was among the first attempts of the new united German Reich, under **Kaiser Wilhelm I** and his chancellor **Otto von Bismarck**, to flex its muscles. The German Empire's prestige was high in the Continent, and all of Europe was eagerly awaiting the unfolding of its foreign policy. Bismarck, convinced that Germany needed a time of peace to develop itself following its recent unification, set about to diplomatically align Europe to Germany's advantage. He sought to isolate France, the largest threat. He worried little about Britain because it was already engaging in a policy of "splendid isolation" from Europe (its interests were elsewhere). Italy was also young and weak and not a major concern. Bismarck concentrated therefore on Russia and Austria-Hungary in his effort to deny France allies. In 1872, Germany, Russia, and Austria-Hungary formed the **League of the Three Emperors**, but the alignment was unnatural and uneasy and fell apart some time after Russia successfully attacked the Ottoman Empire, which frightened Austria-Hungary.

In 1878, the **Congress of Berlin**, which was called by Bismarck to revise the peace treaty between Russia and the Ottoman sultan (see Chapter 10), gave the realms of Bosnia and Herzegovina to Austria-Hungary for administrative purposes, although they remained technically under the overlordship of the Ottomans. Much of Bosnia-Herzegovina was populated by Serbs, whose ancestors had settled the area in the seventh century.

In 1908, Austria-Hungary annexed Bosnia outright, nearly touching off a war with Serbia and Russia, both of which had once supported a Bosnian peasant uprising against Muslim landlords. But German mediation in 1909 averted the fighting with a settlement satisfying Austria-Hungary. Resentment remained among the Serbs in both Serbia and Bosnia.

Meanwhile, the Franco-British Entente of 1904 had prompted another crisis which put Germany at odds with the western European powers. Aimed at settling long-standing differences between England and France, the 1904 *entente* called for France to give up its opposition to British dominance in Egypt in exchange for British support for French acquisition of Morocco. Italy, which also wanted Morocco, backed France in exchange for French support for Italy's acquisition of Tripoli (Libya) which lay between Morocco and Egypt. Never mind that Morocco was an independent Muslim state at the time; its "backwardness" was enough to justify the European powers' desires to take it over anyway.

Kaiser Wilhelm II (who began ruling Germany in 1888 and fired Bismarck in 1890) was miffed that France, Britain, and Russia should presume to grab major colonial prizes such as Egypt, Morocco, and Persia without involving Germany somehow; so he paid a visit to the sultan of Morocco and pledged his support for Moroccan independence. The visit was a sensation which shook Europe. It resulted in the **Conference of Algeciras** in Spain in 1906, which affirmed Moroccan independence but ceded France special interests there. Wilhelm was defeated and sulked for several years about the matter. France finally (in 1912) ceded Germany some interests in the French Congo but at the same time claimed full ownership of Morocco. Thwarted in its expansionist desires in the West, Germany began to eye the Ottoman territories with increasing interest, especially since its ally Austria-Hungary had easy land access to many of them. Germany acquired rights to build a railroad to Baghdad, with possible extension to India, Britain's colonial crown jewel. The whole situation was further made volatile when the Ottoman Empire was weakened by the 1908 Young Turk revolution which overthrew the sultan. As noted earlier, Triple Alliance member Italy, with secret support from Triple Entente member France, invaded Tripoli in 1911, defeating lawless North African desert tribes and taking the territory from the Turks. In 1912 and 1913, the states of the Balkan Peninsula—Greece, Bulgaria, Serbia, Montenegro, Albania, Macedonia, and Romania—successfully battered the Turks in a series of revolts and wars.

The First Shot. In the meantime, Austro-Serb tensions in the Balkans had remained strong, especially with Austria-Hungary's full annexation of Bosnia in 1908. On June 28, 1914, the crown prince of Austria-Hungary, **Archduke Francis Ferdinand**, and his wife drove through Sarajevo, Bosnia. They were assassinated by **Gavrilo Princip**, a member of an underground Serbian nationalist group known as the **Black Hand**. Princip was arrested by Austrian authorities soon after the killing. Austria decided to use this incident to solidify its control over the south Slavs by teaching Serbia a lesson. Austria sent Serbia a harsh ultimatum, requiring a response within 48 hours. Serbia agreed to some of the demands and proposed to submit the rest to the International Tribunal at The Hague. Austria rejected this response, and, on July 28, declared war on Serbia.

The massive alliance system quickly pulled the great powers into the conflict. First Russia came to the defense of its old friend Serbia. Rashly, the Russian forces gathered on the German border, assuming that Berlin would aid its ally, Austria-Hungary. The Germans felt they had to respond with a declaration of war on Russia. France called up its army to come to ally Russia's aid. Germany in turn declared war on France.

The German Plan. Actually, the military-minded Germans under flamboyant Wilhelm II had been working on a war campaign plan for a long time, so certain were they that conflict would come. In 1898 and again in 1900, the German **Reichstag** (parliament) passed two bills to build a massive new navy, acts which irritated the British. The announcement in 1904 of the Anglo-French Entente heightened Germany's suspicion of her western neighbors. Because France's army was well prepared, the German war plan was to deal with the French first, in a two-pronged attack. A small German force would move out from

The Reichstag in Berlin, and Kaiser Wilhelm II, 1859–1941

The Lamps Are Going Out

The German army's ultimatum to Belgium triggered a crisis of indecision in Britain. Should the government honor its word to Belgium or preserve England from the horrors of war? Finally, the British cabinet resolved to fight Germany over the control of Europe, although it would be as dangerous to England as Napoleon's France had been.

To Foreign Minister Edward Grey fell the task of bringing Parliament and the country unitedly into the war. When he came to announce the government position in the House of Commons, extra chairs were placed in the aisles and the room was packed. All England, even Europe, waited for his word.

Borrowing a sentence from Gladstone's 1870 speech supporting Belgian neutrality in the Franco-Prussian War, Grey asked, "Could this country stand by and witness the direst crime that ever stained the pages of history and thus become participators in the crime?" The foreign minister went on to point that "If France is beaten to her knees… if Belgium… then Holland and then Denmark… if, in a crisis like this, we run away from these obligations of honor and interest… we should, I believe, sacrifice our respect and good name and reputation before the world and should not escape the most serious and grave economic consequences."

The House broke into applause, indicating full support for Grey. Two hours later Germany declared war on France. That evening, Sir Edward Grey stood at his window as the lamps in the street below were being lit. His remark to a friend at that moment has been one of the most repeated descriptive phrases of World War I. It captured the feelings of a world on the brink of war. "The lamps are going out all over Europe; we shall not see them lit again in our lifetime."

Alsace, a hilly, well-defended, and long-disputed area between Germany and France. At the same time, more men would advance through Belgium into France. Germany also planned to stall Russia's advance, which would come slowly because Russia needed time to prepare for combat. After taking care of France, Germany could move its forces quickly to finish off Russia.

The Germans expected no trouble from the neutral Belgians, even though Britain had agreed to guarantee Belgium's neutrality. When the German army entered Belgium, the British declared war. So did Britain's ally Japan, which seized some German islands in the Pacific and the German treaty port in China.

European soldiers marched off to war, each side expecting a quick victory. "Home by Christmas" was the slogan of the young men as they mobbed the recruiting stations in 1914.

The Western Front. The German attack moved relentlessly ahead according to plan. They reached the Marne River in France, however, in early September the French checked their advance. That was not according to plan. Although the Germans had captured most of Belgium and part of northern France, the war now bogged down into a stalemate along the so-called **Western Front.**

The Western Front consisted of 400 miles of trenches, long zigzag slits in the ground. Dugouts where soldiers ate and slept led off from the trenches. Between the first line of trenches of each side in the war lay a "no man's land," a thousand yards of shell-pocked ground. An attack began with an artillery **barrage** to silence the machine guns and break up the enemy's barbed wire defenses and trenches. Then soldiers would go "over the top" of their trenches and charge the enemy lines. If they escaped being blown up by land mines and enemy artillery shells, they reached the range of machine guns that were methodically sweeping the battlefield. Finally came the enemy trenches, more barbed wire, point-blank rifle fire, grenades, and hand-to-

hand bayonet fighting. If they killed or drove out the defenders, within a short time they too might be killed, captured, or chased out by fresh forces. It was a ghastly, bloody affair.

New technology increased the horror of the conflict. The German chemical industry introduced poison gas and the flamethrower. Huge railroad-mounted guns lobbed shells into Paris from approximately 76 miles away. Airplanes and zeppelins spotted artillery and did some bombing. In 1916, the British used tanks to carry machine-gun fire closer to the enemy trenches. Millions of men were lost by both sides. For example, about 2 million men died in the **Battles of Verdun** and **the Somme.** Several million more were wounded.

Rail lines supplied both sides with a steady flow of arms, food, and men. The armies could remain in the field indefinitely. No longer did battles have to take place in the dry season or end when the soldiers were exhausted. Weather and ground conditions had less effect than in earlier wars. Once the trench system was established on the Western Front, the battle lines moved very little until the end of the war.

The Eastern Front. On the Eastern Front, there were also huge numbers of casualties, but the location of the fighting moved around from place to place. The Russians did not have enough equipment to dig in and hold their territory. The Russians, however, mobilized more quickly than the Germans had anticipated—a miscalculation akin to their error in understanding the potential extent of Belgian, French, and British resistance in the west. In fact, it was the Russian advance in the east that probably brought about the stalemate at the Marne in the west, as Germany was forced to divert troops planned for the Western Front to meet Russia. This diversion of troops finally helped **General Paul von Hindenburg,** who later became commander of the forces of the

Central Powers, to defeat the Russian invasion of eastern Prussia at the Battles of Tannenberg and Masurian Lakes in 1914. After Russia's initial successes in 1914, the rest of the war was mostly a series of defeats and retreats. The Russians were eventually forced to sign a separate peace treaty in 1918, after the Germans and Austrians had advanced deep into Russia.

The Balkan Front. Though less significant than the Western and Eastern fronts, the war also had a southeastern front in the Balkans. Fighting took place in different parts of the Ottoman Empire, which joined the Central Powers in 1914. Britain tried to capture the entrance to the Black Sea so it could get supplies through to Russia. Even as far from Europe as Iran, fighting went on. The Allies planned how they would subdivide the Ottoman territories after the war. An attack on Serbia drew

This huge Austrian gun was made in Bohemia.

This illustration depicts the violence of hand-to-hand combat.

The use of airplanes in warfare began in World War I. Eduard von Schleich (shown above), a.k.a. "the Black Knight," scored 35 kills. The top-ranking United States ace, Eddie Rickenbacker, shot down 26 enemy planes, while Germany's "Red Baron," Manfred von Richthofen, scored 80 kills.

Bulgaria into the war in 1915 on the side of the Central Powers, since Bulgaria was still angry with Serbia over the loss of Macedonia in the Second Balkan War of 1913. Serbia, Montenegro, and most of Albania were overrun, giving Germany its long-sought connection between Berlin and Constantinople. French and British forces did manage to stake out a base at the Greek city of Salonika, at the head of the Aegean Sea, from which it was able to protect Greece, which reluctantly joined the Allies in 1917. Romania joined the Allies in 1916, only to be brutally overrun and occupied by the Austro-German army.

The Southern (Alpine) Front. Italy, which aligned itself with the Triple Entente nations in 1915, waged a campaign against the Austrians along their mutual border. Italy made some initial

advances, but with German aid, Austria broke through the Italian line and took a considerable amount of territory, men, and equipment. Italy revived its spirits late in 1918 and once again aided the Allied cause near the war's end.

On the High Seas. A different kind of war took place at sea. The Allies began a naval blockade against Germany, stopping all shipments of food, raw materials, and arms into the country. Even imports into its neutral neighbors were closely controlled. But the United States protested that the British were restricting "freedom of the seas."

The Germans responded with a blockade of their own, using a new type of ship, the **submarine**, also called the **U-boat**. They declared the waters around Great Britain a war zone. Allied vessels would be sunk and neutrals would be in grave danger. In May 1915, the Germans sank a British passenger liner, *Lusitania*, which was carrying war supplies from the United States. Despite angry protests from **President Woodrow Wilson**, the Germans did not back off from full use of their submarines until after the torpedoing of yet another liner, the *Hesperia*.

Only one important naval battle occurred in the war, the **Battle of Jutland** in 1916. Germany came out slightly ahead, but it could not manage

The German warship ***Deutschland***

a decisive defeat over Britain. For awhile, the German ships could not leave their ports because of mines set by the Allies.

On the Home Front

World War I touched everyone, not just the men in uniform. The flow of weapons to the front depended on an efficient war industry at home. This in turn required a steady supply of raw materials and manpower. Thus the home front was as important as the fighting front for the first time in history.

War Socialism. Government officials were given almost complete power over industrial production. They could give government contracts, settle labor disputes, and obtain military exemptions for skilled workers. Gradually governments directed their entire national economies toward the war effort. Uses of raw materials and trading with foreign countries were centrally planned.

Trade unions at first agreed not to strike for higher wages. But as the struggle dragged on, patriotic enthusiasm weakened. Some began to feel it was a war of the bosses. Food, fuel, and housing shortages touched the lives of every family.

Women's Status. The war had an adverse impact on women and the home. With millions of men away at war, many women worked in factories and offices, operated streetcars, and became wage earners, the first time for most. Particularly in Germany, women worked in almost every type of job that men had held, including hard manual labor. In 1918, Britain granted women the right to vote and hold national office.

Women swarmed into the war factories to replace the men who went off to war.

Propaganda. Each country cranked out propaganda designed to boost morale and smear the enemy. Newspapers tried to rally the public's fighting spirit by praising the bravery of their soldiers, reporting unending strings of victories, and playing up the virtues of their nations. Strict censorship of information was imposed. This problem was particularly serious in Germany which did not tell its people about its military disasters. They were unprepared for the final collapse in 1918.

Propaganda also taught people to hate the other side. In Germany a new battle song appeared—the "Hymn of Hate." It proclaimed the country's "one and only hate" to be England. The motto, *Gott strafe England* (God punish England), quickly gained nationwide popularity. Stories of brutality on both sides grew more gory with retelling. Propaganda turned the war into a crusade and created hatred and misunderstanding.

The Church and the War. Churches on both sides fully supported the war effort. The English church suggested that Britain acted as the agent of God in this struggle. The German clergy proclaimed that the Almighty was on their side. One pastor said, "God has given us all the weapons to defeat the enemy." American ministers described the Kaiser as Satan.

Few Christians were **pacifists** (those who believe that all war is wrong). Nor could many Christians be found in the movement to end the war by negotiation. The striking exceptions were the **Quakers** and **Pope Benedict XV**, who tried unsuccessfully to persuade the warring powers to make peace. Churchmen usually criticized **conscientious objectors** (people who refused on principle to serve in the military). On the other hand, the church praised the men who served God and country. Thus the church did its part to convince people that this was a "holy war," a righteous conflict to put down evil.

United States Involvement in World War I

During the first years of the war, the United States remained neutral. It continued to trade with many countries, particularly supplying Britain and France with food and arms. President Woodrow Wilson tried to provide leadership in obtaining peace. He appealed to the governments and to the peoples who were at war. In January 1917, he called for a "peace without victory" and

Votes for Women

Women conducted a long, bitter struggle for the vote in both Britain and America. The campaign in England, however, was more violent. Led by the formidable Emmeline Pankhurst and her three daughters, the most vocal part of the movement became embittered by the government's refusal to take them seriously. Losing all faith in legal means to achieve their goals, they began to heckle and harass politicians, interrupt government meetings, and stage demonstrations and parades. As police patience wore thin and arrests increased, the women grew more clever in their attacks. They gained access to meetings disguised as messenger boys or waitresses, by locating roof windows, and jumping out of parked furniture vans. From boats in the river they called to legislators on the House terrace. Ultimately, they turned to arson and window-breaking.

Upon being sent to jail, the women went on hunger strikes. Their captors force-fed them with tubes or released them when their lives were in danger. While these women showed a kind of foolish heroism, a willingness to sacrifice even their health and reputations, many in Britain were shocked by their methods. To a number of legislators, the violence proved that women were irresponsible, unworthy of the vote.

When World War I broke out, the militants and nonmilitants alike set aside their struggle. Volunteering their services to their country, they went to work in hospitals, served on relief committees, assisted the Red Cross, opened emergency workrooms for unemployed women, and took care of more than a quarter-million Belgian refugees.

Soon a shortage of men resulted in many women entering the labor force. The idea of substituting women workers for men, releasing males for combat duty, caught on and spread. The government and the media began to praise the women's hard work and willingness to bear difficult conditions. Public opinion then turned in favor of women's suffrage. When the war ended, so did women's long battle for the vote. They cast their first ballots in England in the election of 1918.

creation of a world organization which would use force to keep peace.

Germany resumed unlimited submarine warfare on February 1, in an attempt to cut off Britain's food supply. Wilson promptly broke off diplomatic relations with Germany. Soon several American merchant ships were sunk, mostly without warning.

Then word came of the overthrow of the Russian czar. A republic formed there, and the United States was the first to recognize it.

The Allied cause was being proclaimed as a struggle between democracy and absolutism. For example, speaking to Congress on April 2, Wilson called the German U-boat blockade "a warfare against mankind." The United States would fight for democracy and the liberation of all peoples. Within four days, the two countries were officially at war.

The 'Lusitania'

Because the **Lusitania** was a passenger liner and carried 197 Americans, no one expected it to be attacked. However, its hold contained ammunition and shrapnel shells, and the Germans knew it. Ten miles off the coast of Ireland they torpedoed the ship. In 15 to 20 minutes, the **Lusitania** sank beneath the waves, carrying 1,260 of the 1,957 people aboard with it. Although this incident did not in itself bring America into the war, it was one of the contributing factors. In the excerpt below, one of the survivors describes what happened when the torpedo hit.

All of a sudden we heard a noise like the boom of a cannon. I rushed through the smoking room to the deck and turned and saw the torpedo making direct for us. The time from the noise of the report until it struck us was less than a minute....

I rushed...to that end of the deck nearest the smoking room on the Irish Coast side. I stood on one of the collapsible boats, which lay on the deck covered with canvas. There were quite 30 or 40 people in the boat already, and I asked why this boat was not launched and put down into the sea. I turned and looked at the front part of the ship, and she was so far settled down in the water that there was no chance that the **Lusitania** would not sink.

One man, who had an axe in his hand, answered that orders had been issued by the Captain not to launch any boat. My reply was..."Don't you see the boat is sinking? And the first man that disobeys my orders to launch the boat I shoot to kill!"

By this time the ship was sinking fast. I was thrown high into the water, free and clear of all wreckage, and I then went down twice with the suction of the steamer. The second time I came up I was 400 to 500 feet away from the ship. I clung to an oar, and just then I saw the **Lusitania** take her final plunge. It sounded like a terrible moan.

Immediately after she sank there were hundreds of people struggling in the water, praying and crying for help. There was wreckage all around—old chairs, wood, all kinds of small items. The water was not so cold and it was a lovely day, the sun shining and not a ripple on the water.

Excerpted from **The New York Times,** June 2, 1915.

I WANT YOU FOR U.S. ARMY

NEAREST RECRUITING STATION

The United States Prepares for War. At first the United States could only supply the Allies with large amounts of money and war materials. It had to create, equip, train, and transport a large army across an ocean. The Germans were sure this could not be done in time to save the crumbling Allies. They gambled that unlimited submarine attacks would soon force Britain and France to ask for peace.

Via the draft, the American army expanded from 130,000 to 3.5 million men within 18 months. The government loaned 7 billion dollars to the allies to purchase goods in America. Farms and factories broke all production records, and people took care not to waste anything so that enormous quantities of goods could go to the war effort.

Germany's submarine campaign almost succeeded. Britain was down to a six-week food supply. But the Allies developed antisubmarine weapons and defenses. They sent freighters to Britain in convoys of a hundred or more. Warships kept submarines away. With the aid of the large American navy, these tactics soon reduced the number of submarine attacks.

Throughout 1917, **offensives** on the Western Front made no significant territorial changes. Hundreds of thousands of men were killed in the slow-paced war. The European Allies realized their need of American troops and weapons. American troops played a crucial role along the Western Front, in such campaigns, for example, as the **Battle of the Argonne Forest** from September to November in 1918.

Motives for U. S. Involvement. At the time the war began, the United States was still somewhat of a novice on the world stage, especially as to its knowledge of and involvement in the affairs of Europe. When the scale and ferocity of the war began to be known in the United States, most Americans were bewildered about how such a terrible conflict could arise. When Wilson proclaimed U.S. neutrality, most U.S. citizens agreed. They could see little reason to believe the conflict between Europe's two alliances had anything to do with America's interests.

Soon, however, American intellectuals began to study the causes of the conflict and concluded that it had resulted from centuries of bitter struggles over competing interests in markets, raw materials, colonies, and military establishments. They decided that the world should be a better place. In their idealism for a better world, they began to discuss ideas and plans for reordering the world in such a way that national hostilities would one day cease. This idealism was matched by many of Europe's liberal elite, who joined their American counterparts in dreaming of and planning for a new world order.

This united liberal **intelligentsia** found a champion in Woodrow Wilson. While Communists in Russia were planning ways to take over the world through violent revolution, President Wilson planned a different kind of utopian, globalist future for the world, with a plan known as the **Fourteen Points**. He wanted freedom of the seas, reduction of armaments, border changes reflecting the self-determination of peoples, and an end to secret diplomacy. Perhaps the most important point was his idea for "a general association of nations" to guarantee political independence of countries and to help keep the peace, a vision

These American troops are advancing against the Germans through a cloud of mustard gas somewhere in France. Most of them are wearing protective masks, but the soldier on the left is suffering the consequence of not using his mask.

which liberals and socialists later pursued with vigor in hopes of establishing a one-world government.

The Western liberal establishment saw the current conflict in Europe as an obstacle to immediate implementation of their plans for global harmony and unification. They began to promote the idea of U.S. entry into the war as a means to bring it to a quicker conclusion, clearing the way for their idealistic agenda. The war, in their eyes, was clearly seen as a "war to end all wars." War had always been predatory; now it was to be a means to peace. As one historian has described the liberals' view of the war: "Its main purpose was to go to the bottom of things by bringing the greedy imperialism of the great powers and the ruinous nationalist rivalries of the great and small states alike under the control of a world conscience and a world law." That "world conscience," of course, was tantamount to the ideals of the liberal, intellectual elite themselves; and "world law" would be written by an international organization, such as the **League of Nations** which Wilson founded after the war.

Though the League collapsed as an organization, the dream behind it never died; and after World War II it was resurrected in the form of the United Nations. **Globalism** became the driving philosophy of liberals for the rest of the century. By the mid-1990s, however, the hollowness of such a structure was becoming more and more apparent, as the United Nations repeatedly faltered and proved ineffectual, even destructive, in the face of a massive new outbreak of nationalism and ethnocentricity worldwide. Ironically, in the 1990s, Bosnia, where the Great War to end all wars began, became a major testing ground for the United Nations and other international alliances; but the world powers failed the test as thousands were killed and brutalized in ethnic conflicts between Serbs and others there.

The Bolshevik Revolution in Russia

In the middle of World War I, events transpired in Russia that would also shape the history of the world for the rest of the century: the Russian Communist Revolution of 1917.

Even before the Revolution, Russia had had many political difficulties. In 1915, the **Duma** (parliament) was suspended, angering the middle class. In addition, discouragement grew as one military defeat followed another.

At this time, a mysterious and legendary Serbian peasant monk named **Rasputin** held great power over **Czarina Alexandra**. Her son, the young crown prince, had hemophilia—a severe bleeding problem. Rasputin claimed magical powers to stop the bleeding. When the young prince's father, **Czar Nicholas II** (1868–1918, reigned 1894–1917), took command of the army, control of the government fell into the hands of Alexandra and Rasputin. Rasputin thus had a major say in government appointments. Several attempts were made on the Russian Orthodox monk's life, but he seemed to mystically avoid death. Finally, he was murdered by nobles.

On March 8, 1917, workers in Petrograd, as St. Petersburg was then called, rioted over food shortages. Soldiers, peasants, and intellectuals joined in what soon became a full-scale revolt. Railway workers struck to keep other soldiers from coming into the city to put down the uprising. Leaders of the strikers and soldiers formed the **Petrograd Soviet** (council), arrested the government ministers, and took over the city.

Meanwhile, the Duma set up a rival government for the nation. It persuaded the czar, a pious leader who had been trying to implement reforms, to step down; and on March 15 the Duma made Russia a republic. The new regime, headed first by **Prince Lvov** and then by moderate socialist **Alexander Kerensky** as provisional premier beginning on July 17, introduced freedom of speech, press, and religion. This approach was supported by the **Mensheviks** (meaning *minority*), a party of moderate socialists who believed Russia must pass through a period of *bourgeois* democracy, like the rest of Europe, before entering a final phase of pure socialism or communism. They backed the Kerensky government, which set a November date to elect an assembly to draft a constitution. The government also promised social reforms and land to the peasants. By agreeing to continue the war against Germany, it won speedy recognition from the Western democracies.

The Petrograd Soviet called for an immediate end to the war and urged the soldiers to elect soviets to run the army. Discipline broke down as peasants swarmed over the countryside seizing land.

This poster encourages the Russian people to support the new Russian republic and the continuation of the war effort. The Bolsheviks, however, exploited the people's war weariness to take control of the government.

Strikes and demonstrations continued in the cities. Then the Russian army suffered yet another crushing defeat in the world war. At this point, **Vladimir Ilyich Lenin** and other exiled radical socialists returned to Russia from Switzerland. (Lenin was born Vladimir Ilyich Ulyanov but took the alias Nikolai Lenin to avoid the police. His alias surname became the name by which history has remembered him.) Upon arrival, Lenin demanded immediate peace, land for peasants, and "all power to the soviets." He focused the anger of the masses upon the Duma's provisional government, which by now was backing off from land reform.

Lenin's group, known as **Communists** or **Bolsheviks** (meaning *majority*), won over the Petrograd Soviet and others throughout the country. On November 6, soldiers and armed workers called

"**Red Guards**" took over the railway stations, power plants, and other strategic points in the capital. The next day, they stormed the Winter Palace and the provisional government.

Once in power, the Bolsheviks launched a drastic policy of "war communism." Hoping to gain support from workers and peasants, they placed large country estates and the urban economy under government control. They also set up a one-party dictatorship. To take care of all opposition, secret police called the **Cheka** under **Felix Dzerzhinsky** and a **Red Army** under Lenin's chief associate **Leon Trotsky** started a campaign of terror. Trotsky was a Jew, born as Lev Davidovich Bronstein, but, like Lenin, took an alias to avoid the police. The new government tried to force the country people to deliver food. Fighting broke out between the farmers and city dwellers.

However, the national assembly to draft a constitution was still scheduled to meet. All the Russian people had elected its members—the only free election ever held in Russian history up to that time and the last until the 1990s. The Bolsheviks won a large number of seats in the assembly but not a majority. The assembly met in January 1918, but Lenin sent troops to dissolve it after one session. Majority rule was replaced by class rule. The Bolsheviks would rule on behalf of the *proletariat,* in keeping with Marx's concept of the *"dictatorship of the proletariat."*

Lenin knew that his regime could not stay in power unless Russia withdrew from the war immediately. Trotsky negotiated a peace treaty, the **Peace of Brest-Litovsk**, the terms of which were largely dictated by the German high command. The treaty was signed on March 3, 1918, requiring Russia to recognize the independence of many sections of western Russia—including Finland, Estonia, Livonia, Courland, Lithuania, Poland, and part of the Ukraine, all territories

Vladimir Ilyich Lenin, 1870–1924

which had been conquered by Russia during the years since Peter the Great. The Germans began to set up puppet regimes in these countries and expected large deliveries of foodstuffs from them.

These events greatly upset the Allies. They did not want to see Russia's one chance for democracy destroyed, and they needed that country's help to win the war. Thus, in 1918, British, French, and American troops entered Russia. Their mission was to aid the various "White" or anti-Bolshevik groups to overthrow Lenin and bring the Russians back into the war. However, the Red Army proved too strong, so the West's intervention ended in failure. When the Germans lost the war six months after Russia had surrendered to them, the Allies forced them and the Russians to abrogate the Brest-Litovsk Treaty, little of which was ever effectuated. The Western powers continued for a time to aid various

counter-revolutionary movements, which launched a civil war in Russia in 1918. The West provided supplies and seized a number of Russian ports. But the Allies were too exhausted from the Great War to put much effort into fighting the Bolsheviks. Besides, with the war over, liberals in the West, especially certain intellectuals and writers, began to voice opposition to anti-Communist sentiment and to support the Communist adventure with propaganda and other forms of aid and comfort.

With Russia out of the war, Lenin and the Bolsheviks were free to continue their revolutionary practices. The intellectuals in the Marxist party could teach the trade unions and the masses about the needed actions. Together they could work out the necessary changes in factories and agriculture. At first force might be needed to rearrange the social order. Indeed, force was used, and great hardships resulted. Eventually, they believed, the Revolution would spread to other countries of the West.

We will look further at developments in Russia later in this chapter.

Conclusion of World War I

The Fighting Ends. Meanwhile, in March 1918, the Germans launched another offensive on the Western Front. They advanced quickly at first, coming within 50 miles of Paris. However, in July, the Allies again stopped the Germans at the Marne River. The Allied commander, French **Field Marshal Ferdinand Foch**, began a counterattack headed by nine recently arrived American divisions. The defenses of the Germans and their allies gradually crumbled. The British routed the Turks in Syria and Mesopotamia, and the Allies

crushed Bulgaria. Austrian soldiers in the east refused to fight any longer and went home. Italy resumed its offensive, causing the collapse of the Hapsburgs rulers, who were deposed. The war ended on the Italian Front on November 3, 1918, when Austria signed an armistice with the Allies. As ferocious battles continued in western Europe, **morale** within the German ranks sank and soldiers deserted. People in Germany suffered from hunger. German officials began to see that peace must be made at once. In the autumn of 1918, **General Erich Ludendorff**, Hindenburg's chief of staff, insisted that a new German government be formed—a liberal constitutional monarchy. He hoped it might obtain better terms, since Wilson had said peace must be signed with representatives of all the people, not just the military aristocracy.

A new cabinet took office under the liberal **Prince Max** of Baden. On October 3, he tried to negotiate with Wilson on the basis of the Fourteen Points. The president demanded that the Kaiser step down as the first condition for a cease-fire. On November 9, the people of Germany revolted, overthrew the imperial government and set up a republic lead by Social Democrats. Kaiser Wilhelm II met Wilson's demand and went into exile in Holland the next day.

The cease-fire went into effect two days later on November 11, 1918, a date which became known as **Armistice Day** (later Veterans Day in the United States). Although the Germans believed it was based on the Fourteen Points, the terms amounted to an unconditional surrender. Germany had to withdraw its troops from occupied territories. It also had to turn over railroad cars, trucks, and the German fleet to the Allies.

Peacemakers Meet. The **Paris Peace Conference** opened in January 1919 with the 25 Allied

This poster expresses the famous French World War I motto, "They shall not pass!" It warns the French not to let down their guard against the Germans.

A World Without War?

As the world disentangled itself from total war, the American president, Woodrow Wilson, suggested specific ways to prevent future conflict. The Fourteen Points partially expressed his blueprint for a new world order, which he believed would be a world at peace.

Wilson saw imperialism as a major cause of war. A number of the Fourteen Points required border changes among countries to undo past imperialism and allow self-determination. "Every people has the right to determine its own form of government," he said. "The countries of the world belong to the people who live in them.... The select classes of mankind are no longer the governors of mankind. The fortunes of mankind are now in the hands of the plain people of the whole world.... I believe in the ordinary man."

Another of the Points called for disarmament. If the world would have peace, then all the nations, not just Germany, should reduce their armaments. The new world order would have no place for balance-of-power politics.

The task of creating a lasting peace at Versailles could only be accomplished, Wilson believed, if the Allies would accept "peace without victory." Severe punishment of Germany would only create hatred that would breed future wars.

But Wilson's greatest hope for peace lay in the League of Nations. It would "operate as the organized moral force of men throughout the world.... Wherever wrong and aggression are planned...this searching light of conscience will be turned upon them." From this statement, it can be seen how the humanist liberal elite sought an institution to replace Christ and His Church as the "moral force" of the world. Through the League, nations could discuss common problems and decide on common action without going to war. In this new world ruled by universal human laws, nations would be guided by the same moral and ethical principles the humanists believed individuals should obey.

To Wilson, moral and spiritual forces had the greatest power in the international realm. "Force will not accomplish anything that is permanent...," he said. "There is a great wind of moral force moving through the world, and every man who opposes himself to that wind will go down in disgrace....Humanity can be welded together only by love, by sympathy, by justice, not by jealousy and hatred...."

When Woodrow Wilson went to the peace table at Versailles, some people hailed him as the savior of civilization. He believed he had made America the moral leader of the world. However, the other men at that table considered Wilson an impractical dreamer. Their view of the Fourteen Points? "After all, the good Lord had only ten," laughed Clemenceau. They ignored most of Wilson's program for peace, and instead sought revenge on Germany.

After the peace conference, the American leader's inflexibility and political opposition to him kept the United States out of the League of Nations. His own country had rejected the cornerstone of his dream for a better world.

nations sending delegates to deal with the pulverized Central Power states. The treaties drafted in 1919–1920 seemed more the sentence of a court than a negotiated settlement. Politicians had to respond to the mob passions aroused during the conflict. Compromise was impossible, for this had been a war of good versus evil as much as a war of nation against nation. The Germans complained about the dictated peace, but in light of the German settlement with Russia, the Allies had good reason to expect that they would have received the same treatment if they had lost.

Although the conference lasted several months, small committees handled all the business. Most of the decisions were made by the "**Big Four**"—**President Woodrow Wilson** of the United States, **Premier Georges Clemenceau** of France, **Prime Minister David Lloyd-George** of Britain, and **Premier Vittorio Orlando** of Italy. When Orlando walked out midway through the conference, the **Council of Four** became the **Council of Three**. While these four men made decisions based on their personal convictions, they, of course, also represented nations whose citizens remained angered over the war and retained a spirit of revenge. Wilson's idealistic Fourteen Point program, which had been set before the Germans as inducement for a cease-fire, was given some lip service; but the conference actually tilted in favor of a tougher realism. Imperialism and nationalism were not yet dead. While the war was still raging, secret agreements had

Can you find the new European countries created after the war?

order, the holdings of the Central Powers were divided as old-style spoils of war. Germany had to give up parts of its territory to other countries. France regained the territory lost to Germany after the Franco-Prussian War, and controlled Germany's rich Saar Basin under the League of Nations mandate until 1935. German colonies were also turned over to the League of Nations and held in trust by the Allied countries. Turkey was divided among Britain, France, and Italy. In this way, the Ottoman Empire ended with the parceling of Arabia, Syria, Lebanon, Palestine, Trans-Jordan, and Iraq. Turkey itself was left as an independent republic. Again, whereas in the secret treaties Russia was originally to have gotten part of the Turkish empire, its share was denied in the final treaty. Japan was awarded the German leases in China and island possessions in the North Pacific. Italy, which had joined the Allies late, was given token parcels which had belonged to Austria-Hungary. In these arrangements, the European Allies stood against Wilson.

Yet Wilson was a formidable factor in both the war and the peace, and the realists found it undesirable to completely repudiate him. With liberal world opinion behind him, he managed to impose his League of Nations proposals upon the conference. Thus all treaties composed in Paris included provisions for the League, which called for future international rivalries to be settled by League-supervised conciliation rather than war.

As to the nuts and bolts of the Versailles Treaty, Germany was forbidden to keep troops or fortifications in the Rhineland, near France. The Allies banned Germany from producing submarines, airplanes, tanks, heavy artillery, and poison gas. The army could only consist of 100,000 men. Furthermore, Allied inspections would see that these military restrictions were followed. The most galling part of the treaty required Germany

been worked out among the various foreign offices (with the exception of the United States, whose Wilsonian program had opposed this very thing) over how the spoils of war would be divided after the victory. The conference thus split between Wilson's idealism and the realism of Clemenceau, Lloyd-George, and Orlando. At first the secret deals had been carefully guarded, but the Bolsheviks discovered the arrangements and exposed them out of malice over the Allied push against them following their surrender to

Germany. The Bolsheviks saw exposure of the deals as an opportunity to lash out against the lingering imperialism of the capitalist countries which had been hypocritically advocated a liberal approach to world reordering.

The final settlement, signed at Versailles on June 28, 1919, largely reflected the arrangements made in the secret documents signed during the war, with the exception that anything Russia was supposed to receive was withheld and given to others. In a triumph for the realists and older

to admit guilt for the war and pay reparations to the Allies. A commission set the figure owed at $33 billion. In addition, they had to surrender much of their merchant fleet as well as property owned by Germans in Allied countries.

The Long Range Impact of the War

For four years of war, the Western nations ripped one another to shreds, leaving their political and social order in shambles. An entire generation of leaders had been destroyed on the battlefields. Those who survived were skeptical about the future. No war had ever had such an emotional and psychological impact. At least 10 million men were killed in action or by disease. Twice that number were wounded. The cost in broken lives, shattered societies, leftover bitterness and hatred cannot be reckoned. However, the direct money cost of the war was estimated at $180 billion; indirect costs (such as property damage) at another $150 billion.

Almost everywhere, the postwar period was an era of disillusionment and discouragement. The economies of the warring countries were unable to absorb into their labor forces all of the demobilized soldiers, leaving widespread unemployment. Nationalism was intensified by the wartime hatreds. Political disturbances were everywhere.

Primarily, however, the disillusionment was a result of a vast gap between the idealism which liberals had promised the world through their utopian new-order schemes and the reality that the world was still pretty much as it had been before the war—marked by rivalry, imperialism,

and other aspects of the troublesome existing order of the day.

The Economy. Domestic economies were transformed. When the war was over, governments did not end their central economic planning, and thus private enterprise was never again fully recovered. Every country sought economic self-sufficiency, and tariff walls sprang up everywhere to protect domestic industries. Both workers and business wanted government involvement in the economy and the high prices and wages that came with it.

Inflation also came with it. The heavy demand for manufactured war goods and serious shortages of consumer goods during the war years drove up prices. Governments went into debt to cover the costs of the war. In 1914, the United States owed $4 billion to European investors. By 1919, Europeans owed $4 billion to the United States. Inflation (an artificial increase in money supplies) made it easier to repay these debts. The middle classes, who lived on salaries and fixed incomes, were hurt the most because as the supply of money increased, the value of each unit of currency decreased. They faced economic ruin. Though one of the most stable groups in pre-1914 Europe, after the war the middle class became **demoralized**. Some joined radical causes hoping to recover what they had lost.

During the postwar period, the socialists grew in strength. As radical-left factions took up the Communist banner, the European moderates, or Social Democrats, carried on the class struggle through peaceful, legislative, and educational means. They formed coalitions in the government and took part in trade union movements.

Through these methods, they influenced social legislation in most European countries. Some of the new laws provided for the eight-hour work-

Woodrow Wilson designed the prototype of a one-world government, known as the League of Nations. His positions on the peace treaty, ending World War I, were opposed by other Western leaders. But he succeeded in getting the ill-fated League of Nations included in the Treaty of Versailles. The League later became the archetype for the United Nations.

ing day, banned child labor, set minimum wage levels, and required collective bargaining between labor and management. Government-sponsored insurance programs against sickness, accidents, old age, and unemployment were either adopted or extended. States undertook public housing programs. The **welfare state** began to take shape.

The League of Nations. In the midst of postwar disillusionment, there was one idealistic innovation—which also eventually failed and thus added to the spirit of discouragement. In April 1919, the constitution of the League of Nations was completed and presented to the potential members. It was obviously not well received by conservative, nationalistic interests in the world. Liberals, who had hoped that a world organization could bring lasting peace, felt the League was not powerful enough. It was not a world government or a superstate, although some may have

The Peace Palace (Vredespaleis, 1913) in The Hague, the Netherlands, houses the International World Court. This court was founded in 1920.

seen it as a foundation for these. The League, headquartered at Geneva, did not technically violate the sovereignty of any nation; it had no armed force of its own, and members could withdraw at any time. And although the covenant provision calling for mutual aid to prevent or punish aggression had sparked controversy, it was little more than a traditional mutual defense treaty depending on the good faith of its signers.

The charter, officially known as the **Covenant**, called for an Assembly for delegates of all member states (forty-three at its beginning) and a Supreme Council initially composed of the United States, Great Britain, France, Italy, Japan, and four rotating members elected annually by the Assembly, nine members in all.

One of the most active of the League's departments was the **International Labor Organization**, designed to deal with relations between capital and labor worldwide. It developed labor legislation which it offered to member states for their adoption, if desired. The League also had successes in various humanitarian endeavors, such as repatriation of some 400,000 prisoners of war and interdiction of international trafficking in women and children for immoral purposes and slavery. The League also resolved a number of international territorial disputes involving smaller nations, notably in the Baltic region, the Balkans, and South America. Failures in the League's mediation efforts usually occurred when disputes involved one or more of the major powers. Major failures included its dealing with Japan's appropriation of Manchuria in 1931 and invasion of China in 1933, Italy's conquest of Ethiopia in 1935–1936, and Nazi Germany's occupation of the Rhineland in 1936. The League also largely failed in its aims of disarmament and naval reductions.

The League's permanent Court of International Justice at The Hague in The Netherlands was created to settle disputes brought to it by member nations. All sides involved in a dispute had to consent to the Court's hearing the matter. The League's steering committee, the Supreme Council, could issue a report on an international dispute, but it required a unanimous vote. If the affected country refused to abide by a decision, the others could impose **sanctions**. Sanctions ranged from a formal rebuke to a declaration of war. The League was powerless to carry out the sanctions, so the enforcement of a decision depended upon the members.

Another factor worked against the League's success. Three of the most important countries did not join. Germany and Russia, now outcast nations, were not invited; and the U.S. Senate voted to keep the United States out. The League was responsible for supervising the former German and Ottoman territories, but in reality it allowed the countries occupying them to treat them as ordinary colonies.

More Alliances and More Treaties. The French were terrified about what might happen when Germany recovered. They had vainly tried in 1919 to have the Rhineland taken from Germany and set up as an independent buffer state between the two countries. Realizing that the League was powerless to prevent German aggression, France took action of its own. It formed military alliances with Belgium (1920), Poland (1921), and Czechoslovakia (1924), and pressed Germany hard for reparation payments.

Germany responded by establishing diplomatic relations with Russia. Russia agreed to cancel claims against Germany for reparations and Germany agreed to cancel demands for payment for property taken by the Bolsheviks. Large Russian orders for German goods followed, plus German technical help for the Red Army, and a secret program to train German fliers and produce illegal armaments on Russian soil.

In 1925, the leading European powers (except Russia) agreed to a series of treaties in the Swiss resort of Locarno. Germany joined the League of Nations after agreeing to recognize present French and Belgian borders and to undertake any boundary changes with Poland and Czechoslovakia only through peaceful means. Great Britain and Italy guaranteed Rhineland borders. Much was heard about the "spirit of Locarno." The major powers even talked about disarmament but did nothing about it except limit construction of battleships.

In the afterglow of this optimism there came the **Kellogg-Briand Pact**, also known as the **Pact of Paris**, in 1928, promoted primarily by France and the United States. The 62 nations who signed it solemnly renounced the use of aggressive war. But because it made no provision for sanctions, it was meaningless.

Postwar Recovery

The United States. In the 1920s, the United States was prosperous and conservative. It enjoyed a highly favorable balance of trade because of high protective tariffs and markets gained during the war. With its own mass market and rapid technological advance, America seemed to have found the key to endless prosperity. Big business dominated political life during the decade. Large industries persuaded elected officials to pass laws favorable to their interests.

People largely ignored the social critics who pointed out disgraceful conditions in urban and rural slums and argued that factory workers and farmers did not share the new middle-class prosperity. These conditions proved to be a fertile ground for socialists to plant their seeds. Socialist agitators infiltrated poor farming and mining communities and labor groups. Yet by European standards, most Americans were doing quite well. And to avoid overcrowding the place with people who did not "fit in," Congress passed laws nearly cutting off the flow of immigrants. The United States was again moving toward isolationism.

Great Britain. Great Britain suffered from economic distress. It had lost many overseas markets because of the war and the Russian Revolution. Its merchant marine was largely destroyed, and its industrial facilities had become outdated and inefficient. Because of high unemployment, millions lived on the **dole** (state relief) with little hope of finding work. That situation was unhealthy psychologically as well as economically.

More and more workers turned to the socialist-leaning Labour Party in hopes of finding a way out. This sharply divided British politics. Property owners tended to vote Conservative; the workers supported Labour; and the middle class was caught in between. In 1926, firm government action put down a coal strike and slapped tight controls on union activity. These actions stirred up bitter class hatred.

Britain also found the ties with its empire loosening. After putting down rebellions in Ireland in 1916 and 1919–1920, the British reluctantly let the southern part govern itself. (In 1937, the Catholic Republic of Eire gained complete independence, while the largely Protestant north chose to stay in the United Kingdom.)

Although the four self-governing dominions had loyally supported Britain in the war, nationalism stirred them too. Finally, a conference in 1926 declared Canada, Australia, New Zealand, and South Africa equal with each other and with Great Britain. They would be united only by a common loyalty to the crown. This created the **British Commonwealth of Nations**.

France. The French economy, balanced between manufacturing and agriculture, withstood postwar economic shocks better. The peace settlement strengthened the economy by giving France the Saar coal mines and Alsace-Lorraine with its potash, iron ore, and textile industry.

France had lost 1.5 million men, and many who survived were permanently disabled. The war had done at least $23 billion worth of damage to towns, factories, mines, and railroads. Billions more had been lost in loans to Russia which the new Bolshevik regime refused to repay. Inflation also undercut the value of French money.

Germany. The new German republic was crippled by the Versailles Treaty, raging inflation, and the violence of political extremists. In 1923, a crisis came. Germany defaulted on its payment of reparations to France. At this point, the French government ordered its armed forces into Germany's industrial heartland, the Ruhr Valley. French authorities were to supervise the industries and turn profits over to the French treasury. Germans there, with encouragement from Berlin, met the French with **passive resistance**, that is, they refused to work, sabotaged projects, and engaged in other acts of disobedience. Berlin promised to pay wages to workers who resisted the French. However, this action sent the value of the German currency, the mark, tumbling until it became almost worthless. It took a large sackful of money to buy even small items such as a loaf of bread. The savings of the middle class and old-age pensioners were wiped out.

It was left to the conservative leader, **Gustav Stresemann**, to stabilize the currency, put down extremism, and secure foreign loans in order to save the economy. Working to fulfill the Versailles Treaty, he wanted to get Germany back on its feet and into a position to ask for a change in the settlement. A group of experts, headed by American **Charles G. Dawes** came up with a plan (the **Dawes Plan**) by which France agreed to withdraw from the Ruhr and German reparation payments were reduced. Although bitterly attacked by rightists for selling out, Stresemann followed what seemed the only possible course.

In a short time, prosperity returned to Germany; and the country became fairly stable. To be sure, nothing had been done to change the prewar social and political character of Germany. The same conservative business groups and landed aristocrats controlled the country, with the old bureaucracy essentially untouched.

Unrest and Change in the Middle East

In the postwar years, vague murmurs of discontent came from the colonial empires. Here and there, the unrest rumbled into rebellion, which in some cases brought modernization or the end of foreign rule.

Turkey. The most spectacular of these postwar revolts occurred in Turkey. As noted earlier, during the world war, Russia, Italy, Britain, and France had secretly agreed to divide the Ottoman Empire among themselves, leaving a small part to become an independent Turkey. At the same time, the British made a conflicting promise of independence to some Arab leaders if they would side with the Allies and revolt against the Turks.

The situation was further complicated by a promise made to the **World Zionist Organization**, a group formed in 1897 by European Jews to deal with growing **anti-Semitism**. Zionists wanted to set up a Jewish homeland in Palestine but could not gain Ottoman approval. So Zionist leaders in England and the United States pressed for Allied help in this goal. In order to win Jewish backing for the war effort, British **Foreign Secretary Lord Alfred James Balfour** had declared Britain in favor of a Jewish state in Palestine. The famous promise became known as the **Balfour Declaration** and later had major implications for Middle Eastern affairs.

At the war's end, only Britain and France decided the Turkish fate. Bolshevik Russia failed to receive its share of the Ottoman spoils, but the Greeks were allowed to seize land in Western Turkey, setting up a long future of tension between Turkey and Greece. The Allies controlled the Turkish government in Constantinople. **Mustafa Kemal**

Atatürk, a powerful Turkish army officer, started a national resistance movement. With some help from Russia, he drove out the Greeks, refused to accept Western control, and in 1923 forced the Allies to change the original peace treaty.

Setting up a dictatorship in Turkey, Atatürk undertook a sweeping political and social revolution. He moved the capital from Constantinople (renamed Istanbul) to Ankara, more in the center of the nation. Following a European model, a constitution and code of law were created for the new republic. Even women could vote. He abolished the position of sultan and with it the office of caliph, the sultan's Islamic religious position. Atatürk also declared the total separation of church and state as he reorganized the state on secular, nonreligious principles. Children had to attend government schools.

These changes affected everyday life. Women were discouraged from wearing the veil and men forbidden to wear the **fez**. People began to use the Western calendar, the metric system, and the Western alphabet for the Turkish language. Polygamy became a crime. Economic development of factories and farms was aided by the government.

Palestine. In Palestine the situation turned into a three-way struggle among Jewish Zionists, Arab nationalists, and British imperialists. The conflict became fierce as Jewish immigrants, now free to settle there, poured into their Promised Land. Jewish population rose from 58,000 in 1919 to 450,000 in 1939. Arabs reacted violently as Jews moved into what had been Arabic land. Why should they lose their country because of Western anti-Semitism? To them, the Jews were Europeans founding a new colony at a time when colonialism was dying in the Middle East. Furthermore, in Islamic doctrine, land once belonging to **Allah** (the Islamic name for God)

A bar mitzvah ceremony at the Western Wall in Jerusalem.

always belongs to Allah; and unending holy wars must be fought to retain or regain it.

Egypt. At the outbreak of World War I, Britain had canceled all remaining Turkish rights to Egypt and made it a British protectorate. Then in 1922, Britain proclaimed Egypt an independent sovereign state but kept control of foreign affairs and some other matters. Dissatisfied nationalists continued the struggle both through legislation and terrorism. Finally in 1936, Britain ended the military occupation and arranged for Egypt to enter the League of Nations. In return, the Egyptians reluctantly agreed to stand with Britain during wartime and allow Britain to station troops along the Suez Canal to protect it.

Persia. Persia set out to throw off Western control. A military **coup d'état** in 1921 brought **Riza Pahlavi** (also known as Riza Khan) in line for leadership. In 1925, he became the **Shah**. Following Atatürk's example, he modernized the army and the economy. He set aside the old Islamic ways as much as possible and encouraged nationalism. In 1935, he renamed the country Iran and sought to identify with Persia's glorious past. But the Shah's attempt to free Iran from foreign influences was not as successful as Atatürk's. When World War II broke out, Russian and British forces made him step down. They took over the country to keep it from siding with Germany, but the Pahlavi dynasty later returned to power until an Islamic Revolution took place in the 1980s.

The Fundamentalist–Modernist Conflict

In 1918, Woodrow Wilson declared: "Why did Jesus Christ not succeed thus far in moving the world to do what He has said?…. I come with a practical plan to perform His purposes." But the war which was hailed as "the war which would end all war" was followed by a period of deep disillusionment, combined with signs of demoralization. The idealism of the 19th century gave way to the pessimism of the 20th century.

Modernism. The theology of New England had moved from Puritanism through Arminianism to Pelagianism and universalism in the 19th century. The Puritans had stressed the importance of the gospel to change individuals and thereby transform culture. This was replaced with the idea that man is basically good and that there is no hell. As more Americans studied in Germany, many absorbed the optimistic idealism of Hegel and combined it with Darwinism. They were especially influenced by the views developed in Germany by Albrecht Ritschl, and in America by Walter Rauschenbusch. Negatively, modernism promoted a critical approach toward the Bible and viewed it as simply the evolution of religious experience, liable to error. Positively, it developed the program of "Christian" socialism known as

Illustration from William Jennings Bryan, *Seven Questions in Dispute* (1924)

the "social gospel." It taught that a moral God was immanent and active in human history through the form of human progress. Men participated in this process by education, humanitarianism, and fighting social evils to establish God's reign in a human brotherhood. Thus liberty, equality and fraternity were disguised as Christian virtues. This movement would become the major force that would replace Evangelical Christianity as the dominant religion in America.

The modernists proclaimed that the 20th century would be the *Christian Century* and published a magazine with the same title, beginning in 1900. But, by the 1920s, gangsters and Mafia organizations infested the country. Hollywood also produced a life style that conflicted with many, if not all, the commandments of God. These factors opened the floodgates to a type of virtual libertinism. In essence, America began to experience the struggle which transpired in Europe when the gospel had been abandoned for humanism.

Dispensational Premillenialism. Prior to WWI there had been a number of revival movements and camp meetings, most notably those under D. L. Moody. The Puritan tradition and ethic had not yet died out. But toward the end of the 19th century and in the early years of the 20th century and the church began to decline and its social impact began to lessen. The perfectionism of the Wesleyan Methodists had stressed moral reformation in society. Now evangelicalism began to focus more to the future than the present.

The neglect of the deep corruption of sin by the Modernists produced a reaction among many Evangelicals. Over against the idea that history was evolving toward a utopia, dispensationalists began emphasized the coming of a thousand-year kingdom, and began to speculate about the fulfillment of these events. Like the Adventist movement, a great deal of attention was devoted to the great tribulation at the end of time: the rapture of the believers, which is invisible to the eye; the coming of the Antichrist; and the future of Israel.

But associated with this were many ideas promoted by John Darby, the father of the Plymouth Brethren, who had visited America no fewer than seven times. His ideas penetrated many circles and prepared the way for C. I. Scofield's reference Bible, which was published in 1909. The Scofield Bible was read eagerly and soon elevated to the status of the standard Bible for many Christians. Scofield distinguished no fewer than seven dispensations. The sixth dispensation was the church age; it is provisional and transitory in character. This affected many in their understanding of the present task of the church.

Their reaction to the social gospel led them to an unbalanced view that tended to overlook the far-ranging significance of the Word of God, which, calls us to service even in such areas as politics, and social and scientific activities. The dispensationalists had their misgivings about science and culture, for they felt they had been deceived too often by scientists. They called for separation—not reformation.

The Pentecostal Movement. There was another force that began to change Protestantism. Since modernism stressed science and reason, the time was ripe for a reaction in the form of an emotional-ecstatic form of experiential religion. Pentecostalism had its roots in the Holiness and perfectionist movement within Methodism. In 1901, Charles F. Parham, an independent Holiness preacher, promoted the baptism of the Holy Spirit and tongues speaking at Bethel Bible College in Topeka, Kansas. Then in 1906, William J. Seymour, a black student of Parham's, carried it to Los Angeles. Subsequently, T. B. Barratt, a Norwegian Methodist preacher, was influential in the spread of Pentecostalism throughout Europe. According to his own testimony, Barratt received the baptism of the Holy Spirit in Los Angeles in 1906. He brought Parham's teachings to Scandinavia, Germany, Britain, and the Netherlands.

The Pentecostal movement promoted a kind of dualism. They recognized a twofold gospel, two kinds of operation of the Spirit, two kinds of believers. While not denying that the gospel was preached in many churches, they brought the full gospel, which included the Apostolic gifts of the Spirit today. They did not deny there are believers outside their own circle, but that victorious believers received the gift of tongues. Some of them even claimed to have conquered sin completely. Pentecostals said that there is no need for a believer to be sick. Yet unlike Christian Science which denies the existence of sickness, however, they promoted the practice of faith healing. The movement also encouraged the leadership of women. Aimee Semple McPherson (1890–1944) was an early woman preacher, involved in various scandals, who promoted healings and tongue speaking at her International Church of the Foursquare Gospel in Los Angeles.

Fundamentalism. Many Christians had shifted from the Puritan stress upon God's sovereignty to a stress on human freedom and experience. Yet the Bible was still stressed by many as the foundation of Christianity. By 1910, Evangelicalism in the United States was lead by such men as **J. Wilbur Chapman**, **William Jennings Bryan** and the converted baseball player **Billy Sunday**, all members of the Presbyterian church. They were not at all a group of narrow-minded, obscure persons, as they have often been depicted as being. But it was a mixed group that reacted against the advancing modernism. Many church members were alarmed when the central facts of salvation of the Christian faith were denied in leading churches. They sought to defense and began talking and organizing. In 1910 conservatives in the Presbyterian Church held sway when five essential points of doctrine were first set forth; the inerrancy of the Bible, the virgin birth of Christ, the substitutionary character of the atonement, the bodily resurrection of Christ and the supernatural miracles of Christ.

Soon a series of booklets were published under the title "The Fundamentals," appearing between 1910 and 1915. The project was organized by the evangelist **R.A. Torrey** and Rev. A.C. Dixon of the Moody Church in Chicago. Among the authors were such scholars as James Orr, B.B. Warfield and H.C.G. Moule. In these booklets the main points of the Christian faith were expounded and defended. The essays were directed against negative criticism of the Bible, against evolution, and against the errors of the Mormons, the Spiritualists, the Christian Scientists, the Roman Catholics and the socialists. They also spoke in a positive way on such topics as sin and grace, the person and work of Christ, revelation, and the spread of the gospel. There were no fewer than three million copies of them in circulation, offering support and comfort to thousands.

The Presbyterian Conflict. In 1922, at The First Presbyterian Church of New York, Harry Emerson Fosdick, a famous orator of the time, and a Baptist in the regular employ of the church, voiced an angry reaction to fundamentalism in a provocative sermon on: "Shall the Fundamentalists Win?" Fosdick proclaimed that there was no

William ("Billy") Sunday (1862–1935), a professional baseball player, was converted at the Pacific Garden Mission in Chicago. He assisted J. Wilbur Chapman, and in 1896 developed evangelistic campaigns held in many American cities in huge wooden tabernacles. While he used florid rhetoric, he down-played emotionalism and preached a down-to-earth gospel.

reason to get so excited about doctrine. The main point after all, he said, was Christian experience. Thus the General Assembly of the Presbyterian Church was forced to respond to modernism. The Presbytery of New York was instructed to require the New York church to teach and preach in accordance to the Bible and the Westminster Confession of Faith. But the Presbytery largely ignored the Assembly's mandate and proceeded to license candidate Henry P. Van Dusen, who refused to affirm belief in the virgin birth of Christ.

The appalling growth of these new ideas, which defied Scripture and the confession, became apparent in 1924 when the so-called Auburn Affirmation was published. This document was initially signed by 150 Presbyterian ministers, and ultimately by 1300 of them. Although the signers of the Affirmation signified their willingness to remain loyal to their ordination vows, they demanded complete freedom of belief about fundamental doctrines.

The most visible and articulate leader of the Fundamentals, was the Presbyterian theologian **J. Gresham Machen** (1881–1937). Like his contemporaries Abraham Kuyper and Herman Bavinck in the Netherlands, Machen had personally wrestled with the problems of modern theology. After studying at Princeton Seminary he studied in Germany under Wilhelm Herrmann. As he struggled with the ideas of modernism he was supported by the prayers of his mother and his daily study of Scripture. Arriving at a solid conviction of the truthfulness and historicity of the Bible, Machen became a became a powerful apologist. He was committed to the teachings of Westminster Confession. He became professor of New Testament at Princeton Theological Seminary in 1915. In 1923, his book *Christianity and Liberalism* demonstrated that, "liberalism on the

J. Gresham Machen, 1881–1937

one hand and the religion of the historic church on the other are not two varieties of the same religion, but two distinct religions proceeding from altogether separate roots." His book was read and praised by thousands.

In the 1920s a number of Southern states, which were still dominated by a more conservative Christian position, made laws against the teaching of evolution in the public schools. In 1925 at Dayton, Tennessee, John Scopes was tried for the teaching of evolution. To his defense came the lawyer Clarence Darrow, affiliated with the American Civil Liberties Union (ACLU), which had been founded in 1920. William Jennings Bryan took the initiative to debate Darrow in defence of the Bible. But in cross-examination, his weak defense gave occasion for the liberal Eastern press to caricature fundamentalists as ignorant rural people. Bryan died five days after

the trial, and fundamentalism seemed to be on the retreat.

In the same year the Board of Directors of Princeton Seminary appointed Machen professor of apologetics. But the appointment had to be confirmed by the General Assembly of the church. Machen was criticized with regard to his personal life when he did not support the views of prohibition. His opponents used this to derail his appointment. Furthermore, the General Assembly dismissed the Directors of the Seminary and placed the Seminary under a new board, with the intention of "broadening" its theological perspective to include modernism.

Convinced that the position of Old Princeton should be maintained and that theological students should not be misled with false doctrines, he joined in the founding of a new theological school—**Westminster Theological Seminary** in Philadelphia in the fall of 1929. It was the eve of the Great Depression. Among its outstanding professors were John Murray and N.B. Stonehouse, who taught New Testament; E. J. Young, who taught Old Testament; the apologist Cornelius Van Til; and R.B. Kuiper, who taught Systematic Theology.

Some of the professors had backgrounds in the Christian Reformed Church. This church, founded by Dutch immigrants in 1857 who were connected with Kuyper and Bavinck, was highly respected by Machen, particularly because of its commitment to a distinct Christian education. During the Modernist controversy, the Christian Reformed Church had maintained a strong commitment to Protestantism. At Calvin College and Seminary in Grand Rapids, Louis Berkhof wrote a standard book on systematic theology which was popular in other schools and seminaries.

The Double Standard

William Jennings Bryan believed that God had given the United States the task of applying the biblical moral code for individuals to the policies of the nation. He expresses this view in the following excerpt:

The universally recognized standard of morals for individuals is built upon the Ten Commandments, and no one disputes the validity of the Commandments against killing, stealing, bearing false witness and covetousness, when applied to individuals; but these commandments are not sufficiently applied to the large groups, called nations and because they are not applied there is no standard of morals which can be authoritatively invoked for the regulation of international affairs.

Men whose consciences would not permit them to take a neighbor's life, as an individual act, think it is entirely proper to take life by wholesale, either through those whom they command or at the command of others—and that, too, without regard to the cause of the war. Nations which long since ceased to imprison their own citizens for debt, do not hesitate to bombard foreign cities and slaughter the inhabitants of foreign countries as a means of enforcing the repayment of international loans— sometimes loans of questionable validity.

Men who would not think of stealing from a neighbor are taught to believe that it is patriotic to defend the taking of territory, if their nation gains by the act. Men who would shrink from slandering a neighbor seem to feel no compunctions of conscience when they misrepresent the purposes and plans of other nations; and covetousness, which is regarded as sinful in the individual, seems to be transformed into a virtue when it infects a nation. This attempt to limit the application of these commandments to small transactions has cost an enormous quantity of blood and has brought confusion into international councils.

From William Jennings Bryan, A Single Standard of Morality," *The Commoner,* XVI (March 1916), p. 9.

In 1932 a book entitled, *Rethinking Missions* appeared, financed largely through John D. Rockefeller, Jr. This opened the eyes of many people to the fact that Modernists were converting the task of missions from the proclamation of the gospel of grace to the promotion of socialism. Machen and his friends founded the Independent Board of Foreign Missions in protest. In 1934 the General Assembly ordered the presbyteries to discipline all church members who were associated with the Independent Board. In 1936 Machen was suspended from the ministry and others were dealt with in the same way.

In 1936, the Orthodox Presbyterian Church came into existence. Among those who left there was agreement on certain essentials, and opposition to modernism served as a unifying factor. But there was certainly not agreement on everything. A number of the separated Presbyterians wanted to rule against the use of alcohol and felt hurt when there was criticism of dispensationalism. They finally formed the Bible Presbyterian Church, in which Rev. Carl McIntire became prominent. In the midst of these events, Machen died on New Year's Day, 1937.

Other secessions also took place, primarily in the North, as the South maintained a more conservative character. In 1932 the General Association of Regular Baptist Churches was founded. In 1946 the Baptist General Conference and in 1947 the Conservative Baptist Association were founded. In Canada, T. T. Shield led in founding of a new Baptist denomination. After the 1930s, fundamentalism was marked by the founding of other churches, Bible Colleges, and stressed separation from modernism and the teachings of the higher life movement.

The Great Depression

The rejection of Protestant Orthodoxy and the public endorsement of Modernism had profound consequences. As the 1930s arrived and wore on, Europe discovered that its postwar prosperity had been built on sand. Unemployment was high in Britain, and the German economy had begun to slow down by the end of 1928. In the United States, agriculture and coal mining had been depressed since the mid-1920s. German prosperity was based on short-term loans which could be recalled at any time. Much of this borrowed money was used for public works projects instead of on productive facilities.

The United States failed to recognize the fragile nature of the international economy. Much of the profit from the industrial boom of the 1920s had gone into investments instead of to the workers in the form of higher wages. Farm income actually declined because agricultural prices fell while taxes and prices of manufactured goods rose. As a result, the U.S. national income became lopsided, with 5 percent of the people receiving one-third of all personal income. People could not buy the output of American industry rapidly enough and unsold goods piled up. Surplus goods could not be sold overseas either because each country had adopted high tariffs, crippling international trade.

Stock Market Crash. But the most serious flaw in the world economy existed in the American stock market. Too many people had purchased stock on credit, expecting a quick gain in value and an easy profit because of the booming industrial development. Stock prices soared to unhealthy heights at a time when other economic factors indicated stocks should be going down. The

The New York Stock Exchange went from boom to bust in the fall of 1929.

number of stocks traded broke all records. Everybody wanted to get in on the bonanza.

But the day of reckoning finally came. On October 24, 1929, "**Black Thursday**," everybody suddenly started trying to sell instead of to buy. In the panic which followed, stock prices collapsed. Many investors, particularly those who had bought on credit, lost everything. Within one month, stock values dropped 40 percent and the decline continued for three years. General industrial production and national income fell by nearly one-half as companies lost their revenue base. In America and Europe, banks and businesses failed, destroying the savings and jobs of millions.

The **Great Depression** had an enormous impact on people's lives. In the United States and Britain, a quarter, and in Germany, a third of the labor force was unemployed. Teachers, engineers, lawyers, and other professional people had to dig ditches and sweep floors. Living standards declined and large numbers of people depended on public charity just to survive. The despair and anxiety of those years scarred a whole generation.

For some, however, the Depression period was a time for learning self-sufficiency and renewing community spirit and family closeness.

Governments Respond. The French regime came under heavy fire from fascist-style political movements. Several leftist parties, including the Communists, put together a **Popular Front** political coalition which tried to cope with **fascism** and the Depression. It adopted an ambitious package of "progressive" labor laws, but this had only limited success. The term fascism, in a general sense, refers to a reactionary autocratic ideology opposed to revolutionary democratic socialism. It emphasizes national pride and prejudice. Although socialism promotes state-directed societies, fascism emphasizes elite-directed societies. It also emphasizes regimentation of life, industry, and commerce. It strictly enforces censorship and restricts opposition through autocratic methods.

The American response to the Depression was the **New Deal**, a program of "reform" designed by **President Franklin D. Roosevelt**. Although it aimed at protecting rather than destroying capitalism, it involved the government in the economy more than ever before in American history. The government put controls on business, helped organized labor, used its powers to redistribute wealth, and set up a social security system. It created jobs in the short-term and gave financial help to the unemployed. The government subsidized public housing and passed laws to regulate the stock exchanges. The New Deal succeeded in doubling the income of farmers and workers. But the long-term implications of the New Deal were destructive to the American economy as private enterprise, with its productive benefits, became hamstrung by government competition and regulation.

Critics complained that the New Deal created a vast expensive federal bureaucracy that choked individual freedom. They worried about the new **deficit spending** policy. Governments, of course, have no income of their own because they are not productive enterprises. To get the money they need, they must borrow it from lenders, take it in the form of taxes, or establish state-owned profit-making enterprises of their own, such as nationalized industries or national forests. When they go into business for themselves, governments compete (often unfairly) with private enterprises, drive private enterprises out of business, and historically have proven to be inefficient because there is no personal pride of ownership as an incentive for good work. When a government spends more money than it receives in revenue, it must either 1) borrow money and pay interest on the debt, 2) raise taxes and thus leave citizens and businesses with less money to spend on productive enterprises, or 3) print more money, meaning the existing money supply will be worth less and people's purchasing power will diminish. In any of these cases, the people are poorer and the national economy is less productive.

That has been the legacy of the New Deal. Even at the time, in spite of Roosevelt's efforts, the job-

Compounding the misery of the Depression, droughts in the Great Plains destroyed crops, and the topsoil blew away in enormous dust storms. Many farmers lost everything and had to leave their farms.

Under Franklin D. Roosevelt (1882–1945), the United States government attempted to solve unemployment by creating many public works jobs. Taxpayers paid the bill.

less figure remained quite high. In fact, some argue that the New Deal programs actually prolonged the Depression. Only the outbreak of war brought back full employment and temporary economic recovery. The real effect of the New Deal was the centralization of power in the federal government, and the concentration of that power in the presidency.

The Rise of Totalitarian Dictators

With the failure of the League of Nations to bring about arms reductions and naval limitations, some of the restrictions of the Treaty of Versailles began to be ignored. Germany left the **Geneva Disarmament Conference** in 1933 and began to build up its weaponry and military forces. In 1935 it announced, in defiance of the Versailles Treaty, that it was instituting a universal military draft. This was seen as a provocation by other nations, who began a new scramble to develop weapons of every kind. As we have seen, numerous new bilateral and multilateral alliances were formed. Italy, Germany, and Japan increasingly consolidated themselves into what appeared to be an aggressor bloc.

Mussolini in Italy. It was clear that all was not well with the democratic regimes so hastily set up in Europe after the war. Postwar Italy had suffered food shortages, rising prices, unemployment, business bankruptcies, and strikes. Many Italians had hoped to gain more land from what had been Austria-Hungary. With disorder and violence sweeping the country, an ambitious politician named **Benito Mussolini** found conditions ripe for building his Fascist Party. After the war, he had formed an anti-socialist military group, the **Black Shirts**, consisting mostly of ex-soldiers and unemployed youths, and promised to end the growing threat of anarchy and communism. Industrialists paid them to break strikes. Dressed in black shirts, they put on elaborate rituals and street parades. Before long the Fascists became one of the major political parties in Italy.

In 1922, Mussolini urged his followers to take the government by force. A few days later, thousands of Fascists marched on Rome. The Italian army could easily have crushed the march, but the weak king, **Victor Emmanuel**, feared Fascist strength. Hoping to save Italy from more violence, he invited Mussolini to become prime minister. In effect, Mussolini was a dictator.

Once in power, Mussolini put his henchmen in key government posts and gained control of the army. Through a campaign of terror, he won a rigged election in 1924. Then he outlawed all other parties and imprisoned or deported anyone who threatened his power. The radio, press, movies, and schools soon came under tight government control. Italians were told only what Mussolini wanted them to know.

To avoid any problems with the Roman Catholic Church, the dictator made a treaty with it, ending the long church-state dispute. The treaty recognized the pope as sovereign ruler over Vatican City, promised him state financial support, and gave the church some control over education. In return, the pope (**Pius XI**) agreed not to interfere in politics and to secure government approval for the appointment of bishops.

Mussolini tried to introduce a new economic plan which was neither capitalism nor socialism. Property could be privately owned, but people's rights were secondary to those of the state. Industries were reorganized into 12 corporations representing workers, owners, and the state. However, the real income of the common worker declined under this system. Mussolini used showy public works projects, propaganda programs, and youth organizations to win the hearts of the Italians.

Hitler in Germany. In Germany, a disgruntled Austrian immigrant named **Adolf Hitler** tried to copy Mussolini's success by staging a *coup d'état*. The venture was a complete flop, and Hitler landed in a jail for nine months. Up to this point, little had gone right in his life. Although he was from a reasonably well-off family, he had failed in his youthful ambition to enter art school, so he became a drifter. He joined the German army in 1914 and left a respectable service record. After the war, he did political surveillance work for the army in Munich. Before long, he formed his own group, the **National Socialist German Workers' (Nazi) Party**.

Calling himself the Führer (leader), he had a large band of hooligans called "Brown Shirts," or storm troopers, who paraded, defended Nazi rallies, and broke up meetings of rival groups. The

Hitler was a master at organizing spectacular rallies and making emotional speeches. Thus he stirred the patriotic feelings of Germans and secured their loyalty.

Nazi symbol was the **swastika**, the crooked cross symbol that had been used in several ancient occult societies.

While serving his nine-month prison term for the 1923 coup attempt, Hitler wrote *Mein Kampf*. In this book, he explained his political views and intentions in autobiographical form. He wanted to turn back the clock to a primitive, idealized German past where the complexities of modern life had no place.

Hitler believed that the Germans were a superior "race." They possessed certain traits, bound up with their homeland and environment, that set them apart from others, he wrote. Hitler traced German ancestry back to the ancient **Aryan** people who had invaded Europe and India. All cul-

ture—art, science, and technology—came from the Aryan race, he said. Other "races," such as Jews, gypsies, and Slavs, were inferior. Their intermarriage with Germans made Aryan blood impure. To Hitler, anything foreign—persons, ideas, or institutions—corrupted German culture. He also accepted the Social Darwinist belief that stronger people should destroy weaker peoples.

From all this flowed the Nazi doctrine of anti-Semitism. In order to regain the lost purity of the past, the Germans should purge the world of corruption—namely the Jews. Hitler blamed the Jews for all modern evils—Marxism, capitalism, and the undermining of the German economy.

Hitler felt that the German racial community needed more room to develop its full potential. They would find this living space in the east. Standing directly in the way of this goal were Poland and Russia.

The Nazis emerged as a major national party in the election of 1930. Two years later, they captured the largest number of parliamentary seats, but then Hitler's popularity began to wane. However, the Communists refused to join with the Socialists to defeat him. Meanwhile, certain conservative, powerful businessmen and aristocrats laid plans to use Hitler to do away with the republic. In a "backroom" political deal, Hitler was legally appointed chancellor on January 30, 1933. He was to share power in a coalition cabinet with the large Conservative Party.

The Führer had other ideas. When he did not win enough seats in a 1933 election to suspend the constitution, he made a bargain with the Catholic Party to protect the church's rights. In return, he received its support for an act which allowed him to rule by decree.

With his position more secure, Hitler moved to strengthen his government, the **Third Reich**. All political parties except the Nazis were dissolved. All youth organizations were forced to become part of the **Hitler Youth**. Labor unions were abolished and their functions taken over by a so-called **Labor Front**. The civil service was purged of Jews and those openly hostile to Hitler's ideas.

Hitler required employers to run their factories and businesses as small dictatorships, subject to close government supervision. The Nazis began a vast program of public works—reforestation, draining of marshes, and construction of superhighways. Along with this came a great rearmament program. In 1936, Hitler launched a **Four-Year Plan** to make Germany completely self-sufficient, independent of imported raw materials, and ready for war.

Although the Germans were not much better off financially than before, most approved of the new order at first. Hitler won the enthusiastic support of the common people by ending unemployment, giving them open-air vacations, and raising their status. They were members of the German national community where all were equal because of their common blood. Businessmen liked the new regime, for it had eliminated strikes and increased production, especially in armaments.

Hitler conducted several purges to strengthen his position by eliminating his enemies. Soon **Heinrich Himmler**, head of the **SS Troops** (protection units), controlled many police organizations, including the **GESTAPO** (*Geheime Staats Polizei*—Secret State Police). The SS operated concentration camps, originally designed to frighten opponents of the regime, and set up special schools to train the Nazi elite. Eventually, the army itself was under Hitler's control.

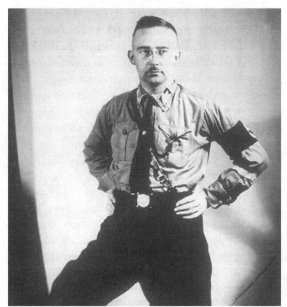

Heinrich Himmler (1900–1945) was a fanatic anti-Semite who directed the Nazi concentration camps.

Some segments of the church put up spirited resistance to Naziism after at first going along with the new order. Although the Nazis had agreed to leave the Roman Catholic Church alone if churchmen would stay out of politics, Catholics soon found they had been deceived. As for the Protestants, many had welcomed Hitler's coming to power as the beginning of a national moral rebirth, but they too were misled. His beliefs conflicted with Christian teachings. Naziism, for example, preached racism, the glory of war, disregard for human life and divinely created rights, and the destruction of the weak.

Some Protestants objected to Nazi efforts to control the church and especially the order to expel clergy with Jewish ancestry. In 1934, a group of churchmen put out a declaration rejecting the claims of the total state in religious and political matters. In a courageous act of resistance, Protes-

tant minister **Dietrich Bonhoeffer** joined a plot to remove Hitler, for which he was imprisoned and later executed. Swiss-born neoorthodox theologian and professor **Karl Barth** was exiled from Germany for his opposition to the regime.

Pope Pius XI criticized Nazi practices in a document smuggled into Germany and read from all Catholic pulpits on Palm Sunday 1937. The bishop of Münster so strongly denounced the Nazi **euthanasia** program in 1941 that it was stopped for awhile. In this program, epileptic and retarded children and adults were killed to prevent them from being a drain on society and a corrupting strain within the German race. The Nazis grudgingly tolerated the existence of the church because they needed it to help keep people's loyalty. Eventually, they planned to abolish it.

The Nazis also developed the "science" of **eugenics**, the study of ways to rid humanity of hereditary "defects" through sterilization, genetic engineering, euthanasia, and abortion. Through these means, "inferior" strains were to be weeded out of the Aryan bloodline. The American eugenics movement, a key advocate of which was **Margaret Sanger**, birth-control promoter and founder of Planned Parenthood Association, influenced the Nazi program. Several other world population control programs which still exist were outgrowths of the program. According to John W. Whitehead,

> American eugenists...were instrumental in getting compulsory sterilization laws passed in a majority of states during those years [1920s]. In fact, the law for the Prevention of Progeny with Hereditary Disease, the basis of Hitler's race purification program, was directly patterned on the model sterilization law proposed by the leaders of the American eugenics movement. (*The Stealing of America*)

The Nazis carried out their most shocking program against the Jews. First they fired Jews from their jobs, took away their rights as citizens, and encouraged them to leave the country. In World War II, when the German armies overran Eastern Europe, which had a much larger Jewish population, the policy became more violent. Nazi death squads killed thousands of Jews on the spot and shipped others to concentration camps such as Auschwitz in Poland. Men, women, and children were taken to these work factories. They were beaten, starved, shot, worked to death, used in medical experiments, and gassed. Estimates by Jewish groups have put the number of Jewish people who died in the **Holocaust** at 6 million.

Chapter 12 considers Germany's expansion into neighboring countries as the prelude to World War II.

Lenin and Stalin in Russia. During the "war communism" period in Russia (1917–1921), Lenin had imposed a rigid dictatorship upon Russia. Other parties were banned and opponents hunted down by the secret police. The government took over factories, banks, land, and foreign trade and confiscated surplus food produced by farmers to supply city dwellers and soldiers fighting in the civil war. Industrial and agricultural production declined drastically. The years 1920 and 1921 brought droughts that, coupled with Communist disruptions and mismanagement, caused terrible famines in Russia. At least 3 million people starved to death, and millions more were barely kept alive by relief shipments from the United States.

In 1921, Lenin introduced the **New Economic Policy** (NEP). It restored some capitalism, especially in agriculture and light industries for the consumer trade. Peasants could sell their goods on the open market and individuals could operate small stores and factories. The state did keep control of the banks, heavy industry, and transportation. The NEP was seen by the outside world as a temporary retreat from socialism to get the country back on its feet. Actually, however, it was part of a program using a new technique of deception known as *dezinformatsiya* (disinformation). By this policy, Lenin sought to portray communism as being in a period of weakness and evolution. As described in 1984 in *New Lies for Old*, by Anatoliy Golitsyn, a former member of the Soviet secret police organization (KGB) who defected to the West:

> Its aim is to calm the fears of the adversaries of international communism by understating real communist strength and to confound the policies of those adversaries by masking the realities of communist policy....

> In order to gain and exploit temporary, tactical political allies and to avoid alarming them, efforts are made to conceal or understate the actual strength and aggressiveness of communism. Factual information favorable to communist regimes is withheld or downgraded; unfavorable information is disclosed, leaked, or invented. Given that communist, unlike democratic, governments are not concerned about their electoral prospects, they can afford to reveal true or false information unfavorable to themselves....

The weakness and evolution pattern was used successfully by Lenin in the 1920s. In 1921 Soviet Russia faced imminent collapse. Industry lay ruined by the war; agriculture was in crisis. The Russian people, disillusioned by the rigid policy of "war communism," were on the brink of revolt; the policy of terror was proving ineffective; there were peasant uprisings in Siberia and along the Volga; nationalist movements in the Ukraine, Georgia, Armenia, and Central Asia were openly proclaiming separatism and posed a serious threat to national unity; the sailors at the Kronstadt Naval Base revolted. Abroad, the hopes of world revolution had faded after communist defeats in Germany, Poland, and Hungary. The major European powers, although not united, were individually hostile to communism and to the new Soviet state; a huge Russian émigré movement, spread across Europe, was plotting the overthrow of the regime. Soviet Russia was in complete political and economic isolation.

It was in this situation, facing a highly unfavorable balance of power vis-à-vis the West, that Lenin conceived and launched a long-range policy that, over the following eight years, was to show spectacular success. It was given the deliberately misleading title of the New Economic Policy, or NEP. In fact, it ranged far beyond the economy, defining also the principal political and ideological objectives and tactics for the regime internally and externally and the strategy for the international communist movement.

The NEP called for creation of a federation of national republics, the Union of Soviet Socialist Republics (USSR), the introduction of long-term economic planning, the construction of an electric power system for the entire country, and schemes to change the balance of power throughout the world in favor of communism. Foreign industrialists were given concessions to operate businesses in Russia. Russian businesses were operated as trusts on a profit basis.

As part of the NEP disinformation plot, Dzerzhinsky secretly devised an organization called **The Trust**. It was purposely portrayed as a counter-revolutionary organization which was appealing to émigrés to return to Russia because the regime was about to be overthrown. Agents of the Trust, claiming to be or to represent monarchists who were on the verge of success, went around the world contacting anti-Communists in the émigré movement and Western governments. In fact, Dzerzhinsky ran the organization. When exiles opposed to the regime returned to Russia to work with The Trust, they were arrested and eliminated. According to one theory, a shadowy British spy, double-agent **Sidney Reilly**, once married to a Russian woman, learned the true nature of The Trust, nearly managed to gain control of it and actually turn it against the regime; but in order to finally expose it, Reilly had to sacrifice himself. According to another theory, Reilly was himself deceived and drawn into the trap unwittingly. Still another theory was the Reilly was actually working for the Russians on behalf of The Trust. Reilly's story is one of the most fascinating in the annals of world espionage. In any event, he disappeared; but shortly thereafter The Trust was put out of business, either through his exposure or because Lenin and company found it had served its purpose of eliminating both internal and outside opposition elements.

> The Soviet leaders...intended that the NEP would not only bring about economic recovery, but would also serve to prevent internal revolt, expand foreign trade, attract foreign capital and expertise, gain diplomatic recognition from noncommunist countries, prevent major conflict with the Western powers, help to exploit the contradictions in and between the capitalist countries, neutralize the émigré movement, and help to promote world revolution through the communist movement.

> Lenin believed that this fundamentally aggressive and ideological policy could prove effective if it was accompanied by the systematic use of misrepresentation and deception, or, to use the current word, disinformation. The characteristics of this disinformation were an apparent moderation in communist ideology, the avoidance of references to violence in communist methods, the exaggeration of the degree of the restoration of capitalism in Soviet Russia, the use of a sober and business-like style in diplomatic and commercial negotiations with the West, and emphasis on disarmament and peaceful coexistence. All of

Joseph Stalin, 1879–1953

this was intended to induce the belief in the outside world that the communist system was weak and losing its revolutionary ardor. Left to itself, it would either disintegrate or come to terms with the capitalist system *(Golitsyn)*.

The country, in fact, did recover under the NEP, but well-to-do peasants were angry because prices for farm products had fallen sharply while prices for manufactured goods had almost doubled. They reduced production and held back food deliveries to the cities in order to force up prices. Thus in the socialist society, capitalist farmers still had considerable power.

When Lenin died in 1924, a power struggle broke out among his close associates. Soon the contest narrowed down to Leon Trotsky and the party general secretary, **Joseph Stalin** (born Iosif Vissarionovich Dzhugashvili), whom Lenin distrusted and opposed as a successor. As an early

follower of Lenin, Stalin had played a major role in the Revolution and civil war before becoming the party secretary. He was not an original thinker, but he had mastered the techniques of political manipulation. Through his position in the party, he learned how to build and use power.

Stalin shrewdly used his comrades' fear of the ambitious Trotsky to outmaneuver him. Rather than lead an armed rebellion against Stalin, Trotsky accepted defeat and was later exiled from the Soviet Union. After moving from one country to another, he wound up in Mexico City, where, in 1940, he was assassinated by a shadowy man wielding an ax and using an alias. The man's true identity was never disclosed, but he was thought to have been an agent of Stalin. By 1928, Stalin had full control of the party. The fate of the Revolution lay in the hands of one of the most ruthless dictators of all time.

Stalin scoffed at the subtle and deceptive methods of Dzerzhinsky's disinformation program and Lenin's New Economic Policy, which he ended. He preferred more direct methods of forcing communism upon the country no matter how brutally that would have to be accomplished. He launched a massive buildup of Soviet industry to make the country self-sufficient and powerful— the first **Five-Year Plan**. All factories were supposed to do as the scheme dictated, and labor unions encouraged productivity and kept discipline among the workers. It provided for the immediate industrialization of the whole Soviet economy.

The manufacturing and commercial part came easily, but the agricultural situation posed problems. Because 80 percent of the rural people were still economically independent, tight control was impossible. Therefore, the state took over all farms and merged them into large **collective farms**. In protest, the peasant capitalists

Leon Trotsky, 1879–1940

destroyed their livestock and property. Soldiers and police killed thousands of peasants and transported millions more to Siberia. After that, the peasants were embittered and worked with little enthusiasm. They gave as much time as possible to the private garden plots which they were allowed to have.

The capital which was squeezed out of the agricultural sector of the economy was used to finance industrial development. Also, the Soviet Union relied heavily on technical aid and equipment from Western countries, some of which was stolen by secret agents. Industrial production grew so spectacularly under the first and second Five-Year Plans that within a decade Russia had risen from fifth to second place in total world output. The emphasis was on heavy industry and later arms production rather than consumer goods. However, piecework pay scales and low wages created a wage slavery worse than Europe's early Industrial Revolution.

Some personal freedom had existed in Russia during Lenin's reign. Artists could express themselves to a point, and Christians could practice their faith, although Lenin repeatedly denounced Christianity and attempted to put the country on the road to atheism. Beginning in 1929, Stalin put the churches under strict controls. He actively promoted atheism. No writer or artist dared express any views which differed in the slightest from the party line. Art degenerated to simply another form of propaganda.

Stalin also set out to destroy all possible rivals to his tyranny. In the **Great Purges** of the 1930s, the **Old Bolsheviks**, pre-1917 party members, were hunted down and relentlessly killed by the secret police. Some of them "confessed" in Moscow show trials to crimes they could not possibly have committed. Fearing also that Red Army leaders would rebel, Stalin had 80 percent of those above the rank of captain removed. The purges reached down to factory and farm managers—even to workers and peasants. At least 8 million people were deported to labor camps in Siberia, above the Arctic Circle. Some 800,000 were executed. Then in 1939, with war clouds gathering on the horizon and nearly all potential rivals out of the way, Stalin halted the purges.

In some ways, Stalin's reign was a throwback to the old Russian system. His hero was not Karl Marx but Ivan the Terrible. Stalin undid the pre-1917 efforts to make Russia more liberal, and turned back to the old pattern of total government control of the economy and serfdom through the collective farm. Communism "succeeded" in Russia for a time largely because the past had conditioned people to submit. But the cost of submission was incredibly high. By some estimates, as many as 30 million Russians lost their lives through starvation, brutality, and execution under Stalin, making him one of the greatest mass killers of all times. Among those to suffer most under Stalin and his "**Stalinist**" suc-

cessors in Russia and other communist lands were Christians. Thousands were martyred or persecuted in terrible ways. Many were beaten, deprived of necessities, imprisoned, separated from families, denied education, scorned, and prevented from worshipping openly. Hundreds of churches were destroyed, and many church organizations were infiltrated and subverted to serve the aims of the atheistic state. Yet the true Church of Christ did not die under these persecutions but actually increased in strength of faith.

Totalitarian Methods. Totalitarianism of both the right and left achieved a level of control over people never before known, through the use of the police power, informers, torture, and execution. Mass media conditioned people's minds by bombarding them with officially approved informa-

tion, and by preventing them from hearing more than one side of a situation. People gained a sense of identity when taught to believe that they were needed to oppose some outside enemy. They participated in well-disciplined militaristic organizations and clubs.

Both fascism and communism use these totalitarian methods. There are, however, some differences between them. For example, fascism tends to emphasize nationalism and often allows traditional middle class institutions and economic arrangements. Communism stresses internationalism and modernization through radical economic and social changes. Ultimately, both of these ungodly systems would be used by devilish tyrants to enslave and ruin millions of people during the twentieth century.

The pro-Bolshevik crew of the cruiser *Aurora* supported the Bolshevik Revolution by firing on the Winter Palace in Petrograd (St. Petersburg) on November 7, 1917.

For your consideration

Questions

1. Do expenditures for weapons and military training prevent war or prepare the way for it?

2. What role did alliances play in starting World War I? In what kinds of alliances is your country presently involved?

3 What were the advantages and disadvantages of trench warfare?

4. What ways are there for a country to survive a naval blockade?

5. Are there some jobs that women should be discouraged from doing?

6. Can you avoid being affected by propaganda? Do you know of some groups using propaganda today? Give examples.

7. How does your church feel about war?

8. Can a country really remain neutral during a war? Should it? What does neutrality mean?

9. How do countries "declare war"? What was the last time the United States declared war on another country? What does the U.S. Constitution say about declarations of war?

10. What conditions in Russia led to the triumph of communism? How were the Bolsheviks able to mobilize their supporters so quickly? Contrast the approach of the Bolsheviks and Mensheviks.

11. Describe how the Versailles Treaty helped set the stage for further unrest.

Projects

1. Read material in a book about economics. Write a brief report on inflation. What is it? How does it come about? How does it effect you?

2. Do some research on the history and nature of the welfare state. What services does it promise to provide for its people? Why are some people so strongly opposed to the welfare state? Describe the status of the current debate in your country about government welfare programs.

3. Write a brief report on the history of anti-Semitism.

4. Write a report on the various new weapons developed and used in World War I, such as tanks, airplanes, zeppelins, and submarines. Collect some pictures of these weapons.

5. The Russian Revolution occurred in 1917. Write a news article about this event as if you were a foreign correspondent from a major European country. Try to evaluate how this revolution would affect the war.

6. Discuss the Jewish-Arab conflict. Trace the problem to its historical root, including its Biblical history and modern history. What claims do the Jews and Arabs each have on Palestine?

7. During the period called the "Roaring Twenties" distinctive styles of clothing, cars, architecture, art, etc. developed. Create some posters illustrating these.

Word List

entente	*coup d'état*
front	Great Depression
barrage	deficit spending
offensives	swastika
soviet	euthanasia
morale	eugenics
inflation	Holocaust
demoralized	collective farms
sanctions	totalitarianism
dole	Third Reich
anti-Semitism	*Reichstag*
fez	U-boat
conscientious objector	intelligentsia
pacifist	globalism
passive resistance	welfare state
fascism	Balfour Declaration
New Economic Policy	*dezinformatsiya*

People and Groups

Triple Alliance	Felix Dzerzhinsky
Triple Entente	Alexander Kerensky
GESTAPO & SS Troops	Vladimir Ilyich Lenin
Heinrich Himmler	Leon Trotsky
Kaiser Wilhelm II	Bolsheviks
Archduke Ferdinand	Mensheviks
Gavrilo Princip	The Trust
Black Hand	Adolf Hitler
Black Shirts	Benito Mussolini
Sidney Reilly	Charles Dawes
Paul von Hindenburg	Vittorio Orlando
Ferdinand Foch	Woodrow Wilson
World Zionist Org'n	David Lloyd-George
Margaret Sanger	Geo. Clemenceau
Emmeline Pankhurst	Franklin D. Roosevelt
Rasputin	Joseph Stalin
Czarina Alexandra	M. Kemal Atatürk
Czar Nicholas II	Dietrich Bonhoeffer
Gustav Stresemann	Karl Barth

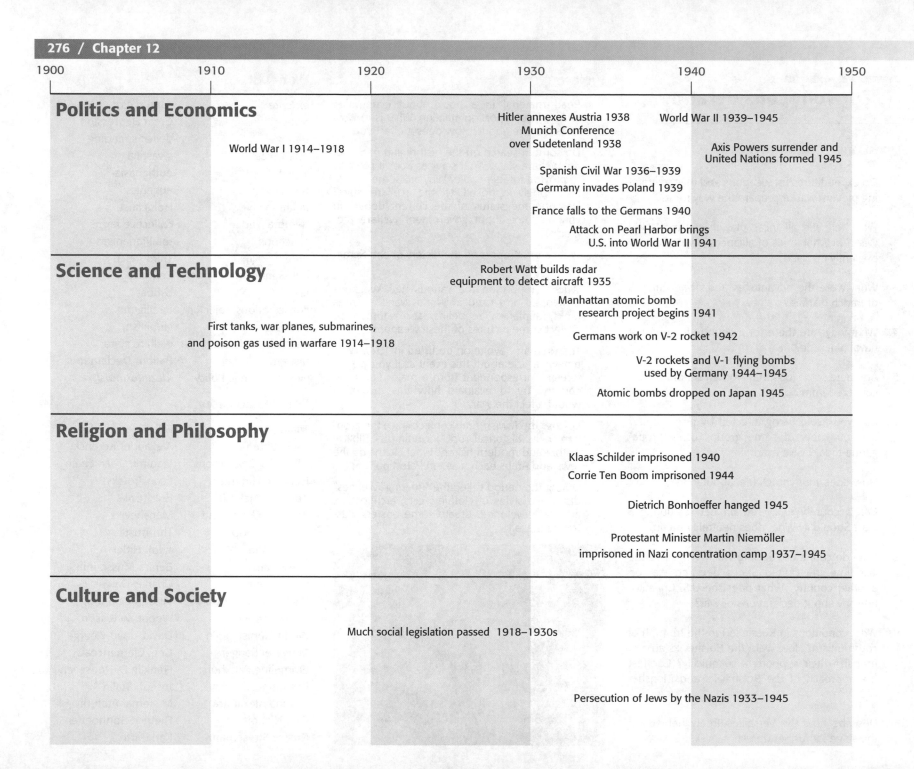

1900   1910   1920   1930   1940   1950

Politics and Economics

Hitler annexes Austria 1938
Munich Conference
over Sudetenland 1938

World War II 1939–1945

World War I 1914–1918

Axis Powers surrender and
United Nations formed 1945

Spanish Civil War 1936–1939

Germany invades Poland 1939

France falls to the Germans 1940

Attack on Pearl Harbor brings
U.S. into World War II 1941

Science and Technology

Robert Watt builds radar
equipment to detect aircraft 1935

Manhattan atomic bomb
research project begins 1941

First tanks, war planes, submarines,
and poison gas used in warfare 1914–1918

Germans work on V-2 rocket 1942

V-2 rockets and V-1 flying bombs
used by Germany 1944–1945

Atomic bombs dropped on Japan 1945

Religion and Philosophy

Klaas Schilder imprisoned 1940

Corrie Ten Boom imprisoned 1944

Dietrich Bonhoeffer hanged 1945

Protestant Minister Martin Niemöller
imprisoned in Nazi concentration camp 1937–1945

Culture and Society

Much social legislation passed 1918–1930s

Persecution of Jews by the Nazis 1933–1945

12 The Rise of Totalitarianism: World War II

During the 1920s and 1930s, western democracies were alarmed by the rise of dictators in Italy, Japan, Germany, and the Soviet Union. Yet avoiding war was very important to countries which had endured so much in World War I. Many people were still committed to the principles of the League of Nations, the Kellogg-Briand Pact, and other agreements. But they had to find some method of dealing with the threats posed by these powerful dictators.

The Nations Respond to Totalitarianism

Some countries tried to contain possible expansion by making security agreements. For example, the Soviet Union had such agreements with France and Czechoslovakia to protect itself from German aggression. Others tried **appeasement.** Britain and France did not want to upset Italy so they did not object very strongly when Mussolini invaded Ethiopia. Still another response was a policy of isolation. The United States again tried to avoid getting involved in European disputes.

Despite these attempts to maintain peace, international relations became more and more strained. Dictators were not content to exercise power only in their own countries. Military lead-

ers in Japan felt that the country needed to control more territory. They wanted Japan to be self-sufficient economically, so they invaded Manchuria, a part of China.

China asked the League of Nations and the United States for help. Japan was strongly criticized, but no force was used—so Japan kept Manchuria. Mussolini and Hitler observed this situation carefully. They saw the weakness of the League. They also found out that the other major powers would not use force to maintain order.

By various acts of international military adventurism during the 1930s, Japan, Germany, and Italy began to show themselves to the world as an aggressor group, even though, at the beginning, there was no specific collaboration among them. Each was seeking to advance its own ambitions on its own initiative. It was not until 1936 that various pacts began to emerge among these aggressors.

Treaty Violations. Soon after coming to power, Hitler decided to build up Germany's military strength. He established an air force, began a military draft, and expanded the army to 36 divisions. An agreement with Britain allowed Germany to build submarines and large ships. In 1934, he attempted to annex Austria but was rebuffed by Mussolini. In 1936 Hitler sent troops into the Rhineland. France did not want to resist Germany's action without British support. Brit-

The cartoon, *Grim Reaper*, from 1933, was very prophetic.

ain did not want to risk a war, just to keep German troops from occupying their own territory. Therefore, nothing was done about these violations of the Versailles Treaty.

In 1938, Hitler again cast eyes upon Austria and this time succeeded in annexing it without a fight. There was political turmoil in Austria at the

Adolf Hitler, 1889–1945

time and many German-speaking Austrians wanted to be part of the German empire. Hitler insisted that a pro-Nazi chancellor be installed in Austria. The new Nazi leader promptly "invited" Hitler to send troops and "establish order." Europe stood by without action. Some leaders thought Hitler was only righting wrongs wrought by the Treaty of Versailles in dividing the German peoples. When Hitler set his sights on Czechoslovakia, he aimed first at the Sudetenland, where there was a large concentration of Germans. The Czechs mobilized their army. Both France and the Soviet Union prepared to aid them. However, the British prime minister, **Neville Chamberlain**, was convinced that Hitler's wish to bring the Sudeten Germans into the Third Reich was a just case of national self-determination. Chamberlain made an all-out effort to settle the crisis peacefully. Hitler, with support from Mussolini,

invited Chamberlain and French **Premier Édouard Daladier** to Munich to discuss the crisis. At length Britain, France, Germany, and Italy signed the **Munich Agreement**, which turned over a large part of the Sudeten area to Germany.

Chamberlain called it "peace with honor." The British and French public enthusiastically welcomed it as bringing "peace in our time." They were lulled into thinking that the Sudetenland would be Hitler's last territorial claim. Czechoslovakia was not even invited to the conference; and its ally, Soviet Russia, was also left out in the cold. Later "Munich" became a symbol of cowardice and shortsightedness in dealing with aggressive dictators.

On October 3, 1938, Chamberlain addressed the British House of Commons and claimed that "the great and imminent menace" of war had been averted and Czechoslovakia was more secure than ever. One member of the House of Commons, **Winston Churchill**, disagreed. Churchill warned, correctly, as history has shown, that no one should think this was the end of Hitler's designs. He added:

> This is only the beginning of the reckoning. This is only the first sip, the first foretaste of a bitter cup which will be proffered to us year by year unless by a supreme recovery of moral health and martial vigor, we arise again and take our stand for freedom as in the olden time.

Ethiopia. Other trouble spots also had appeared around the globe. In 1935, Mussolini invaded Ethiopia, an act which soon indicated a need for German support. The League of Nations called for economic sanctions against Italy. The other countries agreed not to sell them weapons, but other necessary items such as oil were allowed. Finally the sanctions were lifted, and the League of Nations recognized the conquest of Ethiopia.

Neville Chamberlain, 1869–1940

In light of the mild action of the sanctions, Mussolini allied himself with Hitler in the **Rome-Berlin Axis** of 1936. They saw their partnership as the axis around which the other world powers would turn, and they sought to bring their respective foreign policies into harmony. Later that year, Japan joined Germany in a military agreement known as the **Anti-Comintern Pact**, ostensibly an alliance against all communism, but specifically an agreement against Russia. Japan and Italy signed a similar agreement in 1937. During World War II, Germany, Italy, and Japan were known as the **Axis Powers**.

The Spanish Civil War. Trouble had also been brewing in Spain. Torn by unrest for years, the monarchy finally gave way to a republic in 1931. As the depression tightened its grip there, the socialists moved farther to the left in order to hold the desperate workers. After a leftist government took office early in 1936, the rightist middle and upper classes (which included such interests as the Roman Catholic Church, the military, the monarchists, and the new fascist **Falange** party) rebelled. Led by **General Francisco Franco**, the right-wing rebels, known as the **Nationalists**, soon took over much of southern and western Spain.

The liberal **republicans** (also known as **Loyalists**) turned to France and Britain for help, but they were afraid to widen the war. Brigades of idealistic young people from Europe and the United States, especially those with socialist and liberal leanings, came to help the republic. Among them, for example, was the American expatriate writer **Ernest Hemingway**, who came to Spain as a news correspondent sympathetic to the liberal democrats and socialists. His great novel, *For Whom the Bell Tolls*, deals with the Spanish Civil War. Hemingway was typical of the so-called "**lost generation**," men and women living in Europe between the two world wars, who had lost their faith in historic Christian morals and values, adopted a cynical outlook toward life, and sought primarily to satisfy their own emotional needs. They tended to glorify simple people with primitive emotions, who were battling overwhelming circumstances. Many of Hemingway's stories and novels contained such characters.

Communist Russia sent arms, technicians, and political advisers to aid the Loyalist government in Spain. Germany and Italy supplied "volunteers" and war equipment to Franco's forces, so they were much better equipped than the government forces. The bloody struggle ended with Franco's capture of Madrid on April 1, 1939. He became dictator of Spain. Franco's victory owed much to the Axis Powers, and those powers, especially Hitler, gained new confidence through the Spanish war. The Italians had supplied 50,000 combat troops, and the Germans had tried out their new dive bombers and mechanized equip-

This cartoon from October 1939, asks "Wonder how long the honeymoon will last?" The answer is: from 1939 to 1941.

ment. It had been a sort of test run for World War II, although Franco eventually kept Spain neutral and out of that war.

China. Japan also launched a full-scale invasion of China in 1937. The Japanese soon controlled the coast, but the Chinese fought on from strongholds in the interior. From the League of Nations came a feeble rebuke, while the United States remained neutral. (We shall further consider events in China during this period in chapter 14.)

Preparing for War. On March 15, 1939, Hitler's troops marched into Prague. Hitler divided most of the rest of Czechoslovakia outside the Sudetenland, taking land inhabited by non-Germans and breaking the Munich Agreement. He immediately began to eye Poland, demanding a strip of territory known as the "Polish Corridor." Backtracking on his appeasement policy, Chamber-

lain, with French support, committed Britain to help endangered Poland. Meanwhile, Mussolini's forces conquered Albania. Britain responded with promises to help nearby Greece, Romania, and Turkey if they were attacked. In May of that year, Hitler and Mussolini signed the **Pact of Steel**, finalizing their military alliance.

Everyone waited to see what the position of Stalin and the Soviet Union would be. The Russians had no confidence in the strength of the West, and Stalin felt he had been snubbed by Chamberlain and left out of the West's dealings with Hitler. He had no interest in cooperating with Britain. The Soviet Union finally agreed in August 1939 to sign a **nonaggression** pact with Germany (the **Nazi-Soviet Pact**). They pledged to keep from violence against each other for ten years. Together they also agreed secretly to divide Poland and other Eastern European countries between them. Thus the Germans offered Stalin what he wanted most, the recovery of Russian land lost in World War I and a large buffer strip between the Soviet Union and Germany.

The Nazi Invasion of Europe, 1939–1941

Poland and Finland Fall. Without a declaration of war, the Germans marched into Poland on September 1, 1939. The world saw for the first time the awesome effectiveness of their new *blitzkrieg* (lightening war) strategy. First, waves of dive bombers blasted communication lines and spread terror and confusion among the people. Then the armored tank divisions smashed holes in the enemy lines, pushed into the rear, and cut the opposing forces to pieces. Finally, lighter motorized divisions and the infantry

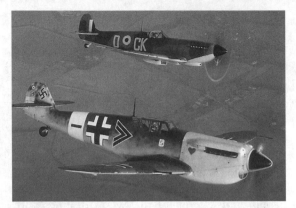
German ME-109 fighter is being chased by English Spitfire.

The Miracle of Dunkirk

The Allied cause hit its lowest point as the Germans closed in on Dunkirk. It was thought that rescue operations could only save about 45,000 men. Churchill warned the House of Commons "to prepare for hard and heavy tidings."

On May 14, the call went out for help from civilian craft on the British coast. More than 600 vessels responded, practically everything that could float. Twelve days later, this strange-looking flotilla, dubbed the "Mosquito Armada," joined some 200 naval vessels, including some from Belgium and France, for the beginning of Operation Dynamo. Protected somewhat by a curtain of naval antiaircraft fire and the Royal Air Force, the rescuers headed across the Channel.

As they neared the beach, thousands of soldiers waded out to meet them. Bombs and artillery shells exploded all around, sinking a number of boats. The others did not hesitate. Some craft capsized under the heavy loads. Many soldiers drowned trying to reach the boats. Machine guns raked the beaches where others waited their turn. But on they came by the thousands.

For nine days, the heroic effort continued, working at night when it was too dangerous in daylight. The results exceeded all expectations. Nearly 350,000 men made it to safety in England. Churchill praised the Royal Air Force for its part in driving off German fighters and bombers, allowing the small boats to do their work in crossing after crossing.

To the Allies, who had feared annihilation, the feat was a moral victory. It had also been an answer to prayer, as Christians everywhere had implored the Almighty for deliverance in this critical hour. As Churchill stated, "We must be very careful not to assign to this deliverance the attributes of a victory. Wars are not won by evacuations. But there was a victory inside this deliverance....

"In the midst of defeat the tale of the Dunkirk beaches will shine in whatever records are preserved of our affairs."

He expressed confidence that Britain would move "through disaster and through grief to the ultimate defeat of our enemies."

---

moved in to "mop up" the splintered enemy forces, supported by air and artillery cover

Hitler had counted on British and French weakness and believed they would not respond to his invasion of Poland. He was wrong. Britain and France declared war on Germany two days later, but they were too far away to save Poland. The German army moved so quickly that on September 17 Stalin ordered the Red Army into eastern Poland to claim the land staked out in his agreement with Hitler. By the end of the month, Warsaw surrendered. Europe was once again at war.

Estonia, Latvia, and Lithuania had to accept Russian military bases; later they were made part of the Soviet Union. Finland refused to accept Soviet demands and fought back; however, it was defeated by March 1940.

Sitzkrieg and Blitzkrieg. After a period of relative calm in Western Europe known as the *sitzkrieg* (sitting war) or "phony war," German forces swarmed unopposed into a surprised Denmark, which surrendered after only a few hours of fighting. On that same day in April of 1940, the Germans attacked Norway, but there a small Anglo-French force tried to help the Norwegians. After two months the Allied troops pulled out in defeat,

and the Germans set up a puppet regime under **Vidkun Quisling**. From that time on any self-seeking traitor who **collaborated** with the enemy was called a "quisling," a term of contempt. The Nazis were aided in Norway by such people, also known as **fifth columnists**, a term coined during the Spanish Civil War to describe persons within a country who aid the enemy by spying, secretly spreading enemy propaganda, or sabotaging their own countrymen's cause. Other Norwegians courageously resisted the Nazis. Civilians, for example, placed their bodies on airport runways preventing German planes from landing.

On May 10, the Nazis unleashed the awesome power of their *blitzkrieg* on Holland, Belgium, and France. Nothing could stand against the German bombers and armored *panzer* divisions. A devastating air attack leveled Rotterdam, and the tank divisions raced across the flat countryside. Within five days, Holland surrendered. Belgium lasted only eighteen days. The Germans surprised the Allies by launching their main attack through the Ardennes Forest region of Belgium, France, and Luxembourg, where tanks supposedly could not operate. This enabled the Germans to avoid the Maginot Line fortifications along the French-German border, and gave them the opportunity to trap the British and French forces that were helping the Belgians.

Charles de Gaulle, 1890–1970

Once the German divisions broke out of the Ardennes Forest into open country, they rapidly drove on to the English Channel and cut off the Allied armies in Belgium. Now in danger of being wiped out, British and French forces retreated to the port of Dunkirk. Their only hope lay in getting across to England. Christians throughout the British Empire launched a concerted prayer effort for the deliverance of the trapped Allied troops. What followed was one of the most remarkable events of the war.

Hitler suddenly halted his powerful land-based *panzer* divisions, believing that there was no hope of escape for the Allies. He planned on finishing off the Allied troops from the air, allowing the *panzers* to turn against France. But bad weather over the English Channel area hampered the German airplanes in pursuing their mission. A general call was issued in England for boats. A **flotilla** of 800 boats, manned by the British army and civilians, rescued some 350,000 men (90 percent of the trapped Allied forces) from the beaches of Dunkirk. The flotilla included every boat the British could find, including motorboats, fishing boats, tugboats, and yachts.

Churchill later referred to the boat brigade as the "Mosquito Armada." Again, the weather providentially cooperated, as the normally choppy English Channel waters were relatively calm and the winds, which had been blowing in the usual northerly direction, began to blow to the west toward the British Isles. Yet fog and haze remained aloft, covering much of the operation and shielding it from the eyes of German pilots. The rescue operation, which was not without considerable attack from the Germans despite the weather, went on for nine days, as troops ashore around Dunkirk valiantly beat back attacks from enemy ground forces and low-flying aircraft. The event became known as "the miracle of Dunkirk."

Sadly, about 40,000 men (the remaining 10 percent of the Allied forces) and all the Allied equipment had to be abandoned in France.

France Collapses. The German armies marched into, and occupied, Paris without a battle on June 13, 1940, and the government fled. **Marshal Henri Pétain**, hero of Verdun in World War I, took over the government and sued for peace. In the surrender, most of France's army was demobilized, and its fleet was rendered useless, although it remained under French control. The empire stayed in French hands. Germany then occupied half of the country, including the entire Atlantic coastline. The French Parliament voted dictatorial powers to Pétain, who dissolved the Third Republic and set up a regime under German control at Vichy, a resort city in central France. Pétain's regime, which effectively controlled only that part of France not occupied by the Germans, was known as the **Vichy government**.

Not all Frenchmen cooperated with the new government. Many escaped to the African territories or Britain, and others supported the liberation movement headed by **General Charles De**

The French Resistance

They started "underground railroads" to take people wanted by the GESTAPO out of France. They cracked coded messages of the Germans and radioed the information to England. They infiltrated the occupation government's postal system, setting up an underground mail system within it. They blew up German troop trains, factories, bridges, and defenses. They rescued French agents and Allied airmen from jails and hospitals. These were only a few of the achievements of the French Resistance during World War II.

A Resistance leader in Toulouse provides an example of the danger facing anyone in this movement. Striking night after night against the Germans, Riccardo's small band of men always managed to avoid capture. The GESTAPO could not infiltrate or find any informers. Increasing patrols, house to house searches, and dragnets all proved futile.

At length the GESTAPO hired a French counterespionage agent to track down Riccardo. The agent set traps but his prey always eluded him. After two months of this, the Germans found out that their new employee was none other than Riccardo himself. Furious at being duped, they printed thousands of wanted posters and placed them everywhere.

Their efforts finally paid off. One day at a roadblock, an official recognized Riccardo from the poster. As he proceeded to take the man prisoner, Riccardo bolted. With bullets whizzing all around him, he ran into a courtyard. The Germans were elated. Now they had him trapped. But when they reached the court, he seemed to have vanished. Just as they were about to start a search of the houses on the court, a tile fell from a roof. The pursuers fired, and the bullets found their mark.

Like Riccardo, many brave men and women played this dangerous game and lost. Their heroism matched that of the soldiers at the front. Part of the credit for winning the war was certainly due the resistance movements.

Gaulle. He was one of the few people in the 1930s who had warned of the inadequacy of French military forces. After Dunkirk, he began to organize the remnants of his country's armed forces in Britain and a few French colonies into the **Free French Movement**. It served as part of the Allied forces. Many who remained in France joined the underground to **sabotage** and spy on German activities.

Britain Stands Alone. Hitler hoped that Britain would make peace. However, the British had had enough of appeasement and had ousted Chamberlain as prime minister on May 10, 1940. His replacement was Winston Churchill, the tough-

R.A.F. pilots scrambled in response to a German air attack during the Battle of Britain.

Winston Churchill (1874–1965) took a heroic stand against the Germans.

minded, outspoken critic of appeasement. Churchill's brilliant speeches and dogged determination rallied the British people to fight. He broadcast words of encouragement and inspiration to his countrymen. In one speech, he said:

> We shall not flag or fail. We shall go on to the end. We shall fight in France, we shall fight on the seas and oceans, we shall fight with growing confidence and growing strength in the air. We shall defend our island, whatever the cost may be. We shall fight on the beaches, we shall fight in the fields and in the streets, we shall fight in the hills. We shall never surrender.

The Führer was not prepared right then to launch a sea operation against the island kingdom. Instead, he called upon his **Luftwaffe** (air force) commander, **Hermann Göring**, to attack the British. In the devastating **Battle of Britain**, the Germans had more aircraft; but British planes were newer and more advanced. Also, Britain used a new tool, **radar**, to sight German planes long before they reached their targets.

The Luftwaffe failed to gain control of the skies and turned to massive bombing of British cities,

especially huge, **vulnerable** London, which was severely damaged. Designed to break British morale, the bombing instead increased British will to resist. The **Royal Air Force (R.A.F.)** destroyed almost 2,500 German aircraft between August and October of 1940 while losing fewer than 1,000 of its own. Churchill praised the R.A.F.'s heroic achievement. "Never in the field of human conflict was so much owed by so many to so few," he said. The feat showed Hitler that his invasion of Britain would have to wait.

The Response of the United States. In November 1939, President Roosevelt had persuaded a reluctant isolationist Congress to allow arms sales to Western European democracies. After the fall of France, the United States began providing arms directly. Congress then approved the first peacetime **draft** in the nation's history.

Roosevelt, whose New Deal programs had failed to completely revitalize the American economy, felt that America must "become the arsenal of democracy." In a speech to Congress on January 6, 1941, Roosevelt declared that **Four Freedoms** should be protected around the world—freedom of expression, freedom of worship, freedom from want, and freedom from fear. In March 1941 Congress practically declared war on Germany and Italy by passing the **Lend-Lease Act**. It authorized vast amounts of food and military equipment for embattled Britain. On May 21, 1941, an American merchant ship, the *Robin Moor*, was torpedoed by a German submarine in the South Atlantic and sank, causing the first American casualties. Other such attacks followed. Roosevelt issued an executive order seizing the American assets of nationals from the Axis countries and their allies. He ordered the U.S. Navy to keep the sea lanes open for shipping in the Atlantic, and warned that American warships would fire upon any Axis warships sighted in channels deemed vital to U.S. interests. In August, Roosevelt met with Churchill on a ship off the Newfoundland coast. There they drafted a statement of peace aims known as the **Atlantic Charter**. In broad terms, it gave their idea of the better world they believed would come after Naziism had been destroyed. Roosevelt's "Four Freedoms" were incorporated into the charter, which later formed the basis for a **United Nations Declaration** in 1942.

More Axis Success. Hitler, meanwhile, was at the crest of his success. He had pressured Finland, Romania, Bulgaria, and Hungary to join the Axis in 1940 and 1941. The oil fields of Romania were a major acquisition of these alliances. The Balkan campaign began in April 1941 with about 550,000 German troops supported by the Luftwaffe, battling alongside the forces of their allies in the area. Croats in northern Yugoslavia defected, and the puppet Axis state of Croatia was created. Serbs in the south were cut off by the Germans from their Greek, British, Australian, and New Zealander allies. In the early spring of 1941, the Germans overran Yugoslavia, despite an ongoing courageous resistance by Yugoslav

guerrillas known as the **Partisans**. With a massive ground and air attack on Greece, they aided the Italian army. (Mussolini had invaded Greece in an effort to exert Italian authority but had been stopped.) Yugoslavia and Greece surrendered in April, and the British were forced to withdraw their troops. To cement their control of the region, the Germans also conquered Crete, giving them a base for operations against the British in North Africa and the oil-rich Middle East. The Axis Powers now controlled the European Continent. They were able to use the resources and manpower of conquered and allied countries.

War in the Pacific 1941–1943

Relations between the United States and Japan had steadily worsened since the outbreak of war in China. After the fall of France, the Japanese built bases in French Indochina. This and the open alliance with the European Axis alarmed American officials, and they banned sales of aviation fuel, ammunition, and strategic industrial products and raw materials to Japan. In July 1941, Japan took full control of Indochina and prepared to attack Malaya and the Dutch East Indies, which contained rich supplies of tin, rubber, and oil. President Roosevelt then ordered a complete halt to trade between the two countries.

The Japanese realized that the United States was the chief obstacle to their goals in the Pacific. By cutting off the sale of scrap iron, steel, and oil products, the Americans could prevent their advance. More and more, Japanese leaders came to feel that direct action was the only answer; but negotiations continued through the year. In April, they protected their border with the Soviet

General Hideki Tojo (1884-1948) was responsible for Japan's war effort while Prime Minister from 1940 to 1944. After the war he was tried and executed as a war criminal.

Union by signing a nonaggression treaty with that country. A few months later, the military, led by **General Hideki Tojo** took over the government. He insisted that American and British influence must be ended in East Asia. The way to do this, he felt, was to destroy the Pacific fleet and occupy the Asian territories before the United States could recover. This would force America to accept the "new order" in Asia. The United States and Japan opened discussions concerning U.S. demands that Japan withdraw from China and French Indochina. The Japanese rejected the U.S. demands, but the U.S. pressed harder with an ultimatum containing eight proposals. In the early morning of December 7, 1941, Japanese diplomats met with U.S. **Secretary of State Cordell Hull** to inform him that Japan could not accept what it considered to be U.S. dominance in China and East Asia. They said further negotiations were impossible.

Japanese Attack the United States. While that meeting was still in progress, unbeknownst to the

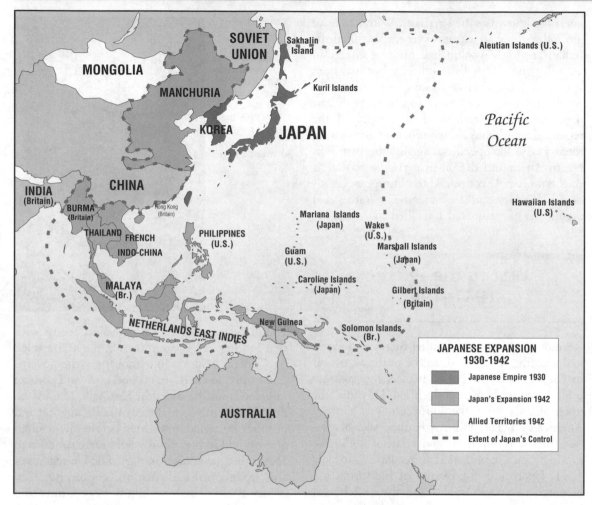

JAPANESE EXPANSION
1930-1942

Japanese Empire 1930

Japan's Expansion 1942

Allied Territories 1942

- - - Extent of Japan's Control

neously, the Japanese attacked the resource-rich East Indies, forcing the surrender of Dutch and Allied forces in March 1942.

At the same time, the American fleet was unable to provide much assistance. Guam and Wake Island were lost in December 1941, and the Philippines surrendered in May 1942. However, prior to the loss of the Philippines, President Roosevelt ordered **General Douglas MacArthur** to Australia to continue the struggle from there. Upon his arrival in Australia, General MacArthur promised the Philippines that "I shall return." By June 1942, the Japanese Empire reached its zenith, stretching from the Indian Ocean to the Aleutian Islands off Alaska.

The Japanese succeeded partly because their venture came at a time when France and Holland were under German occupation, Britain was struggling just to survive, and the United States was only beginning to convert to a wartime economy. Japan exploited anticolonial feelings in

Eight battleships, including the **U.S.S. West Virginia** shown above, were severely damaged or sunk during the Japanese attack on Pearl Harbor. All but two ships returned to service.

Japanese diplomats, a long-planned Japanese air attack on Pearl Harbor, Hawaii, was already under way. The surprise attack, denounced by Roosevelt as a "dastardly" deed of unprecedented "infamy," brought the United States into the war. Almost 2,400 men died, and much of the Pacific Fleet and some 300 aircraft were destroyed or badly damaged at **Pearl Harbor**. Other United States and British bases were also attacked. Germany and Italy responded to Roosevelt's denunciation by a declaration of war against the United States. The United States, on December 11, formally declared war on the Axis Powers.

For a time, the Japanese were unstoppable as neither the Americans, British, or Dutch were able to repel their attacks. Britain surrendered Hong Kong on Christmas Day, 1941. After forcing independent Thailand to accept an alliance, Japan defeated British forces in Malaya, capturing the fortress of Singapore on February 15, 1942, and then overran most of Burma. Simulta-

many places, and was sometimes welcomed as a liberator. The Western imperialists had been beaten right before the eyes of their dependents.

The Allied situation was desperate, not only in the Pacific but also in the Atlantic and in the Mediterranean as well. For awhile, more British and American ships were sunk than were being built. But American industry geared up for rapid production of ships and aircraft. Within two years, the United States had increased the number of aircraft carriers from three to fifty. Similar gains were made in other areas of war-commodity production, far exceeding expectations. The entire American economy had been mobilized and employment was again full.

Allied Victories. By mid-1942, the American naval and air forces began to defeat Japan in major battles in the Coral Sea, at Midway, and in the Solomon Islands. The Americans gained valuable experience in jungle warfare and learned how to coordinate land, sea, and air forces. Both skills played a key role in the westward island-hopping strategy of the next three years which brought the Allies closer to Japan. Meanwhile, in New Guinea, the Australians checked the Japanese advance in September 1942 and launched a counterattack with American help.

During 1943, the Americans worked out their invasion pattern in bitter campaigns in the Pacific. First came **reconnaissance** flights to take pictures of the target, followed by heavy air bombardment to destroy airfields and military installations. Then the naval task force attacked from the sea and air to wreck coastal defenses and to keep the enemy from escaping or sending in reinforcements. Finally, the invasion forces, usually headed by marines, hit the beaches from new types of landing craft. They were joined by tanks while the navy shelled and bombed ahead of the advancing troops.

The War in Europe and North Africa, 1941–1943

Germany Invades Russia. During 1941, the war expanded in Europe. The peace between Germany and Russia had always been uneasy. Both knew that they would one day be at war and worked to build up military and industrial strength. Stalin had hoped the Western powers would wear Germany down, and then Russia would attack at a crucial moment. Waiting almost proved his undoing. By 1941, Hitler had the industrial output of the whole continent at his disposal. Moreover, his armies were larger and more experienced than in 1939.

The Nazis were supremely confident that an attack on Russia would succeed. They massed the greatest invasion army in history, a force of 3 million men. Beginning in June 1941, the German *blitzkrieg* overwhelmed Soviet defenses in an assault that at times included 150 tanks per mile. The Luftwaffe destroyed hundreds of Russian planes on the ground in a surprise strike. Large segments of the Soviet army were surrounded and taken captive. The Germans occupied Kiev, the third largest city in the Soviet Union, and captured the rich agricultural and industrial Ukraine.

Hitler was so sure of victory that he ordered a cutback in arms production. Then the Russian winter, which had defeated earlier would-be conquerors, set in. Heavy rain and snow stopped the German tanks in their tracks, first turning the rough roads into a sea of mud and then freezing engines. One German column did come within 25 miles of Moscow, but on December 3 a severe

The Siege Monument, shown here, commemorates the defense of Leningrad (St. Petersburg) against the German invaders during World War II.

freeze, heavy snowfall, and Russian resistance halted the attack. Since Hitler had assumed the Soviets would be crushed within five months, he had not provided his troops with winter clothing and supplies. The Russians counterattacked on December 6 and pushed the Germans 150 miles back in some sectors.

The Soviet Union suffered huge losses, with much of its best farmland and main industrial areas under German control. Nearly 4 million Red Army soldiers had been captured. Yet the Russian system was able to absorb the shock. During the 1930s Stalin had located a large part of Russia's new industry far to the east, safe from enemy attack. The Russians profited from their enormous resources in manpower and raw materials.

In the spring of 1942, the Germans resumed their attack in the south. They planned to seize the oil fields of the Caucasus and Caspian Sea region and the coal and industry in the Don and Volga River basins. They wanted to capture the large industrial city of Stalingrad (Volgograd). Once it was taken, most of Russia's industry and resources would be in German hands and surrender would be inevitable.

The Germans reached Stalingrad in August. Stalin ordered his army to defend it to the last man. The Russians even fought in hand-to-hand combat. Then **General Georgi Konstantinovich Zhukov**, the Russian field marshal, used two armies to surround Stalingrad. They prevented the Germans from bringing in additional supplies or troops. Both sides lost hundreds of thousands of men. The Germans who survived finally surrendered.

The tide turned and Soviet forces began regaining their territory. The armies were aided by a guerrilla movement of people who were opposed to Hitler. Millions of civilians and war prisoners had perished in German labor camps. The common people discovered that Hitler was not the liberator from Stalin's repression that some had hoped he would be.

In 1942, the stage seemed set for an Axis victory. Germany would march eastward to join forces with its partner, Japan. Britain would pull out of India and the Middle East and accept Hitler's rule over Europe. The United States would come to terms with Germany and Japan and withdraw

The British Lancaster bomber was used extensively in Allied raids over Germany.

General Dwight D. Eisenhower, 1890–1969

to the Western Hemisphere. However, Allied victories on several fronts changed the setting.

North Africa. In North Africa, the Italian army had completely collapsed. Hitler sent an armored unit commanded by **Erwin Rommel** to salvage the situation. The boldest and most colorful of all the German commanders, the "Desert Fox" forced the British out of Libya in 1941. By June 1942, he was 60 miles from Alexandria and heading for the Suez Canal and the Persian Gulf. There he would cut the Allied supply line to Russia and gain control of Middle Eastern oil.

In October 1942, a British force under **General Bernard L. Montgomery** stopped the Germans at El Alamein, Egypt, and launched a counteroffensive. On November 8, a massive Anglo-American force commanded by **General Dwight D. Eisenhower** landed in Morocco and Algeria to put pressure on the Germans from the other direction. Hitler at long last poured men and material into North Africa, an action which a year before would have been decisive, but now

was too late. The German and Italian troops were bottled up in Tunisia and finally surrendered in May 1943.

Italy. The Allied armies moved quickly to knock Italy out of the war. They seized the island of Sicily in 39 days. Mussolini's popularity evaporated, and on July 25 he was overthrown and imprisoned. The king **Victor Emmanuel III**, and **Marshal Pietro Badoglio**, the conqueror of Ethiopia, took control of the government and began peace negotiations.

On September 3, the day Allied forces began landing in southern Italy, an armistice was signed. However, the Germans moved into the country and took over military operations. They rescued Mussolini from prison in a daring commando raid and installed him as puppet ruler of a Fascist republic in northern Italy. From then on, Allied progress northward in Italy was slow and bloody.

The Battle for Europe. In the rest of Europe, the Allies were also making progress. By late 1942,

Christians Under Occupation

In the Netherlands, many Reformed Christians took a stand against the Nazis who occupied their country. Some, like Corrie Ten Boom, hid Jews and escaped prisoners. Others, such as former Prime Minister Hendrik Colijn and Dr. Klaas Schilder, wrote against the German occupation. When Colijn, editor of the highly influential Christian daily newspaper, *De Standaard*, spoke out, he was arrested by the Nazis, and thrown into prison where he died in 1944. Dr. Schilder, a professor at the Theological School at Kampen, had sounded an early warning against Naziism in his book *Not One Square Inch* (1936). During the occupation he wrote many courageous articles in the church paper *De Reformatie.* He exposed Naziism and gave encouragement to Christians, stirring the spirit of resistance. This resulted in imprisonment, yet he was providentially released after five months. He wrote,

Our people in the occupied territory will not take this hour into their own hands but will place it into God's hands. Insofar as they pray, they will want to see this hour "calmed with weapons," but the weapon they will think of is the one mentioned in Revelation 11, namely, the weapon of prayer.

…Only God knows whether they [the Dutch Nazis] will be able to seize 'power' here, using their means. But we know that we will retain the 'authority.' Fortunately, power and authority are not the same thing. Ultimately, the Antichrist will have the power, and the Church will have the authority. And then will come the day of the great harvest. Come, Lord Harvester, yes, come quickly, come over the Channel and the Brenner Pass, come via Malta and Japan, yes, come from the ends of the earth, and bring Your pruning knife along, and be gracious to your people. Your people do possess authority, but only from You, from You alone, for Your eternal good pleasure.

Rudolf Van Reest, *Schilder's Struggle for the Unity of the Church*. Neerlandia, Canada: Inheritance Publications, 1990, p. 260, 271

better convoy and patrol systems reduced the U-boat threat, while a program to build ships in the United States quickly replaced those sunk. Americans then delivered vast amounts of "lend-lease" aid to Britain and the Soviet Union and built up the forces for the eventual assault on Europe.

From bases in Britain and North Africa, the British and Americans began using the German tactic of air power. They built huge four-engine bombers capable of doing far more damage than the smaller German two-motored craft. Precision bombsights, fire bombs, and gigantic missiles called "Blockbusters" completed an awesome array of weapons used during 1942–1945. The bombers hit German industrial and military targets and leveled city after city. In some places, the aerial assault was so intense that terrifying "fire storms" erupted.

The Fragile Alliance

In June 1941, Churchill and Roosevelt had agreed that the Soviet Union must be helped to resist the Germans. The two leaders felt they should lay political differences aside in the common struggle against Hitler. They also agreed on the main points of the Atlantic Charter. These were (1) territorial changes must be in keeping with the wishes of the people concerned; (2) all peoples have the right to choose the form of government under which they will live; (3) all states are to have equal access to the trade and raw materials of the world; (4) all nations will cooperate to gain improved living standards and economic and social security; (5) there must be a state of peace "after the final destruction of the Nazi tyranny" that will allow everyone to live free from fear and want; (6) all will have freedom to

travel the seas unhindered; and (7) aggressor nations are to be disarmed. Idealistic in tone, the charter was an echo of the "Fourteen Points" of Woodrow Wilson which led to the League of Nations after World War I.

The budding "united nations" alliance took more definite form on January 1, 1942. The United States, Soviet Union, Great Britain, along with 23 other countries issued a **Declaration of the United Nations** in which each nation promised to use all its resources to defeat the Axis and not to make individual peace treaties. Following this came a mutual aid pact between Britain and the Soviet Union and the extension of the "lend-lease" program to Russia. From 1942 on, the term "united nations" grew ever more popular.

Meetings of the "Big Three." By 1943, however, serious cracks had opened in the alliance. The Soviets were bearing the brunt of the German attack, and they grumbled because the western Allies would not open a "second front" in France to relieve the pressure. Churchill and Roosevelt knew a successful landing in Western Europe was impossible at this time. To reassure the suspicious Russian dictator, they relayed to Stalin the contents of a statement they had written at their two-party Casablanca Conference (January 1943) in Morocco—that the Allies would fight on until the unconditional surrender of Germany, Italy, and Japan. The statement said that the Allies would never negotiate a peace but would demand unconditional surrender from the Axis. Some historians have felt that this declaration stiffened the resistance of the Axis Powers and prolonged the war.

The Russians were unsatisfied about Allied inaction in Western Europe and even extended some peace feelers to Germany, but nothing came of these. When the three leaders—Roosevelt, Churchill, and Stalin—met at Tehran, Iran, in

The "Big Three," Churchill, Roosevelt, and Stalin at the Yalta Conference in February 1945

December 1943, Stalin was assured that the invasion would take place shortly. They discussed plans for dealing with Germany after the war.

The Americans kept putting off controversial decisions until victory was near. But Churchill realized that without some kind of prior political arrangement the war would end with Russia in control of all of Eastern Europe. On his own, he visited Stalin in October 1944 to work out an agreement. After the war, Romania and Bulgaria would be in the Soviet sphere of influence. Greece would be in the British sphere. Britain and Russia would be equal in Hungary and Yugoslavia.

Further political decisions had to be made, so in February 1945 the "Big Three" gathered at Yalta, on the Black Sea. They agreed to basic outlines on the treatment of Germany but postponed working out the details until after the surrender. The country would be divided into occupation zones, and Berlin would be occupied and admin-

istered jointly. The Soviet border was to be moved westward into Poland, which would be repaid with territory from Germany. Also, the three agreed to create a formal **United Nations** organization to implement the ideals of the Atlantic Charter and the 26-nation United Nations Declaration of 1942.

The most serious problems arose over Poland and Eastern Europe. Now 40 miles from Berlin, the Soviet army controlled all of Eastern and much of Central Europe. Remembering his past unpleasant experience with countries on his borders, Stalin wanted them under "friendly" governments. But neither of the Western leaders wanted Russia to extend totalitarian rule over this vast area. To prevent this, Churchill and Roosevelt obtained a promise from Stalin to help the freed peoples form governments "representative of all democratic elements in the population." These regimes would be pledged to establish through free elections "governments responsible to the will of the people," in the words of the written agreement. These words, however, were interpreted in several different ways. In Communist doctrine, for example, "will of the people" and "representative of all democratic elements" were terms synonymous with the "will of the Community Party."

The most controversial of the Yalta decisions was only revealed after the final victory. This had to do with East Asia. Stalin promised to enter the war against Japan within two to three months after the German surrender. In return, the Soviets were to regain the territories and rights lost to Japan in 1905.

That was the price paid for Soviet assistance against Japan. Most military experts at the time believed this would save hundreds of thousands of American lives. They did not realize how close the Japanese were to surrender (seven months) and that Russian help really was not needed.

Later it seemed apparent that the Yalta agreement had set the stage for the later Chinese Communist victory over Nationalist Chinese leader **Chiang Kai-shek** and for the **Korean War** (1950-1953). It is possible, however, that nothing but outright force could have kept Stalin from moving into Manchuria or from controlling Eastern Europe as he wished. Still, the Yalta agreement did seem to give approval of Soviet expansion.

The Road to Victory 1944–1945

The disaster in Russia and heavy Allied bombing put Germany under tremendous strain. In 1942, Hitler wanted to stage another full-scale offensive, but he did not have the equipment. The country had to use its economic resources more efficiently. To do this, Hitler appointed **Albert Speer** minister of armaments. Speer increased war production and did wonders to sidestep bureaucratic confusion, hallmark of the Nazi system. Despite the air raids, output in mid-1944 was two and one-half times greater than in 1941.

Joseph Paul Goebbels' propaganda played an important role on the German home front. He committed the people to "total war" and constantly assured them of final victory. Hitler seldom appeared in public after 1942, so his propaganda minister became the public voice of the regime, urging the people to accept more and more sacrifices.

Thanks to the watchful eye of the GESTAPO and Goebbels' propaganda machine, the German people obeyed. But some officials doubted the Führer's mental competence and moral right to lead Germany. In 1943-1944, a group of military conservatives, civilian liberals, former socialists, and religious leaders plotted to remove Hitler. Convinced that he was taking Germany to total ruin, they tried unsuccessfully to assassinate him in 1943. By mid-1944, with the GESTAPO closing in on them and the Allies pressing closer, they dared not delay any longer. They worked out a far-reaching plot to plant a bomb in the Führer's conference room and then form a non-Nazi government that would bring peace. The bomb exploded, killing several people, but somehow Hitler escaped with minor injuries. Several thousand opposition leaders were rounded up and many were tortured to horrible deaths. The Nazi tyranny over the Germans became more complete than ever, as even the army became totally submissive to the Führer's personal will.

The Normandy Invasion. The Big Three finally agreed that the invasion of Europe should take place across the English Channel. Eisenhower prepared for it carefully, but he did not underestimate German strength. He knew that the road and railway network was so good that the Germans could quickly rush reserves to the landing site. Moreover, Field Marshal Rommel had been assigned to help in this area. But Hitler's constant interference in military operations caused Germany to suffer one disaster after another. Also, the Germans had no naval forces to help turn back a sea landing, and their air force had been badly crippled in vain efforts to stop Allied bombers.

Commanded by General Eisenhower, British, Canadian, and American forces carried out the **Normandy Invasion** on the coast of France in the gray dawn of **D-Day**, June 6, 1944. During the previous night, Allied troops parachuted into France behind German lines to disrupt communications and capture vital enemy positions. Prior to the actual landing, aerial bombardment and

Allied troops and supplies are being unloaded on the Normandy beachhead during D-Day.

naval gunfire began to pound the German coastal defenses. After the German defenses had been "softened-up," troops began to land. On some beaches, soldiers met heavy enemy fire with little available cover. Allied losses were enormous, but the soldiers kept coming across the beaches, and through an area of mines and barbed wire.

Code-named "Operation Overlord," this was the largest **amphibious** operation in the history of warfare. It was a masterpiece of precision planning and coordination among the air, sea, and land forces of the three participating Allies. Some 4,000 ships and several thousand smaller craft, along with 11,000 aircraft were involved. The Allies landed 130,000 men the first day and 1 million within three weeks. The French underground provided invaluable help in their work against the Germans.

The Final Year. The Allies immediately began offensive operations in France. At first, German resistance was fierce, but the Allies were able to break-out of Normandy by late July. A second invasion force landed in southern France on August 15, and Paris was liberated on August 25 by French Resistance fighters and Free French Forces. De Gaulle, as leader of the Free French Forces, led a parade on the Champs Elysées and established a provisional government in France. By September 1944, the German army had been driven out of most of France and Belgium.

The Italian campaign, however, remained a slow and bloody movement northward. In the east, the Russians forced Finland, Romania, and Bulgaria—all German **satellites**—out of the war. When the Red Army advanced to the Vistula River near Warsaw, the Polish underground launched a full-scale revolt against the Germans. They needed and expected Russian help. However, the Russians stayed out of the conflict while the Germans put down the revolt, killing 200,000 Poles. The country's potential noncommunist leadership was destroyed. The Polish Communists later formed the postwar government.

With the surrender of Romania and Bulgaria, the Germans had to pull out of Greece. In Yugoslavia, a Communist-patriot movement under **Josip Broz Tito** had gained control of much of the country. The Russians freed the rest and then swept north into Hungary where the Germans set up a defense line that held into the winter.

Meanwhile, an Allied airborne landing behind western German lines at Arnhem, Holland, ended in defeat. Had they succeeded in their goal of capturing the Rhine bridges, they could then have launched a strike at the heart of Germany. It was clear that the Allies would have to punch their way through the German lines by land. The Allies reached the Germans' **Siegfried Line** (Germany's western border, also known as the **Westwall**), but paused because their supply lines were overextended and bad weather had set in.

By October, the American First Army, headed by **Lt. Gen. Courtney H. Hodges**, had taken their first German city, Aachen. The U.S. Third Army, under colorful **Lt. Gen. George Patton**, seized Metz on November 22. Strasbourg, on the banks of the Rhine, was taken on the next day by French forces.

Suddenly, in mid December 1944, the Germans counterattacked in Belgium and drove the Allies back 50 miles. The objective was the inland Belgian seaport of Antwerp. The fierce **Battle of the Bulge** was the last gasp of the German military. Germany lost more than 200,000 men and mas-

The Germans fired 3,200 V-2 rockets at Allied targets, killing 5,000 people, but this did not affect the outcome of the war.

sive amounts of equipment. The Allies too suffered huge casualties, making the Battle of the Bulge the second costliest military campaign (U.S. killed: 76,890) in American history (behind the Battle of the Argonne Forest in World War I). Within a few weeks the Allies recovered the lost territory and began moving into Germany. Patton's troops pushed from the south; Hodges' forces attacked from the north. The American north and south pinchers met at Houffalize on January 16, ending the Battle of the Bulge.

The Germans became desperate. In an effort to stem the Allied advance, the Germans expanded the deployment of new weapons. The world's first jet aircraft was the German Me-262. The fighter saw limited service during 1944 and 1945, in part because of a lack of adequate fuel

supplies. Perhaps the most awesome German "wonder weapons" were the jet-propelled flying bombs called the V-1 and V-2 rockets that could strike at targets hundreds of miles away. Deadly though they were, they did not stop the Allies, who drove deeper and deeper into Germany.

In January 1945, the Russians resumed their offensive. Within three months, they captured Warsaw, overran eastern Germany, occupied Budapest and Vienna, and moved into Czechoslovakia. Marshal Zhukov paused at the Oder River, regrouped his forces, and then moved in for the final assault on Berlin.

The Allies broke through the Germans' heavily fortified Siegfried Line defenses on the French border and reached the Rhine, that staunch German landmark which no army had crossed since Napoleon did so in 1806. In early March 1945, in a dramatic crossing of a lone remaining railroad bridge at Remagen, the Americans breached the barrier of the Rhine River. Allied forces poured across that bridgehead and created others, and fanned out into Germany. They continued pushing eastward, and, on April 26, American and Russian armies met at the Elbe River, about 70 miles south of Berlin.

The German defenses in northern Italy collapsed, and they surrendered on May 2. Three days earlier, Mussolini had tried to escape with his mistress to neutral Switzerland. However, they were caught and executed by antifascist guerrillas. Their bodies were hung upside down in front of a gas station.

Hitler committed suicide in Berlin on April 30, 1945, just as the Russians were about to capture the city. On the same day, American forces freed 33,000 inmates of the Dachau concentration camp. The last defenders of Berlin surrendered to Soviet soldiers two days later. On May 7, 1945, the German high command signed unconditional surrender documents at Eisenhower's headquarters in Rheims, France. The following day, May 8, the surrender was also signed at the new Soviet headquarters in Berlin. **V-E Day** (Victory in Europe) had come at last! On June 5, the Four Powers assumed supreme power in Germany.

Progress in the Pacific. In 1944, American forces moved from island to island in the Pacific—through the Marshall, Admiralty, Mariana, and Palau Islands. They knocked out the important Japanese bases and cut their supply lines. In October, MacArthur landed in the Philippines. A major battle in the Philippine Sea destroyed much of the Japanese navy. In 1945, the United States gradually took control of the Philippines, its chief Pacific possession, and conquered the islands of Iwo Jima and Okinawa. Japan began to use a new weapon, the *kamikaze* suicide plane. A pilot would deliberately crash his aircraft loaded with high explosives onto an American ship, killing himself in the process. Gunners found them

General MacArthur is shown here wading ashore at Leyete Island, keeping his promise to return to the Philippines.

almost impossible to stop, and they took a heavy toll of American lives.

On the China-Burma-India front, the Japanese still retained the initiative, launching attacks on India and southern China in 1944. However, once these Japanese assaults had been stopped, the Allies went on the offensive. Chinese troops, with American assistance, reopened the Burma Road in northern Burma in January 1945. No longer would supplies for China have to be flown over the Himalayan Mountains; they could be trucked from India into China. By the war's end, British forces had expelled the Japanese from Burma.

From China came the first bombing raid on Japan by the new "**Superfortress**" bomber, the B-29. With the capture of the Mariana Islands in late 1944, the huge bombers began regular raids on Japan. The Japanese made their houses of wood and paper. When American fire bombs hit the cities, vast areas became an inferno. The destruction was much greater than in Germany.

On July 26, 1945, the Allies sent a note to Japan threatening to destroy it totally if surrender did not come immediately. Although the home islands were now under constant air attack and Japan was almost cut off from its conquests by the American navy, **Premier Kantaro Suzuki** rejected the demand. The United States, now under the leadership of **President Harry S. Truman** (Roosevelt had died on April 12, 1945), responded with something even more terrible than the fire bombings that had reduced cities to ashes.

On August 6, 1945, a lone B-29 left its base in the Marianas with the most fearsome weapon known to mankind. The **atomic bomb** had been developed by the top-secret **Manhattan Project** and built in plants in remote areas in Tennessee,

The atomic bomb that was dropped on Nagasaki caused approximately 35,000 deaths and significant devastation.

Washington State, and New Mexico. The target was Hiroshima, a medium-sized city in southern Japan. In the ball of fire and mushroom cloud that engulfed the town, the **Atomic Age** began. Carrying more power than 20,000 tons of TNT, it destroyed three-fifths of the city and killed 78,000 people.

On August 9, a second atomic bomb was dropped on the southern town of Nagasaki. Some Japanese wanted to fight on, but **Emperor Hirohito**, on the advice of his cabinet, agreed to surrender on August 14. Their only condition, which the Allies accepted, was that the emperor would stay on as nominal head of state. On behalf of the Allies, General MacArthur accepted the Japanese surrender on the battleship U.S.S. *Missouri* in Tokyo Bay. The Second World War of the twentieth century had ended.

The Terms of Peace

The peace settlement after the Second World War was far different from the Versailles Treaty. For one thing, the Axis had been totally defeated and did not expect a negotiated peace. Second, the Allies began drifting apart even before the end of the conflict, and it was impossible for them to unite on a common policy. Third, the victors made no attempt to hold a general peace conference. The arrangements were worked out on a piecemeal basis, and it was a full quarter-century before all of these were accepted. Finally, most people were more realistic in their postwar expectations. Many recognized that the utopian dream of a world without conflict where all people had liberty probably was impossible.

The Allied leaders, nevertheless, moved in the direction of international dialogue by deciding to form the United Nations. Rooted in the 26-nation alliance of 1942, this worldwide peace-keeping body would replace the League of Nations. Representatives of 51 nations gathered in San Francisco on April 25, 1945, and adopted the **United Nations Charter**, or constitution.

Dealing with Germany. At Yalta, the Big Three had agreed to occupy Germany jointly until a final peace treaty could be made. However, they did make one definite decision—to give Germany's eastern provinces to the Soviet Union and Poland. Although these were supposed to be temporary arrangements, both countries quickly united German lands with their own.

The Japanese delegation came on board the U.S.S. Missouri for the official surrender ceremony on September 2, 1945.

The rest of Germany was divided into four zones—British, American, Soviet, and French. Berlin, located deep within the Russian zone, was also divided into four sectors. Russia guaranteed specific road, rail, canal, and air routes through its zone by which the other three could reach their sections of the capital.

It was agreed that the Four Powers could take reparations in the form of factory equipment, livestock, coal, forest products, etc. from its zone. Moreover, each would demilitarize its zone, shut down war industries, and start programs of **denazification** and reeducation of the people. Once Germany had been **rehabilitated**, the country would be reunited and its independence restored.

Much controversy arose over all of these matters, and eventually the Allies reluctantly had to accept the division of Germany into two separate countries, West Germany and East Germany, the latter under the influence of the Soviets. However, they carried out a decision to punish German leaders for "war crimes" immediately. An **International Military Tribunal** was formed to try the major Nazi leaders at Nuremberg in 1945-1946. They were convicted of three types of offenses—war crimes (illegal and inhumane actions), crimes against peace (violation of international treaties like the Locarno Pact), and crimes against humanity (slave labor and mass murders). Many leaders were sentenced to death, but Adolf Hitler, Heinrich Himmler, and Joseph Goebbels escaped the trial by committing suicide. Others fled to locations throughout the world, many hiding in Argentina. Jewish groups and agents tracked down numerous war criminals, including, in 1960, the notorious GESTAPO official **Adolf Eichmann**, who had overseen the mass extermination of Jews since 1940. An Israeli court found him guilty, and he was hanged. Pétain and Quisling were tried and sentenced to death following the war, but Pétain's sentence was changed to life imprisonment, in light of his heroic service during World War I.

Peace with German Allies. On February 10, 1947, treaties were signed with Italy, Romania, Hungary, Bulgaria, and Finland. All of them were to pay reparations, limit their armed forces, and accept changes in their boundaries. Austria was treated as a liberated country instead of an ally of Germany. Until a treaty could be drafted, the Four Powers occupied it also. It was not until 1955 that a settlement over Austria was finally reached. It restored Austrian sovereignty, barred any union with Germany, and pledged the country to permanent neutrality.

Japan was a different case. The European Allies had left matters mostly in the hands of the United States. After the surrender, the Russians took over the lands promised them at Yalta, and Korea was divided into Russian and American occupation zones. Japan gave up its colonial empire, with Formosa (Taiwan) going to China and the Pacific islands made into a U.N. trust territory under American administration. The United States occupied Japan itself, with General MacArthur in charge of setting up a democracy and demilitarizing the country.

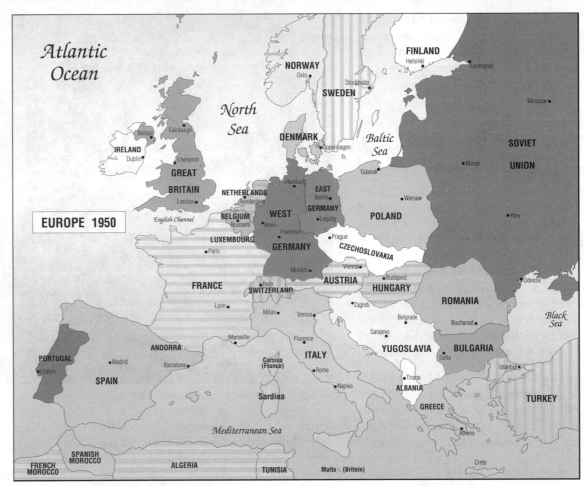

How did World War II change the map of Europe?

MacArthur revised the educational curriculum, encouraged the start of labor unions, and restored civil liberties. He introduced a new constitution in 1947 which gave all adults the right to vote and established a two-house legislature, a cabinet, and considerable local self-government. The document also abolished the state religion. Emperor Hirohito was persuaded to issue a formal statement denying the divinity which he claimed under the **Shinto** faith. MacArthur encouraged

Christian missionary work and urged American churches to send as many workers as possible. Attempts to break up the large industrial firms and redistribute land more fairly were less successful. As in Germany, several wartime leaders were tried and condemned.

The Japanese profited from growing tensions between the Soviet Union and the United States. Needing Japanese loyalty, the Americans pressed for a lenient peace settlement. The treaty signed in 1951 restored Japan's sovereignty but did not impose reparations or drastic limits on armaments. Thanks in large measure to the wise leadership of General MacArthur, the nation of Japan was set on a solid path towards prosperity.

Results of the War

Although peace had returned, the war had taken an enormous toll. Between 17 million and 18 million soldiers had been killed and at least as many civilians. Mass murders in concentration camps destroyed millions of Jews and people of other nationalities. Untold numbers of people were uprooted as 11 million war prisoners and forced laborers were brought to Germany. Nearly 8 million Germans were expelled or fled from the territories taken by Russia and Poland as well as from other areas in Central and Eastern Europe.

The bombing, shelling, and street fighting caused property damage beyond calculation. Major cities such as Berlin, Budapest, Warsaw, Kiev, Manila, Tokyo, and Osaka were reduced to rubble. Also, the war brought widespread devastation to smaller cities. In both Europe and Japan, the economies nearly stood still because of ruined factories, transportation systems, and communications networks. Farm production declined for lack of manpower, fertilizer, and equipment.

Moral Questions Involved. Nagging moral questions remained as well. The massive bombing of civilians was hard to defend. (In fact, more people were killed in a series of air raids on the city of Dresden, Germany, than in either of the two atomic attacks on Japan.) The trial of the defeated leaders for "war crimes" also raised questions. Given the nature of total war, could there be clear-cut lines between guilt and innocence?

The ruins of the Kaiser Wilhelm Church in Berlin is a reminder of the devastation caused by totalitarianism.

For example, some defendants claimed they were only following orders in committing their offenses. Was that a valid defense? This question is still debated.

Another issue was the silence or at least inaction concerning the murder of various groups of people. Western leaders knew of the plight of the Jews in Nazi Germany, but they did not raise a significant outcry. The same silence occurred at the massacres of Poles by the Soviet secret police early in the war.

Further, the alliance between democratic states and totalitarian dictatorships created serious problems. After the war, hundreds of thousands of Soviet citizens who had been German prisoners or who had sided with Hitler against Stalin were forced to return to Russia. Even though the ones who had opposed Stalin were going to almost certain death, Western leaders looked the other way. The West had to honor its treaty commitments, they said.

Finally, the Russians who opposed Stalin and the Germans who opposed Hitler bring to mind another important question. At what point must one decide that he can no longer live under tyranny and turn to armed resistance? And may one join with his nation's enemies to overthrow a brutal dictator? Is the duty to conscience greater than the duty to nationality? All of these issues haunted people after the war, and these questions are just as crucial today.

For your consideration

Questions

1. How should government leaders decide when to negotiate solutions to problems and when to respond militarily?

2. Are young people idealistic today? Give your impressions.

3. Can an international organization enforce peace?

4. It is easy to look back in time and see mistakes that were made. List actions which you consider to be mistakes in international policy, contributing to the outbreak of war.

5. How would you react if your country were conquered by an enemy government? What feelings would you have? What actions would you take? Would you join an underground resistance movement? Explain your reasons.

6. Do you think being an island has helped Great Britain throughout history? Has the airplane removed that advantage?

7. How does industry contribute to military success? Can you think of any ways that climate and weather affect warfare? Explain.

8. Evaluate Roosevelt's and Churchill's responses to the menace of Hitler.

9. How did agreements at Yalta affect the postwar developments?

10. Was it right to use the atomic bomb? Explain your answer.

Projects

1. Read one of the following books and give a brief report on it: *The Diary of a Young Girl* by Anne Frank; *The Hiding Place* by Corrie Ten Boom; *The Battle of Britain* by Quentin Reynolds; *Guadalcanal Diary* by Richard Tregaskis. Alternatively, view a film version of either of the first two books or a film on the war in the Pacific and report on it.

2. Imagine that you were one of the American soldiers taking part in the Normandy landing on D-Day. Write a letter describing the events. A helpful resource is the book *The Longest Day* by Cornelius Ryan, or the film by the same name.

3. Read Ernest Hemingway's *For Whom the Bell Tolls* and write a report. Include your own evaluation of the Spanish Civil War.

4. Find a famous speech by Churchill or Hitler and present it orally to your class or family members.

5. Do some research to find out what advance warning of the attack on Pearl Harbor had been received and why it was ignored. Do a report.

6. Do a report on the role which movies and entertainers in America played on the home front during World War II. Discuss how the war was presented and how the Germans and Japanese were characterized. How has Hollywood continued to deal with the Holocaust?

Word List

appeasement	radar
nonaggression	lend-lease
blitzkrieg	Atlantic Charter
sitzkrieg	Declaration of the U.N.
collaborated	Westwall
sabotage	Siegfried Line
Luftwaffe	Maginot Line
vulnerable	V-E Day
reconnaissance	Atomic Age
amphibious	U.N. Charter
satellites	Four Freedoms
kamikaze	Pact of Steel
Superfortress	Munich Agreement
denazification	Battle of Britain
rehabilitated	Battle of the Bulge
tribunal	Vichy government
fifth columnists	Normandy Invasion
"quisling"	D-Day

People and Groups

Neville Chamberlain	Erwin Rommel
Édouard Daladier	Hermann Göring
Winston Churchill	Joseph Goebbels
Charles De Gaulle	Adolf Eichmann
Axis Powers	Hideki Tojo
Falange	Emperor Hirohito
Francisco Franco	Joseph Stilwell
"lost generation"	Douglas MacArthur
Ernest Hemingway	George Patton
Nationalists	Courtney Hodges
Loyalists	Bernard Montgomery
Vidkun Quisling	Dwight Eisenhower
Henri Pétain	Georgi K. Zhukov
Partisans	Harry Truman
Josip Broz Tito	"Big Three"

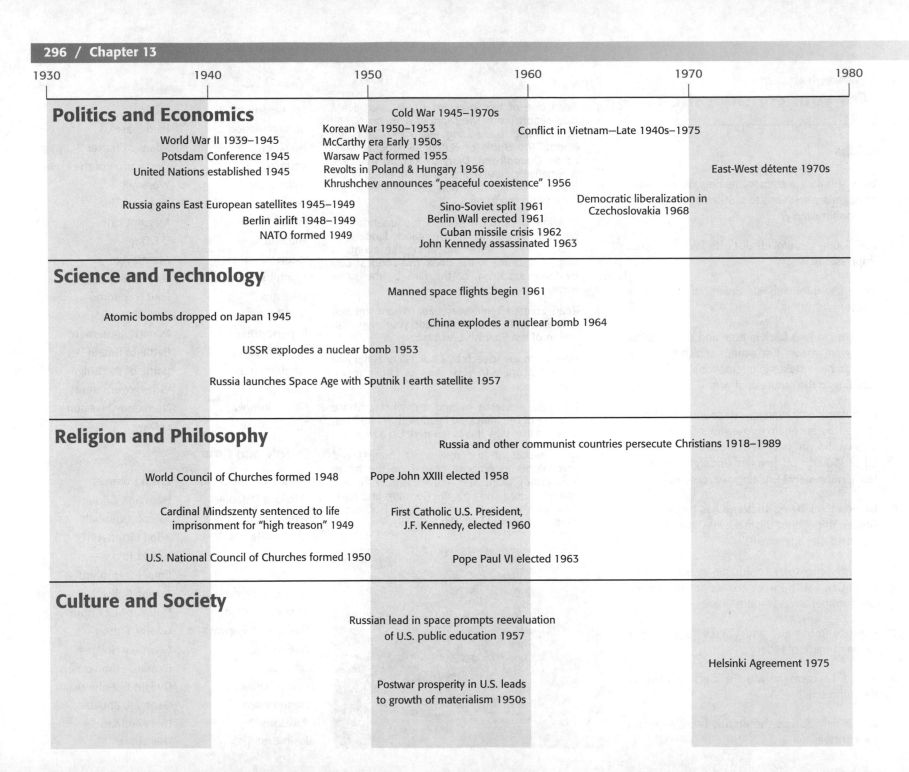

1930   1940   1950   1960   1970   1980

Politics and Economics

Cold War 1945–1970s

Korean War 1950–1953

World War II 1939–1945
McCarthy era Early 1950s
Conflict in Vietnam—Late 1940s–1975

Potsdam Conference 1945
Warsaw Pact formed 1955

United Nations established 1945
Revolts in Poland & Hungary 1956
East-West détente 1970s

Khrushchev announces "peaceful coexistence" 1956

Russia gains East European satellites 1945–1949
Democratic liberalization in
Czechoslovakia 1968

Sino-Soviet split 1961

Berlin airlift 1948–1949
Berlin Wall erected 1961

NATO formed 1949
Cuban missile crisis 1962

John Kennedy assassinated 1963

Science and Technology

Manned space flights begin 1961

Atomic bombs dropped on Japan 1945
China explodes a nuclear bomb 1964

USSR explodes a nuclear bomb 1953

Russia launches Space Age with Sputnik I earth satellite 1957

Religion and Philosophy

Russia and other communist countries persecute Christians 1918–1989

World Council of Churches formed 1948
Pope John XXIII elected 1958

Cardinal Mindszenty sentenced to life
imprisonment for "high treason" 1949
First Catholic U.S. President,
J.F. Kennedy, elected 1960

U.S. National Council of Churches formed 1950
Pope Paul VI elected 1963

Culture and Society

Russian lead in space prompts reevaluation
of U.S. public education 1957

Helsinki Agreement 1975

Postwar prosperity in U.S. leads
to growth of materialism 1950s

13

The Confrontation with Communism

The year 1945 was a great turning point in world history—the end of the European age. From the time Christianity first began to impact the Roman Empire until the end of World War II, Europe had dominated the developing streams of civilization, making Westernism the **linchpin** of world culture. On the fringes of war-torn Europe two superpowers had arisen—the United States and the Union of Soviet Socialist Republics. The United States, of course, was a thoroughly Western nation with a culture deeply rooted in European tradition. The U.S.S.R., despite Russia's longtime interest in Western ways, was not fundamentally in the Western political or cultural tradition. The U.S.S.R.'s new communist ideology was born in Europe, but it had an international vision; and the Soviets found it most expedient to extend that vision in areas of the world where Western culture and religion were weakest. At about the same time, the United States' intellectual and political leadership was beginning to come under the spell of the same globalist ideology, although the heart of the American electorate was still substantially committed to Westernism, democratic idealism, and its own national interests.

Perhaps more significant than ideology, however, was the factor of power. Both superpowers had demonstrated their prowess in World War II, and they soon locked horns in a mighty struggle for

Karl Marx, and the Worker and Farmer Monument in Moscow

global leadership. As the hostility between the two deepened, people began to speak of a "cold war" and worried that it might suddenly erupt into a "hot" or violent war. By 1949, the two superpowers had formed their separate "blocs" and divided the world into two spheres of influence.

The division can be said to have had its beginning at the Yalta Conference (see last chapter) at which Roosevelt, Churchill, and Stalin discussed how the eventual victors in the war would divide up Germany and its European conquests. The general outline prepared at Yalta was finalized in the **Potsdam Conference** (July–August 1945),

attended by the new U.S. president, **Harry S. Truman**, along with Stalin and Churchill (later replaced by new British **Prime Minister Clement Attlee**). The Potsdam agreement divided Germany and its capital, Berlin, into four occupation zones and gave most of Eastern Europe over to Polish and Russian administration. Winston Churchill described the situation in vivid terms when he said in 1946, "From Stettin in the Baltic to Trieste in the Adriatic, an **iron curtain** has descended across the Continent."

Nature of the 'Cold War'

The Cold War can be characterized in several different ways—a policy of **isolation** on the part of the Eastern power bloc, and **confrontations** between the two superpowers, some of which have been in arguments at the United Nations and others in revolutionary-military encounters around the world.

Isolation. Eastern European countries were controlled by the Russian army at the end of World War II. Therefore, the Soviet Union was responsible for them until peace treaties were signed. Local communist leaders were able to take part in forming new governments. They often held key posts, and also prevented anticommunists from voting. "People's democracies" were set up, and

The United States and Great Britain flew urgently needed supplies into West Berlin during the Soviet blockade.

any who opposed the new policies were forced into exile or purged.

By the end of 1946, Poland, Romania, and Bulgaria had been converted into communist dictatorships. Hungary followed in 1947 and Czechoslovakia in 1948. Albania and Yugoslavia were also under communist rule, but their leaders portrayed themselves as independent of the Soviet Union. Stalin began to purge Eastern European patriots in 1947, but Yugoslavia's Marshal **Josip Tito** managed to avoid the purges. Following Stalin's death, Tito and Soviet leader **Nikita Khrushchev** began secret negotiations toward a reconciliation. The reconciliation was interrupted when Yugoslav leaders expressed sympathy for uprisings in Hungary and Poland in 1956 and criticized Stalinist tendencies among other communist leaders in Eastern Europe. Within a year, however, a complete reconciliation between Tito and the Soviets was achieved, but it was not publicly revealed. This was because Tito and other communist leaders had devised a plan of disinformation to deceive the West and bolster

the Eastern bloc's lackluster pace of development. Tito boldly declared Yugoslavia a Marxist state, but one free from Soviet control. The plan paid off. Tito gained promises of help from Western countries eager to see the Eastern bloc split up. Through Yugoslavia, Western aid and technology was filtered into the Soviet bloc. The "independence" ploy worked so well to deceive the West that similar disinformation strategies were devised with regard to Romania and China, as well as China's supposed ally, Albania.

Meanwhile, in 1949, the Soviet eastern zone of Germany became a communist "republic." Germany was again divided. Only Finland was allowed to become a neutral democratic state, possibly because the Soviets feared that a communist takeover there would push socialist Sweden, which had remained neutral during the war, into the Western camp. An international organization called the **Cominform** (Communist Information Bureau) handled affairs of the people's democracies. They were isolated from the free world.

Germany was the scene of several Cold War conflicts. The Allies had pledged to follow a joint occupation policy and treat the country as one unit. But soon they began to disagree over reparations, economic recovery, and forms of government.

In 1948, the Soviets refused to go along with the currency reform which the Western Allies had implemented in their zones and decided to extend to Berlin. The Soviets closed all overland routes to the capital. They assumed that the West would either give in to their demands or pull out of Berlin completely. Instead Allied transport planes brought food, fuel, and other necessities into West Berlin for nine months. The action became known as the **Berlin Airlift**. Finally, the highway to Berlin was reopened. Strong tensions

The Berlin Airlift

Only three minutes apart, the transport planes landed with their loads of supplies. With this split-second timing, a pilot had to carefully calculate his landing. If he misjudged, he had to go all the way back to home base and start over. That this schedule could be kept was even more amazing in view of the fact that West Berlin's Tempelhof Airport had no radar or other modern landing equipment.

Some of the pilots began working with the airlift on the night shift. The first time they drew a day shift they were horrified when they saw the approach to the airport. Jagged ruins of bombed buildings lined the path. Added to this hazard was the occasional buzzing of Russian planes and jamming of electronic equipment.

At first, the Soviet blockade seriously affected West Berlin. Without power or raw materials several thousand factories had to close. Unemployment soared to 150,000. Food was scarce and money to buy it even scarcer. Therefore, when shipments of vegetable seeds arrived, Berliners snapped them up. Little gardens appeared all over the city.

As time went on, the airlift developed ever greater efficiency. Finally, the planes were able to bring in as much as West Berlin had received before the blockade. Factories and businesses reopened and the city functioned normally. At that point, the Russians gave up.

The barriers opened and all West Berlin rejoiced. Flowers decorated the first trains to chug into the city. Schools closed and the children sang and danced in the streets. Hugs and kisses greeted the drivers of the first trucks.

During the airlift, 2.3 million tons of supplies came into Berlin on nearly 278,000 flights. The price tag was half a billion dollars. The United States paid the largest part of this sum, but Britain and the Berliners also paid a share. The Berlin Airlift was a major victory for the West in the Cold War.

remained between the two parts of Germany for years.

One of the most obvious examples of isolation was the **Berlin Wall**. This structure was erected by East Germany in 1961 in an attempt to shore up the shaky regime. Dividing the free and communist sides of the city, it was designed to keep skilled labor and freedom seekers from escaping to the West through West Berlin. It was also designed to protect the weak currency by cutting off economic interchange with the West and to prevent democratic ideas from entering the country.

Western nations, particularly the United States, launched a massive effort to broadcast accurate world news and cultural information by radio from Western points into the isolated countries. **Radio Free Europe** and **Radio Liberty** were among the best such enterprises and were credited for having a major role in the discontent that led to the eventual collapse of the communist regimes. Before that collapse, however, **Radio Moscow** and its various counterparts in Eastern Europe tried to counter with worldwide broadcasts of communist propaganda.

Persecution of Christians Intensifies. As the communist regimes of Eastern Europe tried to prevent access to Western literature and ideas, they gave special attention to the Christian religion. Churches had special problems; they were consistently infiltrated with government spies, and authorities often installed agents into church offices. It was difficult to get Bibles, hymnbooks, and other religious books. Some people were jailed and even tortured because they openly professed belief in God and taught others, in defiance of the officially sanctioned atheism. Some were subjected to ghastly psychological experiments, and thousands were denied education, adequate housing, and other essentials of life.

Christians in Russia

The Communist policy on religion changed with changing times. In the early days, there were massive purges of church members, partly because the Russian Orthodox Church had been a partner in corrupt czarist politics. Then too, Marxists felt that religion hindered their cause.

Communist leaders believed that they could destroy Christianity by persecution. They tore down churches or used them for granaries or stables. Great patriotic rallies were scheduled during the usual church hours. All faithful Communists, and particularly the youth, were expected to attend the rallies. This left only a few elderly folk to attend church. But home prayer and Bible study groups sprang up all over Russia. The church actually became stronger. Giving up the plan to destroy Christianity, party leaders then tried to regulate it.

Some Christian groups in Russia felt that the government controls made it impossible to practice their religion in the manner they thought was right. They refused to comply with the regulations and were considered illegal. Many leaders and members were imprisoned. The government made it difficult for Christians to obtain schooling and get jobs. Yet the believers kept their faith despite great hardship.

Hundreds lost their lives in exile, prisons, or concentration camps. Some church properties were seized by the governments and used as museums or destroyed. One of the most compelling stories of brutality has been told by former Romanian pastor **Richard Wurmbrand**, in his book *Tortured for Christ*. Even high-ranking Roman Catholic officials, including **Cardinal Joseph Mindszenty** in Hungary and **Archbishop Stepinac** in Yugoslavia, were imprisoned. Mindszenty had been a critic of the Nazis and spent years in prison for his opposition. When he began criticizing the communists, he was charged with treason and sent to prison again, where he stayed until the brief revolt occurred in Hungary in 1956. He took refuge in the U.S. legation when the revolt was brutally suppressed with the aid of Soviet tanks.

Small numbers of courageous Western Christians began smuggling Bibles, Christian literature, and relief goods to their brethren in communist countries. Since borders had been sealed off, such couriers ran the risk of discovery at customs checkpoints, but many attested to a seeming miraculous ability to penetrate the Iron Curtain with the Gospel. Among the leaders in this effort was a Dutchman who went by the code name **Brother Andrew**, founder of an organization known as **Open Doors**. Meanwhile, persecution seemed to intensify the faith of Christians in communist lands, although their isolation tended to deprive them of needed spiritual training.

Midnight Easter Service at Joy of All Sorrows Church, Moscow

Confrontation at the United Nations. The founders of the U.N. presented its main function as keeping international peace. Organizationally, it was nearly a carbon copy of the League of Nations. Unlike the League of Nations, it could provide peacekeeping forces voluntarily supplied by its members. These would operate under the U.N. flag. Because the U.N. depended on its member states for financial support and the great powers had veto power, its peacekeeping effectiveness was blunted from the very beginning. Also, it could not legally interfere in the internal affairs of sovereign nations—including civil wars and domestic revolts. It did, however, provide a forum where all nations could air their views on important questions. Disputing nations could quickly gain the services of a U.N. consultant or a mediator.

The Soviet Union saw the U.N. as a potential tool for its international agenda. It filled its delegations with trained espionage agents and influenced or infiltrated enough **"Third World"** delegations to give its perspective a majority position within the body. The U.N. tried to control the use of atomic power, to disarm nations of the world, to create an international police force, and to secure withdrawal of occupation troops in ex-enemy countries. Many measures fell victim to the Soviet veto when they threatened the U.S.S.R.'s revolutionary and expansionist plans. By the end of 1950, the Russians had blocked Security Council action some 50 times. When they were dissatisfied with Council discussions of Cold War issues, the Soviet delegates often boycotted its meetings, sometimes remaining away for weeks. Although the Cold War hindered U.N. effectiveness, the organization dabbled in a number of projects that did not touch on great-power interests. Most of this activity came in the areas of decolonization, cultural and economic matters, and definition of so-called human rights.

Youth Revolt in Hungary

It began as a peaceful demonstration, up to the wooden gates of the radio station in Budapest. Citizens joined the students as they progressed through the streets. A high Communist Party official faced the expectant throng and denied their demands. Some of the students started shouting and pushing angrily. Alarmed, the secret police began firing into the unarmed mass of people, panicking the crowd. A demonstration had turned into a revolution.

Obtaining weapons from the army depots and munitions factories, the Hungarians drove Soviet troops out of the city. Political prisoners were set free. Local councils formed throughout the country, replacing the Communist Party organization. Workers went on strike. Many police and army units joined with the people. The uprising was spontaneous. No primary leader gave directions or planned and coordinated overall efforts.

The most remarkable group among the freedom fighters were the youth. Teenage boys and girls, in an uneven battle with Soviet tanks, devised ingenious and creative methods of stopping the rumbling giants. They hung pans filled with water on overhead tram cables. Mistaking these for antitank weapons, tank drivers stopped. In that moment, people at the windows above threw down grenades and homemade gasoline bombs. Young people covered one city square with silk cloth which they had taken from one of the shops. After spreading it out, they poured oil on it. When the tanks tried to cross, they simply spun their tracks, becoming perfect targets for bombs. In another city square, liquid soap spread over the area had the same effect. As the tanks wallowed helplessly, youngsters dashed up to them beneath the line of fire and smeared their windows with jam.

But bravery was not enough to combat Soviet military might. The Hungarian revolt produced many heroes, but not freedom. Russian forces quickly put down the uprising. But it had exposed the brutal face of communism to the world and invalidated the Soviet claim that its satellites were communist by choice. And the Hungarian revolt demonstrated that years of oppression cannot destroy the desire for freedom.

Though it spent and continues to spend millions of dollars on such activities, little of a positive nature has been accomplished.

Military Confrontations. From time to time, the Western powers responded directly to communist military action as in the Korean and Vietnam wars (see chapter 14). Communist-inspired revolts also took place in many countries which had recently gained independence. On some occasions, the Soviet Union used force in its own satellite countries. In 1956, for instance, riots broke out in Poland and anti-Soviet feelings spread rapidly. The central committee of the Polish Communist Party tried to regain the people's support by appointing **Wladyslaw Gomulka** as party secretary. He had been jailed for a short time after a purge in 1949. Khrushchev threat-ened to send troops, but Gomulka convinced the Soviets that Poland would remain loyal to the communist alliance, the **Warsaw Pact**. Following the "Polish path to socialism," Gomulka had broad public and church backing. He halted further efforts to form collective farms, reduced police terror, and allowed a somewhat freer intellectual atmosphere.

Only a few days after the Polish success, the Hungarians revolted. The moderate Communist, **Imre Nagy**, had returned to power and granted the people's demands, even freeing Cardinal Mindszenty. However, students and workers demanded a democratic regime and an end to ties with Moscow. When Nagy withdrew from the Warsaw Pact, seven Red Army divisions marched into the country. As the wave of tanks and troops rolled over Budapest, Western nations did nothing. In a few days it was all over. Though Hungary had requested Western help, giving that aid probably would have resulted in World War III.

More than a decade later, the Russians again demonstrated that freedom of thought and action within the Soviet bloc was still limited. In January 1968, **Alexander Dubcek** became party leader in Czechoslovakia. His attempts to grant more freedom there aroused fears in Moscow. So in August, 250,000 troops from the Soviet Union, East Germany, and other Warsaw Pact members marched into the country. The Soviets forced the Czech government to restore press censorship, allow the stationing of Russian troops, and remove Dubcek. Some years later, a Soviet intelligence agent who defected to the West claimed, with considerable documentation, that the 1968 Czech "democratization" movement had also been a disinformation ploy to consolidate support for long-range communist-bloc strategies against the West which Dubcek and other Czech "progressives" had actually helped devise.

Western Cold War Strategy

Western nations led by the United States followed several different policies to prevent the dominance of communism throughout the world. In the late 1940s, they used the policy of **containment**. This was the belief that the Russians would withdraw when faced with firm barriers. Containment of Russian aggression did not mean threats, bluffing, or tough talk, but rather meeting force with force at each strategic point. Under this kind of strain, the Soviet regime

Soviet soldiers at the Red Square, Moscow

would eventually either break up internally or change its ways, it was hoped.

The Truman Doctrine. The first move toward containment came in Greece. A communist revolt against the democratically elected government was supported by neighboring countries and apparently had Stalin's blessings. Because of a postwar economic crisis, Britain had withdrawn its troops after the Greek election and could not afford to send any help. Other European nations were also close to financial collapse.

President Truman offered aid to Greece and Turkey, which was also feeling Soviet pressure. In a speech to Congress on March 12, 1947, he laid down the **Truman Doctrine**. There will be no lasting peace, he declared, unless we are willing to help free peoples keep their free institutions and their independence. Aggressive movements that try to impose totalitarian regimes on other countries undermine both international peace and the

security of the United States. He urged Congress to vote economic aid to Greece and Turkey. The Americans quickly scraped together enough men for military missions to Greece and Turkey to train their armed forces. Financial aid followed.

The Marshall Plan. The Truman Doctrine was the political part of containment. A line had been drawn beyond which communist power could not go. The economic part was the **Marshall Plan**, a scheme for European recovery announced by **Secretary of State George C. Marshall** in June 1947.

Europe was economically ruined by the war and recovery came slowly. Two harsh winters had drained relief supplies; production sagged; inflation soared out of control; savings had been wiped out, and living standards remained low. Large communist parties attracted workers in France, Belgium, and Italy. Because communism fed on economic woes, many feared that the Western democracies would fall under its control.

Marshall, former U.S. army chief of staff, offered large-scale American aid to all European countries on condition that they draw up a joint plan to put Europe's economy back on its feet. Even Russia was included, but it refused the offer and forced its satellites to do likewise. Between 1948 and 1952, sixteen noncommunist nations received more than $13 billion in American aid.

The Marshall Plan was a spectacular success. Communist strength in Italy and France declined, and stability returned to war-torn Western Europe. By 1952, industrial production exceeded prewar levels in many countries. Depression and inflation were lessening.

NATO. The military part of containment was a series of alliances. In 1949, a dozen Western nations, including Canada and the United States, formed the **North Atlantic Treaty Organization**

(NATO). The signers agreed that an armed attack upon one would be considered an attack on all, regardless of whether it came in Europe or North America. All would resist by whatever action necessary, "including armed force."

The United States provided most of the equipment and funds for NATO, and member countries contributed units to the joint military forces. West Germany was allowed to form a national army under NATO supervision and join the Western alliance. Similar but less effective mutual defense agreements were set up in the Middle East (**Central Treaty Organization [CENTO],** 1955) and Southeast Asia (**Southeast Asia Treaty Organization [SEATO],** 1954).

Soviet Response. The Soviets tried to bind the East European satellites closer to Moscow. In January 1949, Stalin set up **COMECON (Council for Mutual Economic Assistance),** his own version of the Marshall Plan. The Soviets also had an answer to NATO and the rearmament of West Germany—the **Warsaw Pact** (1955). A mutual defense treaty between Moscow and its satellites, the Pact was supposed to protect Eastern European countries from West German militarism. But it also gave an excuse to station Red Army troops on their soil. Politically, economically, and militarily, Europe had now split into two competing blocs.

Major Powers in the Postwar Period

United States. The United States emerged from World War II as the wealthiest and most powerful nation in history. To everyone's surprise, a postwar depression did not occur. Instead, the returning veterans entered the labor market and

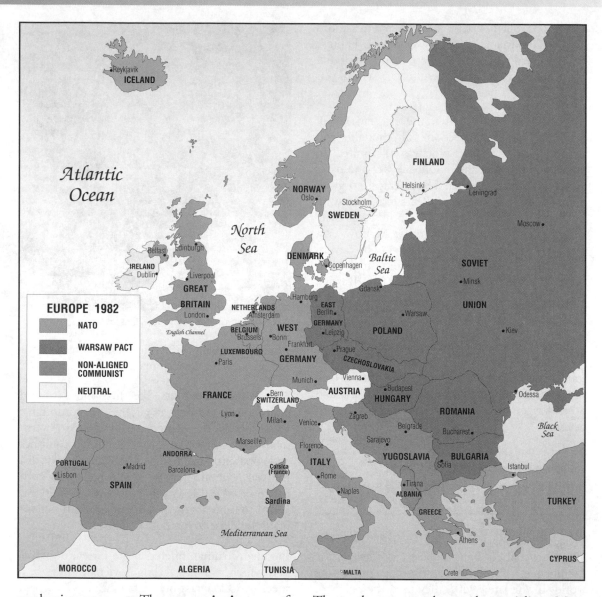

production rates rose. The ***per capita*** income of Americans almost doubled in the first ten years. By 1970, America had only 6 percent of the world's population, but it owned and produced nearly one-half of the world's wealth.

The result was a trend toward materialism. More than ever, owning new homes, cars, and countless gadgets spelled success. Family life and community ties weakened as Americans joined the search for wealth and pleasure. Divorce, juvenile delinquency, and crime rates increased as people tried

McCarthyism and American Communists

On February 9, 1950, an unknown first-term senator from Wisconsin gave a speech in West Virginia. He held up a list of what he said were the names of Communists "working and making policy" in the State Department. That speech made headlines. For the next five years, McCarthy stories appeared in the headlines of major newspapers every week. His continuing charges of Communist infiltration shocked and frightened the American people.

The senator established files on "suspected Communists" and on many who opposed him. Using this information, he attacked the individuals through the press. His critics alleged that the charges were often unfair or based on half-truths, and implied guilt by association. Nevertheless, he succeeded in destroying the reputations of a number of his critics, and some of his colleagues consequently lost elections. After that, criticism from the Senate all but stopped.

McCarthy's attacks were so successful that he became one of the most powerful men in America. For several years, government officials in both the Truman and the Eisenhower administrations made no major decision without considering how McCarthy might react. After a bruising fight over an appointment, the Republican majority leader in the Senate told President Eisenhower that he would never again battle for an appointment McCarthy opposed.

McCarthy even went so far as to accuse the Truman and Eisenhower administrations of treason. He called General of the Army George C. Marshall "a man steeped in falsehood." Marshall was part of a "conspiracy so infamous, so immense, and an infamy so black as to dwarf any previous venture in the history of man." Businessmen, journalists, and politicians feared the senator. Manufacturers were afraid his supporters would boycott their goods.

Some of the issues were aired in spectacular televised hearings. One writer called them the greatest political show on earth.

to "keep up with the Joneses" and searched for happiness in ways other than through true, biblical faith.

At the same time the welfare state appealed to more and more people. The social security, public housing, and minimum wage legislation of the New Deal era became a permanent part of society and expanded under the Truman and Eisenhower administrations. As organized labor operated under the umbrella of official recognition and legal protection, trade unions and collective bargaining increased.

Concern over the possibility of a communist plot to undermine the United States was widespread; some of the concern was well founded as Soviet espionage and the use of **agents of influence** increased. In 1950, a sensational spy case fed that concern. American communists **Julius and Ethel Rosenburg** were arrested as amateur spies who had sold U.S. atomic-weapons secrets to the U.S.S.R. in the mid-1940s. Partisans of the Rosenburgs charged that they were victims of Cold War hysteria and anti-Semitism. Following a much-publicized trial, the Rosenburgs, still maintaining they were framed, were executed. The judge who sentenced them to death called their alleged crimes "worse than murder," and blamed them for the Korean conflict and the predicted deaths of millions who might fall in a Soviet nuclear attack. Defenders argued that their death sentence was illegal, since their activities took place during a time when the Soviet Union was actually a wartime ally of the United States. In the years that followed this case, the attorney general's office prepared lists of **subversive** organizations; public employees were required to sign loyalty oaths. Other espionage trials took place.

Amid this general uproar, Wisconsin **Senator Joseph McCarthy** launched a sometimes excessive crusade to root out alleged Communists in the State Department and other high places. Anyone who opposed nuclear war or McCarthy or held liberal ideas became suspect. Many Americans agreed with McCarthy, and his investigations did uncover several sources of substantial threat, as well as sources of leftist influence in America. One of McCarthy's major thrusts was against leftists in the Hollywood entertainment industry. But some people worried that his "witch-hunting" tactics (which became known as **McCarthyism**) were turning the country into a police state. Eventually his fellow senators condemned his activities, and the public lost interest in exposing communist movements.

USSR. The Soviet Union emerged from World War II much weaker than America because it had suffered such an enormous loss of life (more than 20 million) and property. In order to rally the people behind the war effort, Stalin had relaxed some controls. Most notably, he allowed church organizations to function again and granted the Orthodox and Protestant churches legal status. Once the fighting ended, however, he again lowered the full weight of Soviet totalitarianism on the people. The secret police ruthlessly purged the areas in western Russia that had been under German occupation, swelling the population of forced labor camps to ten million or more.

As rigid rule returned, life in Russia became as harsh and drab as before. Every effort went into rebuilding industry, and by 1950 output had reached the prewar level. But increased taxes and demands for food production oppressed the rural people.

The Russian dictator tightened the screws on his satellite empire as well. While exploiting them economically, he brooded about their loyalty. Sta-

The exercise of Soviet power is from its seat of power in the Kremlin, the former center of Russian Orthodoxy.

lin knew that the East European peoples had never chosen communism. They had been brought into the Soviet orbit by the schemes and actions of communist minorities, and they posed a constant threat to his rule. He mounted another wave of purges between 1949 and 1952. These included the usual mass arrests, **expulsions** from the party, and public trials where people confessed to imaginary "crimes against the people." The purges spread to Russia, where Stalin trusted no one, not even his closest friends.

Great Britain. In Great Britain, a stunning election upset toppled Churchill's Conservative Party in July 1945. The socialist Labour Party leader, Clement Attlee, took over and began a program to **nationalize** (put under government control or ownership) key industries and to extend social services. The Bank of England, public utilities, communications, coal mines, iron and steel industries, railroads, and motor transportation came under public ownership. Since this was only a small portion of British industry, what emerged was not pure socialism but a kind of mixed economy. The Labour government also started a "cradle-to-grave" social insurance system, topped off by the National Health Service

which made medical care available to all regardless of ability to pay.

Economically, Britain was in considerable trouble because it depended so heavily upon foreign trade for survival, and its empire was rapidly vanishing. The government adopted a strict **austerity** program of high taxes, rationing, and controls on imports, foreign exchange, and travel abroad. Unhappy with these measures, the British voted Churchill back into power in 1951. A few industries returned to private control, but the social security and health insurance program remained unchanged. In the 1950s, American aid, an increase in British exports, and economic cooperation with Europe helped Britain to become more prosperous than in the interwar years.

France. In France, **Charles De Gaulle** took charge of the rebuilding but resigned in January 1946 in frustration. Struggles among the many political parties brought one government after another to power. Seemingly, little could be done to bring stability, as the constitution had given more power to the legislative branch than the executive. Also the regime leaned to the left, even though the Communist Party was losing strength. At one point it had been the largest party.

Substantial change, both social and economic, took place, however. Like Britain, France nationalized a number of key industries and received American aid. The French began central planning, which helped to modernize the economy in the short term. Although spectacular growth took place in the 1950s, colonial wars in Vietnam and Algeria drained the country's resources and brought it to the verge of civil war. Finally, in 1958, as public favor shifted to the political right, De Gaulle returned to power and formed the **Fifth Republic.** He built up executive authority and restored a political stability unknown in the

Fourth Republic, which in its 14-year history had had 25 premiers.

Italy. Prosperity returned to the former Axis Powers as well. Italy abolished the monarchy in 1946, and it seemed at first that the Communist Party might gain power in the republic. But in the first election under the new democratic constitution in April 1948, the moderate **Christian Democratic Party** gained the upper hand. Supported by the Roman Catholic Church, this party had a capable leader in **Alcide De Gasperi**, who led the government from 1945 to 1953. During this period came the beginning of an economic boom. By the end of the 1950s, growth rates rivaled those of France and Germany, but a major problem remained unsolved. The poverty of the underdeveloped south contrasted sharply with the well-being of the industrial north, creating resentment among the poor.

West Germany. The most remarkable development occurred in West Germany. The Liberals and Socialists united to create a lasting democracy, something Germans had never been able to do in the past. The **Social Democratic Party** (socialist) and a new party, the **Christian Democratic Union**, both pursued a policy of alignment with the West. The Christian Democrats put their first chancellor into office in 1949. In the hands of the 73-year-old **Konrad Adenauer** rested the fortunes of the new **Federal Republic.**

A strong-willed, patriarchal personality, the shrewd and realistic Adenauer served as chancellor for 14 years. He sought close ties with Western Europe, especially with France, and worked for European political and economic cooperation. Any solution to the question of reuniting Germany he left for the future. Under Adenauer's direction West Germany began to play a role in international affairs. The country strengthened NATO, resisted Soviet policy in Eastern Europe, and stood firm against East Germany. Through Adenauer's efforts West Germany became a major partner in the Western alliance.

Ludwig Erhard, Adenauer's economics minister (and the next chancellor, 1963-1966) directed the rebuilding of West German industry. Through a combination of German ingenuity, hard work, the 1948 currency reform, and Marshall Plan aid, Germany became the leading industrial power of Europe. Unlike Britain and France, West Germany did not nationalize its industry, but the government did give aid through careful economic planning and the lowering of trade barriers.

West Germany joined several European economic organizations (discussed later in this chapter) and by the 1990s, its economic dominance threatened to overpower those organizations.

The Cold War Stalemate
1952–1955

During the early months of the **Korean War** (1950–1953), which was characterized as a United Nations "police action" to settle a violent conflict between communist North Korea and democratic South Korea, President Truman and **Secretary of State Dean Acheson** added more muscle to the containment policy. In order to negotiate from strength with the Communist bloc, they built up armaments including nuclear weapons. The idea was to make the United States so strong that the communists would back down from their campaign to conquer the world and perhaps even set their satellite countries free. But military containment failed to bring freedom to the captive peoples of Europe or unity to Korea and Germany.

Changes in the Cold War Policy. Critics of Truman called this a defeatist approach that only upheld the status quo. President Eisenhower's secretary of state, **John Foster Dulles**, stated that containment was a "cringing policy of the fearful" and proclaimed a new doctrine of "**liberation**." Only unrelenting political, economic, and psychological pressure could peacefully free the Soviet satellites.

The problem with liberation was that no one knew how to carry it out. Thus, when the East Berlin workers rebelled against Soviet rule in June 1953, the United States stood by helplessly. Its small force in West Berlin was no match for the Red Army tanks that brutally crushed the upris-

Visitor's pay homage to Lenin at his tomb in the Red Square.

Red Square, Moscow, with Lenin's tomb in the foreground and the Kremlin in the background

ing. The 1956 revolt in Hungary also showed the liberation policy to be toothless.

Later Dulles shifted his emphasis to "instant and massive **retaliation**." America threatened to use nuclear weapons against future communist aggression. Willingness to go to the "brink of war," if necessary, was to Dulles part of the fine art of foreign policy. He used the threat of atomic attack successfully several times. Both the United States and the Soviet Union tested hydrogen bombs. They developed fleets of bombers to deliver their atomic weapons and reasonably effective early warning systems to guard against enemy attack. They also experimented with long-range guided missiles with nuclear warheads. This race created a balance of terror. Both nations knew a hot war might easily turn into a holocaust.

When Stalin died in 1953, the news sent shock waves around the world. First **Georgi Malenkov** and then **Nikolai Bulganin** became premier of the Soviet Union. However, the real power was now in the hands of **Nikita Khrushchev**, the Communist Party secretary. He was one of the few genuine common people among the communist elite. Still, he was a tough realist who had shown his own ruthlessness by helping carry out Stalin's purges in the Ukraine during the 1930s, purges which he later denounced as crimes.

Attempts at Peaceful Coexistence, 1956–1963

The initiative lay with the Soviets during the later 1950s and early 1960s. They made the new moves, sent the **ultimatums**, and created the crises. Western statesmen usually just reacted to Soviet moves, especially after Dulles's influence

Nikita Khrushchev, 1894–1971

began to fade in 1957. They stumbled from one crisis to the next because their thinking was purely defensive. By now the West seemed to accept the division of Europe into spheres of influence. Soviet leaders, however, took every opportunity to enlarge their sphere. A worldwide Soviet empire began to develop through Marxist revolutions in numerous places.

The Western hesitancy is not hard to explain. In time of peace, democracies always act more slowly than dictatorships. The Americans had to give more attention to their allies' views than the Russians did to their satellites. Also, national interests in Western countries carried more weight than international ones. Some people felt that Stalin's death had ended the Cold War. Others blamed the West for the worsening conditions in Russia after 1945 or claimed that there was no Cold War. They said it was only a myth created by the "military-industrial complex" to put down

"liberation movements" around the world and sell military hardware.

In 1956, at the Twentieth Party Congress, Khrushchev unveiled a new policy—"**peaceful coexistence**." Communist victory would come, not through military might or even the gospel of Marx and Lenin, but through the superior technology and productivity of the Soviet Union. As part of this policy, Khrushchev announced that he would accept the neutrality of the new nations of Asia and Africa. Since Khrushchev's idea of coexistence still left a little room to use force in the non-Western world, he kept alive the threat of nuclear destruction. The Russians (or their satellites) began arming guerrilla movements throughout the world which were carrying out "wars of national liberation." They gave economic and military aid to newly independent countries, urging them to express their grievances against Western "imperialism."

At the Twentieth Congress, Khrushchev also denounced the "crimes" of Stalin. Case by case, he told of the torture and murder of loyal party members. Khrushchev acted partly to consolidate his personal control, but his confession did give a new face to the Soviet Union and improved the regime's image at home and abroad.

Trouble in the Middle East. At this point Khrushchev chalked up a major victory in the Middle East. In July 1956, the Egyptian leader, **Gamal Abdel Nasser**, outraged the British by taking over the Suez Canal. Haunted by memories of past appeasement policies, British **Prime Minister Anthony Eden** decided on military intervention. British forces struck in the Sinai region, together with the French and Israelis (Israel had become a nation in 1948). Khrushchev backed Nasser and threatened to use Soviet missiles against Paris and London if the troops were not withdrawn.

The Americans preferred not to join their NATO allies in what seemed to be old-fashioned imperialism. Still they did not want a Russian Cold War triumph. They turned to the U.N., which persuaded the three countries to pull out of Egypt. But in order to keep the Soviets from profiting from their "defense" of Egypt, the Americans took a more determined stand. Eisenhower announced that the United States was "prepared to use armed force" anywhere in the Middle East against aggression from any communist country. Acting on this restatement of containment, he sent troops into Lebanon in 1958 to block a takeover by pro-Nasser elements.

Sputnik and ICBM's. On October 4, 1957, the Soviet Union announced that it had launched the first man-made earth satellite into space, **Sputnik**. Soon other space spectaculars followed—a rocket which struck the moon and, above all, the first manned space flight. The West's superiority in strategic weapons had ended. Russia had the ultimate weapon, an **ICBM** (intercontinental ballistic missile) capable of a nuclear strike anywhere in the world.

The way was open for Khrushchev's grand diplomatic offensive. Moscow could use the political and psychological threat of ICBM's to paralyze NATO allies in Europe and isolate the United States. The victory of communism was just around the corner. Khrushchev arrogantly predicted, furthermore, that the capitalist West would soon fall like a ripe fruit, due to its own moral corruption.

The Western alliance was in a state of confusion as Europeans began to lose faith in American military might. Some argued for **neutralism** and **unilateral disarmament** ("better Red than dead"). Although it placed a satellite into orbit four months after Sputnik went up, the United

President John F. Kennedy, 1917–1963

States agonized over the "missile gap." It took a searching look at its whole educational system ("Why did we fall behind?") and made a frantic effort to catch up with the Soviets in science and especially rocket technology.

The Cuban Missile Crisis. One of the most serious incidents of the Cold War involved the threat posed to the United States by Russian missiles. During the summer of 1962, Khrushchev began moving military equipment and thousands of technicians into Cuba, the island 90 miles off the southeastern U.S. coast which had fallen to a communist guerrilla revolution under **Fidel Castro** in 1959. The Soviet technicians installed guided missiles which could reach much of the United States. **President John F. Kennedy**, who was elected in 1960, faced a dilemma. If he ordered them destroyed, it might touch off World War III. If he did nothing, the country would be in constant danger.

Kennedy brought the world to the very brink of war. On October 22, he ordered the U.S. Navy to search all vessels headed for Cuba and to turn back any containing "offensive" weapons. He demanded that Khrushchev take down the missile bases and remove all weapons capable of striking the United States. Any Cuban-based nuclear attack, he warned, would be answered by an American attack upon the Soviet Union. Khrushchev blinked in the face-off, and the Soviets agreed to remove the missiles.

Because the **balance of power** policies of the superpowers had become a balance of fear, the Cuban missile crisis led to an easing of Cold War tensions. In August 1963, the Soviet Union, United States, and Great Britain signed a treaty banning nuclear tests in the atmosphere. A direct telephone link (the "**hot line**") was established between the White House and the **Kremlin** for use in any future crisis. But the Cold War had not ended, nor had the Soviets given up the twin strategies of "peaceful coexistence" and revolutionary expansionism. Problems for the Russians

An aerial photograph shows missile erectors and launch stands at the Mariel Port Facility in Cuba.

seemed to be increasing, however, as a supposed rift between them and China opened wider and Khrushchev himself was deposed in October 1964.

The Cold War and Détente 1963–1989

The assassination of President Kennedy in 1963 and the replacement of Khrushchev by **Party Secretary Leonid Brezhnev** and **Premier Aleksei Kosygin** in 1964 seemed to mark a turning point in the Cold War. By then each nation had enough nuclear weapons to destroy the entire world several times over and some limited anti-missile defenses. Also, conflicts developed within each bloc. An ostensibly deep rift opened between the Russians and Chinese, while France weakened NATO by pulling out.

Signs of a Thaw. In 1963, the Americans sold a large quantity of wheat to the Soviet Union, and they agreed to cooperate in space projects involving weather and communications satellites. In 1964, they signed their first two-nation treaty, expanding diplomatic relations between them.

Then direct air service between New York and Moscow started in 1966, followed by an international treaty for the peaceful exploration and use of outer space in 1967. **President Lyndon Johnson** and Premier Kosygin met in June 1967 to discuss world problems. In 1968, the two countries drafted and proposed a **nonproliferation** treaty banning the spread of atomic weapons, which was later approved by the U.N. General Assembly. In 1969, American and Soviet representatives started the **Strategic Arms Limitation Talks (SALT)** in hopes of finding a way to control nuclear arms. In the 1970s, two SALT

treaties were signed by the leaders of the two nations.

An important change in East-West relations came through the efforts of former West Berlin mayor **Willy Brandt**, chancellor of West Germany from 1969 to 1974 and later head of the **Socialist International**. He normalized German relations with Iron Curtain countries, opening lines of communication and trade. In 1970, he signed treaties with Poland and Russia recognizing the boundaries drawn in 1945 and renouncing the use of force. By this act he gave up all claims to the 40,000 square miles of German territory taken by Poland and Russia after World War II. Brandt was later disgraced by scandal after it was revealed that his administration had been infiltrated by East German agents. The Socialist International, which claimed to be promoting democratic socialist ideals against more aggressive

Willy Brandt, 1913–

communist goals, soon joined the Soviets in joint ventures throughout the world.

In 1971, Britain, France, the United States, and the Soviet Union agreed that West Berlin was not part of West Germany, and provided for the free movement of traffic between Berlin and the West through East Germany. The two Germanys were admitted to the United Nations (1973) and also established diplomatic relations with each other.

Cold War Ends in Europe. Because the division of Europe now seemed set, the superpowers began to lose interest in the Cold War. Their main concern by the early 1970s was to avoid nuclear war and curb the costly arms race. Due to frequent grain shortages, the Russians also wanted to import more Western technology and begin trading with the Americans. As for the United States, it had found that the outlay of $1.3 trillion in a quarter century had purchased neither peace nor security, and the end was not in sight. In no way could the Soviet political and territorial gains be undone. So the door was open for *détente* (more friendly relations) between the two.

President Richard Nixon, who as a congressman and vice president during the 1940s and 1950s had been an outspoken anticommunist, played an important role in the new policy of *détente*, primarily designed by Nixon's **Secretary of State Henry Kissinger**. Nixon's representatives made progress in the SALT negotiations and worked out the Berlin settlement. Then he journeyed to Moscow in May 1972 for a summit conference with Brezhnev. There two important pacts were signed limiting both defensive and offensive weapons, agreements which the Soviets proceeded to break repeatedly. Another agreement brought cooperation in space ventures. Two orbiting American and Soviet manned spacecraft linked up in July 1975. Nixon also paid a historic

Leonid Brezhnev, 1906–1982

President Richard M. Nixon, 1913–1994

visit to Communist China in 1972 and was credited with reopening China to the West.

A major landmark was the **Conference on Security and Cooperation in Europe (CSCE)** in Helsinki, Finland, in 1975. Delegates from 35 countries signed a document, known popularly as the **Helsinki Agreement**, accepting the postwar boundaries of Europe. Only by peaceful means could these be changed. In effect, the West recognized Soviet control of Eastern Europe, while the Eastern states agreed to grant their citizens more civil rights and allow a free flow of information between East and West. Families which had been separated by the Cold War could be reunited. Economic, cultural, and educational cooperation would be stepped up. Delegates agreed to broaden *détente* and make it an ongoing process. However, the Helsinki Agreement did not have real binding force, and the Soviet bloc countries largely ignored its human rights provi-

sions, which had received considerable publicity in the West.

Moreover, with its sleek new warships and submarines, Soviet naval power grew remarkably in the 1970s, a fact that worried Western defense experts. With this sea power, the Russians could carry out their global policy. Politicians debated throughout the 1970s whether *détente* had any real bearing on stopping the arms race.

Breakup of the Power Blocs

In the early 1950s, people talked of the **polarized** world. Two tightly organized, massive political blocs were centered around Moscow and Washington. But in the later 1950s, various countries

in both blocs sought more independence, and the so-called underdeveloped Third World became a political force to be reckoned with.

Common Market. Increasingly, West European countries realized they could never gain equal footing with the Soviet Union and the United States unless they united. In 1951, France, West Germany, Italy, Belgium, The Netherlands, and Luxembourg took a major step in this direction by forming the **European Coal and Steel Community (ECSC)**, combining their coal and steel industries and reducing trade barriers against these commodities. In 1957, the same nations signed a treaty expanding their economic cooperation across the board. The result was the **European Economic Community (EEC)**, better known as the **Common Market**. Their goal was to fully merge their economies and create a free-trade area among themselves. In 1967, other European economic groups joined the EEC to form the **European Community (EC)**, which was later expanded to include more nations. The EC, until it was replaced in the 1990s by an even stronger alliance, the **European Union (EU)**, regulated such matters as agriculture, transportation, and business practices. Also, it coordinated legislation in the member countries on health, food, industrial standards, taxation, and social security. The European nations also began working toward a common currency, but that effort remained stymied at least through the mid-1990s. Opposition to a common currency came mostly from Britain, under Conservative **Prime Minister Margaret Thatcher**, and from Denmark.

Not merely an economic group, the EC/EU also had a political nature. In addition to its executive bodies, it had a parliament, elected directly by the people of the member nations. The **European Parliament** did not pass laws; it merely advised on them. But it stood as a symbol of the liberals' hope that European nations would one day lay aside their national self-interests and become tantamount to a single nation, the "United States of Europe."

By 1973, the EC had passed the United States in steel and automobile production. But member nations could not resolve the problems of differing agricultural policies, the weak economies of Britain and Italy, and rapidly changing currency values. The prospect that the community would legally unite in all respects seemed far in the future, especially as nationalist feelings were again on the rise worldwide near the end of the century. It did, however, make Western Europe largely independent of American economic control. And it had proved to be the most effective venture in international cooperation in modern European history.

Defense Arrangements. After 1949, the United States dominated European defense matters through NATO, but the Europeans were unhappy about American reluctance to share control of its nuclear arsenal. Also, some questioned whether the United States really would come to their aid if the Russians attacked. To counter these doubts, President Kennedy signed an agreement with Britain in 1963 providing for an Anglo-American nuclear force. Then came a plan for a fleet of Polaris-missile-firing ships to be manned by mixed crews drawn from NATO members. Thus the European allies would gain at least partial control over the nuclear force.

However, these ideas got nowhere because of French President De Gaulle. He could see little common ground between his country and Britain and America. He saw no need for Atlantic or European unity to hold off a Soviet threat. The ills of Europe resulted, he thought, from its division into two rigid blocs at the end of the war

This T-72 tank was part of the Soviet Union's effort to win the arms race.

and the meddling of two non-European superpowers in its affairs.

To express France's independence, De Gaulle first withdrew all French naval units from the NATO Mediterranean Command in 1959. Then he decided that France would have its own nuclear force, no matter how small. The French president maintained friendly relations with Russia during the Cold War, and in 1964 he gave diplomatic recognition to Communist China. Other Western nations protested, for it was at this time that Chinese Communist leader **Mao Tse-tung** was urging armed struggle against the West and was defiantly exploding an atomic bomb. Then in 1966, De Gaulle pulled all French forces out of the NATO military command.

Political Turmoil. Serious threats to Western unity in the 1960s and 1970s came from dramatic changes in Portugal, Spain, and Greece. Over 40 years of civilian dictatorship in Portugal ended in 1974 with an army coup. Turmoil broke out as socialists and communists jockeyed for power, and the shaky economy virtually collapsed. For awhile, this NATO country seemed to be drifting into the communist orbit. But by giving independence to its overseas possessions and adopting

strict economic measures to check inflation, stability returned by 1977.

Although **Francisco Franco** had set up a fascist-style dictatorship in Spain and was sympathetic to the German side in World War II, he kept the country neutral. Recognizing that Spain could play an important role in the defense of Europe, the United States began giving aid to Franco in the early 1950s and leased naval and air bases in Spain. After his death in 1975, many feared that Spain would be torn to pieces by revolution. However, his handpicked successor, **King Juan Carlos I**, fulfilled a promise to make improvements while keeping a steady hand on the country. **Prime Minister Adolfo Suarez Gonzalez** held free elections, and the Spanish accepted a democratic constitution in 1978.

In Greece, the military seized control in 1967, ended the monarchy, and suspended civil liberties. The military leaders drafted a new constitution which provided for a stable government, but at the expense of democracy. In July 1974, the military group resigned and democratic rule was restored. Just then, Turkey invaded Cyprus. When NATO failed to back Greece, that country angrily pulled its armed forces out of the organization, though keeping political and economic

The worship of man is evident in the many images of Lenin throughout the Soviet empire, such as this one in downtown Tbilisi, Georgia.

ties with Western Europe. Meanwhile, the United States Congress voted an arms **embargo** against Turkey, which improved relations with Greece. Now the Turks were upset and responded by closing down all American military installations on their soil. Eventually, things were smoothed over and Greece returned to the NATO fold, but the alliance had suffered a serious blow on its eastern flank.

The Eastern Bloc. The Soviet bloc also faced threats. Ideological differences arose between China and the Soviet Union over how communism should progress. For example, China emphasized the role of agriculture and the equality of workers on collective farms while the Soviets continued to follow Lenin's views on the importance of the urban industrial workers. Chinese communist leader Mao Tse-tung was careful, however, not to completely spurn communist orthodoxy's claim that the movement was a revolution of the *proletariat* more than of the peasantry. After winning his victory in the countryside, Mao quickly moved his power base to the cities. Maoism, perhaps because of the ori-

ental circular view of history, emphasized the need for endless upheaval and revolution, while Soviet communism stressed a more linear progression to a state of communist perfection.

Yet, as R.N. Carew Hunt, an expert on communist theory, noted in 1962:

> The precise relations between the Soviet Union and China are a matter for speculation. The two countries are united by what is fundamentally a common ideology, and by a mutuality of interest, and neither has anything to gain at the moment by a breach with the other. The Chinese Communists are well aware of their debt to Russia, and as long as they accept the fundamentals of Marxism-Leninism, and anti-imperialism with it, they will remain in the Soviet camp. They will only leave it if they become convinced that Russia offers a greater threat to Chinese national interests than does the West....

The two communist powers did, in fact, quarrel because of differences in their national heritage. Their armed forces even clashed along their mutual border in 1969. Each country had imperial traditions and had claimed superiority over others. Like De Gaulle, Mao Tse-tung was a nationalist who opposed the two superpowers. Chinese nationalism and other developments in China are discussed in chapter 14.

The perceived Sino-Soviet split (again, there is evidence that it was an orchestrated split designed for strategic advancement of the worldwide communist cause) enabled a loosening up in Europe as well. In the mid-Fifties the Italian Communists, the largest Communist Party in the Western bloc, began criticizing Soviet policies and seeking independence from Moscow. Most East European countries remained loyal to Moscow in 1960, with the exception of isolated and impoverished Albania. In 1961, it ostensibly broke with

the Soviet Union, dropped out of the Warsaw Pact, and became China's spokesman in Europe.

However, nationalistic feelings were strong in the bloc countries and large segments of their populations were indifferent to communism. Fearful that division in the communist movement would harm world revolution, the Soviets stopped reforms instituted by Czechoslovakia. But this only divided the movement more. Most communist parties in the West denounced the action; the Chinese and Albanians called it "fascist" power politics, and even Romania was publicly critical. It seemed to indicate that the Soviet Union had to rely on force of arms rather than Marxist doctrine to maintain its place in the communist world.

Nevertheless, industry developed for a time in the bloc countries, although industrialization was dif-

The Marxist dream of creating a glorious workers paradise never materialized.

ficult to maintain as years progressed because of the bankruptcy of communist economic practice. The Soviets allowed some independence among its satellites as long as independence did not challenge the mother country directly. Romania sidestepped Soviet measures that would slow its industrial development and pursued its own foreign policy. (Both the American and Chinese leaders visited there.) At the same time, the country maintained one of the most brutal police states in the world and suppressed religious freedom. Romania's overtures to the West resulted in its ability to acquire some Western technology which the Eastern bloc badly needed. Evidence showed that much of this technology was filtered into the Soviet Union itself, again raising questions about the genuineness of Romanian independence. Romania also was used secretly as a training site for revolutionary and terrorist groups from Third World countries, including the **Palestine Liberation Organization**.

After 1975, a new brand of Marxism appeared on the scene—**Eurocommunism**. After cutting loose from tight Soviet control, several European communist parties took a novel approach to revolution. Rather than trying to gain control through armed class struggle, they worked for votes in democratic elections.

As the Italian Communists scored important electoral gains in June 1976, party leader **Enrico Berlinguer** became the foremost spokesman for the new approach. The Spanish and French parties also came out strongly for it. Most people assumed that within a short time Communists would hold posts in coalition governments in at least one or two European countries.

Both superpowers expressed alarm at this development. At a conference of the European communist parties in 1976, the Soviets seemed to be losing their grip on the world revolution. They could not persuade the other parties to denounce China, nor could they prevent them from declaring each party's right to take its own independent "road to socialism." The United States worried about the possibility of a communist government coming to power in its NATO ally, Italy. Serious discussions took place in the military councils about what to do if this happened, but no decision was reached.

Eurocommunism may have actually advanced the cause of communism for a time. As one analyst, the former KGB officer Anatoliy Golitsyn, described it:

> Mutual criticisms between the Soviets and Eurocommunists would help to dispel fears of the introduction of a Soviet system into Western Europe and confirm the sincerity of the Eurocommunists' conversion to democratic principles. Chinese accusations that Eurocommunists were falling under social democratic influence could further the illusion that this was so. With their credentials thus improved, the Eurocommunist parties would stand to gain new allies among the working classes, the social democrats, the petty bourgeoisie, the intelligentsia, the churches, and the armed forces and thus be able to play a more influential role in overall communist strategy in Europe.

That strategy seemed to be working until 1989, when a series of seemingly miraculous anticommunist revolutions began to sweep through Eastern Europe and the Soviet Union, bringing down one Marxist regime after another, much to the pleasant surprise of many in the West. Those revolutions revealed the bankruptcy of the communist system and severely discredited leftist elements in the United States and Western Europe.

The Berlin Wall Memorial portrays the bondage and misery resulting from Communist rule.

For your consideration

Questions

1. Discuss the main characteristics of the Cold War.

2. Should the United States try to affect the internal policies of other countries? Why or why not?

3. What were the main components of the West's Cold War Strategy? How did the Soviet Union respond?

4. How does economic aid affect the country which receives it? What countries give and receive the most aid today?

5. Consider the growth of the welfare state following World War II. What services, if any, should a government provide for its people?

6. Should a person's political views keep him from holding a job? Discuss this issue in general and in light of McCarthyism.

7. How do you feel about the Cold War motto of some people: "Better Red than dead"? Is freedom worth fighting for? In what situations would you be in favor of starting a war?

8. Is the "peaceful coexistence" of communism and democracy possible?

9. Do you believe there are any fundamental human rights? If so, what are they?

10. Was space exploration a good idea? Explain your position.

Projects

1. Imagine that you are living in Hungary after the Soviets suppressed the 1956 uprising. Write a letter which will be smuggled out to a friend in the West. Describe how your life has changed under Soviet rule and how you feel about it.

2. Do some reading about the McCarthy era and the Communist subversion controversy in the United States. Describe in a written or oral report some of the events, including the black-listing of Hollywood celebrities and other well-known people.

3. Research the Rosenberg spy case. Write a report stating whether you believe the Rosenbergs were treated justly. A good resource is the book *The Rosenberg File: A Search for the Truth* by Ronald Radosh and Joyce Milton (Vintage Books).

4. Contact an organization such as Open Doors with Brother Andrew or Voice of the Martyrs. Compile a report on persecution of Christians in today's world.

5. Do a book report on Richard Wurmbrand's *Tortured for Christ* or one of Aleksandr Solzhenitsyn's books.

5. Make a collection of pictures illustrating space exploration from Sputnik I until now. Create a poster or other display.

6. Interview someone who has traveled to or emigrated from the former Iron Curtain countries. Write a report.

Words

Cold War	McCarthyism
linchpin	peaceful coexistence
Iron Curtain	Potsdam Conference
isolation	Berlin Airlift
Cominform	per capita income
confrontations	Berlin Wall
containment	Third World
subversive	agents of influence
liberation	Marshall Plan
expulsions	Truman Doctrine
nationalize	Fifth Republic
austerity	Federal Republic
retaliation	Sputnik
ultimatums	ICBM
neutralism	neutralism
détente	unilateral disarmament
polarized	National Health Service
embargo	"hot line"
balance of power	SALT
Kremlin	Helsinki Agreement
nonproliferation	CENTO, SEATO
Eurocommunism	World War III

People and Groups

Clement Attlee	NATO, Warsaw Pact
Nikita Khrushchev	Julius & Ethel Rosenberg
Mao Tse-tung	Joseph McCarthy
Richard Wurmbrand	Konrad Adenauer
Cardinal Mindszenty	Willy Brandt
Archbishop Stepinac	John Foster Dulles
Brother Andrew	Dean Acheson
Wladyslaw Gomulka	John F. Kennedy
Imre Nagy	Lyndon B. Johnson
Alexander Dubcek	Richard Nixon
George C. Marshall	Fidel Castro
Ludwig Erhard	Adolfo Suarez Gonzalez
ECSC/EEC/EC/EU	Henry Kissinger
European Parliament	Alcide De Gasperi
Gamal Abdel Nasser	Aleksei Kosygin
Anthony Eden	Leonid Brezhnev

1945　　　　　1955　　　　　1965　　　　　1975　　　　　1985　　　　　1995

Politics and Economics

Cold War between East and West 1945–1970s

Communist regimes overthrown in
Eastern Europe and USSR 1989–1991

India and Pakistan
gain independence 1947

Conflict in Indochina and War in Vietnam 1946–1975

Nation of Israel formed 1948–1949

Great Leap Forward and Cultural
Revolution in China 1958–1969

Egyptian-Israeli peace initiative 1970s

Persian Gulf War 1991

Watergate 1972–1973

Communists take control of China 1949

Sub-Saharan Africa gains independence 1957–1970s

Israel, PLO, Jordan sign peace accords 1994

Korean War 1950–1953

Cuban missile crisis 1962

Arab Oil Embargo 1973

Black majority rule begins in South Africa 1994

Science and Technology

Atomic bombs
dropped on
Japan 1945

Manned space flights begin 1961

Russia launches Space Age with
Sputnik I earth satellite 1957

USSR explodes
nuclear bomb 1953

China explodes nuclear bomb 1964

Religion and Philosophy

Russia and other communist countries persecute Christians 1918–1989

Gandhi applies Hindu philosophy
to politics 1915–1948

World Council of
Churches formed 1948

Archbishop Markarios becomes
president of Cyprus 1960

Lausanne Conference on
world evangelism 1974

China closed to
missionary work 1949

U.S. National Council
of Churches formed 1950

Liberation Theology develops 1973–1980s

Culture and Society

The World Philosophy develops 1950s–1970s

Helsinki agreement 1975

Civil Rights movements
in America 1960s–1970s

Reagan restores U.S. patriotism 1980–1988

Communists restructure
Chinese society 1950s–1960s

Hippie counterculture
in America 1960s–1970s

Apartheid policy in South Africa 1960s–1980s

Western Decline and Third World Crisis

During the two decades following World War II, one-third of the earth's population broke free from colonial rule. At the same time millions of others—influenced, but not directly ruled, by Europe—came to a new awareness of their national identities. The era of unquestioned Western control ended as a tidal wave of nationalism swept through Asia, the Middle East, Africa, and even Europeanized Latin America.

Decolonization came so fast that one tends to lose sight of all the groundwork laid for it before 1945. The modernization of Japan and the efforts of **Sun Yat-sen** in China played an important part. Then, in World War I, Western nations granted greater freedom to their colonies hoping to gain more men and material for the war effort. With the spread of Western education, increased economic development, and the growing political awareness of colonial subjects, the basis for post-1945 nationalist movements was created.

The Russian Revolution presented the most important challenge to imperialism. Backed by the new Soviet might, Lenin's attack on Western colonialism packed dynamite. The activities of local communist parties and the Comintern swelled opposition to Western rule. By World War II, nationalism was well established in the non-Western world and European power had already started to shrink.

The Legacy of World War II

The most truly global conflict in history deeply affected the independence movement. For one thing the chief colonial powers suffered disastrous setbacks during World War II. France collapsed, but even after that it was able to hang on to its possessions in Indochina and North Africa for awhile. Holland was occupied by Germany, which left the Dutch East Indies to shift for itself. Great Britain's shattering defeat at Singapore in February 1942 not only cleared the way for Japan to occupy Southeast Asia and Indonesia, but also warned of the future collapse of the whole colonial system. It especially showed how much England had declined as a world naval power.

A Japanese propaganda slogan, "Asia for the Asians," also undermined Western imperialism. With ease they drove the surprised and ill-prepared Americans out of the Philippines and the British out of Malaya and Burma. By encouraging native military units to form in Burma, Malaya, and Indonesia and allowing local people some role in government in Java and Vietnam, the Japanese raised false hopes that independence was near.

To be sure, most nationalist leaders did not support the Axis cause, and colonial troops willingly joined the Allies. However, they gave their loyalty

Modern Hong Kong

with strings attached, demanding reform in return. Here was a chance for independence, and they wanted more than promises that it would follow after the war.

Nationalism in South Asia

India. In the struggle for Indian independence, **Mohandas K. Gandhi**, often called **Mahatma** or "great soul," provided important early leadership. After receiving his education in England, he practiced law for 20 years in South Africa. There he campaigned against what he called social and economic injustice and began to believe that racial prejudice was a world problem. When he returned home in 1915, he became disillusioned with what he saw as British repression. He began proclaiming a single message—Indians should stop cooperating with the British.

Gandhi's success came from his understanding of the Hindu outlook of the Indian people and from his use of religious terms to which he gave political meaning. He encouraged his followers to use nonviolent passive resistance. This included fasts, sit-down strikes, and other acts of **civil disobedience**. Masses of people followed his ideas in protest against British domination of political and economic life. Some of his views had been adopted from the nineteenth century American writer, **Henry David Thoreau**. Later, Gandhi's techniques were followed by many in the American civil rights struggle.

Gandhi urged the people to boycott British products and use domestic goods such as homespun cloth. He rejected modern technology and felt that Western industrialization was wrong for India. Other Indian leaders, such as **Jawaharlal Nehru**, saw science and technology together with socialism as the means to free people from their misery and ignorance.

In the 1920s and 1930s, the British allowed greater Indian participation in politics, provincial legislatures and cabinets. The Hindu nationalist party, the **Indian National Congress**, became increasingly powerful. During World War II, there were strikes and riots protesting Indian participation in that conflict and demanding that the British leave the country. The British put down this resistance. They needed a stronghold in that area because the Japanese had overrun most of Southeast Asia.

However, by the close of the war the British decided to grant independence. This posed a major problem because of the religious composi-

Mahatma Gandhi

He wore only a homespun loincloth and, to ward off the fierce heat, a wet Turkish towel piled upon his bald head. Thread wound continuously off the spinning wheel he operated. All the while he spoke to the steady stream of dignitaries filing into his hut. This frail man holding court in the poorest district of Bombay did not look like the most powerful man in all India. Yet with only a word, Mahatma Gandhi could send millions of men and women into the streets of India's cities to protest some British action. At his command Indians swarmed the police stations, demanding that the bewildered British arrest them. Many practically worshipped him.

Gandhi believed that a life devoted solely to the service of humanity must be free from possessions. Identifying with the poverty of India's masses, he gave away most of what he owned. His simple diet included no meat. On his many travels, he always went third class. Important trips required several third-class trains to carry him, his followers, and his goats. (Goat's milk was a mainstay of his diet.) An Indian poet once pointed out the high cost of keeping Gandhi in poverty.

The Mahatma's creed of nonviolence had no place for timidity. "I can no more preach nonviolence to a coward than I can tempt a blind man to enjoy healthy scenes," he said. "Nonviolence is the summit of bravery." The nonviolent person must also be humble and loving, Gandhi insisted. Once when in jail, he was ordered to find someone to clean the rest rooms. Instead, he did it himself. He taught his passive resisters that they must not have anger or hate, must not swear or fight back, and they must aid any British officials injured by Indians. According to Gandhi, the most efficient force is the most silent and subtle one. Nonviolence did not aim at destroying the tyrant, but in converting him. He idealistically believed that hard hearts could not fail to be touched by suffering without anger or malice.

After independence, a test greater than alleged British oppression came to Gandhi's philosophy. Indian Hindus and Muslims were killing one another. Could his passive philosophy conquer ancient religious hatred and fanaticism? Gandhi began a public fast for peace between the two groups. Frail and aged, he could not survive a long fast. Religious leaders met quickly and resolved some of their differences. However, this was the Mahatma's last struggle. He was assassinated by a Hindu fanatic a short time later.

tion of India. By far the majority were Hindus, but a sizable minority were Muslims who had different beliefs and ways of life. The Muslims did not want to be part of a country ruled by the Hindus, but wanted to have their own instead.

The British tried to solve the dilemma by dividing the country into two states, **Pakistan** and the **Republic of India**. In July 1947, they both became free nations in the British Commonwealth.

The boundary divisions were unwise. Pakistan had the areas producing jute, cotton, and rice, while India had the factories to process these raw materials but lacked an adequate food supply. The political boundaries cut important canals and river systems. Each area contained large minorities, and a mass exodus of 10 million people occurred in late 1947. Untold suffering resulted as Hindus tried to move into India and Muslims into Pakistan. On both sides, religious fanatics committed terrible crimes that culminated in the assassination of Gandhi in 1948 because of his concern for the welfare of Indian Muslims.

The Republic of India cut its ties with the British crown in 1950 but remained within the "Commonwealth of Nations." (The term "British" was no longer used.) The new nation had a central government like that of Great Britain, and each state in the union also had legislatures and ministers. The constitution provided for the universal right to vote, equality of the sexes, civil rights, and the end of the **caste system**.

India functioned largely as a one-party system. The **Congress Party** dominated all branches of the government with Jawaharlal Nehru serving as prime minister until his death in May 1964.

After his death, the Congress Party lost its monopoly of power, even though Nehru's daughter, **Mrs. Indira Gandhi** (not related to Mohandas Gandhi), became prime minister in 1966. She was a skillful politician in her own right. In the years after 1966, political tensions and pressing social and economic problems chipped away at democracy in India. Though popular abroad, Mrs. Gandhi was unable to overcome these problems at home, and she was temporarily forced from power in 1977. She later returned and ruled with difficulty until she was assassinated in 1984 by two of her own bodyguards who opposed her government's treatment of **Sikhs**, a religious sect. Mrs. Gandhi was replaced by her son, **Rajiv Gandhi**, who was voted out of office in 1989 amid charges of corruption. While he was campaigning to regain office in 1991, he too was assassinated.

Since the murder of Rajiv Gandhi, control of the Indian government has vacillated between multiparty coalitions led by either the Congress Party or the Hindu-nationalist **Bharatiya Janata Party** (BJP). In March 1998, the BJP formed a coalition government led by Prime Minister **Atal Bihari Vajpayee**. Soon afterward, on May 11 and 13, 1998, India conducted a series of underground nuclear tests, resulting in the imposition of economic sanctions by the United States. In 1999 and 2001–2002, India and Pakistan clashed over **Kashmir** and Pakistan's support for Muslim separatists in Indian-controlled Kashmir.

Although India has great supplies of natural resources, most of its people suffer from a miserably low standard of living. Sluggish economic growth, overpopulation, and failure to make land reforms increase the grinding poverty. The Indian economy has seen in recent years, however, significant improvement due to liberalization of foreign trade and investment regulations. India has become a major exporter of software products and workers.

Indira Gandhi, 1918–1984

Pakistan. The problems of Pakistan were even greater. It began not as a nation but as a collection of racial and **linguistic** communities living in two territories separated geographically by 1,000 miles. Religion was the only common bond between East and West Pakistan.

After years of wrangling, a constitution was adopted in 1956 that defined Pakistan as an "Islamic republic." However, political democracy hardly existed here, as a series of strongmen ran the country. Under **General Mohammad Ayub Khan**, head of state from 1958 to 1969, some progress was made in economic development. But little was done to end the widespread political corruption or raise living standards.

Although more than half of the population lived in East Pakistan (formerly East Bengal) and most of the nation's income came from the jute industry there, the major part of the wealth went to

West Pakistan. East Pakistan contributed much to the expanding economy but did not receive its fair share of benefits. As the gap in personal income between the two widened, other problems arose. Political **discrimination**, social neglect, and West Pakistani contempt for the Bengalis further angered people in the East.

India-Pakistan War Creates Bangladesh. In 1971, the Bengalis revolted. In a deliberate campaign of **genocide**, the West Pakistanis murdered potential leaders among the Bengali population. This brought India into the conflict. A full-scale war between India and Pakistan followed, the bloodiest of the century there. Soon gaining the victory, India and the Bengalis set up a new government in East Pakistan in 1971 under the name of **Bangladesh** (Bengal Nation). Its leader, **Sheik Mujibur Rahman**, tried to make it a "secular, democratic, socialist state." So deep was the poverty that real economic development never took place. A famine of world-shocking proportions occurred not long after Bangladesh won independence. Rahman was assassinated in 1975 in a military coup led by **Khondaker Moshtaque Ahmed**, who was in turn overthrown by **General Ziaur Rahman**, who was assassinated in 1981. The nation sank even further into misery as the years passed and the government changed hands time and again through both violence and elections. A woman, **Begum Klaleda Ziaur Rahman**, widow of Ziaur Rahman, became the country's first female prime minister in 1991, the same year that a devastating cyclone left more than 125,000 dead and hundreds of thousands more threatened by famine and disease.

Angered by the British recognition of Bangladesh in 1971, **Pakistan** (the word "West" was dropped from the name) withdrew from the Commonwealth. A new leader, wealthy lawyer **Zulfikar Ali Bhutto**, emerged. Bhutto had held several cabi-

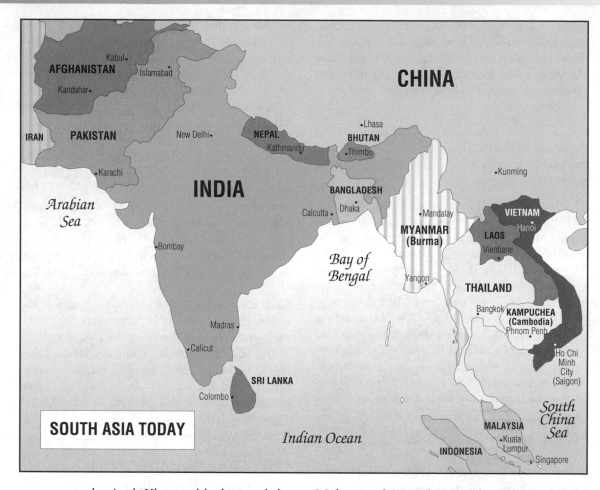

SOUTH ASIA TODAY

net posts under Ayub Khan and had created the opposition Pakistan People's Party (PPP) in 1967. When he came to power in 1971, he restored constitutional and civilian rule, announced a program of economic recovery that included land redistribution and nationalization of certain industries. He eventually **normalized** relations with India and Bangladesh. But political turmoil and economic uncertainty continued, especially in opposition to Bhutto's land redistribution and nationalization policies. He was finally ousted from power in a 1977 military coup led by

Muhammad Zia Ul-Haq. Bhutto was tried for ordering the murder of a political opponent and later hanged.

Bhutto's wife, **Nusrat**, and his daughter, Benazir, assumed leadership of the PPP. Benazir was under house arrest or in exile from 1984 to 1986. In December 1988, after Zia's death and elections won by the PPP, **Benazir Bhutto** became prime minister and the first woman to head a modern Muslim state. She accomplished little and was dismissed by the president in 1990. Her party decisively lost the 1990 elections, but she returned as prime minister after a narrow electoral victory in 1993. Her administration was dismissed again in 1996 over charges of corruption and mismanagement. The succeeding government proved to be unstable and was overthrown by the Pakistani Army. General **Pervez Mushareff** became ruler of Pakistan in 1999.

Pakistan's relationship with the United States in the late 1990s was rocky. Sanctions were placed on Pakistan after it conducted nuclear tests in May 1998—in response to India's earlier tests—and then more sanctions were added after the military overthrew the civilian government in 1999. However, Pakistan has provided significant help to the United States in its **War on Terrorism** since September 11, 2001, and so relations between the two countries have improved markedly.

Sri Lanka. In Ceylon and Burma, the British quickly accepted decolonization after World War II. At the outset, the island of Ceylon had a higher standard of living than India. Ceylon's successful economy was based on producing plantation crops—tea, rubber, and coconuts—for export. British rule had also left a good educational system. Ceylon had the highest literacy rate in South Asia.

The island had enjoyed considerable self-government since 1931, and in February 1948 it received independence and joined the Commonwealth. Then trouble arose between the Buddhist majority—known as **Sinhalese**—and the Hindu minority called **Tamils**, as well as between the rich and poor. When **S.W.R.D. Bandaranaike** was elected prime minister, he worked for socialism, nationalism, and trade with the communist bloc to increase exports. A great deal of violence followed, topped off by his assassination in 1959.

He was followed by his wife **Sirimavo**, the first woman in the world to hold the title of prime minister. Under Madame Bandaranaike, the socialist program unfolded, even as the economy weakened and the population mushroomed. She was defeated in 1965 but returned to power in 1970. The following year, her army and police put down a serious revolt led by young people. A new constitution was adopted in 1972, which renamed the country **Sri Lanka**. Since then little has been done to solve the nation's mounting social and economic problems. Ethnic violence between the Sinhalese and the Tamils emerged in the mid-1980s, with a group known as the **Tamil Tigers** fighting against the government to establish a separate Tamil state in Sri Lanka.

Burma (Myanmar). Burma had been part of British India until 1937 when it received a separate administration and a measure of self-government. In 1948, an independent **Republic of Burma** was founded. It was so strongly anti-Western that it refused to join the Commonwealth. While the strength of Buddhist tradition softened the harshness of this stand, the country looked to socialism to bring about modernization. Burma was deeply divided along political and tribal lines, and the central government was hard-pressed to hold the union together.

In 1962, **General U Ne Win** clamped military rule on the country and proclaimed the hard-line "Burmese Way to Socialism." All major trading and industrial activities and banks were nationalized under the management of army officers. The strict regime was unpopular, but the army was able to put down any revolts. Although politically independent of the great power blocs, it continued to be anti-Western. Even the Christian missionaries were sent home, but the churches thrived under national leadership.

A new constitution in 1974 strengthened the position of Ne Win and his then civilian government. He resigned in 1981 and turned power over to former army chief **U San Yu**, who was reelected in 1985. Ne Win retained his place as head of the ruling socialist party, the BSPP, until 1988. In that year, massive student and urban unrest began to surface. Ne Win stepped down and was replaced by a hard-liner who resigned 17 days later. Unrest continued and successive leaders cracked down hard on dissent.

In June 1989, Burma changed its name to **Myanmar** and its capital of Rangoon was renamed **Yangon**.

The opposition overwhelmingly won an election in 1990, but the military refused to turn over power. Opposition leader **Aung San See Kyi** was placed under house arrest.

From Nationalism to Communism in China

The fall of the Manchu (Ch'ing) Dynasty in China in 1911 marked the start of a long period of instability. A republican form of government was set up, but it had little effective control. Army commanders (often called warlords) divided the country among themselves. A state of anarchy resulted.

The republican leader and reformer, **Sun Yat-sen**, felt that help from the Soviet Union would be useful in rebuilding China. He agreed to remodel his **Nationalist Party** along communist lines in return for military aid. The Russians saw China as a good place to promote the worldwide revolution, so they encouraged the Chinese Communists to join with the Nationalists.

Soviet advisers helped the Nationalists set up a small but effective government in Canton. It was a "state within a state" that collected taxes, regulated commerce, and developed its own army. The officers were trained at the Whampoa Military Academy headed by Sun's trusted friend and chosen heir, **Chiang Kai-shek**. Chiang had helped Sun in the revolution against the Manchus and had been sent to Moscow to learn Soviet skills and tactics. From the very beginning, the academy's secretary, **Chou En-lai**, trained Nationalist soldiers to organize the masses for class struggle, propaganda, and guerrilla warfare. After Sun's death in 1925, Chiang took over the Nationalist movement. In 1928, he led a successful campaign to crush the warlords in the north and finally unified China.

Principles of the People. Although he was not a successful political administrator, Sun became a legend and his ideas spread widely. His political philosophy can shed much light on the revolt of China and other non-Western peoples against the West. Sun believed in what he called the "**Three Principles of the People**." They were *nationalism, democracy,* and *livelihood.*

By *nationalism,* he meant the liberation of China from foreign influence and the transfer of people's loyalty from the family or province to the state. True freedom would come through the new national unity which would result. Lack of Chinese unity had allowed Westerners to control China's political and economic structure.

Democracy meant sovereignty of the people; in particular, government by those with ability. True democracy would come only at the end of the revolutionary struggle. First, military force would have to restore order. Then the people would have to be trained, but power was to be held by the party's revolutionary leaders. Only in the distant future would representative government become possible.

Chinese couple in Beijing

The principle of *livelihood* referred to the need for "material progress" and "social reform." Sun believed that something had to be done to divide China's land and wealth more equally among its people. He also wanted to end poverty and economic injustice.

Nationalist-Communist Conflicts. A split in the party occurred as the right-wing merchants, bankers, and officeholders became uneasy about excesses of left-wing radicals. Because Chiang needed financial help from the right wing, he decided to purge the left. He expelled the Russian advisers, drove the Communists out of the Nationalist Party, and took military action to crush communist groups hiding out in the mountains. Driven underground, the Communists sought support from the peasants with a program of land reform. In 1931, they proclaimed a "soviet republic" in southeast China. Chiang then launched a campaign against them. His forces surrounded them in 1934, but 90,000 managed to break out.

Led by **Mao Tse-tung** (**Zedong**), son of a well-to-do peasant and one of the founders of the Chinese Communist Party, the Communists carried out a trek of epic proportions. Known as the "**Long March**," it took 368 days and covered 6,000 miles of some of the most difficult terrain in the world. They fled to the safety of northwestern China and from there carried on a constant struggle against Chiang's Nationalists.

Chiang moved his capital to Nanking and set up a one-party dictatorship. In spite of the communist threat, he brought more unity to China than had existed since the eighteenth century. The Nationalists secured aid from abroad and worked to get rid of the treaties which had led to the control of China by Western nations. In this they succeeded.

But they did not carry out land reforms which many had demanded since the landlords who controlled the rural areas opposed any change. Chiang's authoritarian government prevented the growth of democracy and left little chance for expression of opposition. Government programs did not satisfy the land-hungry peasants and poverty-stricken city dwellers.

After Japan invaded China in 1937, the Nationalists and the Communists agreed on a temporary truce so they could fight their common enemy. However, the differences between them remained strong and the division became more obvious when Nationalist help slackened as the war against Japan drew to a close. They were saving resources and men for the struggle with the Communists.

The use of propaganda on both sides made it hard to evaluate the policies of Chiang and Mao. But it seemed that the Nationalists' program did not deal with corruption and self-seeking within their own ranks. Because the regime did not allow criticism, it further disappointed many of the intellectuals. Its soldiers, poorly commanded and undisciplined, terrorized the peasants almost as much as the Japanese had.

Communist Gains. The Communists, on the other hand, made a deliberate attempt to gain the backing of as many groups in Chinese society as possible. They were cautious about making outright attacks on landlords. But they created peasant goodwill by lowering rents and interest rates and starting small land "reforms" in areas under their control. Mao's forces took over many areas formerly held by Japan before the Nationalist government could reestablish its authority. Mao also gained large stocks of abandoned Japanese weapons.

After the Second World War, the United States tried desperately to bring the two groups together. **President Truman**, fearing that the Soviets would support the Communists, sent **General George C. Marshall** to China in December 1945 as a mediator. His efforts a failure, Marshall returned home a year later, frustrated and disillusioned. With the help of American forces, Chiang soon regained control over the main cities. But then he made a strategic blunder. Rejecting the counsel of his American advisers, he attacked the Communists entrenched in Manchuria.

A military disaster resulted. Chiang overextended his lines without gaining solid control over the rest of China. Throughout 1948 and 1949, the Communists rapidly pushed the Nationalist forces southward. After pouring in nearly $3 billion worth of military and economic aid, the United States had to give up. Chiang's armies collapsed and took refuge on the offshore island of **Formosa** (Taiwan). There Chiang resettled the government of the **Republic of China**, while in Peking (Beijing) on October 1, 1949, Mao proclaimed the start of the **People's Republic of China**.

In the years after 1949, the Communists rid China of all foreign influences and radically

Making a Society Communist

How can an entire society make a radical break with its past and move in a new direction? That was the challenge facing Mao when he took control of China. He decided to start with the nation's children.

Beginning in nursery school, students learned songs and verses about the goals and values of communism. In elementary schoolrooms decorated with red flags and pictures of Chairman Mao, teachers led their classes in getting rid of old ideas, customs, and culture. Students were encouraged to destroy the three powers of the past—husband's power, father's power, and religious power. If parents told their children anything contrary to the teachings of Chairman Mao, the children were urged to obey Mao and criticize their parents. Many young people persuaded their families to make changes such as replacing tablets of the ancestors (used in ancestor worship) with pictures of Mao. Young people taught their families what they had learned at school, and the revolution thus touched nearly every home in China.

Through constant propaganda and the carefully controlled mass media, people heard the new ideas. Workers had to attend evening classes in Maoist thought. Reeducation centers were opened to correct the thinking of people with "wrong ideas." Criticism by one's fellow workers or family members often caused a person to be chosen for "reeducation." In order to achieve equality in society and to acquaint young people with the basis of the revolution, all students spent two years working on a farm or in a factory. Professional people who showed any signs of bourgeois thinking often received the same assignment for a year or two.

These measures had a profound effect on Chinese life. The people paid a great price in the loss of personal freedom, but the communist revolution there was one of the most thorough in history.

transformed the state and society. Claiming that Christianity was tied both to Western colonialism and American anticommunism, Mao's people wiped out 100 years of sacrificial and fruitful missionary work. They closed the churches, took over the Christian schools and hospitals, and persecuted believers. The new political order extended its authority into every household. Collective farms and industrialization affected family life and economic structures. Confucian ideals were replaced by communist aspirations.

The fall of the Nationalist regime in China started a controversy in the United States. The **"China lobby"** argued for increasing arms and technical aid to Chiang, as well as sending troops to help him defend Taiwan and reconquer the mainland. Another faction wanted to accept the communist victory, recognize the Communist government (as Great Britain did at once), and give it the Chinese seat in the United Nations. They hoped that Chinese nationalism would ward off Soviet domination.

As the years passed, differences between Soviet and Chinese communism emerged. It is likely that the split was primarily a personal power struggle between Mao and Stalin for world leadership of the communist movement. This struggle for leadership intensified after Stalin died and Mao felt that, as leader of the largest communist nation on earth, he should be the helmsman. But there were ideological differences as well. Whereas the Russians clung to Lenin's idea that the urban *proletariat* must lead the movement, Mao assigned the leading role to the peasants. He also had a vision of a communist order where all people were equal and individuals were motivated by a desire to serve society rather than by personal gain. Mao attacked the Soviet Union because of its bureaucratic elite and the great differences in personal income there. During

China's **Great Leap Forward** (1958), and also in the **Cultural Revolution** (1966–1969), Russia was criticized through the use of slogans like "Organization Without Bureaucracy" and "Serve the People."

A major public break came in 1960 at a world conference of communist parties in Moscow. The Soviets withdrew their technical experts from China and all visible cooperation between the two came to a standstill. A propaganda war followed as each side hurled harsh words at the other.

The Chinese had a blueprint for revolution which rejected advanced technology and political caution. Chairman Mao accused the Russians of giving up the class struggle, and he called Nikita Khrushchev's "coexistence" ideas appeasement. "Man, not weapons, decides the issue of war," he declared. Russia had a cowardly and uncharacteristic fear of nuclear war and a selfish desire to rule the world. Chou En-lai even stated in 1973 that the Soviets had backslidden into "social imperialism."

Meanwhile, the prime domestic task of the communists, after coming to power, was to rebuild the country's economy. Severe austerity measures were imposed to slow inflation, restore communications, and impose social order. Collectivization of agriculture and reorganization of industry were given priority in carefully constructed short-term plans. By 1958, however, planning became less cautious; and Mao introduced the fast-paced **Great Leap Forward** campaign. The program was intended to demonstrate that China could catch up with British industrial output in 15 years and surpass the Soviet Union in achieving a perfected communist society. Mao exhorted the masses to heroic efforts. Massive dislocations of agriculture and industry took place as Mao attempted to blast modernization forward with all due haste. Rigid economic controls were imposed, but the

Great Leap was so disorganized and badly planned that the economy fell into chaos. Because farmers had been forced into large-scale and backyard industries, food production collapsed. Famines and other economic dislocations were so severe that more than 30 million Chinese lost their lives, making this experiment one of the worst cases of mass human destruction the world has ever known. Mao was discredited because of the fiasco and was replaced as head of state by **Liu Shaoqi**, although he remained head of the Communist Party.

The **Great Proletarian Cultural Revolution** of the late 1960s, the ideological counterpart of the Great Leap Forward, was Mao's attempt to regain

A Mao personality cult was spread throughout China during the 'Cultural Revolution.'

his former stature as a leading revolutionary. But it had similar disastrous results. By the mid-Sixties, Mao's influence had begun to diminish under competition from those who wanted a more reasoned approach to both economic and political problems. Mao and his supporters used the Cultural Revolution to finally eradicate what they believed to be the vestiges of *bourgeois* thinking within the revolution. Ideas, customs, and daily practices came under glaring scrutiny in every corner. Students calling themselves **Red Guards** sparked street demonstrations, riots, and other violent actions in order to stir up fervor for Mao's radical revolutionary doctrines. Large numbers of government, educational, cultural, political, and party leaders were purged or executed. Thousands of innocent people were saddled with trumped-up charges and often brutalized. Violence and bloodshed swept throughout the country as various factions battled one another. During the height of the radical revolutionary fervor, China tested a hydrogen bomb, sending nervous shivers throughout the rest of the world. Riots inspired by the Red Guards in Hong Kong also provoked fear in other countries of Asia. When some of the attacks were directed at pro-Soviet factions in China, Moscow denounced the whole affair, touching off new denunciations against the U.S.S.R. by Peking. Cross-border skirmishes followed.

As the chaos reached major proportions, the government finally called in **Lio Piao**, a close comrade of Mao, to begin restoring order. The army began to intervene in the street violence, and a network of "revolutionary committees" was set up within the central government and in the provinces and party to restore unity and reason. Red Guard units were disbanded. Yet Mao, who had touched off the fiasco, seemed to have consolidated his power and influence and gained new strength. In fact, his stature was raised to near divinity within Chinese communism and his doctrines were institutionalized as tantamount to a religion. When Mao died, moderate leaders, including **Deng Xiaoping**, purged the most vicious of the Cultural Revolution leaders, whom they called the Gang of Four. These included Mao's widow, **Chiang Ch'ing** (Jiang Qing). She and **Zhang Chunqiao** were sentenced to death, but their sentences were later reduced to life imprisonment. Chiang Ch'ing was released in 1987, but committed suicide in 1991.

After the deaths of Chou En-lai and Mao in 1976, the Chinese tried to strengthen their position against the Soviet Union by establishing friendlier relations with the industrial powers, especially Japan and the United States. Late in 1978, this process reached a climax when U.S. **President Jimmy Carter** announced to a startled world that the United States and China had agreed to normalize relations after almost thirty years of suspicion and hostility. That step opened the door to increased trade and cooperation. In addition, China would receive American technological help in modernizing its industry. Western business interests poured in through the new open door, drooling over the prospect of new markets in the most populous nation on earth, a market with a massive pent-up desire for a better material life.

Renewed Repression. Along with this desire for material development, the new Chinese leaders seemed to be willing to make policy changes, including liberalization of political thinking. Encouraged by this perception, democrats, liberals, and dissidents within China launched new expressions toward reform. By the late 1980s, communist regimes in other parts of the world were beginning to topple and a new wave of hope for political freedom swept through China. Students called for changes in policy and began to

openly act on reforms. In April 1989, a large group of students began to gather in Beijing's (Peking) central **Tiananmen Square**, at first in quiet expressions of hope and soon in joyous outbreaks of democratic fervor. After several days, the hopeful crowd of youths and other citizens, by then numbering in the thousands, were astonished by the sudden appearance of military forces, including tanks. The guns erupted and more than 2,000 of the demonstrators were massacred. There followed several months and years of renewed political repression. Leaders of the democratization movement who did not manage to flee the country were arrested, harassed, tried and imprisoned.

The new crackdown brought cries of disappointment and protest for a time from Western leaders, who attacked China for its repression of human rights. But the earlier opening of China to Western commercial and economic interests had by then become too deeply entrenched, and the leaders of Western nations found it difficult to press the human rights issue too deeply. By the mid-1990s, economic liberalization was again growing substantially in China, especially in the southern provinces, where experiments with small-scale capitalism were again evident.

Some of the economic liberalization may have been related to China's negotiated takeover of the former European colonies of **Hong Kong** (British) in 1997 and **Macau** (Portuguese) in 1999. They have become two of Asia's most prosperous and highly technological free-enterprise centers and stand in stark contrast to much of China's backwardness and repression. Although both territories were given guarantees of a high degree of local autonomy, there are signs that China actually exercises considerable influence over them.

Economic liberalization in China does not seem to be matched by religious tolerance. Substantial

repression of unregistered religious activity continues and is periodically increased. The Christian church in China had been growing into the tens of millions despite decades of persecution. The government sought to control the growth and character of religion by establishing official Protestant and Catholic religious institutions. Unauthorized house churches sprang up by the thousands throughout the country, but a limited availability of Bibles, Christian literature, pastors, and teachers hampered the work of these churches. Christians have also resisted the government's forced-abortion and sterilization policies, all part of a program to limit family size to one child.

Communist Advances in Asia

The Korean War (1950–1953). What had originally caused American attitudes toward communist China to harden was the Korean question. Two generations of Japanese rule had left the Koreans without the needed experience for self-government. At the Yalta Conference, it was proposed that a **trusteeship** consisting of the United States, the Soviet Union, Great Britain, and China be set up for Korea. However, the Cold War froze relations among those powers, and the Far East now had its own version of the Iron Curtain, the **Bamboo Curtain**.

The Soviet-American division of Korea became fixed at the 38th parallel. In 1948, two rival Korean regimes appeared, each claiming sovereignty over the whole country and each supported by one of the superpowers. In the south was the **Republic of Korea** under **Syngman Rhee** and in the north the **Democratic People's Republic of Korea** led by **Kim Il-sung**.

General Douglas MacArthur (1880–1964) was a brilliant military leader and Christian statesman.

In 1950, North Koreans equipped by the Soviet Union invaded South Korea. The United Nations Security Council quickly denounced the move and called upon U.N. members to aid the Republic of Korea. President Truman then ordered American forces into Korea. Eventually 40 countries sent some sort of aid, with 16 actually placing troops directly under U.N. command. The U.N. force was directed by **General Douglas MacArthur**, the hero of the American Pacific campaign during World War II.

At first it seemed that the U.N. forces would be driven out of the peninsula, but on September 15, 1950, MacArthur landed a marine division 200 miles behind enemy lines at Inchon. It recaptured the South Korean capital, Seoul, and cut North Korean communications. After the U.N. General Assembly ordered that a democratic government be established to govern all of Korea, MacArthur's forces moved north, seized the communist capital of Pyongyang, and

reached the Yalu River, the border of Manchuria. MacArthur wanted to carry the fight into Manchuria in an effort to defeat communism once and for all, but his proposals were rejected by President Truman, who preferred a negotiated settlement. Truman's military **Chief of Staff General Omar Bradley**, speaking for the administration, said MacArthur's plan to smash communism beyond Korea would escalate the conflict, provoking "the wrong war, at the wrong place, at the wrong time, and with the wrong enemy." A disgruntled MacArthur stepped outside usual military protocol and publicly criticized the administration. An angry Truman relieved him of duties and replaced him with **General Matthew Ridgeway** as commander of the U.N. forces.

On October 4, 1950, the Chinese politburo decided to intervene in the Korean War, although a full-fledged Chinese attack on U.N. forces did not occur until late November. Over 300,000 Chinese troops, along with limited Soviet air support, came to the aid of North Korea. Long months of bloodshed followed, but eventually a stalemate set in at about the 38th parallel, where the war had begun. Fighting continued through the stormy negotiations until an armistice was signed in July 1953. A **Demilitarized Zone**, a buffer strip along the North-South border, was established in the end, but little else was accomplished by the tragic engagement. More than 54,000 Americans lost their lives in this conflict, the first major war operation conducted by U.S. troops without an official declaration of war, as the American Constitution requires. It was also the first major example of armed conflict under the banner of the new would-be world government, the United Nations.

The war left widespread devastation in the countryside and thousands of orphans, a tragedy

which prompted a number of Western charitable groups and missionaries to enter the country and begin works of mercy and evangelistic outreach. Evangelism progressed slowly at first against entrenched Confucianism, Buddhism, and Shamanism. But important spiritual foundations were laid, and South Korea eventually acquired a large and active Christian population.

The Korean peninsula remained relatively quiet for the next four decades, although there were periodic disturbances across the Demilitarized Zone, leftist student demonstrations in South Korea, and an occasional crisis. One such crisis occurred in 1968 when North Korea captured an American intelligence ship, the USS *Pueblo*, and held its crew hostage for a time, until a committee of American patriots, led by Chicago-area clergyman **Paul Lindstrom** (1939–2002), pressured authorities into securing their release. Tensions increased again in the 1970s when the North infiltrated the South with secret agents in an attempt to establish a grass-roots communist uprising. The attempt failed, and the United States increased military aid to South Korea.

Suddenly in 1994, North Korea again precipitated a crisis when Western sources learned that the repressive and erratic communist regime was developing nuclear weapons, in violation of international accords which it had previously signed. Following threats from the United States, North Korea agreed to negotiate over the nuclear issue. The negotiations resulted in the United States and other nations agreeing to develop new, less dangerous nuclear power plants for North Korea. In exchange, North Korea had to shut down its current nuclear program, and pledge not to develop any nuclear weapons—from which it was already prohibited. In the middle of the crisis, the dictator **Kim Il-sung**, who had ruled North Korea with an iron fist since 1948, died.

He was replaced by his son, who was reputed to be equally repressive but mentally unstable. In October 2002, another nuclear crisis arose when North Korea admitted that it was running a secret nuclear weapons program, violating earlier agreements. North Korea went on to expel United Nations weapons inspectors and, in January 2003, to withdraw from the **Nuclear Non-Proliferation Treaty.**

North Korea's long decades of isolation from the rest of the world and its doctrinaire adherence to communist orthodoxy, revolutionary terrorism, and religious oppression resulted in severely stunted development for the country. In contrast, South Korea's economic and social development soared in the closing decades of the twentieth century, making it a major economic and technological power along the Pacific Rim.

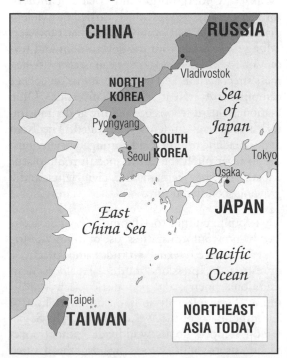

NORTHEAST ASIA TODAY

Evangelical Christianity, finally reaping the fruits of the early missionary efforts, also experienced a period of massive growth in South Korea in the 1970s, 1980s, and 1990s. Some of the largest churches in the world, predominantly Presbyterian, were established in that country, and the church there developed a worldwide reputation for its powerful prayer ministries. Single evangelistic gatherings of more than a million people were reported. Regrettably, South Korea also spawned a troublesome and fast-growing international religious cult, the **Unification Church,** under **Sun Myung Moon,** a staunch anticommunist who considered himself a latter-day Christ figure. Moon became fabulously rich and bought or established major business enterprises, including a leading newspaper and news magazine in Washington, D.C., before he was arrested and imprisoned on various criminal charges. His followers were popularly known as "Moonies."

The Struggle for Southeast Asia. Meanwhile, the communist advance in Southeast Asia had been a matter of deep concern to the Western powers. Communists had been active in Malaya since 1948 and in French Indochina since 1946. The United States made mutual security pacts with the Philippines, Australia, and New Zealand in 1951 and did its best to keep communist China isolated.

Southeast Asia was the flank still uncovered, and the situation there was very complex. After the Japanese surrender in 1945, the French decided to form a union of countries in French Indochina— Laos, Cambodia, and a new independent state to be called Vietnam. This area had rich resources, both human and natural. In the northern part of Vietnam, a nationalist leader with communist leanings, **Ho Chi Minh,** had seized control. Then in 1946, his party won an election there. The French, unwilling to deal with the idea of full

Vietnamese independence, rejected Ho and, in 1949, established **Emperor Bao Dai** (1913–1997) as ruler of Vietnam. Ho naturally refused to accept the new regime and started a long guerrilla war to gain independence from France. The war is known as the **First Indochina War.**

In 1950, the Chinese and Russians recognized Ho as the legitimate ruler of Vietnam, and the Americans began sending economic and military aid to the French. Even with U.S. aid, the French and Vietnamese forces could not stop the guerrillas. Disaster finally overtook the French effort at Dien Bien Phu in May 1954. France then asked the United States for direct help, and **Secretary of State John Foster Dulles** even suggested using nuclear weapons. But **President Eisenhower** decided not to act so rashly.

In June 1954, France sought a cease-fire; and eventually, at a conference in Geneva, a settlement was worked out. Over American protests, even communist China came to the meetings. The United States later refused to sign the final agreement because Dulles did not want Vietnam placed under communist rule. However, the Americans did state that they would not use force to "disturb" the settlement.

The agreement divided Vietnam along the 17th parallel and called for French withdrawal from the entire area. The northern part became the **Democratic Republic of Vietnam** ruled by Ho Chi Minh, while the southern part, the **Republic of Vietnam,** remained under Emperor Bao Dai. Neither one was to join a military alliance or receive new military aid. An international commission was created to supervise the armistice and the all-Vietnam elections to be held in 1956. But in 1955, **Ngo Dinh Diem** overthrew Bao Dai and set up an authoritarian regime in the South. The elections never took place.

The Vietnam War

Soon the conflict turned into a hot war with American arms and advisers helping President Diem in his struggle against the southern-based communist **Viet Cong** guerrillas. Although greatly outnumbered at first, the Viet Cong were aided by public anger over Diem's harsh regime and by supplies from North Vietnam. In December 1960, the Viet Cong formed their own government, the **National Liberation Front**. It set up local councils to govern areas of South Vietnam under its control, built factories to make weapons, and secured ammunition, medical supplies, and money. Arms came from Russia and China over a system of roads and trails known as the **Ho Chi Minh Trail**.

The Viet Cong were so successful that **President Kennedy** stepped up military aid to South Vietnam. American statesmen feared that if the Communists were not stopped here, all the countries of Southeast Asia would fall under their rule like a row of dominoes. The idea became known as the **Domino Theory** and it was advanced as the primary reason for increasing U.S. involvement in the war. Then Diem was assassinated in November 1963 (the same month and year that Kennedy was assassinated), and South Vietnamese army generals put the country under military rule. In 1964, North Vietnamese patrol boats attacked two American destroyers in the Gulf of Tonkin. The United States forces sank two torpedo-boats and bombed their bases and oil storages in the first American attack on North Vietnam.

After this incident, **President Johnson** asked Congress for power to take all necessary steps to stop armed attacks against United States forces

Helicopter-borne troops were used extensively during the Vietnam War.

and to prevent further aggression. Congress voted overwhelming approval. Though it technically fell short of a formal declaration of war, the **Gulf of Tonkin Resolution** became the chief legal basis for American involvement in Vietnam. From this point on, the action grew in intensity as the United States and North Vietnam brought in more and more forces. By 1968, more than a half million American troops were in Vietnam. More bombs had been dropped than in World War II, and large sections of the country had been laid waste. But the will of the North and its client insurgents in the South, the Viet Cong, had not been broken. By early 1968, they launched the dramatic **Tet** (New Year) **Offensive** that took the Americans and South Vietnamese by surprise. While the communist offensive was ultimately defeated, it contributed significantly to the war-weariness in the United States.

The "Revolution" Sweeps America. As the casualties mounted, the Vietnam struggle became increasingly unpopular in the United States. Eventually it became the longest war in American history. Left-wing critics insisted that American

imperialism and sinister business interests had brought the United States into the war, but it is difficult to take their arguments seriously. It is more correct to say that the Americans did not see this was essentially a civil war. Most observers agreed that the regime in South Vietnam was corrupt and undemocratic and had done little to win the hearts of the people. Even the Christian community in Vietnam was divided over which side to support. Supporters of the war were motivated by a desire to contain communism and thwart the revolutionary agenda of the international communist movement. Communist revolutionary spirit, in fact, was just at this time sweeping through the United States. Racial riots fanned by class-warfare rhetoric devastated several major American cities, including Los Angeles, Detroit, and Newark. Certain student groups and other radical youth organizations, such as the **Weather Underground** and **Black Panthers**, formed terrorist groups which carried out violent demonstrations and bombings. Leftist protesters calling for overthrow of the government and revolutionary changes to American society staged mass street actions and demonstrations on college campuses. At Kent State University, Ohio National Guard troops opened fire at demonstrators and several students were killed. The Kent State incident reverberated through society, raising to fever pitch the entire spectrum of volatile debate over the Vietnam War, civil rights, and a growing "counterculture."

This counterculture (or "hippie") was characterized by nonconformist dress, use of mind-altering drugs, depraved sexual attitudes and practices, unrestricted expression, youthful rebellion, nontraditional poetry, and hedonistic "rock 'n' roll" music. Similar disruptions occurred in Europe and other parts of the Western world. The Soviet Union stepped up its worldwide "peace movement" propaganda efforts against the United

States, as communist agents of influence infiltrated university campuses and faculties. A black university professor in California, **Angela Davis**, an avowed communist, became the focal point of the radical intellectual community when she was put on trial for her part in violent protests. Among the sympathizers and activists of the leftist movement were several celebrities, most notable and controversial of whom was Hollywood actress **Jane Fonda**. She outraged servicemen and supporters of the war by traveling to North Vietnam, meeting with communist leaders there, and denouncing American soldiers even as many of her captured countrymen were being brutalized in prisons nearby.

In March 1968, Johnson ordered a halt to bombing of the North and announced his retirement. During his Democratic Party's presidential nominating convention in Chicago that year, a massive violent demonstration broke out in the streets, adding to the nation's agonizing over the war. Pledging to spend his last months in office working for peace in Vietnam, Johnson began negotiating a settlement. In November, **Richard Nixon** was elected president on a platform of peace. He ordered the first withdrawal of American troops in June 1969. He called on the "Silent Majority" of Americans to support his initiatives toward an "honorable peace," but by then Americans were against the war by a ratio of 2 to 1, according to public opinion surveys. Reports of 300 civilian deaths at a village called My Lai at the hand of U.S. troops reinforced claims by opponents of the war that it was a brutal and pointless affair from which the United States should withdraw.

Announcing a new policy, Nixon stated that America would help defend its allies and friends, but would no longer "undertake all the defense." American ground combat troops in Vietnam were to be removed, the South Vietnamese forces strengthened, and more stress put upon bombing and technological warfare. The American strategy of ***détente*** (see chapter 13), which began to govern U.S. foreign policy at this time, was constructed to solve the Vietnam quagmire. Secretary of State Kissinger conceptualized the strategy, believing that by harmonizing relations with the Soviets through trade, cultural exchanges, and arms-limitations agreements, Moscow could be turned into a friend and give up its support for Hanoi. The "China card" overtures were also designed to give the United States an option in Southeast Asia if the Soviets demurred. Nixon and Kissinger believed that this diplomatic strategy would allow the United States to save face and extricate itself from Vietnam, producing "peace with honor." Peace talks over ending the war were set up in Paris; but the North Vietnamese and Viet Cong representatives managed to stall and tied up the talks repeatedly. They refused every attempt to gain concessions. The South Vietnamese also showed little interest in negotiations, though the RVN (Republic of Vietnam) troops remained poorly motivated and ineffective on the battlefield.

Ultimately, the "**Nixon Doctrine**" failed to bring peace, and the war spread into Cambodia and Laos. As peace talks dragged on into 1972, the bombing of North Vietnam and Cambodia was resumed. Finally both sides agreed to a cease-fire on January 27, 1973, and the remaining American ground forces began to pull out. Although an international commission supervised the cease-fire, considerable fighting continued and the North and South both tried to seize territory before the peace terms were to be implemented.

Nixon's position was severely weakened beginning in 1973 when a scandal known as **Watergate** broke loose in Washington, D.C., implicating his administration and possibly himself in illegal political activities. Opponents in Congress took advantage of the situation and passed laws limiting the president's authority to prosecute the war. This virtually guaranteed an end to U.S. involvement, both in terms of military participation and economic aid to the tottering and corrupt South Vietnamese government.

In early 1975, the Viet Cong and North Vietnamese launched a full-scale offensive. The American Congress rejected a request by the new U.S. president, **Gerald Ford** (who took office after Nixon resigned in disgrace), for more aid to the South. This loss of further aid was the crippling blow and South Vietnam's **President Thieu** was forced to capitulate. He resigned and fled the country. Communist troops captured Saigon, the South Vietnamese capital, and thousands of people fled into exile. As the victors were bearing down, the last remaining American personnel were evacuated by helicopter from the roof of the U.S. embassy in Saigon, a humiliating spectacle that was a sad ending to America's first outright defeat in wartime. The two Vietnams were then united into one country, with its capital at Hanoi. (Saigon was renamed Ho Chi Minh City.) At the same time, Cambodia fell to the brutal communist insurgents, the **Khmer Rouge**. The communist **Pathet Lao** took over the government in Laos after South Vietnam fell. There seemed to be some momentary validity to the Domino Theory.

Aftermath of the War. The statistics of the war were bleak: 58,000 Americans were dead; 2 million to 3 million Indochinese were killed; three times more U.S. bombs were dropped than in both theaters of World War II; the countryside in Indochina was laid waste. The war cost the United States more than $150 billion, yet all was lost, even though American troops had never lost a major battle of the war.

At first American citizens seemed to reject the returning Vietnam War veterans as symbols of the nation's defeat in a mistaken war. By 1982, the wounds began to heal. A highly popular new president, **Ronald Reagan**, had been elected in 1980 and rallied the nation with new calls for old-fashioned patriotism. The dedication of a Vietnam Veterans Memorial in Washington, D.C., finally began to bring veterans some belated recognition. Although the slogan "No More Vietnams" was still frequently voiced, Reagan returned the nation to a policy and active course of intervening against communism internationally. He referred to the Soviet Union as an "Evil Empire."

Although Vietnam itself had been officially unified, the country remained in turmoil. Some 200,000 supporters of the former Southern regime were interred in "reeducation camps," where up to 10,000 remained for more than a decade. Agriculture was collectivized, and the usual deepening impoverishment followed. In 1978, China attacked Vietnam. More than 1.4 million Vietnamese, including many of Chinese descent, fled by sea. It was believed that as many as 50,000 such "boat people" perished in the process. Nearly three-quarters of a million Vietnamese resettled in the United States.

In Cambodia, the abjectly brutal despot **Pol Pot** took over after the war. His regime murdered or starved more than 1.5 million of the country's 7.5 million people. Pol Pot's guerrillas began harassing Vietnam, which invaded Cambodia in 1978 and installed a puppet government. The Vietnamese army occupied Cambodia, in violation of the U.N. Charter; the U.N. and many Western countries halted development aid. Vietnam turned for help to its longtime sponsor, the U.S.S.R., which had established military bases there. Vietnam's occupation of Cambodia and its slowness in accounting for 2,500 Americans still missing in action during the war prompted the United States to withhold recognition. In an effort to change recognition and secure aid, Vietnam withdrew from Cambodia in 1989 and agreed to cooperate on the MIA (soldiers "missing in action") issue. When the Soviet Union collapsed in 1991, Vietnam increased its effort to normalize relations with the United States, China, and other nations in Southeast Asia. It opened its war archives in 1992 to improve relations with the U.S. The trade embargo was lifted in 1994, and **President Bill Clinton** normalized relations with Vietnam in 1995. Yet Vietnam remained a thoroughly communist country, with an especially bad record on human rights. Christians and their pastors were frequently targets of persecution as enemies of the revolution.

After the Communists took all of Vietnam, many South Vietnamese attempted to flee by boat.

Independence on the Pacific Rim

Australia and New Zealand. By World War II, only a few places in the southwestern Pacific and Southeast Asia were really independent. Australia and New Zealand were white-settlement areas which had developed much like Canada and the United States. The native people had all but disappeared from the scene, and Asian immigration was not allowed. With almost wholly British populations, the countries kept close economic and political ties with the mother country until recent years. Then they began drawing closer to the United States and Japan. The Australians, however, tended to be more nationalistic and independence-minded than the New Zealanders. Both were strongly committed to political and social democracy.

Thailand. A third independent nation was Siam, or Thailand (Land of the Free). During the 1920s and 1930s, it struggled with the problem of Chinese influence. Fearing its giant northern neighbor and the economic power of its large Chinese minority, it took an anticommunist stand after 1945 and leaned heavily upon American aid. This made the military regime extremely vulnerable to leftist criticism and **subversion**, especially with the end of the Vietnam War and American withdrawal from Southeast Asia. The Thais adopted a more neutral policy after 1975.

Internally, Thailand was a politically divided nation into the 1990s. The government changed hands several times, including through a bloodless coup in 1977 and another in 1991. A non-elected military prime minister was installed after elections under a new constitution in 1992. Widespread protests followed, but they were bru-

The Grand Palace in Bangkok, Thailand

tally suppressed by the army. That forced the prime minister to step down and the king appointed a transitional civilian prime minister to head the government. Pro-democracy parties won a majority in the 1992 elections and a civilian government was formed by **Chuan Leekpai**. In January 2001, telecommunications multimillionaire **Thaksin Shinawatra** won an overwhelming victory on a populist platform of economic growth and development.

The Philippines. After acquiring the Philippines in 1898 from Spain, following the Spanish-American War, the United States put down a bitter native rebellion. Then the Americans began preparing the country for independence. They gave the Filipinos a measure of self-government in 1916. Meanwhile, farmers in the United States, who resented Philippine competition, firmly backed moves to grant full independence. A congressional measure in 1934 provided for a transitional period of American rule which could lead to independence in 1945.

In the meantime, General MacArthur was directed to make the Philippine armed forces strong enough to defend their homeland. In late 1941, the Japanese attacked. Although they put up a good fight, the Filipinos were overwhelmed by the vastly larger Japanese force. The Japanese tried to pose as liberators, but they exploited the Filipinos. After the war was over, the Americans honored their promise by proclaiming independence in 1946, only one year behind schedule.

Although the Philippines received much American aid, powerful landlords and a long, drawn-out struggle with communist rebels slowed economic development. Only halting efforts were made to build real democracy. The country's close ties with the United States gradually loosened in the 1960s and 1970s as it pursued a more nationalist and neutralist course. After **Ferdinand Marcos** was elected president in 1965, the regime actually became more authoritarian in the face of a Muslim revolt in the south, student unrest, and a communist insurgency in many rural areas, particularly in the province of Mindanao. By declaring martial law, he was able to restore law and order as well as social and economic reforms. Martial law was lifted in 1981, by which time Marcos had amassed considerable power. His critics charged that he and his family were enriching themselves at the expense of the poor and the national treasury.

In 1983, Marcos' chief political rival, leftist **Benigno S. Aquino, Jr.**, was assassinated as he was returning from exile. A wave of popular protest arose and Marcos loyalists were accused of complicity in the killing. In legislative elections during 1984, the opposition gained ground. At the same time, the communist insurgency grew. Marcos called for elections in hopes of boosting his political mandate. Aquino's widow, **Corazon Aquino**, who had the backing of the Roman Catholic Church and the business community, claimed victory. But the National Assembly declared Marcos the winner. Mrs. Aquino launched a campaign of nonviolent resistance, and her supporters charged the Marcos regime with political fraud. In February 1984, both Marcos and Mrs. Aquino held presidential inauguration ceremonies. Crowds turned out to protect the dissident leaders, and the United States put pressure on Marcos to resign. Marcos left the Philippines for exile in the United States a few days later. The U.S. government immediately recognized Mrs. Aquino as the head of the government.

Despite popular support, Mrs. Aquino faced substantial obstacles in her attempts to restructure the government, restore civil rights, boost free enterprise, and recover public moneys which she claimed the Marcos family and political cronies had stolen. She was unable to control the insurgents or to halt government corruption. There were several coup attempts after Marcos died in 1989. A six-month state of emergency was declared in 1989, and dissidence was quelled with the help of the U.S. military. Since the Aquino administration, the Philippines has experienced a series of reasonably peaceful, democratic presidential elections.

In 1990, Mount Pinatubo, a volcano near the U.S. Clark Air Force Base, erupted, forcing the base to be abandoned. The Philippine Senate refused to renew a lease for the Subic Bay Naval Base, further loosening ties between the Philippines and its longtime patron, the United States. The last U.S. military and naval units left Philippine soil in 1992, ending nearly a century of presence. In 1996, the government and the **Moro National Liberation Front**, the major Muslim guerrilla movement, signed a peace treaty, ending a 20-year war in which over 50,000 people had died. Not all Islamist groups have made peace, however. The **Abu Sayyaf** Islamic group has continued terrorist activities in the southern islands of the Philippines. The United States has provided assistance to Filipino forces as part of the War on Terrorism.

Malaysia and Singapore. The British had ruled the Malayan peninsula, which was rich in tin and rubber, since the eighteenth century. Large numbers of Indians and Chinese moved there and produced a complex racial mixture. The Japanese captured the peninsula during World War II, but the British regained control after the war. A communist rebellion which began in 1948 was put down nearly a decade later, and an independent **Federation of Malaya**, including Malaya and Singapore, was created in 1957. This became **Malaysia** in 1963 with the addition of British possessions on the island of Borneo. **Singapore** withdrew two years later and became a separate state.

In 1969, rioting between Malays and Chinese brought down the government of **Tanku Abdul Rahman**. Sporadic Chinese-Malay tensions continued into the late 1980s, when the leaders of the unrest were outlawed and imprisoned. They were all released in 1989. A **New Economic Policy**, launched in 1971, was declared a success twenty years later, as the government announced it had alleviated poverty and brought about greater economic unity among rival ethnic groups.

Since 1959, Singapore's politics and government had been completely dominated by **Lee Kuan Yew** and his **People's Action Party**. In 1991, the constitution was revised to increase the power of the presidency. The power of the PAP was diminished somewhat in elections during 1991. In 1993, **Ong Ten Cheong** became Singapore's first directly elected president.

Since its independence in 1965, Singapore has become a major financial and industrial power. It has one of the highest living standards in Asia. The government closely manages the economy and takes a paternalistic approach to law and order. Singapore has maintained a strong pro-Western foreign policy, and its stature increased

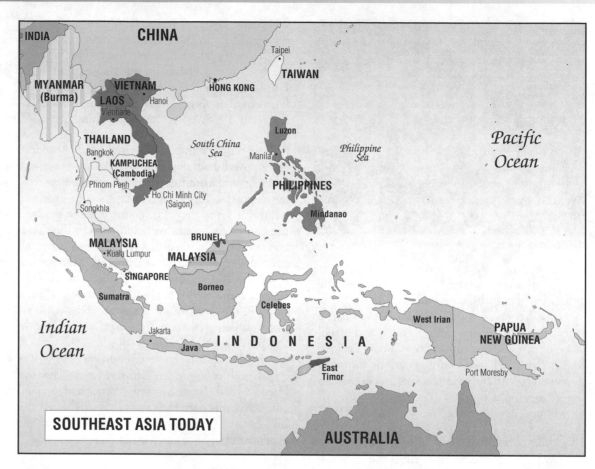

SOUTHEAST ASIA TODAY

as the specter of Chinese communist takeover of the other main capitalist commercial center of Asia, Hong Kong, loomed in the late 1990s.

Hong Kong. The longtime British colony of Hong Kong had been eyed by China for many years. The Chinese staged riots there during the Cultural Revolution in 1967 and declared that treaties governing Hong Kong were invalid because they had been imposed by force. However, China did not disturb Hong Kong to any great extent, perhaps because 40 percent of its foreign exchange earnings came

from trade and commercial transactions with the capitalist enclave.

In 1982, Britain and China opened negotiations about Hong Kong's future. A declaration was signed in 1984 stating that China would resume sovereignty over the colony in 1997. China guaranteed autonomy and agreed to allow capitalism to continue for another 50 years. Under the agreement, Hong Kong was to become a special administrative region of China and was promised a high degree of local autonomy; but only one-third of the municipal legislature was to be popularly elected and the chief executive was to be appointed by the Chinese government. This agreement was put into effect on July 1, 1997, after China took control of Hong Kong.

Indonesia. Holland viewed its Asian colonial possessions as the property of the mother country and an important source of the nation's wealth. Authoritarian colonial rule exploited the islands economically, and problems existed between the Muslim majority and Christian minority. (One of the largest missionary churches in the non-Western world existed among the Batak people on Sumatra.)

Japan's successful war against Russia in 1905 sparked an Islamic revival and the growth of nationalism. In 1927, **Dr. Achmed Sukarno** joined other Western-educated activists in founding the **Indonesian Nationalist Association**. It tried to follow Gandhi's example by organizing massive noncooperation with the regime. The Dutch suppressed this and other political movements and banned the use of the name "Indonesia." Then Sukarno joined forces with the Muslim Socialist, **Muhammad Hatta**, during the Japanese occupation. On August 17, 1945, they proclaimed the **Republic of Indonesia**.

Holland was prepared to permit only internal self-government, keeping foreign policy, defense, and financial questions in Dutch hands. For several years, guerrilla warfare continued. Finally the Dutch agreed to pull out.

Under Sukarno's authoritarian leadership and "**guided democracy**," Indonesia came close to bankruptcy. He nationalized foreign-owned plantations and business firms and practiced his own brand of imperialism on Timor, Borneo, and New Guinea. The influence of the army grew as corruption, inflation, declining exports, and financial mismanagement added to Indonesia's economic problems. Sukarno named himself president for life in 1963 and lived like a playboy, squandering vast sums on sports stadiums and monuments.

At the same time, Sukarno was developing ties with China, and the Indonesian Communist Party was growing in strength. Then in September 1965, a group of renegade army officers tried to seize power. However, forces led by **General Suharto** won a quick victory, accused the rival officers of taking part in a communist plot, and in the next few months killed more than 300,000 **alleged** Communists. The takeover was one of the most successful anticommunist **countercoups** in the postwar world.

Sukarno was gradually eased out of power, and Suharto finally took over as president in 1967. He tried to restore political and economic stability to Indonesia, a country rich in oil and other natural resources. However, the basic problems of unemployment, overpopulation, poverty, and political corruption persisted.

Indonesia's economic problems of the late 1990s brought with it rising economic and political turmoil. Less than three months after being reelected for the seventh time, Suharto resigned from office on May 21, 1998, and was replaced by **Vice President Habibie**. Reforms have been announced and presidential elections have since been held, but much remains uncertain as to what will become of this resource-rich region in the future. Since the fall of Suharto, there has been significant civil unrest, as well as conflicts between Christians and Muslims. In 1999, Indonesia was forced to give up control of the territory of **East Timor**, which it had occupied since the Portuguese left in 1975.

Nationalism and Conflict in the Middle East

Complex situations have faced the peoples of the Middle East in the twentieth century. The division of the Ottoman Empire into several different mandates and an independent Turkey was discussed in chapter 11.

Iran. Another important independent country was Iran, which provided leadership in contacts with the West. During the 1930s, Iran was friendly with Nazi Germany (45 percent of its foreign trade was with the Germans), but it remained neutral at the outset of the war. In 1941, the Allies demanded use of Iran's railroad to send supplies to the Soviet Union. Later they

The Muslim religion dominates life in Iran.

occupied the country. Although the Allies promised to respect Iran's sovereignty and give economic aid during and after the war, the Russians backed movements opposed to the shah in two northern provinces and refused to withdraw their troops. Through political maneuvers by the shah's son, **Mohammad Reza Pahlavi** (1919–1980, who became shah in September 1941), and pressure from the West in the U.N., the Soviets finally pulled out. Nevertheless, communism remained a serious threat.

A strong anti-foreign group then tried to end British ownership of the Iranian oil industry. Their influence peaked in 1951 when the parliament nationalized the huge Abadán oil production facilities. In 1954, Iran signed an agreement with the major companies to market the country's petroleum and share in the profits. After this, the shah aligned himself firmly with the Western bloc and joined the **Central Treaty Organization** (CENTO).

Oil money built irrigation and hydroelectric projects, expanded transportation and communication systems, created industry, and built schools—all part of a seven-year development program. With the help of women who had just been given voting rights, the shah pushed through a land reform measure. By using oil money to obtain the most modern weapons systems, he also made Iran the strongest military power in the Middle East.

However, he bullied the parliament and repressed critics both on the left and the right. Conservatives backed by the **Shiite** Muslim faction opposed his efforts at modernization and his more secular stand toward Islam. Leftists and students resented the shah's authoritarian methods. In 1978, members of both factions took part in the widespread riots that brought down his regime. The **Ayatollah Ruhollah Khomeini**

Khomeini (1900–1989) placed Iran on a path toward Islamic radicalism.

returned from exile in Paris to Iran in 1979 to provide leadership in the establishment of a radical Islamic republic. Hundreds of the shah's supporters and suspected members of the shah's secret police force, the **Savak**, were arrested, tried, and executed. Khomeini denounced the United States as the "Great Satan" and put Iran on a course of undoing the shah's westernization programs. A new constitution imposed **Sharia** (Islamic law) as the legal system for Iran. Khomeini and other Islamic religious leaders became the political government as well.

In November 1979, the U.S. embassy in Tehran was seized and a number of hostages were taken by paramilitary students. The hostage situation became a prolonged international crisis which contributed to the election defeat in 1980 of U.S. President **Jimmy Carter** who appeared weak in his inability to free the American hostages. The hostages were released at the very moment his successor, Ronald Reagan, was being sworn into office in 1981.

A border dispute with neighboring Iraq erupted into a bloody war between the two countries in 1980. The war continued until 1988. Khomeini used both the hostage crisis and the Iran-Iraq

War to consolidate his domestic support, and the Muslim clerics in the government gained increased influence and control over civil affairs. Moderate **President Abolhassan Bani-Sadr** was dismissed in 1981, and his successor was assassinated. **Hojatolislam Ali Khamenei** was elected president in 1981 and reelected in 1985. The iron-hearted Ayatollah died in July 1989 and was succeeded by Khamenei as religious leader and **Hashemi Rafsanjani** as president.

The Islamic government continued to have strong support at home, despite economic problems and political repression, and disapproval abroad, largely due to of its links to **Hezbollah** ("Party of God") and other Islamic terrorist groups. Iran remained neutral in 1991 during the **Persian Gulf War**, after Iraq invaded Kuwait. Following that war, Iraq finally returned Iranian prisoners taken during the Iran-Iraq War. Since the Gulf War, Iran has sought investment from Western Europe and has been trying to develop a nuclear program with assistance from Russia. At the same time, many countries have been concerned about Iran's continued support for Islamic radicalism and the possibility that Iran might be attempting to develop nuclear weapons. Support for the hard-line Islamic government in Iran waned in the late 1990s. Efforts to foster liberalization within Iran through the election of reform governments and public demonstrations faltered, however, in the face of the Islamic clerics' continued influence over the election process, control over the security forces, and the lack of widespread public support beyond the cities and university campuses.

Arab Versus Jew. The focal point of much of the conflict in the Middle East since early in the twentieth century was Palestine, the ancient land of the Hebrews which had been turned over to Britain as a mandate by the League of Nations following World War I. Organized violence by both Jews and Arabs wracked the country as the British were unable to serve the interests of both factions. The British wanted to create an independent Palestinian state which would protect the interests of the two groups, and both would take part in its government. This seemed more feasible in 1919 when less than 10 percent of the total population was Jewish. The **Balfour Declaration** of 1917 expressed Britain's support for a Jewish homeland, and the goals of the declaration were incorporated into a mandate governing Palestine in 1922. By 1947, Hitler's persecution had swelled the number of Jews in Palestine to 614,000 out of a total population of 1,851,000.

Zionists, with strong backing in the United States, kept demanding a separate Jewish state. At the end of World War II, the violence steadily increased as Jewish terrorist groups such as the **Haganah** and the **Stern Gang** acquired modern weapons. They struck at the British as well as at the Arab Palestinians.

Israel Becomes a Nation. Britain was caught between the Zionists with their American allies and the Palestinians supported by the six countries in the **Arab League**—Egypt, Saudi Arabia, Trans-Jordan, Lebanon, Syria, and Iraq. Exhausted and bankrupt from World War II, the British could not afford the large-scale military effort needed to keep the two groups apart. So Britain turned the matter over to the United Nations, which worked out a plan for partitioning Palestine. But neither the Jews nor Arabs were satisfied with it. On May 14, 1948, one day before the partition would have gone into effect, radical Zionists led by **David Ben-Gurion** proclaimed the creation of the independent state of **Israel**. In 1949, the new govenment adopted a constitution that provided for a strong cabinet and parliament (**Knesset**) to run the democratic republic. Both Jews and Arabs would have voting rights.

While the United States and Soviet Union quickly recognized Israel, the Arab League attacked the new nation. Although outnumbered, Israeli troops easily defeated them and captured even more territory than had been assigned in the original division. In July 1949, a U.N. mediator, the American diplomat **Ralph Bunche**, finally worked out a cease-fire. In 1950, he won the Nobel Peace Prize, the first black man in the world so honored. Israel and most of the Arab states remained officially at war, but efforts in the 1970s by Henry Kissinger, and later by President Jimmy Carter, did achieve a peace agreement with Egypt.

The kingdom of Trans-Jordan (independent since 1946 and now renamed **Jordan**) took over the **West Bank** region (west of the Jordan River) and the old part of Jerusalem. The **Gaza Strip**, a narrow territory along the Mediterranean just northeast of Egypt, went to Egypt. About 1 million Palestinians sought refuge in huge, makeshift camps in Jordan, Lebanon, and Egypt, where they lived off U.N. relief and sought to recover their lost lands. Meanwhile, Israel, with massive American aid and contributions from Jews around the world, experienced rapid economic growth. The **kibbutz**, a type of agricultural commune, helped the Israeli people develop the desert lands.

Living under a state of constant siege, the Israelis in 1956 and again in 1967 launched wars to improve their defensive position and lessen the Palestinian threat. In the **Six-Day War** (1967) they overran the **Golan Heights** of Syria, the West Bank, and the Sinai region in a great show of strength. But this only brought more problems—such as an increase in Arab residents and worldwide condemnation by the Soviet bloc and Third World countries. Israel's image of strength was tarnished in the fourth conflict, the **Yom**

ISRAEL TODAY
- Israel Proper
- Palastinian Administrated
- Occupied Territories

LEBANON
GOLAN HEIGHTS
SYRIA
Galilee
Sea of Galilee
Haifa
Nazareth
Mediterranean Sea
Nablus
Tel-Aviv
WEST BANK
Amman
Jericho
Jerusalem
Bethlehem
Gaza
GAZA STRIP
Hebron
Dead Sea
Beersheba
Negev
JORDAN
EGYPT
Elat
Gulf of Aqaba

Kippur War (1973). At that time, Egyptian and Syrian forces temporarily drove the Israelis back and exhausted their reserves of manpower and weapons, although the Israelis managed in the end to hold off the Arab attack.

Strong opposition to the Israelis came from groups such as the **Palestine Liberation Organization (PLO)**, its rival Palestinian terrorist factions, and other militant Islamic groups. Both the U.N. and Arab governments recognized the PLO as the "sole legitimate representative" of the Palestinian people. The PLO and others worked actively to destroy Israel. In 1972, a terrorist massacre of Israeli athletes at the Olympic Games in Munich, Germany, shocked the world. Bombings continue to occur throughout Israel. In response to such activities, the Israelis tried unsuccessfully to wipe out the Palestinian guerrilla units operating among the refugee camps in southern Lebanon.

In 1977, a right-wing government under **Menachem Begin** assumed power in Israel and, with assistance from Jimmy Carter, signed a peace accord with Egypt in 1979, which was denounced by Palestinians and Islamic militants. Begin proclaimed all of Jerusalem the Israeli capital in 1980, annexed the Golan Heights in 1981, and increased Jewish settlement in the West Bank. In 1982, Israel invaded Lebanon to root out PLO guerrilla bases. A coalition government, which came to power in 1984, withdrew most Israeli troops from Lebanon in 1985; all Israeli troops were eventually removed from Lebanon in 2000. In December 1987, Palestinians began an increasingly bloody uprising known as the *intifada*, attacking Jews and Israeli soldiers with sticks, stones, bombs, and other small weapons in the West Bank and Gaza.

Israel remained officially neutral during the Persian Gulf War but was attacked by Iraqi SCUD missiles. Following the war, the United States stepped

Modern Tel Aviv is Israel's major metropolitan center.

up efforts to get regional peace talks moving. In 1993, Israel's new liberal **Prime Minister Yitzhak Rabin** signed a historic peace accord with PLO leader **Yassar Arafat**. The agreement set up an autonomous Palestinian entity in the Gaza Strip and in the West Bank city of Jericho. Sporadic violence continued, but in 1994, Israel completed the withdrawal of its troops from Gaza and Jericho. This treaty was denounced by Iran and opposed by more militant Palestinians and other Muslims.

In July 1994, peace in the Middle East took another significant step forward when Rabin and Jordan's **King Hussein** signed an agreement in Washington, D.C., ending a 46-year state of war between their two countries. As the twentieth century drew to a close, there were increased international hopes that the Jewish-Arab conflict might soon develop into a full-fledged peace.

The Middle East peace process suffered a set back with the assassination of Prime Minister Rabin in 1995. The peace process stalled during a series of Israeli prime ministers after Rabin's murder. He was followed in short succession by **Shimon Peres, Benjamin Netanyahu**, and **Ehud Barak**. Barak attempted to broker a deal with Arafat with the assistance of President Clinton in late 2000, but negotiations failed.

Conflict between Israelis and Palestinians increased significantly after the second *intifada* began in September 2000, contributing to the election of Ariel Sharon as prime minister of Israel in 2001. In an effort to stop Palestinian terrorism, the Israelis began construction of a wall separating the Palestinian territories from Israel. Israeli forces also reoccupied much of the Palestinian lands.

It took changes within the **Palestinian Authority**, however, before any movement toward peace could begin. The position of prime minister for

Yassar Arafat, 1929–2004

the Palestinian Authority was established by the Palestinian Legislative Council in 2003, but it had little effect in helping the peace process or reforming the Palestinian government. It was not until the death of Yassar Arafat in November 2004 and the election of former prime minister **Mahmoud Abbas** as president of the Palestinian Authority in January 2005 that Israelis and Palestinians began to take small steps toward restarting the peace process.

Israel's determination to remain in Palestine is reinforced by the memory of the Holocaust. Jewish theologians regard this tragedy as an event second only to the Exodus in importance. Jews have resolved that they will never allow such persecution again. For nearly 2,000 years they had been a people without a land; now they had reclaimed their former homeland. Even though the majority of the world's Jews have not settled in Israel, most regard it as their spiritual home.

The Palestinian issue put some Christians in a difficult position. In the West, many liberals, especially among the Protestants, were tormented by a deep sense of guilt for the Holocaust. Yet they wanted the Palestinians who were driven from their homes to receive justice. They were afraid to criticize Israeli policy lest they be considered anti-Semitic. Fundamentalist Protestants, however, were among the most enthusiastic supporters of the state of Israel, largely due to certain doctrinal beliefs that the rise of Israel signaled the imminent return of Christ to set up a supposed thousand-year earthly reign in Jerusalem. Even though Christian missionary work in Israel is forbidden, they saw events in Palestine as the fulfillment of biblical prophecy—proof that God is at work in history. On the other hand, almost all Eastern Christians—Assyro-Chaldean, Catholic, Coptic, Maronite, Orthodox, etc.—firmly back the Palestinians. Like Muslims, they considered Israel an outpost of Western colonialism.

Lebanon. Lebanon, to the north of Israel, has been a crossroads of history since ancient times. Christianity (including some offshoot Christian sects such as the Maronites and Jacobites) became well established there by the fourth century, but Islam (with its Shiite and Sunni divisions, and an offshoot cult called the Druze) also made major inroads. Lebanese Christians fought alongside European knights during the Crusades against the Muslims. From 1516 until 1918, Lebanon was part of the Ottoman Empire, under which the country developed religious, educational, and commercial ties with the West. These ties led to political rivalries among various powers, including France, England, and Russia, each assuming a role to protect certain ethnic and religious interests there. After World War I, Lebanon became a French mandate and remained so until 1946, when it gained independence.

For a time, Lebanon was a unified and progressive nation. But its many internal divisions began to unravel that harmony in the 1950s. The Arab-Israeli conflicts, from which Lebanon refrained directly, brought many Palestinians into the country, and it was used as a base of action against Israel. A revolt broke out in 1958, and the United States sent marines to establish order. A civil war erupted in 1975 between the **Nationalist Movement** (a mixture of socialists, communists, and followers of Egypt's Gamal Nasser) and the **Lebanese Front** (a group of right-wing Maronite-Phalange Christians and right-wing Muslims). The PLO sided with the Nationalists and nearly won the war until Syria, with the backing of the Arab League, intervened on the side of the Lebanese Front. The Arab League helped arrange a cease-fire in 1976. Syria continued to dominate Lebanon until 2005.

Syria's intervention failed to halt the violence and factional strife. Israel invaded southern Lebanon in 1978 in response to PLO attacks but withdrew when a United Nations peacekeeping force arrived. Israel again invaded in 1982, occupied Beirut, and forced the PLO out of its headquarters there. Another multinational peace force arrived in 1982 and a new Christian Phalange leader, **Amin Gemayel**, concluded a security agreement with Israel. Syria refused to withdraw, however, and the government was unable to halt fighting between the armed militias of Lebanon's various internal factions and between rival Palestinian groups. There were terrorist bomb attacks on the American-led multinational force (250 American marines were killed in a terrible explosion in October 1983), and the force was withdrawn in 1984. Gemayel backed out of the Lebanese-Israeli Accord and installed a pro-Syria cabinet, which did little after Gemayel rejected a Syrian peace plan in 1986. This rejection escalated the turmoil, and terrorist activities, especially by Hezbollah, increased. Prime Minister **Rashid Karami** was assassinated in 1987. In 1988, the legislature's inability to find a successor to Gemayel led to the formation of rival Christian and Muslim governments. However, an Arab-brokered peace in 1989 led to the election of Maronite **Rene Moawed** as president, but he was assassinated almost immediately. Christian Prime Minister **General Michel Aoun** launched a war against the Syrian forces in Lebanon. New hopes for peace arose when Aoun surrendered in 1990, political equality was granted to Muslims, the Lebanese militias were disarmed, and a number of Western hostages held by Shiite terrorist groups were released. Syria and Lebanon signed a treaty in 1991. A year later, parliamentary elections were boycotted by Christians, but the country began to rebuild under the leadership of **Rafiq al-Hariri**, who served as prime minister from 1992 to 1998 and 2000 to 2004. His murder in February 2005 led to widespread demonstrations, which led Syria to withdraw from Lebanon.

Egypt. After World War II, overall Arab unity encountered problems—growing nationalism in various countries, competition between the Cold War blocs, and new military regimes in many places. Egypt, the most populous nation and intellectual center of the Arab world, had a deep impact on other parts of the Middle East. It tried unsuccessfully to negotiate an end to British control of the Suez Canal and the Sudan. Finally in 1952, a military coup overthrew the corrupt and ineffective **King Farouk**. Among the group was **Colonel Gamal Abdel Nasser**, who after two years would emerge as leader. He became the dominant personality in the Middle East until his death in 1970.

Nasser established single party rule and worked for economic development, socialism, and the end of foreign influence. He obtained agreements with Britain which led to the withdrawal of troops from the canal zone in 1955 and to the independence of the Sudan in 1956. Displeased with some of Nasser's actions, the United States canceled the loan it had promised for Nasser's grand scheme, the **Aswan High Dam**. The Egyptian president then turned to the Soviet Union, even though he followed an anticommunist policy.

The Soviets helped him because they hoped to stop American influence in the Middle East. At the same time, Nasser formed close links with his Arab neighbors and used the Arab League to back revolutionary movements in the North African French territories. His status grew when he nationalized the Suez Canal (1956).

By joining forces with Syria in 1958, Nasser seemed finally to have found the way to Arab unity. But the **United Arab Republic** which they formed lasted only three years. Meanwhile, poverty in Egypt increased in spite of the Aswan project.

Nasser died in 1970 and was succeeded by his vice-president, **Anwar Sadat**. Two years later, Sadat ordered 20,000 Soviet military advisers and other experts out of Egypt because the Soviets, he believed, were not willing to supply modern weapons needed to roust Israel out of captured territories. When Sadat delayed actions against Israel, students agitated and clashed with police. Sadat assured the dissidents that he would soon take military action against Israel, which he did in the surprise attack on October 6, 1973, at the same time Syria attacked through the Golan Heights. The action raised Sadat's stature in the Arab world. However, it was he who eventually joined with Israel's Begin in signing the peace accord in 1979. That **rapprochement** soon isolated Egypt from the rest of the Arab world. Sadat found new opposition at home from militants and was forced to order a crackdown on them in September 1981. Some 1,600 religious (most Islamic fundamentalists) and secular dissidents were arrested. A month later, while attending a military parade, Sadat was assassinated by gunmen associated with a militant Muslim group.

Hosni Mubarak

He was succeeded by **Hosni Mubarak**, who was reelected in 1987 and 1993. Mubarak continued Sadat's policies toward Israel but also improved relations with other Arab states. He led Arabs to join the United States against Iraq in the Persian Gulf War of 1991. He also was active in promoting the 1993 peace accord between Israel and the PLO. While cracking down on radical Islamic fundamentalists, he sought to cooperate with Egypt's activist Muslim Brotherhood.

Iraq. As the position of Egyptian leaders diminished somewhat within the Arab world, that group lacked strong leadership. One figure who attempted to fill the void was Iraq's strongman, **Saddam Hussein**, who came to power in 1979.

Like Palestine, Iraq had become a British mandate under grant from the League of Nations following World War I. **Faisel I** of the **Hashemite** family was installed as king. The mandate was ended following disturbances in 1932, but the British remained a strong influence in Iraq until 1958. During the 1940s and 1950s, Iraq took a strong pro-Western stance under **Nuri es-Said**, who sought to modernize the country. Iraq joined CENTO in 1955, the only Arab state to do so. But radical nationalists caused trouble which led to a military coup under **General Abdul Karim**

Kassem in 1958. A pro-Communist republic was proclaimed and es-Said and the royal family were murdered. Violence continued until the Kassem regime collapsed in 1963. Another coup took place in 1968 when **Ahmad Hassan al-Bakr** took power. He was succeeded in 1979 by Saddam Hussein, a rising member of al-Bakr's **Ba'ath Party**. Saddam took a strident anti-Israel stand, participating in the Arab-Israeli War of 1973. Israel attacked an Iraqi nuclear reactor in 1981, fearing it might be used to create atomic weapons.

In 1972, Hussein signed a treaty with the U.S.S.R. and received military aid. It resumed diplomatic ties with the United States in 1984, partly because it was fighting Iran, whose relations with the United States were highly strained. After the Iran-Iraq War ended with a United Nations-brokered cease-fire, Hussein's regime launched a chemical weapons attack upon Kurdish rebels in the north of Iraq. Two years later, in 1990, Hussein accused Kuwait and the United Arab Emirates of violating oil cartel regulations and driving oil prices down, thus reducing Iraq's all-important oil revenues. He also charged that Kuwait had stolen Iraqi oil, and he demanded that Kuwait and other Gulf States cancel about $30 billion in loans they had granted to Iraq during its war with Iran. He said they owed Iraq this consideration because Iraq had been fighting for the cause of all Arabs against the Persian Iranians.

When his demands were not met, Iraq invaded Kuwait. On August 28, 1990, Hussein annexed Kuwait. Nearly universal international condemnation followed, including from fellow Arab countries. The PLO and Libya supported Hussein's action, while Jordan tried to maintain its safety, being situated between Iraq and Israel, by both condemning Western reaction against Hussein and allowing vital movements by Western interests in Jordan.

The militaries of many nations fought in the war against Iraq.

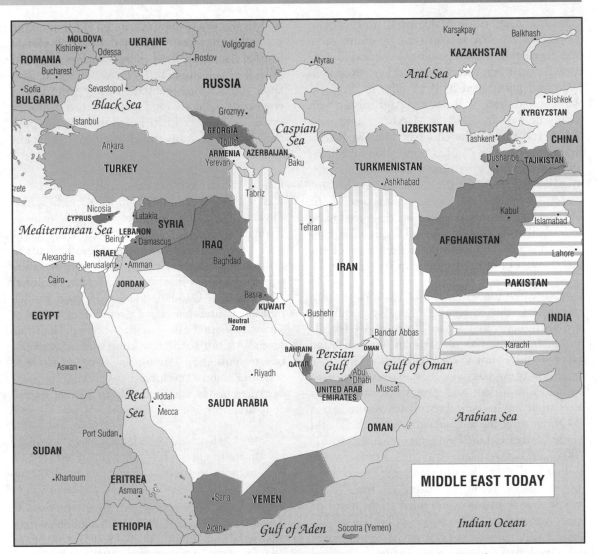

MIDDLE EAST TODAY

In 1991, the Persian Gulf War began after Hussein failed to comply with United Nations' orders to withdraw from Kuwait. A coalition led by the United States under President **George H. W. Bush**, attacked Iraq with massive aerial bombardments and swift-moving ground troops, forcing it to accept peace terms within a month. Hussein remained in power and immediately turned on Kurds in the north and dissident Shiites in the south. "No-fly-zones" were established by U.S. and other allied forces in the north (1991) and south (1992) of Iraq to prevent Iraqi aircraft from attacking the Kurds and Shiites. The northern zone enabled the Kurds to establish an autonomous region in northern Iraq. Iraq continued to suffer under economic sanctions, as well as occasional allied air attacks for Hussein's failure to comply with all U.N. peace terms and violations of the "no-fly-zones." Hussein, in turn, periodically flexed his muscles in attempts to shake that embargo.

Hussein's failure to live up to the terms of the Persian Gulf War treaty and various U.N. resolutions—especially with regard to Iraq's possession of weapons of mass destruction—as well as Iraq's ties to terrorist organizations, eventually led to the overthrow of his government. In March 2003, the United States and Great Britain—with help from

Australia, Poland, and Kurdish rebels—invaded Iraq, capturing Baghdad and all other major Iraqi cities in a month-long conventional war. Hussein was captured in December 2003, but a serious insurgency continues against U.S.-led coalition forces and the new Iraqi government. In spite of terrorist threats, a large number of Iraqis voted in parliamentary elections in January 2005.

Rest of the Middle East. Developments in some Middle Eastern and North African areas were marked by tensions while elsewhere decolonization went smoothly. **Turkey** aligned with NATO after World War II in order to check the growing Soviet threat, but still it suffered from political instability and low economic growth. **Cyprus** gained independence from Britain in 1960 with

Orthodox **Archbishop Makarios III** as president. The island republic was so torn by ethnic strife (the population was 80 percent Greek and 20 percent Turkish) that forces from Turkey invaded in 1974 and partitioned it. Both sides in the Cold War courted strategically located **Afghanistan** with economic aid. In 1978, a Marxist regime took power and moved the country closer to Russia. Resistance from its Muslim population and instability within the government provoked a Soviet invasion in December 1979. The Soviets became deeply embroiled in a protracted war against the Muslim rebels in Afghanistan, which proved to be so costly that they eventually pulled out of Afghanistan in 1989, in a manner reminiscent of the withdrawal of the United States from Vietnam.

However, fighting within Afghanistan continued; first against the remaining Afghan communists and then between Afghan factions. An Islamic movement known as the **Taliban** arose to bring order to the country, eventually gaining control over most of Afghanistan. It established a militant Islamic government and gave shelter to **Osama bin Laden** and his radical terrorist group known as **al-Qaida**. After the al-Qaida attacks on the **World Trade Center** and the **Pentagon** on September 11, 2001, the United States launched attacks on the Taliban and al-Qaida. With the assistance of local Afghan forces, **Kabul** was captured, the Taliban regime was overthrown, and many of the terrorists were captured or killed, although bin Laden has yet to be apprehended. A new Afghan government was established and the country's first democratic election was held in 2004.

The French tried to hold on to their North African empire, but nationalist movements in **Tunisia** and **Morocco** forced them to withdraw and grant independence in 1956. In **Algeria**, the situation was complicated by the presence of 1 million European settlers who regarded the territory

as their homeland. The result was a bloody eight-year-long conflict. It had a deep psychological impact upon the French, much like the Vietnam War was to have in the United States a decade later. Those who wanted "victory" in Algeria engineered General De Gaulle's return to power in 1958. However, he surprised them by stopping the bloodshed and permitting Algerian independence in 1962.

Libya, which received independence in 1951, was the poorest of the North African states. However, the discovery of rich oil reserves changed everything. In 1969, an army coup ended the monarchy and added another radical military regime, this one headed by the unstable, egocentric, hard-line Muslim leftist, **Colonel Muammar al-Qaddafi**. He was known for his radicalism and hatred of Israel. He has been accused of interfering in the internal affairs of several African states, providing support for various revolutionary groups, engaging in terrorist activities, and developing weapons of mass destruction. He has been able to survive several coup attempts.

Colonel Qaddafi has been largely unsuccessful in his efforts to export his radicalism. He failed in his attempts to merge Libya with neighboring countries, and his activities have provoked international opposition. In 1986, President Ronald Reagan ordered U.S. warplanes to raid Libya after a Libyan-sponsored attack in Berlin killed two American servicemen. Qaddafi's palace was hit and members of his family were killed, but he escaped. He became an international outcast after Libya was implicated in the destruction of two civilian airliners and the resulting death of several hundred people in 1988 and 1989. Sanctions against Libya did not begin to be lifted until 1999 when the two Libyan security agents who were implicated in the deadly Pan Am airliner

bombing over Scotland were turned over for prosecution and compensation was agreed to for both airline bombings. All remaining sanctions were lifted in 2004 when Libya revealed its weapons of mass destruction program and agreed to give up all such weapons.

Along the Arabian coast, the British surrendered their protectorates, beginning with oil-rich Kuwait in 1961, followed by Aden in 1967, and Bahrain, Oman, Qatar, and the United Arab Emirates in 1971. Each of these nations joined the Arab League and backed the effort against Israel.

By 1989, the only Muslim population still under colonial rule was in the Soviet Union. In spite of communist talk about national liberation, in 1924 the Islamic peoples were divided into five "republics"—**Kazakhstan**, **Kirghiza**, **Tadzhikistan**, **Turkmenistan**, and **Uzbekistan**. The boundaries were drawn more or less according to language groups, but the republics lacked any national consciousness. Instead, many of the Muslims in Central Asia espoused an ancient ideology known as **Pan-Turanism** ("All-Turkism"), which included a vision for dominion of Turkic peoples from the Pacific to Europe. This vision was particularly strong in an ongoing conflict between Muslims (Azeri Turks) in the Soviet republic of **Azerbaijan** and neighboring **Armenia**, the oldest officially Christian nation on earth. During the Soviet period, the Muslim peoples were transformed overnight from "oppressed masses" into "younger brothers" in the struggle for peace and equality. Although they had the outward form of self-government, they were politically, economically, and culturally ruled by Moscow. But with the rising tide of Muslim identity following the revolution in Iran, it became clear that these territories might be the source of great weakness in the Soviet system. Following the breakup of the Soviet Union in late 1991, these Muslim republics gained independence, although they remained part of the **Commonwealth of Independent States** which formed among the former Soviet territories.

Independence and Instability in Africa

Leading the struggle for independence in Africa were political parties modeled after European organizations. The party leaders were Western-educated, middle class, urban Africans who understood how the colonial state worked; and they believed that the way to independence was to work through that state and eventually take it over. They transformed what were originally elite black groups into mass parties by adopting goals which appealed to as many different ethnic groups and economic classes as possible. However, their chance to practice **electoral** politics in a democratic way had been limited. Africans learned how to use political groups to gain power, but they had no experience in the more difficult art of giving up power after an election defeat.

Many of the newly independent countries suffered internal struggles between different ethnic and linguistic groups. Earlier European colonial boundaries had not always followed ethnic divisions. Consequently, the new countries had difficulty trying to establish unity among diverse groups of people. Africa experienced numerous ghastly conflicts with the tragic results of widespread starvation, disease, and ethnic bloodshed. Several of them, the worst of which were in Ethiopia, Mozambique, Somalia, and Rwanda, led to international crises.

Ghana. Decolonization south of the Sahara came first to the Gold Coast where more political development had taken place in the interwar years.

Kwame Nkrumah, left, exchanges views with Prime Minister Nehru of India before a U.N. General Assembly session in 1960.

Kwame Nkrumah, an American-educated Marxist and skillful politician, founded an organization in 1949 that took the lead. The British agreed to a constitution allowing self-government for the colony, and he campaigned from prison for the new assembly. Because the party won, he was released and later named prime minister. He used this position to negotiate independence for the country, renaming it **Ghana**. It became the first black African member of the Commonwealth of Nations.

Once Ghana had gained freedom in 1957, Nkrumah set up a one-party dictatorship with himself as president for life. He argued, as many after him elsewhere have done, that having only one party would help national unity. A poor, developing nation could not afford the luxury of political opposition. He then tried to become the spokesman for all of Africa, but his lust for power and extravagant living proved his undoing. When a military group seized control in 1966, he fled into exile and died six years later.

The colonial dike rapidly crumbled. The British gave the rest of its African colonies independence in the 1960s. De Gaulle dismantled the vast French empire in west and central Africa between 1958 and 1960, and Belgium gave independence to its African territories in 1960 and 1961.

Nigeria. Nigeria, the most heavily populated territory in Africa, became an independent nation in 1960. Nigeria's government since then has been characterized by corruption and frequent military coups. Its society has also been plagued by ethnic and religious conflict. The worst example was the **Biafran War** during the late 1960s, which resulted from clashes between the Hausa and Ibo tribes. This war produced widespread starvation with as many as a million deaths before the Biafrans surrendered in 1970. Since the war, Nigeria has played an important role in regional affairs, championing the establishment of the **Economic Community of West African States** in 1975 and sending peacekeeping troops to help settle crises in other west African nations.

Congo. A dangerous crisis developed in the Belgian Congo. The Belgians had smothered any sense of Congolese nationhood, but people there could see what was happening elsewhere in Africa. By 1959, protest movements had become so widespread that the Belgian government realized it faced a long struggle. Even though they had done nothing to train the Congolese in self-government, the Belgians suddenly announced that independence would be granted on June 30, 1960.

Civil war broke out almost immediately, and anarchy spread through the land as the European army officers and civil servants fled. Belgian troops occupied the cities to protect Europeans and the copper-rich **Katanga** (Shaba) province which had declared itself independent of the rest of the country. Katanga's leader was **Moïse Tshombe**, who was backed by the mining interests. Then the Russians threatened to step in on behalf of the elected government and its prime minister, **Patrice Lumumba**. However, Lumumba was removed from office and assassinated in 1961.

The United Nations sent a peacekeeping force (made up largely of Africans) which tried to bring the factions together. After five years of conflict, a military group led by **General Joseph Mobutu Sésé** seized power and gradually united the republic. It was renamed **Zaire** in 1971. By the 1990s, however, corruption became rife in Zaire and order began to break down.

In late 1996, a rebellion under the leadership of socialist **Laurent Kabila** began in eastern Zaire. On May 16, 1997, Mobutu gave up power and went into exile. Kabila declared himself president of Zaire and then renamed the country the **Democratic Republic of the Congo**. The removal of Mobutu, however, did not end the Congo's troubles. Kabila suppressed political opposition and hindered investigations of alleged human rights abuses. In addition, a falling-out with some of his earlier supporters led to another rebellion in eastern Congo. This rebellion, however, had an international flavor with Zimbabwe, Namibia, and Angola supporting the Kabila government, and Rwanda and Uganda supporting the rebels. Zambia sponsored peace talks, but the ultimate fate of the Congo remains uncertain.

Rwanda. In 1994, a vicious ethnic conflict broke out in Rwanda between members of the ruling majority Hutu and minority Tutsi tribes. A holocaust of killing resulted in nearly a million civilian deaths (mostly Tutsi), including infants and children who were massacred, burned, or thrown into rivers. As one missionary observed, "There are no demons left in hell. They are all in Rwanda." As Tutsi rebels gained the upper hand, up to two million of Rwandan Hutus fled to refuge camps in neighboring countries, where epidemics broke out

and even more thousands died daily. Western powers stood by for the most part, although private relief organizations stepped into the refugee camps to check the starvation and epidemics. Most Hutu exiles have since returned to Rwanda, but suspicion still lingers between the Hutus and Tutsis.

The "Horn of Africa." British and Italian Somaliland were combined into the republic of **Somalia** in 1960. In 1992, President George H. W. Bush sent American troops into Somalia to join a United Nations force in distributing food to starving people caught in a civil war between rival warlord factions after the collapse of its socialist government. The mission quickly turned into a military conflict when some of the local warring militias began attacking the U.S. and U.N. troops, killing a number of them. The U.S. backed out of the mission.

Tiny French Somaliland became the independent country of **Djibouti** in 1977. **Ethiopia** regained its independence from Italy as a result of Britain's conquest of the "Horn of Africa" during World War II. The monarchy was overthrown by Marxist military officers in 1974. A communist government was then established, but was eventually overthrown in 1991. **Eritrea**, a former Italian col-

American soldiers in Somalia

ony, was incorporated into Ethiopia as part of a federation in 1952. However, a war broke out in 1962 after the federation, with Eritrean local autonomy, was ended. Ethiopian forces were finally driven out and Eritrea was recognized as an independent country in 1993.

Uganda. In Uganda, several small strong kingdoms wanted to become separate states; instead they gained freedom as a single entity in 1962. In 1971, **General Idi Amin Dada** came to power. He launched a reign of terror against political opponents and Ugandan Christians that caused the world to view him as an African "Hitler." Eventually, in 1979, Ugandan exiles and **Tanzanian** troops overthrew Amin's tyrannical regime. Since the demise of Idi Amin, Uganda has been characterized by political instability and strife.

Tanzania. In the mandate territory of Tanganyika, the British were as committed to African self-government as they were in Uganda. The principal political figure was **Julius Nyerere**, a liberal Christian schoolteacher, who led it to independence in 1961. Three years later, it merged with Zanzibar and was renamed **Tanzania**. Nyerere was the advocate of "African socialism," a doctrine that emphasized cooperation within local village communities and the priority of rural development over industrialization.

Kenya. In Kenya, the situation was complicated by a large community of white settlers, by Indian and Arab minorities, and by African tribal jealousies. A serious conflict erupted in 1952 known as the **Mau Mau Rebellion**. Militant members of the Kikuyu tribe, angry at losing their ancestral lands to European settlers, struck against whites and Africans who sympathized with the colonial government. The bloodletting cost more then 13,000 lives, mostly blacks. It was basically a nationalist movement which aimed at African control of land use and government.

Jomo Kenyatta, a journalist and scholar, was the chief African political figure. He was blamed (falsely, it turned out) for the Mau Mau atrocities and spent seven years in prison. There he developed his philosophy of socialism which would involve all citizens fully and equally in public affairs and prevent individuals or groups with economic power from seizing political power. The British tried to move Kenya in the direction of a politically balanced, **multiracial** state, but Kenyatta's party called for African majority rule. After an election victory in 1961, he was released from jail and accepted the leadership of the new state created in 1963, which he retained until his death in 1978. Kenya became a fairly progressive one-party state but suffered from tribal jealousies and occasional political violence.

Sudan. In Sudan, the land known to antiquity as Cush or Nubia, ethnic conflicts and ancient religious rivalries have continued throughout Sudan's history. Christianity came to Sudan in the sixth century, but Arab Muslims moved in a century later. In the late 1880s, a self-proclaimed Muslim "messiah" conquered the country, but his regime was overthrown by British and Egyptian forces, and Sudan was jointly governed by them until independence in 1956. A succession of civilian and military regimes failed to resolve ethnic conflicts within the nation. A civil war began almost immediately between the south, inhabited by Christians and animists, and the north, which was under Muslim control. There was a coup in 1968 and a briefly successful communist coup in 1971. In 1972, ruler **Gaafar Mohamed el-Nimeiry** granted the south a regional government and some local autonomy, bringing peace to the country. But the south again rebelled in 1983 when he imposed Islamic law and ended regional self-government. Nimeiry was overthrown in 1985 after there were nationwide riots protesting his austere and erratic policies. A mili-

tary coup led by Muslim radicals known as the **National Islamic Front** occurred in 1989. The United States began to work toward bringing peace to southern Sudan in 2001, resulting in the signing of a peace treaty, with autonomy for the South and the possibility of independence in six years, between the Sudanese government and the southern rebels in January 2005.

Even as the war in southern Sudan was being settled, war erupted in the **Darfur** region of western Sudan. While not religious in nature, it involved a similar conflict between Arab and non-Arab tribes. Fighting began in 2003 when non-Arab groups attacked government forces. The Sudanese government responded by supporting attacks by Arab militias known as the **Janjaweed**. These militias have been accused by many of committing genocide against the black population of the Darfur. Many thousands have fled to refugee camps both within Sudan and in neighboring Chad.

Southern Africa. African nationalists in Nyasaland and Northern Rhodesia demanded one-man, one-vote rule from Britain. They finally received self-rule with African prime ministers in 1964. Nyasaland gained independence as the state of **Malawi**, and the copper-rich area of Northern Rhodesia became **Zambia**. The political leaders of both countries, **Dr. H. Kamuzu Banda** of Malawi and **President Kenneth Kaunda** of Zambia, eventually established one-party governments with democratic facades. Recently, however, unrest in both nations forced them to allow free elections, which resulted in their downfall.

But Southern Rhodesia, renamed simply Rhodesia, was ruled by a white African minority which refused to allow black Marxists any part in the government. To prevent Britain from granting black rule, the white minority led by **Prime Minister Ian Smith** declared Rhodesia independent of Britain in 1965. Britain protested; the United

Nations started a boycott to bring Rhodesia to its knees; and Africans began Marxist guerrilla warfare against the Smith regime. In 1979, black rule came to the country, now renamed **Zimbabwe**. Within a few years, this revolution, quite predictably, produced a "one-man, no vote" Marxist state in Zimbabwe. One of the leaders of the black revolt was a missionary-trained Methodist minister named **Canaan Banana** who espoused a socialist liberation brand of Christianity based on the thesis that all people should be the masters of their own destiny. In a book called *The Gospel According to the Ghetto*, Banana wrote a revision of The Lord's Prayer which read:

> Our Father which art in the Ghetto,
> Degraded is your name
> Thy servitude abounds,
> Thy will is mocked,
> As pie in the sky.
> Teach us to demand,
> Our share of gold,
> Forgive us our docility,
> As we demand our share of justice.
> Lead us not into complicity,
> Deliver us from our fears.
> For ours is the sovereignty,
> The power and the liberation,
> For ever and ever..., Amen.

South of the Zambezi River, the Portuguese ruled Angola and Mozambique and argued that they were not colonies but overseas provinces of Portugal. Nevertheless, they had to deal with increasing guerrilla activity.

The most startling development of the 1970s was the end of Portuguese colonialism. South Africa, which wished to see Angola and Mozambique stand as a barrier against spreading leftist African nationalism, strongly supported Portugal. Despite this backing, revolutionary activity increased in all Portuguese possessions. However, in April 1974, the Portuguese government back home was overthrown by a military coup. The new regime

Agestino Neto declared that within twenty years Christianity would be eradicate from Angola. Instead, Marxist rule died.

promptly negotiated settlements with African guerrilla leaders in **Angola**, **Mozambique**, **Guinea-Bissau**, and the offshore islands. For some time, a bloody civil war raged in Angola, with troops from communist Cuba fighting on the guerrilla side. The Cuban presence remained in Angola for a decade and a half, making Angola a base for other Marxist liberation efforts in Africa.

South Africa. After World War II, the **Nationalist Party** had come to power in the Republic of South Africa and started a far-reaching program of racial separation known as *apartheid*. This program denied political participation to nonwhites, legalized racial discrimination, and **segregated** employment, transportation, and public facilities. The government planned to move Africans from their homes in white areas (whites made up 19 percent of the population), to permanent homes in self-governing territories where they could work out their own destiny. In the late 1960s, the government began to carry out this idea. However, since South Africa's economy depended on black labor, only a token effort went into the project.

Antagonism against South Africa grew rapidly as more and more Asian and African nations became free. In 1961, the country withdrew from the Commonwealth of Nations because of the disapproval there of its racial policies. Criticism in the United Nations was intense, and most countries eventually joined a boycott against trade with South Africa. Anger mounted as a sense of black consciousness developed, largely through agitation by communists and leftists.

Partly through the efforts of the Organization of African Unity (OAU), established in 1963 for the promotion of African unity in the areas of government, defense, trade, and world affairs, the colonial era and white rule throughout the rest of Africa was brought to an end. South Africa was left to face the world alone. No longer able to withstand the pressure from within and without, the last chink in African solidarity was sealed with South Africa's modification of its *apartheid* policy.

The modifications failed to satisfy the South African Communist Party and its partners in the militant **African National Congress** (ANC) and other terrorist organizations such as the **Pan-African Congress**. In the 1980s, the ANC, financed by millions in grants from socialist Sweden, and other Marxist and liberal interests around the world, launched a massive international propaganda campaign aimed at overthrowing the white government. The organization's president, **Nelson Mandela**, had been in prison for insurrection since 1962, and had been portrayed as a martyr for the cause of economic justice and black rule in South Africa. The ANC lobbied successfully throughout the world to get other nations and businesses to withdraw or withhold investments in South African enterprises, an action which actually damaged the interests of black workers in those enterprises.

The ANC was first formed in 1912 under the name **South African Native National Congress** with the aim of representing the interests of black people in South Africa. It consisted of conservative tribal chiefs, clergymen, and educators who had a genuine Christian interest in the needs of native peoples. By the 1930s, however, members of the South African Communist Party began to take part in the affairs of the organization (renamed African National Congress in 1923) and gradually took it over, turning it toward revolutionary aims. In 1961, an agent of the Soviet KGB (secret police) and key operative within the South African Communist Party, **Joe Slovo**, organized a military wing of the ANC, **Umkhonto we Sizwe (MK)** ("Spear of the Nation") and put it under Mandela's control. The MK and other violent elements within the ANC, along with other terrorist groups, launched a campaign of violence, resulting in thousands of deaths of both black and white South Africans. Propagandists and the international news media consistently blamed the violence on the South African security forces (ignoring the fact that most of the members of the police and defense forces of the country were blacks). The ANC also became involved in violence against blacks who refused to cooperate with its actions. Thousands of black town counselors, mayors,

Nelson Mandela

policemen, businessmen, and teachers were murdered. Special targets were members of the conservative black **Inkatha Freedom Party** under Zulu **Chief Mangosuthu Buthelezi**. More than 800 of these victims were burned to death by the ANC's brutal "necklace" method—victims were trussed around the neck with a tire soaked in gasoline and ignited. More than 15,000 murders were committed per year after the campaign of violence began. Despite the fact that *apartheid* was substantially dismantled during the 1980s and Mandela was freed from prison, the campaign of violence and international propaganda continued. A Marxist Anglican bishop, **Desmond Tutu**; a leftist Reformed minister, **Allen Aubrey Boesak**; and the liberal South African Council of Churches were among the religious leaders supporting the revolutionaries. Tutu was awarded a Nobel Peace Prize by the Swedish Academy for his part.

In its effort to seize power, the ANC set forth four strategic goals: (1) convince the U.N. to support their cause and possibly intervene, (2) neutralize Inkatha, (3) neutralize the police and defense forces, and (4) secure a new constitution and the establishment of an interim government leading eventually to black majority rule. By 1994, the campaign harvested its fruits. In the first all-race national election, the ANC was swept into power and Mandela became president of the country. The change in government did not lead to any significant improvement in the economic condition of the poor in South Africa, and a year later Mandela found it necessary to call for further patience. The once rich and self-sufficient South Africa was soon becoming a subsidized client state of rich, liberal Western powers, demonstrating once again the hollowness of the socialist liberation claims. Mandela retired from public life in June 1999 and was succeeded as president of South Africa by **Thabo Mbeki**, who had already replaced Mandela as head of the ANC in 1997.

AFRICA TODAY

Dictators and Marxism in Latin America

Although Europeanized and having a large white population, Latin America, in the middle-to-late twentieth century came to identify with the Third World. To be sure, it shared some common characteristics of Africa and Asia: a low standard of living in some areas, domination of the economy by foreign interests, rapid population growth, widespread illiteracy, political instability, military dictatorships, and revolutionary guerrilla movements. The level of prosperity in some parts of Argentina, Venezuela, and Mexico was low. In Paraguay, Bolivia, and Haiti, people lived in utter poverty.

Racial Make-up. Latin America's history has been shaped by several factors. First, it has one of the most varied populations of any major section of the globe. Roughly 15 million whites from Europe and 10 million blacks from Africa reached Latin America and the Caribbean islands. There they mixed in with the existing Indian population. Intermarriage was so common that a new class of people known as **mestizos**, the offspring of Indians and Europeans, developed. Mestizos moved in the sphere of European culture even though some whites looked down on them. They had a lower social and economic standing than the whites, but a higher one than the Indians.

Economic Imbalance. Ever since the colonial period, a minority of whites owned most of the wealth while the vast multitude of peasants lived on the brink of starvation. Thus the peasants raised a clamor for a share of the lands belonging to the rich, and most revolutionary movements in the twentieth century have demanded land reform. Yet in 1970, at least 65 percent of the land was held by only 15 percent of the people.

In some places a central economic institution was the **hacienda**. This was a large piece of land on which a group of Indian peasants or slaves had been settled. The owner would allow them to use some of the land, providing them with simple houses, a store where they could purchase needed goods, and with spiritual care. The peasants, or **peons**, were required to work a certain number of days on the owner's land. The peons were also expected to build and repair such buildings on the hacienda as the owner's house and barns and the chapel. Peons received a home, some land, and the basic necessities of life. They were frequently in debt to the local store, as they received little pay for their labor. If peons were disloyal or disobedient they could be whipped or sent away from the hacienda.

Some economic problems have been blamed on foreign involvement. Capital from abroad developed Latin America's natural resources, such as bananas in Central America, tin in Bolivia, copper in Chile, oil in Venezuela, and timber in the rain forests. Critics of the foreign companies charged that little of the profit was plowed back into these countries to raise the economic and social level of the great majority. Thus foreign-owned firms became popular targets of revolutionary movements. It was difficult to develop industrial production because most people raised or made everything they needed and had little money to buy manufactured goods.

Roman Catholicism. A key element of Latin American life is the influence of the Roman Catholic Church. The Spanish and Portuguese who settled colonies in Latin America had made the native peoples a part of the colonial economies and converted them to Roman Catholicism. This church became a major landowner. After independence, it firmly supported the status quo in the various countries. With the growth of secularism in the twentieth century, the church began losing economic and political power. But it still has enormous influence. Late in the century, Protestant evangelism through large-scale revivals began to have a major effect, and Protestantism grew rapidly in some South and Central American countries.

Unstable Governments. Political instability was also common. Almost every Latin American country has been torn by repeated "revolutions," which usually meant that one military clique was replaced by another. Further, the states have frequently waged bloody and destructive wars against each other. Most regimes allowed little freedom and brought little progress. Their huge military budgets and their use of force to wipe out any opposition drained the countries' resources. At the same time, guerrilla groups received aid from supporters in other countries and used terrorism in their efforts to overthrow the governments they disliked.

Dictatorships were frequently established. Some, such as that of **General Alfredo Stroessner** (elected president of Paraguay in 1954, 1958, and 1963), brutally exploited the people. But others, such as that of **Getúlio Vargas** in Brazil (1930–1945; 1951–1954), had considerable popular support. Vargas improved working conditions; built schools, highways, and airports; promoted coffee exports; and established the giant Volta Redonda steel mill complex, all at great cost and with soaring inflation. He committed suicide in 1954 after being forced to resign.

From 1946 to 1955, **Juan Perón** headed a fascist-leaning dictatorship in Argentina that appealed to the poor with promises of wage increases and land reform. In the later part of the century, a conservative government came to power and began a massive privatization program, with positive economic results.

Castro's Cuba. An idealistic group of young communist revolutionaries led by **Fidel Castro** overthrew the dictatorship of **Fulgencio Batista** in Cuba in 1959. At once Castro's regime nationalized American-owned property and launched a great land "reform" in which the state took over 40 percent of the cultivated land. He eliminated the wealthy upper class and the business middle class, most of whose members went into exile. After the Castro takeover and through the mid-1990s, more than 1.5 million Cubans left the country, most of them establishing themselves in southern Florida.

In 1961, Castro began openly calling himself a "Marxist-Leninist" and threw in his lot with the communist bloc. The United States, which at first had viewed him as a romantic liberator-hero, was uneasy about his socialist program, and tried to isolate his regime. President Kennedy inconsistently backed a poorly planned military action by exiles to overthrow Castro (**Bay of Pigs Invasion**). Following that, in the dramatic "missile crisis" of 1962, the United States made it clear that it would not tolerate the Soviet Union's use of Cuba as a base for offensive weapons in the Western Hemisphere.

Castro hoped to make agriculture, not industry, the basis of Cuba's prosperity and economic development. Manual labor was glorified over intellectual effort, and farm workers were considered the nation's leading citizens. Starry-eyed American liberals went to Cuba to help in the sugarcane harvests. Castro tried to slow the growth of cities, allowing once-beautiful Havana to fall into ruin. Thus his movement rejected urbanization as well as industrialization.

Castro actively exported his revolutionary ideas. Young Marxist fanatics throughout Latin America admired and copied him. Cuban aid went to

Fidel Castro

guerrilla movements in various places. His closest associate, **Ernesto (Ché) Guevara**, was killed in Bolivia in 1967 while leading a guerrilla band trying to overthrow the government there. The Cuban revolution was also exported to Nicaragua, where **Sandinista** rebels seized power in 1979 and drove the country into ruin before they lost their Soviet support and were voted out of office by democratic forces in the early 1990s. The Sandinista regime was under constant attack from right-wing **Contra** rebels who were supported, sometimes clandestinely, by the United States.

When Castro lost his Soviet sponsorship in the early 1990s, Cuba became poorer and more isolated. Most other Latin America countries had diplomatic relations with Cuba and they encouraged Castro to move toward democracy and a free-market economy. But Castro continued to

Ché Guevara, 1928–1967

reject fundamental change and remained blindly committed to communism. Cuban exiles in the United States were optimistic that communism would eventually collapse in Cuba as it did in Eastern Europe, the Soviet Union, and Nicaragua.

Meanwhile, in recurrent intervals, Cubans still on the island made attempts to escape to freedom and better economic opportunities. Using small boats and makeshift rafts, they tried to float across the Straits of Florida. While the United States once welcomed and encouraged refugees to escape communist countries, President Bill Clinton actually pressured Castro to keep his people in Cuba, reversing a 28-year-old policy of accepting nearly all Cuban refugees. The Castro government said in August 1994 that it would prevent the departure of refugees only if the United States would agreed to new talks about immigration policy and lifting the long-standing U.S. trade embargo of Cuba. The Clinton administration agreed to process only 20,000 Cuban refugees annually but said that substantial democratic reforms in Cuba would have to be a prerequisite for any change in the economic embargo.

The United States and Latin America. To counter Castro's influence in the 1960s, Kennedy founded the **Alliance for Progress** in 1961, intended to be a kind of Marshall Plan for Latin America. However, it gave aid chiefly in the form of loans which were supposed to be used to buy U.S. exports. For this reason, the aid helped only the groups already controlling economic life in these countries. Instead of bringing development, the Alliance for Progress actually widened the gap between rich and poor and made governments more dependent than ever upon foreign investors. By the early 1970s, about three-quarters of Latin America's raw materials and one-half of its industry, banking, and foreign trade were controlled by North American corporations.

The United States also acted directly to stop Castro-like movements. In the **Dominican Republic** a long struggle took place after dictator **Rafael Trujillo** was deposed in 1961. President Lyndon Johnson sent American troops there in 1965 to keep order and prevent alleged Communists from taking over.

In another revolt, this time in **Chile**, the United States Central Intelligence Agency took part in a 1973 military coup which overthrew the elected Marxist government of **Salvador Allende Gossens**, who then reportedly committed suicide. The coup was led by right-wing **General Augusto Pinochet Urgarte**, who served as president from 1974 to 1990. His government instituted conservative economic policies, but it was accused by critics of stifling dissent and violating human rights, even with death squads. In 1981, Pinochet was sworn in as president under a new constitution, but in 1988, he lost an election on a measure that would have allowed him to continue as president beyond the end of this term in 1990. The leader of the opposition party, **Patricio Aylwin**, replaced him and tried unsuccessfully to limit Pinochet's remaining power as chief of the army. **Eduardo Frei Ruiz-Tagle** succeeded Aylwin in 1994 but faced a political crisis when courts ordered investigations into past government involvement in various murders and other crimes.

In 1983, United States troops again ventured into the Caribbean to overthrow a new Marxist government, which had opened the doors to another Western-hemisphere Soviet and Cuban military buildup. The action took place in the tiny island of **Grenada**, which had been under French or British rule alternately since 1650 (Columbus landed there in 1498). In 1979, the **Marxist New Jewel Movement** led by **Maurice Bishop** overthrew the Commonwealth-related government. Bishop set up a **People's Revolutionary Government**, but was ousted and murdered in 1983 by another New Jewel faction. U.S. intelligence sources discovered that a major military airport was being constructed there and alleged that the Soviets were attempting to do what they had tried to do in Cuba in the early 1960s—establish a military foothold near the United States. President Ronald Reagan ordered a U.S. military task force to invade the island. Within a few hours, the island had been taken and a new government installed. U.S. troops left within two months.

In 1977, the United States began to deal with another dangerous situation by agreeing to give up control of the **Panama Canal** by the end of the century. After a series of changes in the Panamanian government, military strongman **Manuel Noriega** came to power in the host country. Anti-American demonstrations took place in 1987, and the United States suspended aid and imposed economic sanctions. In 1988, U.S. courts indicted Noriega on charges that he was involved in illegal drug trade and other forms of corruption. After a 1989 coup attempt failed, United States armed forces invaded Panama and, after a brief operation, deposed Noriega. He was arrested, jailed, and tried in the United States, where he remained in prison during the 1990s.

Another trouble spot is Haiti, a Caribbean country steeped in poverty and voodoo religion. The United States had occupied Haiti militarily from 1915 until 1934. In 1957, **Francois "Papa Doc" Duvalier** came to power and established a brutal dictatorship until he died in 1971. Repression diminished somewhat under his lavish-living son, **Jean Claude "Baby Doc" Duvalier**, but economic woes, civil rights abuses, and government corruption continued to produce popular resentment and international criticism. As protests mounted, Duvalier fled the country in 1986 and took up exile in France. Unstable military rule followed the Duvalier government until an election in 1990 brought a Marxist-oriented Catholic priest, **Father Jean-Bertrand Aristide**, to power. He was deposed and exiled in 1991 after eight months in office. A military junta took control, defying international condemnation and hemisphere-wide trade sanctions which followed. The United States led an effort through the United Nations to get the junta to step down. In 1994, the United Nations authorized the United States to take necessary actions to restore Aristide to power. The junta intensified its resistance to international intervention. U.S. President Bill Clinton announced that an armed invasion might be necessary. In September 1994, U.S. warships and aircraft headed for Haiti. As the invasion force neared the island, former **President Jimmy Carter**, retired **General Colin Powell**, and **Senator Sam Nunn** formed a last-ditch negotiating team which succeeded in getting the junta, headed by **General Raoul Cedras** to step down and leave the country. U.S. troops landed in Haiti anyway and remained there as a security measure until they could be replaced by an international force which was supposed to assure the success of democracy. Aristide, by now defrocked as a priest, returned to complete his term of office. In 1996, **René Préval**, an ally of Aristide was elected president. Préval and Aristide soon became political opponents, leading to political turmoil in Haiti. Aristide ran for president again in 2000, winning an overwhelming election. Artistide was accused of corruption and using violence by his opponents. Finally, a revolt against Aristide erupted in February 2004; and by the end of the month, he had resigned from office and gone into exile. Some controversy exists about whether he resigned voluntarily or was pressured by the United States to resign. After Aristide left, peacekeeping troops from the United States and others in the region landed in Haiti to maintain order and help establish a new government.

The most complex and controversial U.S. involvement in Latin American affairs took place in **Nicaragua**. This Central American country had been the scene of revolutionary ferment since the late nineteenth century. A liberal revolution occurred in 1893, but in 1909 the United States supported another revolution which restored conservative rule. An uprising in 1912 led the United States to invade with marines who stayed until 1925 to complete training of a National Guard. U.S. marines returned a year later to halt another revolution. **General Augusto Cesar Sandino** conducted a guerrilla war against the U.S.-backed government until the marines left in 1933. He was killed in 1934 by the National Guard under **General Anastasio Somoza**, who seized power in 1936 and stayed in power until

he was assassinated in 1956. His two sons, **Luis** and **Anastasio**, followed him into power.

Nicaragua's economy improved under the Somozas but there was evidence of widespread corruption which produced growing resentment. When opposition leader **Pedro Joaquin Chamarro** was murdered in 1978, a nationwide uprising occurred. The United States tried unsuccessfully to negotiate the ouster of the Somoza regime while a Marxist guerrilla group, the **Sandinista National Liberation Front (FSLN)** waged a civil war. The Sandinistas took power in 1979 and set up a coalition government with a communist agenda. The Sandinistas conducted bloody repressions, especially against Christians. The Roman Catholic Church, moderate politicians, the business community, and the United States opposed the regime, which increasingly tightened controls. An opposition guerrilla military force known as the **Contras** continued attempts to bring down the Sandinista government, which by 1984 was headed by **President Daniel Ortega Saavedra**. The government channeled more and more of its scarce resources into the military effort against the Contras, further impoverishing the country. The Soviet Union and other communist regimes, especially East Germany, dominated Nicaragua's tottering economy, which was boycotted by the United States and its allies. In 1987, Ortega and leaders of four other Central American nations signed an idealistic regional peace plan (similar leftist guerrilla conflicts were occurring in countries neighboring Nicaragua). As international communism was toppling in 1989, Ortega agreed to elections. The Sandinistas were thrown out of power in the vote in 1990. They were replaced by a broad-based coalition government headed **Violetta Barrios de Chamarro**, widow of the slain Pedro Chamarro. She worked to reconcile the nation and end devastating economic problems. By 1993, however, her

efforts had had only limited success and there were new threats of civil war by ex-Contras who were angry at her conciliatory approach to the Sandinistas.

The Iran-Contra Scandal. Behind the open political turmoil in Nicaragua during the 1980s, the makings of an international scandal were brewing—at least it was called a scandal by critics of the operations involved.

In November 1986, President Ronald Reagan confirmed that the United States had secretly sold arms to Iran in an effort to improve relations with that country. He at first denied but later admitted that the deal had turned into an exchange arrangement for the release of U.S. hostages being held in the Middle East by various groups of Iran-backed terrorists. Critics of the Reagan administration, especially opposition party members in Congress, expressed outrage that the administration would provide arms to a hostile government. The affair was escalated when **Attorney General Edwin Meese** discovered that some of the profits from the arms sales to Iran had been diverted to aid the anticommunist Nicaraguan Contra freedom fighters. This allegedly occurred at a time when Congress had prohibited aid to the Contras. A special prosecutor was appointed to investigate the matter, and Reagan appointed a special review commission. The commission criticized Reagan for being too passive in controlling members of his administration's security agencies. Congress launched an investigation. The central figure of the investigations soon became **Marine Lt. Col. Oliver North**, a member of the National Security Council's staff, who appeared to have been the central link in the Iran-Contra financing exchanges. North's supervisor **John Poindexter** took responsibility for the affair and was later convicted of criminal charges associated with the affair, as were other figures involved. North too was convicted of several alleged crimes, including lying to Congress; but his convictions were overturned in various court appeals. In 1994, he ran unsuccessfully for the U.S. Senate, but in the interim, he had become a highly popular figure among conservative Christian political activists because of his outspoken interest in Christianity and in patriotism. President George H. W. Bush pardoned former **Defense Secretary Caspar Weinberger** and other principals for their alleged parts in the affair. Critics charged that the pardons were intended to cover up Bush's own complicity in the Iran-Contra transactions. The so-called Iran-Contra Scandal seemed to weaken the otherwise popular presidency of Ronald Reagan and tarnished U.S. prestige abroad. The drawn-out investigation, which largely fizzled in the end, cost taxpayers many millions of dollars. By the time it was over, the Sandinistas were well out of power and the Middle East hostages had been released through other means.

The Growth of a Third World Consciousness

The term "Third World" began to be applied in the 1950s to the newly emerging non-Western countries. It implied they would not be tied to either the "First World" or "Second World," the blocs centering around Washington and Moscow, but would remain **neutral**, or "nonaligned."

Twenty-nine of these states from Asia and Africa held a general conference at Bandung, Indonesia, in 1955. The main idea behind the meeting was neutralism. Denouncing colonialism in all of its forms, the delegates implied disapproval of Soviet actions in Eastern Europe, as well as alleged

The United Nations has played an increasing role in policing third-world conflicts.

Western imperialism. They supported the complaints of individual members that did not cut across the interest of others—the liberation of French North Africa, the Arab states against Israel, Yemen against Aden, Indonesia against Holland. In addition, they called for general disarmament, recognition of all races and nations as equal, and economic cooperation. In most cases, leftist causes tended to get the support of the nonaligned group, betraying the thinly cloaked infiltration efforts of the communist bloc. Yugoslavia played a major role in influencing the **nonaligned movement**. Also, the prominent role played by Premier Chou En-lai at the meeting showed that China had again become a factor in the international power struggle. The "neutralism" of the 1950s was thus deceptive. With its strong anticolonialism and policy of taking Eastern aid in order to reduce dependence on the West, many Third World countries found themselves aligned much closer to the communist bloc than they publicly admitted.

Bandung was significant because it provided a meeting ground for nations which before had had little in common. Now they could think of themselves as a force in international affairs. Leaders could seek aid from both West and East without being officially tied to either. Instead of a negative refusal to take sides, neutralism became seen as a positive policy linked with nationalism. From this point on, neutralism attracted many newly independent states. It seemed to help them gain the maximum advantage from each side in the Cold War with a minimum commitment.

The nonaligned nations held other conferences after Bandung, but none was as important as the first. Although they regularly condemned Israel, supported revolts in white-ruled parts of Africa, urged world disarmament, and championed the right of underdeveloped countries to control their natural resources and take over foreign-owned companies, they could not agree on what **nonalignment** meant. And they could not agree on how to get the wealthier states to help the poorer ones.

In the 1960s, the political power of neutralism declined. However, by then the Third World nations had a large majority in the United Nations, and they concentrated their diplomatic efforts there. A focal point of Third World action was the **United Nations Conference on Trade and Development**. At the first UNCTAD meeting in 1964, a bloc of 77 countries, over the protests of Western participants, made what was supposed to be a one-time conference into a permanent organization. Through it they could challenge the developed states on economic issues. The group later attracted over 130 members (including the Palestine Liberation Organization) but continues to call itself the "**Group of 77**." It serves as a major means by which the

Third World exerts its power in the United Nations.

Many of the Third World powers are active in regional groups as well, such as the **Organization of African Unity**, the **Association of Southeast Asian Nations**, and the **Organization of American States**.

The Oil Weapon. In late 1973, a few developing countries in the Middle East did with one bold stroke what most had dreamed of doing for many years. An oil cartel they had formed, the **Organization of Petroleum Exporting Countries (OPEC)**, almost succeeded in bringing the industrial nations to their knees. First, Arab members stopped the shipment of oil to those nations which had sympathized with Israel in the Yom Kippur War. Then in just one year, the cartel raised the world price of crude oil fourfold.

The steep hikes in oil prices hurt developing countries more than the West, although retail prices for gasoline and other petroleum fuels and products skyrocketed in the industrial countries as well. The developing countries needed oil for making fertilizer and operating irrigation systems to increase food production. Also, in order to pay for oil, Western nations had to cut back purchases of raw materials and other goods, many of which would had come from the Third World. In only three years, OPEC's share of world trade rose from 7 to 13 percent. The so-called **Arab Oil Embargo** touched off significant inflation of prices and wages worldwide. In the United States, President Richard Nixon finally imposed nationwide wage and price controls, which further damaged the U.S. economy. Attempts by other producers of primary goods (except for aluminum ore) to use the potent weapon of price-fixing failed.

Third World Viewpoint. A Third World "philosophy" seemed to accompany the sense of identity

Market in Turkey shows that food distribution in many Mideastern countries has not been influenced by technology.

these peoples had. It was a mixture of anti-white racism; resentment against wealthier, developed countries; and a vague socialism. Using the idea of "class struggle" to justify their actions, they were prepared to eliminate traditional authorities, the educated classes, or any other obstacle to wielding power, in the name of the "people."

Nations of the Third World struggled to achieve and maintain their political independence. They expressed a concern over Western economic ties which have continued and even increased as the twentieth century moved toward its close. Some identified this problem as "neocolonialism" or "dependency." In order to resist what they considered Western exploitation, they wanted a "New International Economic Order" to reorganize the world's economic system so there will be less dependence on Western capital. Yet they continued to welcome giveaways of foreign aid from Western nations. Studies by Britain's **Lord P. T. Bauer** have documented how foreign aid severely hampered the natural economic development of Third World countries. He showed that hand-

outs have not promoted the interests of the donors but often were "counterproductive, by arousing suspicions of undisclosed motives or by encouraging recipients to thwart donors to show their independence." He argued that the best thing for the West to do would be to reduce trade barriers against Third World exports, thus encouraging Third World productive enterprises and investment, reducing unemployment, and increasing the spread of skills.

Marxism was an underlying idea in Third World thinking, but it was not identical to Western Marxism or Soviet communism. China's Mao Tse-tung developed one form, and liberation movements in Vietnam, Cuba, Peru, Algeria, and elsewhere adopted it. Maoism made the peasants, rather than the *proletariat*, the social basis of the revolution. The Communist Party takes the lead, but it is a people's "democracy" which unites the peasants, workers, lesser *bourgeoisie*, and intellectuals in a revolutionary organization. Using the tactics of closely organized guerrilla warfare, the movement chipped away at the existing order. But, according to studies by conservative Swedish economist **Sven Rydenfelt**, Third World socialism consistently harmed the economic and social development of emerging nations. When the Soviet Union collapsed and China grew more interested in involvement with the West, the concept of a "Third World" began to diminish in much of the world's thinking. The United States emerged as the single world superpower, and the world scene witnessed fragmentation into narrower and narrower national, ethnic, and tribal interests as the century drew to a close.

Religious Response to Third World Demands. One form of Third World belief joined Marxism and liberal Christian theology. It was called **liberation theology.** Held mainly by a number of important Roman Catholic thinkers in Latin

A cathedral located in the center of Cuzco, Peru. Roman Catholicism is one of the greatest influences in South America.

America, it saw salvation mostly as political and economic liberation. They argued that the gap between the rich and poor nations could never be closed by Western economic aid and the workings of the capitalist system. To these thinkers, China and Cuba demonstrated that Marxism was the key to the future. Cuba's deterioration and China's continued backwardness without capitalism tended to deflate that claim.

Some Roman Catholic priests in Latin America felt strongly that the church had been too closely tied to existing governments and European imperialism. A few actually joined revolutionary guerrilla movements. Others, such as **Archbishop Dom Helder Camara** of Brazil, publicly defended the rights of the poor but stressed nonviolent action.

Liberation theologians believed that one must begin not with theology or the Bible but with one's own place in the world. The Bible becomes relevant only when it speaks on practical world issues, they said. Thus they said the Exodus was an act of political liberation, and "salvation" means struggle against misery and exploitation. Also, they claimed that the teachings of the Old Testament prophets and Jesus attack private property. These theologians felt that Western Christians had failed to realize these things because they read the Bible through capitalist eyes and stressed theory rather than practical matters.

The **World Council of Churches (WCC)** had become thoroughly infiltrated by leftists and even communist agents by the 1960s, and it turned its prestige against the West, supporting scores of revolutionary causes in the Third World. WCC documents were laced with accusations that Western capitalist democracies were "colonial tyrants, capitalist aggressors, warmongers, oppressors, exploiters, imperialists, *bourgeois* class dominators, racists, bloody suppressors," and "scandlers of social, economic and political justice."

As Australian researcher-author Henry R. Pike described it in 1978,

> The WCC "experts" have taken hold of the biblical doctrine of "salvation" and its various relative terms, e.g., "reconciliation," "freedom," "forgiveness," "redemption," etc., and have emptied these terms of their original God-intended and [God-]given meanings. Now, in WCC pro-left theology, they have become instruments for "revolution," "change," "restructuring of society," "world socialism," "identity-finding," for "the humanization," for the "destruction of capitalism," etc. (From *Religion: Red and Rotten*.)

Most Protestant evangelicals would not go so far. However, at the **Lausanne Conference on World Evangelism** in 1974, Protestant leaders from around the world agreed that evangelism and sociopolitical action were part of their Christian duty. They recognized the task of spreading righteousness in an unrighteous world, and they condemned oppression and discrimination.

Although rejecting the Marxist basis of liberation, more and more Protestants in the West came to believe Third World demands were just.

Other Christians argued, however, that the very real plight of the poor nations of the world has a spiritual cause—they have been inhabited for generations by peoples who have spurned God's social and economic order as outlined in the Bible. As David Chilton has written,

> The central fact about the heathen is that they are living in willful rebellion against the one true God, and are therefore under God's curse. The economic issue is a symptom of their condition; but the problem with pagans is primarily religious and ethical. To neglect this central point in order to focus only on their poverty is radically unbiblical and immoral.
>
> If pagans are truly to be helped, they and their culture must be converted to the Christian faith. If we seek merely to neutralize the effects of God's righteous judgment upon them, we are manifesting contempt for Him, and our efforts will not be blessed. Our major concern must be to reconcile the heathen to God whom they have offended. The problem is religious; the solution is religious as well....
>
> The fact that the poor nations are suffering under the judgment of God does not mean we should disregard the real misery of these people. But it does require that we approach them carefully, with a biblical, theologically informed mind. Our actions toward them must be concerned with transforming their cultures by the Word of God. (From *Productive Christians in an Age of Guilt Manipulators*, ICE.)

For your consideration

Questions

1. How do a person's religious ideas affect his political and economic decisions? Would your answer be different if you were considering a Hindu, a Jew, or a Christian?

2. How do you feel about the idea of civil disobedience? Have you ever boycotted a particular product or company? Why or why not?

3. What are the advantages and disadvantages when a political party remains in power for a long time?

4. Why did newly independent countries experience political instability?

5. How does a dictator gain control of an army and government?

6. Why is Christianity often called a Western religion although it started in the Middle East?

7. If Marx were alive during the twentieth century, would he likely have sided with Russia or China? Explain. Is it wise to adapt a political system to conditions within different countries and to changing times? Explain. Does the Bible favor any particular type of political system for all men?

8. How should the United States relate to countries with authoritarian governments? What is the best way to deal with terrorists?

9. What causes poverty?

Projects

1. Read Thoreau's essay "Civil Disobedience" and report on it.

2. Use a recent atlas to locate countries mentioned in this chapter. Choose a country and study its geography, language, people, history, religions, and natural resources. Read some recent publications to find out what is happening there now.

3. Research and report on one of these female leaders: Golda Meir (Israel), Margaret Thatcher (Britain), Benazir Bhutto (Pakistan), Sirimavo Bandanaike (Sri Lanka), Eva Perón (Argentina), Begum Rahman (Bangladesh), Indira Gandhi (India), Corazon Aquino (Philippines).

4. Interview someone who served in the military in Vietnam. What are his or her feelings about the war?

5. Interview a missionary who has served in a Third World country. Find out his or her feelings about the struggles in that country and about changing social customs.

6. Do a report on the history of the African National Congress in South Africa.

7. View the film *China Cry* about the Christian evangelist Nora Lam's experiences during the Cultural Revolution, if it is available to you.

8. Research reasons for the West's failure to defeat communism during the Korean and Vietnam wars.

Word List

mahatma	kibbutz
civil disobedience	electoral
linguistic	multiracial
discrimination	*apartheid*
genocide	segregated
normalized	mestizos
trusteeship	hacienda
subversion	peons
alleged	neutralism
countercoup	nonaligned
caste system	Great Leap Forward
Three Principles of the People	Cultural Revolution
	Nixon Doctrine
Domino Theory	Sharia
guided democracy	Iran-Contra
Pan-Turanism	rapprochement

People and Groups

Mohandas Gandhi	Hezbollah
Jawaharlal Nehru	David Ben-Gurion
Indira Gandhi	Menachem Begin
Deng Xiaoping	Yassar Arafat
Chiang Ch'ing	Anwar Sadat
Red Guards	Jimmy Carter
Kim Il-sung	Gerald Ford
Ho Chi Minh	Ronald Reagan
Ngo Dinh Diem	George H. W. Bush
Jane Fonda	Bill Clinton
Viet Cong	Muammar Qaddafi
Khmer Rouge	Patrice Lumumba
Pathet Lao	Amin Dada
Pol Pot	Nelson Mandela
Ferdinand Marcos	The Duvaliers
Corazon Aquino	Sandinistas
Sukarno & Suharto	Oliver North
Ayatollah Khomeini	OPEC

1945	1955	1965	1975	1985	1995

Politics and Economics

Cold War between East and West 1945–1970s

India and Pakistan
gain independence 1947

Conflict in Indochina and War in Vietnam 1946–1975

Communist regimes overthrown in
Eastern Europe and USSR 1989–1991

Korean War 1950–1953

Great Leap Forward and Cultural
Revolution in China 1958–1969

Egyptian-Israeli peace initiative 1970s

Persian Gulf War 1991

Nation of Israel formed 1948–1949

Keynesian economics developed 1936

Watergate 1972–1973

Communists take control of China 1949

Sub-Saharan Africa gains independence 1957–1970s

Israeli, PLO, Jordan sign peace accords 1994

Great Depression 1930s

Cuban missle crisis 1962

Arab Oil Embargo 1973

Black majority rule begins in South Africa 1994

Science and Technology

Man lands on the moon 1969

Automobile assembly
line developed 1901

Information theory developed
by Bell Labs 1940s–1950s

Discovery of the
vacuum tube 1920s

First supersonic flight 1947

Manned space flights begin 1961

Polio vaccine developed 1950s

Antibiotics developed 1930s

Russia launches Space Age with
Sputinik I earth satellite 1957

First Test tube baby 1978

First electronic
computers 1939–1945

DNA molecule structure discovered 1953

AIDS epidemic begins 1981

Religion and Philosophy

Russia and other communist countries persecute Christians 1918–1989

Ghandi applies Hindu philosophy to politics 1915–1948

World Council of
Churches formed 1948

Lausanne Conference on
world evangelism 1974

Archbishop Markarios becomes
president of Cyprus 1960

China closed to
missionary work 1949

Liberation Theology
develops 1973–1980s

U.S. National Council
of Churches formed 1950

Rise of cults 1945–present

Culture and Society

Increased emphasis on welfare 1945–1990s

Organized crime mushrooms 1920s

Abortion legalized in many countries 1920s–1970s

Public education quality deteriorates 1950s–present

Civil Rights movements
in America 1960s–1970s

Period of rapid changes in all areas of life 1945–present

Hippie counterculture
in America 1960s–1970s

Technological Innovation in the 20th Century

Science and Technology

After World War I, scientific and technological knowledge increased at an incredible pace, even more rapidly than in the Industrial Revolution of the late nineteenth century. By the 1970s industrial societies were more dependent on science than at any other time in history. Science and technology had joined hands—"pure" or "theoretical" science had united with "applied" science or "practical" technology. Until the late nineteenth century, science and technology had commonly remained apart. The scientists were usually university professors who were not really interested in technology—the effective combination of tools, machines, materials, skills, and sources of energy in order to make work easier and more productive. The practical matters were left to the technicians and engineers who, for the most part, were trained on the job and operated on the basis of trial-and-error experimentation. Thus, most useful applications of earlier scientific discoveries were by-products of curiosity.

By 1900, a few scientists and a number of industrial firms realized that directed, concentrated research to develop new products was worthwhile. As mentioned in chapter 7, the chemical industry took the lead in establishing research laboratories. Generally, however, the separation of science and technology continued until the late 1930s, when scientific research and technical skills began to be directed toward solving military problems. War and international rivalry prompted governments to spend huge amounts for scientific research and development. What followed were spectacular breakthroughs such as radar, jet propulsion, and the atomic bomb. Still other experiments in chemistry and biology resulted from the prospect of commercial uses in agriculture, industry, and medicine. From the space program, all sorts of "spin-offs," that is, new products with commercial value, have been fringe benefits.

The field of transportation illustrates the **acceleration** of technological knowledge. Until the nineteenth century, the speed of movement had not increased since ancient times. By the beginning of the twentieth century, the steam locomotive traveled at the remarkable speed of 80 miles per hour. But what happened in the next three generations? The automobile and airplane were developed. They went faster and farther and were more flexible than trains. The jet plane further revolutionized air travel. Later the liquid fuel rocket enabled humans to circle the earth in 90 minutes and also to travel to the moon. All this occurred in the span of one generation

Acceleration of Available Data. One of the most significant changes of the twentieth century was the explosion in the amount and availability of

High-tech bullet trains at a Tokyo station

information. The rapid increase has led to the necessity of **specialization**. Although vast amounts of data have been compiled, a person can only absorb a small percentage of it. As a result, he concentrates his education on a very narrow field. Very few people acquire a thorough understanding of a given area, much less a firm grasp of the vast volume of new and old general knowledge; and they thus often have trouble seeing relationships between their subject and others. Specialization affects not only the scientific researchers but also the worker who repeats the same task on an assembly line without ever acquiring an awareness of the complete product.

This specialization also affects people as they vote, buy a car, select foods to eat, or choose their doctors. They have to rely on information given

The Electronic Servant

A few short years ago, it was a science-fiction fantasy. Today, millions of homes, businesses, schools, and research facilities have an electronic servant that performs thousands of daily chores. It is the digital computer.

The home computer is getting smaller and cheaper, making it a common tool in ordinary households. It may serve as a master control center, turning on heat and lights, regulating appliances, opening and closing doors and windows, and performing security functions. The housewife may go to her screen for a readout of comparative prices at on-line shopping outlets. Pressing a button on the terminal, she can order what she wants. Another key may call up from a data bank the recipes she needs for the evening meal. Meals may be planned by the computer to provide a balanced diet.

Hooked up to the telephone, television set, bank, stores, and library services, the computer may form the basis for a home communications, educational, or research center. The computer may keep track of family finances and perform banking functions. Specialized news reports and other data can be retrieved from information exchange centers. Users may call for information on the weather, the price of stocks, consumer information, or virtually any item of knowledge. Global networks open the entire world of knowledge to any individual user.

Researchers engaged in experimental work may communicate with colleagues in other locations concerning work in progress. Messages may be exchanged until work is completed, whereupon a report may be prepared and transmitted to an editor for publication. The publication may become part of an electronic forum where experts and other interested persons may contribute their ideas and feedback.

Libraries are becoming access points for electronically stored information, not just repositories for books. A person may telephone or go to the library to locate information on community agencies and services, on jobs, on the stock market, or any other need. If the library does not possess the information, it is likely to have network connections with other libraries or agencies that do. The potential for accessing information resources by means of computer terminals within the home, business, school, college, or laboratory is growing rapidly. Various systems permit viewers to have interactive access to data bases.

Adapted in part from Jessica L. Harris, "Information Science—Future Techniques," *AcademicAmerican Encyclopedia* (Grolier's Electronic Publishing, 1994), via CompuServe Information Services.

them by experts. Often the views of experts conflict, so the individual becomes frustrated as he is forced to make decisions without data he can understand. He sometimes gives up and just follows whatever the television, radio, newspapers or other "gatekeepers" of information are saying.

This problem was not only a result of specialization but also a result of the sheer volume of available information. Even though a larger amount of information existed than ever before, many people remained uninformed or misinformed because they were not able to receive the right information at the right time, were not aware of the availability of the information they needed, and did not know where to find it or how to retrieve it. While much of the information was available through electronic means, many people were insufficiently trained in the use of information storage and retrieval technology. This fact led some people to feel the world was moving too fast and was passing them by—a feeling that produced frustration and anger. Workers whose lives had been geared to the world of heavy industry, for example, suddenly found that the world had changed, and their skills and knowledge were no longer relevant to the mainstream of life.

The explosion in the availability of information in the last decade of the twentieth century caused the world to believe that a new historical epoch had arrived. It was called the **Information Age**, and life was said to be traveling an **Information Superhighway**. By 1995, about half of all U.S. workers were engaged in some form of information processing, rather than industrial production.

The era spawned a new field of knowledge known as **information science**. In its broadest sense, information science encompassed a wide variety of disciplines, including biology, physics, computer science, psychology, sociology, and library science. Information science was defined by experts as the study of ways in which people, groups, and other living organisms process information. It might explore, for example, how genetic information is processed in living cells. It might study how an individual organism uses information concerning its environment, or it might consider methods of human learning and how information is generated. The primary emphasis, however, was on human information processing at the conscious level.

The knowledge expansion led information scientists to concentrate on means of making information more readily available (**indexing**) and of transferring information. One of the earliest indexing tools was developed by **Hans Peter Luhn** and a team at International Business Machines Corporation (**IBM**) in 1959. It was called "Keyword in Context" or **KWIC** indexing. This method involved using a computer to generate entries from title words in documents. An additional tool, known as "Selective Dissemination of Information" or **SDI**, involved preparation of electronic lists or profiles of topics of

Computer technology touches all of our lives.

continuing interest to a user. These lists are then compared to index terms related to specific documents in currently available literature, which are continually updated, and the user is informed of the documents that match his needs. These techniques were dependent upon another foundational tool called a **data base**, a body of information, usually stored in a computer, which can be searched and manipulated in various ways. **Bibliographic** data bases are primarily based on published or printed materials, transferred from "hard copy" to electronic media through computer keyboarding. These are the primary data bases for general public use. Some of the information for the book you are now reading, for example, was retrieved from electronic data bases and reference libraries. It was then studied by the researcher-writer of the book and written in the writer's own words on a computer which generated "output" used to print the book. **Numeric** data bases consist of any sort of data, usually of a sophisticated variety useful only to highly trained technicians for specific private uses.

Electronically stored information is dependent on various items of "**hardware**"—magnetic tapes, electronically or magnetically charged drums,

disks, and diskettes, as well as the machines used to access these devices. Microfilms are also used to store large amounts of printed information in a very small amount of space.

In the twenty-first century, information science is expected to develop even further. One of the key tools, already in fairly widespread experimental use in the 1990s, was **computer conferencing**, which uses complex computer networks for the exchange of messages among users. This suggests that the world may soon become what early communications theorist **Marshall McLuhan** called "the global village." Others suggested that computer communication would create greater social isolation as people no longer interact face to face but only via machine. By using these networks, citizens will be able to interact directly with their governments, with fellow researchers, with libraries, with business colleagues, with merchandisers, with friends and relatives, and with any other element in a developed society. On higher official levels, the bulk of industrial and military operations will be based on these technological means.

The History of Automation. The distinctive initial feature of the third phase of the industrial-technological revolution was, as we have seen, **automation**. First came the development of mechanization, followed by mass production and the assembly line. After World War II, automation transformed the factory from a collection of machines into a single, integrated unit with a greater capacity than before but with less involvement of human labor. With the advent of electronic equipment that regulates and coordinates the quantity and quality of production, the new equipment is actually capable of performing decision-making tasks, whereas the older machinery merely did physical labor. Just as man's early machines extended his muscle power, so electronic devices extend his brain power.

Two factors that contributed most to the technological explosion after 1945 were the electronic computer and the larger numbers of highly trained people. Although mechanical computers were invented in the nineteenth century, the first simple electronic ones appeared during World War II. These computers, usually huge, room-filling devices, performed thousands of complicated calculations in a split second, some of which would take a person working alone many years to do. Since then, computer technology has grown so rapidly that even the most sophisticated equipment becomes outdated within a few years or even months.

Remote **sensing devices**, **photoelectric cells**, and **miniature computers** have also been developed. The modern automobile, for example, is run almost entirely by dozens of miniature computers and computerized parts which calculate millions of operations every minute. Some cars have electronic guidance systems that use space-based communications technology. These kinds of devices also are used to operate industrial machinery, military weapons, underwater survey equipment, trains, airplanes, broadcast stations, and even entire factories with little human help. Governments and businesses can bill customers, write letters, and make plane reservations with computers. These marvelous inventions have great potential for good as they have enriched lives, ended humdrum work, and expanded knowledge. But they can just as easily be put to evil uses in an invasion of **individual privacy**, through acquisition of personal records, the use of "bugging" (electronic eavesdropping) devices, or for immoral or destructive purposes. Data bases filled with pornography, for example, are now widely available.

In individual countries, basic literacy rates have neared the 100 percent mark, while in others, even advanced countries such as the United States, *functional* literacy rates have dropped severely. Opportunities for study in colleges and technical schools are readily available. In fact, a college degree has become almost essential in the new scientific-technological order, not only for work as a scientist but also for positions in business, commercial, and government bureaucracies. Through heavy investment in education, governments and private industries have sought, unsuccessfully in many cases, to make sure that schools turn out the brain power needed for the technological age. However, as modern secular education has lost its spiritual foundation and has been subverted to the creation of a new humanistic social order, it has increasingly deteriorated in the basic areas of knowledge and skills. Just when the world's new technologically based economic order was demanding more and more sophisticated skills, a major portion of the population was failing to acquire even the most rudimentary educational skills such as reading, writing, mathematical calculation, and logical reasoning. Christians were among the first to see this problem and were in the vanguard of revitalizing education in the basic areas of God-given knowledge.

Poor quality secular and state-operated education has thus often widened the gap between the skilled and unskilled and the rich and poor nations of the world. Because industrial societies have more money to invest in technological training and basic research, their economic growth continues to accelerate. The poorer countries have low literacy rates and little money for education. In addition to seeking direct technological aid, they often have to send their students to study abroad.

However, higher education all too often downgrades or ignores literary, historical, religious, and artistic studies. Yet, these humanities courses are needed to provide the intellectual, philosophical, and moral framework in which scientific decisions must be made. Frequently, practical applications have been required without a clear understanding of the purposes or moral implications of particular actions. For this reason, some people in the 1990s were beginning to ask such questions as: "Even if we are *able* to do a given thing, *should* we do it?"

Innovation in Transportation

The new scientific technology has had a remarkable impact on human life. Major advances in transportation resulted from developments in the automobile and aviation industries.

Automobiles. Gasoline, electric, and steam-driven carriages were in operation even before the beginning of the twentieth century. In 1901, **Ransom E. Olds** set up the first assembly line in Detroit, the city which soon became the motor capital of the world. **Henry Ford** so improved the assembly line technique that his Model T (15 million sold between 1913 and 1927) put automobile ownership within the reach of even the lower middle class. As the years passed, continuing improvements in automotive technology made cars faster, safer, more comfortable, and easier to operate. Many companies producing cars grew into massive, worldwide corporations such as Ford, Chrysler, and General Motors in North America; Toyota, Mitsubishi, and Nissan in Japan; Hyundai in Korea; Volkswagen-Audi and Mercedes Benz in Germany; Leyland in Britain; Renault in France; Volvo and Saab-Scania in Sweden; and Fiat in Italy.

Sharp increases in auto production occurred in Japan and Europe in the decades after World War

Henry Ford, 1863–1947

II, but one-third of all cars in the world were still made in the United States and Canada. One-half of all vehicles currently registered were in these two countries. To accommodate the cars that increasingly clog the roads of the industrial nations, millions of miles of highways have been built. Following the lead of Germany, which in the 1930s built a nationwide network of superhighways, the United States has constructed its own 42,500-mile interstate highway system.

Effects of Automobiles. The impact of the automobile has been enormous. Because it provides even common people with freedom of movement, something which in the past ages was possible for only the very wealthy, it is one of the major liberating forces of modern times. It opens vast new opportunities for finding employment and enjoying leisure time. It made possible suburban living, so that now people often live some distance from where they work. The auto business and related industries provide employment for several millions of people, and the economies of the Western industrial countries are heavily dependent on it.

Critics claim, however, that the auto's influence on society is more negative than positive. They argue that auto exhaust fumes help to pollute the air of the world's large cities and endanger the health of their residents. They say the need for highways diverts funds away from private use and social programs and removes valuable farmland from food production. Moreover, they say, the manufacture and operation of autos is consuming the earth's so-called nonrenewable resources, especially iron and petroleum, at an alarming rate. The drastic effects when oil-producing countries increase prices demonstrate clearly how dependent the economies of industrial nations are upon motor vehicles. People spend such long hours commuting to their jobs that time with their families is limited. Motorist accidents are now one of the leading causes of death in the industrial countries. Finally, critics say that the presence of so many cars discourages the development of energy-efficient systems of mass transportation which the cities need if they are to survive.

Airplanes. In 75 years, what was once a vision of dreamers and a hobby of flight enthusiasts became a decisive factor in warfare and also the chief form of long-distance travel. Airplanes were first widely used in World War I, and after the return of peace they were utilized on a limited scale for mail, freight, and passenger service. Small, privately owned airlines sprang up everywhere. Except in the United States, these gradually passed into government ownership. During the 1930s, large planes known as Flying Boats began passenger flights to Europe and Asia.

Supersonic jets, like this F-15A *Eagle*, are now a standard part of a modern military arsenal.

During World War II, several hundred thousand aircraft were produced for the warring countries by firms in the Soviet Union, Germany, Japan, Great Britain, and the United States. In the United States alone, the annual output of planes reached 100,000 by 1944. The Germans used the first jet-propelled fighter planes in combat in 1944–1945, but with little effect. Not until the Korean Conflict did jet fighters finally play a key role.

A desire for planes that could make nonstop transoceanic flights caused manufacturers to develop more powerful gasoline engines and then jet airliners. The latter carried large loads quickly and safely everywhere, and contributed to the enormous jump in passenger traffic in the 1960s. The introduction of the jumbo jet in 1970 resulted in even greater increases in airline business.

Meanwhile, as aircraft technology improved, **supersonic** flight became possible. This required designing more powerful jet engines and aircraft that would stand up under the tremendous air pressure reached at the speed of sound (760 miles per hour at sea level). The sound barrier was first shattered in 1947, and supersonic jet fighters and bombers were used by the late 1950s. Both a

Russian (the *TU-144*) and a jointly built British-French (the *Concorde*) supersonic transport were put into passenger service in the early 1970s. The United States worked on it own *SST* for a time but abandoned the project due to high costs and objections from environmentalists. Other types of aircraft that are now in wide use include the helicopter and the Hovercraft, which rides on a cushion of air a few inches above the ground or water.

Effects of Air Travel. The airplane has reduced distances around the globe to only a few hours flying time. Because light goods and passengers can be transported swiftly and efficiently by air, ships and railroads are now used primarily for bulk goods like coal, mineral ores, oil, nonperishable foodstuffs, and manufactured items. Although air travel is quite expensive, the large planes bring costs within the reach of people of moderate means. When the United States government deregulated airline service in the 1980s, fare prices became more competitive and prices were generally lowered. International travel has expanded to an extent never thought possible. Many ordinary people can now actually visit faraway places.

On the other hand, critics note that airplanes cause extensive air and noise pollution, especially around large metropolitan centers. The airlines are particularly vulnerable to the efforts of oil producers to force up prices by reducing fuel supplies. Airports occupy large amounts of land that otherwise could be used for agriculture and housing. The airplane, along with the automobile, has contributed to the decline in railroad service and the sense of isolation felt by smaller cities without airline connections.

Albert Einstein, 1879–1955

Development of Atomic Energy

One of the spectacular developments of the twentieth century concerned atomic or nuclear energy. In the 1930s, **Enrico Fermi** and other researchers discovered how to split the nucleus of the uranium atom and unlock the energy in it. Splitting an atom of uranium (**fission**) produced a particle called a **neutron**, which could be used to crack other uranium atoms. Scientists predicted this would set off a "chain reaction" in the atoms and release enormous amounts of energy. Several scientists (including **Albert Einstein**, who had come to the United States) persuaded President Franklin D. Roosevelt to support atomic research. Fermi and his associates built a **reactor** (also called an atomic pile), and in December 1942 produced the first man-made nuclear chain reaction.

Weapons. The top secret **Manhattan Project** developed the bombs dropped on Japan in 1945. These weapons gave a terrifying new dimension to warfare. If man at last had gained control over the basic forces of the universe, had he also created a Frankenstein monster that would ultimately destroy all human life? This question became even more pointed with the development of the **hydrogen bomb**, which works through nuclear **fusion** (union of atomic nuclei to produced enormous energy releases) and unleashes far more destructive power than the early atomic bombs. By the late 1960s, people talked of building even more dreadful weapons—the **neutron bomb** that would kill people but not destroy property, and the **cobalt bomb** that could wipe out all life on the planet. For some interpreters, the biblical description of the coming "day of God" where "the heavens being on fire shall be dissolved, and the elements shall melt with fervent heat" began to take on an awesome sense of reality. And because the highly antagonistic world political superpowers, the United States and the Soviet Union, both possessed the capability of building and delivering such weapons, a kind of nuclear-destruction hysteria began to sweep over the world during the 1950s through 1980s. The Soviets exploited and encouraged this hysteria through propaganda designed to prod their enemies into unilateral disarmament, but the United States and European powers insisted upon mutual disarmament. While several treaties were signed to this effect, enormous stockpiles of weapons of mass destruction and missiles to carry the warheads remained in place for years to follow. When the Cold War ended with the collapse of Soviet communism, the nuclear-war hysteria began to fade, some weapons were destroyed, missiles were disarmed, and targets were deprogrammed. However, much of this activity was deceptively superficial, since rearming missiles and reprogramming targets was a quick and simple operation, as long as the weapons themselves remained available for use by fanatical elements within hostile governments.

Other Uses. However, numerous peaceful uses for nuclear energy have been found. The heat from fission operates electrical generating plants in many countries, and reactors provide power for ships and spacecraft. Radioactive material has thousands of applications in medicine, industry, and agriculture. Nevertheless, the possibility of explosions or leakage of radioactive substances always poses a danger. Disposal of atomic wastes is also a critical matter, as some emit deadly levels of radiation for thousands of years.

Electronic and Computer Technology

As we have already seen, electronics was and is another area of spectacular achievement. In the early part of the twentieth century came a key development—the discovery of the **vacuum tube**. It greatly improved the radio and aided the earliest experiments in television in the late 1920s. The **magnetron**, invented in 1939, made possible microwave radar and long-distance telephone and television communications. The next great electronic advance was the development of the **computer** based on the **binary** numerical calculation system. Further, right out of the pages of science fiction emerged the **laser** (amplified light beam) in 1960. On this highly concentrated beam of light can travel thousands of telephone messages, for example. Lasers are also used to perform delicate surgical operations such as those on the eye, to operate space ships and satellites from the earth, and to destroy enemy rockets at a great

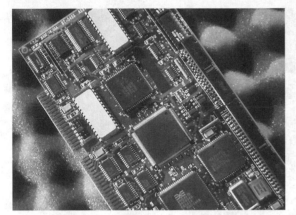

Integrated circuit board with individual microchips

distance. They are also used in fusion energy research.

The invention of the **transistor** in 1948 made it possible to reduce the size of electronic units. Printed wireless **integrated circuits**, invented in the 1950s, and **microchips**, which combined several minuscule electronic components, further revolutionized the field, making possible stereophonic sound systems, color televisions, pocket-size radios, communicating and animated toys, efficient kitchen appliances, and desktop and portable computers, some small enough to fit easily within a briefcase or clothing pocket.

Electronic devices transformed human life in countless ways. Computers now keep track of **credit card** transactions, and people use these plastic rectangles as money to purchase everything from an airplane ticket to a tank of gas or even a pizza. Financial indebtedness has become a significant aspect of life for people who want to "buy now, pay later." Individual miniature calculators simplify record-keeping and mathematical processes for people. Telephone service has improved to the point that one can dial a few numbers on his home, business, or portable unit and instantly speak with people on other conti-

nents or transfer data from computer to computer. Cellular telephones, which transfer messages by radio, microwave, or laser beams through thousands of strategically located stations (cells) linked through space-based satellites, make interpersonal communication possible from virtually any location. In some places people were developing phones which transmit a picture as well as sound. Long-range facsimile transmission of printed material also changed patterns of business transactions and scientific research. Reports, news photographs, and telegrams are among the materials that can be sent by electronic means, often via wireless and laser linkups through space satellites. Transmission of "live" television pictures and sound via satellite has given virtually the entire world instant access to information about momentary events anywhere as they happen.

The Space Age

Space exploration was one of the most exciting achievements of technological progress. As with atomic energy, military concerns motivated development of the space program. World War II experiments in rocketry laid the groundwork for long-range missiles and orbiting satellites. The new electronic devices were also crucial ingredients of successful space flight. During the intensive program to put an American on the moon, scientists created complex computer systems, gigantic rocket engines, and equipment to help humans cope with weightlessness.

Man's venture into deep space makes an interesting contrast with the earlier voyages of discovery. New developments in space exploration took place over a very short period of time. Only eight

Neil Armstrong, 1939–

years passed between **Yuri Gagarin**'s first orbital flight in 1961 and **Neil Armstrong**'s first step on the moon in 1969. Because of modern technology, space exploration is much safer than the sea travel of 500 years ago. Space adventures have been communicated to people all over the world. At Christmas in 1968, millions heard on their radios or television sets the voice of an American astronaut reading the Bible's creation story and describing the earth while his spacecraft circled the moon. On July 20, 1969, people on six continents watched **Neil Armstrong** and **Edwin Aldrin** set foot on the lunar surface.

After several additional manned moon landings, space ventures shifted to unmanned flight and space-based scientific research aboard orbiting laboratories and space shuttle ships. By 1980, unmanned landings had been made on Mars and

Venus, and space probes were winging their way toward the far reaches of the solar system. At the same time gigantic reflector and radio telescopes were exploring the vast distances of outer space, collecting data on the universe. A fleet of automated spacecraft met Halley's Comet when it neared our solar system in 1986.

Numerous satellites now orbit the earth, taking pictures which improve the accuracy of weather forecasting, aiding television and amateur radio transmission, and monitoring the levels of radiation in the atmosphere. Others provide navigation aids so that aircraft can plot their courses more carefully. Satellites are also used for military purposes such as spying and reconnaissance. Space-based antimissile systems were designed during the last years of the Cold War, but they were not deployed when the apparent threat of nuclear war between the United States and Russia appeared to dissipate in the 1990s. Also planned are colonies of people living in orbit so that they can do research.

Apollo 15 astronauts used the Rover to explore the moon's surface in 1971. Astronaut James Irwin stands by the flag. Irwin, a devout Christian, formed the High Flight Foundation and became an evangelical lecturer after retiring from the space agency.

The Mass Media

With the advent of the electronic and space ages has come a revolution in mass communications which has insured that the present generation is better informed than any that preceded it. Not only is there now an abundance of information, but, as we have seen, there are also many means of storing this information and of transmitting it to others. Instant telecommunications have drawn the world closer together. Microcircuit radios and television sets and digital television satellite "uplinks" and "downlinks" have opened new horizons of knowledge and understanding. Once-local news items now are broadcast world-wide. Communications satellites have made it possible for people everywhere to see major events taking place around the earth.

New technology in printing enables the rapid publication of books, magazines, and newspapers to provide information in depth. One of the most significant developments was the advent of desktop publishing systems using personal computers and small mechanical or laser printing devices. Desktop publishing gave the common man the ability to publish and disseminate his ideas directly to anyone he chooses. In the past, there were great cost and logistical limitations which kept publishing within the reach of only those with large professional printing presses and the money to finance mass publishing ventures.

The desktop publishing opportunity generated thousands of new publications, making the **newsletter** a major alternative to the mass, establishment newspapers and magazines of the past, which were often controlled by powerful, elitist interests with limited (usually liberal) points of view.

In schools, many electronic devices—motion pictures, audio and video tape recorders, video cameras, stereophonic sound systems, computers, and closed-circuit television systems—aid the learning process.

One of the positive contributions of advances in electronics and communications is in the area of religion. Evangelists, who in the past could only reach hundreds or thousands, now reach millions

Cameramen are quick to get a photo of a news event.

via television. Christian networks have their own communications satellite systems, or access to commercial systems, to send programs to other parts of the world. Churches and missionary societies utilize computers and data banks to solicit contributions, inform their supporters, and plan new evangelistic efforts. Computers are also used to aid in making new translations of the Bible into languages for which no version of the scriptures had earlier been produced.

Not all the advances in communications have had positive effects, for devices which produce an informed public serve just as easily to control thinking. Dictatorial governments utilize the media to shape public views by filtering out all "undesirable" data. The concept of propaganda has taken on new meaning. Previously it meant the dissemination of information—now it is the systematic use of all forms of communication to bring public thinking into line with what a ruler desires. This includes the continuous repetition of lies, half-truths, disinformation, misinformation, and one-sided views.

Mind-control Techniques

Many people think that brainwashing happens only in totalitarian countries or in special situations, such as the North Korean POW camps in the 1950s. They would be shocked to learn that a number of brainwashing tactics are being used by groups in the United States today in the process of gaining and indoctrinating members. These cults often persuade a person to accept ideas and behavior totally foreign to him, in fact, unacceptable to him before coming under the cult's strong influence.

The approach to a prospective member is important. Cult members offer him love and attention. Then they try to draw him into their indoctrination program. According to psychologist Robert Jay Lifton, who studied mind-control techniques, most indoctrination programs utilize the following principles:

Control of the environment. The cult tries to disorient the recruit by separating him from his old environment and providing a new, carefully controlled one. For instance, the cult may invite him to a retreat where there is no telephone, radio, or newspapers. He is discouraged from contacting friends or family. With less than normal sleep, no privacy, a strange diet of low-protein food, a highly emotional atmosphere, and constant group pressure to conform, the recruit soon finds himself entering into the activities. The singing, prayer, meditation, dancing, and chanting tend to change his state of mind and make him more open to new ideas. Then comes the second step.

Mystical manipulation. The teaching which prospective members receive usually includes some of the following ideas. God has chosen the group for a special purpose in the world. Each member has a responsibility in the achievement of that goal. The leader presents a simple solution to the world's problems. When recruits try to ask questions, group members silence them with the warning to think more positively.

Need for purity. Cult members zero in on the recruit's former life. They impress him with the sinfulness of certain actions, playing upon his feelings of guilt. Bearing down hard on the point in his life about which he is worried and anxious, eventually they cause more stress than he can bear. His patterns of behavior and belief weaken under this attack. Now he is ready for **confession**. Through this means, the recruit makes a definite break with aspects of his past life.

Indoctrination. The cult develops around itself an **aura of sacred science**. Its doctrines are absolute and must be followed without question. Members hear that these ideas are more important than anything else. Further, the cult has its own special vocabulary, which serves to set it apart.

Salvation. The group is told that **only cult members will be saved; all others are lost**. Again this increases the distance between the cult and society. This belief presents a psychological barrier to anyone considering leaving the group. By the time a person has gone through these steps and accepted all these ideas, he usually no longer thinks for himself. He is in the control of the cult.

Examples of some or all of these features have been seen in such cults as The People's Temple (Guyana), the Unification Church (Moonies), the Church of Scientology, and the Branch Davidians (Waco, Texas). Mass deaths occurred in Guyana (1978) and Waco (1993).

Techniques discovered by modern psychology have increased the effectiveness of "brainwashing." An individual is deprived of food and sleep while constantly hammered with simple ideas and falsehoods until his will is completely broken. Then his mind is filled with the new concepts that the group or leader had decided upon,

and he no longer exercises control over his will. Although this bears some similarity to the methods of the medieval Inquisition, it was sophisticated during Stalin's purges in the 1930s and the Korean Conflict 20 years later. Today it is most widely used by cults such as the Unification Church and the Hare Krishnas. It has ominous implications for human freedom, as the tragic suicide of 900 cultists in Jonestown, Guyana, in November 1978, and similar later episodes so dramatically illustrated.

The "**mind benders**," as some refer to the mass entertainment and news media, affect all people, even in countries with a high level of political freedom. In these nations the "media barons" or "information gatekeepers" decide what will or will not appear in the press, on television, and in motion pictures. They determine the kinds of values that will be communicated, and the only real alternative in the past for the ordinary person was to stop his subscription to the paper, shut off his TV set, or stay home from the movies. Those who directed the media decided what was news, what the people should be told about current issues, and for all practical purposes what is right and wrong. However, as we have noted, personal communications systems, such as desktop publishing, camcorders, duplicating devices, and the Internet, have now given ordinary people the opportunity to bypass these media controllers. Christians have also increasingly moved into the media to affect the values carried thereby. More and more Christians are becoming journalists; film producers, directors, critics, and screenwriters; radio and television station owners; and publishers.

A further concern is the effect of **advertising** on society. In Western countries, people have more leisure time than ever before, and new industries cater to their recreational needs. As gadgets have been developed and marketed at a dizzying rate of speed, advertisers have played a major role in causing readers and viewers to believe that these products are desirable, regardless of whether they are really needed or worthwhile. For even common people in the industrialized countries, a moderately affluent standard of living has become the norm. While advertising often produces materialistic covetousness and envy, it also may serve a legitimate purpose, when used in nonexploitive ways, in the marketing of useful and worthwhile goods, thus bolstering productive enterprises.

Developments in the Life Sciences

Chemistry and Medicine. Chemistry has also played an important role in the technological revolution. New fabrics such as nylon, dacron, rayon, orlon, and polyesters; a wide range of plastics and **acrylics**; synthetic substances like rubber and motor fuel; and artificial fertilizers and pesticides became commonplace. The greatest increases came in the use of drugs, plastics, and **petrochemicals**. The enormous quantity of new products from the chemical industry affected everyday life in a multitude of ways.

The field of **materials engineering** creates new materials with unusual properties. In the 1990s, this field saw the advent of **nanotechnology**, which creates microscopically miniaturized sensors that promised to improve medical diagnosis and treatment.

Advances in the field of medicine were truly remarkable. In the 1930s, penicillin and sulfa drugs, the first **antibiotics**, were developed. **Aspirin** was found to be an all-purpose painkiller. The number of other such "miracle drugs" multiplied rapidly. **Insulin** enabled diabetics to live normal lives, and tranquilizers aided the treatment of mental patients. The scourge of polio was attacked in the 1950s through the Salk and Sabin vaccines. Insecticides helped in the struggle against malaria and typhus. By the 1990s, however, there were frightening reports that overuse of antibiotics may be producing a threat of new or stronger diseases. Scientists found evidence that some disease-producing microorganisms were developing immunities to certain common antibiotics and were thus becoming more powerful and deadly. New strains of these "superviruses" were discovered and some sensational reports predicted the possibility of widespread unstoppable epidemics.

In the early 1980s a newly recognized disease began to sweep the world and caused thousands of deaths. **AIDS** (acquired immune deficiency syndrome), a complex and largely misunderstood malady involving deterioration of the immune system due to a virus known as HIV (human immunodeficiency virus), infected millions of people. By the mid-1990s there was still no known cure. The disease was almost exclusively limited to those involved in illicit sexual behavior, users of contaminated needles, sexual partners of infected individuals, and a few innocent victims who came into contact with contaminated blood. Great controversy arose over the disease, the causes, how research should be conducted and financed, and what society's attitude should be toward those infected. The disease soon became more a political concern than a medical one. Homosexual groups—demanding government research and freedom to continue their unbridled, detestable sexual practices—staged violent and disruptive demonstrations. Because many of the victims who acquired the disease through illegal-drug use and prostitution were members of nonwhite racial groups, militants introduced racism into the discussion. A law was passed in the United States naming HIV infection a "physical disability," thus prohibiting discrimination against infected persons.

By 1993, some 194,000 AIDS-related deaths were reported in the United States alone. More than 1.5 million people were reported to be infected with HIV, meaning their deaths could be expected within a decade unless a cure was found. Additional infection was growing at an alarming rate. By 1990, the United States government was spending more than $2 billion for medical research about AIDS. AIDS was also reported in 208 other countries worldwide. In sub-Saharan Africa, estimates were that as much as half of the population of some counties was infected, with a potential death rate in the early twenty-first century in the tens of millions.

Meanwhile, doctors and researchers worked to gain control over other age-old maladies such as heart disease, cancer, high blood pressure, kidney disease, asthma, and multiple sclerosis. Many researchers complained that the large amount of money being spent on AIDS research limited the resources available for these older diseases which were claiming far more lives. Researchers were sought to develop new drugs, as well as chemically produced hormones, and electronic monitoring devices. New research and experimentation produced knowledge which enabled doctors to transplant organs and create and install artificial organs, even basic organs such as the heart. Advanced radiology techniques such as **magnetic resonance imaging** (MRI) and **positron emission tomography** (PET) came into use. The sophisticated devices using these technologies cost millions of dollars and added to the high cost of health care, making such care difficult for many people to obtain. These costs, which also soared when governments began subsidizing health care, became a source of major political and social debate in the 1980s and 1990s. In some countries, health care was financed totally by the government through staggeringly high tax collections. In virtually every case, this so-called **socialized-medicine** approach led to a deterioration in the quality and comforting aspects of traditional private care.

Genetics. Related to medicine was research on the chemistry of genes, the mysterious factors that cause biological inheritance from one generation to another. In 1953, **James D. Watson** and **Francis Crick** discovered that the structure of the **DNA** molecule, the basic substance found in the nucleus of the cells of all living matter, is a **double helix** (spiral chain). Biologists quickly realized that if the two strands of the double helix were split apart, each one would match the other. Also they became aware that small changes in this molecule determine the differences in the genetic inheritance of every living creature.

They learned that all the cells in an organism's body contain the same amount of DNA. Since the cells can multiply, a few scientists began experimenting with **cloning** lower forms of life in the late 1970s. The DNA from a body cell of an organism injected into the egg cell of that same being, results in the exact reproduction of the parent organism. Some people have considered producing human clones, but so far this is a distant and improbable prospect. This understanding of DNA has led to other "advances" in genetic science. Some biologists have investigated the possibility of treating crippling hereditary diseases and birth defects by replacing the defective DNA in the genetic scheme of a fetus with material that has been chemically corrected. The conception of a child outside the body of the mother, a procedure first carried out successfully in 1978, also seemed to some as a way in which genetic defects could be treated.

Ethical Implications. Many ethical questions have been raised by these medical achievements. Science now possesses the technological means to keep a sick person alive long after the point when

Biological research continues to open the door to the wonders and complexity of the human body.

physical death would have previously occurred, but at enormous financial expense. Should the failure to maintain the life-support system of a terminally ill patient be regarded as **euthanasia** (so-called "mercy killing") or would it be murder? Should it be acceptable for the state to order the elimination of the chronically ill, severely handicapped, and very aged on the grounds that they are of no value to society and it costs too much to keep them? Should tests be run on all expectant mothers, and those who seem to have a genetically deficient fetus be forced to undergo an abortion since the state may ultimately have to support the child? For that matter, should abortion be used as a method of birth control to help stem population increases? Would genetic engineering (the scientific altering of a person's genetic make-up) remove a tendency to particular diseases or would it create "monsters"? Would such changes violate the integrity of the human as a divinely created being? Should some people be bred almost like animals to serve as eventual organ donors or as sources of material for cloning experiments? Are biomedical scientists trying to "play God"? These difficult questions have given rise to an entire new specialty, the field of **biomedical ethics**.

Sadly, this field has largely ignored the only true source of moral direction, the Christian Scriptures, and "ethical" decisions are now being made on the foundation of the sinful human mind and imagination. When moral and ethical questions arise, one response has been to deal with them through civil law, since all systems of civil law are codifications of an underlying moral perspective (what is right and wrong). This has plunged medicine further into the political arena, where the debate often became highly charged during the late twentieth century.

The Abortion Holocaust. One of the most significant debates of this nature centered around medically induced abortions and euthanasia. Between 1920 and 1967, the U.S.S.R., most Scandinavian countries, Japan, Great Britain and some Eastern European countries legalized abortion on demand, and the world began to witness a new holocaust that far outstripped the destruction of the Nazi's ethnic Holocaust of the World War II era. The United States joined this hall of infamy in 1973 when the Supreme Court overturned historic laws in all states which had made induced abortion a crime. Now about half of the world's people live in countries were abortion is available on request, and another one-fourth live in areas where abortion is permitted to protect a

Genetics and Playing God

Genetic research has triggered the creative imagination of the science fiction writer like few other subjects. Dr. Frankenstein fails in his efforts to create a beautiful being in his laboratory. Instead he turns loose upon the world a hideous monster who destroys everything the doctor loves, and eventually even the doctor himself. The novel ***Brave New World*** describes a human assembly line in a totalitarian world. Test tube babies are produced on a conveyor belt solely for the "good of society." Each baby is assigned a function in society—such as an engineer, doctor, workers, garbage man, or athlete. Raised in a laboratory, the child's entire upbringing conditions him to fulfill that function. In ***The Andromeda Strain***, a deadly new microbe threatens the earth.

The disasters envisioned by these writers have worried some people. There is no assurance that some of these nightmares could not really happen. For example, it is possible that gene-transplantation experiments might give bacteria found in the human body immunity to antibiotics. These bacteria could spread through the population. A greater danger might occur with bacteria to which genes from cancer-causing viruses have been added. Some accident might allow such bacteria to escape from the laboratory. Scientists were so fearful of these possibilities that they voluntarily called a halt to gene-transplanting experiments until they had drawn up guidelines for this work. In the mid-1990s some limited accidents of this nature were reported.

If genetic research is so risky, why continue it? Some scientists believe that the prevention of diseases such as cancer, multiple sclerosis, birth defects, rheumatoid arthritis, viral infections, allergies, and many others may be achieved through gene-transplantation. This research may also provide new tools to control viruses and uncover future uses for enzymes and hormones, its supporters say. Scientists in favor of genetic research believe that adequate safeguards can be developed to prevent a Frankenstein slip or a ***Brave New World***. In the 1990s government-backed researchers sought authority to use tissues from aborted babies for genetic and disease control experiments. Some wanted to actually create embryos and fetuses for the sole purpose of "harvesting" tissues and organs for experimentation. Aldous Huxley's ***Brave New World*** was becoming a reality.

Some important questions remained, however. What about the ethics of designing humans according to specifications? Who decides what kind of humans society needs? Would artificial production of humans replace the family? Is cloning of humans ethical? Further, who should make all the ethical decisions connected with genetic research—the government: scientists? theologians? the people? God's Word says all of life is in His hands alone. Fallible and sinful human beings are simply not equipped to play God.

women's health. Only in ultraconservative Islamic countries, sub-Sahara African countries, and predominantly Roman Catholic Latin American countries was abortion still outlawed or restricted. In many of these countries, however, practitioners perform abortions without prosecution. In the 1980s, about 40 million to 60 million unborn children were slaughtered worldwide every year, about 33 million of these deaths being legally sanctioned. In the United States, about 27 women out of every 1,000 women of childbear-

ing age had induced abortions each year, a rate higher than in some other Western nations but about half of the worldwide rate. In China, abortion was mandatory for every child conceived beyond one per family!

"Right-to-life" interests in the United States succeeded in convincing legislatures, administrations, and courts to reestablish or apply minor new restrictions on the availability of abortion, but by the mid-1990s, these curbs were fairly insignificant in the face of the ongoing tragedy.

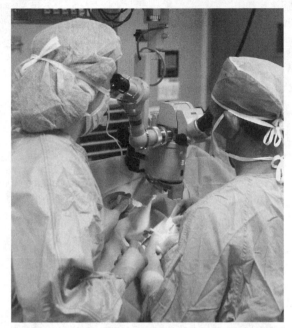

Doctors have the technology to save lives or to destroy them.

Many such attempts to control abortion through government decree proved transitory and seemed to depend on the changing political climate and personal convictions of politicians.

In the 1960s, deaths from illegal abortions reportedly amounted to one-fifth of all deaths related to pregnancy and childbirth in the United States. After legalization, mortality and hospitalization of women due to abortion-related complications dropped *proportionately*, although *actual numbers* of women harmed by abortions increased because far more abortions were being performed. Moreover, studies of long-term consequences of abortion indicated increases in risk of breast cancer, other physical problems, and long-term psychological damage among women who had abortions.

Most significant, however, was the moral issue. Opponents of legalized abortion demonstrated both from the Bible and through science that human life begins at conception and that abortion is therefore the intentional killing of a human being—namely, murder. Supporters of abortion "rights," even some who conceded the reality of human life in the womb, elevated "personal choice" and political rights above all other considerations and insisted that women have a right to destroy their unborn children for any reason. In some cases, abortion advocates also attempted to make cases for the legitimacy of infanticide and involuntary killing of the infirm, elderly persons, and people whose "quality of life" is inferior (as they see it).

For the first 30 years of the debate in the United States, the controversy was largely peaceful, if not always civil, and was largely carried out through publications, political lobbying, and "crisis pregnancy" counseling. Then some pro-life forces began employing civil disobedience methods such as blocking entrances to abortion clinics and picketing that involved trespassing violations. Police often responded brutally and thousands of antiabortion demonstrators were arrested, jailed, and heavily fined. Beginning in 1994 and 1995, some fanatical individuals on the fringes of the antiabortion movement took the drastic step of killing several abortion doctors and abortion clinic personnel. They argued that the Bible and common law allow or require the use of force, even deadly force, to prevent murder and mayhem. But others within the pro-life movement argued that it was neither legitimate nor moral to take a life in order to preserve a life.

Many of the same issues raised in the abortion debate also applied to the growing debate over **euthanasia** (a term from the Greek for "easy death"). Euthanasia takes several forms: *active, passive,* and *voluntary,* all of which were being employed increasingly in the 1980s and 1990s amid considerable social and political controversy. Passive euthanasia means the discontinuing of life-sustaining or extraordinary treatment of the ill. Active euthanasia is the deliberate ending of a life to prevent suffering due to disease, distress, or old age. Voluntary euthanasia is suicide (including medically assisted suicide) for the same reasons.

Many physicians consider it good medical practice not to artificially prolong life for those suffering from diseases considered to be ultimately fatal. Instead, they aim to provide comfort and relief while the patient awaits natural death. Passive euthanasia gained legal stature in the United States only in the 1970s when courts began to rule that doctors may disconnect medical equipment sustaining the life of terminally ill persons. After that, more than 30 U.S. states passed "right-to-die" laws allowing patients, relatives, friends, legal guardians, religious advisors, or courts to grant authority to remove life-support equipment in such cases. In 1990, the U.S. Supreme Court ruled that people have a right ahead of time to make their wishes for such action known. Medical technology, however, has blurred the medical definition of death. Now

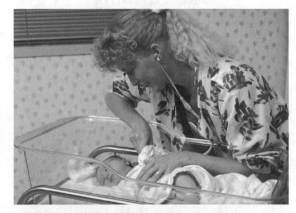

The Bible teaches the sanctity of life.

most authorities consider the cessation of brain waves on electronic monitors to be the legal indicator of death.

Active euthanasia remained a crime in the United States through the mid-1990s. In The Netherlands, however, the practice of active euthanasia, often without the knowledge or consent of a patient, was a widespread practice. Doctors were not prosecuted if they followed certain guidelines, but a 1992 survey showed that many physicians were not following the legal guidelines. In some other countries, euthanasia is a crime with only light punishment. In Uruguay, it was not a crime at all.

In the United States, so-called "assisted suicides" generated controversy in the 1990s. An unlicensed Michigan doctor, **Jack Kevorkian**, was a pioneer in the activity and was repeatedly convicted of crimes for helping patients commit suicide. In a 1994 state-wide vote, Oregon became the first state in the United States to officially legalize doctor-assisted suicide.

Changes in Agriculture and Farming

Other questions are raised by developments in food production, or agriculture. Many of the facets of technological change already discussed are especially important in their effects on farming and on the world's food supply.

Mechanization. Farmers began to use machinery to accomplish tasks previously done by humans. Planting, fertilizing, irrigating, and harvesting of many crops were done by machine. Efficiency in mechanization demanded larger acreage, so one farmer often bought out the smaller holdings from his neighbors. The numbers of traditional "family farms" began to decline. Some human labor is still needed and in many areas this need is met by a supply of migrant workers who move from one place to another following the ripening crops.

Increased Yields. Crops have become more plentiful, not only because of the effective use of machinery but also because of increased knowledge of genetics and farming techniques. The right characteristics are selected so that a larger quantity of wheat, for example, can be grown on the same number of acres. Chemical nutrients are often added to the soil or are replenished more naturally through crop rotation. Livestock and poultry bred with a higher percentage of meat than before have also been developed scientifically.

Farming as a Business. When fewer workers were needed, farm families began to have fewer children than they used to. Instead of a family enterprise, running a farm increasingly was seen as a business venture. The owner of a large farm must now know more than agriculture; he must also be a good businessman. He needs to be able to gauge market trends, to interpret governmental policies and restrictions, and to keep up with scientific information to prevent disease from devastating his crops or his herds.

Many small farmers have given up on this task. Faced with the uncertainties of climate, inflation, cost of loans, and rising taxes, many have sold their fields, either to larger farming enterprises or, more commonly, to yet another housing development. As a result, fewer acres are devoted to agriculture now than in the early part of the twentieth century.

What is Hunger?

At Siuli Bari village, 170 miles northwest of Calcutta, India, Adary Mal hunched over the little pot where the family's one meal for the day was cooking.

Bubbling in the pot was a wad of weeds.

One of her six children squatted beside her, picking through a handful of snails gathered from the fields that day.

This would be the only protein they would have.

"I am eating these things every day," said Dukhu Mal, looking at his wife's weeds. "What else can I eat? I have no choice. Look at my skin. Look at my bones."

Hunger has overtaken this village of 150 families. The landless laborers now have nothing to do except pick the weeds in front of their mud-and-thatch hovels to fill the swollen bellies of their starving children.

Rice prices have doubled and the farmers have sold their stock to the traders for cash. There is nothing left for the local hungry at prices which they can afford.

Not far away at Bankura town, Habu Baury picks up cow dung, pats it into little cakes and sells it for fuel.

"Some days it's sold and some days there's no buyer," he said. "The day there is no sale, we starve. When there is no food, the children cry. How can they live without food? That's why they cry."

Excerpted from W. Stanley Mooneyham, *What Do You Say to a Hungry World?* (Waco: Word, © 1975), p. 175. Used by permission of Word Books, Publisher, Waco, Texas 76703.

The Environment and Environmentalism

This loss of farm acreage together with the harvesting of large tracts of forest land increased the number of people concerned about conservation. They wanted to make sure that land is maintained for agricultural uses, that forests are replanted, and that wilderness areas are available for the next generations. These legitimate concerns, however, were often overshadowed by fanatics within the so-called **Environmental Movement** which became a major social force in the 1960s. Many of those involved in this movement had socialistic beliefs and a hatred for capitalism. Environmental preservation became a means to deny capitalistic industries the raw materials they need, which supposedly would lead to the demise of such industries. Among the early propagandists for this movement was the Soviet Union, which, ironically, had one of the worst environmental preservation records on earth.

Others in the movement had pagan religious motivations. They believed that all living things share a common world spirit received from some divine force such as **Gaia** or **Mother Earth**, and it is immoral to destroy or harm living things for any purpose. Oddly, many of these environmentalists elevated animals, birds, insects, trees, flowers, fish, microorganisms, and other living specimens to a place of high honor, but considered mankind, the true crown and steward of God's creation, to be a scourge which must be removed from the earth. For this reason, many environmentalists shared the philosophy and active agenda of people and organizations dedicated to limiting or stopping worldwide population growth.

Despite record crops in many areas of the world, other parts have been subject to droughts and famines. Some problems result from natural causes, while others stem from revolutionary or governmental actions which disrupt the natural food supply. "Zero-population-growth" zealots

Hazardous waste needs to be disposed of properly to protect the environment.

argued that overpopulation leads to famines and other hardships such as overcrowded urban areas, diseases, and various kinds of human suffering. They insisted that people in wealthier countries must reconsider how much they consume of the world's resources. These zealots sought to implement their ideas through a series of worldwide population control conferences. At one such conference in Cairo, Egypt, in 1994, U.S. President Bill Clinton's administration supported population control. But the advocates of control met strong opposition from representatives of **Pope John Paul II**, an ardent foe of abortion and birth control, who managed to curb some of the conference's agenda.

How food and other goods should be distributed will be less of a problem if men are willing to follow economic principles God has outlined in His Word to sustain the world He has created. To be sure, the Bible sets forth man's responsibility for his fellow man's material needs. Furthermore, good stewardship of limited resources is essential as part of man's duty to have dominion over creation. People have already begun to be aware of the need for careful individual planning in the

use of renewable resources such as forests. Other areas must also be identified for intelligent and godly management as well as for beneficial use. Responsible and reasonable conservation of world resources is perfectly consistent with Christian ethics.

Economic Experiments

Even as governments and individuals have been concerned about the natural or physical environment, so have they tried to observe, predict, and control trends in the economic arena. Their task has been complicated by the fact that the application of science to industry has had wide-ranging effects on businesses and corporate growth, affecting economic relationships and behavior worldwide. Besides technological variables, economists have also begun to include political and social goals as part of their calculations.

Keynesian Approach. The work of Englishman **John Maynard Keynes** has had an enormous but seriously adverse impact on modern economic thought. He argued in *The General Theory of Employment, Interest, and Money* (1936) that during a depression the government should spend more than it collects in taxes. This money would be used to employ people in public works projects. They would in turn spend their wages for consumer goods and thereby supposedly stimulate the **private sector** of the economy. Then, when times are good, the government should take in more and spend less. This would hold down consumer demand and check inflation.

The **Keynesian** approach was offered as a middle way between capitalists who emphasized the free market and socialists who wanted the state, con-

This cartoon illustrates the idea that liberty is enslaved by a tax on income.

classical theories advanced by Adam Smith and his disciples through the nineteenth century. Classical economics emphasized a "hands-off" approach which allowed "natural" market forces of supply and demand to govern economic activity. One of its most recent advocates was the Austrian scholar **Ludwig von Mises**.

The revival of a form of classical economics was led by an American economist, **Milton Friedman** of the University of Chicago. This approach was known as the **neoclassic synthesis** or **monetarism**. The monetarists emphasized a *laissez-faire* philosophy, rejected Keynesian government intervention, and called for central bank manipulation of the money supply to encourage stable economic growth. They believed that inflation—the general rise of all prices in a period when resources are not fully employed—could be kept in check by controlling the amount of money available in an economy. Historically, when resources are underutilized, wages and interest rates have fallen to levels low enough to encourage the reemployment of labor and material resources. For reasons not fully understood, this did not happen during the 1970s and 1980s when conditions suggested it should happen. High interest rates recommended by monetarists did not curb inflation. Government antipoverty and economic-stimulation programs did not reduce unemployment. Neither approach seemed to be working.

Beginning in 1981, some governments, notably in the United States, under Ronald Reagan, and Britain, under Margaret Thatcher, tried another approach—cutting both government spending and taxes. This was supposed to encourage private savings and investment, which in turn would increase production and employment. By 1984, inflation was substantially under control and unemployment was decreasing. This rise in eco-

nomic fortunes lasted until 1990 when the country and much of the world again slipped into a deep and prolonged recession. Government spending, despite conservatives' wishes, had remained extremely high and national debts—public and private—were soaring out of control. The economic uncertainty resulted in a major political upheaval in late 1994 in the United States as citizens again turned to conservatives in search of relief from government involvement in the economy.

Effects of Technology. Despite efforts to control the economy in a way which would benefit everyone, many problems have not yet been solved. For example, even though productivity increased enormously in recent years, automation left many permanently out of work because their skills were no longer needed. This was certainly the case with manual laborers having little training in specialty skills. There was a high unemployment rate among minority racial groups who failed to keep pace with advancing economic trends.

The necessity to market mass-produced goods led to a "**consumer society**." People filled their homes with items that they believed they must have if they were to maintain their social status and a high level of comfort. This was especially a problem in the area of nutrition. People ate widely advertised "junk foods" which had little nutritional worth. Even in remote areas of the world one could find American soft drinks used as popular beverages. In the 1980s and 1990s, however, there was a new trend toward healthier diets, natural foods, and physical fitness, although experts were constantly revising ideas about which substances and practices were beneficial or harmful.

The shift from manufacturing industries to information-based industries also shifted employ-

trolled by the workers, to seize control of the means of production. By carefully expanding and contracting public works programs, Keynes believed, it would be possible to moderate the extremes of the business cycle. His views on management of the economy were adopted, at least in part, by most Western capitalist nations after World War II. The results, however, were disastrous. Government interference with natural market forces disrupted economies everywhere, exaggerated business cycles, created staggering public debt which will economically ruin untold generations to come, and led to the expansion of government oppression in every aspect of private life.

The Neoclassic or Monetarist School. The miserable record of Keynesian economics gave rise to a backlash in economic thinking, the revival of

ment to a so-called **service economy** where wages tended to be lower and jobs more transitory than in the older industrial setting.

Business firms continued to grow larger in spite of antimonopoly legislation. The more efficient and lower-priced supermarkets, department stores, discount chain stores, and franchise operations tended sometimes to squeeze out small shops and grocery stores throughout Europe and North America. Gigantic **multinational corporations** conducted a wide range of business activities in many countries and exercised political influence as well. Their defenders saw them as a vital source of investment capital and technical assistance for less-developed countries, while their opponents claim they exploit poorer nations for the benefit of riches.

Inflation. As the range of goods available to consumers increased markedly, so did inflation. Inflation often started when governments increased money supplies to pay for their own overspending, thus making the previous supply of money worth less. This decrease in money's buying power required that consumers needed a larger amount of money to pay for the same commodity they had earlier purchased for less. Workers and managers then demanded higher wages, which were customarily paid for by higher prices rather than reduced profits (because profits were needed to sustain the businesses operation), and an **inflationary spiral** developed. Thus, much of the economic growth in the 1970s was an illusion. Whenever one obtained a reasonable increase in wages, he found that the cost of living had risen and he had gotten nowhere. Much of the economic gain of the previous decades had resulted from increased productivity, but this is often no longer the case.

Peoples in the Third World were very hard hit by inflation, since the Western countries were pay-ing the same dollar prices for their raw materials but charging much higher prices for finished industrial products due to higher production costs at home. Resentment between the nations of the "northern" and "southern" hemispheres increased. Finally the latter retaliated by forming cartels to monopolize the production of raw materials needed by the industrial nations, thereby artificially forcing up the price paid for them (see chapter 14).

A New Social Order?

Twenty-first century technology requires highly skilled labor.

Position and Status. The expansion of science and technology created a whole new society after World War II. For one thing it was **technocratic**; that is, the people who were specialists in managing productive enterprises became the leaders of society. The old ideal of the middle class, the self-employed individual who owned a business or who worked in a profession like law or medicine, declined in the face of the rising prestige of scientist-technicians. Before, people who owned property had wealth and status which they expected to pass on to their children. After 1945, a new breed of managers and scientific experts rose to the top. Within the large bureaucratic structures which now make up corporations and governments, men and women move up as individuals largely on the basis of their own merit or influence. The ability to serve the needs of a large organization rather than one's family connections and inherited wealth often determines a person's position in society.

This means that education in such fields as science, engineering, or accounting has become more important. The new middle-class experts and managers might be able to provide their chil-dren with education, but they cannot pass on their positions as the older wealthy classes could pass on their estates through inheritances. The new class is based on specialized skills and training, and thus it is more open and competitive.

In the United States in the later years of the twentieth century, women and minority groups exerted pressure on the social order. They sought access to education and vocations formerly reserved for white males, who traditionally believed it was their duty to be providers and heads of their households.

Crime. In many parts of the world, rising crime rates accompany a lack of respect for law. As people have concentrated in large cities and moral restraints have declined on all fronts, it has become easier to commit violent crimes such as rape, armed robbery, and murder without fear of punishment.

During the 1920s, organized crime mushroomed in the United States when the government attempted to ban the manufacture and sale of alcoholic beverages. Many people found ways to obtain liquor anyway, and lawlessness swept over the country. Bootlegging became a complex business along with gambling and prostitution, and profits were enormous. After World War II, traffic in narcotics and pornography helped to stimulate the growth of huge criminal empires. A new kind of organized crime emerged in the 1980s and 1990s—urban gangs, marauding bands of young people attempting to exercise power in their neighborhoods and accumulate wealth through robberies and dealing in illegal drugs. Senseless gang violence became a major social scourge in most large cities and even spilled into the countryside.

"White collar crime" became a major problem when the number of stock swindles, embezzlements, and robberies by computer arose alarmingly. Shoplifting and employee thefts cost businessmen billions of dollars and forced them to invest heavily in security measures. Governmental bureaucracies at all levels seemed riddled with corruption and graft.

Fear of crime gripped many people and became the No. 1 social concern late in the century, according to surveys. Citizens demanded tougher penalties for criminals, and prisons everywhere were packed beyond capacity. There was also a resurgence in demand for capital punishment, which had fallen into decline during the idealist years of the social revolution of the 1960s and 1970s. In desperation, governments took steps to ban certain types of firearms in an effort to give the impression that problems could be solved by fighting the symptoms of crime. However, many Americans still understand that gun control is not crime control.

Welfare. Another aspect of twentieth-century life has been the increased emphasis on welfare. In all industrialized countries, free public education, old-age pensions, unemployment insurance, and health care are regarded as of utmost importance—even more than fundamental rights. Some countries, especially in Europe, provided such welfare programs as cheap housing for the poor, cash bonuses for newlyweds and babies, and subsidized vacations for housewives. These **social security** programs, financed by high taxes (especially on the wealthy), were intended to level the extreme differences within society. However, they created a sustained sense of dependency among the lower classes, and the high costs crippled public economies and the working classes whose taxes finance welfare programs. By the mid-1990s it was clear that the welfare state simply could not be sustained.

By that time, however, government involvement extended into the lives of all its citizens and provided a great deal of financial support for scientific and technological ventures. Money for research was generously allocated in hopes that with enough manpower and investigation many of society's problems could be solved. In recent years, however, disillusionment has set in. Many claim that governmental bureaucracies put a stranglehold on meaningful research because scientists had to satisfy those who dispense the funds. Others felt the new technology was incapable of coping with (and in fact causes) social problems. Some critics argued that science is oriented mainly toward stimulating and satisfying consumer demands for mass-produced goods and services, and neglects more important matters like the quality of life, balance of nature, and spiritual concerns.

Still others admitted that technology has caused some problems, but they emphasized the advances which have been made. Careful use of technological data and processes can continue to provide a positive asset for the world's future. Making the society responsive to real needs will require answers of a spiritual and ethical nature, rather than from the material realm alone.

"HEY, NO PRAYING HERE ... THIS IS A PUBLIC BEACH!"

For your consideration

Questions

1. Has the government been effective in managing the economy? Discuss.

2. Is specialization a good thing? Explain.

3. What "spin-offs" of the space program do you know about.? Do some research before you answer.

4. How do you choose which experts to believe?

5. Have you decided what kinds of formal education to pursue? Do you plan to study how to live as well as how to make a living? What is the difference between these two ideas?

6. What is the best way to lower the rate of automobile accidents?

7. Is it good for people to visit foreign countries? Explain.

8. What is the best solution to the problem of rising crime? Should people obey all laws without question?

9. Should people use credit cards? If so, what guidelines would be good to employ? If not, explain.

10. Would you like to go to the moon or travel in outer space? Tell why or why not. Is space exploration worthwhile?

11. How much of what you see on television do your believe? Can you verify the truth of what is presented? If so, how?

12. Who, if anybody, should make decisions about genetic engineering?

Projects

1. Study the Help Wanted section of the classified ads in a major newspaper. What kinds of skills are mostly needed in your area?

2. In a brief report, discuss the advantages and disadvantages of nuclear energy.

3. Write an essay projecting further technological developments in the twenty-first century. You may wish to limit your topic to a particular subject area.

4. Make up questions and interview your grandparents or others of their generation to find out their responses to the technological innovations that have taken place in their lifetime. You could also ask a doctor or other professional about changes in their fields.

5. Write an essay expressing your opinions and the opinions of others who have written on the subject about whether it is right or wrong to break laws (including trespassing and murder) to stop abortions. Talk to your pastor, parents, or a "right-to-life" advocate about this issue.

6. Write a letter to a newspaper or magazine expressing your opinion about some current event or public issue.

7. "Natural foods" are highly praised by some people. Is it desirable to use chemicals to prevent disease or to increase crop yields in a hungry world? Do disadvantages of chemical use outweigh the advantages? Do a report on organic growing and pesticides.

Word List

acceleration	Information Age
specialization	information science
automation	indexing
individual privacy	data base
supersonic	hardware
fission	computer conferencing
fusion	sensing devices
reactor	photoelectric cells
vacuum tube	neutron; neutron bomb
binary	cobalt bomb
laser	magnetron
transistor	microchips
integrated circuit	credit card
"mind benders"	newsletter
acrylics	AIDS, HIV
petrochemicals	MRI, PET
antibiotics	socialized medicine
insulin	genetic engineering
DNA	biomedical ethics
cloning	environmentalism
abortion	Keynesian
euthanasia	monetarism
private sector	service economy
technocratic	inflationary spiral
social security	multinational corporation

People and Groups

Hans Peter Luhn	James Watson
Marshall McLuhan	Francis Crick
Ransom E. Olds	Jack Kevorkian
Henry Ford	Gaia
Enrico Fermi	Pope John Paul II
Albert Einstein	John Maynard Keynes
Neil Armstrong	Ludwig von Mises
Edwin Aldrin	Milton Friedman
James Irwin	Pro-life movement

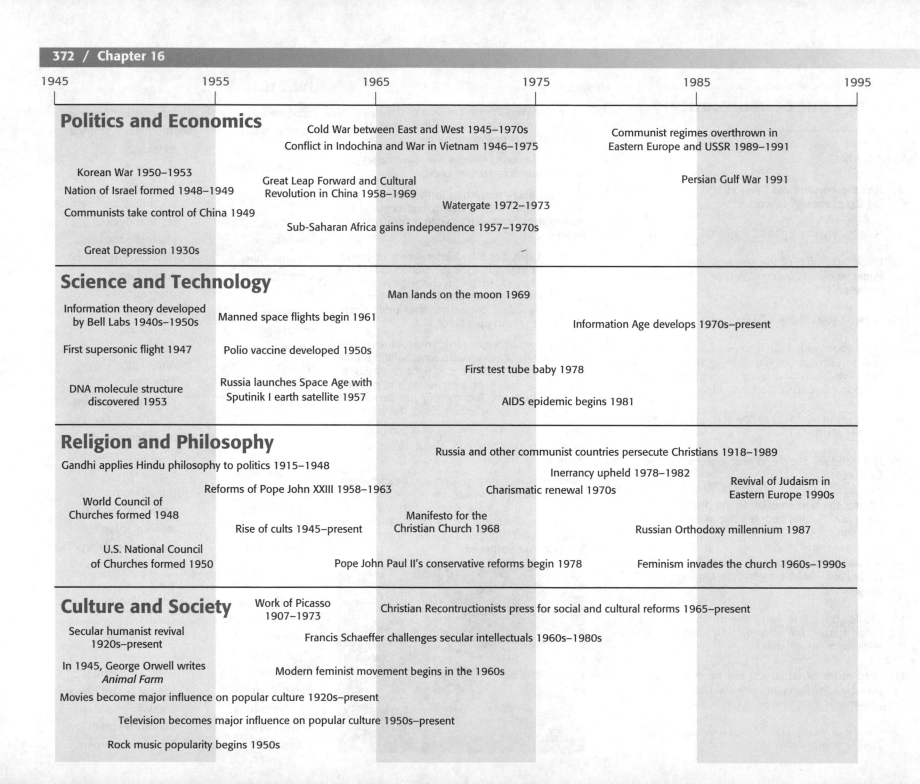

1945　　　　　　1955　　　　　　1965　　　　　　1975　　　　　　1985　　　　　　1995

Politics and Economics

Cold War between East and West 1945–1970s

Conflict in Indochina and War in Vietnam 1946–1975

Communist regimes overthrown in
Eastern Europe and USSR 1989–1991

Korean War 1950–1953

Nation of Israel formed 1948–1949

Great Leap Forward and Cultural
Revolution in China 1958–1969

Persian Gulf War 1991

Watergate 1972–1973

Communists take control of China 1949

Sub-Saharan Africa gains independence 1957–1970s

Great Depression 1930s

Science and Technology

Man lands on the moon 1969

Information theory developed
by Bell Labs 1940s–1950s

Manned space flights begin 1961

Information Age develops 1970s–present

First supersonic flight 1947

Polio vaccine developed 1950s

First test tube baby 1978

DNA molecule structure
discovered 1953

Russia launches Space Age with
Sputinik I earth satellite 1957

AIDS epidemic begins 1981

Religion and Philosophy

Russia and other communist countries persecute Christians 1918–1989

Gandhi applies Hindu philosophy to politics 1915–1948

Inerrancy upheld 1978–1982

Reforms of Pope John XXIII 1958–1963

Charismatic renewal 1970s

Revival of Judaism in
Eastern Europe 1990s

World Council of
Churches formed 1948

Rise of cults 1945–present

Manifesto for the
Christian Church 1968

Russian Orthodoxy millennium 1987

U.S. National Council
of Churches formed 1950

Pope John Paul II's conservative reforms begin 1978

Feminism invades the church 1960s–1990s

Culture and Society

Work of Picasso
1907–1973

Christian Recontructionists press for social and cultural reforms 1965–present

Secular humanist revival
1920s–present

Francis Schaeffer challenges secular intellectuals 1960s–1980s

In 1945, George Orwell writes
Animal Farm

Modern feminist movement begins in the 1960s

Movies become major influence on popular culture 1920s–present

Television becomes major influence on popular culture 1950s–present

Rock music popularity begins 1950s

Conflict Between Secular Culture and the Church

If the nineteenth century can be termed the Age of Optimism, then the twentieth century can be called the Age of Uncertainty. The optimism of the nineteenth century, with its high hopes for science and technology and the progress of humanity, gave way to **pessimism**, despair, and anxiety in the twentieth century. This pessimism was reflected in philosophy, theology, the arts, and in popular culture.

The factors influencing this change were many. The secular philosophies of the nineteenth century—Darwinism, behaviorism, materialism, socialism, communism—all had, at their base, a loss of biblical absolutes. The worldview and values they promoted were humanistic, materialistic, and socialistic, rather than biblically **theistic**, that is, the absolutes which God had established in Scripture.

In addition, the many achievements of science and technology in medicine, communications, transportation, and electronics were neutralized by the abuse of these new tools to promote evil. Moreover, the belief that these achievements could save man from his basic problems, which are caused by sin and unbelief, became suspect. The loss of **absolutes**, along with the rise of dictators, and the growing fear of technology gone out of control—all affected the crises of the twentieth century. The restraints developed over centuries of biblical law and Christian values had been ripped away, and human life was reduced to an evolutionary and materialistic struggle for survival.

The philosophy of humanism which developed during the Renaissance came to full expression in the optimism of the eighteenth and nineteenth centuries. But by the twentieth century, non-Christian thought descended to its logical level in pessimism and a sense of the absurdity about life. Yet humanists in the twentieth century sought desperately to revive their hopeless philosophy by issuing two *Humanist Manifestos*. They called for what one leading humanist, **Paul Kurtz**, described as a "more humane world, one based on the methods of reason and the principles of tolerance, compromise, and the negotiations of differences." But the humanistic twentieth century, if it was anything, was a century in which the very opposite of those goals was achieved.

Roots of Secular Culture

Secular Philosophy. With the loss of belief in biblical absolutes—those basic, divinely established principles which hold true and are applicable in all times and places, under any circumstances, philosophy divided into many streams. The number of books and articles on such topics as logic, mathematics, **aesthetics**, knowledge, and linguistics increased greatly since

Francis Bacon, *Study after Velazquez: Pope Innocent X*

all areas of study were opened to questioning and debate.

The most influential school of thought was **existentialism**. Originating in the philosophy of the Germans **Arthur Schopenhauer** (1788–1860) and **Friedrich Nietzsche** (1844–1900) who in turn introduced Eastern mysticism, pessimism, and atheism into Western humanism. The nineteenth-century Danish thinker, **Søren Kierkegaard** (1813–1855) held that reason leads not to optimism but to pessimism, and that meaning can be found only by a blind "leap of faith." Twentieth-century existentialists, such as **Martin Heidegger** and **Karl Jaspers** focused on the anxiety of the contemporary individual whose freedom has been crushed by science and technology. They rejected all traditional explanations of the meaning of life and questioned the value of progress. In fact, they did not deal with ultimate meaning or purpose because they did not believe there was anything beyond our present existence. They claimed that an individual must assert his own freedom by a sheer act of will in an irrational world, engaging in actions even though his deeds have no ultimate significance.

Existentialism had a vast influence on the arts. The most widely known existentialists were the French writers **Albert Camus**, **Simone de Beauvoir**, and **Jean-Paul Sartre** and the Swedish film maker, **Ingmar Bergman**. Their writings, expressed in drama, fiction, autobiography, and essays, reflected concern with man's inability to cope with human freedom and responsibility in a world without guidelines. In one of Bergman's films, *The Seventh Seal*, a Knight speaks to Death,

> My life has been a futile pursuit, a wandering, a great deal of talk without meaning. I feel no bitterness or self-reproach because the life of most people are very much like this. But I will use my reprieve for one meaningful deed.

This view of life without the God brings true misery and despair. It is a life without hope.

In Austria and England another school of philosophy arose which focused on whether language conveys meaning. Ludwig Wittgenstein (1889–1951), Alfred J. Ayer, and others developed linguistic analysis, teaching that language has no

Jean-Paul Sartre, 1905-1980

created meaning but men give it meaning in the moment. The British philosopher **Bertrand Russell** (1872–1970), sought to give philosophy a mathematical base. Russell was an outspoken opponent of Christianity but could not escape irrationalism.

Secular Humanism. In the face of such disenchantment, the groundless optimism of humanism is demonstrated in its continuing 'religious' belief that man, and only man—man in and of himself—is able to cope with the problems of life. They expressed their philosophy in several **propositions** which they considered essential, according to Paul Kurtz in *A Secular Humanist Declaration*:

> **Total freedom of inquiry.** "We oppose any tyranny over the mind of man, any efforts by ecclesiastical, political, ideological, or social institutions to shackle free thought. In the past, such tyrannies have been directed by churches and states attempting to enforce the edicts of religious bigots. In the long struggle in the history of ideas, established institutions, both public and private, have attempted to censor inquiry, to impose orthodoxy on beliefs and values, and to excommunicate heretics and extirpate unbelievers…. Sectarian ideologies have become the new theologies that use political parties and governments in their mission to crush dissident opinion."

> **Separation of Church and State.** "A pluralistic, open democratic society allows all points of view to be heard. Any effort to impose an exclusive conception of Truth, Piety, Virtue, or Justice upon the whole of society is a violation of free inquiry. Clerical authorities should not be permitted to legislate their own parochial views—whether moral, philosophical, political, educational, or social—for the rest of society." (Apparently, humanists believe they should have complete freedom, but no one else, especially Christians, should.)

> **The Ideal of Freedom.** "We stand not only for freedom from religious control but for freedom from jingoistic government control as well…. Where it is necessary to limit any of these rights in a democracy, the limitation should be justified in terms of its consequence in strengthening the entire structure of human rights." (This seems to say that some people's freedoms may be curtailed if doing so gives the humanists greater ability to do as they please.)

> **Ethics Based on Critical Intelligence.** The humanists argue that it is possible, indeed necessary, to establish a system of right and wrong without appealing to revealed religion. "…[H]uman beings can cultivate practical reason and wisdom and, by their application, achieve lives of virtue and excellence."

> **Moral Education.** "We do not believe that any particular sect can claim important values as their exclusive property; hence it is the duty of public education to deal with these values…. Although children should learn about the history of religious moral practices, these

young minds should not be indoctrinated in a faith before they are mature enough to evaluate the merits for themselves."

Religious Skepticism. "Secular humanists may be agnostics, atheists, rationalists, or skeptics, but they find insufficient evidence for the claim that some divine purpose exists for the universe. They reject the idea that God has intervened miraculously in history or revealed himself to a chosen few, or that he can save or redeem sinners. They believe that men and women are free and are responsible for their own destinies and that they cannot look toward some transcendent Being for salvation. We reject the divinity of Jesus, the divine mission of Moses, Muhammad, and other latter-day prophets and saints of the various sects and denominations. We do not accept as true the literal interpretations of the Old and New Testaments, the Koran, or other allegedly sacred religious documents, however important they may be as literature."

Reason. "We are committed to the use of the rational methods of inquiry, logic, and evidence in developing knowledge and testing claims to truth. Since human beings are prone to err, we are open to the modification of all principles, including those governing inquiry, believing that they may be in need of constant correction." (This means that, in humanism, there is no such thing as a fixed truth. There are only ever-changing opinions.)

Science and Technology. "We believe the scientific method, though imperfect, is still the most reliable way of understanding the world. Hence, we look to the natural, biological, social, and behavioral sciences for knowledge of the universe and man's place within it… While we are aware of, and oppose, the abuses of misapplied technology and its possible consequences for the natural ecology of the human environment, we urge resistance to unthinking efforts to limit technological or scientific advances."

At a news conference, Bertrand Russell reads a statement by nine eminent scientists, most of them Nobel Prize winners, calling on mankind to renounce war. Russell won a Nobel literature prize for defending humanism and free thinking.

Evolution. "[W]e deplore the efforts by fundamentalists (especially in the United States) to invade the science classrooms, requiring that creationist theory be taught to students and requiring that it be included in biology textbooks. This is a serious threat both to academic freedom and to the integrity of the educational process…. [I]t is a sham to mask an article of religious faith as a scientific truth and to inflict that doctrine on the scientific curriculum."

Education. "In our view, education should be the essential method of building humane, free, and democratic societies…. Indeed, there is a broader task that all those who believe in democratic secular humanist values will recognize, namely, the need to embark upon a long-term program of public education and enlightenment concerning the relevance of the secular outlook to the human condition." Humanists

called on the mass media to stop trying to educate people with "… a pro-religious bias. The views of preachers, faith-healers, and religious hucksters go largely unchallenged, and the secular outlook is not given an opportunity for a fair hearing," Kurtz said. In the late twentieth century, the mass media seemed to have heeded the humanists' call completely.

Religious Compromise with Secular Culture

The secular philosophies of humanism were combined by some with Christianity. Each new philosophy found a counterpart in new 'theologies' taught in various seminaries. These new philosophical and theological trends affected more than just the thinkers and the professors in seminaries. Eventually, many people who professed to be Christians also tended to adopt these liberal views. Such church members gave up any real belief in the supernatural, thought mainly about **temporal** matters, and felt that their religious activities were primarily of social rather than spiritual significance. Their 'churches' provided them with a feeling of identity and with an outlet for their humanitarian desires for social reform or for their inner desires to feel religious sentiment.

Secularism and materialism continued to increase their hold over people in Western Europe following World War II as interest in the church fell to an all-time low. Most people neglected spiritual pursuits as they devoted their leisure time and increased purchasing power to getting ahead in the world. In some formerly Christian countries of Europe, fewer than three percent of the people even claimed to be Christian, much less were they active in churches serving Christ.

The New Modernism. Liberal Protestantism reflected secular thought and culture as it continued into the later years of the twentieth century. Some denominations abandoned belief in a supernatural revelation from God. They viewed Jesus merely as a good man who can provide an example for other humans. Primary religious activities were often seen as service to humanity. They no longer considered the Bible to be the infallible, inerrant, reliable Word of God, but merely a collection of religious writings that contained some measure of useful moral guidance and much material which should be rejected as irrelevant or even detrimental.

One of the most influential movements was called **neoorthodoxy** or the theology of crisis. Developed in Germany and Switzerland by **Karl Barth** (1886–1968), **Emil Brunner** (1889–1966), **Rudolf Bultmann** (1884–1976), **Paul Tillich** (1886–1965) and the American **Reinhold Niebuhr** (1893–1971). These men incorporated existentialism into theology. While using Christian terminology they gave new existentialist meaning to these terms. They taught that the Bible becomes the Word of God when we experience it. They actually denied the teaching of the Bible while claiming to affirm the Scriptures. They saw the Bible as basically myth, yet useful to modern man to enable him to deal with life. Their teachings set aside confessional Protestant orthodoxy—even to the extent of denying the existence of God Himself.

Subsequently, a number of Roman Catholic theologians were influential in laying the groundwork for the ecumenical movement. **Jacques Maritain** (1882–1973), an eminent French Roman Catholic thinker, proclaimed Christian humanism, the idea that man is both a natural being and a child of God. The natural man was able to make spiritual progress only when he took advantage of his divine nature.

'Christian Atheism.' Perhaps the logical conclusion of neo-liberal theology was expressed in the 1960s as some thinkers used Nietzsche's shocking phrase, "God is dead." It began in the teachings of **Dietrich Bonhoeffer** and the followers of Barth, such as Paul Van Buren. **John Robinson**, whose book, *Honest to God*, a bestseller in the 1960s, said that we must have a new idea of god. **Harvey Cox** wrote that the secularization of Christianity was a good thing. They claimed there was no deity governing the universe who made the rules by which people must live and to whom they could turn in moments of need. They argued that modern man has outgrown his need of God in this "**post-Christian era.**" People must reject the way of religion and make their own choices and commitments. It can be seen from this that 'theology' was little more than religious humanism. But the result was that many left the churches who taught this, and some spoke of the lost generation of the 1960s.

Reinhold Niebuhr (1893–1971) promoted neoorthodoxy in the United States and was active in the founding of the National Council of Churches and New York's Liberal Party. In 1930 he ran for Congress as a Socialist.

Ecumenical movement. Throughout the century, liberal and modernist church leaders and many of the major denominations encouraged the growth of the **ecumenical movement**, which culminated in the formation of the World Council of Churches (WCC) in Amsterdam in 1948. Because doctrinal beliefs varied so much among the denominations, some saw this kind of cooperation as lowering the level of Christianity to the least common denominator. Indeed, the religion of most of the members of the WCC could barely be considered Christianity at all, by the end of the century. Some recent "Christian" ecumenical gatherings included delegates from non-Christian religions and prayers to pagan goddesses.

Modern Roman Catholicism. Catholicism made gains in Spain and France in the 1940s, but the most important "renewal" movement came under **Pope John XXIII** (1958–1963). He caught the popular imagination by stressing that the church must "engage in a dialogue with the world in which she lives." With that in mind, Pope John encouraged the hitherto unthinkable—seeking ways to work together with liberal Protestants and Jews, and perhaps someday even to unite the world's religions.

He convened the **Second Vatican Council** which brought about many changes, including the celebration of the mass in the language of the people

Liberation theology has been promoted in South America since the 1960s by the Roman Catholic order of the Jesuits. Rooted in the Marxism of Ernst Bloch, it was endorsed by the World Council of Churches in 1972.

rather than in Latin. Another was an emphasis on Bible translations which could be easily understood.

Under his successor, **Paul VI** (1963–1978), the Catholic Church again took a more conservative turn, especially holding to a historic position on birth control and clerical celibacy. However, many Catholics in Latin America were dissatisfied because of the church's continued ties with harsh political regimes. They wanted a greater degree of church participation in revolutionary liberation movements. When Polish Cardinal Karol Wojtyla, an ardent anticommunist, became **Pope John Paul II** (1920–2005) in 1978, the influence of socialism in the Church was diminished, and he fought hard to return Catholicism

to many traditional positions. Liberals in the Church and elsewhere in society strongly criticized him as a relic of a bygone era, but his influence reached far and wide by the mid-1990s. A major news magazine even named him its "Man of the Year" for 1994, a designation given to a person who the publishers believe most effected the course of human events at that time. After the death of John Paul II in April 2005, German Cardinal Joseph Ratzinger was elected as the next pope (Benedict XVI) and is expected to carry on the traditional values of his predecessor.

In the Third World as a whole, the number of priests increased, but in the West, church attendance and the number of people entering religious orders plummeted. A **charismatic** renewal in the Catholic and Episcopal churches in the 1970s helped to slow the decline but was not a return to sound biblical Christianity.

The Charismatic Movement. This movement, which had roots in Pentecostalism, has cut across most of the traditional divisions of Christendom. Churches in both the Catholic and Protestant traditions were deeply affected by an increased emphasis on the "gifts of the Holy Spirit," particularly speaking in tongues and miraculous healing, and by demonstrations of Christian love, joy, and help for other members of the body of Christ. In an impersonal world, some people responded positively to such emotions.

This movement contributed to part of the dynamic church growth in Latin America, Asia, and Africa, and among some of the disillusioned young people in the West. In a number of European countries, where the traditional church seemed all but dead, charismatic groups grew rapidly and became the primary center of religious life. In the United States, Korea, Sweden, and other places, "**megachurches,**" with thousands, even tens of thousands, of members worshipping in multimillion-dollar structures, often reflected a charismatic theology and approach to worship. Some megachurch complexes included bookstores, schools, nurseries, retail shops, broadcast studios, gymnasiums, workshops, hobby centers, hotels, escalators, and even swimming pools.

Although charismatic doctrines brought much emotional "heat" into Christianity, it brought considerably less light. Like Roman Catholicism, the charismatic movement insisted upon emphasizing extra-biblical revelation, in neglect of the Holy Scriptures. The Roman Catholic religion has consistently held that the traditions of their church leaders and the pronouncements of their popes are equal with Biblical truth. In a similar fashion, most charismatic churches proclaim that Christians can experience direct revelation from the Holy Spirit, in a manner similar to the Apostles of Christ's era, by way of a "word of knowledge." The charismatic movement has spawned a number of powerful leaders who claim apostolic authority and the power to heal the sick as God's special agents. Nevertheless, orthodox Christianity has always proclaimed that in all matters of faith and life it is *sola scriptura*, "scripture alone," that is to be followed under the guidance of the Holy Spirit.

Rise of Modern Cults. By the latter part of the twentieth century, as liberal mainline churches were dwindling in size and significance, many people were seeking to find spiritual truth outside of the traditional church environment. In the spiritual vacuum of Eastern Europe and the rest of the world, religious cults continued to spread. These groups hold beliefs that are rooted in pagan religions and heretical Christianity. Usually, they are characterized by deep devotion to a charismatic leader and by distinctive beliefs. The **Jehovah's Witnesses**, **Mormons**, **Christian Scien-**

tists, **Scientologists**, and several others have taken their message from the United States to the rest of the world. Some elements of their strategies as well as their personal involvement have been effective in making many converts.

Judaism. There were also developments in **Judaism** in Eastern and Central Europe, where the Jewish faith had been severely decimated in successive decades of Naziism and communism. By 1995, there were reports of an increase in interest in Judaism, especially among the young. New and stronger Jewish communities were growing in Budapest, Prague, Warsaw, Moscow, Bratislava, Berlin, and hundreds of villages and towns from the Baltic Sea to the Black Sea. Synagogues and Hebrew schools were rising again, some in old quarters dating back to the Middle Ages. Germany, the home of the Holocaust, saw a major resurgence of interest. Berlin ranked with New York City and Los Angeles as a center for certain aspects of the Jewish cultural renaissance. Even numbers of people with no Jewish background were converting. The official population of the Jewish community in Germany was 34,000 in 1992. By 1995, another 20,000 had arrived from Eastern Europe and the expected growth rate was reported to be about 10,000 a year for the foreseeable future.

Eastern Religions. Due to the secular vacuum, Eastern religions moved into Western society. An emphasis on mysticism appealed to many young people who were rejecting a materialistic view of society. The **Hare Krishnas**, an offshoot of Hinduism, were one of the most visible Eastern cults during the 1970s, after a number of popular musicians and prominent figures became interested in Eastern mysticism. Sun Myung Moon's **Unification Church** came from Korea as a blend of biblical terminology used with new meanings and Eastern elements. The zeal and dedication of these groups caused phenomenal growth for a time.

The New Age Movement. There was also a resurgence of ancient paganism during the 1980s and 1990s, particularly in Russia and Europe. Interest in gnomes and pagan deities grew. A related development was the rise of the **New Age Movement**, which resurrected old mythologies and generated interest in the world of spirits and cosmic forces. The term "New Age" applied to a whole spectrum of ideas involving a **holistic** approach to life. New Agers believed in unity of the body, mind, and spirit, and emphasized nutritional awareness, ecological integration, and even changes in business perspectives. New Age ideas were often spread through business seminars which claimed to provide spiritual insights into creativity and productivity. Hundreds of major corporations subjected their employees to these heretical religious notions.

Fundamentalist Christians, particularly those with prophetic visions, strongly opposed the growth of New Age thought. One of the leading antagonists was **Constance Cumbey**, who regularly debated New Age advocates before standing-room-only gatherings. A New Age Church was established in several locations. Seattle's Unity Church, for example, claimed some 25,000 interested families. New Age ideas seemed to find a ready market in young, "upwardly mobile," affluent, well-educated professionals, popularly known as "Yuppies." Two-thirds of Americans in the mid-1990s reported to pollsters that they had had "extrasensory perception" (ESP) experiences and nearly one-half said they had had "contact with the dead."

Secularization in the Social Sciences

Social Engineering. The twentieth century saw increasing attention paid to the social sciences around the world. Research in fields such as sociology, anthropology, psychology, and archeology, was stimulated by the growth of a secular global consciousness, which caused interest in creating a New World Order. Researchers believed that knowledge of historical trends was important in understanding the present, and knowledge of present life could help in making predictions for the future. In this way secular man sought for truth in statistics apart from the Bible. In many cases the goal was to control society through manipulation and social engineering.

Many of these secular social scientists, as well as philosophers, tried to accumulate data about humanity. They made ready use of new technology, especially computers, to assist in the recording and analyzing of information about individuals or groups of people. They believed that charting the trends could lead to better use of resources and to an awareness of human characteristics which affect behavior. People are not as predictable as chemical elements, for example, so much more variation of interpretation could result. Some critics pointed out that so-called social sciences were not really science at all.

Relationships between people in society and factors affecting social patterns are the primary concerns of **sociology**. Unlike Marx, who saw economics as the sole cause of social behavior, the German sociologist **Max Weber** emphasized that particular patterns resulted from multiple causes, such as religious beliefs, personal ideologies, and powerful leaders. He explained American society, for example, on the basis of the Calvinist work ethic. After World War II, Marxism increasingly influenced sociology. In recent times, sociology has become extremely diverse, with no single school of thought, nation, university, or subject matter providing a central focus. The field has become highly **esoteric**, as scholars involve themselves in such layman-befuddling subjects as "symbolic interactionism," "systems theory," "structural-functionalism," "phenomenology," and "ethno-methodology."

Anthropology involves the study of racial and cultural characteristics of particular groups of people. American researchers emphasized *cultural anthropology*. **Ruth Benedict** and **Margaret Mead** claimed to demonstrate that environment rather than race shapes different cultures. Their conclusions were based on studies of American Indians and the Asian peoples of Oceania. Margaret Mead studied primitive people in Samoa and claimed that their pagan, primitive life-style kept them free of behavioral problems which civilized people experience. She argued that a society can deal with its destructive cultural influences by changing its environment toward a more primitive approach. Her anti-western, anti-Christian ideas gained acceptance among members of the counterculture in the West during the 1960s. British researchers emphasized *social anthropology*. **Sir Alfred Reginald Radcliffe-Brown**, a professor at Oxford University, devoted much study to patterns of family structures, which affect the structures of nations as well. In most recent times, anthropology has become concerned with meaning and symbolism. The French anthropologist **Claude Levi-Strauss** advanced complex theories on how the structures of the human mind manifest themselves in cultural designs. The field has also become increasingly international with contributions from researchers in Japan, India, Nigeria, Mexico, Brazil, and Indonesia. Evolutionary

Controlling Behavior

According to a survey of American university professors in the 1970s, the individual who had the greatest impact on modern psychology was B.F. Skinner. Skinner tried to make behavior study an objective science. He learned to predict and control the behavior of laboratory animals by using a system of rewards and punishments. His techniques became the standard procedure for studies in this area, and his books on the subject were required reading for most psychology students. Well-known Christian psychologist James Dobson adapted behaviorism to traditional morals in his popular books and radio programs counseling parents about the raising of children. The idea that behavior should be based on a system of incentives or disincentives does not follow the biblical prescription for behavior—that it should be guided simply by God's revealed and fixed standards of right and wrong. A given act should be chosen or rejected only on the basis of whether it is in keeping with God's moral standard, not on the basis of whether it produces some benefit or penalty.

B.F. Skinner was also one of the most controversial figures on the American scientific scene. Applying his findings on animal behavior to humans, he urged scientific control of human behavior, claiming there is no such thing as free will. Skinner further believed that by controlling environment, behavior can be controlled. He believed that parents, teachers, advertising, and the government are shaping people in an unplanned, inefficient manner. He believed that control should be put into the hands of scientists because they alone know how to design a good environment and to condition behavior. He felt that the majority of parents are incapable of effective parenting. Skinner would put it into the hands of professionals who would then condition and train the children for specific roles in society.

In the 1980s some scholars called for government licensing of parents to ensure they meet government standards. Parents who could not qualify for a license would lose their children. Consequently, these children would be turned over to government-selected professionals.

views of culture reemerged in recent years in studies of how cultures supposedly adapt to ecosystems, how biology and culture interact, and how human social organizations relate to behavior among apes. Marxist ideas have also increasingly slipped into anthropology. Another recent controversy was whether anthropologists are improperly affecting the very cultures of the groups they study. This debate generated a critical reassessment of the relationships between the Third World and Western scholars.

Secular Psychology. Modern psychology is divided into two branches, **clinical** and **experimental**. Clinical psychology is concerned with the diagnosis and treatment of mental disorders. Experimental psychology is concerned with theory and procedure. Computer models and information processing are important influences on modern experimental psychology. The role of heredity and small brain abnormalities, revealed through brain scans, became important areas of research in the 1980s. Some theorists suggested that genetics may predispose certain people to emotional disorders.

Psychological studies in the twentieth century proceeded in various directions. **Freudian** psychology (see chapter 8) led to the development of psychoanalysis for the treatment of personal problems. Unlike the Freudians' emphasis on the "unconscious," **behaviorism** studied external influences on human actions and choices. The founder of behaviorism was **John B. Watson**, an early twentieth-century American psychologist who adapted the work of Russian psychologist **Ivan P. Pavlov** on conditioned reflexes. **B.F. Skinner**'s invention of the teaching machine encouraged the use of programmed learning as a means of instruction. He became controversial because of his interpretations of society and his prescriptions for controlling it. Some psychologists, such as **Paul Tournier**, used religious insights to try to help people.

Confused and bewildered by the complexities of modern, godless life, men and women have turned to a vast array of psychological counselors for help, even though no firm agreement exists among these experts about which theory is correct, if any. Secular psychological counseling methods also became used by some who professed Christianity. **Norman Vincent Peale**, came from a Methodist background and taught the power of 'positive thinking' in a number of books and on the radio and television.

Non-Christian Views of History. Reinterpreting history from a secular humanistic viewpoint, such historians as **Arnold J. Toynbee** and **William H. McNeil** suggested that the separate histories of peoples, nations, and civilizations should be seen as parts of the sum of mankind's experience. They looked for comparative patterns in the continuing rise and fall of civilizations.

A German historian, **Oswald Spengler**, claimed to demonstrate in *The Decline of the West* (1918) that each culture goes through a life-cycle of youth, adulthood, old age, and finally death. He announced that Western civilization was in the midst of the last phase. Like the others that preceded it, European culture would soon disintegrate and pass away, he claimed. Spengler asserted that the vital forces of the West were dying. While faith and social discipline were disappearing, anarchy was increasing, he said.

In the past, historians approached the story of mankind and civilization from a narrative standpoint and tended to emphasize political events. In the twentieth century, the study of history was more and more integrated with modern social sciences. Historians became concerned with exploring how geography, the economy, society,

and culture provided the framework for historical life. Some historians began to analyze history as **psychohistory**, emphasizing individual biographies isolated from broader social contexts. Others of the **historical social science** school emphasized social structures over development of societies, culture over politics, and collective behavior and attitudes over the ideas of individuals. Marxist historians emphasized social conflict. Analysis and explanation played a far greater role in modern historical studies than in the older narrative method.

Humanistic Political Theories. Political science is the study of the activities and structures of government. In recent years, it has also encompassed studies of private and public activities which influence governments and government decision-making. Three fields of study are fairly common in political science: international politics (including international law), domestic (home-country) politics, and comparative politics, which contrasts governments in various countries. Some political science programs include the study of such things as public policy analysis, the formulation and evaluation of governmental policies related to education, criminal justice, energy, health care, welfare, transportation, environmental protection, public administration, budgeting, personnel management, data collection and processing, statistical analysis, and decision-making processes.

Archeology and Paleontology. Archeology is the study of individuals and nations in ancient and so-called prehistoric times. It investigates remains of cultures such as bones, pottery, and even parchments which have been preserved in dry climates. Paleontology is the study of fossils. **Louis S.B. Leakey**, his wife **Mary**, and son **Richard** found bones in Africa which they claim to be several million years old. They were among the lead-

ing advocates of evolution, but some of their discoveries proved to be other than what they claimed. Middle Eastern excavations have increased knowledge of biblical backgrounds. Cities such as Nineveh, Ur, and Jericho are among the sites which were extensively studied.

Political Theory. The greatest modern changes in political science occurred in between the 1930s and 1950s, when men such as **Harold Lasswell**, **Walter Lippmann**, **Charles Merriam**, **Graham Wallas**, and **Arthur Bentley** brought behaviorism into political studies. They sought to form generalizations about political behavior in order to predict the recurrence of certain events in political life. During the revolutionary turbulence of the 1960s, political scientists focused on pressing contemporary social problems such as the Vietnam War, urban rioting, assassinations of public figures, and other evidences of crisis. A number of scholars began calling for new emphasis on moral and factual issues as traditional political science had done. By the 1990s, political science was dealing with so-called humanistic values such as "peace," the abolition of hunger and disease, "social justice," and "human rights."

Secularization of Society

Underlying intellectual currents of philosophy and theology affect the way in which people approach the study of social sciences such as sociology, psychology, history, and political science. In turn, the results of investigations in these fields affect goals which people try to achieve within their own societies.

In the twentieth century, the relatively new assumption has been made that all people can benefit by formal education. At the same time, there have been changes in the status of women and in the role of the family which have resulted in dramatic social differences. The opinions and involvement of youth in some significant political and social confrontations has also had wide influence. Time-tested biblical wisdom has taken a back seat.

Humanistic Education. Education of the masses is a recent phenomenon. Previously, in some settings, education was confined primarily to the rich and to those entering religious service. Christians were among the first to provide widespread education as they sought to create a society that was literate in its understanding of the Word of God and its call for mankind's dominion over creation. By the end of the nineteenth century, however, the impulse for universal education had shifted. Socialists saw state schools as the best avenue to divorce children from their Christian past and to recreate a new socialized man. Eventually, attendance became compulsory so that indoctrination in secular social values would be more complete. Governments began to play a larger role in dictating curriculum. Moral and ethical values became humanistic and collectivistic rather than biblical in origin. The ultimate goal of statist educators was to condition children to accept the lordship of the state over their lives.

Basic theories of learning changed from the idea that students should acquire factual knowledge by committing it to memory and being able to reproduce it through recitation. Instead, educators believed that students had to become self-motivated to learn. The American socialist philosopher and educator **John Dewey** insisted that students should be prepared to live in modern society, by which he meant a socialistic and secular society; they should "learn by doing" instead of being instructed with facts by knowledgeable persons. This **progressive education** led to a

broadened curriculum which included more utilitarian courses such as business, industrial, and vocational arts, rather than the classical fields of arts, humanities, mathematics, and rhetoric.

The International Student Rebellion. Since 1950 the ideas of European secular ideology and Marxism replaced the more biblical views in many of the universities in the United States. In 1964 the Free Speech Movement at the University of California at Berkeley, near San Francisco, was part of the larger 'hippie' movement which demanded absolute freedom in every area of life. Such leaders as Allen Ginsberg, Alan Watts, Gary Snyder, and Timothy Leary led those who protested against various aspects of political, religious, or social life in the revolutionary days of the 1960s. **Herbert Marcuse** became the political inspiration of the New Left while a professor at the University of California at San Diego. He was a German professor of philosophy associated with neo-Marxism. All around the world, students exerted pressure on their political leaders and other authorities to remove restrictions on their activities. Some **dissidents** took up international revolutionary causes. In some instances, their protests were put down by military force such as at Kent State in 1970. Student rebellions became more widespread and were transported worldwide through coverage by the mass media.

Some youths in the 1960s attempted to reject the materialism of society and the institution of marriage in favor of communal life-styles. Many following the teachings of **Aldous Huxley** and **Timothy Leary**, a psychology professor at Harvard, experimented with illegal hallucinogenic drugs such as LSD. Claiming to find spiritual enlightenment, many became addicted and others died. The peak of the drug culture and the hippie movement came in 1969 at the **Woodstock Music Festival** in New York State. This

Aldous Huxley (1894–1963), the grandson of evolutionist Thomas Huxley, settled in California and followed mysticism, Hindu philosophy and experimented with drugs. His novel *Brave New World* (1932) gave a picture of a secular society.

three-day rock festival attracted a crowd of 400,000 young people. One of the largest musical gatherings in history, it both reflected and set the cultural tone for the era of youthful rebelliousness and drug use in which it occurred. But the initial idealism of the 'Woodstock Nation' subsided when the evil side of the drug culture and its connection with the occult became evident. At Altemont, California and at the Isle of Wight, England, the dark side of the youth movement became clear. By the early 1970s some of the great musicians of the movement such as Jimi Hendrix, Jim Morrison and Janis Joplin died of drugs and sinful living.

By the 1990s, narcotics were a major cause of social disintegration and serious crime. Suicide was rising among the young who had been taught evolutionary materialism and were

Jimi Hendrix, rock guitarist, died from drug abuse.

encouraged to take on adult responsibilities. To a large extent, this aimlessness could be attributed to a loss of a Christian understanding and lifelong indoctrination in moral relativism during their public education. Millions of children were raised in single-parent homes, dependent upon public subsidies, and constantly living under the threat of violence and death.

The Feminist Movement. The two world wars, which took millions of men to the battlefield and to death, were particularly instrumental in taking women out of the home into the workplace. Between the end of World War II and the mid-1990s, the number of working women in the United States increased 200 percent. During the 1980s and 1990s, women took two-thirds of the new jobs created in the fast-growing information field. Overall, women were no longer a minority in the working world: in 1994, for example, 74 percent of men were working while 79 percent of women without children under age 18 were working; 67 percent of women with children under age 18 had jobs outside the home; 50 percent of women with small children were working.

The percentage of professionals who were women was 10 percent in 1970, but 30–50 percent twenty years later. And women were starting their own businesses twice as often as men.

It was predicted that women would increasingly assume positions of leadership in business during the twenty-first century because most of them were in careers in the information and service industries, the pool from which business and social leadership usually comes.

The influx of women in the workplace brought about, in part, a change in the way businesses were run. In the past, management followed somewhat of a military or directive model. By the 1990s, the style had changed to one of "leadership" designed less to direct than to "bring out the best" in people, to inspire commitment, and to respond quickly to change. Successful managers were less like generals and more like teachers, coaches, and "facilitators." As analysts John Naisbitt and Patricia Aburdene described it:

> Leaders recognize that while capital and technology are important resources, people make or break a company. To harness their power, leaders inspire commitment and empower people by sharing authority. Responding to labor shortages with flexibility, they enable their firms to attract, reward, and motivate the best people. But effective leadership must also monitor the external environment, tracking trends, markets, technological change, and product cycles in an increasingly global 1990s (From *Megatrends 2000*).

Throughout the nineteenth century, women also began to work for access to public education and voting rights. Some American states such as Wyoming (1869) granted the vote to women, but it was not until 1920 that women across the United States could vote. New Zealand (1893) was a forerunner in this movement, but many other countries did not give political rights to women

until after World War II. Some women have used their increased educational opportunities and political leverage to move into professions and careers previously reserved for men. Accompanying this move was the **women's liberation movement**, also known as **feminism**, a militant movement which at first claimed to want equality between the sexes but soon sought to totally reorient society to make women and feminine power central. Feminism also swept through the church. Its advocates attempted to portray God and Christ in female terms and to overturn the divine order of male headship in church, family, and society.

During the last decade of the century, however, a renewed interest in the historical roles of the genders was appearing. Many career-oriented women confessed to having failed to realize the hollow feminist promise of fulfillment outside the home and were turning to childbearing and nurturing of their households.

Attack on the Family. Changes in the status of women and in the number of children per household were accompanied by other changes in family life. Attacks on family stability came from several directions, stemming in part from current philosophies and from modern technology. The modern emphasis on the importance of the present with little concern for long-range effects of an action or decision encouraged the desire for immediate physical gratification. This gave rise to the promiscuous **sexual revolution** which caused illegitimate births to soar.

When marriage was no longer thought of as a lifelong commitment based on a spiritual covenant with God, but merely a civil or social contract, there was less hesitation about dissolving the relationship. As a result, divorce rates in many countries rose sharply. Laws were changed to make divorce simpler. By the end of the 1970s, some statistical analysts found that there was one divorce for every two marriages.

When a marriage is broken, the family structure changes. Children are awarded by court decisions to the custody of one parent or the other. Or there might be joint custody, subjecting children to two, sometimes very different, home environments and value systems. When remarriage takes place, family relationships are further complicated, and ties with grandparents and other relatives are often weakened.

The rise in the number of working women led unavoidably to a change in the method of raising children. More than three-quarters of working women were of prime childbearing age, and that meant that children were increasingly being raised by unrelated baby-sitters and day-care professionals, often without the necessary nurturing love that only a mother can provide. Since women traditionally were responsible for care of elderly family members, the increased incidence of working women also shifted the care of the elderly outside the home. In 1994, there were more than 1,500 adult day-care facilities in the United States, supervising more than 60,000 elderly people. Some companies were creating day-care centers on their premises for both children and the aged.

Family problems are also resulting in a rising incidence of child abuse. Feminist thinking and the trend toward abortion caused children to be generally devalued. Thousands of children were beaten by parents or other adults or were neglected and abandoned. Courts, rather than parents, were increasingly involved in determining the "best interests" of children, not only to insure freedom from physical abuse but also in other areas such as overall conditions of life and types of education available. Anti-Christian forces began to use trumped-up charges of child

The traditional family unit is the bedrock of a culture.

abuse to get children removed from Christian homes where godly discipline was practiced or where children were kept out of state education or where children were compelled to do things against their wishes. Sweden led the way in this; children there were even spirited away from their families when parents insisted that reluctant children attend church.

Contributing to family instability was the rise in **mobility** of people who changed their residences, often because of job demands. Many families averaged a move once every two years or so. They constantly faced readjustment of social, religious, and educational ties.

Living patterns contributed to the isolation of one generation from another. Couples and their children might be in one area, with grandparents in small apartments and eventually in nursing homes almost completely separated from the rest of the family.

One of the most devastating developments late in the twentieth century was the rise of homosexuality. Advocates of this diabolical and sinful lifestyle began to agitate for the right of same-sex "marriage" and child-rearing. Liberal churches began to sanction such marriages, and governments in some areas extended legal recognition to "domestic partner" arrangements. The entertainment and news media increasingly sought to pique interest in these perversions.

Despite all these pressures, many people remained hopeful about the future of the family. People marry and have children. Many feel incomplete without participation in husband-wife and parent-child relationships, and believe that raising children to successful adulthood is one of life's most rewarding callings.

Secularization of the Arts

The despair, confusion, and frustration which had their base in modern philosophy and theology affected not only human social relationships and behavior, but also human artistry. In serious art and in more popular culture as well, twentieth century artists showed how much they felt adrift in a sea of uncertainty.

In the late nineteenth century, many writers had attacked social ills with the attempt of bringing about reforms. Such naturalists as **Émile Zola** (France), **Henrik Ibsen** (Norway), and **Gerhart Hauptmann** (Germany) and even the "**muckrakers**" in the United States, who exposed governmental and political corruption, believed progress was possible.

However, following World War I, writers and other artists openly acknowledged the shallowness and emptiness of life. Gloom and pessimism characterized the works of those without a solid biblical foundation. The writers were disillusioned because they could only see life as meaningless.

In popular culture, **escapist** activities began to fill the increasing amount of leisure time. Sports and pleasure-seeking were on the rise. (See the section on Popular Culture later in this chapter.) In the final years before the new millennium, however, there was a resurgence of interest in the fine arts. Attendance at museums, operas, plays, and musicals was increasing dramatically. Wherever the affluent, Information-Age economy flourished—from the United States to Europe to the Pacific Rim countries—the need to scrutinize life for *meaning* returned, and many turned to the arts in their search for meaning. Tragically, contemporary art was at its most meaningless stage by then and could provide no answers. Because of the sorry state of modern art and music, people pressed their search for meaning by returning to ancient art forms. There was a renaissance of interest in music of the Middle Ages and the Renaissance. One of the best-selling musical recordings of 1994, for example, was one featuring one of the earliest forms of Christian music—Gregorian Chant—performed by Benedictine monks. The music of the ancient Celts was also highly popular, as was so-called "New Age" or "space" music, which sought to probe the mystic realms of the spirit world and the natural cosmos.

Earlier in the twentieth century, serious composers reacted and responded to the romanticism of the nineteenth century. In France, impressionist **Claude Debussy** often turned to nature as subject material, and served as a transition composer between nineteenth-century romanticism and

Igor Stravinsky (1882–1971) was a Russian composer.

twentieth century **atonalism**. His music had a key center, but the inner musical process was clouded over with different scale systems and the freer use of dissonance. Typical examples of his work are *Prelude to the Afternoon of a Faun* and *La Mar (The Sea)*. **Igor Stravinsky's** work was a revolt against the **chromaticism** of the romantic era. One of his most popular works, *The Rite of Spring*, is an expression of primitive violence.

Arnold Schönberg, in Vienna, started composing in the romantic tradition but soon felt that he could go no further within the traditional tonal system. After a decade of searching, he developed a system using 12 tones in a fixed series. This 12-tone music was considered **atonal** (without a key center) and proved to be the most significant change in music since the advent of polyphony a thousand years earlier. An example is the *String Quartet No. 4* which, although highly structured in itself, appears to the average listener to be irresolute and chaotic because of its lack of traditional harmony.

Composers who followed also turned to dissonance, chaos, and nothingness. One composer, **John Cage**, believed that music should be totally random, with chance determining what sounds should be created. At one point, he "created" a "composition" that contained no notes at all. He "performed" it by sitting in silence before a piano. Cage's work was the epitome of the emptiness to which mid-twentieth century music had come before people could no longer live with the emptiness and began their search once again for meaning.

The innovative techniques of composers served as inspiration for new directions in ballet and modern dance. Both in music and dance, these developments transcended national boundaries. Some of the foremost artists created and performed their works in many places and often did not uniquely reflect their national heritage as artists in the past did.

Dance. Twentieth-century dance was given new life through the efforts of the Russian impresario **Sergei Diaghilev**, who founded the **Ballet Russe** in Paris in 1909. Among his famous dancers were **Anna Pavlova** and **Vaslav Nijinsky**. This company, a permanently traveling troupe popularized Diaghilev's revolutionary choreographic techniques of asymmetry and perpetual motion and emphasized the importance of set design as well. These ideas were followed by other ballet companies which formed following his death in 1929. Among them were companies in Russia, Monte Carlo, Britain, France, Denmark, Germany, and

America, featuring such performers as **Margot Fonteyn**, **Antoinette Sibley**, **Lynn Seymour**, **Anthony Dowell**, and **David Blair**. The Russian schools associated with the **Bolshoi Ballet** of Moscow and the **Kirov Ballet** of St. Petersburg were the most prominent, and produced such great performers as **Galina Ulanova**, **Maya Plisetskaya**, **Irina Kolpakova**, **Vladimir Vasiliev**, and a number of sensational dancers who defected from the Kirov to the West during the repressive Soviet days—**Rudolf Nureyev**, **Nataliya Makarova**, and **Mikhail Baryshnikov**.

George Balanchine, a dancer and choreographer with Diaghilev, later founded the famous New York City Ballet. For more than 40 years, Balanchine attracted performers of exceptional caliber to dance under his direction. Many of Balanchine's works focused on interpretive dance techniques rather than following the earlier practice of depicting a plot.

In these abstract innovations, ballet choreographers approached the experimentations found in **modern dance**. Pioneers in this field included **Isadora Duncan** and **Ruth St. Denis**. Later **Martha Graham** continued the process of innovation as she used angular, harsh motions and developed themes from history and mythology. Still later, dancers further departed from the traditional forms as they have reflected the confused human predicament.

A form of dance which gained increasing popularity in the mid-1990s was **ice figure skating**. This blended the period's interest with sports with the arts. Growing out of the Olympic Games and related competitive athletic events, figure skating came into its own as an independent art form.

Literature. Despite the discouragement experienced by early twentieth century writers, many

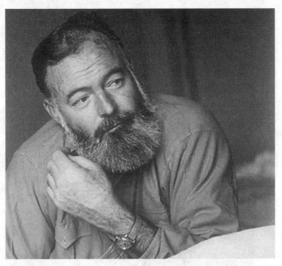

Ernest Hemingway (1899–1961) was a highly influential American writer who lived in Cuba. He was a heavy drinker, and a womanizer, who ended his life by committing suicide.

T. S. Eliot (1888–1965), an American-British poet and critic, was one of the most distinguished literary figures of the 20th century. In 1948, he won the Nobel Prize for literature.

produced classic works displaying creativity and originality. Among these were such works as *Main Street* by **Sinclair Lewis** and *The Magic Mountain* by **Thomas Mann**. **Marcel Proust** pictured society as breaking down because of the inner corruption of outwardly respectable people. In novels about war, **Ernest Hemingway** (*A Farewell to Arms* and others) and **E.M. Remarque** (*All Quiet on the Western Front*) gave readers a compelling view of the **futility** of war. **Aldous Huxley** in *Brave New World* (1932) revolted against the pressure of the modern industrial system to make every person think and act alike. **George Orwell** wrote remarkably prophetic satiric novels in the 1940s examining the horrors of totalitarianism (*Animal Farm* and *1984*).

Characters in novels by **William Faulkner** and **John Steinbeck** were depicted trying to cope, usually unsuccessfully, with social pressures, economic situations, and historical patterns which limited their choices. Novelist **Upton Sinclair**, author of *The Jungle* and other works, protested

conditions from his perspective as a socialist. (He once ran unsuccessfully for governor of California as a socialist on the Democratic Party ticket.)

Particular social conditions are not the only factors which affect human beings, of course. Some writers such as **T.S. Eliot** and **Franz Kafka** explored more universal elements. In his poem *The Waste Land* (1922), T.S. Eliot described human life as a living death, ground out in boredom and frustration. People were shown treating one another impersonally, with no significant communication between them. Although Eliot continued to write complex poetry after his conversion to Christianity, his poems became much more hopeful, with significant images of spiritual refreshment. In the novels *The Trial* and *The Castle*, Kafka shows a semi-anonymous man who finds himself in a living nightmare. His efforts to understand the situation only lead to further confusion and eventual destruction. The term **Kafkaesque** eventually was coined to describe this view of the human predicament.

Similar ideas were presented in drama. **John Millington Synge** focused attention on the bleak struggles of Irish fishermen in *Riders to the Sea*. **Tennessee Williams** and **Arthur Miller** show complex situations with no easy solutions and sometimes no human solutions at all. Contemporary writers have reflected the continuing influence of Freud as they dramatize the role of sex as a major force in man's actions.

The emptiness of much of human existence led some writers to abandon traditional techniques of structure and narrative. The **stream of consciousness** technique used by **James Joyce** in *Ulysses* reflected current interest in the psychological workings of the human mind. In the **theater of the absurd**, writers such as **Samuel Beckett** (*Waiting for Godot*) cast aside comprehensible characterization and traditional plot development in an attempt to present an existential view of life. The feeling is that if no cause and effect relationship can be seen in the universe, then it has no place in serious writing either. The poet **E.E. Cummings** decided to buck convention by writing without capital letters and with only limited punctuation.

Other positive authors who exercised a significant influence were novelists such as **Graham Greene** and **Alan Paton**, whose works present human responsibility in contemporary settings.

The Visual Arts. The mixture of uncertainty and creativity was seen in modern visual art as well. Like the writers, the painters and sculptors were concerned with self-expression, novelty, and searching analysis. They rebelled against recognizable subjects, unlike their immediate forerunners, the impressionists (see chapter 8).

In the early twentieth century, art began to follow the trends of humanistic ideas in rebelling against creation and seeking to create the world from

Aleksandr Solzhenitsyn

In 1945, a Russian soldier and writer who was falsely accused of a political crime began spending the next eleven years in labor camps and in exile. After his release, Aleksandr Solzhenitsyn, considered by many of his countrymen to be the greatest living Russian writer, wrote of his prison experiences and life in Russia. The result was a Nobel Prize for literature in 1970. However, because his books were critical of the Soviet system, in 1974 the government revoked his citizenship and deported him. Solzhenitsyn found sanctuary in the United States, living for many years in seclusion on a farm near Cavendish, Vermont. During his first years in exile, he continued to speak out on trends in both Eastern and Western societies.

As an observer of the West, Solzhenitsyn believes that it has declined from its position of strength, reasoning that Western society took a wrong turn at the very foundation of modern thought—the Renaissance. The humanism of the Renaissance viewed man as independent of any higher force and made him the center of all.

According to Solzhenitsyn, the error was not surprising. During the Middle Ages, philosophers had denied man's physical nature. In reaction, Renaissance humanists went to the other extreme, denying man's spiritual nature. Closing their eyes to the evil in man, they recognized no "task higher than the attainment of happiness on earth.... Everything beyond physical well-being and the accumulation of material goods, all other human requirements and characteristics of a subtler and higher nature, were left outside the area of attention of state and social systems, as if human life did not have any higher meaning."

Solzhenitsyn went on to point out the results of such a philosophy. The individual is losing his sense of responsibility to God and to society and is becoming increasingly selfish, seeking unlimited freedom to satisfy his own whims. The Christian ideals are fading from national life, he said. Rather than depending on belief in God to restrain human passions and irresponsibility, the West has looked to social and political factors. They have not worked, he said.

While he was still a dissident in Russia, intellectuals in the West considered him a hero for opposing the authorities. When he came West, criticized its humanism, and expressed his Christian faith, leftist intellectuals began to shun him. After the Soviet Union collapsed in 1991, Solzhenitsyn returned to his beloved Russia and was welcomed by many of his countrymen; others were unfamiliar with his views.

Pablo Picasso, *Weeping Woman*, 1937

within man. No longer was the artist seen as dependent upon God's creation, but he could create out of nothing with absolute freedom. Among such movements was **fauvism** (also known as the art of the "Wild Beasts") which emphasized spontaneous and subjective expression in the use of color. Artists using this style included **Henri Matisse**, **Maurice de Vlaminck**, **Georges Rouault**, and **Raoul Dufy**. **Futurism** sought to find in motion the idea of change as central. They composed dynamic renderings of such things as racing cars or crowded streets. Italian artists favored this style. Finally, there arose in Spain and France the movement called **cubism**, the most radical departure from traditional art forms and a specific reaction to fauvism. Cubism reduced all life forms, indeed all forms, to geometrical shapes and planes. Even people were

broken down into a series of geometric surfaces. This stylistic movement which was the beginning of abstract art was led by **Pablo Picasso** and **Georges Braque**.

They poured out their feelings and emotions in their art works in styles that reflected the chaotic world in which they lived. The fragmented nature of the modern age was sharply revealed in the schools of **abstract expressionism**, **cubism**, **Dadaism**, and **surrealism**. One of the best-known surrealist works is **Salvador Dali's** *The Persistence of Memory*. To some observers, the works of men like **Wassily Kandinsky**, **Paul Klee**, Pablo Picasso, and **Jackson Pollack**, seemed to attack the very concept of art itself. Kandinsky (1866–1944) was one of the key figures in the development of modern secular art. He was born in Moscow, Russia but studied in Munich, Germany. He was one of the first to paint a purely 'abstract' painting in 1910. In 1911 he was one of the founders of the 'Blue Reiter' group in Germany, and published his work, *Concerning the Spiritual in Art* (1914), which formulated the ideas behind abstract art. He returned to Russian in 1914 and was there during the Bolshevik Revolution, serving the communist government in the arts. His influence there along with others led to the development of the style of **constructivism**, fusing cubism with abstraction, which is now popular in graphic design in the United States. In 1922 he returned to Germany where he taught at the Bauhaus, the famous German art school that promoted modernism in design and architecture, until it was closed by Hitler.

Such ideas as Kandinsky's influenced many artists to create paintings that were completely nonobjective, focusing upon the arrangement of color, line, and form as ends in themselves. They expressed a burning desire to have complete freedom. Yet portrayed in their works were the absur-

Pablo Picasso

The artist most characteristic of this century, Pablo Picasso, responded greatly to its changing conditions, moods, and philosophies. Beginning his work in Paris, he struggled to find his own style. His first paintings were considered second rate, and Picasso slept on bare floors, ate rotten sausages, and burned his own drawings to keep from freezing to death in his makeshift studio. Then in 1907, he branched out from his almost conventional work and co-invented with Georges Braque the visual style now called cubism. Subjects of cubist painting could scarcely be recognized. Looking rather like a geometry exercise, the canvases were filled with colliding curves and angles and tilted planes. The public was horrified.

Early in 1912, Picasso began including newspaper clippings, pieces of junk, and stenciled words in his paintings. He hoped to break down the distinction between art and non-art and make the viewer rethink his relationship to traditional art. But his viewers at first were more outraged than stimulated.

After cubism, Picasso shifted rapidly from one style and subject to another, always experimenting, trying to escape reality. He explored the world of nightmare and imagination. He tried to reveal factors hidden within the unconscious mind. His art challenged traditional views of life.

Though some people refused to consider Picasso's experiments art, the art world came to consider him a creative genius. During his long career, he had center stage "as the master showman of modern art." He probably made more money than any other artist of our time and enjoyed success and recognition without equal. Picasso was considered by some as the most influential artist of the twentieth century.

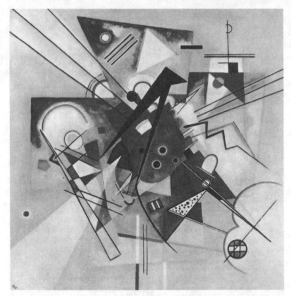

Wassily Kandinsky, *Yellow Accompaniment*. 1924

dity and alienation of modern life, the frustration which the artist experienced as he tried in vain to find true freedom and true humanity.

One modern artist who did utilize the modern style to portray human life in a loving and compassionate fashion was **Georges Rouault**, a French Roman Catholic.

By the 1970s however, another movement arose called the **New-Realism**, which painted with photographic exactness. Considering themselves as abstract painters, these artists sought to show that reality itself is abstract. Such art, however, has become so esoteric, that few follow it. Yet many of these movements have had an impact on culture in general through graphic design and film.

Architecture. The architecture of the nineteenth century emphasized the need for economical, utilitarian buildings combining the handsome, classical elements of earlier days. Late in that cen-

tury, such men as engineer **Alexandre-Gustave Eiffel** designed structures like the **Eiffel Tower** which became the forerunners of our modern skyscrapers with their use of steel.

The **Bauhaus** style of architecture had the greatest influence on modern structures. It began in Germany in the 1920s and spread around the world. It was distinguished by the free use of steel, concrete, and glass walls, and by simple rectangular, "functional" building designs.

Modern architects now take into consideration the climate, physical environment, and patterns of building use, adapting structures to their locations and providing creative surroundings. Awareness of the aesthetic values of bridges, shopping malls, and plazas is often combined with the desire for efficient function.

The effects of increased population density can also be seen in the desire for better urban design. At the beginning of the twentieth century, only ten cities in the world had populations in excess of 1 million, but by 1950, there were 49 such urban areas. Architects now have to deal with masses of people using buildings for work, shopping, entertainment, and other purposes. Some buildings combine all of these uses with living space. They also try to consider the overall effect of a group of structures.

Two of the leading artists of the twentieth century were the Americans **R. Buckminster Fuller** and **Frank Lloyd Wright** They stressed the environment as related to the building site and the use of natural and man-made materials. A prime example of Wright's work is the **Imperial Hotel** in Japan, which withstood one of Tokyo's worst earthquakes a year after it was built, firmly establishing his reputation. He and his family were deeply involved in Unitarianism, and he reflected a modernist worldview in his work and life.

Frank Lloyd Wright created the basic design, "prairie style," for homes of the twentieth century. As his ideas spread, boxy houses gave way to ranch-style and multilevel structures.

To some, modern architecture was cold and uninviting. This feeling gave rise later in the century to interest in **historic preservation**. Older, elegant buildings were designated as historical landmarks and legally prevented from being razed or significantly altered. On occasion, this designation frustrated the rights of private ownership of certain old buildings with lesser historical significance, and historic preservation laws were used as political devices to prevent economic development.

Government Funding of the Arts. Controversy also attended the move, beginning in the 1960s for government financing of art. At least this was the case in the United States and the Netherlands. Kings and governments had been patrons of the arts in the past, but when people's taxes began to be used to fund unpopular public artworks, a revolt developed. This was particularly true among Christians who objected to use of their taxes in government endowments and grants for vulgar, obscene and anti-Christian expressions, particularly at a time when there was pressure to censor and suppress traditional expressions of Christian faith in the public arena.

Secularization of the Entertainment Industry

While many artists produced works which were pessimistic and showed frustration, they often gave up trying to explain either form or content to large audiences. They were content to work without being understood or appreciated by people in general.

Andy Warhol, 1928–1987

Pop culture often leaned toward a more ordinary view of life, sometimes escapist in nature and sometimes just enjoying the good or common elements of living.

The use of technology provided the masses with leisure time never before available, and rising wages left them with more money for recreation. With an increasingly secular and hedonistic view of life, many people were wrapped up in movies, radio, and eventually television. The traditional arts, festivals, and other amusements of small towns rapidly declined in the face of standardized, commercial entertainment carried from Hollywood into homes in the hinterlands of the world via television and videotape. Even remote jungle huts were outfitted with satellite receiving dishes, and natives gathered around television sets to view the latest popular show, with content often far removed from the viewers' experiences.

There was also a blurring of the lines between fine art and popular culture. One of the leaders of this movement was the American artist of the 1960s and 1970s, **Andy Warhol**, whose paintings of such ordinary items as soup cans were exhibited in fine-art galleries.

Movies and Theater. Some early film makers were highly creative. Still, most movies were a shallow form of entertainment that provided the viewers with a temporary escape from the hard realities of life. The same was true of the radio dramas and comedies of the 1930s and 1940s and television programming beginning in the 1950s. Some star performers appeared in dozens of productions and attracted loyal fans by the millions. Not all films were insubstantial, however. Many were based on great literature of the past or present, and some skilled film-makers were able to create significant works of art in their own right. During the 1950s, Biblical themes

were often depicted in such epic films as *The Ten Commandments* and *Ben Hur.*

Although the theater did not attract the crowds that movies did, playwrights and theater companies in the larger cities were kept busy. Several festivals in Canada and the United States produced Shakespeare's plays for capacity audiences. Musicals were also well attended and the songs from these were popularized by radio and television.

Television. Television did much to shape mass tastes. Millions of people watched the same shows at the same time every week. Variety and music shows, comedies, and dramatic series, as well as game shows and soap operas, appealed to a wide audience. In the 1990s television turned to "reality" programming featuring harsh, on-the-scene coverage of police activities or courtroom

Walt Disney (1901–1966) built an entertainment empire beginning with film animation and moved into television. He also developed a theme park in California, and envisioned additional parks in Florida and other countries.

proceedings as a form of entertainment. There was an explosion of "talk shows" in which ordinary people were paid to appear before a studio audience and air the sordid details of their sinful lives or to publicly quarrel with spouses, neighbors, and enemies. It was not uncommon for fights and brawls to break out, to the perverse delight of audiences. Radio "call-in" talk shows became a major political force in the 1990s. Populist and conservative public opinion found an outlet with such popular radio program hosts as **Rush Limbaugh** and Christian radio's **Marlin Maddoux**.

Television also presented news coverage and documentaries designed to inform viewers around the world. Because of the power of the camera's on-the-spot coverage, most people felt that they were receiving an accurate report. However, only a small segment of the action is actually shown on television, thus giving a limited picture of the full reality of events. Regardless of this, television has expanded participation in world events. Riots, military battles, and major crimes, as well as presidential inaugurations and explorations by scientists can be part of everyday life for people around the globe.

The formal educational values of television were still being explored as the twentieth century drew to a close. Some courses were developed so that lectures, exhibits, and laboratory experiments could be seen in more than one location. Public-interest television stations often presented concerts and plays produced by professional symphony orchestras and drama troupes. As video cassettes became more available, the instructional possibilities multiplied. Some television technology was linked to computers, giving users the opportunity to "interact" electronically with programming.

Some critics conceded the value of television entertainment, news, and instruction, but they also voiced concerns. For example, some people were afraid that parents, schools, and churches were having less effect on children than television was having. Viewers became wrapped up in the lives of television characters and lost track of the real world around them. Television also encourages passivity, some studies showed. For example, millions of viewers watched sports events but never took time to participate for themselves. A popular phrase in the 1990s described such sedentary viewers as "couch potatoes." There was concern, on the other hand, that television and movies inspired imitation, particularly among children and youths. Critics fought against violence and sexual content on television, citing studies and anecdotes revealing that crimes and immoral activities were inspired by television programming.

Popular Music. The "big bands" and "crooners" of the 1940s and the rock music groups of the 1950s and thereafter played to large and enthusiastic audiences. Band leaders, such as **Glenn**

Jazz musician, Louis Armstrong, 1900–1971

The Beatles

Miller and **Tommy Dorsey**, joined with singers like **Bing Crosby** and **Frank Sinatra**. Black Americans also contributed several original musical forms—the most influential being **jazz**, which originated in the ghettos of New Orleans, Memphis, and other cities. White performers picked it up in the 1920s, and interest in jazz soon became widespread. Among the leading artists were trumpeter **Louis Armstrong**, pianist **Thelonious Monk**, and band leader **Duke Ellington**. Forms of African-American music that also attracted great attention included spirituals, "rhythm and blues," and "soul music." Music of blacks from the Caribbean—the calypso and reggae styles—also became popular internationally.

Rock-and-roll music became popular beginning in the 1950s with such memorable performers as **Elvis Presley**, who imitated "rhythm and blues." In England a number of groups such as the **Beatles** became international celebrities. They were not only musicians but also prophets of the "hippie" movement. Music and "rock" concerts became for many a kind of religious worship.

After the 1960s "rock" music divided into many types. Restless musicians developed "disco" music which was quite materialistic. "Hard rock" and "heavy metal" bands were followed and imitated by a subculture that often promoted death. Many black youths turned to "**rap**" music, which was not really music at all, but usually some form of biting, vicious, social commentary spoken over a throbbing beat. Again, the search was for some sort of meaning; in this type of "music," however, the meaning was often profoundly wicked, violent, and despairing.

Dancing. Various styles of pop music also affected the types of social dancing done by many people. Here too several traditions contributed to the practices of the twentieth century. In earlier times, there were folk dances and elaborate court dances which were succeeded in the nineteenth century by ballroom dances such as the **waltz** and the **polka**, the latter related to the **mazurka**. These dances in turn gave way to the swaying rhythms of Latin America as the **rumba**, **conga**, and the **tango** came into vogue. In the 1920s, the **Charleston** was the forerunner of the popular teenage dances that began with the **jitterbug** in the 1940s and progressed through the many **rock-and-roll** variations of the 1950s and 1960s. In the 1970s, the "**disco**" dances of discotheque night clubs were popular. Later, dances with highly suggestive sexual movements became popular among the young. In the 1970s through 1990s, country and western dance forms were popular, following a trend toward lyrical and harmonious country-style music which may have been a reaction to the hardness and noise of rock.

Reading. Although the audio and visual media captured people's attention, there was still some limited interest in reading on the popular level. Libraries expanded to include paperback books and common magazines. Romances, westerns, science fiction, and detective stories were enjoyed by large numbers of people. Other best-sellers included a variety of "how-to" manuals for such tasks as raising children, improving marriages, and repairing one's home. Children's literature

was recognized as a literary form in its own right, while a host of new characters like Winnie the Pooh and Charlie Brown came to populate a child's world.

Sports and Recreation. In addition to leisure time used for cultural interests such as movies, television, music, or reading, competitive sports appealed to the masses around the world. The most popular was soccer (known outside the United States as football). Soccer matches drew capacity crowds throughout Europe and the Third World countries. Fans frequently became frenzied in their enthusiasm. On a number of occasions, the frenzy turned to rioting or stampedes as crowds surged in and around stadiums. Frequently deaths occurred. In the United States, basketball, football, and baseball stars were numbered among the country's most highly paid people, together with entertainers and astute businessmen. America's "favorite pastime," baseball, was dealt a blow in 1994 when the season was canceled because of a labor strike by players demanding an end to salary limitations. Many players were already earning salaries in the tens of millions of dollars annually. For the first time in baseball history, the annual **World Series** playoff between the American League and National League champions, which had earlier survived world wars, great depressions, and other national calamities, was canceled.

The modern **Olympic Games**, revived in 1896 from the ancient Greek athletic contests, were designed to encourage international competition in many kinds of summer and winter sports. Athletes worked hard to qualify for a position on their national teams. As their accomplishments became well known, some observers became interested in physical fitness, participating in such activities as running, swimming, skiing, and ice skating. Fitness centers and bodily exercise

became a near craze in the 1980s and 1990s. During the Cold War era, Soviet bloc athletes began to dominate the Olympics, in part because they were given the best possible training and unique social privileges because the communist leaders wished to use them as instruments of propaganda demonstrating the alleged superiority of the socialist system. The Olympic Games, designed to encourage sportsmanship and a healthy competitive spirit, instead became the focal point of bitterness and controversy in recent years. Some athletes, lured by the rewards of high stipends for such things as endorsing athletic equipment and other products, turned to illegal substances like steroids to boost their physical prowess. In the 1994 winter games, the fierceness of the competitive spirit led to a scandal. Thugs related to American figure skater **Tonya Harding** physically attacked a leading competitor, **Nancy Kerrigan**, injuring her knee and threatening to put her out of the contests. Miss Harding later pleaded guilty to criminal charges. Her cohorts were convicted and jailed. Miss Kerrigan went on to win a silver medal.

The high salaries, bitterness of competition, and labor strikes led some people to believe the sports and leisure world had been ruined by materialism and greed, one more evidence of the loss of civility in Western civilization.

Evangelical Christian Responses to Secularism

Evangelical and Reformed Protestants continued working to maintain and promote orthodox beliefs. In the earlier part of the century, some denominations divided and new ones were formed over the issue of biblical orthodoxy. This concern affected seminaries and mission organizations as well. Institutions such as Westminster Theological Seminary and Dallas Theological Seminary were founded to provide conservative education after older schools adopted more liberal views.

The New Evangelicalism. After WWII there were a number of changes that took place in fundamentalist Christianity. There arose a new generation that had not been participants in the Fundamentalist-Modernist Controversy of the 1920s. Many of them desired to leave behind the scorn of being labeled fundamentalists.

The neo-evangelical movement was closely associated with Wheaton College, near Chicago and Fuller Theological Seminary in California. Wheaton, founded in 1848 by Wesleyan Methodists, came under the influence of Congregationalism in the person of Jonathan Blanchard, who was a fervent abolitionist and temperance leader. From 1926–1940 J. Oliver Buswell, Jr. (1895–1977) became the third president of Wheaton College. He was a leader in the Bible Presbyterian Church associated with Carl McIntire, who had led a split from Westminster Seminary and the Orthodox Presbyterian Church in 1937 over temperance and premillenialism. In 1936 **Gordon H. Clark** became professor of philosophy at Wheaton, and became a powerful influence on many of his students. Clark stressed

Billy Graham, 1918–

the law of noncontradiction and the priority of the intellect. Many of the leaders of the new-evangelical movement had been trained or taught at Wheaton such as Billy Graham, Carl Henry, Harold Lindsell, Merrill Tenney, Kenneth Kantzer and Leighton Ford. Its interdenominational fundamentalism spawned numerous missionary and para-church organizations in its circle of friends.

Men such as **Harold J. Ockenga**, pastor of Park Street Church in Boston, became the first president of the National Association of Evangelicals, which was founded in 1942. He had studied at Westminster Theological Seminary and was an assistant pastor under Clarence E. Macartney at the First Presbyterian Church of Pittsburgh. With the Baptist theologian **Carl F. H. Henry** he called for a 'New Evangelicalism.'

Under the evangelistic work of **Billy (William Franklin) Graham** (b. 1918), signs of revival were evident in North America. Born in North Carolina and raised in the Associate Reformed Presbyterian Church, he was educated at Bob Jones University and Wheaton College and was ordained in the Southern Baptist Church. In 1943 he served as the first evangelist for the newly founded **Youth for Christ**. He became nationally known in 1948 in the Los Angeles Crusade. By 1954 he obtained world notability in the first Greater London Crusade. These crusades made the most powerful impact in North America and Britain since the work of Moody. But Graham's methods included a cooperative use of both conservative and liberal churches, for which he received much criticism. Also his emphasis on making a decision for Christ, shifted the focus more on man's choice than on God's grace, though he did stress the importance of being born again. His influence was widespread through the Billy Graham Evangelistic Association and the numerous Crusades they organized in many countries. His books *Peace with God* (1952) and *World Aflame* (1965) became bestsellers. In 1966 he was involved in the World Congress on Evangelism in Berlin, which inspired other meetings to promote worldwide evangelism. He became one of the most well-know figures representing Evangelical Christianity and was in contact with many of the presidents of the United States. In 1956 Graham supported the founding of *Christianity Today* under the editorship of Carl Henry.

Apologetic Compromise. In 1947 Fuller Theological Seminary was founded in California under the support of **Charles E. Fuller** (1887–1968), a pioneer Baptist radio evangelist. Ockenga became the first president of Fuller. In 1954 **Edward J. Carnell** (1919–1967) became president. A student of both Wheaton College and Westminster Seminary, Carnell obtained doctorates at Harvard and Boston University, where he came under the influence of Boston Personalism. His views on apologetics led to compromises with secular thought. By the end of his life he was a harsh critic of fundamentalism and showed signs of compromise with liberal thought.

Men such as the Baptists, Carl Henry and **Bernard Ramm** thought they could challenge critics of the Scriptures on their own ground of biblical scholarship. They believed that careful study of the ancient manuscripts and of archeology could produce evidences for the validity of Christianity. By this approach, however, they erroneously sought to subject God's revelation of Himself in Creation and His written Word to human testing—to the requirements of empirical science and human scholarship. Ramm, who had studied under Karl Barth, showed compromises with secular science and critical views of the Bible in his *The Christian View of Science and Scripture* (1954). The neo-evangelical American Scientific Affiliation, founded in 1941, was eventually dominated by theistic evolutionists. Ramm went on to promote the theology of Karl Barth. Clark H. Pinnock, a Baptist, abandoned his early commitment to an evangelical view of the Bible and rejected the inerrancy of the Bible. This opposition to inerrancy was fed not only by the ideas of Barth but also the European G.C. Berkouwer, who promoted a kind of 'Christian' skepticism. In 1962 Daniel Fuller, son of the founder, who had studied under Barth in Switzerland, became president. By 1967 Fuller Theological Seminary removed the doctrine of inerrancy from its Statement of Faith.

The Battle for the Bible. Evangelical and particularly Reformed and Presbyterian theologians, sought to maintain a commitment to the doctrine of inspiration and inerrancy. Among their efforts to restore inerrancy was a movement that became known, as Harold Lindsell described it, as the **Battle for the Bible.** The neo-evangelical compromise with a liberal/critical view of Scripture had so infiltrated the church, evangelical colleges and seminaries, publishing houses, and Christian organizations that they felt a stand had to be taken. Led by such confessional Presbyterians as James Montgomery Boice, John H. Gerstner, R. C. Sproul, and Francis Schaeffer they helped organize the **International Council on Biblical Inerrancy (ICBI)** in 1977. In 1978, some 300 evangelical theologians and church leaders from a wide variety of religious backgrounds met in Chicago, Illinois. At this conference, they defended the historical view of the Scriptures against wavering evangelicals and neoorthodoxy. The conference gave new courage to conservatives who had for several years been fearful of losing their denominational or academic positions for swimming against the tide of liberalism. The ICBI produced a document known as the **Chicago Statement on Biblical Inerrancy** and, in 1982, a companion document outlining the historic Christian approach to interpreting the Bible. As a result, the pendulum swung the other way, at least within evangelicalism; and, for the next decade, the Bible was again viewed as God's inerrant Word. However, by the 1990s, there were signs that this historical position was again being seriously eroded throughout much of the church.

The Jesus Movement. Since the late 1960s the neo-evangelical movement had begun to fragment as a result of its confusion over Biblical Authority. There was a failure to challenge the "hippie" movement and student rebellion of the period with the gospel. Many of these alienated counterculture young adults had left the empty liberalism of mainline Protestant churches in which they were raised. But a new revival broke out in the early 1970s as many saw the new-materialism and emptiness of the "Age of Aquarius." By God's grace a revival known as the "Jesus Movement" swept many Western countries. In North America it consisted of many widely scattered converts in unorganized diverse groups. Some became associated with traditional fundamentalist and evangelical churches, while others sought to develop a Christian counterculture and Christian communities. Characteristics of this movement were an intense evangelistic zeal, an apocalyptic fervor as well as a spontaneous joy in finding new life. As with many revivals there were false manifestations. Several "spiritual communities" were formed to follow what they felt were the patterns of the early New Testament church. A number of cults such as the Children of God, The Way and the Local Church led many astray. Yet under the direction of such men as Chuck Smith at Calvary Chapel in California and elsewhere, these new converts were incorporated into established denominations, though many embraced the Charismatic movement. Many went on to attend Christian colleges and seminaries and brought new life into the church. Because many had been involved in the counterculture agenda of the international student rebellion, they sought for a Christian answer to the dilemmas of their time.

Presuppositional Apologetics. An alternative to the compromising character of neo-evangelicalism was being promoted at Westminster Theological Seminary by **Cornelius Van Til (1895–1987).** Born in the Netherlands, he immigrated to the United States in 1905, and as a member of the Christian Reformed Church he studied at Calvin College and Seminary. He then went on to Princeton Theological Seminary to study under C.W. Hodge, Jr., the grandson of Charles Hodge. Building on the views of Abraham Kuyper, Herman Bavinck, and B.B. Warfield, Van Til sought to develop an apologetic that could stand against secular philosophy. He was an associate of J. Gresham Machen in the fundamentalist conflict of the 1920s, and from 1929–1975 he taught apologetics at Westminster Theo-

Cornelius Van Til, 1895–1987

logical Seminary and promoted a consistently Christian and biblical philosophy.

Van Til's teachings in apologetics created a great deal of controversy among evangelicals who were used to compromising with secular philosophy and the 'neoorthodoxy' of Karl Barth. Van Til's critique of Barth in *The New Modernism* (1948), exposed Barthianism as but a dangerous form of humanism. Van Til stressed the need to bring all areas of thought into subjection to Scripture. In so doing he not only refuted the fundamental ideas of modern humanistic philosophy since Kant but provided the basis for other Christians to develop a consistent biblical worldview.

One of his early students, **Francis Schaeffer** (1912–1984), popularized much of Van Til's presuppositionalism after he moved to Switzerland in 1948 and established L'Abri. This study center and evangelistic outreach to students and intellectuals was located near Lake Geneva, Switzer-

land. The first ordained minister in the Bible Presbyterian Church, Schaeffer became perhaps the best known evangelical Christian to explore and challenge the secular intellectualism of the twentieth century. His books, which stem from his encounters with inquisitive students intellectuals in the 1960s, show that existentialism is inadequate and that orthodox Christianity is able to provide the only basis for living. His early books *The God Who Is There* and *Escape from Reason* (1968) provided many of the converts of the Jesus Movement with a Christian worldview. Schaeffer argued that there are only two alternatives for society and culture—chaos restrained only by "imposed order" (totalitarianism) or the freedom that comes through the Divine Grace and social order revealed in God's Word. As he put it in his great opus on the rise and fall of Western civilization which was also released as a film, *How Should We Then Live?*:

> The biblical message is truth and it demands a commitment to truth. It means that everything is not the result of the impersonal plus time plus chance [evolution], but that there is an infinite-personal God who is the Creator of the universe, the space-time continuum. We should not forget that this was what the founders of modern science built upon. It means the acceptance of Christ as Savior and Lord, and it means living under God's revelation. Here there are morals, values, and meaning, including meaning for people, which are not just a result of statistical averages. This is… truth that gives unity to all of knowledge and all of life. This second alternative means that individuals come to the place where they have this base, and they influence the consensus….
>
> [T]he universe and its form and the mannishness of man speak the same truth that the Bible gives in greater detail. That this God exists and that he has not been silent but has spoken to people in the Bible and through

Christ was the basis for the return to a more fully biblical Christianity in the days of the Reformers. It was a message of the possibility that people could return to God on the basis of the death of Christ alone. But with it came many other realities, including form and freedom in the culture and society built on that more biblical Christianity. The freedom brought forth was titanic, and yet, with the forms given in the Scripture, the freedoms did not lead to chaos. And it is this which can give us hope for the future. It is either this or an imposed order.

Schaeffer argued that people function on the basis of their **worldview** more than they realize. "The problem is having, and then acting upon, the right worldview—the worldview which gives men and women the truth of what is," he said. Schaeffer, following Van Til, said that people live according to their **presuppositions**, the basic ways they look at life—whatever they consider to be the truth of what exists. "People's presupposi-

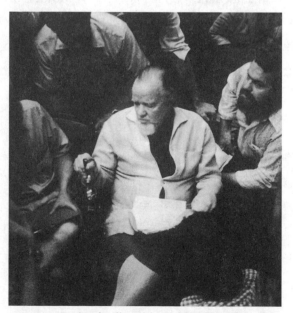

Francis Schaeffer ministered to students.

tions lay a grid for all they bring forth into the external world. Their presuppositions also provide the basis for their values and therefore the basis for their decisions," he said, adding:

> There is a flow to history and culture. This flow is rooted and has its wellspring in the thoughts of people. People are unique in the inner life of the mind—what they are in their thought world determines how they act. This is true of their value systems and it is true of their creativity. It is true of their corporate actions, such as political decisions, and it is true of their personal lives. The results of their thought world flow through their fingers or from their tongues into the external world. This is true of Michelangelo's chisel, and it is true of a dictator's sword.

Schaeffer's influence became widespread and became one of the key influences in the development of the new Christian Right, in its opposition to totalitarianism and abortion on demand. **John Whitehead**, building on Schaeffer, wrote *The Second American Revolution* and other books promoting a Christian view of society and politics. He organized The Rutherford Institute to defend the First Amendment rights of Christians. Others, such as **James Dobson** and his organization Focus on the Family did much to inform Christians of the secularization of society and promote Christian activism.

The Moral Majority. In 1952 **Jerry Falwell** (b. 1933) was converted in Lynchburg, Virginia under the influence of the radio preacher Charles Fuller. After attending a Baptist Bible College he founded the Thomas Road Baptist Church in Lynchburg in 1956, which became one of the largest fundamentalist churches in the United States. In 1968 The Old Time Gospel Hour was broadcast on television, and in the early 1970s Liberty University was begun. In 1979, Falwell became one of the leading spokesman of a new

fundamentalism which promoted Christian political action through the Moral Majority. This organization had a strong influence on the political involvement of evangelical Christians and became a target of attack on the part of secular humanists and compromising evangelicals in the United States.

Christian School Movements. By the late 1960s, concerned parents began to reject the efforts of the government schools to indoctrinate children in the religion of secular humanism. The early 1970s saw a surge in the establishment of private, Christian schools. Christians schools had been pioneered by the Christian Reformed Church in North America and conservative Lutherans since the turn of the century. But from the 1970s there was an even more substantial reaction to humanistic education as millions of families began to educate their children at new Christian schools which sprang up all over the United States. There also arose an interest in home schooling, integrating family life with learning. Organizations such as the Illinois-based Christian Liberty Academy School System, Bob Jones University in South Carolina, and Pensacola Christian College in Florida, were some of the most influential groups promoting Christian homeschooling.

By the year 1997, there were an estimated 1 million students involved with home schooling in the U.S. alone. Additional reports from Canada, Europe, and Australia, all indicated a noticeable growth in home education in these nations as well. As tests revealed an increasingly poor record of education in the public schools, they began to show a substantial record of improvement among students educated in Christian and home schools. In the mid-1990s, there were increasing calls for massive reform of public education, and a number of experimental programs began,

Christian Liberty Academy near Chicago, Illinois

including the privatization of some public schools and changes in the methods of school finance which gave parents a greater choice in the education of their children.

Christian Worldview. By the mid-1980s, many Christian leaders saw a need for calling the church back to a biblical worldview. On July 4, 1986, they called a Solemn Assembly ceremony at the Lincoln Memorial in Washington, D.C. In a three-day **Congress on the Christian Worldview** that preceded the assembly, some 460 Christian leaders from nearly all denominations signed *The Manifesto for the Christian Church*. This document included a confession of the church's **apostasy** and set forth a list of *Essential Truths and a Call to Action*. The document declared what the signers believed to be the central demands of historic Christianity, and it called for opposition to a number of prevalent social evils. These evils included: abortion, infanticide, euthanasia, adultery, fornication, homosexuality and other sexual perversions, pornography, prostitution, drug abuse, unjust treatment of the poor, criminal injustice, racial discrimination, theft, fraud, certain forms of violence, state abuse of parental rights and God-given liberties, atheism, moral relativism, evolutionism, communism, socialism, fascism, the New Age Movement, and the drive for one-world government. In the years that followed many activist Christian leaders began to battle in the public arena against these ills.

The creators of the *Manifesto*, organized under a group known as the **Coalition on Revival**, headed by theological networker **Jay Grimstead**, developed separate documents setting forth the biblical worldview for seventeen key areas of life. These included law, government, economics, business and professions, education, art and media, medicine, science and technology, psychology and counseling, Christian unity, local and world evangelism, discipleship, helping the hurting, marriage and the family, pastoral renewal, and others. In the early 1990s, the Coalition on Revival began working on another project, a series of national and international church councils, patterned after those in the early centuries of Christianity, to deal with basic doctrinal errors which had crept into the church.

Christian Reconstruction. Another movement to revive Christianity and rebuild society and culture according to the teachings of the Bible was the **Christian Reconstruction Movement**. It was led initially by an independent scholar, **Rousas John Rushdoony** (1916–2001) of California, who had learned much from Van Til. In the mid-1960s, he began publishing treatises and books calling on the church and the world to conform itself to the entire volume of the law of Moses as declared in the Old Testament. Rushdoony taught that obedience to Biblical law is the only foundation upon which any society or culture can be successful. He described the Bible as the law system of the Kingdom of God, which he said extends to every area of life through all time and eternity. Biblical law provides the only standard for measuring spirituality and the best foundation of civil law, he argued. He introduced the word **theonomy** to describe the rule of God's law. He taught that if the church would be committed to biblical law, and if civil government leaders would voluntarily utilize biblical principles to govern their societies, the world would one day reach a kind of golden age. He thus revived postmillennialism which saw a dominion of Christianity at the culmination of history, at which time Christ would return and bring time to an end in judgment. Critics argued that the Bible does not describe history as becoming progressively better and that an unregenerate world does not have the spiritual ability to be obedient to God's Word.

British Evangelicalism. In England a reviving of evangelical Calvinism was spurred by the ministry of **David Martyn Lloyd-Jones** (1899–1981). Born in Wales, he became a highly successful medical doctor, but decided to enter the Christian ministry. At the time Christianity was at a low ebb in England, as it was in North America. But in his regular expository preaching of Scripture at Westminster Chapel in London from 1938–1968 he promoted a revival of evangelicalism. A strong Calvinist, his influence spread through many published books of his sermons and lectures. He was influential in the founding of the Evangelical Library in London and the Banner of Truth Trust. Under his leadership, several Puritan and Reformed Studies Conferences were held in London which led to a revival of Puritanism. Ian Murray who has been involved in the work of the Banner of Truth, not only reprinted many writings of the Puritans and other Reformed theologians and preachers, but provided a source of influence for Reformation thought in North America and in many European countries.

David Martyn Lloyd-Jones, 1899–1981

Developing Christian Culture

In the 20th century, while culture in general was moving away from a Christian basis, there developed many alternate forms of Christian culture which became a witness to the world.

In Britain, a number of literary circles formed called the Inklings. The most notable writers among these was **C.S. Lewis** (1898–1963), a professor at both Oxford and Cambridge, appealed intellectually to both Christians and non-Christians alike. Through his essays, fantasies, and novels, he expressed a powerful defense for Christianity. One of his most widely read works is the outstanding apology for the faith, *Mere Christianity*. His essays focus on basic aspects of Christian doctrine and of the importance of human life. His science-fiction space trilogy and his children's stories, *The Chronicles of Narnia*, depict a universe filled with order and meaning. **Dorothy L. Sayers** (1893–1957), wrote essays, religious drama, and detective stories. **J. R. R. Tolkien**

(1892–1973), born in South Africa was a close friend of C.S. Lewis. He wrote masterful fantasies in which his characters cope with evil and discover their position in a cosmic struggle. In recent years, his *The Lord of the Rings* trilogy, *The Hobbit*, and *The Silmarillion* have enjoyed a wide following, especially among youth. Some writers turned to Christianity later in life as they discovered that Jesus Christ provided a meaningful answer to terror and anxiety. Among these was the well-known editor of the British humor magazine *Punch*, **Malcolm Muggeridge** (1903–1990). He became an outspoken defender of the faith.

Christian Publishing. In North America, Christian publishers provided many books for Bible study and self-help books with devotional or counseling advise. By the 1980s Christian novels also gained popularity. Among the most widely read were novels by **Frank Peretti**, who frequently wrote about demonic influences in modern society. James Dobson authored several bestselling books on family and child rearing, while popular author Charles Swindoll wrote about pressing issues regarding true spirituality and doctrinal purity.

The Christian book business also tackled social issues such as abortion, drugs, marriage, and relationships. There was a major rush of new Bible translations in the 1960s and the decades that followed. These were usually copyrighted and sold millions of copies. Many editions of the new Bibles included study aids and commentaries, leading some critics to warn against confusing the ideas of men with the Word of God. Harsher critics blasted many of the new translations themselves as perversions of the original texts.

Christian Music. "Gospel" music gained a wide acceptance and influenced other musical forms, including early rock-and-roll. In large part, it stemmed from traditions beginning in slave churches in the American South. Enthusiastic unison singing was combined with a lead voice which set the tone and the pace. It included an expression of human response to God and a desire for spiritual attainment. This music was often sung by choirs, quartets, and soloists in churches and in musical concerts as well. Two African-American singers, **Mahalia Jackson** and **Marian Anderson**, gained international fame through Gospel music. Miss Anderson, whose first successes were in Europe, later gained stature as the first black singer with the Metropolitan Opera in New York City.

In the Jesus Movement, Christian music began to adopt the popular rock-and-roll style, pioneered by musicians such as Larry Norman, Chuck Girard, the Maranatha Singers and the Second Chapter of Acts. Some conservative Christians decried this development, considering it a sinful compromise with worldliness and immoral sensuality. Nevertheless, "contemporary" Christian music eventually became a multimillion-dollar industry, and the newer forms swept through many churches, replacing more traditional hymns and psalm-singing. In some cases, the great hymns of the ages have been replaced, while many great hymns have been redone in a contemporary style.

The Church and the Media

The advance of communications technology offered new opportunities for religion. Christian broadcasting became a major industry in countries which allowed private access to airwaves. The **National Religious Broadcasters** association in the United States claimed more than 1,600 members by 2005. In Europe, where governments maintained a monopoly on broadcasting in many countries, religious broadcasters took advantage of the new space-satellite technologies and cable-TV outlets to bypass the regulations. In North America, various Christian networks reached millions households via satellite or cable, 24 hours a day. The **Vision Interfaith Satellite Network**, a religious cable network, carried programs with preaching, music, films, and social issues. Mainline religious groups offered alternatives to the normally evangelical broadcast fare on **The Faith Channel**. One of the leading evangelical/charismatic enterprises was the **Christian Broadcasting Network** headed by popular religious figure, businessman, and political activist **Pat Robertson**. His multimillion-dollar, Virginia-based operations used satellite technology to reach around the world, including the Middle East. The **Church of Christian Liberty** in suburban Chicago supported Christian broadcast outreaches in the Middle East, Russia, and Armenia. The **Far Eastern Broadcasting Company**, a pioneer in religious shortwave broadcasting, brought the Word of God into Asia, including largely closed China. New media outlets seemed to spring up everywhere.

Church Growth Movement. Pioneered by Donald McGavran at Fuller Theological Seminary, the Church Growth Movement incorporated secular marketing methods into evangelism and church planting. Marketing consultants were hired by some churches to help them "target" specific groups. These consultants often promised to bring thousands into the fold in short periods by using mass advertising, by emphasizing "product benefits," and by appealing to growing interest in entertainment. One of the leading churches to employ this technique was the **Willow Creek Community Church** in suburban Chicago, where 20,000 people attended weekly services in a $70 million complex featuring Christian rock music and multimedia shows with split-second timing and scripts. The program was designed on the basis of results of community surveys to see what people wanted out of a church. Church growth experts used **telemarketing** and direct mail devices to attract "converts" like customers.

Scandals. During the mid-1980s and early 1990s, a number of scandals rocked the Christian church in the United States. Most of these were from a Pentecostal/Charismatic background. A popular television evangelist **Jim Bakker** was convicted of fraud and imprisoned for raising money through his **PTL Club** television program to build a mansion for himself, a "Christian" amusement park, and other enterprises. Investigations revealed that Bakker had also engaged in illicit sexual activities and tried to bribe persons involved to cover up his activities. His wife Tammy divorced him while he was in prison. Not long thereafter, another **televangelist**, charismatic preacher **Jimmy Swaggart**, an ordained minister in the Assembly of God, was arrested for soliciting prostitutes. Christian radio commentator and preacher **Bob George** was also arrested for alleged similar activities and pleaded "no contest" to related criminal charges. Charismatic Faith-healer **Oral Roberts** shocked many by claiming that God told him that he would take his life within months unless supporters sent him millions of dollars to keep his university, medical complex, and television ministries going. Several other lesser known religious figures also fell in similar scandals, all of which severely damaged the reputation of the church and brought disgrace upon the name of Christ. Such scandals hurt the cause of the new Christian Right, which sought to bring America back to its historic Christian roots.

The Church in Communist Countries

Christianity has often proved to be the main spiritual alternative to communism. In communist nations, a faithful core of believers endured years of persecution; and where communism still survived toward the end of the twentieth century, such persecution continued. It was clear that true religion does not die in spite of atheistic propaganda and oppression. In the Soviet Union, about 10 percent of the population openly professed Christianity during the years of opposition. When communism collapsed in the Soviet empire, Western Christians flooded into the former Soviet republics and Eastern Europe; and a major revival was under way, although some of the older faithful believers expressed alarm about the influx of what they saw as a watered-down version of Christianity from the West.

In East Germany, Czechoslovakia, and Hungary, a moderate amount of religious freedom existed in spite of official disapproval. In Romania, however, Christianity was heavily suppressed, and believers were frequently subjected to brutality and discrimination. In tiny Albania, the only officially atheistic state in the world, Christianity (which had been a minority religion in comparison with Islam) was all but wiped out during the communist years. Yet even there, a tiny faithful remnant remained; and in the 1990s that fledgling church was again beginning to make headway into a society which virtually knew no religion. Asian Christians, however, saw little relief from communist oppression.

Following the anticommunist revolutions of 1989-1991, the former Soviet bloc saw a massive resurgence of interest in Christianity. New

These South African Christians are laboring to translate the Bible.

churches were being established; Bibles, Christian literature, and films were being published, produced, and distributed; Christian schools were being founded; Christian organizations were being formed; universities were welcoming Christian teachings; and numerous other signs of revival were present.

Summary. As one considers the state of human society in the closing decades of the twentieth century, there is cause for both optimism and pessimism. As we look at the development of secular humanistic culture we have reason to be only pessimistic about what man will become apart from Christ. Human relationships and the families seem to be breaking down, and society is becoming increasingly impersonal, even violent.

Yet when we look at the God of the Bible and how he continues to manifest His grace in the lives of people from all nations, we have reason to be optimistic. Christians can be encouraged to be faithful to follow their duty to spread the gospel and thus promote Christ's dominion. His people need to grow in developing a Christian worldview so that they will be able to serve Him more faithfully in all areas of their lives and callings. In this way alone, we can fulfill the Great Commission of Christ to disciple the nations.

For your consideration

Questions

1. What is existentialism? Critique this philosophy from a Christian perspective.

2. Why did people become more pessimistic during the twentieth century?

3. Do many people in your area participate in religious activities? Which churches seem to attract the most interest? Why are these churches popular and other are not?

4. Are any cults active in your area? How do they contact potential followers?

5. How would archeological discoveries add interest to the study of ancient history or the Bible?

6. Should education be compulsory? Why or why not? Who should decide what subjects ought to be taught?

7. Discuss the differences in the roles of men and women.

8. What means should be used to bring about social change? Political action? Confrontation? Revolution? Evangelism? Other means? Discuss.

9. What are presuppositions? Discuss how they operate in behavior, in thinking, in writing, in other areas of life.

10. Do you like modern art? Why or why not?

11. Give your evaluation of "contemporary" Christian music.

Projects

1. Early in this chapter, some quotations are found by Paul Kurtz explaining some of the key tenets of secular humanism. Write a Christian rebuttal to each of these points.

2. Interview several people and write down their definitions of some significant words such as love, loyalty, religion, happiness. What elements do the definitions have in common. How do they differ. Use this experiment to see how important definitions are for good communication.

3. Do some research to find out current Christian attitudes toward one of the social issues mentioned in this chapter, such as the role of women or the breakdown of the family.

4. Visit an art museum if one is available to you and view some recent art works.

5. Listen to some music by Debussy, Stravinsky, Schönberg, or other modern composer. How do you react?

6. Keep a log of the television programs and amount of time TV is watched in your home for a week.

7. Write an essay about whether people should be optimistic or pessimistic as they observe today's society.

8. Read a novel or some poetry by a twentieth-century writer and write a brief report.

L'Abri

Word List

pessimism	propositions
theistic	worldview
absolutes	presuppositions
aesthetics	ecumenical
existentialism	post-Christian era
dehumanizing	inerrancy
temporal	apostasy
renewal	theonomy
charismatic	megachurches
mobility	Judaism
dissidents	New Age Movement
communal	holistic
futility	telemarketing
esoteric	televangelist
theater of the absurd	behaviorism
chromaticism	feminism
atonal	dissidents
escapist	rap music
progressive education	liturgical dance
abstract expressionism	Bauhaus style
pop culture	Kafkaesque

People and Groups

Bertrand Russell	Lech Walesa
John-Paul Sartre	J.R.R. Tolkien
Francis Schaeffer	Franz Kafka
Cornelius Van Til	Max Weber
ICBI	Margaret Mead
C.S. Lewis	Leakey family
Andy Warhol	B.F. Skinner
Billy Graham	Oswald Spengler
Pope John Paul II	James Dobson
T.S. Eliot	Sergei Diaghilev
Frank Lloyd Wright	Aleksandr Solzhenitsyn

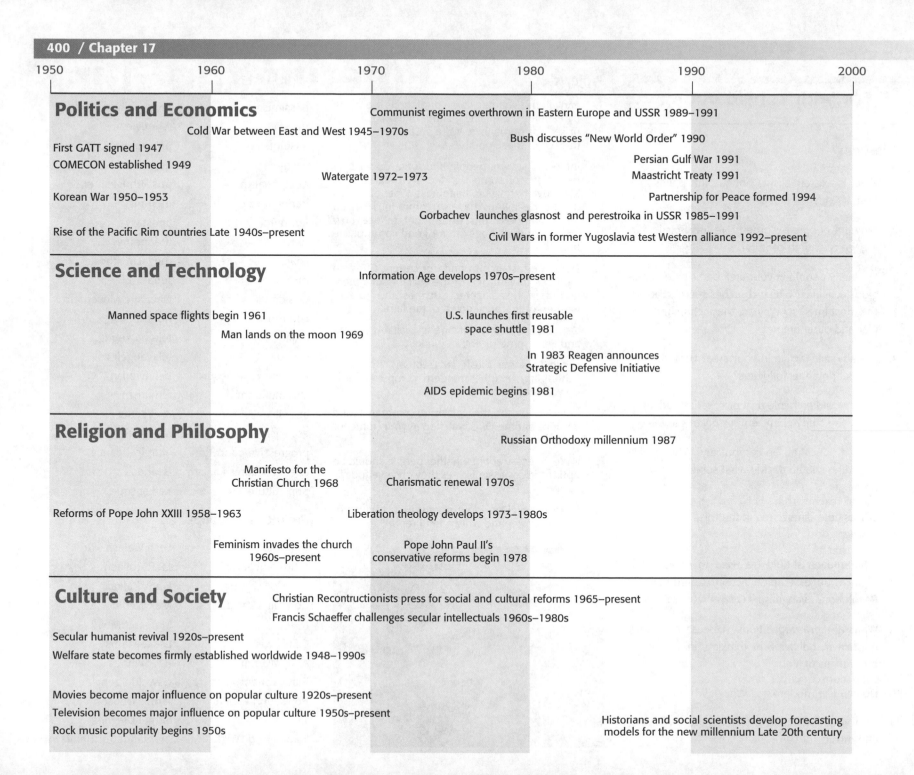

1950   1960   1970   1980   1990   2000

Politics and Economics

Communist regimes overthrown in Eastern Europe and USSR 1989–1991

Cold War between East and West 1945–1970s

First GATT signed 1947
COMECON established 1949

Bush discusses "New World Order" 1990

Persian Gulf War 1991
Maastricht Treaty 1991

Watergate 1972–1973

Korean War 1950–1953

Partnership for Peace formed 1994

Gorbachev launches glasnost and perestroika in USSR 1985–1991

Rise of the Pacific Rim countries Late 1940s–present

Civil Wars in former Yugoslavia test Western alliance 1992–present

Science and Technology

Information Age develops 1970s–present

Manned space flights begin 1961

U.S. launches first reusable
space shuttle 1981

Man lands on the moon 1969

In 1983 Reagen announces
Strategic Defensive Initiative

AIDS epidemic begins 1981

Religion and Philosophy

Russian Orthodoxy millennium 1987

Manifesto for the
Christian Church 1968

Charismatic renewal 1970s

Reforms of Pope John XXIII 1958–1963

Liberation theology develops 1973–1980s

Feminism invades the church
1960s–present

Pope John Paul II's
conservative reforms begin 1978

Culture and Society

Christian Recontructionists press for social and cultural reforms 1965–present

Francis Schaeffer challenges secular intellectuals 1960s–1980s

Secular humanist revival 1920s–present

Welfare state becomes firmly established worldwide 1948–1990s

Movies become major influence on popular culture 1920s–present

Television becomes major influence on popular culture 1950s–present

Rock music popularity begins 1950s

Historians and social scientists develop forecasting
models for the new millennium Late 20th century

17

Entering the Third Millennium after Christ

In this volume, we have observed many events in the historical developments of man's intellectual, political, scientific, industrial, religious, and cultural life. Biblical Christians have observed that the key to understanding history focuses on God's central activity of building His kingdom. As Daniel the prophet wrote,

> "It is He who changes the times and the epochs; He removes kings and sets up kings .... For His dominion is an everlasting dominion, and His kingdom endures from generation to generation. And all the inhabitants of the earth are accounted as nothing. But He does according to His will in the host of heaven and among the inhabitants of earth." (Daniel 2:21, 34–35)

The Bible teaches that there are ultimately only two forces in history; the kingdom of darkness and the kingdom of light. It is the kingdom of darkness that brings revolution and destruction. It is the kingdom of light that brings reformation, revival, and reconstruction. Someone has observed that "ideas have consequences." Those ideas that are contrary to God's word have evil consequences for men and nations. But the Truth—how God has provided the solutions for man's dilemmas in the gospel of Jesus Christ— has good consequences not only for individuals but also for nations.

The unifying factor in history is the Sovereign Triune God as he rules history by His providen-tial plan. He knows and sees all of history from the perspective of His eternal purpose. As men and nations have sought to understand and develop His plan they have been blessed by Him. As they have forgotten or departed from His will, they have experienced the curse and miseries that He promised would attend such disobedience.

God fully knows the entire spectrum of history from the beginning until the end of time. However, man, without the eye of faith, can only know his past. Throughout the various civilizations in history, men have attempted to see beyond the present. For early man, these attempts involved various forms of divinations, such as astrology. For man today, the scientific techniques of statistical trend analysis have been employed. Christians have sought to understand the future by looking into the Master Plan. This Plan gives us a certain knowledge as to how history will end; yet in our creaturely finiteness, we cannot always or fully ascertain the details of the unfolding of the Plan as it leads to that end. Still, God has given us the gift of historical knowledge and interpretation to guide us, if we will only learn the lessons He has sought to teach us through our history. Recently, some historians have noted that:

> Even though we cannot know the future, we can use history to develop a framework for evaluating it and partially anticipating it as it unfolds: We can know what factors to moni-

tor. Recent patterns and their relationship to older themes in world history allow an orientation toward what is to come.

Isolated events in themselves may or may not establish historical directions. But events in context of broader history may be indicators of the future, if interpreted in the light of divine revelation.

We will, in this final chapter, discuss some of the major events in the last few decades as they affected the West. While such events by definition take on the flavor of current affairs rather than true history, we consider them here for their possible impact on the future.

Twentieth-century Patterns

As we have seen, the twentieth century began with massive internal decay within the West itself and an attendant marked decline in the domination of the West in the world arena. Some historians have noted this as a major break in history—the beginning of a new phase or epoch. Since the events that suggest this break are relatively recent, however, it is difficult to predict whether this seeming new direction is a lasting one. Among the critical trends of the twentieth century which may or may not be permanent patterns for the future were these:

◆ The loss of a single center of political, cultural, and economic dominance—the position held by the West since the 1500s.

◆ The decline of colonialism.

◆ A utopian attempt to establish a "new world order" based on universal civil government and brotherhood.

◆ Growing secularization, i.e., a world without a dominant religion.

◆ A surge in technology and material achievement.

◆ The rise of the welfare state.

◆ An unprecedented shift toward feminization.

These patterns were clearly recognizable during the first three-quarters of the twentieth century. As the century drew to a close, however, there were indicators that each of them was beginning to be modified or reversed.

Events in the Eastern world in the early 1990s, for example, suggested a revival of influence for the European-American (Western) worldview. Many analysts were describing a new kind of colonialism, not territorial as in the nineteenth century, but cultural and economic (although

there were certainly economic dimensions to the earlier imperialism). The dream for universal peace and world order appeared to be dashed at the peak of its vision as fragmentation, nationalism, ethnocentrism, racism, and tribalism suddenly experienced a resurgence at the end of the twentieth century. The century's trend toward secularization also began to wane late in the century in the face of a massive resurgence of Islam, substantial new Christian missionary efforts, and a revival of age-old pagan ideas in New Age spiritual clothing. While there seemed to be no end in sight for advances in technology, *faith* in technology and material things was declining as the ecological movement surged to the forefront along with religious revival. As the century drew to a close, there was increasing dissatisfaction with the welfare state as the ark of human security; it was increasingly apparent that its cost was not sustainable. Although feminism remained a major theme as the century drew to a close, there were increasing signs that this doctrine was detrimental to the social order and the nurturing of the individual. Even **Mikhail Gorbachev**, in the midst of his reforms during the closing days of the Soviet Union, noted that the historic com-

Mikhail Gorbachev with Prime Minister Margaret Thatcher

munist drive for women's equality had overburdened them. He suggested a "return to their purely womanly missions" of homemaking, raising of children, and "the creation of a good family atmosphere."

The Fall of Communism

The twentieth century saw a number of remarkable events of history-making proportions—the two world wars being among the most obvious. But there was one event that perhaps was among the most pivotal in that it touched nearly every one of the major themes just described. That was *the rise and fall of communism.*

The triumph of the Communist Revolution in Russia in 1917 was the practical outgrowth of at least three centuries of development, beginning with the Enlightenment ideas of the seventeenth century (which had its roots in the humanist elements of the earlier Renaissance), the liberalism and revolutions of the eighteenth century, and the paradoxical combination of idealism and economic disruption in the nineteenth century. It was therefore remarkable that in only about seventy years, the great theories of these centuries proved so utterly bankrupt and unworkable in their implementation.

The failure of the communist ideal and system came to widespread recognition during the regime of Soviet leader Mikhail Gorbachev, beginning in the mid-1980s; but the failure of the system cannot be attributed to him. The failure was inherent and the weight of that failure only grew too heavy during his term in power. It was Gorbachev who more clearly recognized it from within than any other communist leader had. The swift collapse had such a careening quality that those outside the system seemed to fully grasp its significance only after it had happened. While Gorbachev was perhaps the first to realize the failures, he was unable to reverse them, *first,* because they were **innate** and, *secondly,* because (even if they had not been innate) they had become too deeply **entrenched** within the structures of the Soviet system. One of the fatal flaws was the central **tenet** of communist ideology that communism was the final state of history and therefore its ultimate triumph was inevitable. After the initial zeal of the Russian Revolution, it was not long before faith in the ideology began to wane. By the 1970s and 1980s, few of those living under communism, including the leaders, believed the promises of the communist faith. Yet the leaders had invested their lives, fortunes, and thirst for power in the system and had convinced themselves that history would move unavoidably toward a triumph for socialism. This idea became so ingrained in the thinking of Soviet leaders during the century that it blinded them to many of the harsh realities of their own circumstances and environment. Because communism was at its heart a revolutionary ideology, its progress depended to a great extent on armaments and the tools of coercion. Soviet leaders from Stalin onward invested heavily in military might. In fact, as the decades passed, expenditures for military hardware, military adventures, space programs with military potential, and international revolutionary and terrorist activities knew no bounds. While the Soviet budget listed specific figures for these expenditures, the figures were merely theoretical. No one really knew how much was being spent, but later estimates were that as much as one-third of the entire national income was being dedicated to military production. An ill-fated but costly military adventure in Afghanistan proved to be

one of the last straws making the military expense burden unbearable by the Soviet economy.

But the mortal blow was delivered by sources outside the Soviet empire—the policies of the West, especially of the United States. U.S. President **Jimmy Carter** announced during the late 1970s that the United States would begin developing the **neutron bomb**. This weapon would be designed to destroy people, including soldiers inside armored vehicles, but leave physical objects unharmed. Soviet leaders were disturbed because this weapon threatened to undermine the heart of the Soviet ground attack system, its tank forces, which the Soviets held in superior numbers over

The United States threatened to deploy a space-based missile defense system.

the West. Unable to afford development of a similar weapon, the Soviets decided to counter Carter's announcement with propaganda. They launched a massive international "peace" movement. Soviet-inspired leftists throughout Europe, Asia, and the United States organized mass rallies, marches, demonstrations, international conferences, and media campaigns demanding disarmament and warning of an impending nuclear cataclysm. The pressure eventually succeeded, as the U.S. Congress called a halt to the bomb's development, and other Western leaders began to speak of unilateral disarmament.

Emboldened, the Soviet leaders began to deploy a new generation of short-range ballistic missiles (SS-20s) with nuclear warheads aimed at the heart of Western Europe. President Ronald Reagan countered with the deployment of similar missiles (Pershings) within the NATO countries and aimed at the Soviets. The new threats led to an escalation of the arms race, further crippling the Soviet economy. Reagan finally delivered the crushing blow when he announced the development of a space-based missile defense system, known popularly as "Star Wars" and officially as the **Strategic Defense Initiative**. This proposed high-tech laser system threatened the heart of the Soviet airborne military strike force, its intercontinental missiles. Gorbachev realized that the Soviet economic system simply could not afford the cost of developing countermeasures, and he sued for real, multilateral disarmament. He and Reagan met several times. In one remarkable meeting in Iceland, major agreements were suddenly written to halt the arms race and destroy large amounts of existing weapons stockpiles.

The lopsided Soviet emphasis on military production adversely affected an economic system which was already bound for disaster because communism provided no incentives for productivity. Soviet propagandists and duped sympathizers in the West continued to boast about the achievements of communism, claiming great progress in education, industry, and general welfare. Unperceived in the West and among the ideologically blinded Soviet leadership was the depth of the stagnation of the Soviet economy and the desperation of the people. The same was true for the Eastern European satellite countries in the Soviet orbit.

Forced industrialization and poor stewardship over the industrial process had brought about an unprecedented ecological disaster throughout the Soviet empire. Official Soviet estimates themselves indicated that 50 percent of all rivers were severely polluted, more than 40 percent of agricultural land was crippled by pollution, and one-fifth of all Soviet citizens lived in regions of ecological disaster. Infant mortality rates and serious respiratory and other diseases were rising at alarming rates. Housing was increasingly inadequate and unavailable. Commonly needed consumer goods, including staples, were in ever-smaller supply. Morale among the citizenry was extremely low, and this further eroded their economic performance. Yet there was still no limitation on military and revolutionary expenditure. Old, doctrinaire leaders failed to appreciate the widening gap between basic economic need fulfillment and the underwriting of the revolutionary cause. But younger leaders began to realize quietly that the system was nearing collapse. According to post-collapse studies, Gorbachev was among the first to understand this.

Glasnost and Perestroika. When he came to power, Gorbachev was determined to make an attempt to revive the nation. He realized that to do so, he would need assistance from the West, to which he had acquired somewhat of an **affinity**, not unlike that of Czar Peter the Great. He and

his much-publicized wife wore stylish Western clothing, and his public political style reflected the mannerisms of Western politicians.

But Gorbachev knew that getting assistance from the West would require more than style changes; it would require some fundamental changes in the Soviet system to satisfy the demands of Western liberal democrats. His solution was *glasnost*, a policy of "openness," which did away with many of the repressions and oppressions which had marked the Soviet police state from its beginning. Political and religious prisoners were freed. Newspapers and broadcast stations were given the right to speak freely. Freedom of movement was instituted and border barriers were lowered. The terroristic practices of the secret police were curtailed.

The policy of political openness was accompanied by a plan for economic "restructuring," known by its Russian name, *perestroika*. This policy included more opportunities for private ownership and decentralized control of industry and farming. Farmers were given the chance to lease up to 50 acres, with the right to pass the lease on to heirs. State industries were allowed to purchase from both private and state sources. Limited foreign investment was encouraged, the most sensational evidence of which was the opening of a McDonald's "fast-food" restaurant in Moscow. Gorbachev called for reductions in military expenditures and reallocation of resources into production of consumer goods. He called on Russians to lessen their drinking habits. He told Soviet citizens he wanted "to rid public opinion of… faith in a 'good czar,' the all-powerful center, the notion that someone can bring about order and organize *perestroika* from on high."

Gorbachev added political changes to *glasnost* and *perestroika* by advocating a new constitution in 1988, increasing the power of a new parlia-

ment and the Congress of People's Deputies, and abolishing the Communist Party's monopoly in elections. These measures caught Gorbachev in a vice between liberal forces demanding more change and hard-line conservatives demanding a halt to change. The combination of reform-mindedness and continued economic **deprivation** increased dissatisfaction among minority nationalities in other Soviet republics. Asian Muslims and Armenian Christians rioted and fought both each other and the central state. Baltic republics demanded independence. In 1991, a number of regions, including Lithuania and Georgia, actually voted for independence. Others followed suit. Gorbachev himself had sparked much of this ferment by declaring, contrary to the long history of Soviet imperialism, that "any nation has the right to decide its fate by itself."

Reverberations. The relaxation of totalitarianism in the motherland of the revolution was immediately welcomed and imitated in the daughter nations of Eastern Europe. In fact, the satellite countries took positive **initiatives** even while changes were only still stirring in the U.S.S.R. Restrictions came crashing down in a mere matter of weeks, beginning in 1989, in Eastern Europe. Thousands of Eastern European citizens streamed across borders to the West, sometimes moving through more liberalized communist countries first and then to full freedom.

Bulgaria had tried economic liberalization in 1987 but the Soviets squelched it. By 1989, however, the Communist Party leader in Bulgaria was ousted and free elections were scheduled. In 1989, **Hungary** installed its first noncommunist leader in decades. The Communist Party renamed itself the Socialist Party but soon lost elections. Hungarian reformers resurrected the spirit of the 1956 revolt and glorified it. Hungary moved swiftly toward a free-market economy, the foundations for which had been laid in previous years.

In **Poland**, the **Solidarity** labor movement, which had pressed for reforms since the late 1970s, drew together noncommunist leaders and Catholic intellectuals to bring down the communist government in 1989. The new government sought to dismantle the state-controlled economy, but prices rose sharply as subsidies were ended.

East Germans ousted their communist government in 1989 and moved swiftly to unify with West Germany the following year. In perhaps the most symbolic act signifying the anticommunist explosion, jubilant East and West Germans tore down the Berlin Wall amid wild celebrations.

In **Czechoslovakia**, a new government, headed by a former dissident playwright, was installed in 1989. A free-market economy and political freedoms were introduced. In a short time, the country was peacefully divided into **Slovakia** and **The Czech Republic**, reflecting the ethnic make-up of the region.

The Berlin Wall Memorial

While changes in all of these countries had been accompanied by public demonstrations, **Romania**'s experience was unique. There, an especially brutal dictator, **Nicolae Ceauçescu**, had been ruling with the worst of old-style Stalinist terrorism and repression. In December of 1989, a Hungarian Reformed Church pastor, **Laszlo Tokes**, in an interview broadcast by Hungarian television, publicly criticized the Romanian regime's repressions, especially as they affected the Hungarian minority in western Romania. Authorities approached Tokes' home in Timisoara to arrest him, but parishioners and other residents of the city suddenly swarmed into the streets and surrounded his home. Additional crowds soon gathered in that city and in other cities across the country, as many Christians joined in concerted prayer for freedom. Secret police forces and army units opened fire on the crowds and drove tanks over many protesters, including children. That action produced an explosion of popular fury, and the army inexplicably turned against the secret police forces to join the cause of the people. Battles and riots ensued. Thousands were killed and wounded. A massive rally arose outside Ceauçescu's palace in the capital, Bucharest. When the dictator tried to speak, he was suddenly met by a barrage of furious shouting which drove him from his balcony. A bloody street battle followed, and Ceauçescu attempted to flee. His bodyguards eventually turned against him. He and his egotistical wife were arrested, given a superficial trial, and summarily executed by a firing squad. Old-line allies seized power, claimed to have reformed, and established a new central government. In various regions of the country, Christians came to power through local elections or appointments; but many were later muscled out of their positions. Romania remained in turmoil and severe poverty well into the late 1990s as changes came slowly.

Another communist country which was not considered to be within the Soviet orbit, **Albania**, also overthrew its government; but its severely crippled economy and social structures were slow to recover.

The most troubling situation was in **Yugoslavia**, a region inhabited by a number of rival ethnic and religious groups with ancient hatreds. A series of bloody civil wars developed in the region which threatened to undermine the security of all of Europe. We shall examine that situation further in a later section of this chapter.

The Collapse of the U.S.S.R. Meanwhile, in the Soviet Union, Gorbachev's attempts to reform the mortally ill communist system were proving to be too little too late. As noted earlier, Gorbachev had launched his changes as part of a necessary appeal to the West. But in doing so, he sowed the seeds of destruction for the Soviet system. By lifting domestic restrictions through *glasnost,* he had removed one of the last remaining elements holding the system together, *internal fear.* In addition, he had been forced to call for international disarmament because his country could no longer compete in the arms race. But this move removed another of the last remaining consolidating forces, fear of destruction by *external* enemies. Thus, with both internal and external fears removed, the people of the Soviet Union saw no reason to continue tolerating their desperate circumstances.

The uncertainties of the situation prompted a last-ditch *coup* attempt in the late summer of 1991 by a small group of hard-liners with some degree of police and military support. Gorbachev was briefly forced to step down and flee Moscow. But this new threat to liberalization resulted in massive popular demonstrations, reasserting the strong democratic tide that had been flowing since 1986. One of the populist leaders of the pro-democracy demonstrations in Moscow was the city's freely elected mayor **Boris Yeltsin** (who later was elected president of the new Russian Federation). The August 1991 coup failed; Gorbachev returned to Moscow and banned the Communist Party. There were new independence movements in the republics. This time, the independence movements gained quick international recognition. As one region after another split away, the Soviet Union collapsed entirely, producing shock waves throughout the world. The false dream of the inevitable triumph of communism had evaporated. Virtually overnight, Soviet-inspired revolutionary movements worldwide lost their patron and their punch.

The new republics, including Russia, begged for aid from the West, which in turn became deeply involved in the economic restructuring of the former communist lands, sometimes to the resentment of anti-Western elements remaining within them. With the stakes high for success in the move toward free market economies, Western countries, especially the United States, committed themselves heavily to political democratization in the former Soviet bloc. Those commitments increasingly became problematic. The U.S. commitment to Boris Yeltsin in Russia, for example, was becoming a source of embarrassment as Yeltsin increasingly exhibited signs of severe alcoholism and inability to govern. During 1998 and 1999, Yeltsin fired four different prime ministers and their governments. On December 31, 1999, Yeltsin resigned and appointed **Vladimir Putin**—who had been a prime minister earlier in 1999—as acting president. Putin went on to win the election as president of the Russian Federation in 2000. As internal discontent with slow economic progress grew, communists and hard-core nationalists formed opposition groups seeking to restore Russia's former stature in the world.

NATIONS OF THE FORMER U.S.S.R.

▓ RUSSIAN FEDERATION

☐ FORMER SOVIET REPUBLICS

The 'New World Order'

A Single Superpower. The collapse of the Soviet Union, one of the two so-called "superpowers" of the Cold War era, left the world with only one superpower, the United States. It is true that an increasingly consolidated Europe and a rapidly developing Japan were clearly economic giants in the world, along with the United States. But only the United States had the political and military clout added with its economic prowess to qualify it for the superpower designation.

The United States emerged from World War II without damage to its landscape and physical **infrastructure**. It was also by then the most powerful economic force in the world. For the rest of the century, its wealth enabled it to assume global responsibilities—from President Harry Truman's Marshall Plan to President John Kennedy's **Peace Corps** humanitarian volunteer service to the massive foreign aid and international monetary programs of subsequent administrations. Under President Richard Nixon and his close advisor Henry Kissinger, the United States took an especially large step in becoming an organizer of globalist strategies. President Jimmy Carter portrayed an image of weakness internationally, and during his presidency the Soviet Union reached the pinnacle of its international stature (deceptive though its true power was) and Islamic radicalism became a major international force.

Carter's foreign policy became a source of humiliation in the eyes of American voters, and Ronald Reagan, promising to restore U.S. prestige on the world scene, won an overwhelming victory in his presidential bid in 1980. In large part, he did restore the U.S. position by using or threatening to use American troops in the face of a series of crises around the globe. He supported anticommunist "freedom fighters" and stood up to terrorists. His powerful challenges to Soviet nuclear power, as we have seen, were one of the most significant causes of the Soviet collapse.

Reagan's successor, President George H. W. Bush—an experienced foreign policy expert, having served as ambassador to China and to the United Nations and as director of the U.S. Central Intelligence Agency—held to a globalist ideology and was highly criticized by nationalists and isolationists within his own Republican political party. He sought to build upon Reagan's moves toward better relations with the Soviet Union. He worked closely with American allies to maintain world political stability during the remarkable changes in Eastern Europe and the Soviet Union beginning in 1989. It was when Saddam Hussein invaded Kuwait in 1990, however, that Bush first publicly used a controversial term to describe where he believed the world should be headed historically. In an address to a joint session of Congress, Bush referred to a "new world order"—a phrase which sent shivers up the spines of conservatives who had feared the establishment of a single world political and economic order ever since the idea first surfaced in modern times with the League of Nations. After outlining four objectives of the U.S.-led multinational effort against Iraq, Bush told Congress:

President George H. W. Bush, 1924–

We stand today at a unique and extraordinary moment.... Out of these troubled times, our fifth objective—a new world order—can emerge: a new era, freer from the threat of terror, stronger in the pursuit of justice, and more secure in the quest for peace....

A hundred generations have searched for this elusive path to peace, while a thousand wars raged across the span of human endeavor. Today that new world is struggling to be born.

To some Christians, such talk seemed like a revival of the ideas which led to the construction of the ancient Tower of Babel, man's first attempt to construct a humanistic world power to challenge the universal rule of God. Advocates of the New World Order argued that the United Nations should be given a stronger role in securing international peace and cooperation. They said its "peacekeeping machinery" should be strengthened by the deployment of troops under U.N. command throughout the world in anticipation of possible crises. They noted that the U.N. Charter had always included strong provisions for enforcing U.N. decisions, but these Charter provisions had been mostly ignored during the Cold War. The Charter envisioned converting national military forces into a system of worldwide, collective "security."

"Such a system would be a giant step forward from the belated and impoverished efforts to which the United Nations has so far been limited...," said former U.N. Undersecretary General **Brian Urquhart** in 1991. "Governments, if they want the United Nations to be respected and taken seriously, will also have to respect its decisions, and make decisions that can if necessary be enforced. Such changes in attitude would be the best practical test of a commitment to a 'new world order.'"

The End of History? An official in the U.S. State Department during the first Bush administration went so far as to describe the alleged New World Order as the "end of history." **Francis Fukuyama** wrote a widely publicized article in which he said, "What we may be witnessing is not just the end of the Cold War, or the passing of a particular period of postwar history, but the end of history as such: that is, the end point of mankind's ideological evolution and the universalization of Western liberal democracy as the final form of human government." These words were as idealistic as any ever expressed by any proponent of Western liberalism. Though he claimed to be a conservative, Fukuyama reflected a Marxist view when he defined *history* as the record of human conflict and *ideology* as the framework for historical action. He said that each epoch in history develops it own contradictions and conflicts, but this process was now coming to an end with the triumph of Western liberal democracy. He said that all the possible ideological constructions had been tried and none remained to be explored—meaning that the "theoretical truth" of Western-ism had proved to be "absolute, and could not be improved upon." His claim was the opposite of Marxism's claim that perfected communism would be the absolute end of history, but his method of historical analysis was essentially the same as that of Marx.

Fukuyama's thesis must be rejected on the basis of both the evidence and the Bible. As the twentieth century grew to a close, the world remained, as one group of secular historians put it, "a hodge-podge of conflicting beliefs." They noted correctly that one of the most basic characteristics of Western democracy is its own contradictions: "It is precisely because democracy derives from the point of view that absolute truths are unreachable that it is necessary to consult majorities on a continuing basis over what they consider to be right."

The Bible rejects this central doctrine of liberal democracy by revealing that absolute truths have always existed. Furthermore, it shows history moving neither to an end of perfected communism nor perfected democracy but toward an ultimate triumph of those absolute truths that govern the Kingdom of God. As Psalm 86:9 states "All nations whom thou hast made shall come and worship before thee, O Lord; and shall glorify thy name." In that those truths were still widely rejected as the world enters the third millennium since Christ, it was clear that history had not yet come to its end.

History enables mankind to view the past as past and to see both the past and present as the prologue for the future. Both past and present allow us not only to plan for the future but also to rethink history's social goals and value systems in light of the unchangeable Word of God.

Alliances. By the close of the twentieth century, several crises began to test whether government of, by, and for the New World Order would long endure. This testing could be seen in the handling of the crises by various world alliances, particularly the United Nations and the North Atlantic Treaty Organization (NATO).

While both organizations were repeatedly called to respond to conflicts and catastrophes during the last three decades of the twentieth century, a crisis in Yugoslavia and some of its former provinces threatened to expose them as costly irrelevancies. NATO was particularly tried and found wanting in the conflict in Bosnia.

It will be recalled that the NATO alliance was established in 1949 by twelve nations in Western Europe and North America and was expanded several times through 1982. It began in the era of the Cold War and was intended to protect the West militarily against Soviet bloc aggression. Over the years, NATO expanded from a strictly military organization to include committees and offices through which the sixteen member nations could cooperate on economic, cultural, scientific, and environmental matters. But its primary focus remained military defense.

With the collapse of the Soviet bloc, its military alliance, the Warsaw Pact, also disintegrated. NATO faced new questions about whether it was still relevant or necessary. Some leaders in Europe believed that the European nations should begin to assume a larger role, as compared to the United States, in the defense of the continent; and they looked to the Conference on Security and Cooperation in Europe (CSCE), an alliance of 33 nations, as a potentially more logical organization to integrate both political and military defense strategies. The United States announced in 1991 that it would reduce the number of its armed forces participating in NATO.

United Nations vehicle in Eastern Europe

But the next year, Bosnia—following the example of Croatia and Slovenia—declared its independence from Serbia-controlled Yugoslavia and touched off a bloody civil war that took hundreds of thousands of lives. Bosnia was divided among three ethnic-religious groups: Orthodox Serbs, Catholic Croatians, and Muslim Slavs. Fighting among these groups resulted in atrocities (included the reported rape of 20,000 Muslim women by Serbian soldiers), terrible destruction of cities (especially the capital Sarajevo), displacement of more than 3 million people from their homes, and untold suffering. By 1994, more than 300,000 persons had died. Humanitarian, civic, and women's groups throughout Europe pleaded with authorities in their countries to stop the suffering and hold war-crime trials, but governments reacted slowly and cautiously, fearing that the conflict would drag them into a unwinnable **morass**.

Former U.S. Secretary of State **Cyrus Vance** (later replaced by Norway's **Thorwald Stoltenberg**) and Britain's **Lord David Owen** led a negotiation effort in Geneva to end the fighting by partitioning the country. A U.N. peacekeeping force was deployed and sanctions were imposed against the warring factions. NATO warships were sent to the Adriatic Sea to enforce an arms embargo. But Serbia and its Bosnian-Serb partners repeatedly undermined or defied international efforts to bring peace. U.N. forces and relief agents were frequently threatened or attacked, but the U.N. forces did not fight back. In February 1994, NATO ministers delivered an ultimatum to Bosnian Serb forces to lift their siege of Sarajevo. They did so temporarily, after additional appeals from sympathetic Russian diplomats. Later that month, NATO planes, with United Nations blessing, shot down four Bosnian Serb warplanes, and in mid-April, U.S. planes bombed Serbian and Bosnian Serb positions near the Muslim city of Gorazde. For the first time in NATO's history, targets had been attacked by alliance forces. Nevertheless, the war in Bosnia and Croatia continued into 1995. In December, the Dayton Peace Accords were signed, paving the way for NATO peacekeeping troops to enter Bosnia.

The Balkans heated up again in 1998. Conflict arose between ethnic Albanians and Serbs in the Serbian province of Kosovo. Efforts to resolve the dispute failed and, in March 1999, NATO for the first time attacked a sovereign nation when its planes bombed Yugoslavia. The air war lasted into June when the Yugoslav forces pulled out, allowing NATO troops to enter Kosovo. During the air war, the Serbs practiced a form of ethnic cleansing, killing an estimated 10,000 Albanians and forcing hundreds of thousands from their homes. On February 4, 2003, Yugoslavia was changed into a loose commonwealth of Serbia and Montenegro.

In January 1994, a NATO summit meeting endorsed a U.S. proposal to welcome former Warsaw Pact members into a new NATO **adjunct** organization, the "**Partnership for Peace.**" This would allow former Soviet bloc nations to partici-pate in various cooperative measures, informa-tion-sharing, military exercises, and peacekeeping consultations; but they would not benefit from the full protection of NATO membership. In June 1994, Russia, the West's old nemesis, became the twenty-first member of the Partnership for Peace. By the turn of the century, NATO itself was expanding through the addition of former communist countries. In 1999, the Czech Republic, Poland, and Hungary became members of the alliance, and seven others—including former Soviet states Estonia, Latvia, and Lithuania—joined in 2003.

The New World Economic Order

It seemed clear that the end of the Cold War and collapse of the Soviet Union spelled the end of a **bipolar** world *politically* and *militarily*, as the United States alone rose to the pinnacle of world power. Some argued, however, that the world was not yet **unipolar** *economically*. In this view, Japan had emerged as a victor in the Cold War. While the United States had invested heavily in arma-ments, Japan had concentrated on automobiles, electronics, and robotics and had developed highly efficient industrial techniques. In addition, the economic consolidation of Europe under the 1991 **Maastricht Treaty** also promised to make the old continent a powerful economic rival of the United States, by continuing the process of European eco-nomic integration. It created the **European Union (EU)** and established a process of economic and monetary union within the EU. This process resulted in the introduction of the European cur-rency known as the Euro in 1999. While many hoped that this economic union would result in greater prosperity for Europe, it had the effect of subverting certain nationalistic interests to central-ized European authority.

During the twentieth century, commerce, com-munications, science, technology, migration, tourism, and environmental problems began more and more to cross national boundaries, making the nations of the world increasingly **interdependent** economically. As the century drew to a close, global strategists sought to bring this *economic interdependence* into line with pro-posals for world *political interdependence*. But nationalism, ethnocentrism, and tribalism, as we have seen, remained a powerful force; and world economic goals often clashed with national or regional political interests. Interestingly, two of the greatest economic powers, Japan and Ger-many, were not members of the **United Nations Security Council**, the center of would-be world government; and the United States, through a newly conservative Congress, was threatening in 1995 to withdraw from unlimited participation in U.N. "peacekeeping" activities.

The "North-South" Gap. In spite of growing eco-nomic interdependence, the economic *gap* between the countries of the Northern and South-ern Hemispheres remained wide in the 1990s. About 70 percent of world income was produced and consumed by 15 percent of the world's popu-lation, which stood at 5 billion in 1995, up from 1.7 billion in 1900 and 2.5 billion in 1950. In the industrial world, per capita income averaged $14,500 a year, while in the forty-one least-devel-oped countries the average was under $300 a year. Each year, some 14 million children were dying before age five in the underdeveloped world and another 150 million were listed as malnourished, according to U.N. figures.

The nations of the South received most of their foreign exchange income from exports of agricul-tural products, whose prices were controlled by commodity exchange rates set by the North. At the same time, manufactured goods from the North were available to the South at prices also set by the North. Underdeveloped countries borrowed more than a trillion dollars from developed nations, and the interest on that debt alone exceeded the amount of foreign aid grants they received—in 1988 the interest was $43 billion more than the amount received. Critics used such figures to claim that the poor nations of the world were still subsidizing the rich ones. Developing countries tried for many years to work through the United Nations to create a world economic order which they felt would be more equitable.

The world economic imbalance posed major threats to the rich nations as well as the poor ones. Many of the poorer countries were unable to repay loans, leaving international bankers extremely vulnerable to disaster. When this situation was realized by the banking community, money was tightened. This fact led some countries to seek funds through illegal measures, such as dealing in cocaine, heroin, and marijuana at very high prices for users in developed countries.

Demographics. Population figures also indicated that the developed nations were at a disadvantage in the world. By the year 2000, experts predicted, more than three-fourths of the world's estimated 6.25 billion people would be living in developing countries, with most of those in urban areas having limited employment and other economic opportunities. It was claimed that by 2025, the world's resources would have to support 8.2 billion people, with 6.8 billion of those in less-developed countries. At the same time, the industrial countries were projected to reach zero population growth by 2025. The developed world would thus have stagnated demographically, while the Third World continued to expand. This fact, it was believed, would continue to esca-

Pollution is a serious problem in many countries.

late another problem that was surfacing in the late twentieth century—massive migrations of economic refugees. Migration was becoming a volatile political problem in the developed countries, the kind of problem which historically has led to political conflict.

Doomsday scientists and environmentalists also expressed alarm about the world population explosion's effect on the earth's food supply and environment. They spoke hysterically about "global warming" caused by depletion of the earth-atmosphere's protective ozone layer from industrial pollution and about catastrophic worldwide weather changes brought on by cutting and burning of tropical rain forests. Authoritative studies by U.S. government agencies disproved the global warming theory. Nevertheless, in June 1992, the countries of the world met in Rio de Janeiro, Brazil, to discuss ways to "save the planet" from predicted environmental disaster. The so-called **Earth Summit** attempted to construct a global treaty for environmental protection, with the industrialized nations footing the

bill. A world conference on population growth in Cairo, Egypt, in 1994 predicted similar disasters.

Others claimed that doomsday scenarios were misplaced. They pointed out that from 1965 to 1990, according to **World Bank** figures, average growth of **gross national products** per capita worldwide was at least 1.5 percent annually. At that rate, they noted, annual production per capita would double every 48 years. They noted that the substantial rate of increase in labor productivity would lead to increasing quantities of goods selling at lower prices, making them more and more affordable. They also demonstrated historically that the percentage of income spent for basic necessities was continuing to diminish. American sociologist **Charles Murray** pointed to studies which indicated that the greatest threat to such economic growth was the welfare state, which he said was hurting the poor more than helping them.

The Rise and Fall of the Welfare State. The leftward drift of the world politically during the first three quarters of the twentieth century resulted in new activism by the state in economic and welfare policies. Central planning during wartime added to this trend. By 1948, the basics of the modern **welfare state** had become well established in Western Europe. By the 1960s, they were also becoming entrenched in the United States, Canada, and Australia. Most Western European governments provided payments to families with children. Most provided "free" health care to everyone. Many launched massive public housing or housing-subsidy programs. Usually, significant portions of the middle class benefited from welfare-state schemes, making it difficult after a while to effect changes in the system politically—too many people had a stake in the benefits. Most governments in Europe after World War II nationalized some sectors of industry. They set up expensive new central-planning offices responsible for developing long-term economic projections and finding ways to meet the goals. Government planners directed the flow of capital from state banks and determined tax concessions. State planning also covered agricultural production and marketing. Many of these features also characterized the U.S. economy, although there was less direct nationalization of industry.

The welfare state proved terribly expensive, not only in terms of direct payments and subsidies, but also due to the fact that government bureaucracies exploded in size and cost. By the 1950s, as much as 25 percent of the gross national product of some European countries was going for welfare purposes, and that figure continued to rise as time went on. A new breed of government officials, known as **technocrats**, emerged. These bureaucrats usually were educated in engineering, economics, or some scientific or technical field; but they often lost sight of real human circumstances in their zeal to apply their expertise under

Most countries have moved away from the use of gold as the basis for their currency.

the power and authority of government regulatory agencies. This caused considerable resentment among enterprising individuals in the general population, who felt hamstrung in their productivity by heavy-handed regulation. The combination of "red tape," oppressive taxation, and the creation of a dependency mentality among the unproductive led to a backlash against the welfare state. This backlash simmered for several years and finally became a major political trend in some industrialized countries, especially the United States, by the middle 1990s.

Welfarism also prevailed on an international level. In 1989, Japan provided $42 billion to help underdeveloped nations, finally joining efforts by the United States and others that had pumped untold billions of foreign aid onto the world scene for years. The major nations worked through the 1980s to bring about debt relief, reschedule loan payments, open their markets to goods from poor countries, and provide technical assistance. But by the mid-1990s, international welfarism seemed only to be widening the gap between the developed and less-developed nations. Wars, political instability, droughts, and, most of all, socialist economic policies continued to create food shortages in sub-Saharan Africa.

The International Monetary Fund. As World War II was coming to a close, the Allies laid plans which they thought would preclude the kind of economic chaos which followed World War I. In 1944, representatives of forty-four nations met in Bretton Woods, New Hampshire, to plan a peacetime world economy. At the heart of the plan were measures to ensure a free flow of capital and trade internationally. One of the mechanisms to accomplish this was the **International Monetary Fund**. It was designed to restore and stabilize money systems that had floundered in recent decades when countries dropped the **gold stan-**

dard. The IMF established a worldwide system of fixed exchange rates, based on the American dollar, which could be exchanged for gold at $35 an ounce. Member states paid into the IMF, which served as a world savings account from which they could withdraw money to make debt payments without having to devalue their currencies or manipulate exchange rates. Although the Bretton Woods agreement brought some monetary stability allowing businesses to carry on their international affairs with confidence, the system faced problems because of the weaknesses of some member states' economies. Several other organizations grew out of the Bretton Woods program, including the **International Bank for Reconstruction and Development** and the **Organization for Economic Cooperation and Development**. In 1971, President Nixon ended the U.S. policy of convertibility of the dollar to gold. His action dealt a serious blow to the foundation of the Bretton Woods arrangement.

WTO. A further effort to integrate the world economically was the establishment of the **World Trade Organization (WTO)** in 1995; its purpose is to supervise and liberalize world trade. It succeeded the **General Agreement on Tariffs and Trade (GATT)**, established in 1947 under U.S. leadership, which was very successful in liberalizing world trade over its fifty-year history. Under the GATT, world trade increased at an amazing rate of 7 percent annually during its first twenty-five years of existence. A key feature of the GATT was its "most-favored-nation" provision. This clause in the agreement said that all members of the GATT would honor trade advantages worked out between any individual members. Though trade increased overall, member states gave up some of their national sovereignty on trade matters because many conflict resolutions and binding decisions governing trade were made by international commissions. In 1994, the U.S. Congress enacted laws

UNITED STATES OF AMERICA

CANADA

MEXICO

The North American Free Trade Agreement (NAFTA) includes the United States, Canada, and Mexico.

allowing the United States to withdraw whenever such decisions ran counter to U.S. interests.

A year earlier, the Congress approved a similar free trade agreement with Canada and Mexico, the **North American Free Trade Agreement (NAFTA)**, a counterpart to the 1991 Maastricht Treaty which sought to eliminate trade barriers in Europe. Like the NAFTA parties, leaders of the European Union (sometimes called the United States of Europe) sought to assure the world that the union would not become a **protectionist** bloc in world trade. The EU members collectively enacted more than 300 directives, which would serve as the laws of the union. The union was designed to open national borders to the free movement of goods and people and to establish continent-wide standards for such things as electrical current, pressures, safety, and health. In addition to economic rules, the union sought to establish a "social dimension" defining "the rights of ordinary people in the great market and to help the poorer among them." The effort to create a common European currency and central bank caused a lingering controversy over national interests. Conservatives in Britain and Germany, both countries with strong national currencies, opposed the common currency idea. Japan and the United States welcomed the idea of a major new unified market, but they feared they might be harmed if the EU favored its own industries in the purchase of supplies and equipment, in internal industrial subsidies, and in pricing policies that included the value-added taxes common in Europe.

Traditional liberal-conservative alignments grew fuzzy during debate over these free-trade measures, because, while they purported to follow *laissez-faire* doctrines dear to conservatives, they also jeopardized national-sovereignty prerogatives in favor of global unity, a doctrine dear to liberals.

Recession. The integration of the world economy sometimes meant that economic cycles were experienced far and wide. For example, the world economy stagnated during a major global recession that lasted roughly from 1978 to 1985. Unemployment rates skyrocketed, especially in underdeveloped countries where population was rapidly growing at the same time.

The world economy suffered a series of currency crises beginning with Mexico in the mid-1990s. Late in the 1990s, many countries of the Pacific Rim experienced significant devaluations of their currencies which caused them great economic hardship. As a result, international investors became wary about doing business in the unstable economic climate of Asia and Eastern Europe. This made it difficult for their economies to grow.

Political Developments in the West

Great Britain. Britain emerged from World War II amid the glow and glory of victory, but underneath the prestige attending that victory the country was near bankruptcy. Its poor economic performance persisted through the next three and a half decades and a succession of Conservative and Labour Party leaders. When Labour Party leader **Harold Wilson** resigned in 1975, he was succeeded by the moderate **L. James Callaghan**, who mourned that Britons were "still not earning the standard of living we are enjoying. We are only keeping up our standards by borrowing, and this cannot go on indefinitely." During the following year, Britain was forced to borrow $5.3 billion from ten other countries. Callaghan proposed massive cuts in welfare, social services, and the military, but unions balked and Callaghan's government failed.

In the spring of 1979, Conservatives returned to power under a woman who was to dominate Great Britain and much of the world scene for more than a decade. **Margaret Thatcher** (known as "The Iron Lady") led her government and the nation through radical changes in economic and social programs. She sold off many nationalized industries, cut social services and welfare, reduced public housing expenses, and boosted private enterprise. Her successes gained her overwhelming re-election victories in 1983 and 1987. She demanded and received more favorable treatment for Britain in the Common Market (now known as the European Union). She and U.S. President Ronald Reagan, friends and kindred spirits ideologically, cooperated successfully on numerous foreign policy initiatives. Her chief domestic adviser—a follower of the American Christian

Reconstructionist theologian R. J. Rushdoony—designed programs in keeping with biblical laws, including a proposed flat-rate (or head) tax. That proposal, as well as other fundamental restructuring measures, eventually led to a backlash against Thatcher, who was forced to resign in 1991 and was replaced by fellow Conservative **John Major**. Despite his party affiliation, Major took much more of a globalist position than Thatcher had.

By 1995, Major's popularity had plummeted to one of the lowest points for any prime minister since World War II. Major's decline in popularity resulted in an overwhelming victory by the Labour Party in 1997, bringing **Tony Blair** to power. One key development during Major's tenure, however, was a cease-fire in the bloody, centuries old, religious conflict in Northern Ireland. Major opened talks in 1994 with **Gerry Adams**, leader of **Sinn Fein**, the political arm of the outlawed Catholic **Irish Republican Army**, which had been battling Protestants in Northern Ireland for many years.

Tony Blair became the first Labour prime minister to serve two consecutive terms in office when his party won the 2001 election. His stated goal in British politics has been to establish a "third way"—one that is less socialist and more open to private initiative than the old Labour Party. He has created regional legislative bodies in Scotland and Wales and encouraged the peace process in Northern Ireland. Blair also sent British forces to participate in the Kosovo War and to assist the United States in Afghanistan and Iraq.

France. The Free French hero of World War II, **Charles De Gaulle**, left a strong imprint on his country as its president until 1968. During his tenure, he sought to restore France to its historic grandeur in Europe. In his memoirs he once wrote, "France cannot be France without greatness." To that end, he made France an independent nuclear power. In 1966, he withdrew French forces from participation in NATO, although the country remained a consulting member. De Gaulle opposed membership in any international superagency with governing powers. Although France joined the Common Market, he fought attempts to give it political authority.

In 1968, domestic difficulties came to a head in widespread strikes by university students and workers. De Gaulle lost a vote-of-confidence referendum and retired to his country estate, where he died eighteen months later.

He was succeeded by an able administrator **Georges Pompidou**, who died in 1974. The country then elected young **Valery Giscard d'Estaing** as president. He initiated a series of major reforms related to urbanization, land ownership, divorce, and the voting age. But economic problems, some related to the worldwide recession, persisted; and in 1981, a coalition of leftist parties brought socialist leader **François Mitterand** to power. Mitterand and the Socialist-controlled National Assembly proceeded to decentralize a government apparatus which had been essentially in place since Napoleon. He

German Chancellor Helmut Kohl with Margaret Thatcher

nationalized large businesses and banks. By 1985, when the world recession ended, the French economy improved. The Socialists lost their majority in the National Assembly in 1986. This was the first time in the history of the Fifth Republic, when the executive and legislative branches were held by different parties, beginning a period of political fluctuation between the parties of the left and the right.

The Socialist Party made a comeback in 1988, when Mitterand won reelection as President of France and the Socialists regained control of the Assembly. After that victory, however, the left steadily lost power to the right. Conservative parties won control of the Assembly again in 1993, and gained complete control over the government when **Jacque Chirac** defeated the Socialist presidential candidate in 1995. The left, however, again won control of the Assembly in 1997. President Chirac's overwhelming victory in 2002 also resulted in control of the Assembly by his supporters. He was one of the leading opponents of war with Iraq in 2003, along with Germany's Gerhard Schröder and Russia's Vladimir Putin.

Germany. West Germany's postwar leaders, **Konrad Adenauer**, **Ludwig Erhard**, and **Willy Brandt**, were succeeded in 1974 by moderate socialist **Helmut Schmidt**, who led Germany through the strong economic growth that put Germany near the top as a world economic power. In the late 1970s, Schmidt asked the United States to counter the Soviet deployment of SS-20 short-range missiles aimed at Western Europe. That stance was highly controversial in Germany. Soviet-inspired "peace" groups clamored against nuclear weapons and disapproved of the proposed Pershing missiles. At the same time, conservatives disapproved of Schmidt's close economic ties to the Soviet Union. By 1982, the pressures from both sides led to the defeat of

Schmidt's party, and power reverted to the Christian Democratic Union, led by **Helmut Kohl**.

Kohl was a strong ally of the United States and succeeded in getting the Pershing missiles deployed, in the face of strong Soviet protests. Kohl was easily reelected in 1987 and played a leading role in European and world affairs thereafter. He masterfully handled the rapid reunification of Germany after the 1989 demise of the German Democratic Republic, but the absorption of the East Germans proved to be a major drain on resources of the stronger half of the new Germany. He became a major advocate of environmental issues when the **Green Party** gained popularity in Germany. He remained in office until 1998. The Social Democratic Party won the most votes in the 1998 election and, in coalition with the Green Party, selected **Gerhard Schröder** as the new chancellor of Germany.

Italy. Italy's postwar leader, **Alcide De Gasperi**, was a strong advocate of democracy and European unity. He led his country to economic recovery, more so in the north than the south. After he resigned in 1953, Italian politics fell into disarray through a series of cabinet crises, government turnovers, and uneasy coalitions. Between World War II and 1990, there were forty-nine different governments. Corruption and inefficiency seemed **endemic** to the political system, which was dominated by the Christian Democratic Party. In the 1970s, inflation, unemployment, and labor unrest plagued the country. In 1978, an anarchist group calling itself the **Red Brigades** kidnapped former premier **Aldo Moro** and assassinated him. Terrorists and the **Mafia** spread chaos until the government of **Bettino Craxi** and **Ciriaco De Mita** reestablished a measure of order and improved conditions. Corruption investigations in the 1990s have created political uncertainty, due to the fact that many

politicians have been convicted and traditional parties have become discredited. Italians have recently begun to turn to new political parties. Wealthy businessman **Silvio Berlusconi** took advantage of Italy's new political realities. He originally became prime minister in 1994 as leader of a short-lived center-right coalition government. He became prime minister again in 2001 as the leader of a similar coalition. In 2003, he provided political support to the United States and Great Britain prior to their invasion of Iraq.

Portugal. The countries of the Iberian Peninsula have been marked by both dictatorships and radicalism. Portugal was ruled from 1932 until 1968 by strongman **Antonio de Oliveira Salazar**, an austere Catholic who avoided social life and lived on a small salary. He censored the press and neglected education. Although there were some economic improvements, Portugal remained one of the poorest countries in Western Europe. A five-year economic plan was launched in 1955 but proved ineffective in the face of budget drains caused by colonial wars in Africa. In 1974, a group of junior army officers overthrew the government. Workers seized many businesses, farms, and other properties. In 1976, elections gave a victory to moderate socialists. A new constitution was written and democracy established, but economic problems persisted. Unemployment was heightened when 600,000 refugees from Portuguese Africa entered the country. During the 1980s, a socialist coalition led by **Mario Soares** returned a measure of political and economic stability to Portugal.

Spain. Spain was ruled from 1939 until 1975 by the dictator **Generalissimo Francisco Franco**. Some years after World War II, Spain began to rapidly industrialize and modernize. The Cold War led the Western nations, who were eager for anticommunist allies, to welcome Spain into their fold. Spain entered the United Nations in 1955,

and the following year, in the **Pact of Madrid**, Spain became a base for American armed forces in exchange for $1 billion a year in aid. In the 1960s and 1970s, literacy and affluence improved, but discontent arose in the mid-1970s. Franco died in 1975 after naming **King Juan Carlos** as his successor, thereby restoring the monarchy to Spain. The king helped establish a reform government, which granted new civil liberties and helped ease ideological tensions. In May 1982, Spain joined NATO, a move which was highly controversial. Later that year, the Socialist Party led by **Felipe González Márquez** came to power. He supported NATO and the U.S. bases against the wishes of some on the left, brought Spain into the Common Market, and welcomed investors for high-tech industries. The Socialists were defeated by a

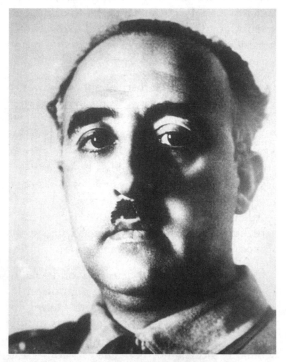

Generalissimo Francisco Franco, 1892–1975

coalition of more conservative parties led by the Popular Party in 1996, and **Jose Maria Aznar** became prime minister. The Aznar government provided significant political support for President George W. Bush's Iraq policy, but that came to an end with the Socialist Party's election victory in 2004, shortly after the March 11 al-Qaida train bombings that killed 191 people. As a result, Spanish troops were withdrawn from Iraq by mid 2004.

Greece. For most of the period following World War II, Greece was politically unstable. Its governments were inefficient and its economy was backward. The **Greek Civil War** of 1946–1949 saw pro-Western forces defeat communists. A monarchy, military junta, and republic followed in succession. In 1981, Greece was admitted to the **European Community** after pledging to accept the European democratic tradition. In November of that year, Socialists came to power under **Andreas Papandreou**, who led the country until 1989. He vowed to oust U.S. forces from Greek bases and to lead Greece away from a western orientation, but Greece remained in NATO and the EC nevertheless. Economic stagnation, poverty, and scandals drove Papandreou and the socialists from the government in 1989. They were replaced briefly by an unlikely coalition of communists and conservative parties. In 1990, the conservative New Democracy Party gained a one-seat majority in parliament, and its founder and former premier **Constantine Karamanlis** was elected president by the parliament.

In 1992, the government sought international support for its campaign to stop the former Yugoslavian republic of Macedonia from using that name following its independence. Greece has a northern province by the same name. The two regions, along with Bulgarian Macedonia, were united in ancient times under the name Macedon.

Sweden. Sweden, which remained neutral during World War II, had been the most left-leaning

socialist democracy in Europe since early in the twentieth century. Forty-four years of socialist government ended briefly in 1976 with the election of a conservative coalition led by **Thorbjörn Fälldin**. He resigned in 1978 in an intramural controversy over use of nuclear power. His conservative successor, **Ola Ullsten**, lasted for only a year after failing to achieve consensus on the same issue. Fälldin returned to power and submitted the issue to a referendum. But in 1982, the socialists regained the government under **Sven Olof Palme**, who antagonized the West by backing the communist side in the Vietnam War, by supporting Marxist revolutionaries in South Africa and elsewhere, by making friends with Castro, and by advocating numerous radical-left causes. He opposed full Swedish participation in the European Community (now known as the

European Union). During his second term in office, the Swedish economy sagged amid labor unrest. Palme was mysteriously assassinated by an unknown assailant as he emerged onto a Stockholm street after attending a movie. Sweden applied for EC membership in 1991. Later that year, the Social Democratic Party was ousted from power. A new coalition of four moderate and conservative parties, including a new evangelical Christian party, launched a program to cut taxes and reduce the massive welfare state. Unemployment benefits were shaved and old-age pension allowances were restricted. There were also cuts in a number of other social service programs. These were seen as remarkable measures for the world prototype democratic socialist state to take, especially at a time when many former communist countries in Eastern Europe had been examining the Sweden model.

Norway. Despite severe losses during its occupation by Nazis during World War II, Norway recovered quickly after the war. It engaged in innovative social experimentation and entered NATO in 1949. The Conservative Party government of **Jan Peder Sysé** resigned in 1990 over the issue of Norway's relationship with the European Community. A minority Labor Party government under **Gro Harlem Brundtland** took over. The government of Norway applied to join the EU, but this effort failed in 1994 when a referendum supporting this application was defeated.

Canada. Following World War II, Canada underwent remarkable economic development. Its gross national product rose from $12 billion in 1946 to $61 billion in 1966. Much of the prosperity was tied to development of oil and gas reserves and iron ore and to the opening of the St. Lawrence Seaway, a joint U.S.-Canadian project completed in 1959. Controversy over construction of a transcontinental natural gas

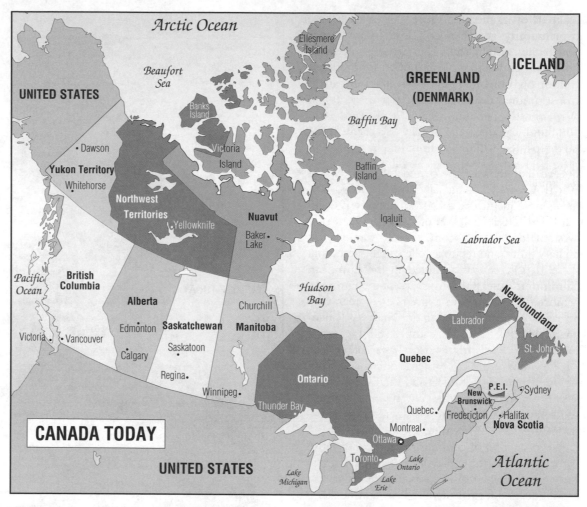

pipeline led to the defeat of the Liberal government of **Louis St. Laurent** in 1957 and the ascension of the **Progressive Conservative Party** under **John Diefenbaker**. In 1958, the dynamic Diefenbaker won the largest election victory in Canadian history. But an economic recession caused the Progressive Conservatives to lose their majority in 1962. The Liberals took over under **Lester Pearson**, who retired in 1968. Pearson was succeeded by the somewhat flamboyant **Pierre Elliott Trudeau**, an intellectual who had to deal with a growing influx of U.S. capital.

Trudeau also faced the rise of French factions demanding independence for Quebec. A pro-independence group known as the FLQ began a terrorist campaign in the 1960s, while others favoring independence engaged in electoral politics. The secessionist **Bloc Québécois** party gained ground in Quebec in 1976. The threat from Quebec, along with economic problems, led to defeat of the Liberals in 1979. A Conservative minority government under **Joseph Clark** lasted only until 1980, when Trudeau and the Liberals returned to power. In May 1980, a referendum on Quebec independence was rejected. Constitutional changes took place in 1982, but were not accepted by Quebec. Trudeau retired in 1984 and was succeeded briefly by **John Turner**. In September 1984, the Progressive Conservatives, led by **Brian Mulroney**, won 211 of the 282 parliamentary seats. By 1987, Mulroney convinced Quebec to accept the 1982 Constitution Act by proposing an amendment recognizing Quebec as a "distinct society" within Canada. The amendment failed nationwide. In 1992, Mulroney and provincial premiers agreed to new constitutional changes guaranteeing Quebec's special status, giving greater autonomy to Canada's Native Americans, and providing for popular election of members of the national Senate. But a referendum later that year was defeated by six of Canada's ten provinces, including Quebec itself. Mulroney retired in June 1993 and was succeeded by the country's first female prime minister, **Kim Campbell**. But in October 1993, a division within the political right resulted in the

Ottawa, the capital of Canada

crushing defeat of the Progressive Conservatives, who were reduced from 154 to 2 seats in parliament. Liberal **Jean Chrétien** gained a landslide victory to become Canada's twentieth prime minister. A new populist party based largely in western Canada known as the **Reform Party** (later called the **Canadian Alliance**), became the main conservative party in Canada. In 2003, the Canadian Alliance and the Progressive Conservative parties merged to form the **Conservative Party of Canada**. Chrétien resigned the same year and was replaced by **Paul Martin**, who led the Liberals to a narrow electoral victory the 2004.

The highpoint of secessionist politics was from 1993 to 1995. In the 1993 federal elections, the Bloc Québécois became the chief opposition party in parliament because of the split among conservative voters. In Quebec, Bloc Québécois leader **Jacques Parizeau** narrowly defeated Liberal provincial premier **Daniel Johnson** in 1994 and promised to call a referendum on independence, which was held in 1995. The independence referendum was narrowly defeated, however, stalling the secessionist movement. The Bloc Québécois lost its position as the primary opposition party in Parliament in subsequent federal elections to the Canadian Alliance and lost its hold on power in Quebec when it was defeated by the Liberals in the 2003 provincial election.

Japan. Though Japan is geographically and historically within the Oriental orbit, its development since World War II places it substantially within the Western tradition. Its rise from a conquered nation to a world economic power in less than a half century was remarkable. The foundations for that recovery were laid by General Douglas MacArthur, who headed the occupation force following Japan's defeat in 1945. In exchange for its demilitarization, the Allies gave aid to rebuild the island nation's economy. New

Tokyo during the rush hour

educational and political systems were instituted with sufficient flexibility to allow radical transformation of the nation. By 1951, Japan had regained full sovereignty. Except for only brief periods, conservatives controlled the Japanese government. The **Liberal Democratic Party** has been friendly to the United States and favored limited rearmament. Yet, the Communist Party was never a significant factor, and the Socialist Party has rarely taken a part in the government.

Japan experienced rapid urbanization. Three metropolitan areas, Tokyo, Osaka, and Nagoya contained more than one-quarter of the population by the 1990s though occupying only 1 percent of the land. In the cities, traditional values and attitudes were Westernized; and Western materialism, with its emphasis on changing fashions, television, sports, and rock music, began to overpower the traditional culture. The status of women was also substantially changed. By the 1980s, nearly half of the nation's work force was female, and nearly one-third of female high school graduates entered colleges and universities.

It was necessary for Japan to adapt its system to fit its circumstances. It had to import most of its industrial raw materials and much of the food needed to feed its population of 123 million (1990 census). Business leaders developed new management techniques, and workers channeled their traditional discipline into efficient use of new technologies and compliance with managerial designs. This combination of leadership innovation and discipline within the work force had spectacular results. In 1950, the gross national product (GNP) was $10 billion; by 1973, it was $300 billion. By 1980, Japan was building half of the world's tonnage in shipping and was the world's largest producer of transistor radios, sewing machines, bicycles, and motorcycles. Japan soon surpassed the United States in automobile production and drove the American television-set industry out of business. By the 1990s, Japan's per capita GNP was nearly $22,000, compared with $19,800 in the United States, making Japan one of the world's strongest economies. Tokyo became the leading world financial and banking center after 1987.

Among the few negatives ever faced by Japanese industry was the 1973 Arab Oil Embargo that drove energy prices up 400 percent, touched off soaring inflation, slowed economic growth, and led to a negative balance of trade. In the late 1980s, another challenge arose when South Korea, Taiwan, Hong Kong, and Singapore began to adopt the Japanese industrial formula and to give strong competition in the high-technology and automotive fields.

Although Japan's economic growth had been spectacular up through the 1980s, the image of Japan as an economic juggernaut was sorely tested in the 1990s. Overinvestment in stock and real estate markets caused a recession that began in 1992 and continued throughout the decade and into the twenty-first century. The severe monetary crisis, which affected much of the

The Development of the Pacific Rim

The rise of coastal areas in eastern Asia to world importance forms one of the major facets of the rebalancing of major societies in the 20th century. The dynamism of Asia's Pacific Coast centered in several societies long in China's shadow as East Asian civilization was redivided and redefined, and the same societies began to influence international patterns in unprecedented ways. Societies that had been shaped by Confucian influence began to take very different paths.

The Pacific Rim states also reflect some common heritage that had included considerable Chinese influence. The Pacific Rim category was still tentative by the 1990s, for it was not clear how much these different nations would prove to have in common, or how permanent their splitting away from other East Asian societies would be, notably China and Vietnam. Yet the Pacific Rim states were undeniably important in their own right, becoming along with the West the center of the world's greatest economic strength, and challenging the West through new competition. The Pacific Rim states also shared a fascinating effort to blend successful industrial forms with a distinctive cultural and political tradition—providing the clearest alternative to the West of what a vigorous modern society might look like.

The key actor was Japan, which had diverged from Chinese patterns in the previous period. Japan became a leading factor in international markets of all sorts—in banking, in foreign investment both in raw materials in the United States, and in foreign economic aid—as the relatively small, resource-poor island nation reached toward control of almost one-fifth of total world trade. Japanese competition challenged the United States and Western Europe, while its demand for raw materials figured prominently in Canada, Latin America, and the Middle East as well as Asia.

After World War II, Japan's success was mirrored by the rapid rise of other centers in eastern Asia, some of which became the first successful entrants to the ranks of industrial economies for virtually a century—since Japan and Russia had begun their surge. South Korea, Taiwan, and the city-states of Hong Kong and Singapore, though not yet attaining Japanese levels of prosperity and influence, gained ground rapidly, challenging the Japanese lead in certain export sectors and making a profound impact on international markets.

The rise of the Pacific Rim nations commands attention in 20th-century history because of their success in breaking the previous Western monopoly on industrial leadership—not only in sheer volume of production and export trade, but in technological innovation as well. Many observers predicted that coastal East Asia, perhaps joined by parts of China and other areas, would replace the West in world leadership. The emergence of the Pacific Rim also commands interest because it has formed such a challenging exception to the general difficulty faced by 20th-century societies that were still to enter into a genuine industrial revolution. And it commands interest because successful industrialization has not led to full Westernization.

Overall, the Pacific Rim has formed a distinctive grouping of societies amid the larger patterns of the 20th-century world.

Adapted from Stearns, Adas, and Schwartz, *World Civilizations: The Global Experience.* (Harper Collins; Bureau of Electronic Publishing, 1992)

Pacific Rim during the late 1990s, had the effect of deepening Japan's existing economic problems.

The United States. We have already considered, in piecemeal fashion, most of the major political and economic developments in the United States dur-

ing the late twentieth century. Until 1981, most of those developments arose on a foundation built upon the legacy of Franklin D. Roosevelt's New Deal. Both Democratic and Republican administrations constructed policies featuring expanded central government, welfarism, and liberal social changes. Democrat Harry Truman fought communism and crusaded in homespun fashion for the "common man" and against the "fat cats." Republican war hero Dwight Eisenhower fought communism and watched the federal bureaucracy balloon. Democrat John F. Kennedy fought communism and advocated idealistic programs for the poor and racial minorities. Under Democrat Lyndon Johnson, who also fought communism, the welfare state in America experienced explosive growth.

Republican Richard Nixon, an old communist fighter, warmed up to the communist world and, while talking conservative talk, involved the central government in direct wage and price controls and oversaw new forms of government regulation before he was forced to resign from office, the first American president to do so. The cause was the **Watergate Scandal**. During Nixon's 1972 reelection campaign, a group of shadowy men with ties to the campaign were arrested and charged with an illegal break-in at the headquarters of the Democratic Party in the Watergate office-apartment complex in Washington, D.C. Nixon at first denied any knowledge of the affair and related political "dirty tricks," but the discovery of White House tape recordings led to disclosure of the extent of his knowledge and his administration's attempts to cover up the activities. A special prosecutor, a grand jury, congressional hearings, and incessant newspaper reporting caused the scandal to reach a fever pitch and all but paralyzed the national government. At the same time, Nixon's vice president, **Spiro Agnew**, resigned from office under charges of bribery, extortion, and kickbacks dating to his time as governor of Maryland. Several Nixon associates were convicted of crimes and imprisoned. In the summer of 1974, a committee of the House of Representatives recommended that the Senate impeach the president. Disgraced and overwhelmed by the scandal, Nixon

announced his resignation. He was succeeded by **Gerald R. Ford**, who had been appointed by Nixon to replace Agnew. Ford continued Nixon's basic policy directions domestically and in foreign policy. Nixon, later in life, remained active as an elder citizen-statesman in foreign affairs. It was in this arena that he had excelled during his presidency, and it was this that helped to rehabilitate his image before the nation and world before he died in 1994.

Economic problems, including high inflation, high unemployment, and the falling value of the dollar internationally, plagued the one-term presidency of Democrat **Jimmy Carter**, who was perceived as weak and inept, particularly in foreign policy. This was despite the fact that he brokered the first major step toward peace in the troubled Middle East by bringing Israel and Egypt together for a peace treaty. Yet he failed in securing release for American hostages held in Iran, and he seemed unable to address the challenge of international communism, which appeared to reach the zenith of its effectiveness during his administration. Carter's status as a "born-again" Christian and Baptist Sunday school teacher was highly publicized during his campaign, and he had come to office with support from a newly active bloc of evangelical Christians and other voters disturbed about a perceived moral decline in the presidency as seen in the Watergate Scandal. Like Nixon, Carter conducted himself as an elder citizen statesman after he left office. During the mid-1990s, he negotiated crucial temporary agreements in a series of international crises in North Korea, Haiti, and Bosnia. He also distinguished himself as a volunteer in humanitarian causes and as an election observer in various Third World countries.

Ronald Reagan, a movie actor and former governor of California, overwhelmed Carter during the election of 1980. A former admirer of Frank-

President Ronald Reagan, 1911–2004

lin Roosevelt, he promised to reverse decades of increasing federal involvement in American life and economics. He promised tax cuts and reduction of federal bureaucratic regulation. His economic theory—derisively called **Reaganomics**, "trickle-down economics," or "voodoo economics"—was that if the government took less money from individuals and businesses, they would have more to invest in productive enterprises which in turn would cause the general economy to expand. National economic problems marked his first administration, but the economy showed signs of significant growth during his second term. At the same time, however, the federal budget soared and the national debt increased to staggering proportions.

In spite of generally good economic news during the Reagan years, there were some troubling signs. The United States racked up huge **trade deficits** (more imports than exports). A Democratic Congress refused to make the necessary cuts in federal spending, and thus a key component of Reagan's plan was never implemented. High government spending continued to outstrip revenue income, creating massive federal budget deficits. This practice generated a staggering national debt in the trillions of dollars. Interest obligations related to that debt will siphon money from generations to come.

Reagan proved highly successful, however, in foreign affairs. Calling Soviet communism an "Evil Empire," he challenged leftist revolutionaries and terrorists wherever they appeared. He restored a sense of patriotism at home and America's image as a determined world power abroad. His emphasis on increased military preparedness brought the arms race to heights that the rival U.S.S.R. could not match in the end, and his pressures against the Soviets finally forced them to make accommodations to the West that led to the Soviet collapse which we discussed earlier in this chapter.

Largely on the Reagan legacy, his more liberal-minded vice president, **George H. W. Bush**, was swept to an easy election victory in 1988 against a lackluster Democratic candidate, **Michael Dukakis**. Bush built on Reagan's late-term improving relations with the Soviet Union and led the Western world's celebration over the end of the Soviet Empire. His domestic popularity skyrocketed to more than 90 percent approval after his highly successful prosecution of the Persian Gulf crisis of 1990–1991, which he used to boost the role of the United Nations in the world, at least briefly.

At home, however, economic and social problems continued to tear at the fabric of American life. Productivity was declining, the federal budget continued to soar, America's trade balance was increasingly negative, financial institutions failed at an alarming rate, unemployment remained a problem, crime rates were up, fears of recession loomed, racial tensions were growing, and there were signs that America's morality had deteriorated to all-time lows. These factors gave the American electorate a feeling of uneasiness and anger.

During the election campaign of 1992, Democrats sought to capitalize on this feeling of largely undefined discontent, with Arkansas Governor **Bill Clinton** as the party's candidate to challenge Bush. An outspoken but erratic independent candidate, billionaire businessman **Ross Perot** also entered the race and capitalized on the discontent. The first President Bush ran an ineffective reelection campaign, and on Election Day was narrowly defeated. Clinton actually received less than half of the popular vote, and won by only a 5 percent plurality over Bush. Perot, who financed his campaign from his own pockets, grabbed 19 percent of the vote, the highest for an independent candidate in 80 years. Perot's participation probably cost Bush his re-election. Voter turnout was exceptionally high that year, up 26 percent among the educated classes, 27 percent among self-proclaimed liberals who voted overwhelmingly for Clinton. Conservative voter turnout dropped 10 percent, largely because conservative Christians were displeased with Bush's seeming disregard for their perspectives.

When he came to office, Clinton immediately launched a series of radical social-policy initiatives, including an effort to allow homosexuals

U.S. President Bill Clinton speaks outside the White House in 1994 about the Partnership for Peace program.

into the military and to remove numerous restrictions related to abortion. He appointed several homosexuals and other controversial liberals to government positions. He named his outspoken, liberal wife **Hillary Rodham Clinton** to spearhead a high-profile legislative effort to enact a complex and costly socialized medicine program. The program was rejected by Congress, even though Congress was controlled by his own party. During the 1994 elections, voters showed their disapproval of the directions which Clinton and a scandal-ridden, Democrat-controlled Congress had been taking by sweeping Republicans into a majority in Congress and state offices. The Republican Congress, led by House Speaker **Newt Gingrich** launched a major conservative legislative program dubbed "**A Contract with America**" in 1995. The election and legislative program was hailed as a virtual "revolution" in the direction of the country. One of the initiatives passed by the new Congress was a major reform of the nation's welfare system.

One part of the "Contract with America" was the enactment of a constitutional amendment requiring the federal budget to be balanced in the future. Although the proposed amendment failed to pass Congress, the budget deficit problem improved significantly because of modest limits placed on federal spending by the Republican Congress and increased tax receipts due to the strong American economy.

The Republican "revolution" stalled in 1996 and 1998. In the election of 1996, President Clinton again won a plurality of the vote over Republican **Robert Dole** and independent Ross Perot. The Republicans were only able to maintain a narrow margin of control over Congress after the 1998 election. After that election, Newt Gingrich resigned from Congress.

Throughout his presidency, Clinton had sought to establish an enduring legacy. The 1994 election, however, forced him to retreat, causing him to focus on small, incremental programs instead of large, grandiose projects. His foreign policy initiatives, in the Balkans and elsewhere, provided him with little public acclaim. Much of Clinton's energy was spent dealing with the various scandals in his administration. He and his wife were accused of questionable financial deals in the **Whitewater Scandal** while he was governor of Arkansas. In addition, individuals associated with his reelection effort were involved with obtaining illegal contributions for the Democratic National Committee. The scandal, which possibly had the greatest consequences for the United States, was the Chinese nuclear espionage case; lax security by the Department of Energy enabled the espionage to continue even after the President was warned.

The best-known scandals, however, had to do with President Clinton's sexual misconduct both before and during his presidency. At least three women accused him of misconduct while governor. **Paula Jones** even brought a civil suit against him for sexual harassment. Although this suit was eventually settled out of court, it brought to light the President's immoral relationship with White House intern **Monica Lewinsky**. In an effort to prevent disclosure of his affair, Clinton lied to the American people and perjured himself before the courts, but the entire affair became public in August 1998. As a result of his perjury, President Clinton became the first elected President in American history to be impeached in December 1998. Although not convicted by the Senate, he became the first President to be fined ($90,000) for perjury by the courts. It seems that President Clinton's enduring legacy was that of scandal—not greatness.

In part as a result of President Clinton's scandals, Republican **George W. Bush**, son of former President George H. W. Bush, won one of the closest elections in American history. George W. Bush narrowly won the national electoral vote in November 2000 and, therefore, the presidency, while still losing the popular vote to Democrat **Al Gore**. President Bush's time in office has proved to be a difficult one. A recession, which had begun toward the end of the Clinton administration, became worse. Then, early in President Bush's administration, America became engaged in the **War on Terrorism**. On September 11, 2001, Islamist terrorists hijacked four airliners, crashing two into the World Trade Center in New York City and one into the Pentagon in Washington, D.C., while the fourth crashed in a Pennsylvania field due to resistance by passengers and crew. Almost 3,000 people were killed as a result of these attacks.

It was determined that these attacks were carried out by the al-Qaida Islamist terrorist organization led by Osama bin Laden, which had been granted safe haven by the Taliban government in Afghanistan. When Afghanistan refused to extradite the leaders of al-Qaida to the United States, war was begun against the terrorists and their Taliban supporters in October 2001. With the assistance of allies and Afghan opposition groups, the Taliban regime was overthrown. Although bin Laden and some of the leaders of the Taliban have yet to be captured, the terrorists are no longer protected in Afghanistan. Later, in March–April 2003, the United States, with the assistance of others, invaded Iraq—deposing the regime of Saddam Hussein. Although Hussein was captured in December 2003, a significant armed opposition continues against coalition forces and the new Iraqi government. In November 2004, President Bush won a clear reelection victory in a campaign that focused heavily on the Iraq war.

Whither the West?

The present book is part two of a two-volume set examining the history of world civilizations by tracing the major political, economic, scientific, technological, religious, cultural, and social streams through which civilizations have flowed. This volume has concentrated on the rise of Western Civilization, which dominated the world for most of the second millennium. As we enter the third millennium after Christ, questions have been raised by historians and social analysts whether Western Civilization would endure much longer.

Contemporary Observations. Our examination of the twentieth century indicates an undeniable *relative* decline in the position of the West within the broader world during that period. Since the 1980s, some observers have been pointing to the emergence of a "Pacific century," dominated by the nations of East Asia, beginning somewhere around A.D. 2000. While Japan and some other Asian entities clearly were rising as important economic forces in the world, there was scant evidence that this economic prowess was uniquely non-Western or that it was the foundation for a comprehensive new form of civilization. Yet, as we has seen, Europe and North America, the heartlands of the Western tradition, faced substantial challenges and competition during the twentieth century, causing Western *dominance* to suffer relative setbacks.

Other observers predicting an end to Western Civilization claimed to note more than a *relative* decline. They claimed to have detected signs of profound internal decay which they said evidenced an *absolute* decline in Western vitality, a portent of its eventual demise. Historians Peter

N. Stearns, Michael Adas, and Stuart B. Schwartz described these observations as follows:

> Some focused on cultural trends, bemoaning the lack of standards in art—the tendency to play with novel styles, however frivolous, simply to win attention. Or they might bemoan popular culture for what they claimed was a shallow materialism and vulgar sexuality; some critics saw analogies between Western commercialism and the Roman "bread and circuses" approach to urban masses that, they argued, had weakened the empire's moral fiber and reduced its capacity for work and military valor.

Stearns, Adas, and Schwartz suggested that the various evidences of Western decline during the twentieth century were insufficient, at the present early stage of analysis, to pronounce Western Civilization dead, however. Paraphrasing Mark Twain, they argued that reports of the death of the West seemed premature. But they added the following word of caution based on past examples from world history:

> Social decline, if it does set in, typically takes a long time to work through. Rome declined for three centuries before it "fell"; the Ottoman Empire began to turn downward two centuries before it became known as "sick." The first century of decline may be hard to perceive, yet particularly important to monitor in case restorative measures are necessary.

Among the observers who saw a fatal, *absolute* decline were those who saw the twentieth century as a time of such debased philosophical futilities and acts of barbarism that the decline could not be undone by any superficial means. Among the debased behaviors were the atrocities of war and revolution; the tragic tide of abortion, infanticide, child abuse, euthanasia; the soaring incidence of divorce and family disintegration; and the despicable inclination toward homosexuality and pornography.

Others suggested that there may be merely a gap in *perceptions* about the condition of the West. On one side of the gap were **intellectuals** who insisted on using their humanistic reason to falsely portray, through art and literature, a picture of a civilization gone mad. On the other side of the perception gap, it was argued, were the **common people** of the West who remained substantially committed to disciplined work, to control over their emotions and biological urges, and to historic standards of morality and family life.

In any event, it seemed clear near the end of the millennium that Western Civilization stood at a crossroads of confusion. As the above-named historians described it:

> Poverty and job boredom coexisted with affluence and continued appeals to the essential value of work. Youth protest—including defiant costumes and pulsating rock music—family instability, and growing crime might be signs of a fatally flawed society. Rising rates of suicide and increasing incidence of mental illness were other troubling symptoms. At the least, Western society continued to display the strains of change.

Western civilization, in sum, continued to be distinctive for a mixture of old and new reasons. Headed by the United States, it led the world, by the 1960s, in the use of mind-altering drugs. The burgeoning leisure culture involved many Westerners with an interest in sexuality and sexual symbolism profoundly shocking to people from many other societies. The West also maintained a distinctive commitment to liberal democracy...[but, on the other hand,] remained closely tied to larger world currents. It continued to organize much world trade, as its economy fairly steadily expanded. Western developments in technology, science, and popular culture continued to have international impact. Western feminism, a newer force, helped inspire feminist interest in other societies, such as Japan. At the same time, growing rates of immigration to the West and the increasing impact of economic competition from industry in other societies made it clear that the West's links to the rest of the world were not entirely determined by the West itself.

War on Terrorism. Since Soviet communism has collapsed, a new threat to the West has emerged—independent terrorist organizations and the nations that support them. Terrorism has existed for decades, but a new form of transnational terrorism has arisen—organizations that are associated with militant, radical Islam. While many groups are still focused on the Arab-Israeli conflict, others like al-Qaida seek the eradication of Western influence from the Middle East and the reshaping of Muslim countries into what they consider to be in strict accordance with the Koran. Such groups have proven since the late 1990s to be threats to Western interests throughout the world, with attacks staged against Western targets, Jewish sites, and friendly Muslim governments in such places as the Middle East and North Africa, Argentina, the Philippines, Indonesia, Pakistan, and Russia. Al-Qaida's most spectacular attack occurred in the United States on

The Twin Towers of the World Trade Center in New York City were destroyed in the terrorist attack of September 11, 2001.

September 11, 2001, with the attacks in New York City and Washington, D.C. Contributing to this threat are those countries that support terrorism and are seeking to acquire weapons of mass destruction. President George W. Bush, in his 2002 State of the Union speech, said such countries were part of an "**Axis of Evil**" and identified Iraq, Iran, and North Korea as prime examples.

Many countries, including some that are Islamic, helped the United States after the September 11 attack by stepping up law enforcement and intelligence activities against terrorist groups, and some helped America with its assault on al-Qaida and its Taliban supporters in Afghanistan. However, when the United States and others decided to deal with Iraq in 2003, a number of countries—led by France, Germany, and Russia—opposed any effort against Iraq without the approval by the United Nations Security Council while at the same time preventing approval of action by the Security Council. In fact, some countries seemed more concerned about the United States as the sole superpower—or "**hyperpower**" as some call it—than Iraq. As President George W. Bush stated in his speech to the nation on March 17, 2003: "These governments share our assessment of the danger, but not our resolve to meet it." Iraq was soon after invaded and the Saddam Hussein regime overthrown by a "coalition of the willing" led by the United States but without the support of the UN and a number of traditional American allies. In light of these events, how will the West respond to such threats in the future? Will a united West confront its enemies or will it be divided between the United States and those countries of "**Old Europe**" that wish to use multilateral organizations like the United Nations to restrain the United States and enhance their influence?

Forecasts. Mankind has always had a desire to see into his future, a realm which God seems to jealously reserve for Himself. He warned the ancients against divinations and declared that He would reveal only those things which He sovereignly chose to reveal to man for the accomplishment of His divine purposes. In Deuteronomy 29:29, Moses reminded the ancient Hebrews: "The secret things belong to the Lord our God, but those things which are revealed belong to us and to our children forever, *that we may do all the words of this law*" (NKJV, emphasis added).

Yet, in the late twentieth century, scientific man sought to perfect new ways to know the future. Using sophisticated trend analyses and computer modeling, they searched the past for clues to the future.

One common approach was called the "**Zippy Forecast.**" This method involved trying to identify some *single, overwhelming, causal factor* that would fundamentally alter the framework upon which civilization operates and thus revolutionize the future. Among the blockbuster factors which some claimed would produce that result were the following:

◆ The "population bomb." Gloomy forecasters argued that if current trends in population growth were not checked, the sheer number of people would soon outpace available resources, produce unmanageable environmental catastrophes, create conflicts over territory and living space, and lead to terrible wars and poverty.

◆ "Exhaustion of frontiers." This was a close variation of the population bomb theory just examined. This theory suggested that human societies would run out of room, unless space travel provided a new outlet as the Age of Exploration had done at the middle of the second millennium.

◆ Urbanization. Again, this idea was related to the above concepts. It was argued that overcrowding in cities affects the overall quality of life and contributes to the anonymity of urban societies, making individuals feel they are not responsible for what goes on in their environment.

◆ Racism. It was argued that unless the people of the world overcome their racial and ethnic hatreds, there will never be a common solution to mankind's problems and the globe will once again become a fragmented world of barbaric antagonisms.

◆ "Post-industrialism." Some forecasters said that the late twentieth-century's technological revolution involving computers, genetic engineering, robotics, and new energy devices would generate a change far more dramatic than that brought on by the Industrial Revolution. They predicted that social status would depend on technical knowledge and skills, not on money or property. They envisioned that cities would become centers of information sharing and recreation, rather than centers for exchange and production as they have been in the past. They saw major changes in the nature of man as routine types of work are eliminated by automation and computers cause labor to become more individualized.

Most historians reject this "one-cause-determines-all" **deterministic** approach. They argue that major changes in history are the result of a confluence of several factors. The streams of civilization flow into a single ocean of history. As the historians we have previously quoted put it:

The analysis of the past shows the power of considerable continuity, rather than some single-minded transformation.... Though some **cataclysm** is always possible, most historians assume that complexity will continue. Eye-catching forecasts can help organize thinking about what makes history tick and how the present relates to past, but there are other orientations toward the future as well.

The more common approach to forecasting is **trend analysis**. Based on studies of trends, forecasters usually develop both optimistic and pessimistic cases for the future—sometimes referred to as "best-case scenarios" and "worst-case scenarios." Experience with this method has shown, however, that much of the so-called scientific forecasting has been little more than guesswork, distorted by **myopic** visions of the present. Some past fears have proven unfounded, while some idealistic expectations have never been realized. On the one side, for example, the great hopes for peace through world unity (League of Nations, United Nations, etc.) based on Enlightenment philosophies have not worked out. On the other side, long-standing predictions that world population would by now have wiped out the food supply or that the United States and Soviet Union would one day end the world in a nuclear holocaust have not been realized.

The Providence of God

The Christian's best answer to understanding the future is found in the historic doctrine of the Providence of God. The word *providence* itself, though strange-sounding to the modern ear, is full of meaning. It consists of the Latin parts *video*, "the see," and *pro*, "before." This tells us that God "sees beforehand," a fact which Scripture confirms. The Word of God adds a further dimension to the concept of Providence when it speaks of God's Sovereignty. The Westminster Confession of Faith describes both a **first cause** for history—God's sovereign will—and a **second cause**—human responsibility:

> God from all eternity did, by the most wise and holy counsel of his own will, freely and unchangeably ordain whatsoever comes to pass: yet so, as thereby neither is God the

A Warning Against the Spirit of the Age

... Unless men's every thought is brought into captivity to the obedience of Christ, neither knowledge, nor ingenuity, nor experience, nor a study of all the lessons taught by the horrors of the French Revolution—in a word, nothing at all will prevent them from being dragged along the same path to the same abyss, from holding Reason to be an infallible criterion of divine Revelation, from passing censure on institutions based on higher than human approval, from admiring the faint glimmerings of a dim lantern or the hot flames of a hell-torch as if they were lights of heaven. Men will laud a Revolution whose blood and tears, whose inhumanity and absurdity are the very proof of the impracticability of its principle. They will hail this unholy and unwholesome revolt against nature and law as the initial triumph of ideas sacred and sublime, in the wholesale application of which alone the happiness of the nations is to be sought. And, as though everything were forgotten and nothing were learned, they will speak in poetic rapture of the French Revolution as of a volcano, yes, but a volcano issuing forth imperishable truths—a beacon for humanity amid the storms to be anticipated on the ocean of human errors and passions.

... Unbelief has no outlet save in the Revolution principle. The great variety of opinions, when once subjected to logical and historical analysis, narrows down to the simple contrast between divine truth and human invention. One either becomes a Christian, by unconditionally submitting to Holy Scripture, or else, by reasoning it away, a Jacobin and a radical. And so the few who do not shrink back from being consistent are the first to reveal the character of the awesome struggle that is to come, the struggle that will herald the return of Him to whom is given all power in heaven and on earth and Whose words, "Fear not, little flock, for it is your Father's good pleasure to give you the kingdom; I am with you always, even unto the end of the world," (Luke 12:32) are addressed not only to His apostles but to all who through their testimony would come to believe on Him.

Over against all the wisdom of men and in awareness of my own frailty, my motto consists of two words that assure me of victory: *It is written!* And *It has come to pass!*—a foundation that will stand against any artillery, a root that will hold against every whirlwind of philosophic unbelief. History—which is also the flaming script of the holy God. Scripture—which is also the historical Scripture since what comes to pass is inseparable from what is taught. History—as it is formed, not just by the succession of deeds, but especially by the unfolding of ideas. History—as it receives its beginning and meaning and direction and unity from the facts of Revelation. Scripture—as it gives the law to scribes, in the foolishness of the Cross confounding the wisdom of the philosopher with the humble faith of little children. Scripture—as it bears witness to the Lamb that was slain, to the rod out of the stem of Jesse and the unconquerable Lion from the tribe of Judah, David's son and David's Lord, God and man, Mediator or Judge, who after holding out the staff of grace in vain, has in His hand a rod of iron to smite a stiffnecked people. —August 1847

Groen Van Prinsterer, ***Lectures on Unbelief and Revolution***, Edited by Harry Van Dyke (Jordan Station, Ontario, Canada: Wedge Publishing Foundation, 1989), pp. x–xii.

author of sin, nor is violence offered to the will of the creatures, nor is the liberty or contingency of the second causes taken away, but rather established.

At the heart of Providence is the gift of Redemption through Christ, by which mankind may be rescued from the consequences of his own folly and brought into line once again with the revealed will of God. The Scottish theologian John J. Murray has noted that we may not understand our present condition because God's Providence works on a grander scale than our minds can sometimes comprehend. But he adds: "We must look to the end of everything."

For your consideration

Questions

1. What is the basic unifying factor of history? What has happened to civilizations when they remember this factor and when they forget it?

2. In which way can humans truly know the future? Discuss scientific ways in which men seek to see into the future.

3. Do you believe the world is overpopulated? Why or why not? Discuss.

4. What are the advantages and disadvantages of urbanization?

5. Should rich countries help poor countries? Discuss acceptable and unacceptable methods of international economic aid. How can Christians help their fellow believers and non-Christians in poorer nations?

6. Define racism. Is racism sinful? Can people maintain racial and ethnic distinctives without becoming racists?

7. In the 1960s through 1980s many people feared extinction through nuclear war? Is this still a fear in your generation? Why or why not? How can people, especially Christians, work to diminish the causes of war?

8. How should Christians feel about the kind of "New World Order" advocated by internationalists in the late twentieth century and beyond? Compare this vision with Christ's Great Commission in Matthew 28:18-20 and with other Scriptures dealing with the Kingdom of God.

9. Discuss how the West will respond to terrorist threats in the future. Also explain what governments are already doing to protect their citizens from international terrorism.

Projects

1. Read the Charter of the United Nations and summarize it in a report. Conclude with an evaluation of it from your personal perspective.

2. Research some 1991-1992 magazine articles about the Maastricht Treaty and European Union. In a report, summarize your findings and tell whether you think European unification is a good or bad step.

3. Review the books *Megatrends* (1982) and/or *Megatrends 2000* (1990) by authors John Naisbitt and Patricia Aburdene. (See your local library.) Develop a set of five "megatrends" which you envision as occurring during the next decade.

4. Research current or recent literature describing the Japanese industrial management style and formula. Write a brief report on your findings.

5. This chapter gives brief descriptions of the postwar development of several European, North American, and Pacific Rim countries. Choose one of these and write a more detailed report on the modern history of the chosen country.

6. Research the history of the Watergate Scandal. Write a brief report.

7. Pretend you are running for the office of the head of government (president, premier, etc.) in your country. Outline in writing the chief points of your proposed foreign policy.

Word List

millennium	interdependent
innate	demographics
entrenched	Earth Summit
tenet	gross national product
neutron bomb	welfare state
glasnost	technocrats
perestroika	gold standard
infrastructure	WTO and GATT
affinity	NAFTA
morass	initiatives
adjunct	trade deficits
bipolar	Pacific Rim
unipolar	Reaganomics
New World Order	relative decline
Maastricht Treaty	absolute decline
Strategic Defense	Zippy Forecast
Initiative	deterministic
cataclysm	myopic
trend analysis	first cause
forecasts	second cause
deprivation	population bomb

People and Groups

Mikhail Gorbachev	Olaf Palme
Boris Yeltsin	John Diefenbaker
Peace Corps	Pierre Elliott Trudeau
Canadian Alliance	Brian Mulroney
Laszlo Tokes	Bloc Québécois
N. Ceauçescu	Ross Perot
Francis Fukuyama	Newt Gingrich
Margaret Thatcher	Spiro Agnew
John Major	Antonio Salazar
Helmut Schmidt	Green Party
Helmut Kohl	Gerhard Schröder
Francois Mitterand	Partnership for Peace
Tony Blair	Bill Clinton
Sinn Fein	Hillary Rodham Clinton
Ronald Reagan	Jimmy Carter
George H. W. Bush	George W. Bush

Jesus said to his disciples, "You are the light of the world. A city set on a hill cannot be hidden. Nor do men light a lamp, and put it under the peckmeasure, but on the lampstand; and it gives light to all who are in the house. Let your light shine before men in such a way that they may see your good works, and glorify your Father who is in heaven." Matthew 5:14–16

God moves in a mysterious way
His wonders to perform;
He plants His footsteps in the sea
And rides upon the storm.

Deep in unfathomable mines
Of never-failing skill,
He treasures up His bright designs
And works His sovereign will.

Ye fearful saints, fresh courage take;
The clouds ye so much dread
Are big with mercy and shall break
In blessings on your head.

His purposes will ripen fast,
Unfolding every hour;
The bud may have a bitter taste,
But sweet will be the flower.

Blind unbelief is sure to err
And scan His work in vain;
God is His own Interpreter
And He will make it plain.

—WILLIAM COWPER

Index

CREDITS

INDEX OF MAPS